STRATEGIC MARKETING

Creating Competitive Advantage

Douglas West, John Ford,
and Essam Ibrahim

OXFORD
UNIVERSITY PRESS

OXFORD
UNIVERSITY PRESS

Great Clarendon Street, Oxford OX2 6DP

Oxford University Press is a department of the University of Oxford. It furthers the University's objective of excellence in research, scholarship, and education by publishing worldwide in

Oxford New York

Auckland Cape Town Dar es Salaam Hong Kong Karachi Kuala Lumpur Madrid Melbourne Mexico City Nairobi New Delhi Shanghai Taipei Toronto

With offices in

Argentina Austria Brazil Chile Czech Republic France Greece Guatemala Hungary Italy Japan Poland Portugal Singapore South Korea Switzerland Thailand Turkey Ukraine Vietnam

Oxford is a registered trademark of Oxford University Press in the UK and in certain other countries

Published in the United States by Oxford University Press Inc., New York

First published 2006

British Library Cataloguing in Publication Data

Data available

Library of Congress Cataloging in Publication Data

Data available

Typeset by Laserwords Private Limited, Chennai, India
Printed in Great Britain
on acid-free paper by
Ashford Colour Press Ltd, Gosport, Hants.

ISBN 978–0–19–927398–0

10 9 8 7 6 5 4 3 2

Dedicated to Lynda, Alexandra and Olivia and the memory of my parents. **DCW**

This book is dedicated to my wife, Sarah, and my children, Lisa, Kimberly, John, and Jamie. They have been a constant source of encouragement and support. **JBF**

I dedicate this book to the memory of my father, Mr Bakr, and my two beloved daughters, Wasyla and Sondos. A smile on their faces was like a magic word for me to continue when it was hard. **EI**

Preface

The three of us have known each other for many years. When we met up a few years ago at a conference in the USA the discussion turned to teaching strategy, and by twists and turns, marketing strategy textbooks. There are some great books on the shelves, but marketing strategy is a topic where we felt writers often fall into the trap of erring on the side of marketing planning or marketing management rather than keeping the focus on strategy. Some years later, after shaking hands on the book project, this book has emerged and you can judge if we did indeed manage to keep the focus on strategy.

We have tried to remain true to our initial ideas. In particular we discussed at great length what would be the best strategic 'hook' to provide for the book. After all, there is a comprehensive set of offerings to choose from. In the end we felt that Porter's framework of cost, differentiation, and focus, the tried and tested, provided that best point of view that much of the book could be hung upon. Yes, many marketers argue, quite rightly, that organizations of all kinds often need to both reduce costs and differentiate. Nevertheless, as a framework it seemed second to none in finding the essence of strategy.

One thing to emphasize at the beginning is that the book cites a number of cases of success and failure, but please bear in mind that hindsight is a wonderful thing. Marketing strategy is not an exact science. If it were, there would not be any failure. Marketing strategy is underpinned by the behaviour of buyers who make decisions in response to a multitude of personal and environmental factors. The 'tectonic plates' of the market are continually shifting and so this quarter's winning strategy can be next quarter's disaster. The cases cited are for illustrative purposes only and are not in any way tied to any judgements about marketing strategy. To paraphrase the famous phrase about history: 'marketing strategy is often like looking in the rear view mirror of a car: things get clearer the further away from them that you are'.

We hope that some sense of the multinational nature of this endeavour will be apparent. All three of us have lived and worked abroad and we reside in different parts of the world, albeit two of us in the UK. It was for this reason that we decided an 'international marketing strategy' chapter would largely be redundant given our combined national and cultural perspectives.

The book's structure entailed a long debate at the beginning of the project. We looked at a variety of frameworks and had some discussions with contacts in business and amongst our students and further debate after receiving advice from some anonymous reviews. Eventually we returned to the most popular framework (more on this in Chapter 1):

1. Where are we now?
2. Where do we want to be?
3. How will we get there?
4. Did we get there?

We concluded that there was no point in choosing a different framework just for the sake of being different. This works, and in our view it doesn't need fixing. However, we would argue that the content of the book, using this framework, draws (where appropriate) on both the traditional and the modern, if not the leading edge. The book also draws upon marketing strategy and the strategy literature (where the latter is oriented to a marketing context).

Each chapter contains two mini cases and one longer end of chapter case with questions for class discussion or assignment work. There are also three much longer cases at the end of the book with questions that integrate the central themes of the book.

The book is designed for postgraduate students and undergraduates in the final year of their studies. It is not intended for those looking for an introduction to marketing. Each chapter is packed with concepts, theories, and practice and a driving narrative with a strong and prescriptive point of view. This is our account of strategic marketing and we hope that you enjoy it.

Acknowledgements

A wider team supports the production of a book like this. A special thank you to all the staff at OUP: they have had a significant affect on the shape of the book and its evolution. In particular thanks to Sacha Cook at OUP for her vision and for her professional management of the process, as well as for her complete dedication to helping us see it into print. Thanks also to Professor Leyland Pitt at Simon Fraser University, Canada, who provided a great deal of help and advice. In addition, there was a small group of anonymous reviewers who provided guidance on the book's structure and specific content. Thanks to *Market Leader* for use of some of the reviews of articles that appeared in the magazine. Finally, we would like to thank our research and business colleagues and students over the years who have helped shape our thinking.

Publisher's acknowledgements

The authors and the Publisher would like to thank the following for permission to reproduce copyright material.

The American Marketing Association for permission to abstract Charles H. Noble and Michael P. Mokwa, 'Implementing marketing strategies: Developing and testing a managerial theory', *Journal of Marketing*, vol. 63 (4), 1999, pp. 57–73; and Rajan Varadarajan, Satish Jayachandran, and J. Chris White, 'Strategic Interdependence in organizations: Deconglomeration and marketing strategy', *Journal of Marketing*, vol. 65 (1), 2001, pp. 15–28. Reprinted with permission from *Journal of Marketing*, published by the American Marketing Association, Charles H. Noble and Michael P. Mokwa, vol. 63 (4), 1999, pp. 57–73 and Rajan Varadarajan, Satish Jayachandran, and J. Chris White, vol. 65 (1), 2001, pp. 15–28.

The Economist for 'Relentless Competition in the Car Industry—what car makers are doing to counter', *The Economist*, 4 September 2004. © The Economist Newspaper Limited, London, 4 September 2004.

Elsevier for Russell Abratt and Patience Motiana, 'Managing co-branding strategies: global brands into local markets'. Reprinted from *Business Horizons*, Sept–Oct 2002, Russell Abratt and Patience Motiana, 'Managing Co-branding Strategies: Global Brands into Local Markets', pp. 43–50, © 2002 with permission from Elsevier.

The Financial Times for Alan Cane, 'Seeking New Angles: Digital Camera Mania has Forced Film Suppliers Such as Kodak to find new ways to build their brands', *Financial Times*, 7 December 2004; Tom Foremski, 'Intel Counts the Cost of its partnership with Rambus', *Financial Times*, 18 October 2000; John Griffiths, 'Flash Rat Shows its teeth', *Financial Times*, 30 July 2005; Mure Dickie, 'Global Brand Strategy Key for Lenovo', *Financial Times*, 13/14 August 2005; 'Who Practised the Bargaining Power over the other—is it Safeway or Morrison?', *Financial Times*, 15 December 2003; 'Something in the Air: European Airline Consolidations is Edging Forward', *Financial Times*, 24 March 2005; 'UK Banks Lag

Behind the Rest of the World in Reporting their customers', *Financial Times*, 14 April 2005; Jonathan Birchall, 'Rich, but not fortune's fools', *Financial Times*, 13 December 2005; Emiko Teranzo and Mark Odell, 'BT signs licensing deals for pay-per-view television service', *Financial Times*, 8 December 2005; Simon London, 'Faulty customer data and the faux-royal slipper syndrome', *Financial Times*, 7 December 2005; Kathrin Hille, 'Taiwan research team learns how to be genuinely creative', *Financial Times*, 2 December 2005; Jonathan Guthrie, 'Pricing reflections on the wonder and woes of a new inkjet printer', *Financial Times*, 26 October 2005; Claire Dowdy, 'Marketing: Smoking Out Images of Pipes and Slippers', *Financial Times*, 7 November 2005; Andrew Ward, 'The 1997 Asian Crisis Forced Samsung to switch its focus from cheap consumer electronics to the top end of the market', *Financial Times*, 6 September 2004; Jeremy Grant, 'We Can Build a Juggernaut', *Financial Times*, 4 February 2005; Susanna Voyle, 'E-tailing comes of age as Women Spend More than Men', *Financial Times*, 1 February 2004; Richard Waters, 'Yahoo Advances into Traditional Territory', *Financial Times*, 18 October 2005; Jonathan Birchall, 'How Wal-Mart is swapping tired for tidy', *Financial Times*, 10 November 2005; Meg Carter, 'Big Business Pitches Itself on Fair Trade Territory', *Financial Times*, 25 October 2005; and Elizabeth Rigby, 'New Look plans trial stores abroad', *Financial Times*, 17 November 2005.

Harvard Business School Publishing Corporation for Erich Joachimsthaler and David A. Aaker, 'Building Brands without Mass Media', *Harvard Business Review*, Jan–Feb, 1997, pp. 39–50. Reprinted by permission of *Harvard Business Review*. © 1997 by the Harvard Business School Publishing Corporation. All rights reserved;

Haymarket Publications Ltd for Robert Gray, 'The Changing Faces of Man', *Marketing*, 27 March 2003; Daniel Rogers, 'Brand Britain Goes Regional', *Marketing*, 27 March 2003; Ben Carter, 'Freedom Fighter', *Marketing*, 19 May 2004; Alexandra Jardine, 'Banks Suffer Identity Crisis', *Marketing*, 6 May 2004; Mark Ritson, 'Black, White and Grey are the Three Colours of a Free Market', *Marketing*, 13 June 2002; W. Bruce MacDonald, 'The Art of the Brief', *Marketing*, 27 October 2003; and 'Nike Shows the Way to Return from the Wilderness,' *Marketing*, 20 April 2005. Reproduced from *Marketing* magazine with the permission of the copyright holder, Haymarket Business Publications Ltd. Casper van Vark, 'Persil Gets Playful', *Revolution*, 1 February 2003; reproduced from *Revolution* magazine with the permission of the copyright holder, Haymarket Publications Ltd.

Christopher Klenner for 'Demand Exists for Premium Airlines', *Financial Times*, 5 September 2004; Winston Fletcher, Visiting Professor of Marketing, Westminster University, for 'In Search of Integration: Campaigns must combine all marketing options', *Financial Times*, 23 February 1998.

California Management Review for the material used in: Figure 3.5 Copyright © 1991, by The Regents of the University of California. Reprinted from the *California Management Review*, Vol 33, No. 3. By permission of the Regents; Figure 3.7 Copyright © 1991, by The Regents of the University of California. Reprinted from the *California Management Review*, Vol 33, No. 3. By permission of the Regents; Figure 6.2 Copyright © 2001, by The Regents of the University of California. Reprinted from the *California Management Review*, Vol 33, No. 3. By permission of the Regents; Figure 7.4 Copyright © 1991, by The Regents of the University of California. Reprinted from the *California Management Review*, Vol 33, No. 3. By permission of the Regents.

Crown copyright material is reproduced under Class Licence Number CO1P0000148 with the permission of the Controller of HMSO and the Queen's Printer for Scotland.

Every effort has been made to trace all copyright holders, but if any have been inadvertently overlooked the publishers will be pleased to make the necessary arrangements at the first opportunity.

Outline contents

Contents

Online Resource Centre

Visit the *Strategic Marketing* Online Resource Centre at

http://www.oxfordtextbooks.co.uk/orc/west/

to find an extensive range of teaching and learning resources, including:

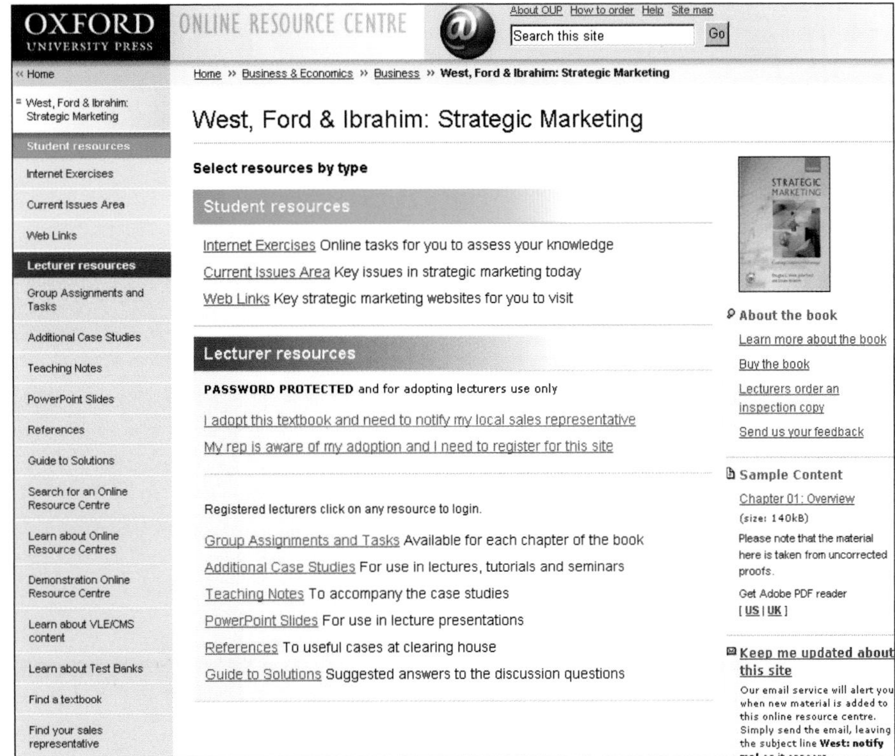

For students:

- Current issues area—providing information on the latest developments in the field of marketing
- Internet exercises—a variety of tasks and assignments to be carried out online
- Annotated web links—websites of relevant organizations and sources for each chapter

For lecturers (password protected):

- PowerPoint slides—for use in lecture presentations and handouts
- Teaching notes—for use alongside the case studies
- Guide solutions—tips on how to answer the discussion questions
- Group assignments and tasks for each chapter
- Additional case studies
- References to useful cases at clearing house

Part I Introduction

I. Introduction

1. Overview
2. Marketing strategy: analysis and perspectives

II. Where are we now?

3. Environmental and internal analysis: market information and intelligence

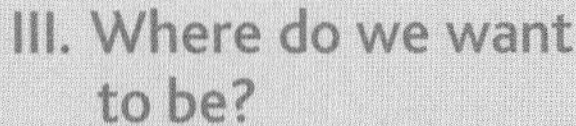

III. Where do we want to be?

4. Strategic marketing decisions and choices
5. Segmentation, targeting, and positioning strategies
6. Relationship strategies

IV. How will we get there?

7. Product innovation and development strategies
8. Branding strategies
9. Service marketing strategies
10. Pricing and distribution strategies
11. Marketing communications strategies
12. E-marketing strategies

V. Did we get there?

13. Strategy implementation and control

VI. Conclusion

14. Social marketing and CSR

1

Overview

LEARNING OBJECTIVES

- Be able to define marketing strategy
- Understand the essential differences between the main approaches towards marketing strategy
- Review the structure of the book
- Assess the importance of marketing strategy to a business and identify the kinds of things that can go wrong

CHAPTER AT A GLANCE

Introduction

Competitive marketing strategy occurs within departments, across organizations, and within people's heads as a way of doing business. Competitive marketing strategy is defined in this book as a market-oriented strategy that establishes a profitable and sustainable market position for the firm against all forces that determine industry competition by continuously creating and developing a competitive advantage from the potential sources that exist in a firm's value chain. The key elements are:

- **Market-oriented:** the strategy is based upon the needs and wants of the marketplace.
- **Establishes a profitable market position:** the end goal of the strategy is to make a profit in the for-profit sector or to meet alternative metrics such as in the not-for-profit sector. In the latter case for example, a road safety campaign based on a particular marketing strategy might 'make a profit' if there is a decline in road injuries and deaths attributed to it.
- **Establishes a sustainable market position:** marketing strategy is not about one-off transactions. The aim is to reach a point where an organization finds a place in the market that fits its available marketing resources.
- **Forces that determine industry competition:** these are all the complex mix of ingredients that create the marketing 'whirlwind', such as government regulation, global competition, or the extent of buyers' knowledge and understanding of a particular market.
- **Continuously creating and developing a competitive advantage:** few (if any) organizations can just rest on their laurels, so the idea is to find a spot where, if need be, the primary challenges can be tackled. Not all organizations have to do this on a continuous basis of course, but if it had to, an organization with a sound competitive marketing strategy would be able to. A simple example: you might make the best tomato ketchup in the best-recognized glass bottles, but if the market moves towards plastic 'squeezy' bottles you need to be able to adapt.
- **Potential sources that exist in a firm's value chain:** competitive marketing strategy relates to what value any organization wants to create using its available marketing resources.

Thinking First

This definition and wider perspectives and analyses relating to marketing strategy will be examined in Chapter 2. This chapter seeks to examine the kinds of thinking that can underpin marketing strategy and its practice. The book takes rational 'Thinking First' as the basis for marketing strategy and is logical, sequential, and largely linear in its exploration of marketing strategy. Thinking First is about cognitively analysing a strategic marketing problem and developing the solution (the strategy) through a carefully thought-out process. Instant views and decisions are not made, though it can help to see the big picture occasionally throughout the process. It can involve some inspiration and insight, but largely the process is one of painstakingly doing your homework to arrive at a solution.

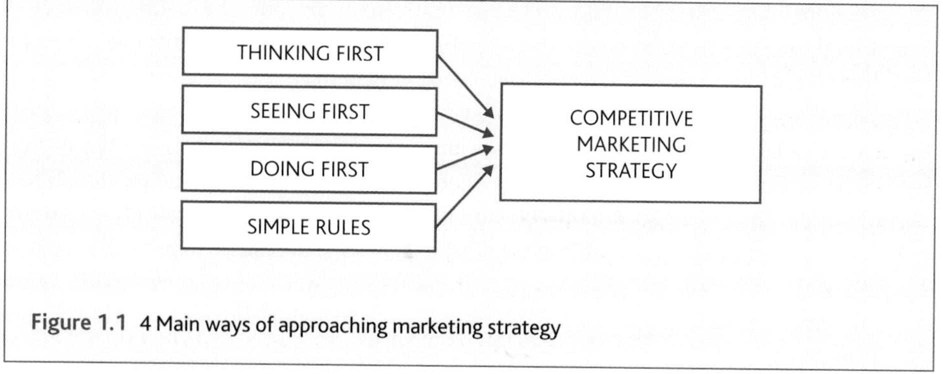

Figure 1.1 4 Main ways of approaching marketing strategy

Business, just like life, for that matter, is rarely quite so rational. Decisions can be taken from a variety of perspectives and logic and rationality may provide only one perspective. The main alternatives are (see Figure 1.1):

- Seeing First
- Doing First
- Simple Rules

Each of these will be considered in turn in this chapter.

Another area to be explored in this chapter is how important marketing strategy is to a business. This is a difficult area to investigate given the problems of isolating strategy from other variables that affect any business but some new research on the topic will be highlighted. Finally, the chapter examines some of the reasons why marketing strategies fail as well as some of the important organizational issues that can affect strategy.

Seeing First

Seeing First reminds us that the importance of seeing the overall decision is sometimes greater than thinking about it. As Mozart noted, the best part of creating a symphony was to 'see the whole of it at a single glance in my mind' (Mintzberg and Westley, 2001). Seeing First is basically insight and insight often only comes after a period of preparation, incubation, illumination, and verification in the cold light of day (Wallas, 1926) so the best way of Seeing First might, arguably, be after a process of rational analysis! The 'eureka' moment has been often known to come after sleep, as rational thought is generally switched off during sleep.

Some inspirational leaders can scan the signals in the environment, sense what is going on before it is articulated, and rely upon their intuition (Gofee and Jones, 2000). For example, Franz Humer, the CEO of Roche, easily detected changes in climate and ambience and sensed underlying currents of opinion. Such leaders are skilful at sensing and keeping on top of changes in the company and the environment. However, sensing skills can be dangerous if overly relied upon. It is especially difficult to sense how far you can lead when it comes to major change. For example, the various leaders in the Kyoto Protocol talks had many difficulties in sensing how far they could take the process without losing support. The danger of not being able to distinguish key issues from the peripheral is another danger. A leader might be able to sense a whole range of issues, but not be able to sift out the really important ones. This might lead to confused decision-making.

Are some organizations more likely to See First than others? According to Hamel (1999) there are two kinds of companies: stewards and entrepreneurs. Stewards are the incumbents who conserve by 'polishing the silver', cutting costs, outsourcing, and selling off bad business units. Entrepreneurs are the revolutionary wealth creators who capture the future riches. In this sense, they are capable of 'Seeing First'. In most industries newcomers, such as Amazon.com, Cisco, Charles Schwab, and SAP, are creating much of the new wealth. These are well-known names, but across lots of industries unorthodox start-ups are challenging the incumbents.

Stewards have only one option if they are to survive—they have to 'out-entrepreneur' the entrepreneurs. Hamel suggests that the solution for big companies is to move from what he sees as resource 'allocation' to resource 'attraction' by developing internal markets for ideas, capital, and talent. Places like Silicon Valley are 'refugee camps' for frustrated entrepreneurs who could not get a hearing elsewhere. In Silicon Valley, if an idea has merit it will attract capital and talent—there is no CEO to allocate resources.

Can the Silicon Valley approach be grafted on to big rational-thinking companies? According to Hamel the answer is a resounding 'yes' and he cites several good examples such as GE Capital, Monsanto, Royal Dutch/Shell, and Virgin. The principles employed by these big companies involve (1) ideas, (2) capital, and (3) talent.

A flow of new ideas is essential for wealth creation and the best way to encourage this is to reward internal entrepreneurs handsomely. Big companies must be willing to create a slew of 30-year-old millionaires in the process instead of preserving the usual 'long on risk and short on reward' status quo that exists in most companies. Few companies are willing to do this, so why should employees battle for their ideas? Another problem with big companies and innovation is that there is normally only one buyer for any new idea, so the chances of it being turned down along the way are high. In Silicon Valley there are lots of sources of capital. To replicate this, for example, Shell invites internal entrepreneurs to present their business plans to a wide cross-section of senior executives in the hope that at least one might say 'yes'.

The second aspect relates to capital. Silicon Valley's venture capitalists are prepared to relax traditional financial screens. In big companies if the estimates of market size and growth are shaky and the analyses weak, the idea gets stifled. One senior auto executive admitted that its entrance into the minivan market was delayed because a business case could not be made with any certainty. By the time the company amassed enough supporting evidence, the market was dominated by Chrysler. Venture capitalists in Silicon Valley ask simple questions like: 'who will care and what kind of difference will this make?' The basic problem with capital allocation in big companies is that lost money is highly visible whereas forgone money is, by its nature, invisible. One example of how to tackle this is Shell, which has addressed the problem by creating a panel to whom innovators can present a business case at any time. They are guaranteed an almost instantaneous response.

Silicon Valley's talent market is the third element of wealth creation that can be adapted internally by big companies. Every CEO in Silicon Valley knows that employees need exhilarating work or they will 'turn in their badges'. Big companies need to reduce any barriers that hinder staff from going to work on whatever fires their imagination. Shell lists available jobs on its intranet and anyone, with two months' notice, can go and work on anything that interests them. The bottom line is that if highly creative and ambitious people feel trapped in dead-end positions, they will leave and if they do so they may create wealth somewhere else and not for you.

Even if larger companies do start to See First more easily through developing their flow of ideas, capital, and talent, many companies still face a problem as the competition from the 'left field' has grown more intense since the mid-1990s. As a result of consumer tastes, globalization, and unrelenting technological change, competition boundaries have blurred significantly. For example, a decade ago retail banking in the UK was comfortably dominated by the 'big four'. Intense rivalry has now appeared from former building societies like the Halifax, supermarkets such as Tesco, and high street retailers like Marks & Spencer. How many bankers would have predicted such an outcome 15 years ago? Telecommunications has undergone a similar experience. Previously separate sectors such as computing, entertainment, telephony, and utilities are now locked in fierce competition. For example, BT has formed a partnership with BSkyB to develop digital TV and telephone services via satellite and Northern Telecom is working with several electricity companies to provide broadband communications over power lines.

How can firms See First and diagnose the likelihood of a new entrant from an unexpected place? According to Geroski (1999), a couple of observations can be made. One is that successful unexpected entrants are not like aliens in the marketplace. They behave rationally by applying basic product and/or process innovations and generally use sound business planning. However, the second observation is that incumbents often have problems seeing outside their boxes and rarely cope with unexpected entrants.

Wherever the new entrant comes from, they need to understand the marketplace and the nature of innovation in that marketplace to be successful, and this is the key to spotting them. Few goods or services are consumed in isolation: consumers buy packages of complementary products.

Producers of similar products are known as 'complementors' and these are the firms most likely to mount unexpected entrances into your marketplace. They also offer the best opportunity for you to form alliances with them and to mount your own unexpected entrances into other firms' markets. For example, book publishers, cinema chains, newspaper groups, magazines, and TV companies are complementors—they all compete for our sedentary leisure time and 'feed off' each other for content and publicity.

Each good or service is also a package made up from specialist suppliers and distributors. These too are part of the complementor group that might mount an unexpected entrance into your market. Thus, Tandy entered the personal computing industry from retailing and Microsoft has attacked applications from its operating systems base.

Having a related competency is another route to unexpected entrance. For example, Racal and Ericsson's understanding of cellular technology in the defence sector enabled them to enter as competitors in telecommunications and Nike's expertise in athletic shoes has enabled it to branch out into sportswear, equipment, and managing sports events.

Similarly, supermarkets have skills in managing cash transactions, which has enabled their entrance into financial markets.

So how can you see what kinds of firms might enter your marketplace? Look to firms who know your customers and are familiar with your value chain. Firms with the necessary skills to compete with you and possess such knowledge are especially a threat. Throughout such scanning, keep in mind that such an entrance is the hardest to predict of all types of rivalry. Cannibalization is preferable to losing market share to unexpected rivals and such strategies will help fend off unexpected entrance.

To maintain control of your market Geroski (1999) recommends five steps:

1. Begin by identifying who might take advantage of the flows of information from your market.
2. After that, you need to imagine that you are the potential new entrant and think coherently about them.
3. Then organize your thoughts coherently from the point of view of attacking your own market position.
4. Think through the what, who, and when aspects of market entry and assess the required competencies.
5. Finally, pre-empt potential entrants by introducing the new process or product developed in (4) yourself!

Summary

'Seeing First' has most relevance with new ventures or dramatic changes of direction. The reality with Seeing First is that, invariably, you need to do your homework. That is, you also need to be able to Think First. Mozart may have been able to See First before he wrote his symphonies, but the application of this to marketing strategy is less obvious. You might occasionally have luck with Seeing First, as with the insight for a market for no-frills low cost airlines. For the most part marketers need to examine the trends and the evidence and be able to develop some sense of what is important within the mass of actions and events. A more accessible alternative approach is to see the 'big picture' which does involve Thinking First. Successful marketing strategy requires the ability to move from tactical detail to a big picture overview of the market to place a strategy in context. Seeing First is rarely of much relevance to day-to-day marketing.

Doing First

When you cannot think it through and you do not see it, what do you do? 'Doing First' happens when marketing managers experiment and learn from the mistakes and successes. The process is: (1) do something, (2) make sense of it, and (3) repeat the successful parts and discard the rest. Instead of there being a marketing strategy, the reality is often that 'doing' drives. For example, many companies that have successfully diversified their businesses have done so by a process of figuring out what worked and what did not (see Mini Case Study 1.1).

MINI CASE STUDY 1.1

'Intel counts the cost of its partnership with Rambus: What seemed a marriage made in heaven has become a nightmare'

When Intel teamed up with Rambus in 1996 it seemed to be a marriage made in heaven. But the relationship has soured, costing the world's largest chip manufacturer hundreds of millions of dollars and several high-profile chip problems.

Intel's support of the high-speed Rambus memory chip technology is directly related to the recent cancellation of its Timna microprocessor, the recall of more than 1m PC motherboards in May and the scrapping of about 1m PCs a year ago. 'We made a big bet on Rambus and it did not work out', Craig Barrett, Intel chief executive admitted. 'In retrospect, it was a mistake to be dependent on a third party for a technology that gates your performance.' But back in 1996 the partnership seemed to make sense. Intel was producing ever faster microprocessors but PC memory chips could not keep up. It did not matter how fast the microprocessor became since PC performance would be constrained by trailing memory speed.

Enter Rambus, with memory chips that produced a sharp improvement in memory speed. Given Intel's powerful position in influencing the direction of future PC systems, Rambus-based memory chips were widely expected to dominate memory chip markets, producing a royalties bonanza for the tiny company. Unfortunately, memory chip makers were hit by falling chip prices, profits were under pressure and paying royalties to Rambus was the last thing chip makers wanted to do.

In addition, making Rambus-based memory chips was difficult and expensive, with yields of good chips low at first. Intel stepped in with money and marketing muscle. Two years ago it paid $500m for a 6 per cent stake in Micron Technology, the top US memory chip maker, to help it make Rambus-based chips. And three months later it invested $100m in Samsung, the leading Korean chip maker, to help it produce Rambus memories.

In addition, Intel tried to push the overall market towards Rambus with plans for microprocessors that would only work with that type of memory. Despite its best efforts, the promise of Rambus's technology led to a nightmare for Intel.

First of all, the first PC boards for Rambus contained a serious flaw. According to some estimates, this forced leading PC makers to withdraw as many as 1m systems last September, just weeks from launch.

Intel was then confronted by the problem of chips that would allow cheaper memories to be used with its Rambus-only microprocessors. This led to the recall of about 1m PC boards earlier this year, and a profits warning related to the costs involved. Then, more recently, Intel scrapped its delayed low-end Timna microprocessor after customers showed little interest in a low-cost PC microprocessor that required expensive Rambus memory chips.

Rambus, meanwhile, smarting from the poor support from memory chip producers, and PC makers which favoured slower but cheaper types of memory, decided that rival memory chips violated its patents and filed the first of a series of patent infringement lawsuits. This began in January with a lawsuit against Hitachi and grew to include complaints against virtually every leading memory chip producer. It triggered several counter-suits.

Intel became disgruntled with the company's strategy. 'We hoped we were partners with a company that would concentrate on technology innovation rather than seeking to collect a toll from other companies', Mr Barrett said.

It is clearly a relationship Intel is unhappy with but one it cannot change easily. Mr Barrett said the company has a contractual obligation specifying that its Pentium 4 microprocessor, due for release next month, should support Rambus memory. Yet Rambus memory chips significantly raise the cost of PCs—never a good thing especially with Wall Street already concerned about slowing PC markets. Intel is trying to remedy this with rebates to PC makers to make up for increased manufacturing cost, further adding to the expense of its Rambus support.

However, there is something of a silver lining for Intel. The company's investments in Micron and Samsung have produced a generous return as the shares have appreciated significantly in value. And it stands to profit from sales of its higher margin server microprocessors—a product area that is not dependent on the use of Rambus-based chips.

Source: Tom Foremski (2000), *Financial Times*, 18 October, p. 39.

Take the case of Manchester United Football Club. Of all the English clubs, Manchester United's performance on (and off) the pitch has been tremendous. According to Szymanski (1998) its success is rooted in its exceptional 'brand image' which has been developed over a century. Manchester United entered the football league in 1892, staved off bankruptcy ten years later, and thereafter has rarely looked back. As an institution, it entered the collective psyche in the 1950s and 1960s when Matt Busby's 'Babes' dominated the game and in between, the Munich air crash of 1958 stunned the nation. The club's success has not been based on the outcome of strategic marketing planning. Instead, it has been based on the vagaries of fortune and the maintenance of its brand character over time through investment in its management, facilities, and players. In recent years the club won several Premier League Championships and FA cups. Between 1992 and 1997 it generated income of £249 million, of which £69 million was spent on wages and £66 million was profit. Manchester United is the 'Coca-Cola' of English football. Even when its pitch performance has been below that of its rivals, it has been able to attract higher attendances to its fixtures than its rivals.

The key aspect of football economics is that there is no significant link between profits and league position. As clubs improve their league position, their profits are just as likely to go up as down. The reason is simple. Better league performances lead to higher revenues with better attendance, higher ticket prices, and TV rights. However, increased expenditure on wages leads to sustained league performances. Thus, to move up the league, and stay there, a football club has to spend out on the better players in order to consistently win matches. Consequently, successful clubs cannot harvest profits—they are forced to maintain spending to replace players over time. So how has Manchester United managed to combine profitability with pitch performance?

Amongst the fans, the decision to support the club is straightforward. As it is the leading brand name, a costly information search by fans for the best club to follow is reduced.

Fans know that the games will be entertaining and the likelihood of winning will be high. Additionally, fans often make lifetime 'once-for-ever' decisions on which clubs to support. Manchester has demonstrated its commitment to maintaining its quality over time, much as Nescafé does. Both of these factors are essential to fans shunning their local teams in favour of Manchester. A final factor is that the choice of which team to support for many football fans is often random. Fans unable to make an immediate choice are influenced by which teams are doing well at the time of the decision, and over the century Manchester has been one of the most successful. Manchester United is well supported because it has always been well supported and that is the value of a strong brand.

Summary

'Doing First' is a credible and viable strategic approach. There are often circumstances and issues in which it is virtually impossible to disentangle the best course of action or outcome. Doing First enables organizations to try out marketing strategies and, with careful monitoring, assess the results. This is the way to test the boundaries of stretching a brand, the viability of new kinds of distribution channel, and so on and so on. However, Thinking First is still a necessity in establishing how you will define and measure the success of any Doing First strategy.

Simple rules

Marketing strategy as simple rules is about selecting a few key marketing strategic processes, crafting a handful of simple rules, and 'jumping in' rather than avoiding uncertainty. In many respects the approach is related to 'Doing First' aside from the main difference in that the rules are predefined. Companies like Vodafone and Yahoo! have excelled without the traditional advantages of superior resources or strategic positions. According to Eisenhardt and Sull (2001) the key to their success has been the use of simple rules.

On the surface companies pursuing simple rules appear to be have no strategy at all. For example, AOL has been called the 'cockroach of the Internet' for scurrying from one opportunity to the next. However, AOL has been pursuing a simple rules strategy unique to the company and such rules are hard to see from the outside. There are five kinds of simple rule: how-to, boundary, priority, timing, and exit.

How-to rules are about keeping managers organized enough to be able to seize opportunities. For example, Dell applies a rule that when any customer segment's revenue reaches $1 billion, the segment must be split into two halves.

Boundary rules help managers to pick the best opportunities based on geography, customers, or technology. Thus when Cisco decided on an acquisitions-led strategy its boundary rule was that any company acquired would have a maximum of 75 employees of whom 75 per cent had to be engineers. Another example is when Miramax, known for its creative and innovative films, decides on a film project. It has to satisfy four boundaries: (1) the film must revolve around the human condition such as love; (2) the main hero must be flawed in some way; (3) there must be a clear beginning, middle, and end; and (4) a firm cap on production cost must be established (e.g. the films *Shakespeare in Love*, *The Crying Game*, and *The English Patient*).

Priority rules are about allocating resources amongst competing opportunities. For example, Intel allocates manufacturing capacity based on a product's gross margin. This simple rule was the basis for the company's move from its traditional memory business to highly profitable microprocessors.

Timing rules relate to the rhythm of key strategic processes. For example many Silicon Valley companies set timing rules for NPD. When developers approach a deadline they are often forced to drop features in order to meet the schedule. Other companies have been known to set deadlines for geographic expansion, such as one new country to be targeted every two months. Timing rules help maintain momentum.

Exit rules are about pulling out from past opportunities. New initiatives might be dropped if set sales and profit goals are not being met. Some rules can be specific. At the Dutch hearing aid company, Oticon, product development is halted if any key team member decides to leave for another project.

How many rules are optimum? It would be ridiculous to have a thick manual of rules. Ideally companies should develop between two and seven rules and none should be complex—marketing strategic rules should be easy-to-follow directives. It is better to have fewer rules when the market is unpredictable and you need flexibility. The point about following simple marketing rules as a strategy is that once established the rules must be followed slavishly (Ten Commandments rather than options!). Also, when the rules go stale, they need to be changed. The basic tenet is that when business is complicated, marketing strategy should be simple.

Scenarios and Simple Rules

Scenarios are especially useful for Simple Rule (not just Thinking First) approaches as they can be used as triggers—that is, when events happen, the rules come into place. For example, Microsoft famously operationalized a long-standing scenario to develop and introduce its Explorer Web browser when Internet activity reached a crucial level. However, according to Schnaars and Ziamou (2001) writing scenarios has become an idiosyncratic process much like writing a novel—there are no standards for writing good scenarios.

There are three defining characteristics to scenarios. First, they are normally written as narratives, like Hollywood scripts, that provide an image of some kind of future end-state. Such scenarios are based on plots with beginnings, middles, and ends. The second characteristic is that scenarios are usually written in sets of three or four. The final element is that most scenarios provide a progression from the present to the future, rather than provide a single-point forecast. They weave a plot that connects a series of interrelated events. While there is a great deal of variety in scenario writing, when viewed as an aggregate, four steps can be observed.

The length of a scenario depends very much on the topic at hand. Generally they range from a few paragraphs to a few pages. Occasionally a very detailed scenario might run to 10+ pages, but that is rare.

The starting point for most scenarios is normally to identify the key drivers that will affect the issue at hand, thereby generating a list of trends or factors.

The next stage is normally to rank or combine all the identified drivers into a smaller, more meaningful set that can be used for structure. One popular scheme ranks by uncertainty and impact.

The third part is to write the scenario. Three scenarios remain the most popular ('best guess', 'base case', and 'middle ground'). However, the recent trend has been to broaden this to between two and five scenarios to avoid the good/bad/middle ground and to present more independent stand-alone options. Drilling down to just two scenarios overcomes the problem of focusing on the middle ground. Good practice is to identify the most likely scenario.

Finally, a single strategy has to be created to cope with the identified scenarios.

One of the key problems in scenario writing is the 'reduction problem' of reducing the multitude of plausible scenarios to between two and five. An easy way of doing this is to keep the initial analysis simple and to combine trends and events into logical themes. There is little to be gained from trying to separate the two approaches of 'future backward' and 'future forward' to solve reduction, as scenario writing is inevitably iterative of both. Users have the final problem of what to do when presented with a multitude of strategies. The options are: 'straddle'—develop a strategy that fits every eventuality; 'multiple'—pursue all scenarios until the outcome is clear; 'flexible'—target the best-guess outcome while making contingencies for the rest; and finally, 'focus', which is to pick one scenario alone, the most likely.

Summary

'Simple Rules' is an approach particularly well suited to complex markets. But how do you identify the Simple Rules to use? Clearly you need to Think First and establish your business model and propositions. Once you have done this you can identify, establish, and put your simple marketing strategy rules into place. To do this the much-neglected Thinking First art of scenarios can be utilized. Scenarios are often misunderstood as part of competitive marketing strategy but can aid a Simple Rules marketing strategy.

Postmodern

A completely different view of strategy is provided by the postmodern school. Underpinning the approach of postmodern marketing strategy is the proposition that buyers are increasingly sophisticated and cynical about 'regular' marketing. Wright (1985) has argued that consumers have to interpret and withstand marketers' sales appeals and that they develop knowledge and coping tactics to do so. 'Persuasion knowledge' helps consumers identify how, when, and why marketers try to influence them and helps them adaptively respond to persuasion attempts to achieve their own goals (Friestad and Wright, 1994). Developing this notion that consumers have developed 'schemer schema' or intuitive theories about marketers' attempts to influence them, they draw marketers' attention to 'folk' models of persuasion. These observe that consumers learn about persuasion in many ways: from everyday social encounters, from observing marketers and other persuaders, and from media commentary on marketing and advertising tactics. The diffusion of psychological concepts and language into our culture also plays a role, as does formal education in schools about marketing issues. Developing over time, consumers' persuasion knowledge is an important factor shaping their response to attempts to persuade (O'Donohoe, 2001). Individuals develop context-specific persuasion knowledge in situations that they frequently encounter. Marketing persuasion knowledge has migrated widely within our culture. Thus, when commercial television first appeared in 1955, its persuasive attempts were novel and powerful. People had never before experienced moving black and white commercials inside their own homes. However, since then cultural knowledge about television advertising and other marketing techniques has developed in greater depth. This knowledge has been based on the first insights that people had about the early commercials, derived from shared conversations as well as what they learnt from the occasional commentaries of professionals on marketing. With knowledge having passed between and within generations there is now a high degree of understanding of how marketing 'works' and postmodern marketing strategy argues that if you ignore this you run an increased risk of failure.

One of the leading proponents of the postmodern view, Stephen Brown (2001) argues that customer-centric marketing has gone too far and now places many companies in the position of Uriah Heep: 'unctuous, ubiquitous and unbearable'. His view is that people do not want the truth, the whole truth, and nothing but the truth. They certainly do not expect truth from marketers. People want marketing to be about glitz and glamour and to be mischievous and mysterious. Marketing should be fun, but in the current politically correct climate any nastiness is forbidden. Contemporary consumers find marketing's obsession with 'love, honour, and obey' embarrassing. They would prefer a lovable rogue to the Disneyfied version that is the norm of today. Retromarketing harks back to the 'good old bad days' when marketers were pranksters and proud of it. To go retro, marketers need to practice TEASE: 'tricksterism', entertainment, amplification, secrecy, and exclusivity.

Tricksterism has to be played as a postmodern joke. The film, *The Blair Witch Project* is a perfect example. Was it a snuff movie? Moreover, sneaky sales promotions are allowed where the gregarious round-buying barfly in the cool club turns out to be a sales rep. Tango's numerous attempts to trick its customers, leaving them 'Tango'd', qualifies, especially its bogus hotline for customers to notify the company of knockoffs of the brand that were not fizzy. It turned out to be a new non-carbonated version of the drink.

Entertainment is one of the major elements in retro's armoury according to Brown. Modern marketing is basically dull, as eschewed by Philip Kotler. Being the backbone of business and having to integrate all the other functions has left marketing a lacklustre enterprise. Marketing has forgotten how to flirt. The surreptitious and ambitious Web-based promotions to promote Spielberg's AI were highly entertaining. It involved using a Web-search discovery of a murder and a 'body' of clues to provide a perfect example of entertaining consumers rather than boring them.

Amplification is about ensuring that the hot ticket or cool item is talked about and especially that the talking about is talked about. The idea is to turn a tiny advertising spend into a megabudget monster. Examples include Benetton, the Citroën Picasso, Calvin Klein, and Pizza Hut paying to place its logo on the side of a Russian rocket.

Secrecy in retro is the opposite of upfront and above board. It is best seen in 'secret' recipes for Coca-Cola, Heinz Ketchup, Kentucky Fried Chicken, and Mrs. Field's Cookies but can also be found in cosmetics and hideaway holiday packages. The consumer is engaged by secrecy and selling is enhanced.

Exclusivity is central to retro. 'Get it now while supplies last' replaces 'There's plenty for everyone'. It is practised for example by Beanie Babies, De Beers diamonds, Disney's videos, Harley, Harry Potter, the Honda Odyssey, and Mazda Miata. The end result is less inventory and consumers who luxuriate in feeling that they are the lucky few.

Brown (2003) offers another view of postmodern marketing strategy illustrated by an assessment of the marketing of Madonna. He argues that her phenomenal success relies upon the fact that people like to be shocked rather than upon her ability to shock them, as they enjoy being affronted and expressing outrage at her transgressions. Her marketing model is therefore antithetical to the traditional 4Ps model (of product, price, promotion, place), being based upon what he coins to be the 'Seven Ss' of subversion, scarcity, secrecy, scandal, sell-ebrity, storytelling, and sublimity.

Subversion relates to Madonna's contemptuous regard for her audience. Her approach is very much 'forget the consumer' and 'the customer isn't king'. With her 2001 'Drowned World' tour she regularly swore at the audience, refused to perform any of her greatest hits, and ended the show with a giant video clip telling the audience that she wasn't coming back and that they should go home.

Scarcity conveys her attempts to restrict supply to the marketplace. Rather than raise supply in response to demand, Madonna has done the opposite. She has only had five major tours in 20 years and performs on stage for about 90 minutes. As a result of this undersupply, her shows instantly sell out, she charges the highest ticket prices in the business, and her tours are extremely profitable despite the elaborate stage sets.

Secrecy relates to Madonna's carefully manufactured mystery. She constantly changes her image, has ambiguous lyrics and cryptic song titles, has married twice in extreme secrecy, and has 'predictably unpredictable' offstage behaviour.

Scandal is an essential ingredient in marketing Madonna. She is a master at scandal selling, that is, making a scandal carefully timed to coincide with the launch of a new product. For example in 1990 MTV banned her lesbian kiss video 'Justify My Love' with a publicity eruption that helped sell 400,000 copies of the $9.99 video. Ten years later her 'What it Feels Like for a Girl' video was banned on the basis of the amount of violence depicted in the film and the song duly went to number one in a chorus of cash registers.

Sell-ebrity refers to Madonna's ability to sell the selling of scandal rather than just selling scandal alone. For example when she attended the Academy Awards in 1991 with Michael Jackson on a 'date' it was clear to both the media and the public that the whole event was simply a stunt to publicize their latest projects. Nevertheless, it worked and attracted a media frenzy in its wake.

Storytelling or the creation of legends is an essential part of Madonna's marketing prowess. She has created a rags-to-riches myth that people buy into, along with a parade of personalities that go with her changing plots from 'Monroesque movie siren' to 'earth mother hippie chick'.

Sublimity relates to Madonna's ability to straddle different worlds from sacred and profane, gay and straight, parent and child, street chic and haute couture, material and ethereal and commerce, avant-garde and mainstream.

Summary

A 'postmodern marketing strategy' can provide insight into markets that strategists ignore at their peril. Most markets, be they business-to-consumer or business-to-business, have enormous levels of 'savvy.' Buyers are smart and have a good appreciation of the motives and methods of marketing strategies. The vast majority of marketers set out to create genuine value for their customers but strategies faced with increased suspicion and cynicism need increasingly to take into account the postmodern perspective. This can be achieved within a 'Thinking First' approach. The twist is that the end point of the strategy needs to engage, be interactive, and take into account the buyer's perspective.

Market-oriented strategy

Market-driven firms, such as Tesco and BMW, stand apart through their devotion to customer value and their culture, process, and abilities. Many firms attempt to adopt a market-oriented strategy, but according to Day (1998) many adopt one of three less successful orientations: the 'self-centred,' the 'customer compelled', and the 'sceptical'. Each orientation is a form of myopia that inhibits organizations from realizing the potential from their marketing strategy.

Successful organizations are the most prone to the self-centred trap as they take their place for granted. Generations of managers emphasize maximizing returns and have an increasingly inward focus until the original value proposition is distorted beyond recognition. IBM's orientation of the 1980s is a classic example: its strong profitability masked a total loss of focus as the company became distant, arrogant, and unresponsive. By 1990 it had squandered its trust with customers, with IBM-compatible competitors educating them on the alternatives.

Customer-compelled organizations try to be all things to their markets. This trap leaves most organizations unable to set priorities on which markets to serve. Compelled by customers, each function acts separately and tries to find new segments, features, or points of differences. Thus, IBM attempted to satisfy large and medium-sized customers in every industry in the early 1990s with a total offering that was incoherent.

The scepticism trap is a curious backlash to the customer focus. The assertion is that customers cannot envision breakthrough products and seldom ask for products that they later come to value. Customer research leads to bland offerings and is a distraction to the real work. For example, Motorola's research on the cellular phone concept was met with discouraging customer feedback. While such examples abound, Day considers that they miss the point. Truly breakthrough products require an intimate understanding of customer behaviour, latent needs, changing requirements, and deep-seated dissatisfaction with current alternatives. Thus, the potential fax machine market of the early 1970s was estimated based on the need for urgent written messages given existing technologies.

The desire to satisfy customers has a commonsense appeal as well as being likely to lead to greater loyalty and higher future profits than otherwise. Lots of companies have extensive and rigorous customer satisfaction measurements, but it is not always clear that the right variables are being measured or that the data are being used in anything other than a reactive way. The focus for many firms has been 'internal' (preventing dissatisfaction) rather than 'external' (increasing satisfaction). Too great an internal focus can lead to getting stuck in a customer satisfaction rut (Dahisten, 2003).

Volvo is generally regarded as a company at the forefront of customer satisfaction practices. Product quality is seen as equivalent to customer satisfaction within the company as noted in their policy: 'Customer satisfaction is the way we measure quality'. However, interviews amongst managers have revealed divergent views about what constitutes customer satisfaction. For example Dahisten (2003) found one manager who asserted that customer satisfaction 'equals no mistakes' whereas another saw it as more closely aligned with customer delight by defining it as: 'positively surprise the customer'. Other views were that it was, 'having the right range of attributes in the product profile', and somewhat tautologically, customer satisfaction 'is what is being measured'.

Unfortunately there is a range of variables that can influence customer satisfaction and measurement itself can sometimes take precedence. Volvo's measures are primarily quantitative (as with other car manufacturers) and it only uses qualitative measures occasionally, such as when designing new vehicles. Topics surveyed include satisfaction with the car, and sales and workshop experience. Owners are the primary subjects and comparisons with rival brands are made, in order to show Volvo's position. A huge volume of data is produced and largely analysed in a descriptive way. Managers rarely question the validity of the data. The data are used in an action-oriented approach rather than to enhance knowledge. Actions are generally focused on the short term and mainly on complaints.

Recognizing the need for a greater extrinsic focus to provide greater customer satisfaction insight, Volvo has recently added a more proactive approach to its research. Principally, qualitative measurement has been added to the mix with much greater direct customer contact involving engineering teams, senior managers, and dealers. Interactions with customers on the Web and through local workshops in different markets are being made so that customers' shifting perceptions of issues, such as safety, are being more strongly tracked. Lost-sales analyses have been instigated to capture the perceptions of customers who decided not to buy Volvo. Product development projects capture customer satisfaction issues at the development stage rather than only at production. This has been exemplified by Volvo's recent SUV, the XC90, which was developed from the beginning with customer satisfaction in mind, with the aid of a group of female customers in California.

Summary

A 'market-driven marketing strategy' has its weaknesses, but remains the primary approach. Marketing is an activity that continues to rely largely upon the successful generation and dissemination of, and response to market intelligence (see for example Matsuno and Mentzer, 2000). Marketing strategy, as suggested in this book, is part and parcel of a market-driven approach.

The book's perspective

The book takes a 'Thinking First' view of competitive marketing strategy from a market-driven perspective. The central structure of the book rests on the four central questions:

1. Where are we now?
2. Where do we want to be?
3. How will we get there?
4. Did we get there?

This is the most widely used competitive marketing strategy framework. See Figure 1.2, which identifies how the chapters fit the framework. The particular value of the where/where/how/did framework is that the four stages neatly define the necessary mindsets and place the associated key tools to develop the marketing strategy.

Another way of looking at the book's structure is provided in Figure 1.3. Here you will see a similar framework presented as a funnel. You can see that the key tools at **phase one** represent a narrowing of analyses and options. Every organization has to grapple with thousands of activities in its markets every day and so the starting point of any marketing strategy must be to gain a clear understanding of the key ones to include in the plan (events that are important and likely to happen) and items that are best to be cognizant of, and that are not necessarily to be included in the plan at the moment (events that are important but unlikely to happen), but that could become part of a scenario. **Phase two** continues with a further narrowing of options as the strategy is decided upon in terms of objectives, financial

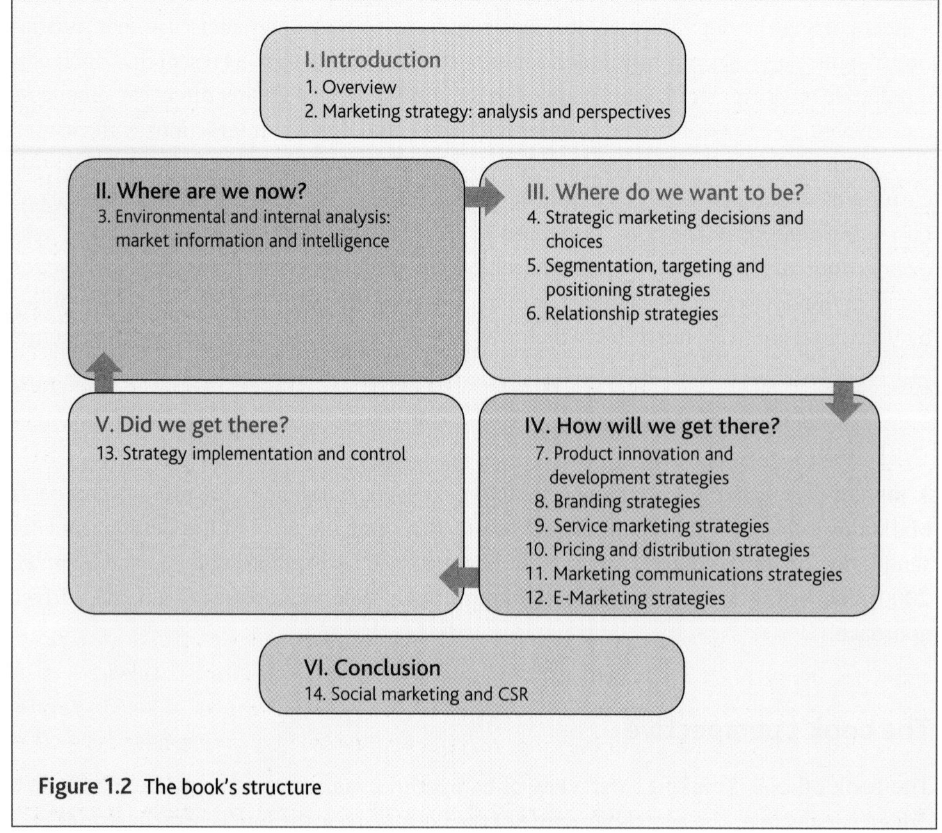

Figure 1.2 The book's structure

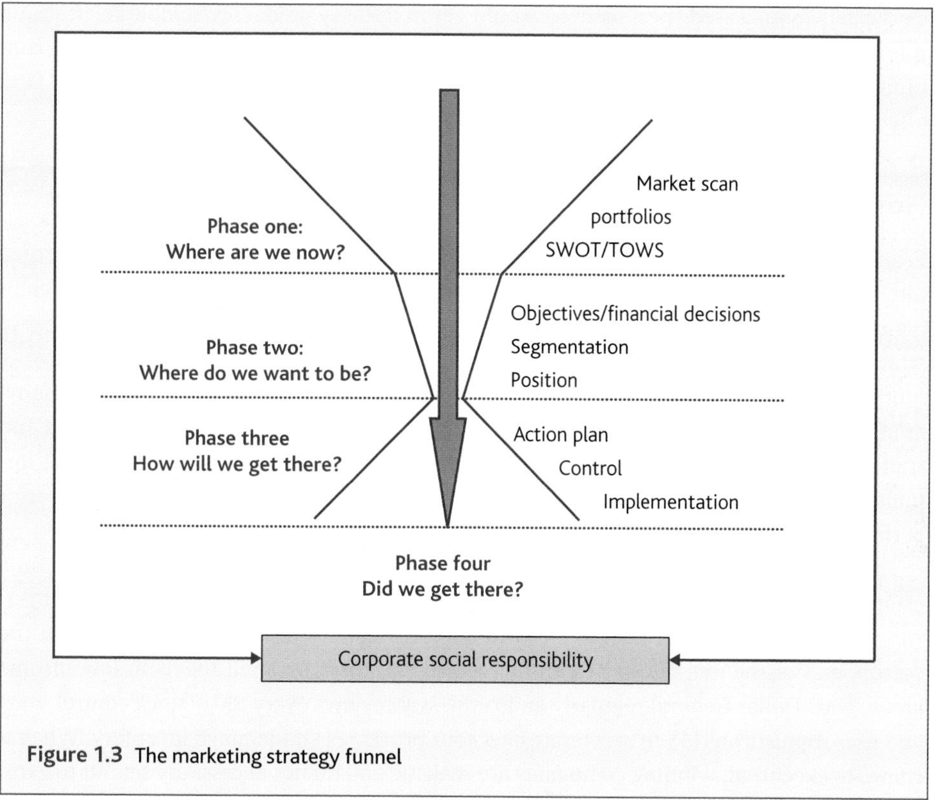

Figure 1.3 The marketing strategy funnel

decisions, segmentation, and positioning. These are the crucial and central decisions in the development of any competitive marketing strategy. The concern of **phase three** is, how will we get there? The focus in the book is on product innovation and development, branding, services, pricing and distribution, marketing communications, and E-marketing. Each of these is examined from a strategic rather than a tactical perspective. Finally, having decided on how to get there, the question of how to establish whether or not we got there is reviewed in **phase four**. Please also note that there is no separate consideration of international marketing strategy as it pervades the entire book. However, there is a focus upon Corporate Social Responsibility (CSR), see Chapter 14, given its rising importance in recent years.

What to choose

Considering marketing strategy overall, the key issue is to recognize the appropriate approach. Thinking First/Market orientation works best when the issues are clear, the data are reliable, the context is structured, thoughts can be pinned down, and discipline can be applied. On the other hand, Seeing First works best when many elements have to be creatively applied, commitment to solutions is key, and communications across boundaries are needed (e.g. in NPD). Doing First or Simple Rules work best when the situation is novel and confusing, complicated specifications would get in the way, and a few simple relationship rules can help move the process forward. The postmodern orientation needs to be continually borne in mind to provide a check on how, in reality, buyers will interpret the final offering.

How important is marketing strategy?

From a study of 160 companies between 1986 and 1996 Nohria et al. (2003) provide some interesting insights into the importance of strategy to any business. They found that companies that outperformed their rivals excelled at the four primary management practices of strategy, execution, culture, and structure. These were then supplemented by any two of four secondary management practices of talent (holding on to talented employees), innovation (industry-transforming), leadership (finding leaders committed to the business and staff), and mergers and acquisitions. They called this winning combination the '4 + 2 formula' for business success, and it was found to provide a 90% chance of sustaining superior performance.

The hallmark of effective strategy was found to be the ability to devise and maintain a clear focus. Success was be achieved by competing on low price, top quality, or great service. Dollar General, for example, consistently sold quality products at low prices at the bottom end of the market and carefully located its stores in small towns in low income areas. Thus Dollar General regularly and ruthlessly reviews every SKU (stock control unit) and uses sophisticated IT to accelerate checkout processes and manage inventory. When it comes to execution, winning companies are realistic and do not necessarily set out to excel at everything. They identify the key processes and make sure they efficiently meet customers' needs.

Winners developed and maintained a performance-oriented culture. Home Depot, for example, gives associates (a term applied to all employees) a sense of ownership of the stores. Store managers are allowed to determine their own layout and there is no sense of command-and-control leadership. In aggregate, 90% of winners linked pay to performance. With regard to structure, winners built and maintained fast, flexible, and flat organizations. Procedures and protocols were used, but winners trimmed as much red tape as possible for everyone, including vendors and customers.

Surprisingly, while winners were found to excel in the four primary areas, it did not make any difference which two secondary areas they chose (talent, innovation, leadership, and mergers and acquisitions) and there was no improvement if they went beyond 4 + 2. That is, whether they performed well in three or all four secondary areas, success only in two was all that was required. Strategy is thus at the core of business success.

Things that can go wrong

The reality is that the textbook approaches to strategy do not always work. Sometimes the problem is the strategy and sometimes the implementation, which begs an interesting question as to whether it would be better to have a great strategy with weak implementation or a weak strategy with great implementation. Let us assume you have a great strategy in place. Beer and Eisenstat (2000) have identified what they call 'six silent killers' of great strategy. These relate to management style, unclear strategy, ineffective management, vertical communications, cross-functional coordination, and down-the-line leadership. (See Mini Case Study 1.2.)

MINI CASE STUDY 1.2 'Flash rat shows its teeth'

'Flash as a rat with a gold tooth.' That description, applied to Cadillacs by the once-anarchic *Car* magazine, has stuck with me over the years as the most evocative label ever applied to retired Florida golfers' favoured mode of transport. *Car* magazine had a point.

The Cadillacs of the 1970s and 1980s it was describing had been progressively toned down from Cadillac's wildest excess: the Eldorado Biarritz convertible of 1959. That was nearly 20ft long, had more rocketship tailfins than Apollo 12 and might have made even Batman envious were not the usual colour a rather whimsical shade of pink. The smaller Sevilles and Eldorados that followed shrunk their tailfins and lost much of their bulk. But in European eyes they remained bad taste, badly-built and requiring a yacht skipper's certificate rather than a driving licence to lurch around in one.

By the mid-1990s, however, the powers-that-be within Cadillac's parent, General Motors, had convinced themselves that the then-latest edition of the Seville, with front wheel drive, a reasonably potent engine and (by US standards) restrained styling was ready to do battle with BMW and Mercedes-Benz in their own backyard. It wasn't. The build quality had improved but ride, handling and refinement were not a patch on European rivals. Anything resembling a marketing strategy was notable by its absence. The resulting flop—only a few hundred were sold—saw the humiliated Cadillac men rowing back across the Atlantic to the safety of Market America.

It has taken a decade for them to pluck up courage to come back—and only then by hiding behind the Dutch. Well, one Dutchman in particular: a hearty, jovial character called Gerard Jansen. Jansen is chief operating officer of Cadillac and Corvette Europe. His task is to convince sceptical/bored/desperate European drivers of the more affluent persuasion that the last thing they need is yet another bloody BMW. And that what they really want is to be bold, different and dashing behind the wheel of Cadillacs like no others that have gone before.

Jansen's stylish mode of dress—much more Milan than Motown—makes him appear an unlikely GM 'suit'. His business card confirms it. Cadillac and Corvette Europe is owned not by General 'Junk Bond' Motors but by an independent Dutch group, Kroymans. GM, its confidence shot to pieces by the 1990s Seville debacle, has recruited expert mercenaries to lead Cadillac back into Eurobattle.

It looks a good choice. Kroymans is long-established and one of Europe's biggest retailers of other premium car brands, including Ferrari, Maserati, Jaguar and Aston Martin. It is also prepared to put its money where Cadillac's grille is, investing, alongside dealers, in a network of large, glitzy 'experience centres' to show GM's presumed finest at their best.

Quite how many Euro-drivers might be won over is exceptionally hard to tell. For a start, there's the styling—all highly subjective, of course, but in this case first impressions will most surely count. Without question, the two models forming the heart of the range and expected to provide the bulk of sales, the CTS saloon and its larger stablemate, the STS, proved real head turners on both Dutch and British roads. The trouble is, the double-takes could have stemmed from admiration, amazement, puzzlement, disbelief, derision—or anything in between.

You are either going to like the grinning Cheshire cat looks of the Cadillac 'family' front end or, if not quite loathe it, be left absolutely cold by it. The same goes for the odd angles and creases that make up the body styling not just of the CTS and STS, but of the roadster, sports-utility vehicle and Swedish-built BLS medium saloon all soon to join the range. For me it's the Kryton school of styling; a bit too much like the creased cranium of the robot in space TV series 'Red Dwarf'.

On other major counts—performance, ride and handling, refinement, interior design—both cars make a case for themselves to European buyers stronger than anyone had a right to expect after the Seville letdown.

Pushed hard by leaden-footed motoring hacks, the 2.8 and 3.6 litre V6 engine options available in the CTS and the 4.6 litre additional option for the larger STS, have a more raucous, hard-edged note than the BMW 5 Series, E-Class Mercs and similar, which make up the European opposition. In real world usage however, with the engine not bouncing off the rev limiter, all versions are satisfyingly swift and more than acceptably quiet.

The big surprise is in ride and handling. Be unwise enough to say, 'hey, it's pretty good' to an engineer on the Euro-Cadillac team and he will nail your ears to the wall for an hour while he tells you how it's been honed to perfection by four years of thrashing prototypes, not in the US, but on demanding European roads and race tracks such as the Nurburgring.

Human capacity for self-delusion is infinite; and perfecting the cars' dynamic performance certainly is not. But the crucial point is that it's near enough to the Euro-pack not to be badly embarrassed. Leaving the styling issue aside, so is the rest of the package. Not least, no longer should anyone feel the need to wear checked trousers and white fringed brogues to match the CTS and STS interiors.

Where the cars punch their greatest weight is in price. All versions come loaded as standard with the equipment most companies list as options. In the UK the CTS starts at a list price of £ 24,850 and [is] now produced with right-hand drive; the STS at £ 29,850. The like-for-like price advantage over Eurorivals is about £ 5,000; higher for top-spec versions of the STS.

The downside is that there will be far fewer dealers than [for] BMW or Mercedes, making maintenance more complicated and steeper depreciation more likely. The situation should be helped in the UK, by Pendragon, the country's biggest multifranchise dealer group, having taken on sales and after-sales responsibility.

In any case, GM's European ambitions for Cadillac appear modest enough. The intention is to sell 4,000 across Europe in the current year, through a network of 175 dealers, which should be in place by the start of 2006.

By the end of the decade, says Jansen, that number should be up to 20,000 at least. 'What we're doing today is not for the short term. We are part of a growth strategy to make Cadillac a credible premium brand world-wide. We know it will take five to 10 years.'

Source: John Griffiths (2005), *Financial Times*, 30 July, p. 5.

Take the case of Apple Computers, which, according to Beer and Eisenstat, up to the late 1980s illustrated the issue of lack of strategic consensus and clarity and how this undermined effective upward communication. Until 1990 senior managers failed to seriously consider opening up the architecture by licensing the operating system or moving from high-end to middle to low-end customer-driven strategies. This failure to act occurred against the backdrop of the opening up the PC architecture since the early 1980s. Unfortunately there was no open dialogue at Apple. One manager reportedly said: 'For two and a half years I wanted to do low cost Macintoshes. I was always yelled at by senior managers that this was wrong.' A 1990 survey of the company revealed that many Apple employees saw senior managers as unconnected.

Many CEOs avoid open discussion, which may challenge their authority, and down-the-line managers are often too worried to tell. Managerial replacement can be effective because new managers are not directly implicated in the problems of the 'old regime'. They do not share the same mental models and often initiate a new direction. At first organizations embrace such change, but over time the silent killers re-emerge and the 'honeymoon' ends. The new leaders become identified with the new difficulties and, once again, employees at lower levels will be fearful to talk and enter into open discussion. Replacing the CEO is a short-term measure but does not build new embedded organizational capabilities.

Engagement is the only sustainable approach where both senior and lower-level staff together confront the silent killers. Each silent killer has its own strategic response:

1. Top-down or laissez-faire leadership needs to be turned into engaged leadership, creating an enabled, delegated, and accountable structure of authority.
2. Unclear strategy and conflicting priorities need compelling business direction.
3. An ineffective senior management team needs to transform itself into a truly effective one—which may take time.
4. Poor vertical communication needs to be turned into an honest and fact-based one.
5. Poor coordination across functions, businesses, or borders needs to be replaced with teamwork, by realigning roles and responsibilities and accountability—get the right people together to work on the right things.
6. Inadequate down-the-line leadership skills need to be transformed into strong leadership with a general management perspective. This might need just-in-time coaching and targeted recruitment. Those unable to make the grade will need to be replaced.

The evidence suggests than when the top team follows the six principles to overcome silent killers it has a chance of succeeding. However, not all organizations overcome them. There must be a compelling business reason or it simply will not happen.

A note on organization

It is extremely difficult to develop and implement a successful marketing strategy without a sense of direction as managers, in order to lead effectively, need to find ways to motivate and gain commitment to organizational goals. At the same time there is a great deal of confusion about what does and does not work, and several thousand books on leadership are published each year. It is well known that leaders need authority, strategies, energy, and vision. Take the case of Microsoft. Until the mid-1990s Microsoft was a freewheeling environment—with some hallmarks of innovation and speed—but other practices that generated pure chaos and impeded quick decisions and creativity, according to Herbold (2002). Planning was a mess and finances were ad hoc. Apparently at one meeting Bill Gates asked the Chief Financial Officer and his team where Microsoft stood. 'So where are the results? I know they're in your laptop somewhere. Come on, guys, do you want me to go in there and figure out how to piece it all together myself? Do you want me to write the code? I'll do it over the weekend!' Furthermore, globally, when it came to financial reporting, Microsoft's operating units acted independently. They did things their own way. Weeks had to be spent harmonizing disparate data before the quarterly books could be closed. Procurement practices were equally diverse. Just about anyone at Microsoft with a *Yellow Pages* and a phone was a purchasing agent. Their primary goal was to get the goods in to do a job rather than paying vendors, which meant suppliers often remained unpaid for up to nine months. Human resource management was equally eclectic. At one sales meeting, the then Head of Sales found his managers did not know how many staff they each had. On receiving various answers he pointed out: 'Look, maybe we should suspend the meeting for three hours. All of us can go back to our building and count heads to find out how many people you actually have.'

A single, global, financial reporting system was created in the mid-1990s and implemented in a year, based on packaged software from an outside vendor. The books could now be closed in three days instead of 21. Two standardized procurement systems were put in place. One was based on the Web and allowed employees from all over the world to order what they needed. The second system automated the invoices and matched the order. Both were run on one database with very few people required to oversee it. An HR system was implemented to track the number of employees, their status, business unit, and function. It also enabled the integration of new employees. The system went further and introduced a new evaluation and reward system for employees. This enabled Microsoft to put in place strategic planning processes with a rolling three-year plan based on a range of performance indicators.

Conclusion

Developing a marketing strategy is a largely subjective activity. This book suggests that 'Thinking First' is the best model to adopt based upon rational and linear thinking. Nevertheless, this chapter has recognized from the outset that while Thinking First dominates our view of marketing strategy, there are alternative approaches. Seeing First suggests a single glance at the organization and its market to produce the key flash of insight into the central strategy. For example the flash of insight from Stelios with his easyGroup was that the market wanted something simple. The Group has kept to this formula with its stable of companies such as easyJet, easyInternetCafe, easyCinema, easyCruise, and easyHotel. Doing First recognizes that seeing first is rarely straightforward. Quite often in strategy there is no clear way forward and so the best solution is to make a decision and to try and make sense of it. Then repeat the successful bits and leave out the rest. A number of companies have undertaken acquisition and mergers (A&M) on the basis of Doing First. Sometimes they work and sometimes they do not and it is not always clear what makes the difference. Often it is culture but it can be resources or market issues and it is only by trying out the A&M that such aspects are revealed, such is the complexity of the activity. Simple Rules have emerged as a strategic approach in recent years, particularly with the so-called new economy of the dot.coms. They are especially relevant to complex markets where triggers can be established to set strategies in motion. Thus a tea manufacturer might decide to introduce a herbal tea range if the market reaches a certain size or a rival does something similar. Once established such rules are not matters for debate but should be followed to the letter. Postmodern strategy offers a completely different view to Thinking First. The postmodern view of marketing is that the modern/scientific twentieth-century view of marketing is waning in impact as buyers know all the tricks of the trade. Even on the business-to-business side buyers are more aware of the techniques and practices of marketing, and more wary. With buyers being increasingly cynical and suspicious, the argument is that the tried and trusted tools of marketing strategy no longer have such saliency and certainly there are numerous examples where more irreverent approaches to the marketing of mainstream products have been successful (for example Tango). Postmodernism reminds us that Thinking First and the logical and rational development of marketing strategies can neglect the all-important question of how the intended audience will respond to the strategy. For example, a claim that a dishwasher tablet is 'new and improved' (even if true) may be greeted with tired derision. Having said that, there is nothing to stop a Thinking First approach arriving at a postmodern solution to a problem, if that is what is deemed best in the market.

Overall, the market-oriented strategy is the one preferred in this book based on the framework of: (1) Where are we now? (2) Where do we want to be? (3) How will we get there? and (4) Did we get there? Nevertheless, as shown in this chapter, in the rush towards a market-oriented strategy firms might adopt a less appropriate self-centred, customer-compelled, or sceptical orientation. Each one is a form of myopia that might inhibit marketing strategy. Furthermore, in the desire to satisfy customers, firms may not use the right kinds of measures to drive strategy.

Strategy has been shown to be a fundamental component of business success along with execution, culture, and structure. Of course all four elements are strongly intertwined. Things can go badly wrong—such as with poor vertical communications or conflicting priorities and, as noted towards the end of the chapter, it is vital to have well-run reporting systems that work.

Summary

This chapter has taken a somewhat 'left field' and alternative view of strategy to that taken in the rest of the book. Given that the book is devoted to a 'Thinking First' and rational view of marketing strategy, this opening chapter has taken the opportunity to review and discuss alternative approaches that are less mainstream. A bit like running before you can walk, 'Seeing First' or 'Doing First' are approaches to decision-making that normally need a sound understanding of 'Thinking First' to be successful. You need to know the rules before you should break them—you can break all the rules once you know what they are!

KEY TERMS

Thinking First Rationally addressing marketing strategy problems with a view to finding a solution.

Seeing First Appreciating the wider strategic picture with one glance based upon insight.

Doing First Making experimental strategic marketing decisions and learning from mistakes and successes.

Simple rules Identifying market triggers that set in motion key changes in strategy.

Scenarios Plausible written narratives based upon problems that exist in some small form today that may become unexpectedly important marketing problems in the future.

Postmodern A reaction to the 'modern' marketing practices of the twentieth century favouring a more ironic, cynical, and less scientific view of marketing.

DISCUSSION QUESTIONS

1 Examine the pros and cons of the Seeing First approach to strategy.

2 Imagine a chocolate manufacturer is going to launch an ice-cream based on its leading brand. It has decided there are too many uncertainties to be sure of the outcome and so is just going to 'do it' and see what happens. What kinds of things might it measure to see what did and did not work?

3 Would it be fair to say that there are more examples of postmodern approaches to strategy in consumer than in business markets? If so, why?

4 Write a short (single) scenario on one of the following markets with implications for marketing strategy:

   (a) The personal digital audio player.
   (b) The hybrid (part petrol engine/electric battery) car.
   (c) Convenience food.

ONLINE RESOURCE CENTRE

Visit the Online Resource Centre for this book for lots of interesting additional material at: **www.oxfordtextbooks.co.uk/orc/west/**

REFERENCES AND FURTHER READING

Beer, Michael, and Russell A. Eisenstat (2000), 'The Silent Killers Of Strategy Implementation and Learning', *Sloan Management Review*, Summer, 41 (4), pp. 29–40.

Brown, Stephen (2001), 'Torment Your Customers (They'll Love It)', *Harvard Business Review*, October, pp. 83–8.

Brown, Stephen (2003), 'Material Girl or Managerial Girl?', *Business Horizons*, July–August, pp. 2–10.

Dahisten, Frederik (2003), 'Avoiding the Customer Satisfaction Rut', *MIT Sloan Management Review*, Summer, pp. 73–8.

Day, George S. (1998), 'What Does It Mean To Be Market-Driven?', *Business Strategy Review*, Spring, pp. 1–14.

Eisenhardt, Kathleen M., and Donald N. Sull (2001), 'Strategy as Simple Rules', *Harvard Business Review*, January, pp. 107–16.

Friestad, Marian, and Peter Wright (1994), 'The Persuasion Knowledge Model: How People Cope with Persuasion Attempts', *Journal of Consumer Research*, 21, pp. 1–31.

Geroski, Paul A. (1999), 'Early Warning Of New Rivals', *Sloan Management Review*, 40 (3), pp. 107–16.

Gofee, Robert and Gareth Jones (2000), 'Why Should Anyone Be Led By You?', *Harvard Business Review*, Sept–Oct, pp. 63–70.

Hamel, Gary (1999), 'Bringing Silicon Valley Inside', *Harvard Business Review*, September–October, pp. 70–84.

Herbold, Robert J. (2002), 'Inside Microsoft: Balancing Creativity and Discipline', *Harvard Business Review*, January, pp. 73–9.

Matsuno, Ken, and John T. Mentzer (2000), 'The Effects of Strategy Type on the Market Orientation-Performance Relationship', *Journal of Marketing*, 64 (4), pp. 1–16.

Mintzberg, Henry, and Frances Westley (2001), 'Decision Making: It's Not What You Think', *MIT Sloan Management Review*, 42, Spring, pp. 89–93.

Nohria, Nitin, William Joyce, and Bruce Robertson (2003), 'What Really Works', *Harvard Business Review*, July, pp. 42–53.

O'Donohoe, Stephanie (2001), 'Living With Ambivalence: Attitudes to Advertising in Postmodern Times', *Marketing Theory*, 1 (1), pp. 91–108.

Schnaars, Steven, and Paschalina (Lilia) Ziamou (2001), 'The Essentials of Scenario Writing', *Business Horizons*, 44 (4), July–August, pp. 25–31.

Szymanski, Stefan (1998), 'Why Is Manchester United So Successful?' *Business Strategy Review*, 9 (4), pp. 47–54.

Wallas, G. (1926), *The Art of Thought* (New York: Harcourt Brace).

Wright, Marian (1985), 'Schema Schema: Consumers' Intuitive Theories about Marketers' Influence Tactics', in *Advances in Consumer Research*, 13, Richard J. Lutz (ed.) (Provo, UT: Association for Consumer Research), pp. 1–3.

END OF CHAPTER 1 CASE STUDY

'Seeking new angles: Digital camera mania has forced film suppliers such as Kodak to find new ways to build their brands'

The rapid transition to digital media is throwing up some new brand winners, with Samsung and Apple among the most obvious beneficiaries.

But the shift has also claimed numerous victims. In the photography market, while camera makers such as Sony, Canon and Olympus have managed to establish themselves as digital photography brands, the move to digital has proved tumultuous for many film suppliers and photo-service providers such as Kodak.

Sales of digital cameras have soared in the past few years. Eight million digital cameras were sold in Europe in 2002: some 24m will be sold both in Europe and North America this year, according to industry estimates.

This has meant the need for photographic film has declined, as has the demand for professional photofinishing: in the past month, Kodak has been forced to close five laboratories in the UK alone, with the loss of 500 jobs. And Kodak plus other major photographic brands, including Fuji Film and Agfa, have been forced to take a careful look at their marketing strategies.

Fuji, for example, has never been in the retail film-processing business but has, for the past 20 years, concentrated on mini-labs, both analogue and digital, for high street photoshops, and now has some 20,000 installed.

With most of the digital photos being printed at home, computer printer brands such as Hewlett Packard, Epson and Lexmark have become strongly associated with digital photography.

According to Mette Eriksen, analyst with the consultancy Infotrends/CAP Ventures, some 70 per cent of European customers printed their photographs at home in 2003: 'At home, most consumers are using inkjet printers, and a small proportion are using dye sublimation printers.' (The latter are more expensive, but produce a result that is much closer to professional photofinishing.)

The emergence and rapid growth of unfamiliar brands such as Snapfish is symptomatic of the turmoil surrounding the photographic industry. Virtually unknown only four years ago, Snapfish now claims to be the leading online photoservice in North America, with more than 10m customers. It has just opened for business in the UK, where it clearly sees a void crying out to be filled.

Managing director Helen Vaid says: 'Online photoservices are not as established here as in the US, and customers are not so aware of the options open to them.' Snapfish's photofinishing processes are based on software developed by the company, but it still makes a marketing point of the fact that the digital images will be printed on Kodak paper.

Eriksen says that in the US, digital camera owners turn to retailers for print orders of 10 or more photos and use their home printers to make a small number of prints rapidly. She expects that the European market will follow the same trend. This is good news for the commercial photofinishers such as Snappy Snaps or Jessops, or online services such as BonusPrint or Ofoto (Kodak's own).

A more recent development, however, has been the advent of supermarkets' own-brand photoservices. Pixology, for example, a UK software company best known for a technology for eliminating 'red eye' in digital images, is providing the processing power for photokiosks in stores belonging to Dixons, Currys, John Lewis and, most recently, Tesco.

Pixology software is used to power digital photo kiosks in 165 Tesco stores: customers can insert their smart media cards, preview the images on screen and process their orders at a mini-lab in the store. The service, however, is Tesco branded.

David Honey, Fuji's UK general manager for photofinishing, admits the current situation is difficult for big film suppliers trying to maintain the strength of their brand. He says innovation, revenues and profit margins are all needed to provide the marketing that supports the brand.

Meanwhile Research group IDC forecasts home printing of digital photos will fall to 42 per cent by 2007. Honey also predicts that the novelty of printing at home will quickly wear off, and that only 10 per cent of photographs will be printed at home in the future: 'You can do it, but it's expensive, difficult and fiddly.'

So can the likes of Kodak and Fuji resurrect themselves as digital brands? James McConnell, head of Kodak in the UK, believes the company name is providing retailers with a measure of comfort: 'The Kodak brand is more important than ever. Retailers want a brand that means imaging.'

So Kodak is riding on all the horses: home printers and internet processing on the one hand, and in-store mini-labs and kiosks branded with the Kodak name on the other. Boots the chemist alone has some 1,400 Kodak-branded kiosks.

McConnell has just written to some 9,000 retailers in the UK outlining the company's plans to develop its kiosk business. And the own-brand operators? 'We've always had people who operated their own-label processing and printing,' he retorts.

Of course, the branding issue is just one of a number which are keeping the industry in ferment: how quickly will digital replace film? To print at home or via the net? Will cameraphones take the place of single-use cameras? 'These are lively topics, but we have far too many to discuss,' says Fuji's Honey, wearily. 'They're getting in the way of work.'

Source: Alan Cane (2004), *Financial Times*, 7 December, p. 14.

QUESTIONS

1. Write a brief statement providing your assessment of Kodak's strategic marketing options from a Seeing First perspective.
2. Make the hypothetical assumption that Kodak is unsure what it should do next. What strikes you, top-of-mind, as a good idea for Doing First? How might Kodak monitor whether or not it worked?
3. Look at the variety of data in the case. Using your judgement, develop a simple marketing strategic rule for Kodak that would affect the degree of its involvement in the home printing market.
4. From a postmodern perspective, might there be a role for any elements of TEASE or the Seven Ss in Kodak's digital strategy?

2

Marketing strategy: analysis and perspectives

LEARNING OBJECTIVES

- Provide an overview of the 'marketing' and 'strategy' concepts and discuss how the term strategy has migrated from military planning to the business field
- Review the nature and various definitions of marketing strategy
- Discuss the possible orientations of marketing strategy and establish what competitive marketing strategy is
- Review the linear models/frameworks for the strategy-making process

CHAPTER AT A GLANCE

Introduction

Marketing strategy has been the subject of considerable research in both the business and the marketing literature for the last three decades. It has become an area of primary concern to all organizations, depending critically on a subtle understanding and analysis of the market. The development of marketing strategy is essential for success not only in developed markets, where the competition can be intense and with every player attempting to gain market share, but also in emerging markets, where the elements of product, communications, and distribution are recognized as valuable sources for competitive advantage. This importance becomes even greater in the case of developing markets where local producers are coming under increasing pressure to become more competitive in order to face the intense competition from their foreign counterparts. No doubt the presence and success of such global companies as McDonald's, Toyota, Vodafone, and HSBC in the Middle East countries have forced local companies to search for new competitive advantages through the effective use of their marketing resources. In fact increased competition from abroad, coupled with environmental uncertainties, present a formidable challenge to the business community in these markets to formulate and implement their marketing strategy more effectively.

Marketing strategy: different perspectives

The starting point, before we review some of the available definitions of marketing strategy, is to look at the nature and concept of the two terms 'marketing' and 'strategy'.

What is marketing?

Under this question Baker (1992) describes marketing as an enigma that 'at the same time is both simple and complex; straightforward and intricate, a philosophy or state of mind and dynamic business function; it is new and it is as old as time itself'. Marketing is therefore precisely what you want it to be, and thereby everything or nothing. People would respond to this question with a variety of descriptions: selling, advertising, promoting, and targeting but without doubt marketing encompasses many more activities than these.

Marketing has been defined as 'individual and organisational activities that facilitate and expedite satisfying exchange relationships in a dynamic environment through the creation, distribution, promotion and pricing of goods, services and ideas' (Dibb et al., 2001). This definition looks at marketing as a set of functional activities. From a different perspective, marketing has been defined as 'a social process by which individuals and groups obtain what they need and want through creating, offering, and freely exchanging products and services of value with others' (Kotler, 2000). Marketing in this definition is a process of exchanging benefits.

It should be emphasized that the marketing concept is not a second definition of marketing. The marketing concept is 'a way of thinking—a management philosophy guiding an organisation's overall activities. This philosophy which holds the key to achieving organisational goals consists of the company being more effective than competitors in creating,

TABLE 2.1 Contrasting operational and strategic marketing

Operational marketing	Strategic marketing
Action-oriented	Analysis-oriented
Existing opportunities	New opportunities
Non-product variables	Product market variables
Stable environment	Dynamic environment
Reactive behaviour	Proactive behaviour
Day-to-day management	Longer range management
Marketing department	Cross-functional organisation

Source: Lambin Jean-Jacques, Strategic Marketing Management, 5/e. © 1997. Reproduced by permission of McGraw-Hill Education, Inc.

delivering, and communicating customer value to its chosen target' (Kotler, 1994). The view of marketing as a business philosophy stimulated marketing researchers (e.g., Kohli and Jaworski, 1990; Narver and Slater, 1990; Morgan et al., 1998; Slater and Narver, 1994, 2000) to examine the contribution of marketing orientation to business performance (see p.39).

Marketing has also been defined and categorized as **operational marketing**—that is the classical commercial process of achieving a target market share through the use of tactical means related to the 4Ps, and **strategic marketing**—its task is to specify the firm's mission, define objectives, elaborate a development strategy, and ensure a balanced structure of the product portfolio (Lambin 1997). The roles of operational and strategic marketing are shown Table 2.1.

What is strategy?

The word *strategy* comes from the Greek word *strategos*, meaning a general in command of an army; it is formed from 'stratos', meaning army and 'ag', meaning to lead. Therefore, it was first defined in the ancient military dictionaries. Strategy was defined in military literature as 'a plan of attack for winning' or 'a plan for beating the opposition'. Similar definitions are still in use today. Researchers are still examining the effective application of strategy in the military field (Frentzel et al., 2000). The militaristic roots of the term strategy are well documented, with some key components of the military view of strategy having been transferred to business usage. In reflecting upon the link between military and business usage of the strategy concept, it has been claimed that the discourse and practice of strategy is distinctively a mechanism of power whether seen from either perspective (Horton, 2003).

The word 'strategy' appeared for the first time in business literature in 1952 in a book by William Newman. At the time strategy was implicitly seen as a plan for achieving organizational goals. The increasing pace of environmental change over the last three decades has forced management to make their strategies explicit and to change them frequently. Responding to such circumstances, academic interest in strategy has grown rapidly. It is not surprising today to find a profusion of books and articles on strategic planning, corporate strategy, business strategy, and marketing strategy—a fashionable word in business language.

There were a number of early attempts to present the concept of strategy in the business literature. Most notable are the pioneering contributions by Ansoff (1965), Andrews (1971), and Hofer and Schendel (1978). The contributions of those writers and others can be classified into three categories. In the first category are writers who produced analytical or rationalistic models, which, while precise, are neither sufficiently comprehensive nor useful enough for practice. In the second category are other writers who were more eclectic and introduced a range of frameworks that collectively define the underlying notion of strategy in business management. Finally, some writers have been primarily 'verbal' in presenting their understanding of strategy.

Early in the 1990s, strategy was defined as the means an organization uses to achieve its objectives. This definition did not establish a clear boundary between strategy and tactics and ignored the environmental dimension of strategy. What types of decisions are strategic, and what distinguishes these decisions from other operational decisions taken by organizations? This question is central in any discussion of strategy. For example, how could we describe the decision taken by Dell to adopt the 'direct-to-consumer' mode of delivery? Was it a strategic decision or something else?

Taking two dimensions into consideration, Grant (1995) defined strategy as 'the overall plan for deploying resources to establish a favourable position, while a tactic is a scheme for a specific action'. The task of strategy, in Grant's view, is to determine how the firm will deploy its resources within its environment and satisfy its long-term goals and how it will organize itself to implement that strategy. Adding a competitive dimension, Fifield and Gilligan (1998) defined strategy as 'the broad statement of the way in which the organisation sets out to achieve its objectives. Included within this would be a series of decisions on the markets in which the organisation will operate, the type of products/services it will offer and the basis of the competitive stance'. From a multi-angular view Mintzberg and Quinn (1996) proposed five definitions of strategy (5Ps)—as plan, ploy, pattern, position, and perspective—and looked at some of the interrelationships between them. The preceding definitions of strategy reflect that successful strategies typically consist of four key ingredients:

1. They are directed toward unambiguous long-term goals.
2. They are based on insightful understanding of the external environment.
3. They are based on intimate self-knowledge by the organization or individual of internal capabilities.
4. They are implemented with coordination and effective harnessing of the capabilities to achieve the competitive position targeted.

In similar vein, Fifield (1998) highlighted the most significant aspects of strategy as:

- longer term
- not changed every Friday
- not another word for important tactics
- not top management's secret
- not a public relations exercise

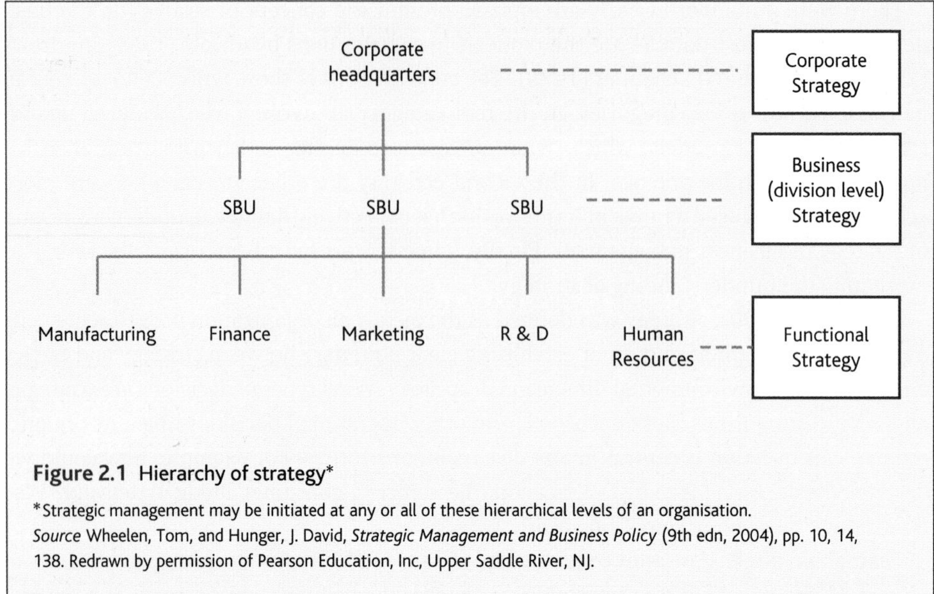

Figure 2.1 Hierarchy of strategy*

*Strategic management may be initiated at any or all of these hierarchical levels of an organisation.
Source Wheelen, Tom, and Hunger, J. David, *Strategic Management and Business Policy* (9th edn, 2004), pp. 10, 14, 138. Redrawn by permission of Pearson Education, Inc, Upper Saddle River, NJ.

- based on analysis, not straws
- essential to an organization's survival

Having reviewed the definitions of strategy, more generally, in terms of its dimensions and components, we can also define strategy in terms of three organizational levels: the *corporate, business*, and *functional* levels. Figure 2.1 shows this hierarchical relationship.

Corporate strategy

This describes a company's overall direction in terms of its general attitude toward growth and the management of its various businesses and product lines to achieve a balanced portfolio of products and services. Additionally, it is (a) the pattern of decisions regarding the types of business in which a firm should be involved, (b) the flow of financial and other resources to and from its divisions, and (c) the relationship of the corporation to key groups in its environment. In a drastic change to the company corporate strategy, AT&T decided to obtain local access for its long-distance customers and chose to acquire the USA's biggest cable operators, TCI and Media One, for $110 billion. These acquisitions put AT&T directly into the booming Internet business. This was a significant advantage stemming from the company's corporate strategy.

Business strategy

Sometimes called competitive strategy, business strategy is usually developed at divisional level and emphasizes improvement of the competitive position of a corporation's products or services in the specific industry or market segment served by that division. Just as corporate strategy asks what industry the company should be in, business strategy asks how the company or its strategic business units (SBUs) should compete or cooperate in each industry. In order for AT&T to achieve its corporate objective described above, should the company purchase more cable companies (very expensive), form strategic alliances with cable companies (many of which are not interested), or should it try something different? Business strategies should also integrate various functional activities to achieve divisional objectives.

Functional strategy

This is concerned with maximizing resource productivity. Within the constraints of the corporate and business strategies under which they work, functional departments, such as marketing, finance, R&D, and production, develop strategies to pull together their various activities and competencies to improve performance. But where should a function be housed? Should it be integrated within the organization or purchased from an outside contractor? Some writers suggest that organizations should purchase from outside only those activities that are not critical factors in the company's distinctive competencies. Otherwise the company may give up the capabilities that made its success in the first place. Therefore, outsourcing decisions are at the top of the agenda of major corporations. A recent survey in the USA showed that 94% of US firms outsource at least one activity. The outsourced activities found are general and administrative (78%), human resources (77%), information systems (63%), distribution (66%), manufacturing (56%), marketing (51%), and finance and accounting (18%) (Wheelen and Hunger, 2004).

The three levels of strategy form a hierarchy of strategy development within any large corporation. They interact closely and constantly and must be well integrated for corporate success.

Marketing strategy: nature and definitions

Most writers on the subject of marketing strategy typically start with a broad encompassing statement of what they consider it to be, then move on to explain the detailed issues which they prescribe as constituting a marketing strategy. In the early 1980s, marketing strategy was defined as an indication of how each element of the marketing mix will be used to achieve the marketing objectives. This view gave prominence to the marketing mix and, therefore, saw the utilization of the mix elements as the marketing strategy.

Forbis and Mehta (1981) also emphasized an orientation to the marketing mix, but broadened the definition to utilize the concept of positioning by introducing the term economic value to the customer (EVC). Their definition advocates the use of market segmentation and hence includes market positioning. Four major bases have frequently been used in explaining the detail of marketing strategy: the marketing mix, the product life cycle, market share and competition, and positioning. Marketing strategy was seen as part of the long-term operational planning of the marketing function.

Focusing on the functional level of planning, marketing strategy was defined as 'the broad conception of how product, price, promotion and distribution are to function in a co-ordinated way to overcome resistance to meeting marketing goals' (O'Shaughnessy, 1995). This view shows how the proposed key features of the firm's offerings (the 4Ps) are intended to achieve the marketing and company objectives. Another view sees marketing strategy as a means that defines the specific market toward which activities are to be targeted and the types of competitive advantages that are to be developed and exploited (Dibb et al., 2001).

This definition advocates the use of the market segmentation concept and, hence, the competitive advantages are directed to the specific market segment/s.

All the above definitions see marketing strategy as one of the firm's functional strategies. The differences between the definitions may be attributed to the type of marketing strategy being defined. Baker (1992), for example, at a very simple level, isolated and defined three basic marketing strategies—undifferentiated, differentiated, and concentrated. The three strategies are similar to the generic strategies suggested by Porter; low-cost, differentiation, and focus. The classic 2×2 matrix introduced by Ansoff enables two marketing strategies to be identified: the market-penetration strategy and the market-development strategy. In terms of targeting and positioning, the marketing targeting strategy selects the people (or organizations) that the management wishes to serve in the product market. Once the company's product markets are identified and their relative importance to the firm determined, management selects the targeting strategy. This decision is the focal point of marketing strategy. The marketing positioning strategy is the combination of product, channel of distribution, price, and promotion strategies a firm uses to position itself against its key competitors in meeting the needs and wants of the target market. The positioning strategy provides the unifying concept for deciding the role of each component of the marketing mix.

Earlier Ries and Trout (1981: 219) stated that 'positioning strategy is thinking in reverse. Instead of starting with yourself, you start with the mind of prospect. Instead of asking what you are, you ask what position you already own in the mind of prospect'. Thus the concept of positioning goes beyond image creation, which merely identifies the attributes that are strengths, to provide guidance on which attributes should be used in the positioning/repositioning strategy.

Pulling all these together, it has been suggested that numerous marketing strategies exist in the categories of market, product line, distribution, pricing, advertising, and promotion. When market and product are combined this will produce a *market penetration/development strategy* by which a company can capture a large share of an existing market for its current products or develop markets for its current products. Producers of consumer products such as P&G, Unilever, and Colgate-Palmolive are very experienced in using advertising and other communication tools to implement a market-penetration strategy to gain the dominant market share in a market. By means of a *product-development strategy* a company can develop new products for existing markets or develop new products for new markets. The Sara Lee Corporation uses its successful brand name 'Sara Lee' to promote other products such as premium meats and fresh baked food products.

Adopting the same way of classification enables other marketing strategies to be used. For example, combining promotion and distribution, a company can choose between a *push* and a *pull* marketing strategy. Most of the large fast-moving goods (FMG) companies follow a push strategy by spending a great amount of money on a particular trade sector to gain/hold shelf space in major retail outlets. Also, with pricing and distribution, a company may adopt either *skim pricing*, that is, charging differentiated (high) prices to customers who are willing (and can afford) to pay a premium for top-quality products/services (e.g. BA which—arguably—targets particular segments of the market and charges them differentiated prices) or *penetration pricing*, that is, charging lower prices to gain market share (e.g. KLM which adopts a range of prices that suit most customers) (Wheelen and Hunger, 2004). (For another example see Mini Case Study 2.1.)

MINI CASE STUDY 2.1 'Demand exists for premium airlines'

In his article, 'Low fares are the only way to an air passenger's heart', Mr Aline van Duyn raises a number of interesting issues regarding the situation of the global airline industry. I think, however, that some of the views expressed need to be put into perspective. It is claimed that the industry has lost its glamour and, strangely, the established airlines seem to get the blame for this, whereas they are the only ones that still offer a product for the more demanding traveller. Mr van Duyn claims that air travel should be all about getting from A to B. Untrue, as it is the consumer who decides what air travel should be about.

It is everyone's right to take a bet and ride on a low-cost jet full of noisy holidaymakers. And without any doubt, low-cost travel in some form or another will also go long-haul sooner or later. But if our more demanding travellers want extra flexibility, premium comfort, or just a superior experience, be it short- or long-haul, why should they not be able to have it? And why should an established airline not be allowed to offer them the product they are prepared to pay for?

The tremendous success of upmarket premium economy products, of business class-only flights, and in general of prestigious carriers from the Middle East and Asia proves that there is a solid demand for something else than plain low-cost travel. Why else would we have luxury hotels if all one cared about was getting a night's sleep? And what would be the purpose of top-notch restaurants if it was all just about downing a meal?

Contrary to claims, the discrepancy between the high margins of low-cost carriers and the poor profitability of established airlines has nothing to do with the culture of flying. The problem is that network carriers, as opposed to low-cost carriers, need a much higher critical mass to break even. Bringing their fares down will not save them. In the end, only a further consolidation will.

Source: Christopher Klenner (2004), *Financial Times*, 5 September.

Marketing Strategy Development

The development of marketing strategy can be seen at three main levels. At the first, the core strategy of the company is selected, and the marketing objectives and the broad focus for achieving them are identified. At the next, market segments and targets are selected and the company's differential advantage in serving the customer targets better than the competition is identified. Taken together the identification of targets and definition of differential advantage constitute the creation of the competitive positioning of the company and its offerings. At the third level, a marketing department capable of putting the strategy into practice must be created. The marketing department, at this stage, is responsible for developing the marketing mix programmes that can convey both the positioning and the products/services to the target market (Hooley et al., 1998). Applying this structural concept of marketing strategy development to British Airways (BA), we can see that at the first level the company's core strategy and marketing objectives have been set to ensure

TABLE 2.2 Selecting and developing marketing strategies for different market and competitive situations

	Important issues	Major actions/Decisions
Product-market definition and analysis	• Evaluating the complexity of the product-market structure. • Establishing product-market boundaries	• Defining product-market structure • Customer profiles • Industry/distribution/ competitor analysis • Market size estimation
Market segmentation	• Deciding which level of the product-market to segment. • Determining how to segment the market	• Select the basis of segmentation • Form segments • Analyse segments
Define and analyse industry structure	• Defining the competitive area • Understanding competitive structure • Anticipating changes in industry structure	• Sources of competition • Industry structure • Strategic group analysis
Competitive advantage	• Deciding when, where, and how to compete	• Finding opportunity gaps • Cost/differentiation strategy/focus • Good/better/best brand positioning strategy
Market targeting and positioning strategies	• Deciding market scope • Good/better/best brand positioning strategy	• Selecting targets • Positioning for each target • Positioning concept • Marketing mix integration

Source: Cravens, David W, *Strategic Marketing*. © 1994. Reproduced by permission of McGraw-Hill Education, Inc.

that BA is the customer's first choice through the delivery of an unbeatable travel experience. At the next level, BA has elected to provide overall superior service and good value for money in every market segment in which it competes. At the third level, BA's marketing programmes (including advertising, pricing, distribution, and customer service) have been designed to support its product/service positioning at the forefront of the globalization of the airline industry. BA's marketing strategy is geared to sustaining a significant presence in the world market by emphasizing consistent quality of customer service and the delivery of value for money.

Cravens (1994) has suggested a step-wise approach to the development of marketing strategy for different markets and competitive situations. This approach is shown in Table 2.2, which presents the sequential steps to developing a marketing strategy, a summary of the important issues to be considered at each step, and the major actions/decisions that are required.

Table 2.2 also illustrates the role marketing can play in creating a competitive advantage and developing a marketing strategy. This role has been acknowledged by Weinrauch et al. (1991)—in small industrial manufacturers—and Quinn and Humble (1993)—in the service industry.

Marketing strategy orientation

It is useful at this point to shed light on the different orientations of marketing strategy. Should the development of marketing strategy be oriented by consideration of customers, competitors, or both? Luck et al. (1989) distinguished between consideration of consumers and the competitive orientation of marketers observing what rival firms or brands are doing, anticipating their moves, and setting objectives for surpassing them. In the late 1970s, a competitive orientation was seen as preferable to a customer orientation. In the early 1990s, it was argued that companies need to pay equal attention to both customers and competitors, that is, to adopt a *market* orientation.

How significant is the adoption of a *market orientation* on firms' performance? The results of empirical research in this field vary. For example, Kohli and Jaworski (1990) found that a market orientation provides a unifying focus for the efforts and projects of individuals, thereby leading to superior performance. Similar results were found by Narver and Slater (1990), who concluded that a market orientation has, in some cases, a substantial positive effect on profitability. A subsequent study by Slater and Narver (1994) found that a market-oriented culture provides the foundation for value-creating capabilities which enable businesses to consistently deliver superior value (that is, competitive advantage which leads to the achievement of superior performance) to customers.

On the other hand, Armstrong and Collopy (1996) examined the relationship between a firm's profitability and a competitor orientation and claimed that the development of competitor-oriented objectives is detrimental to profitability and, therefore, firms should look beyond their competitors when setting objectives and focus directly on profit maximization!

What is competitive marketing strategy?

The answer to this question is not as easy as it seems at first sight but requires further analysis and discussion. The starting point is to dismantle the term 'competitive marketing strategy' and define what 'competitive strategy' is. We then look at the preceding definitions of 'marketing strategy' before establishing what we mean here by 'competitive marketing strategy'. Is it a typical marketing strategy orientated by competition in the marketplace? Or is it a competitive strategy with a marketing orientation?

The definition of competitive strategy

In the hierarchy of strategy development business unit strategy sits between the high level of corporate strategy and the detailed strategies for individual functions. Based on this and for the purpose of defining business strategy, Doyle (1998) pointed out that while corporate strategy sets the broad direction for the company, business strategy details how a sustainable competitive advantage (SCA) can be achieved, allowing the strategic business unit

(SBU) to contribute to the overall corporate objectives. While this view implicitly refers to the competitive dimension of business strategy, other authors have explicitly defined business strategy as a competitive strategy. El-Morsy (1986), for example, suggested that 'competitive strategy is a business strategy that discerns the basic forces affecting competitive conditions and their underlying structural causes, identifying the particular strengths and weaknesses of the firm vis-à-vis each underlying structural cause and determining offensive and defensive tactics for creating and maintaining a competitive position over time'.

Aaker (2001) pointed out that business strategy, which is sometimes termed competitive strategy, can be defined in terms of six elements or dimensions. These dimensions are: (1) the product market in which the business is to compete, (2) the level of investment, (3) the functional area strategies needed to compete in the selected market, (4) the strategic assets or skills that underlie the strategy and provide the SCA, (5) the allocation of resources to the business units, and (6) the development of synergistic effects across the businesses. Wheelen and Hunger (2004) explicitly addressed the competitive dimension of business strategy in their definition: 'business strategy which is often called competitive strategy focuses on improving the competitive position of a company's products or services within the specific industry or market segment that the company or business unit serves'. In this context, it is worth noting the alternative orientations of competitive strategy.

Marketing-oriented competitive strategy

A marketing-oriented competitive strategy allows marketing to decide the direction pursued by a business, as well as adopt a supporting role in relation to strategy. Marketing can help to establish a match between firms and their environment by deciding: (1) what kinds of business firms may enter in the future, and (2) how the chosen field of endeavour may be successfully conducted in a competitive environment, by pursuing product, price, promotion, and distribution perspectives to serve target markets.

A marketing-oriented competitive strategy recognizes some alternative approaches for achieving differential advantage over competitors, such as concentrating on particular market segments, offering products which differ from competitors' offerings, using better approaches to distribution and promotion activities, and putting more emphasis on price or non-price aspects. IKEA has been transformed from a local mail-order furniture business into one of the key retail furnishing businesses in the world by having a clear differential advantage over competitors and providing value-for-money products. The success of the company derives from the unique benefits it offers customers and its consistent implementation of an effective marketing-oriented competitive strategy. Successful implementation of a marketing-oriented competitive strategy requires, in the first place, a sound organizational structure that places a major emphasis on the marketing concept as an overall business philosophy. Research has examined the importance of marketing orientation as a competitive advantage for organizations (e.g., Cravens and Shipp, 1991; and Gummesson, 1991).

Technology-oriented competitive strategy

This strategy involves serving high-income markets with a flow of new, preferably unique, high-performance and high-technology products. Microsoft, Mercedes-Benz, and Sony are typical examples of the large corporations that pursue technology leadership in their respective industries. Competitive strategies adopted by those companies have been developed to flag up their substantial investment in technology and R&D activities. Technological innovation provides an opportunity to develop an advantageous position for the longer term. The power of technology as a competitive weapon lies in its ability to alter competition through changing industry structure. Several studies have acknowledged that technology and competitive strategy are inseparable and technological decisions are of fundamental importance to businesses as a valuable source of competitive advantage (Schlie and Goldhar, 1995; Schroeder, et al., 1995; Price, 1996).

On deciding which strategic orientation to adopt, a firm should construct its own criteria and guidelines as there is no universal formula. The choice of strategy is not a routine task. Strategic choice, like all decisions, should be made in the context of the decision situation and the requirements of the decision-makers.

From the preceding review of the nature and various definitions of 'competitive strategy' and 'marketing strategy', we can conclude that:

- **competitive strategy** is a business strategy which exists at the SBU level, and deals primarily with the question of competitive position
- **marketing strategy** is a functional strategy which is limited to the actions of specific functions within specific businesses

Following on from the latter point, it can be suggested that an organization's development of a functional strategy is dictated by the SBU strategy of its parent. For example, a business unit following a competitive strategy of differentiation through high quality requires a manufacturing functional strategy that emphasizes an expensive quality assurance process, a human resource functional strategy that emphasizes the hiring and training of a highly skilled workforce, and a marketing functional strategy that emphasizes distribution channel 'pull' using advertising to increase consumer demand, rather than 'push' using promotional allowances to retailers. If a business unit, however, is to follow a low-cost competitive strategy, a different set of functional strategies would be needed to support the business strategy. As a company may decide to adopt different competitive strategies in different regions of the world, functional strategies may have to vary accordingly (Wheelen and Hunger, 2004). Ford, for example, has a different set of functional strategies in the Middle East from the ones adopted in the UK. Ford is seen as a differentiated car producer in the Middle East, while this is not the case in Britain.

The differences between competitive and marketing strategies are shown in Table 2.3. From this table several aspects can be noted.

Competitive strategy, in most cases, is developed at a higher strategic level (the SBU) than marketing strategy which develops at the operational level of functional areas. Most discussions of strategic planning are focused upon the concept of the strategic business unit which has been defined as a competitive strategy centre (Baker, 1992).

Competitive strategy development involves four key factors: determination of mission statement, evaluation and selection of generic strategies, objective setting, and policy-making. On the other hand, marketing strategy development involves choosing the target

TABLE 2.3 Illustrative comparison of business and marketing strategies

	Corporate and business units strategy	Marketing strategy
Perspective	Organizational and/or competitive focus, often with a heavy industry orientation	Customer and/or product focus, often with a heavy end-user orientation
Decisions	• Mission determination • Allocation of business resources to business units • Acquisition/diversification • Elimination of business units • Product development and management • Selection and implementation of SBU strategies	• Identification of market opportunities • Choice of target market(s) • Marketing program positioning strategy • Product, distribution, price and promotion strategies
Strategic focus	• How to gain and keep strategic advantage • How to determine business strategies • How to organize the business for planning/control	• How to divide product/markets into segments • What segment(s) to serve • How to position for each segment
Information needs	• Financial performance • Business opportunity assessment • Market performance and forecasts • Competitors' strategies and performance	• Financial performance by market target and product type • Customer/prospect description and requirements • Market position and forecasts • Competitors' marketing strategies and performance

Source: Cravens, David W, *Strategic Marketing*. © 1994. Reproduced by permission of McGraw-Hill Education, Inc.

market/s, assessing competitors' marketing strategies, and designing the marketing mix strategies.

Responsibility for competitive strategy development is borne by all managers in the company, by following either bottom-up planning or top-down planning as modes of strategy formulation. Responsibility for marketing strategy development is borne by the marketing manager in the marketing department.

These differences and dimensions help decide whether marketing strategy and competitive strategy represent two different types (or levels) of strategy. Therefore, the inclusion of the two terms *competitive* and *marketing* with *strategy* must be based on the fact that one refers to the type of strategy and the other to the orientation of the strategy. In light of this, we must ask:

1. Does competitive marketing strategy refer to the SBU strategy which is oriented by the market? Or
2. Is it a typical functional strategy with a competitive orientation?

Before answering, we should address some considerations about the orientation of the two types (levels) of strategies.

In the competitive orientation of marketing strategy, the marketer observes what rival firms or brands are doing, anticipates their moves, and sets objectives for ways to surpass them. While this approach was seen in the 1970s and early 1980s as the opposite of the consumer orientation, some current marketing literature views the competitor orientation as having many disadvantages, so that there is no need to choose it exclusively. Companies have been recommended to consider both consumer and competitor and to attempt to have a balanced outlook in the marketplace (Hooley et al., 1998; Kotler, 2000).

In the marketing orientation of competitive strategy, marketing plays a pivotal role for strategy development by linking the organization with the environment. Because of marketing's position at the boundary between the organization and its customers, channel members, and competitive forces, it becomes central to the competitive (business) strategy planning process and is seen as a responsibility of the entire business rather than as a specialized function.

Perhaps the link between marketing orientation and competitive strategy can be made clearer if the major contributions of marketing to strategic thinking and competitive analysis, in particular, are discussed. El-Morsy (1986), for example, pointed out that marketing has a perspective which is critical to competitive strategy development. This perspective is captured by the marketing concept, which provides competitive strategy with both a philosophy and an operational method of resolving some of the strategic issues and for the integration of the activities of the business.

Baker et al. (1986) also examined the practice of marketing and its contribution to competitive success and classified the contribution in terms of three factors: (1) attitudinal marketing factors, (2) strategic marketing factors, and (3) tactical marketing factors. This study looked at the dimensions of marketing and corporate success, taking account of both empirical and anecdotal evidence suggesting an association between a marketing orientation and competitive success.

Brooksbank (1991) examined successful marketing practices and came up with a checklist of contributions by marketing which have been found to be commonly associated with companies' high-performance competitive strategies. This checklist includes: (1) marketing as a philosophy; (2) marketing's contribution to a situation analysis; (3) marketing's contribution to objectives setting; (4) marketing's contribution to achieving competitive advantage; and (5) marketing's contribution to performance evaluation.

The role of marketing in both large corporations and small businesses has changed over the past decade. Marketing can no longer be the sole responsibility of a few specialists. Rather, everyone in the firm must be charged with responsibility for understanding marketing because the formulation and implementation of a market-driven business strategy requires marketing skills in designing, developing, managing, and controlling strategic alliances (Webster, 1992; Hart, 2003).

The above comments on the orientation of strategy serve as strong evidence that marketing plays a focal role in developing and implementing the competitive strategy of a firm. Lambin (1997) pointed out that the absence of a strong marketing orientation culture may have significant impact on the competitiveness of the firm and several potential problems may arise. Wilson and Gilligan (1997) also claim that there is a strong interdependence between strategic planning and marketing which, in their view, can be used to develop an effective competitive strategy.

The preceding perspectives have influenced our view that 'competitive marketing strategy' cannot be reduced to a lower level of strategy development nor to a functional strategy developed to serve the 4Ps. Competitive marketing strategy should be seen as a marketing-oriented business strategy. This view highlights the importance of marketing as a business philosophy that should guide all of an organization's activities. Against this view one might argue marketing's role in formulating and implementing the three generic strategies (lower cost, differentiation, and focus) which are developed at the SBU level. Looking at the generic strategies suggested by Porter (1980), we can argue that at least two of them are, in principle, marketing-oriented strategies. Focus strategy, for example, by its nature is a marketing strategy. Marketing scholars, in general, deal with the concept of segmentation, its procedures, and the major basis for segmentation, as well as the requirements for effective segmentation. With reference to differentiation strategy, differentiation can take many forms, including brand image, design technology, customer services, and dealer network. It is obvious that the successful implementation of such a strategy needs, in the first instance, strong marketing abilities to create brand image and maintain consumer loyalty, to provide the customer with sufficient service, to help in choosing and motivating a capable dealer network, and to push new or improved products to the marketplace. Thus, the perceived uniqueness as a major dimension of differentiation strategy is a marketing mission and responsibility (Levitt, 1980; Baker, 1992) (see Mini case study 2.2).

Marketing can play a significant role in achieving success for the low-cost strategy through rational spending on salesforce, advertising, market research and other marketing activities. Also, marketing contributes to achieving, at optimum, competitive costs through the way it selects the markets and customers.

Generally speaking, in the search for competitive advantage which represents the core dimension of the above competitive strategies, marketing is a major area that is able to assess customer needs and preferences, anticipate competitive moves and reactions, and, consequently, the firm's potential for gaining competitive advantage. Porter (1985) highlighted the role of marketing when he suggested his value chain concept; at least four of the five primary activities are marketing's responsibility.

Finally, bearing the above in mind, we propose the following definition of competitive marketing strategy:

Competitive marketing strategy is a marketing-oriented competitive strategy that establishes a profitable and sustainable market position for the firm against all forces that determine industry competition by continuously creating and developing a competitive advantage from the potential sources that exist in a firm's value chain.

Planning frameworks for the strategy-making process

There is a difference between strategy (as an outcome) and the process by which strategy is developed, approved, implemented, and evaluated. This process of strategy making has

MINI CASE STUDY 2.2 'Global brand strategy key for Lenovo'

Lenovo, the world's third-largest computer maker, is drawing up a new global brand strategy that will use the Think trademark, recently acquired along with IBM's business unit for high-end products and its own corporate name for mainstream offerings. Lenovo, the first Chinese company to acquire a global technology business, expects to launch the strategy this year (2005).

Effective brand management will be essential if Lenovo is to successfully adjust to life as a global company. Yang Yuanquing, Lenovo chairman, said an 'extremely clear' approach to branding was essential to guide the integration of Lenovo and IBM business units following the completion in May of its $1.75bn purchase of the US company's iconic but anaemic PC business.

The Think name used for IBM's Thinkpad laptops and Thinkcentre desktop PCs would be adopted around the world as Lenovo's premium brand aimed in particular at major corporate customers, Mr Yang said in an interview with the FT. The Lenovo name would be used for computers and other products competing with PC global market leaders Dell and Hewlett-Packard for smaller corporate and retail consumers.

The focus on two product lines marks a decision to play down use of the IBM brand for products made by the US company's former unit, even though Lenovo acquired the right to use the IBM name for five years. By moving to establish Think as standalone brand that it is required to, Lenovo may deflect recent criticism that some of its post-acquisition promotions have lacked focus.

However, Mr Yang said Lenovo had decided not to try to separate Think products completely from its mainstream brand in the way that Japanese carmaker Toyota has done with its luxury Lexus vehicles. Some colleagues had been concerned that marketing Thinkpad laptop computers as made by Lenovo might put off buyers, he said.

'However, research showed that such doubts were not removed by just using Thinkpad without making clear what company produced the product, so it's better to be clear that the company's name is Lenovo', he said.

Lenovo adverts in the US and elsewhere are intended to establish it as a recognized corporate name. However, Mr Yang said that under the *new strategy*, Lenovo's focus would be on promoting products that enhanced its image rather than on direct corporate brand-building. Lenovo's IBM PC purchase has made it the poster-child for China's 'Go Global' strategy of outward corporate expansion.

Source: Mure Dickie, (2005), *Financial Times*, 13/14 August, p. 8.

been described over the years in such terms as, 'budgeting', 'long-range planning', 'strategic planning', 'strategic market planning', 'strategic management', and 'strategic market management'. All these terms have a similar meaning and they are often used interchangeably. If these terms are looked at in historical perspective, it is possible to see four phases in the evolution of the management planning discipline (Marx, 1991; Wheelen and Hunger, 2000). For the purpose of our discussion, we will concentrate on the third and fourth phases: strategic planning and strategic management.

Strategic planning

Although numerous studies have been published on strategic planning, it should be said that strategic planning and its associated concepts were born amid a flurry of optimism and industrial growth in the 1960s and early 1970s. There are several reasons for this, perhaps the most notable of which is that, largely because of the growing and continuously buoyant markets of the 1950s and 1960s and the turbulence of the early 1970s, many managers needed to find a radically different approach to the running of their business (Porter, 1987).

Ansoff (1965) was one of the first to define strategic planning (which he then called strategic decisions). Strategic planning has recently been defined as the process which defines the long-term objectives of a company and the means by which these objectives are to be obtained (Greenley, 1989). Planning horizons may, however, vary from one company to another and from industry to industry. For example, in a retail company, a three-year plan may be appropriate. In companies operating in the oil industry, however, planning horizons may be as long as 10–15 years. The above definition may also give the impression that strategic planning and strategic thinking are similar. They are not.

Whereas strategic thinking involves creative and entrepreneurial insights into a company and its environment, strategic planning has often degenerated into frameworks for the systematic and comprehensive analysis of known options. Liedtka and Rosenblum (1996) supported this view. Strategic thinking, in their view, is a shaping process in which a reflective conversation with a situation takes place in order to reduce the complexity of such a situation, while strategy making is a process of continuous adaptation between the industry environment and organizational capabilities. For example, the management of Hewlett-Packard (HP), after a careful study of trends in the computer and communications industries, noted that the company needed to stop thinking of itself as a collection of stand-alone products with a primary focus on instrumentation and computer hardware. Instead, the top management felt that the company needed to become a customer-focused and integrated provider of information appliances, highly reliable information technology infrastructure, and e-commerce services. A comprehensive framework of strategic planning and its related components, which illustrates the two dimensions of external environment and organizational capabilities, is shown in Figure 2.2 (Mintzberg, 1994a).

Strategic planning as a model of strategy making has its supporters, as evidenced by the number of surveys undertaken to assess the validity of the model (e.g., Haspeslagh, 1982; Hamermesh, 1986; Greenley, 1987; McDonald, 1989, Ansoff, 1991, 1994). However, there are a number of criticisms of the theory and application of strategic planning (Powell, 1992; Mintzberg, 1990, 1994b). In the case of small businesses, research shows that strategic planning is strongly related to their financial performance. A survey of the high-growth *Inc. 500* firms revealed that 86% undertook strategic planning. Of those 94% reported improved profits. Nevertheless, many small businesses still do not use the model. The reasons often cited (Wheelen and Hunger, 2004) for the apparent lack of strategic planning practices in many small-business companies are:

- not enough time
- unfamiliarity with the strategic planning model

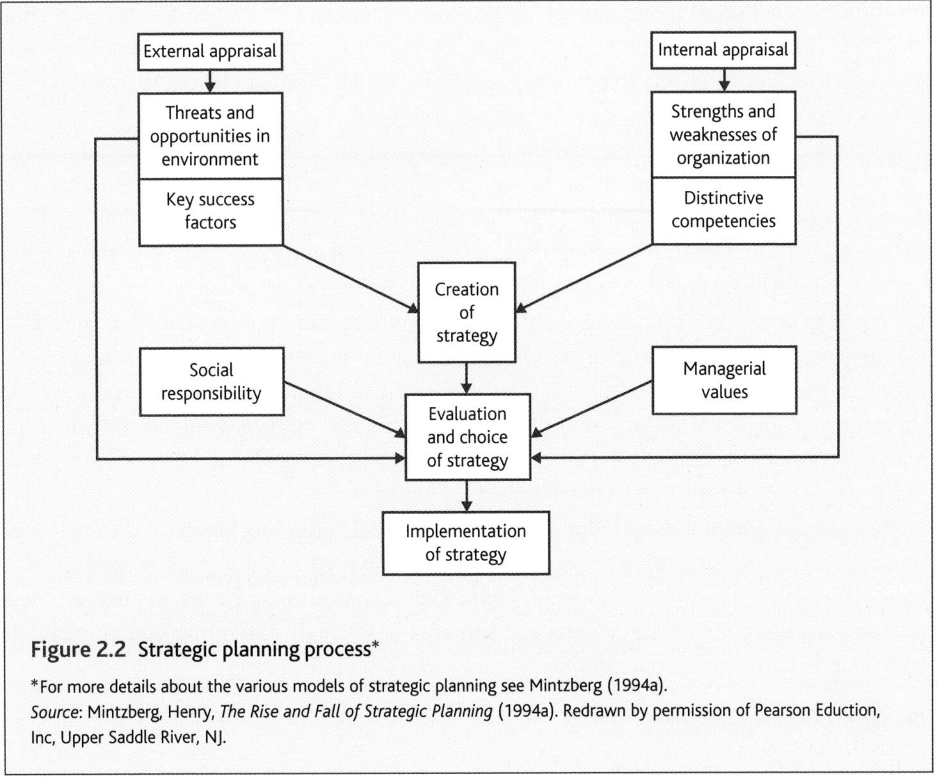

Figure 2.2 Strategic planning process*

*For more details about the various models of strategic planning see Mintzberg (1994a).
Source: Mintzberg, Henry, *The Rise and Fall of Strategic Planning* (1994a). Redrawn by permission of Pearson Eduction, Inc, Upper Saddle River, NJ.

- lack of skills
- lack of trust and openness

Strategic market planning was added to the lexicon of strategic concepts by Abell and Hammond (1979). The inclusion of the term *market* in strategic planning serves to emphasize that strategy development needs to be driven by the forces of the market environment rather than by internal factors. Strategic market planning is defined as the managerial process that entails analysis, formulation, and evaluation of strategy and that enables an organization to achieve its objectives by developing and maintaining a strategic fit between the organization's capabilities and the threats and opportunities arising from its changing environment (Kerin et al., 1990).

There is also a need to distinguish strategic **market** planning from strategic **marketing** planning. Whereas the first prepares a firm to develop a strategic response to its changing market environment, strategic marketing planning is concerned with functional decisions related to the elements of the marketing mix. In that capacity, marketing competes with other functional areas for the firm's resources. This distortion and minimization of the role of strategic marketing planning is reviewed and discussed by several authors. Kerin et al. (1990), for example, articulated the strategic role played by marketing and pointed out that the primary responsibility of strategic market planning is always to look outward and keep the business in step with its expected environment. The lead role in meeting this responsibility is played by marketing. As a general management responsibility, marketing embraces the interpretations of the environment and the crucial choices of which customers to serve, which competitors to challenge, and with which product characteristics the business will compete.

In fact the need to justify consideration of marketing as a distinct function is not to deny the importance of marketing as an orientation guiding the discipline of formal strategic planning in an organization. Baker (1992) distinguished strategic marketing planning from marketing planning by stressing that the latter is seen as dealing primarily with the marketing mix, while the former is seen as planning for all aspects of an organization's strategy in the marketplace. Based on this view strategic marketing planning is described as the establishment of the goal or purpose of an SBU and the means by which this is to be achieved.

In fact, marketing has a presence at the three organizational levels of any corporation. At the corporate level marketing can influence organizational culture, while at the SBU level marketing guides the company's competitive positioning, and finally at the operational level marketing is responsible for the development of 4Ps tactics.

The concepts and practicalities of strategic and tactical marketing planning and their relationship to strategic planning are comprehensively covered in the literature (see Brooksbank, 1991; Webster, 1992; McDonald, 1996; Fifield and Gilligan, 1998). In general, there is wide agreement about the process and contents of strategic marketing planning and its contribution to the development of the organization's overall strategy.

Strategic management

Following on from phase three of the planning discipline, with its emphasis on *strategic planning,* phase four, *strategic management*, involves and highlights the importance of strategy implementation, evaluation, and control. Strategic management stems from an assumption that the planning cycle is inadequate to deal with the rapid rate of change that can occur in the environment facing the firm. To cope with strategic surprises and fast-developing threats and opportunities, firms' strategic decisions need to be made outside the planning cycle (Aaker 2001).

In the academic literature, Ansoff et al. (1976) were the first to transform strategic planning into strategic management. In the world of business, General Electric Corporation (GEC), one of the pioneers of strategic planning, led the transition from strategic planning to strategic management during the 1980s. Because strategy formulation and implementation are now considered to be of equal importance, and interdependent (a key concept of strategic management), it has been suggested that the largest companies in the world all have to take strategic management seriously. Strategic management has been defined as a set of managerial decisions and actions that determines the long-run performance of a corporation (Wheelen and Hunger, 2000). The strategic management process in terms of four basic elements: environmental scanning, strategy formulation, strategy implementation, and evaluation and control is shown in Figure 2.3.

Research in the area of strategy has supported the validity of the strategic management concept and revealed that strategic management, in general, leads to improved performance far more often than it results in no change or in even poorer performance (e.g., Ansoff, 1991; Armstrong, 1991; Waalewijn and Segaar, 1993; Hopkins and Hopkins, 1997).

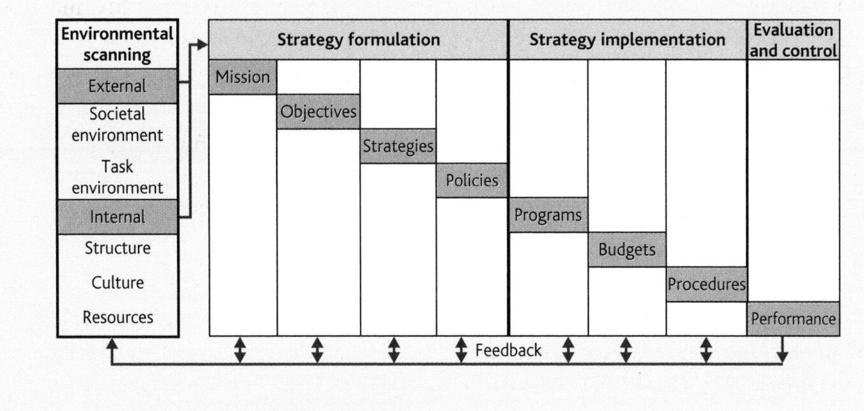

Figure 2.3 Strategic management framework

Source: Wheelen, Tom, and Hunger, J. David, *Strategic Management and Business Policy* (9th edn, 2004), pp. 10, 14, 138. Redrawn by permission of Pearson Education, Inc, Upper Saddle River, NJ.

The term strategic *market* management emerged as an extension of the term strategic management, the inclusion of the term *market* serving (a) to emphasize that strategy development needs to be driven by the market and the external environment rather than being internally oriented; and (b) to underline the fact that the process should be proactive rather than reactive and that the task should be to attempt to influence the environment instead of simply responding to it. Strategic market management has been defined as a system designed to help management in developing, evaluating, implementing, and changing business strategies. Such a system will (1) provide vision to businesses, (2) monitor and understand a dynamic environment, (3) generate strategic options, and (4) develop strategies based on sustainable competitive advantages (Aaker, 2001). It is beneficial, at this point, to illustrate the contents of that system as shown in Figure 2.4.

The term strategic *marketing* management is introduced to highlight the lead role of marketing as the link between the organization and its environment and the pivotal importance of marketing in formulating and directing the implementation of the overall organization strategies. The role of marketing in strategy development and implementation and its contribution to business performance have been acknowledged in the marketing and strategy literature (see, for example, Brownlie 1989; Narver and Slater, 1990; Kerin and Peterson, 1993; Wong and Saunders, 1993; Slater and Narver, 1994; Doyle 1998). Brownlie (1989) summarized the role played by marketing in leading the migration of ideas from strategic management to strategic *marketing* management. Marketing is likely to play an analytical and diagnostic role in the search for competitive advantages where the business's unique capabilities match the key success factors of one or more product markets. And since strategic marketing activity generates imperatives for organizational transformation, marketing considerations are also the starting point for the strategic management process. In fact, marketing as a relatively mature discipline has the potential to contribute viewpoints, concepts, and methodologies to the field of strategic management.

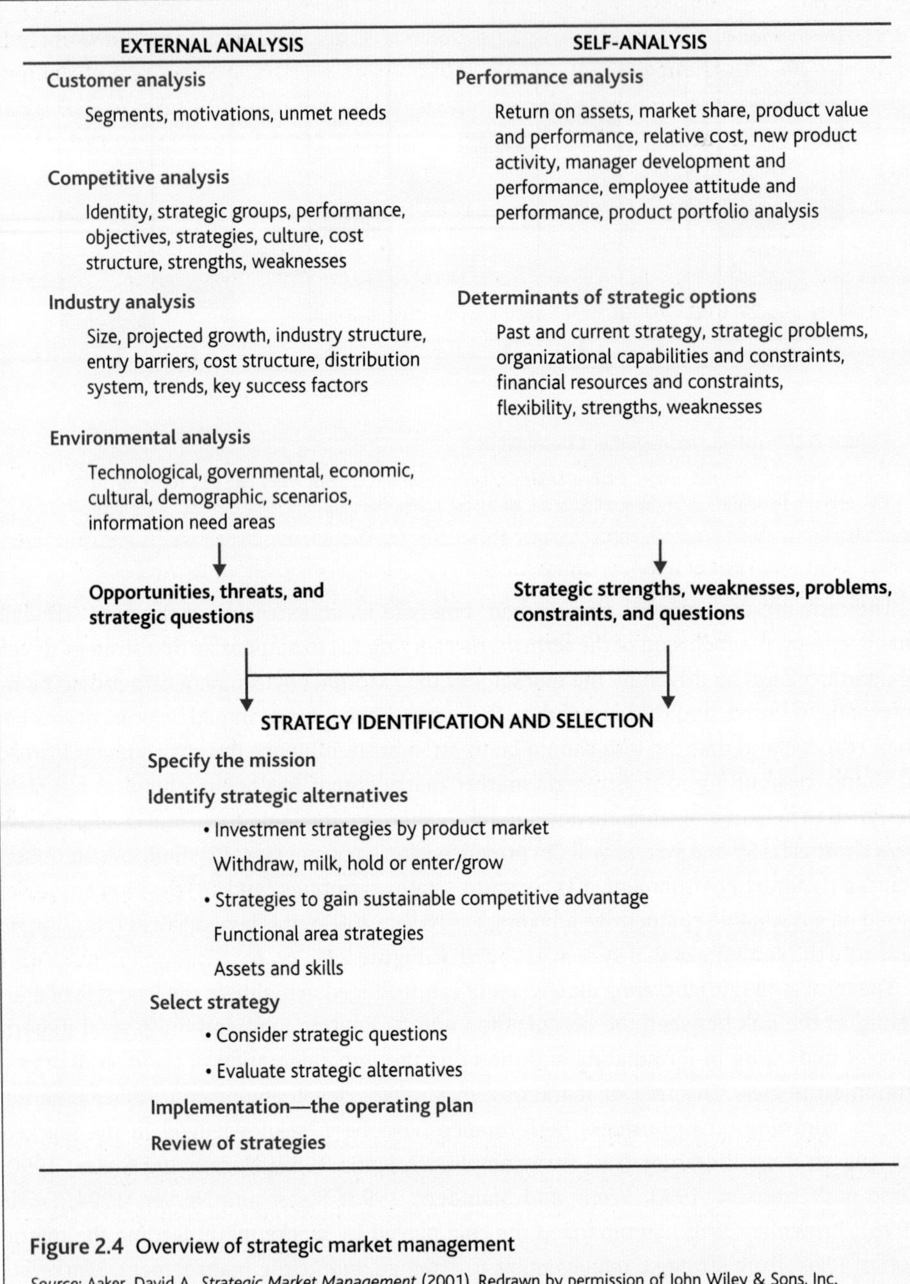

Figure 2.4 Overview of strategic market management

Source: Aaker, David A., *Strategic Market Management* (2001). Redrawn by permission of John Wiley & Sons, Inc.

Strategic marketing management has also been defined as the analytical process of seeking differential advantage. This process includes the analysis and choice of the firm's product-market relationships and the formulation of management strategies that create and support viable relationships consistent with the firm's capabilities and objectives (Kerin and Peterson, 1993). As the part of the organization which interacts most directly and immediately with the environment, there is an obvious need for marketing expertise and planning to investigate, analyse, and respond to any environmental changes that take place. Because of this, the term 'strategic *marketing* management' was introduced as a substitute for 'strategic *market* management'.

Acknowledgement of the lead role of marketing in the context of strategic marketing management is coupled with the key concept of the framework, which integrates the formulation and implementation processes of competitive strategy, to add significant value to the framework, compared with other strategic planning models.

Conclusion

The current view of the development of marketing strategy is consistent with the early literature about the marketing concept, which recognized marketing as not only a set of functions but also a guiding philosophy for all of an organisation's activities. At the functional level, the major task of a marketing manager is to influence the level, timing, and character of demand in a way that will help to achieve the organization's marketing objectives. The marketing manager is the organization's primary link to the customer and the competition and must, therefore, be concerned in particular with the development of the organization's positioning strategy and marketing mix programmes.

At the strategic (SBU) level, marketing as a business philosophy can play a significant role in guiding all of an organization's activities. Therefore, we suggest that competitive marketing strategy is not an upgraded version of the marketing strategy that is oriented by competitors, but rather:

> *A marketing-oriented competitive strategy that establishes a profitable and sustainable market position for the firm against all forces that determine industry competition by continuously creating and developing a competitive advantage from the potential sources that exist in a firm's value chain.*

Summary

This chapter has reviewed the nature and various definitions of marketing strategy, a topic that has been the subject of extensive analysis and discussion in the marketing literature. Marketing strategy is typically seen as having developed through three sequential steps/phases. First, the core strategy of the company will be selected, and the marketing objectives and the broad focus for achieving them will be identified. Secondly, market segments and targets (both customers and competitors) are selected, and the company's differential advantage in serving the customer targets better than the competition is identified. Together, the identification of targets and the definition of differential advantage constitute the creation of the competitive positioning of the company and its offerings. Finally, a marketing manager capable of putting the strategy into practice must be elected. The marketing department, at this stage, is concerned with establishing the marketing mix programmes that can convey both the positioning and the products/services themselves to the target market (Hooley et al., 1998).

KEY TERMS

Corporate strategy Describes a company's overall direction in terms of its general attitude toward growth and the management of its various businesses and product lines to achieve a balanced portfolio of products and services.

Business strategy Usually developed at the strategic business unit (SBU) level and emphasizes improvement of the competitive position of a corporation's products or services in the specific industry or market segment served by that SBU.

Functional strategy Concerned with maximizing resource productivity. Within the constraints of the corporate and business strategies around them, functional departments, such as marketing, finance, and production, develop strategies to pull together their various activities and competencies to improve performance.

Competitive marketing strategy A marketing-oriented competitive strategy that establishes a profitable and sustainable market position for the firm against all forces that determine industry competition by continuously creating and developing a competitive advantage from the potential sources that exist in a firm's value chain.

DISCUSSION QUESTIONS

1. What are the key differences between the three levels of strategy: corporate, SBU, and functional?
2. Do you agree that marketing strategy is the same as competitive marketing strategy?
3. To what extent do you agree that marketing strategy is central for large corporations as well as small firms?
4. What is the difference between strategic market planning and strategic market management?
5. To what extent do you agree that marketing should be seen as a business philosophy rather than a set of activities?

ONLINE RESOURCE CENTRE

Visit the Online Resource Centre for this book for lots of interesting additional material at: **www.oxfordtextbooks.co.uk/orc/west/**

REFERENCES AND FURTHER READING

Aaker, David A. (2001), *Strategic Market Management* (New York: John Wiley & Sons, Inc.).

Abell, Derek F., and John S. Hammond (1979), *Strategic Market Planning: Problems and Analytical Approaches* (Englewood Cliffs: Prentice-Hall, Inc.).

Andrews, Kenneth R. (1971), *The Concept of Corporate Strategy* (New York: Dow Jones-Irwin, Inc.).

Ansoff, Igor H. (1965), *Corporate Strategy* (New York: McGraw-Hill, Inc.).

Ansoff, Igor H. (1991), 'Critique of Henry Mintzberg's The Design School: Reconsidering the Basic Premises of Strategic Management', *Strategic Management Journal*, 12 (6), pp. 449–61.

Ansoff, Igor H. (1994), 'Comment on Henry Mintzberg's Rethinking Strategic Planning', *Long Range Planning*, 27 (3), pp. 31–2.

Ansoff, Igor H., Roger P. Declerck, and Robert L. Hayes (1976), *From Strategic Planning to Strategic Management* (New York: John Wiley & Sons, Inc.).

Armstrong, Scott J. (1991), 'Strategic Planning Improves Manufacturing Performance', *Long Range Planning*, 24 (4), pp. 127–9.

Armstrong, Scott J., and Fred Collopy (1996), 'Competitor Orientation: Effects of Objectives and Information on Managerial Decisions and Profitability', *Journal of Marketing Research*, 33 (May), pp. 188–99.

Baker, Michael J. (1992), *Marketing Strategy and Management* (London: Macmillan Press Ltd).

Baker, Michael J., Susan Hart, Caroline Black, and Tawfik M. Abdel-Mohsen (1986), 'The Contribution of Marketing to Competitive Success: A literature Review', *Journal of Marketing Management*, 2 (1), pp. 39–61.

Brooksbank, Roger W. (1991), 'Successful Marketing Practice: A Literature Review and Checklist for Marketing Practitioners', *European Journal of Marketing*, 25 (5), pp. 20–9.

Brownlie, D. T. (1989), 'The Migration of Ideas from Strategic Management to Marketing on the Subject of Competition', *European Journal of Marketing*, 23 (12), pp. 7–20.

Cravens, David W. (1994), *Strategic Marketing* (New York: Richard D. Irwin).

Cravens, David W., and Shannon H. Shipp (1991), 'Market-Driven Strategies for Competitive Advantage', *Business Horizons*, 34 (1), pp. 53–61.

Dibb, Sally, Lyndon Simkin, William M. Pride, and O. C. Ferrell (2001), *Marketing: Concepts and Strategies* (New York: Houghton Mifflin Company).

Doyle, Peter (1998), *Marketing Management and Strategy* (Harlow: Prentice-Hall, Inc.).

El-Morsy, Gamal E. M. (1986), Competitive Marketing Strategy: A study of Competitive Performance in the British Car Market (Unpublished PhD, University of Strathclyde, UK).

Fifield, Paul (1998), *Marketing Strategy* (Oxford: Butterworth-Heinemann).

Fifield, Paul, and Colin Gilligan (1998), *Strategic Marketing Management: Planning and Control, Analysis and Decision* (Oxford: Butterworth-Heinemann).

Forbis, John L., and Nitin T. Mehta (1981), 'Value-Based Strategies for Industrial Products', *Business Horizons*, 24 (3), pp. 24–9.

Frentzel, Y. William, John M. Bryson, and Barbara C. Crosby (2000), 'Strategic Planning in the Military', *Long Range Planning*, 33, pp. 402–29.

Grant, Robert M. (1995), *Contemporary Strategy Analysis: Concepts, Techniques, Applications* (Oxford: Blackwell Publishers, Inc.).

Greenley, Gordon (1987), 'An Exposition of Empirical Research into Marketing Planning', *Journal of Marketing Management*, 3 (1), pp. 83–102.

Greenley, Gordon (1989), 'An Understanding of Marketing Strategy', *European Journal of Marketing*, 23 (8), pp. 45–58.

Gummesson, Evert (1991), 'Marketing-Orientation Revisited: The Crucial Role of the Part-Time Marketer', *European Journal of Marketing*, 25 (2), pp. 60–75.

Hamermesh, Richard G. (1986), 'Making Planning Strategic', *Harvard Business Review*, 64 (July–August), pp. 115–20.

Hart, Susan (2003), *Marketing Changes* (London: Thomson Learning).

Haspeslagh, Philippe (1982), 'Portfolio Planning: Uses and Limits', *Harvard Business Review*, 60 (January–February), pp. 58–73.

Hofer, Charles W., and Dan Schendel (1978), *Strategy Formulation: Analytical Concepts* (St. Paul, Minnesota: West Publishing Company).

Hooley, Graham J., John Saunders, and Nigel F. Piercy (1998), *Competitive Positioning: The Key to Market Success* (Harlow: Prentice-Hall International Ltd).

Hopkins, Willie E., and Shirley A. Hopkins (1997), 'Strategic Planning—Financial Performance Relationships in Banks: A Causal Examination', *Strategic Management Journal*, 18 (8), pp. 635–52.

Horton, Keith S. (2003), 'Strategy, Practice, and Dynamics of Power', *Journal of Business Research*, 56 (2), pp. 121–6.

Kerin, Roger A., and Robert A. Peterson (1993), *Strategic Marketing Problems: Cases and Comments* (Boston: Allyn and Bacon, Inc.).

Kerin, Roger A., V. Mahajan, and Rajan P. Varadarajan (1990), *Contemporary Perspectives on Strategic Market Planning* (Englewood Cliffs: Prentice-Hall, Inc.).

Kohli, Ajay K., and Bernard J. Jaworski (1990), 'Market Orientation: The Construct, Research Propositions, and Managerial Implications', *Journal of Marketing*, 54 (April), pp. 1–18.

Kotler, Philip (1994), *Marketing Management: Analysis, Planning, Implementation and Control* (Englewood Cliffs: Prentice-Hall, Inc.).

Kotler, Philip (2000), *Marketing Management* (Englewood Cliffs: Prentice-Hall, Inc.).

Lambin, Jean-Jacques (1997), *Strategic Marketing Management* (Maidenhead: McGraw-Hill International Ltd.).

Levitt, Theodore (1980), 'Marketing Success through Differentiation–of Anything', *Harvard Business Review*, 58 (January), pp. 83–91.

Liedtka, Jeanne M., and John W. Rosenblum (1996), 'Shaping Conversations: Making Strategy, Managing Change', *California Management Review*, 39 (1), pp. 141–57.

Luck, David J., O. C. Ferrell, and George H. Lucas (Jr.) (1989), *Marketing Strategy and Plans* (Englewood Cliffs: Prentice-Hall, Inc.).

McDonald, Malcolm H. B. (1989), 'Ten Barriers to Marketing Planning', *Journal of Marketing Management*, 5 (1), pp. 1–18.

McDonald, Malcolm (1996), 'Strategic Marketing Planning: Theory, Practice and Research Agenda', *Journal of Marketing Management*, 12 (1–2) pp. 5–27.

Marx, Thomas G. (1991), 'Removing the Obstacles to Effective Strategic Planning', *Long Range Planning*, 24 (4), pp. 21–8.

Mintzberg, Henry (1990), 'The Design School: Reconsidering the Basic Premises of Strategic Management', *Strategic Management Journal*, 11 (3), pp. 171–95.

Mintzberg, Henry (1994a), *The Rise and Fall of Strategic Planning*, (Englewood Cliffs: Prentice-Hall, Inc.).

Mintzberg, Henry (1994b), 'Rethinking Strategic Planning Part I: Pitfalls and Fallacies', *Long Range Planning*, 27 (3), pp. 12–21.

Mintzberg, Henry, and J. B. Quinn (1996), *The Strategy Process: Concepts, Contexts, Cases* (Harlow: Prentice-Hall International, Inc.).

Morgan, R. E., C. S. Katsikeas, and K. Appiah-Adu (1998), 'Market Orientation and Organisational Learning Capabilities', *Journal of Marketing Management*, 14, pp. 353–81.

Narver, John C., and Stanley F. Slater (1990), 'The Effect of a Market Orientation on Business Profitability', *Journal of Marketing*, 54 (October), pp. 20–35.

O'Shaughnessy, John (1995), *Competitive Marketing: A Strategic Approach* (London: Routledge).

Porter, Michael E. (1980), *Competitive Strategy: Techniques for Analyzing Industries and Competitors* (New York: The Free Press).

Porter, Michael E. (1985), *Competitive Advantage: Creating and Sustaining Superior Performance* (New York: The Free Press).

Porter, Michael E. (1987), 'Corporate Strategy: The State of Strategic Thinking', *The Economist* (May 23), pp. 21–8.

Powell, Thomas (1992), 'Strategic Planning as Competitive Advantage', *Strategic Management Journal*, 13 (7), pp. 551–8.

Price, Robert M. (1996), 'Technology and Strategic Advantage', *California Management Review*, 38 (3), pp. 38–55.

Quinn, Michael, and John Humble (1993), 'Using Service to Gain a Competitive Edge—The PROMPT Approach', *Long Range Planning*, 26 (2), pp. 31–40.

Reeves, S. (1991), 'Leadership and Technology: Creating A Competitive Advantage', The Published Proceedings of International Management Conference, The Society of Advanced Management, pp. 23–32.

Ries, A., and J. Trout (1981), *Positioning: The Battle for Your Mind* (New York: McGraw-Hill Book Company).

Schlie, Theodore W., and Joel D. Goldhar (1995), 'Advanced Manufacturing and New Directions for Competitive Strategy', *Journal of Business Research*, 33 (2), pp. 103–14.

Schroeder, Dean M., Steven W. Congden, and C. Gopinath (1995), 'Linking Competitive Strategy and Manufacturing Process Technology', *Journal of Management Studies*, 32 (2), pp. 163–89.

Slater, Stanley F., and John C. Narver (1994), 'Market Orientation, Customer Value, and Superior Performance', *Business Horizons*, 37 (2), pp. 22–28.

Slater, Stanley F., and John C. Narver (2000), 'The Positive Effect of a Market Orientation on Business Profitability: A Balanced Replication', *Journal of Business Research*, 48, pp. 69–73.

Waalewijn, Philip, and Peter Segaar (1993), 'Strategic Management: The Key to Profitability in Small Companies', *Long Range Planning*, 26 (2), pp. 24–30.

Webster, Frederick E. (Jr.) (1992), 'The Changing Role of Marketing in the Corporation', *Journal of Marketing*, 56 (October), pp. 1–17.

Weinrauch, Donald J., O. Karl Mann, Julie M. Pharr, and Patricia A. Robinson (1991), 'Marketing strategies of Small Industrial Manufacturers', *Industrial Marketing Management*, 20 (3), pp. 251–9.

Wheelen, Thomas L., and David J. Hunger (2000), *Strategic Management and Business Policy* (New York: Addison-Wesley Publishing Company, Inc.).

Wheelen, Thomas L., and David J. Hunger (2004), *Strategic Management and Business Policy*, International Edition (Englewood Cliffs: Pearson Education, Inc.).

Wilson, Richard M. S., and Colin Gilligan (1997), *Strategic Marketing Management: Planning, Implementation and Control* (Oxford: Butterworth-Heinemann).

Wong, Veronica, and John Saunders (1993), 'Business Orientation and Corporate Success', *Journal of Strategic Marketing*, 1 (1), pp. 20–40.

KEY ARTICLE ABSTRACTS

Tadepalli, Raghu and Ramon A. Avila (1999), 'Market Orientation and The Marketing Strategy Process', *Journal of Marketing Theory and Practice*, 7 (2), pp. 69–82.

This paper looks at the adoption of the marketing orientation concept in the process of strategy formulation, implementation, and evaluation.

Abstract: Market orientation refers to the generation, dissemination, and responsiveness to market intelligence by organizations. The focus of this study is on the process of strategy formulation and implementation in a market-oriented organization. Using the 'rational' approach to strategy formulation as a framework, and drawing on literature from the 'incremental' and 'political' approaches, an attempt is made to describe how strategy is formulated, implemented, and evaluated in a market-oriented organization. The 'key variable' concept is suggested as an alternative means of strategy evaluation to the marketing audit. Implications for marketing managers are discussed.

Fodness, Dale (2005), 'Rethinking strategic marketing: achieving breakthrough results', *The Journal of Business Strategy*, 26 (3), pp. 20–34.

This is a useful paper, which encourages marketing managers to look forward to embrace a new application of the traditional strategic marketing planning framework.

Abstract: Strategic thinking offers marketers the opportunity to move beyond the automatic application of traditional strategic frameworks to identify and to achieve breakthrough marketing strategies. The real power of thinking strategically about marketing lies in its potential as a source of competitive advantage that is equally applicable to creating superior value for customers, erecting barriers to competitors, or enabling more rapid adaptability to change. The strategies proposed here are all designed to reduce the risks of marketing strategy failure. The raw materials of strategic thinking (creative and critical thinking, decision-making, and problem-solving) can be transformed into a practical system for enhancing the strategic promise and performance of marketing and its practitioners. In addition, using visualization to communicate marketing strategy in a concise, articulate, and compelling manner significantly increases its likelihood of success. The marketing profession has long neglected to apply the same attention and rigour to strategic thinking that it applies to strategic planning.

Hunter, Jeffrey G. (2003), 'Determinants of Business Success Under "Hypocapitalism": Case Studies Of Russian Firms and Their Strategies', *Journal of Business Research*, 56 (2), pp. 113–20.

A case study based paper, which examines different strategic factors of business success in Russia in the post-transformation economy.

Abstract: This study examines the strategies adopted by selected firms in the post-transformation economy in Russia. The aim was to determine: (1) if there were substantial commonalities among the strategies employed, and (2) if so, was it likely that a theory of the firm could be found which persuasively explained and predicted success under the unusual characteristics of the present Russian economy? This question is pursued through an analysis of the strategies followed by 'successful' firms. Almost always present in successful firms was some form of diversification, and a variant of network capitalism was prevalent among market share leaders. The study describes the economy which resulted from the political and economic changes the Russian Federation experienced between 1991 and 1998. This economic state is referred to as 'hypocapitalism'.

Voss, Glenn B. and Zannie Giraud Voss (2000), 'Strategic Orientation and Firm Performance in an Artistic Environment', *Journal of Marketing*, 64 (1), pp. 67–83.

This is an interesting article, which examines the impact of a market orientation that includes three alternative strategic orientations (customer orientation, competitor orientation, and product orientation) on the measurement of performance in not-for-profit organizations.

Abstract: Conventional marketing wisdom holds that a customer orientation provides a firm with a better understanding of its customers, which subsequently leads to enhanced customer satisfaction and firm performance. Building on the market orientation research stream, the authors examine the impact of three alternative strategic orientations—customer orientation, competitor orientation, and product orientation—on a variety of subjective and objective measures of performance in the non-profit professional theatre industry. The results indicate that the association between strategic orientation and performance varies depending on the type of performance measure used. However, the most unambiguous result is that a customer orientation exhibits a negative association with subscriber ticket sales, total income, and net surplus/deficit.

END OF CHAPTER 2 CASE STUDY Smile.co.uk—The Internet Bank

Background to the Market

The financial service industry provides goods and services that help people to manage their money and prepare for the future financially. Organizations in the industry can focus on one type of financial product, for example mortgages or insurance, or they can provide a combination of products, as do, for example, retail banks and building societies. The introduction of the Internet in this sector has allowed for the creation of a new financial service—Internet banking, and a multitude of new organizations. As a result, the retail banking sector has been further divided into two groups of organization: online-only banks and the traditional high street banks. Online-only or stand-alone Internet banks offer various financial services to customers via the Internet only. Examples of these stand-alone banks include Egg, Smile, IF, Cahoot, and many more. Since 1998, the number of accounts accessible via computer has grown dramatically, from 375,000 in 1998 to approximately 11 million in 2002 (*Annual Abstract of Banking Statistics*, 2002). And since the emergence of online banking the number of online accounts in the UK has grown dramatically. It was estimated previously that there would be 10 million accounts in 2002, expected to rise to 11.5 million by the end of 2003. These figures tell us that there are numerous people who both have joined and are willing to join the online banking market.

Key players in online banking in the UK

Egg Plc was one of the first online-only banks to be launched in the UK. It was set up in October 1998 by Prudential, a leading international financial services group, in response to rapidly changing technology. Egg offers a number of financial services including the Egg credit card, saving accounts, loans, mortgages, insurance policies, as well as investment products such as ISAs and PEPs. Prudential clearly responded to the Internet faster than any other financial organization. Its quick response would have initially given »

Egg a competitive advantage, as it was able to offer lower interest rates on its credit card and higher interest rates on its saving accounts compared with the high street banks. This particular advantage only lasted until other financial organizations responded and were able to offer similar rates. Therefore, although the response of Prudential was to create Egg Plc, the response of Egg was to utilize the low set-up and running costs of Internet banking to offer highly competitive interest rates that would encourage consumers to bank online. This in turn forced some financial institutions and high street banks not only to set up their own Internet banks but also to compete on both price and convenience.

The Royal Bank of Scotland is one of Europe's leading financial service groups. By market capitalization it is the second largest bank in the UK and ranks fifth in the world. In March 2000, the Royal Bank of Scotland Group completed the acquisition of NatWest in a £21 billion deal that was the largest takeover in British banking history. It has 2,287 UK branches and had total assets of £412 billion at 31 December 2002. The Group employs over 110,000 staff worldwide (**www.rbs.co.uk**).

After a period of intense organizational and business change, the Royal Bank of Scotland began focusing on more direct customer requirements in sectors such as commercial, retail, and corporate. It launched Direct Banking in 1994 to be Britain's fastest 24-hour telephone banking operation. It further diversified its services delivered to customers in 1997 by being one of the first high street banks to offer online banking service over the Internet.

Soon after this, online-only banks, such as Egg, Smile, and Cahoot were established. The launch of these banks increased competition considerably for the traditional high street banks. In fact, the introduction of Internet-only banks changed the nature of banking, mainly in favour of customers. These relatively new banks have consistently offered their customers better value for money than the high street banks, forcing them to rethink their offerings and update their products (**www.guardian.co.uk**). In response to this change in the market, Royal Bank of Scotland offers a wide range of e-banking and online banking services in its personal finance, small business, corporate banking, and financial markets sections.

NatWest Bank is an established bank with over 1,600 branches and 31,000 cash machines in the UK. To maintain its leading position in the market it has had to compete with key players in the online banking industry, such as Egg, Smile, and Cahoot, by providing its customers with similar online banking services. NatWest designed its website to provide financial services focusing on three main areas: personal, business, and commercial banking. The personal banking site provides information on day-to-day banking matters, such as current accounts, credit cards, savings and investment, and borrowing. The business banking site provides information to support businesses and help them grow by offering free business advice, insurance, finance, and current accounts. Commercial banking serves corporate customers and provides up-to-date information on finance, investment, payment and cash management, international services, e-banking and risk management. Because of the increasing use of advanced technology, NatWest has recently evaluated its Internet banking strategy by providing a comprehensive list of accounts and services for existing and new customers.

Smile.co.uk online banking services

Smile was launched on 28 October 1999 and since then has achieved a leading position within the online banking industry. Its financial products are competitively priced and include a current account which pays one of the highest credit interest rates in the market, as well as offering no-fee, low-cost overdraft facilities. Current account customers are offered preferential rates for their Smile saving accounts and Visa cards to encourage them to develop a broad relationship with the bank. The bank has also realized the importance of acquiring students at an early stage, since they will be a major source of profits in the future. Therefore they offer a student current account with the same high rates of interest on credit card balances as well as completely free authorized student overdrafts. Investment products such as Cash Mini ISAs are available and customers can also book holidays, shop for insurance, drinks, and green power.

When it was launched Smile differentiated itself from the other online banks by being the only UK clearing bank with an ethical policy. This was done to attract and satisfy customers who wanted to know that their money was not invested in companies that pursued profits at the expense of their social and environmental responsibilities. It was decided that the ethical policy should reflect the concerns of the customers rather than that of the management. The policy is reviewed every three years to make sure that customer views are reflected as accurately as possible.

Smile has a high level of customer satisfaction. A recent survey reveals that 90% of their customers would actively recommend Smile to a friend or colleague. As a consequence of their customer awareness they have received many awards. It was also the first Internet bank to be accredited with the British Standard BS7799, Information Security Standard.

Since its launch, Smile has targeted the younger, Internet-oriented customers. The bank offers, through its award-winning secure website, a range of typical banking products as well as mortgages, motor insurance and investment opportunities in areas such as funds, stocks, and shares. The bank has established a distinctive character and provides a combination of value, convenience, and services that resulted in its being named 'Best Internet Banking Provider 2002/2003' by *Your Money*. The bank was also voted top in the UK's league table for electronic banking customer satisfaction.

The key drivers that have influenced Smile's *marketing strategy* can be summarized under four subheadings.

Market drivers

Smile has differentiated itself from its main competitors by adopting a unique organizational philosophy which is broken down into five elements: value, transparency, service, commerce, and accountability. It prides itself on and bases its *strategy* around comprehensive customer service and ethical practice. The company aims to create a different online experience and acquire and retain customers by placing emphasis on customer service rather than aggressive pricing. The products offered by Smile may not be the cheapest but the overall aim is to retain its customers via the quality of service provided and the degree of customer satisfaction. All products and services are provided mainly via the company's website, the security of which has been acknowledged by the British Standards Institution Kitemark. This is partially a result of the company's focus on getting things right first time. Its strict testing and examination of products help Smile to avoid the problems that most online banks, such as Egg and Cahoot, have suffered from. For instance, while Smile successfully launched its site right from the start, Cahoot was unable to accept account applications for the first two days of its launch. Learning from its mistakes, at the expense of customer convenience, has never been a part of the business philosophy of Smile.

Customer drivers

Being oriented by customers is believed to be a win-win situation. Smile realizes that the main reason customers use online banking is convenience, and hence they ensure their customers are able to gain access to their accounts and conduct financial transactions 24/7. Smile also offers a full telephone banking service to back up its online customer service. Using the information provided by customers when opening an account, Smile has built a comprehensive database that is used for their benefit. Smile uses this information to target and personalize products and services.

Economic drivers

One important reason customers adopt online banking is its lower cost (hence price) in comparison with traditional banks. This is attributed to the fact that online banks do not have the huge costs associated with physical branches. Price, however, is not enough to satisfy and retain customers. Life-time value and short-term selling are of great importance to the company because they deliver exceptional customer value and build customer relationships. This means that Smile can use the knowledge it holds on its customers to target the most valuable customers, the ones who create major profits for the company (the 80/20 rule). As the online banking service is still a rather 'new' service, Smile believes that it should focus on acquiring advanced technology and improving its services to attract new customers as well as retaining the existing ones.

Technology drivers

People's knowledge of using the Internet is increasing and Smile never underestimates its customers. Online banking customers are very knowledgeable and therefore demanding, Smile believes. The convenience of Smile Internet banking is that customers are able to contact staff 24/7 to make general enquiries via telephone and/or e-mail. Enquiries are sorted by subject, and, to satisfy customer requests quickly and promptly, staff and suppliers of Smile services are supported by sophisticated technology that gives them access to the information they need, easily and quickly.

It might be difficult for an Internet-based company to differentiate itself in terms of the products and services it offers as these can be easily copied by competitors. Customers have to be at the heart of the business. To be successful in the new Internet era requires effective strategic planning and a successful customer-led strategy that is based on sound analysis and customer mapping. Strategies and actions should involve integration and coordination of people, culture, processes, and technology. Being customer led should drive the entire business; the decisions that are made will influence all functional areas of activity including marketing, sales, human resources, R&D, and IT.

Source: This case was prepared by Dr Essam Ibrahim (2003) for class discussion and not to illustrate either effective or ineffective handling of an administrative situation.

QUESTIONS

1. Identify and discuss the key success factors and strategic forces that drive the online banking industry.
2. What are the major attributes that differentiate Smile from the other key players in the UK online banking market?
3. Critically evaluate the marketing strategy of Smile and advise the management on how to strengthen the company's competitive position in the online banking industry.

Part II Where are we now?

3

Environmental and internal analysis: market information and intelligence

LEARNING OBJECTIVES

- Provide an overview of the three stages (areas) of the Strategic Marketing Management (SMM) process.
- Define the marketing environment and discuss the relevant types of market information that are required for market scanning and analysis.
- Review the analytical models/frameworks that can be used in the strategic analysis stage.
- Outline the potential outcome of the strategic marketing analysis stage and the possible implications on the subsequent stages of the SMM process and future strategic choices.

CHAPTER AT A GLANCE

Introduction

Building on the discussion in Chapter 2, where the analytical models and frameworks of strategic marketing planning/management were briefly reviewed, this chapter and Chapter 4 discuss in greater detail the first two stages of the strategic marketing management (SMM) process for strategy development. The remaining chapters of the book are devoted to the third stage of the SMM process, namely, strategy implementation. In other words, the remaining chapters discuss the implementation aspects of the various elements of marketing mix and activities. Porter's generic strategy typology (low-cost, differentiation, and focus) form the backdrop to the discussion in every chapter in the book. Although other typologies of generic strategy are suggested in the literature (e.g., Utterback and Abernathy, 1975; Miles and Snow, 1978), Porter's typology is still the one that has received wide acceptance and appreciation from both academicians and practitioners. The SMM process involves, arguably in a linear way, three subsequent stages—strategic analysis, strategic choice, and strategy implementation (see Figure 3.1).

Johnson and Scholes (1999) described the three stages of the process as follows. *Strategic analysis* is concerned with understanding the strategic position of the organization in terms of its external environment, internal resources and competencies, and the expectations

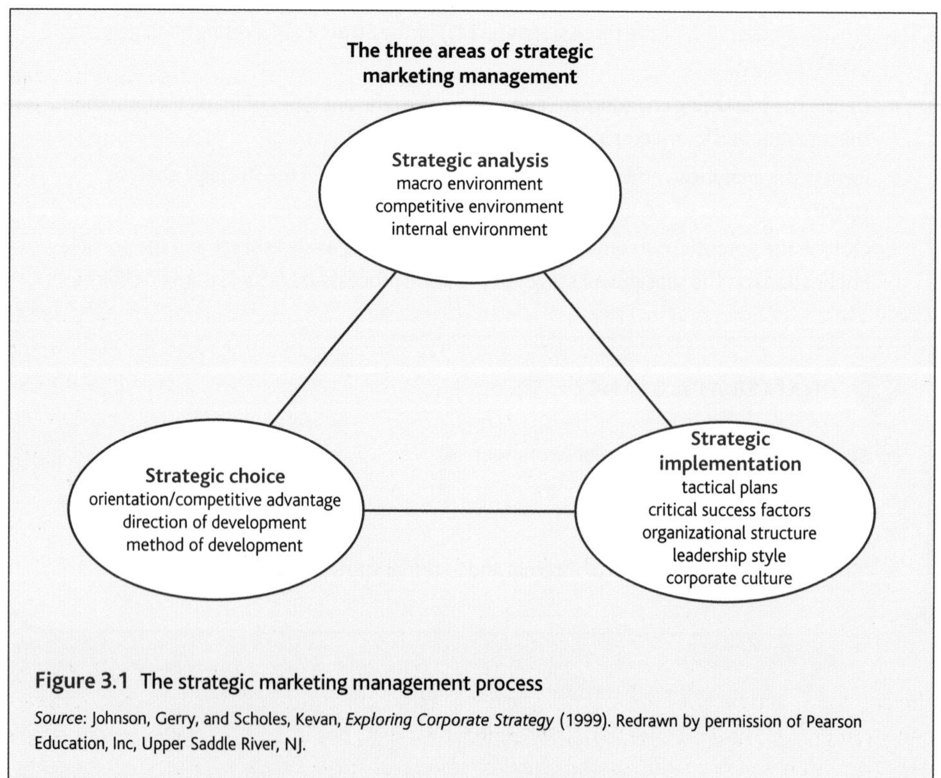

Figure 3.1 The strategic marketing management process

Source: Johnson, Gerry, and Scholes, Kevan, *Exploring Corporate Strategy* (1999). Redrawn by permission of Pearson Education, Inc, Upper Saddle River, NJ.

and influence of stakeholders. *Strategic choice* involves understanding the underlying bases guiding future strategy, and generating strategic options for evaluation and selecting from among them. *Strategy implementation* is the translation of strategy into organizational action through organizational structure and design, resource planning, and the management of strategic change. The purpose and importance of the SMM model as well as the major criticisms have been extensively debated in the marketing and strategy literature (e.g., Mintzberg, 1990, 1994a; Ansoff, 1991, 1994).

Strategic analysis and market environment

Any organization is a creature of its environment. Strategy formulation is, therefore, seen as the development of long-range plans for the effective management of the environmental opportunities and threats while taking into account the organization's strengths and weaknesses. Strategic analysis, as an integral stage of strategy formulation, involves the collection and analysis of relevant types of information about the environmental forces and trends on the one hand, and organizational resources and capabilities on the other. The firm's environment involves two distinct levels, the internal environment, consisting of variables within the organisation but not usually within the long-run control of top management, and the external environment consisting of variables outside the organization and not typically within the short-run control of top management. The external environment is further divided into two sub-environments: the 'macro' or remote environment and the 'micro' or competitive environment. The potential output of scanning and analysing the external environment is the identification of opportunities and threats, both present and potential, which face the organization. On the other hand, the key output of analysing the internal environment is the identification of strengths and weaknesses that exist within the organization's culture and structure (see Figure 3.2 for the marketing environment).

External environmental analysis

To be successful over time an organization must be in tune with its external environment. There must be a 'strategic fit' between what the environment wants and what the organization has to offer, as well as between what the organization needs and what the environment can provide. While most airline companies saw the horrific events of 9/11 as a major threat affecting the whole industry and started to slow down their businesses, a low-cost airline, Easyjet, responded differently. Two months after 9/11, it was reported that the market share of Easyjet was not only in a good shape but actually increasing.

A step towards achieving such strategic fit is scanning and analysing the variables and forces that exist in the two sub-levels of the external environment: remote and competitive.

The macro (remote) environment

The 'macro' or remote environment includes general forces that do not directly touch on the short-run activities of the organization but that can, and often do, influence its long-run strategic decisions. These variables generally affect, but in different ways, every single organization in the marketing environment regardless of the industrial sector in which the

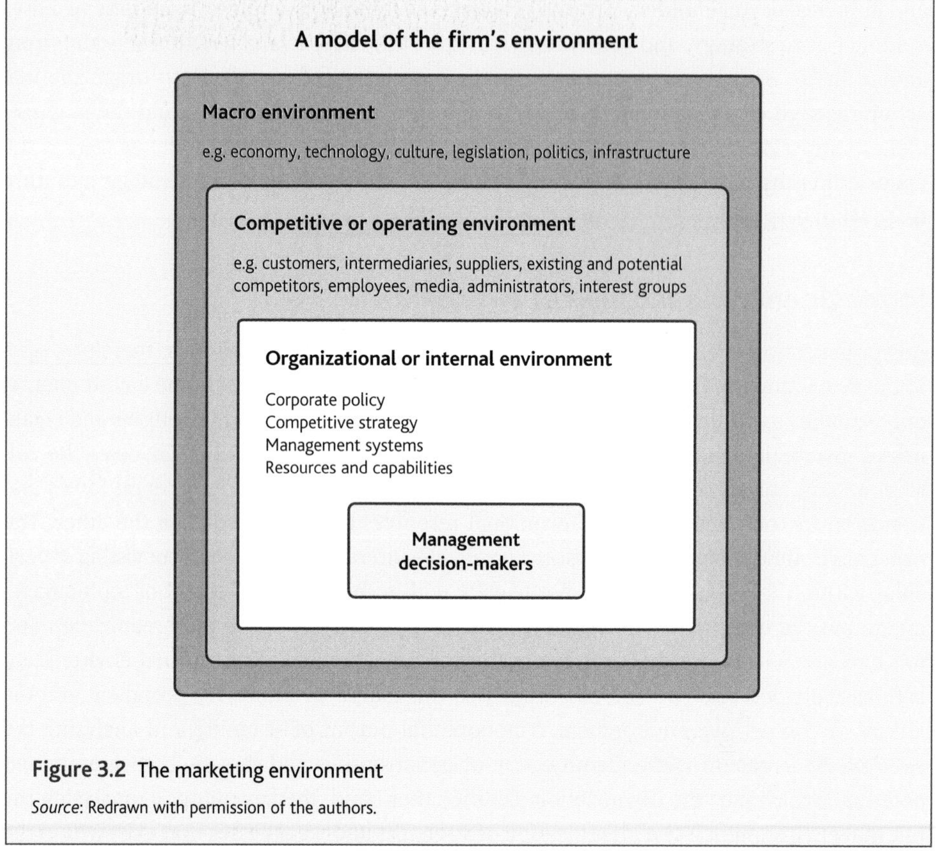

Figure 3.2 The marketing environment

Source: Redrawn with permission of the authors.

organization operates. The number of possible strategic variables in the macro environment is enormous, given the fact that each country has its own unique set of macro variables. For example, although China, Thailand, Taiwan, Hong Kong, and Japan are parts of Asia's Pacific Rim, they have different views on the role of businesses in society. It is generally believed in China, for example, that the role of businesses is primarily to contribute to national development, whereas in Hong Kong and Thailand the role of business is primarily to make profits for shareholders. Needless to say such differences may translate into different trade regulations and varying degrees of opposition to foreign competitors.

The variables of the macro environment are categorized in different ways, the most notable being the PEST framework (political/legal, economic, socio-cultural, and technological) (see Table 3.1 for the PEST variables).

In order to identify and examine the possible impact of the strategic variables of the macro environment, organizations should systematically scan and analyse the environment. Dibb et al. (2001) defined environmental scanning and analysis as follows. **Environmental scanning** is the process of collecting information about the forces in the environment. Scanning involves observation, perusal of secondary sources, such as business, trade, government, and general interest publications, and marketing research. Motorola, the mobile handset producer, has its intelligence department to monitor the

TABLE 3.1 The PEST framework for environmental analysis

Political/legal factors
Legislative structures
Monopoly restrictions
Political and government stability
Political orientations
Taxation policies
Employment legislation
Foreign trade regulations
Environmental protection legislation
Pressure groups
Trade union power
Social-cultural factors
Demographics
Lifestyles
Social mobility
Educational levels
Attitudes
Consumerism
Economic factors
Business cycles
Money supply
Inflation rates
Investment levels
Unemployment
Energy costs
GNP trends
Patterns of ownership
Technological factors
Levels and focuses of government and industrial R&D expenditure
Speed of technology transfer
Product life cycles
Joint ventures

Source: Adapted from Wilson and Gilligan (1997) and Johnson and Scholes (1999).

latest technology developments introduced at scientific conferences, in academic journals, and in trade gossip. This information helps it build 'technology roadmaps' that assess where breakthroughs are likely to occur, when they can be incorporated into new products, how much money their development will cost, and which of the developments is being worked out by competition. **Environmental analysis** is the process of assessing and interpreting the information gathered through market intelligence and environmental scanning.

In scanning and analysing the macro environment Johnson and Scholes (1999) suggested a step-wise approach which involves an initial audit of environmental influences followed by a series of increasingly focused steps that are designed to provide the strategist with a clear understanding, not just of the current state of the environment, but also of how it is most likely to develop. Another approach has been suggested by Wheelen and

Hunger (2000), who put together the variables of the macro environment and the competitive environment to form a matrix. This approach enables strategic managers to estimate how future developments of the macro variables may affect the firm via their impact on forces in the firm's competitive environment. In responding to macro environmental variables organizations can either accept environmental forces as uncontrollable and remain passive and reactive towards this environment, or, if they believe that environmental forces can be shaped, they can adopt a more proactive direction. (See Mini Case Study 3.1.)

MINI CASE STUDY 3.1 'New Look plans trial stores abroad'

New Look, the UK's third-largest retailer, is planning to open six trial stores in France and Belgium, following Hennes and Mauritz and Zara into overseas markets.

Phil Wrigley, chief executive, said New Look would spend about £6 m opening four stores in France and Belgium next spring. The move will come ahead of a wider roll-out of the New Look label. Mr Wrigley said New Look could run 50 to 60 outlets in France and up to 10 stores in Belgium. He also said the retailer had more ambitious plans for Europe, citing Belgium, the Netherlands, Luxembourg and eastern Europe.

He said he was also considering opening New Look franchises in the Middle East and Asia. He said: 'Eastern Europe is growing very quickly, there is demand in countries like Poland and H&M have opened some stores [in Eastern Europe]—it is nice to not be at the leading edge.'

New Look, which already has a 212-strong chain of smaller fashion boutiques trading under the name of Mim in France, said it was comfortable that the New Look and Mim labels could trade side-by-side. Inditex, which runs Zara, has another six brands trading under its name including Bershka and Pull and Bear, which caters for younger customers.

New Look's international ambitions reflect the growing trend among UK retailers to seek new markets amid fierce competition and price deflation on their home turf.

Tesco, the UK's biggest retailer, has been pushing into eastern Europe and south-east Asia over a decade. So have DSG International, formerly Dixons Group, and Kingfisher, owner of B&Q.

This month, Marks and Spencer said it was expanding its international franchise operations by adding Russia to its portfolio. M&S's decision to extend its franchise operations came just four years after it retreated from Portugal, Spain and France.

Mr Wrigley said UK retailers could succeed abroad. He said: 'It is not true that UK retailers don't do well overseas. Look at what Mothercare has done in Russia. Credit to Napoleon when he said we were a nation of shopkeepers. We are not just a nation of shopkeepers in the UK—we are a nation that does well outside as well when we listen to consumers.'

Mr Wrigley insisted that the international push was not a precursor to New Look returning to the public market, having been taken private in 2004 for £699 m. He said the business was now worth £1bn to £1.5bn. But, when asked whether New Look may float next year, he said: 'Nothing has been ruled in and nothing has been ruled out.'

Permira and Apax both have a 30 per cent holding in the retailer, with the remainder being held by Tom Singh, New Look's founder, and the management team.

Source: Elizabeth Rigby (2005), *Financial Times*, 17 November.

Despite the difficulties of environmental scanning and analysis that act as deterrents to the development and implementation of an effective scanning system, there are several principal benefits. The essence of strategy formulation is relating a company to its environment. The competitive dimension of the environment is strongly influential in determining the competitive rules of the game as well as the competitive strategy that is to be pursued. Empirical studies have examined the influence of environmental scanning on business activities in general and strategic decisions in particular. Diffenbach (1983), for example, carried out a survey on 500 US corporations and identified a number of benefits gained by adopting an effective environmental scanning system. Other research, by Daft et al. (1988) and Thomas et al. (1993), showed a positive relationship between environmental scanning and the outcomes of business performance. Jennings and Lumpkin (1992) also examined the influences of environmental scanning on strategic decisions. The results of their research indicated that businesses following a differentiation strategy tend to scan the environment primarily for opportunities and closely monitor customer attitudes, while firms following a cost leadership strategy tend to scan the environment primarily for threats and closely monitor competitors' activities. In short, environmental analysis is regarded as a key component in any planning system, without which a company cannot expect to develop an effective strategy. All firms should engage in systematic and continuous scanning of the whole range of external variables and analyse them thoroughly to find out what influence such variables have upon their performance and strategic decisions. Organizations usually develop strategies on the basis of both environmental analysis and scanning to find the 'strategic fit' between external opportunities and threats, on the one hand, and internal strengths and weaknesses, on the other. IKEA's experiment with housing trends in Europe in the late 1990s was presumably the result of its ability to identify a possible market opportunity and also its attempt to capitalize on its skills in developing kit-form products at reasonable prices to customers.

The role marketing can play in environmental scanning relies on the specific activities of market research and marketing audit. Marketing audit involves a formal review of the organization's products, markets, customers, and forces and trends in the external environment. Marketing research has been successfully used by companies such as Procter & Gamble and Microsoft to identify new market opportunities. Procter & Gamble, for example, create a market advantage by spending a great amount of money on advertising and promotion to build entry barriers in the face of a new entrant. This company and others believe that market research is an especially useful tool in directing incremental improvements to existing products.

The micro (competitive) environment

The 'micro' or competitive environment includes those forces or groups that directly affect, and are affected by, an organization's major operations. An organization's competitive environment is often referred to as the industry in which the organization competes. A fundamental step in strategy development is anticipation and analysis of the major structural elements of the industry. Such structural elements of any industry are identified by Aaker (2001) as industry size, growth, competitive structure, cost structure, channels, trends, and key success factors. The analysis of the industry's environment, however, should include not only the characteristics and trends of the industry but also the forces that influence such characteristics and trends. A number of analytical models and frameworks have been suggested for analysing the micro (competitive) environment in which any organization operates. In a linear model, Cravens (1994) focuses on the most important aspects that should be examined when analysing the industry environment (see Figure 3.3).

Industry can simply be defined as a group of firms producing similar products or services. From a competitive perspective, industry can also be defined as a group of competitors producing products or services that compete directly with each other. However, one of the most difficult problems in industry analysis is defining the specific industry to which the company's product belongs. This might be because no clear boundaries exist between industries in terms of either products or geographical area. In practice, many organizations compete for the customer's money, e.g., Coke versus Pepsi versus Irn Bru versus Crisps versus a lottery ticket versus a hamburger versus whatever we can spend our money on, at the same price. Kotler (1994) suggested that instead of looking at industry as an aggregate group of companies that produce similar products, we can look at industry as different sets of companies that satisfy the varying needs of customers. Using an illustrative example, Kotler

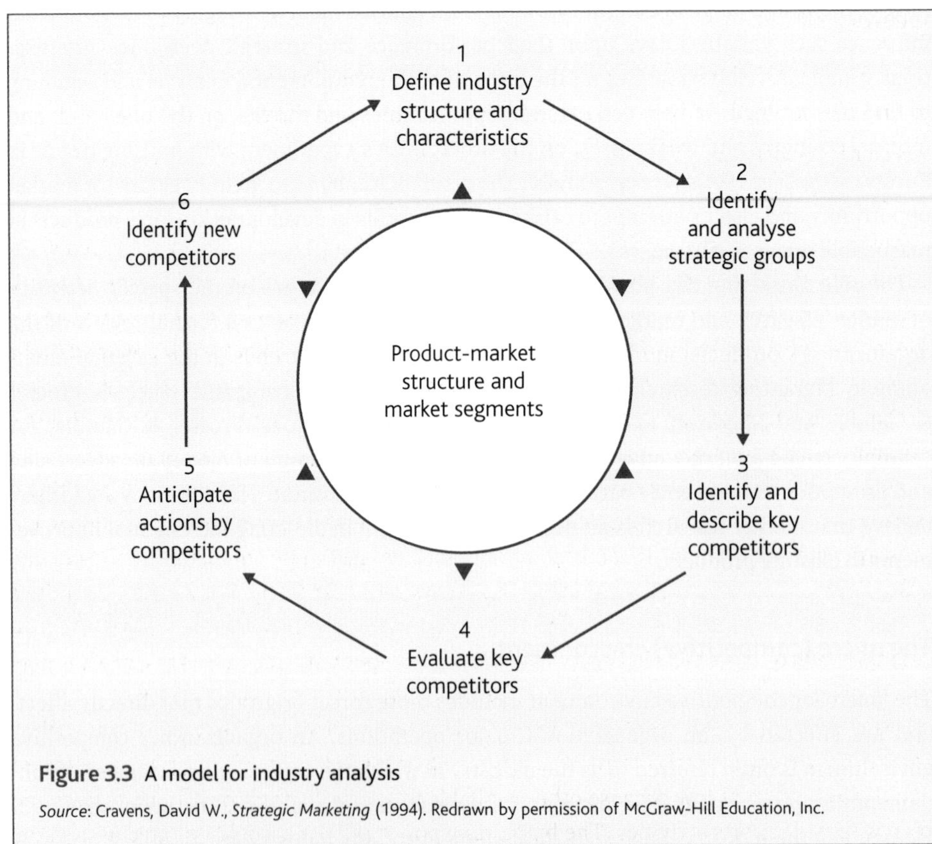

Figure 3.3 A model for industry analysis

Source: Cravens, David W., *Strategic Marketing* (1994). Redrawn by permission of McGraw-Hill Education, Inc.

suggested that industry can be defined and analysed in terms of four levels of competition within an industry:

- **Industry definition based on brand competition:** here Buick might compete against Ford, Toyota, and Honda but not against Mercedes.
- **Industry definition based on product competition:** here Buick competes against all automobile manufacturers.
- **Industry definition based on form competition:** here Buick is competing against not only other automobile manufacturers but also manufacturers of motorcycles, bicycles, and trucks.
- **Industry definition based on generic competition:** here Buick is competing with companies that sell major consumer durables, foreign holidays, and new homes.

The potential companies (new entrants) that may come on the scene should also be considered when undertaking industry analysis. Ten years ago no one would have imagined that Asda may compete in other product lines than food, beverages, and grocery goods. Today Asda displays under one roof a variety of clothing products, appliances, and insurance policies alongside its conventional grocery goods. Although identifying the potential new entrants to an industry is not an easy task, they can often be expected to come from the following groups:

- firms not in the industry but which could overcome entry barriers
- firms for which there is obvious synergy from being in the industry
- firms for which competing in the industry is an obvious extension of the strategy
- customers or suppliers who may integrate backwards or forwards

Another way of analysing the micro environment, which takes full account of the competitive forces that shape the industry structure, is Porter's five forces model (1979). According to Porter's view the state of competition in an industry depends on five basic competitive forces, the collective strength of these forces determining the ultimate profit potential of the industry and the ability of firms in an industry to earn rates of return on investment in excess of the cost of capital (Porter, 1985). The five forces and the elements related to each force are shown in Figure 3.4.

To illustrate the linkage between the five forces and strategy development, Porter (1980) pointed out that the goal of competitive strategy for a business unit is to find a position in the industry where the company can best defend itself against these competitive forces or can influence them in its favour. A strategist can analyse any market by rating each competitive force as high, medium, or low in strength. Looking at the sportswear industry in the UK, for example, we could rate the five forces as follows. Competition among existing rivals is high as key players such as Adidas, Reebok, Nike, and Puma compete closely and strongly in the market. The threat of new entrants might be seen as low since the UK market has reached the maturity stage and sales growth is not as high as it used to be. The threat of substitutes could also be seen as low because other available products do not appeal to customers and do not sponsor sports activities. The bargaining power of buyers could be rated as medium in strength as buyers are interested in buying trendy sports products (well-known brands)

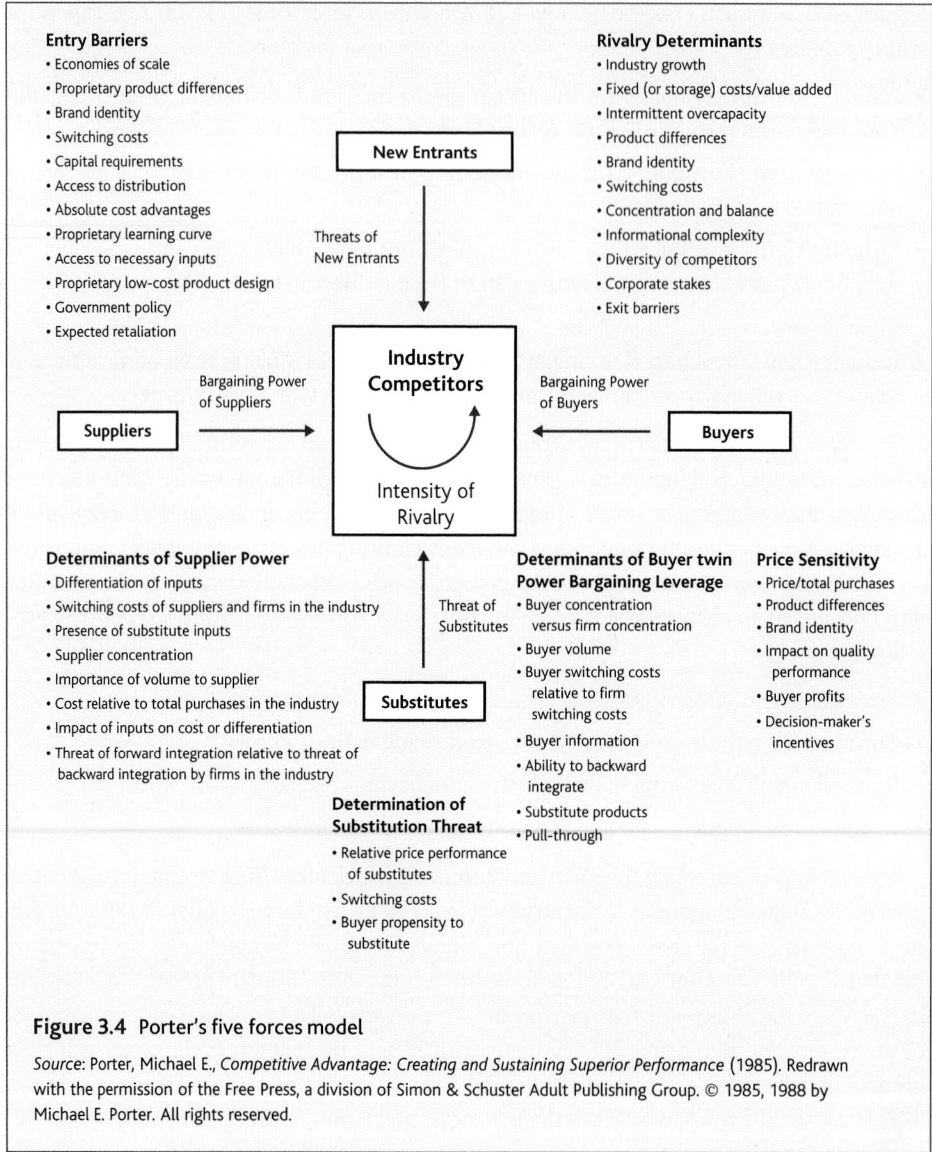

Figure 3.4 Porter's five forces model

Source: Porter, Michael E., *Competitive Advantage: Creating and Sustaining Superior Performance* (1985). Redrawn with the permission of the Free Press, a division of Simon & Schuster Adult Publishing Group. © 1985, 1988 by Michael E. Porter. All rights reserved.

but they cannot influence the price in their favour. Such an assessment of each competitive force will help strategists in analysing the competitive environment in which their companies compete.

Although widely used, Porter's five forces model has been subject to a number of criticisms. Speed (1989) claims that the principal criticism of Porter's work is methodological in that many of his points do not appear to be justified. O'Shaughnessy (1995) criticizes the five forces model on two grounds. First, he says, there is little to suggest that Porter's list is necessarily an exclusive or exhaustive one. Freeman (1984), for example, suggested a sixth force including a variety of stakeholder groups. In Freeman's view, analysis of the relative power of stakeholders fits quite well with Porter's theory and helps in formulating generic strategy. Secondly, O'Shaughnessy says, Porter gives no indication of how to operationalize any analysis based on these forces. In fact, there is no indication of how to assess the relative power of the forces, or how to determine what reactions to take. See Mini Case Study 3.2.

MINI CASE STUDY 3.2

'Who Practised the Bargaining Power over the other—Is it Safeway or Morrison?'

What was all the fuss about? After 11 months of brawling in the aisles, the UK supermarket industry is back where it started. Wm Morrison looks poised to buy Safeway for almost exactly the same price as the two agreed in January—before the rest of the industry piled into the fray and knocked the deal off course.

Safeway was badly hobbled by the Competition Commission's decision to block Tesco, Wal-Mart and J. Sainsbury from bidding. That ruled out an auction. But Safeway can still, almost, claim that it pushed Morrison slightly higher. Instead of the all-share bid worth 277p, it has negotiated a cash and shares bid worth 283p.

In reality, Safeway did get squeezed. Morrison's share price rise means that the share exchange terms of its original bid would now be worth 249p. Safeway shareholders are getting slightly less of the cake than before. But they do get to take some of the proceeds in cash. And David Webster, Safeway Chairman, deserves credit for avoiding a more brutal cut from Morrison—given this need to sell Safeway and his weak negotiating position. Sir Ken Morrison, meanwhile, has bowed to pragmatism. He knows he is getting a good deal. The 53 Safeway stores he is required to sell will fetch a strong price. By offering a cash component he, personally, also retains a bigger equity stake in the combined business.

As the only credible bidder, he could have tried slashing the price. But that would have risked losing out on a Safeway recommendation and having to go hostile. Importantly—assuming the deal goes through as expected—it avoids a bitter ending to the battle for the UK's fourth largest grocer. Morrison is already taking a huge risk by spending £3bn on a group twice its size. It will need all the co-operation it can get from Safeway management to give the complex integration a reasonable chance of success.

Source: *Financial Times*, 15 December 2003.

The five forces model suggests that competition extends beyond the companies within the industry to include new entries, substitutes, suppliers, and buyers. The stronger the force is, the greater the restrictions on companies to raise prices and earn greater profits. In other words, a strong force may be regarded as a threat because it is likely to reduce profits, whereas a weak force may be viewed as an opportunity because it may allow the company to earn higher profits.

Another approach for analysing the competitive 'micro' environment is to categorize the various competitors within the industry into strategic groups. Strategic group analysis is essential for identifying the group of companies with which the organization will compete. A strategic group can be defined as a group of firms pursuing the same or a similar strategy with similar resources. For example, although McDonald's and Subway are both in the fast food industry, they may have different objectives and strategies, and thus they belong to different strategic groups. They generally have very little in common and pay little attention to each other when planning competitive action. Burger King, however, has a great deal in common with McDonald's in that both have a similar strategy of serving low-priced fast food targeted for sale to the average family.

A firm's strategy can be distinguished using several dimensions that differentiate it from the strategies of other firms in the industry and which, in turn, should contribute to its relative performance in the industry. Such strategic dimensions include those strategic decision variables that best distinguish the business strategies and competitive positioning of the firms within an industry. Two approaches are frequently used for forming strategic groups. The first is a two-dimensional analysis by which a firm selects two strategic variables or characteristics that differentiate the companies within an industry and draws them on the vertical and horizontal axes. The second approach is a multidimensional analysis by which the difficulty of selecting the best two strategic factors can be overcome by incorporating several strategic variables. Figure 3.5 shows seven strategic groups in the world automobile industry.

The strategic group approach is an analytical device designed to aid in industry structural analysis. It is an intermediate frame of reference between looking at the industry as a whole and considering each firm separately. We should emphasize here that strategic groups are not equivalent to market segments of segmentation strategies but are defined on

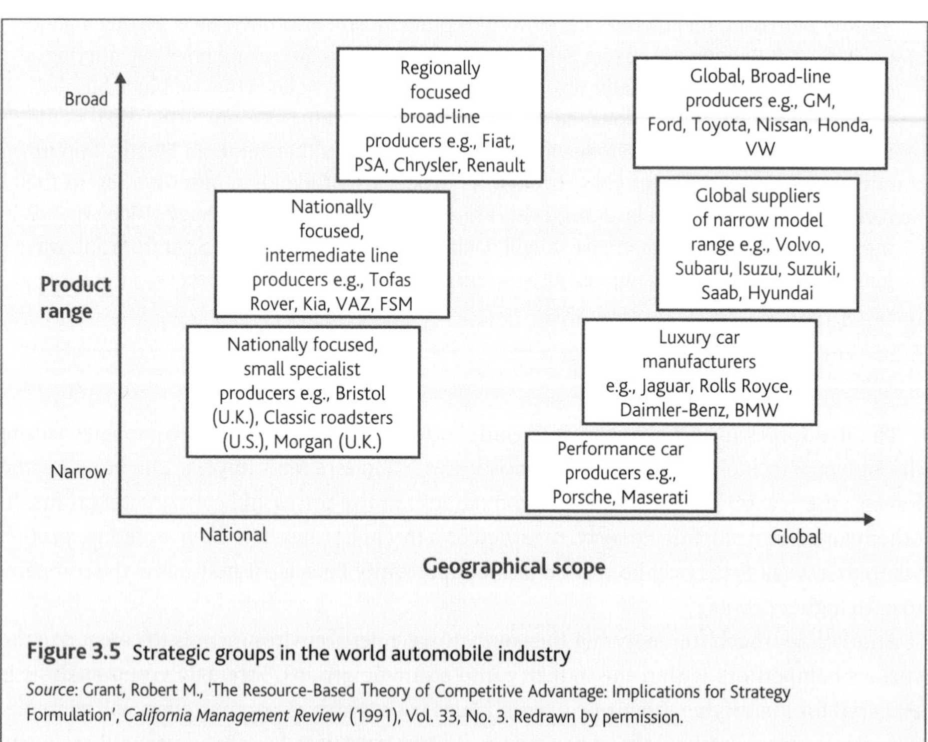

Figure 3.5 Strategic groups in the world automobile industry

Source: Grant, Robert M., 'The Resource-Based Theory of Competitive Advantage: Implications for Strategy Formulation', *California Management Review* (1991), Vol. 33, No. 3. Redrawn by permission.

the basis of the broader concept of strategic posture. While segmentation analysis focuses on the characteristics of customers and products as the basis for dividing the market, strategic group analysis uses the characteristics of firms and producers as the basis for division.

The benefits of identifying strategic groups are twofold. The first is that the height of the barriers to entry and exit can vary significantly from one group to another. The second is that the choice of a strategic group determines which companies are to be the principal competitors. Despite these benefits, a number of criticisms have been made. Issues related to identifying appropriate dimensions upon which to develop groups, their number, and the dynamic versus static analysis of strategic group formation remain problematic. Most of the empirical studies of strategic groups analyse differences in profitability between firms within one strategic group (Fiegenbaum and Thomas, 1990; Cool and Dierickx, 1993; Reger and Huff, 1993). The findings of these studies may reflect the fact that the members of a strategic group, while pursuing similar strategies, are not necessarily in competition with one another. While the strategic group is a useful concept, the value of that analysis is as a descriptive rather than a predictive tool. It is unlikely to offer much insight into why some firms in an industry are more profitable than others (Kerin et al., 1990).

Competitor analysis

Another central aspect of strategic analysis is perceptive competitor analysis. The objectives of undertaking competitor analysis are twofold. First, a company may have to develop a profile of the nature and success of the likely strategy changes each competitor in the market might make. Secondly, the company may also have to anticipate other competitors' probable response to the range of feasible strategic moves other firms could initiate and each competitor's probable reaction to the array of industry changes and broader environmental shifts that might occur. Competitor analysis is not a luxury task. It is necessary for a company to survive, grow, and to stay competitive. The purpose and importance of competitor analysis have been extensively discussed in the marketing literature (e.g., Taylor, 1992; Kotler and Armstrong, 2000; Hooley et al., 1998). Wilson and Gilligan (1997) defined competitor analysis as a set of activities which examines the comparative position of competing enterprises within a given strategic sector. The set of activities that organizations might undertake when analysing competitors are:

- identifying the company's competitors
- understanding competitors' objectives
- identifying competitors' strategies
- assessing competitors' strengths and weaknesses
- estimating competitors' reactions
- selecting competitors to attack and those to avoid

The key to identifying competitors is to link the industry perspective of competition and market perspective of competition by mapping out product/market segments. Such a map is the competitive arena in which a company can identify actual and potential competitors (Kotler, 2000). In identifying the company's competitors, a company should not be restricted to the current competitors but should also take into account potential competitors. Aaker (2001) pointed out that, among the sources of potential competitors are firms that might engage in market expansion, product expansion, backward integration, forward integration, and the export of the asset of skills. Shell, for example, has introduced mini-supermarkets to its forecourts in order to compete with supermarket petrol stations and 24-hour opening for convenience. This has been countered by Tesco with the introduction of 24-hour opening in selective sites around the country. There has been extensive research examining the competitive reactions to market entry from both existing rivals and new entrants (e.g., Lambkin, 1988; Gatignon et al., 1989; Haverty and Kyj, 1991; De Castro and Chrisman, 1995).

Having identified the principal competitors, a company needs then to focus upon each competitor's objectives. What drives each competitor's behaviour? Companies might begin by assuming that each competitor aims for profit maximization. In practice, however, profit maximization is an unrealistic objective which, for a wide variety of reasons, many companies are willing to sacrifice. The management of Ryanair, 'the no-frills airline', may have decided in the first three years after its launch not to adopt profit maximization as a strategic objective; instead they were interested in achieving a sustainable market share in the domestic and Western European market. Therefore, one must assume that each competitor has a variety of objectives, each of which has a different weight. These objectives might typically include cash flow, market share growth, technological leadership, or overall market leadership. Gaining an insight into this mix of objectives allows the strategist to arrive at tentative conclusions about how a competitor will respond to a competitive thrust. For example, a firm like Volkswagen pursuing market share growth in the world car market is likely to react far more quickly and strongly against a price cut or a substantial increase in advertising spending than a firm like Microsoft aiming for technological leadership.

The starting point for understanding competitors' strategies is identifying each competitor's assumptions. These assumptions generally fall into two major categories: (a) the competitor's assumptions about the industry and other companies, and (b) the competitor's assumptions about itself. A competitor's assumptions about the industry and other companies may well be subtly influenced by, as well as reflected in, its current strategy. Knowing a competitor's assumptions will guide a firm to identify the basis of the competitor's strategy, e.g., the competitor may see itself as socially aware, an industry leader, a low-cost producer, or as having the best salesforce. These assumptions will influence how the competitor behaves, the way it reacts to events, and how it formulates its own competitive marketing strategy.

Having identified the competitors' assumptions, the firm is in a position to develop statements of the current strategy of each competitor. This strategy is most usefully thought of as a key operating policy in each functional area of the business. The firm needs to know each competitor's product features, quality, customer services, pricing policy, distribution coverage, salesforce policy, advertising, and other promotion programmes. The firm has also to estimate competitors' future strategies. These strategies may simply follow the general direction already established, particularly if there are no major external influences requiring them to change their strategies. Nevertheless, it is not wise to assume that an existing strategy will continue to be effective. Competitors' current actions may only signal probable future actions.

By this stage it should be apparent that the identification and evaluation of competitors' strengths and weaknesses is at the very heart of a well-developed marketing strategy. Understanding a competitor's strengths and weaknesses provides insight into the firm's ability to initiate and/or react to strategic moves, respond to environmental or industry events, and pursue various strategies. The Japanese car producers were able to dominate the world automobile market during the 1970s and 1980s by analysing and understanding competitors' strategies and appreciating competitors' strengths and weaknesses. Such a thorough understanding enabled them to provide customers with better value than the competition.

As a first step, companies can gather secondary data on each competitor's goals, strategies, and performance over the past few years. They can also conduct primary marketing research with customers, suppliers, and dealers in order to understand more about competitors' strengths and weaknesses. Two pieces of empirical research by Smith and Prescott (1987) and Cvitkovic (1989) have suggested different approaches to profiling competitors within an industry in terms of their strengths and weaknesses. The approach suggested by Cvitkovic (1989) began by suggesting four key areas of competitive strengths: marketing, technology, management, and manufacturing; and their respective measures of success: sales, R&D, ROI, and capacity utilization. By defining the linkage between each of these pairs, the author illustrated how different profiles of a firm's competitors can be developed.

According to Aaker (2001), competitors' strengths and weaknesses are based upon the existence or absence of assets or skills. Thus, to analyse competitors' strengths and weaknesses, it is necessary to identify the assets and skills that are relevant to the industry. For example, an intangible asset like Nike's well-known brand could present a major strength as could a skill like the company's ability to manufacture top quality goods. Conversely, the absence of a unique asset or distinctive skill can represent significant weaknesses. The knowledge of a competitor's weaknesses can often be used to great effect by a strategist. Wilson and Gilligan (1997) listed several factors that make a competitor vulnerable, such as lack of cash, low margins, poor growth, and limited market share.

A growing number of companies have used benchmarking to assess and trace competitors' strengths. Benchmarking has become a powerful tool for increasing a company's competitiveness. It is the continuous process of measuring products, services, and practices against the toughest competitors or those recognized as industry leaders (Shetty, 1993). The UK Customs and Excise department won the 1996 European best practice benchmarking award for an innovative adaptation of benchmarking to the requirements of a public sector organization market testing the value of its activities. Drew (1997) investigated the links between benchmarking and improvements in organizational performance. This study revealed that benchmarking can actually generate broadly-based change in organizational thinking and action and lead to better understanding of competitors' strengths.

A company's survival depends on anticipating the actions and reactions of rivals. How a competitor is likely to behave in future should be examined from two sides: first, how a competitor is likely to respond to any changes taking place in the external environment; and secondly, how the competitor is likely to respond to specific competitive moves other organizations might make. Four common reaction profiles among competitors in terms of type and time of response have been suggested by Kotler (2000):

- **the laid-back competitor:** does not react quickly or strongly to a given assault
- **the selective competitor:** might react to certain types of assault and not others
- **the tiger competitor:** reacts swiftly and strongly to any assaults
- **the stochastic competitor:** does not exhibit a predictable reaction pattern

This issue of competitors' response has been investigated in numerous research studies. For example, Smith et al. (1991) investigated how firms build competitive advantage by focusing on the actions and responses of rivals in the US market. They identified four attributes of competitive response: propensity to imitate, likelihood of response, average response lag, and average response order. The findings of this study supported the idea that a firm's response can be predicted from the manner in which it interprets and processes information.

While competitors can surely be threats, the right competitors can strengthen rather than weaken a firm's competitive position in the market. Companies that learn to live with competitors and even benefit from them will clearly be better positioned for the future. Microsoft and Apple Macintosh are examples of two companies competing in the same market (PC market) and contributing to market development and improving customer knowledge. A good competitor is not one that performs beneficial functions and challenges the firm not to be complacent, but one with which the firm can achieve a stable and profitable industry equilibrium without protracted warfare. Bad competitors, on the other hand, have the opposite characteristics (Porter, 1985). It is often desirable for a firm to have one or more good competitors. At the same time, a firm should concentrate its efforts on attacking bad competitors. In terms of the strategic benefits of a competitor, Porter (1985) identified four general categories: increasing competitive advantage, improving current industry structure, aiding market development, and deterring entry. Hooley et al. (1998) also identified a number of characteristics of a good competitor. These are:

- able to perceive own weaknesses
- holds realistic assumptions
- accepts its current profitability
- formulates a strategy that improves industry
- understands the rules
- has knowledge of cost structure
- has reconcilable goals
- is risk-averse

In order to undertake competitor analysis that will be of value, a company needs to collect relevant information in an effective manner. Such information should be collected, organized, interpreted, disseminated, and used in a systematic way. Specifically, two basic categories of information are required for marketing strategy development: information about the company itself and relevant information about the company's environment and its competitors. The latter set of information is generally collected through a competitive intelligence system. The marketing intelligence system first identifies the vital types of competitive information and the best sources of this information. The system then continuously collects the data from the field. The information should be checked for validity and reliability before key information is communicated to relevant decision makers. The process and functions of a competitive intelligence system are shown in Figure 3.6.

The effectiveness of any marketing intelligence system is dependent on the frequency of collecting, interpreting, and disseminating the required information about the market environment and competitors. While large corporations have to design an intelligence system, smaller companies, which cannot afford to set up a formal intelligence system, may assign specific executives to watch specific competitors.

Strategic analysis of remote and competitive environments can be concluded by developing what is known as an 'environmental impact matrix' in which the potential impact of major opportunities and threats is identified, assessed, and weighted (see Table 3.2).

Internal environmental analysis

Internal analysis aims to provide a detailed understanding of those aspects of the organization that are of strategic importance. Although the external information and

TABLE 3.2 Environmental impact matrix

Factor	Impact of factor	Potential opportunity or threat
Macro-environment		
Political/legal	Increased legislation on product liability	Mild threat (−1)
Economic	Recession in key overseas markets	Major threat (−4)
Technological	Little innovation likely from competitors	Neutral impact (0)
Socio-cultural	Increased awareness of environmental protection issues	Significant opportunity (+5)
Competitive environment		
Competition	Intense rivalry in industry/marketplace	Critical threat (−5)
Buyers	Convergence of customer requirements worldwide	Significant opportunity (+5)
Suppliers	Few suppliers dominate industry	Critical threat (−5)
Threat of new entrants	Industry barriers to entry are low	Threat (−3)

Source: Reprinted with permission of the authors.

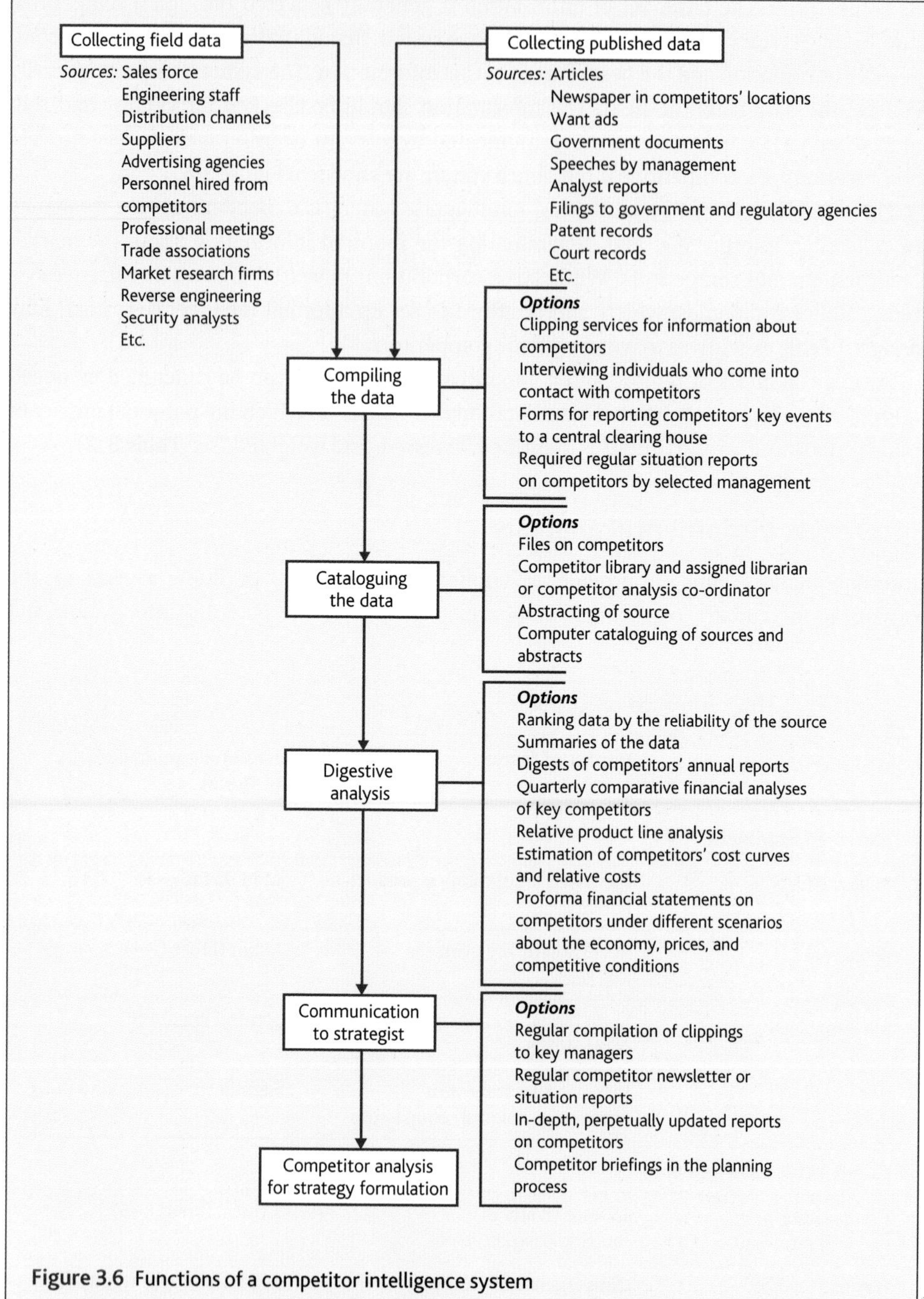

Figure 3.6 Functions of a competitor intelligence system

Source: Porter, Michael E., *Competitive Strategy: Techniques for Analyzing Industries and Competitors* (1980). Reprinted with the permission of the Free Press, a division of Simon & Schuster Adult Publishing Group.

analysis are essential to success, they are not sufficient to achieve the required success unless they are accompanied by a thorough analysis of the organization's internal environment. The internal appraisal has a pivotal role in formulating marketing strategies and plans with which a firm can trace its success. It has been suggested that differences in performance among companies may be best explained, not through differences in industry structure identified by industry analysis, but through differences in the firm's assets and resources and their application (Grant, 1991). It has also been claimed that a considerable amount of thinking in the 1980s on marketing strategy focused upon the nature and structure of the organization's external environment and upon the ways in which this environment is the principal influence upon strategy development (Fifield and Gilligan, 1998). More recently, however, it has been argued that the significance of the external environment has been over-emphasized and that a more appropriate focus for strategy development is the organization's resource base.

Resource-based approach

The resource-based approach to internal analysis is a well recognized framework for strategy development (see Figure 3.7). Figure 3.7 illustrates the role of the firm's resources

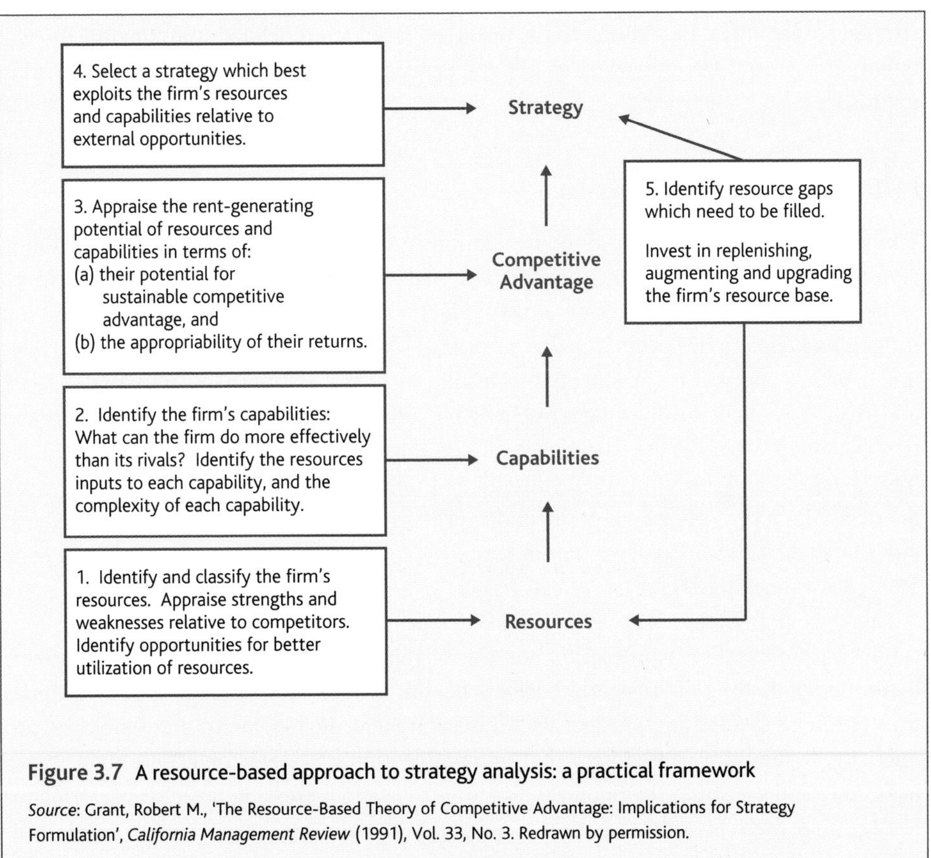

Figure 3.7 A resource-based approach to strategy analysis: a practical framework

Source: Grant, Robert M., 'The Resource-Based Theory of Competitive Advantage: Implications for Strategy Formulation', *California Management Review* (1991), Vol. 33, No. 3. Redrawn by permission.

as the foundation for formulating marketing strategy. This framework shows how a firm's resources and capabilities can create a competitive advantage.

The elements of this framework are: (1) defining the firm's resources that present internal strengths and weaknesses; (2) the organization's combined resources form a number of capabilities; (3) these resources and capabilities provide a sustainable competitive advantage; (4) this sustainability derives from linking the organization's unique resources to different types of strategies that exploit these resources and capabilities across time; and (5) the characteristics of resources and capabilities (i.e. durability, transferability, and replicability) are important in sustaining competitive advantage and in identifying resource gaps. Research on the resource-based approach has shown that a company's sustained competitive advantage is primarily determined by its resources and capabilities. The resource audit identifies the unique resources available to an organization to support its strategies. Some of the resources may be unique because they are difficult to imitate, e.g. a world class brand, patented products, or location. A study by Williams (1992) focused on the time-based interdependencies between an organization's resources and its environment, and on the role of strategy in creating these links. In Williams's view, strategic managers must link their organizations' unique resources and capabilities to different types of strategies across time and they must also learn how to create and sustain these links proactively. By their very nature, resource-based strategies demand a clear understanding of the organization's strategic capabilities. In addition to the resource-based approach for analysing the internal environment, strategic managers can adopt/apply one or a combination of other distinct approaches.

Performance analysis approach

The most notable work being done in relation to this approach is the PIMS programme (*Profit Impact of Market Strategy*) conducted by the American Strategic Planning Institute to help pinpoint relevant internal strategic factors for business corporations. The PIMS programme aims to discover empirical principles that determine which strategy variables, under which conditions, produce what results in terms of return on investment (ROI) and cash flow. Specifically, PIMS research has identified nine major strategic variables that account for 80% of the variation in profitability (ROI) among businesses in the database (Buzzell and Wiersema, 1981; Buzzell and Gale, 1987). Much work has been carried out to highlight the importance of the PIMS approach (Chussil, 1991; Gale, 1992; De Castro and Chrisman, 1995). However, a number of criticisms have also been made (Kerin et al., 1990; Schwalbach, 1991).

There are many other ways to evaluate the performance of a business. While the most common is financial measures, other non-financial performance measures can also provide better understanding of long-term business health. A number of such non-financial measures are market standing, product value, management development, and employee productivity. It should be noted here that an organization's strategic objectives may change over time, and so should the financial measures to use for assessing business performance. For example, at the introduction stage of a new product, the key measure to use may be sales growth, whilst at maturity stage, ROI may be used to assess company success. Given the importance of both financial and non-financial measures, Kaplan and Norton (1992, 1996) introduced the balanced scorecard as a tool that measures and evaluates a company's performance. This approach suggests four perspectives by which to integrate the financial and non-financial measures of a company's performance: the *financial perspective*, the *customer perspective*, the *internal business perspective*, and the *innovation and learning perspective*.

Apart from categorizing the internal variables they use as either financial or non-financial, strategic managers must generally look within their organizations to identify the internal strategic factors that have the greatest effect (positive or negative) on the company's performance. In other words, strategic managers should identify the internal variables that may be significant strengths or weaknesses. A variable is a strength if it provides a competitive advantage; it is of value to customer; and the firm does or has the potential to do particularly well relative to the abilities of existing or potential competitors. On the other hand, a variable is a weakness if it is also of value to a customer but the firm does it poorly or does not have the capacity to do it well, although its competitors have that capacity (Wheelen and Hunger, 2000). In evaluating the significance of such variables, the management of an organization should ascertain whether they are a company's particular strengths and weaknesses, which will help determine its future performance. One way of doing this is to compare the measures of these variables with similar measures of: (a) the company's past performance, (b) the company's key competitors, and (c) the industry as a whole. When using the financial statements of a company to measure its performance, we should take into account the fact that multinational corporations follow the accounting rules of their home country. As a result, their financial statements may be somewhat difficult to understand or to use for comparisons with competitors from other countries. For example, British firms such as Body Shop and British Petroleum use the term 'turnover' rather than 'sales revenue'.

Value chain analysis

This framework was developed by Porter (1985) as a way of examining the nature and extent of the synergies, if any, among the internal activities of a firm. According to Porter, every firm is a collection of activities that are performed to design, produce, promote, deliver, and support its product. All of these activities can be represented in five primary activities and four support activities using a value chain concept (see Figure 3.8). The main idea of a value chain is that it is a systematic way of examining all the activities a firm performs and how they interact to differentiate a firm's value chain from its competitors' value chains. This differentiation is recognized as a key source of competitive advantage.

Value chain analysis has been widely used as a means of analysing the internal activities of an organization and relating them to an assessment of the competitive strength of the organization. One of the key benefits of value chain analysis is the recognition that organizations are much more than a random collection of machines, money, and people because these resources are of no value unless deployed in activities and organized into systems which ensure that products and services are produced and valued by the final customer/user.

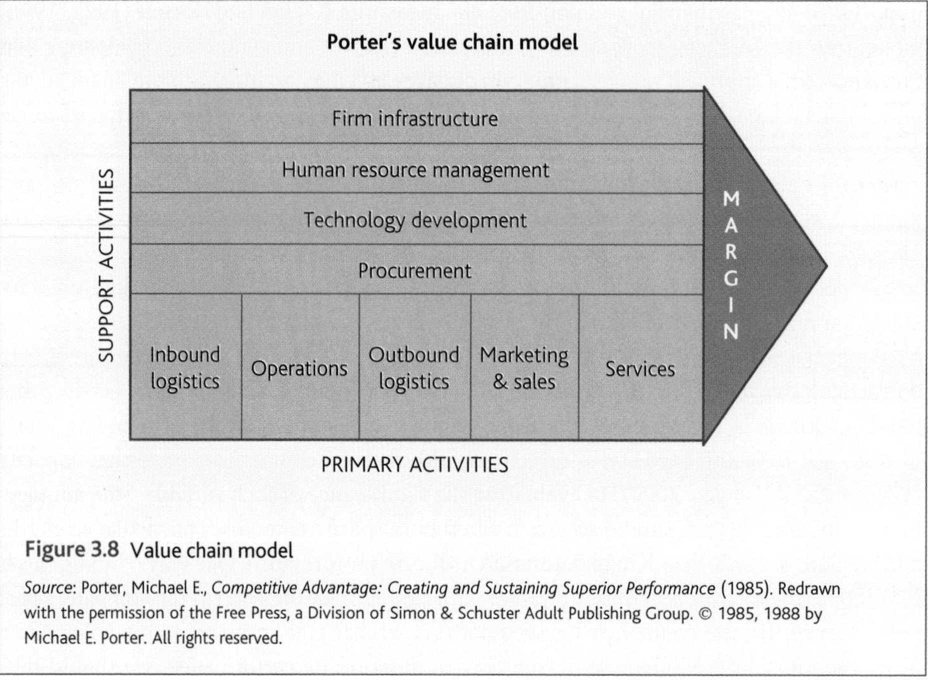

Figure 3.8 Value chain model

Source: Porter, Michael E., *Competitive Advantage: Creating and Sustaining Superior Performance* (1985). Redrawn with the permission of the Free Press, a Division of Simon & Schuster Adult Publishing Group. © 1985, 1988 by Michael E. Porter. All rights reserved.

Because most companies produce several products or services they may have a different value chain for each of the company's product lines. Thus the internal analysis of the company involves evaluating a series of value chains. The internal analysis of an organization can be undertaken as follows.

- examination of each product line's value chain in terms of the various activities involved in producing that product
- examination of the linkages within each product line's value chain
- examination of the potential synergies among the value chains of different products

In addition to the above, it should be noted here that much of the value creation occurs not only inside the organization but also in the supply and distribution channels. For example, the quality of a passenger car is not only influenced by the activities undertaken within the manufacturing plant but also determined by the quality of spare parts, components, and the performance of distributors.

Functional analysis approach

One of the simplest approaches for analysing an organization's internal environment is functional analysis. A company's skills and resources can be organized into a competence profile according to the typical business functions of marketing, finance, R&D, and production, among others. The firm's resources include not only the financial and physical resources in each functional area but also the ability of people in each area to formulate and implement the necessary functional objectives, strategies, and policies. The resources

TABLE 3.3 Strategic capability profile

Internal area	Resource/Competence	Evaluation
Strategic capability profile (A) based on resource audit		
Physical resources	New facilities incorporating latest technology	Major strength (+4)
Human resources	Highly trained technical staff	Minor strength (+2)
	Top scientists recruited	
Financial resources	High gearing	Mild weakness (−2)
Strategic capability profile (B) based on Value Chain activities		
Intangibles	Strong corporate image in the marketplace Well-established brand names	Significant strength (+3) Significant strength (+4)
Inbound logistics/procurement	Over-reliance on a limited number of suppliers	Significant weakness (−4)
Outbound logistics	Ineffective warehouse automation	Weakness (−3)
Human resource management	High levels of absenteeism/poor industrial relations record	Significant weakness (−4)

Source: Reprinted with permission of the authors.

include knowledge of analytical concepts and techniques common to each area and the ability of the people to use them effectively. Used properly, these functional resources serve as strengths to support strategic decisions. In addition to the functional resources the organization's culture and structure should be regarded as key parts of the organization's internal environment.

Whatever approach is used or variables examined, the analysis of the organization's internal environment can be concluded by developing what is known as a 'Strategic capability profile' in which the potential strengths and weaknesses of the organizational resources and capabilities are identified, assessed, and weighted (see Table 3.3).

'Strategic fit': an integration of internal and external strategic analysis

In any model of strategy development a successful strategy arises from a firm's strategic analysis of emerging opportunities and threats while taking into account the firm's internal strengths and weaknesses. SWOT analysis (looking at strengths, weaknesses, opportunities, and threats) is usually suggested as a systematic way of integrating internal analysis and external analysis to find a 'strategic fit' between what the environment wants and what the organization has to offer, as well as between what the organization needs and what the environment can provide. Basic SWOT analysis is just as relevant to small entrepreneurial businesses as to established large ones. SWOT analysis, or situation analysis, is an important foundation for any plan helping to produce realistic and meaningful strategic recommendations for an organization's future direction. Situation analysis provides an appraisal of the difference between the company's current performance and its past stated objectives in the light of the relevant information obtained from the company's external and internal environments (Dibb et al., 2001). The four headings of SWOT analysis can be very useful for summarizing many of the elements of the internal analysis and combining them with the key issues arising from the external environment analysis. In fact SWOT analysis aims to identify the extent to which the current strategy of an organization and its more specific strengths and weaknesses are relevant to, and capable of, dealing with the changes taking place in the business environment.

SWOT analysis is a particularly well-known model and frequently used as a strategic analysis tool. However, it has been argued that there are many limitations to the use of this tool in practice. One of the principal criticisms of SWOT, make by Weihrich (1982), is that, having conducted the analysis, managers frequently fail to come to terms with the strategic choices that the outcomes demand. Weihrich (1982) proposed a SWOT (TOWS) matrix which, while making use of the same inputs as the SWOT matrix, recognizes them and integrates them more fully into the strategic management process. This matrix, which is shown in Figure 3.9, illustrates the alternative ways in which an organization can use its specific strengths to capitalize on opportunities or to minimize threats and invest in available opportunities to overcome its weaknesses. The SWOT/TOWS matrix, in our view, is a very useful tool for generating a series of strategic alternatives that the decision-makers of an organisation might not otherwise have considered.

Internal elements / **External elements**	**Organizational strengths**	**Organizational weaknesses**
	Strategic options	
Environmental opportunities (and risks)	**SO**: Strengths can be used to capitalize or build upon existing or emerging opportunities	**WO**: The strategies developed need to overcome organizational weaknesses if existing or emerging opportunities are to be exploited
Environmental threats	**ST**: Strengths in the organization can be used to minimize existing or emerging threats	**WT**: The strategies pursued must minimize or overcome weaknesses and, as far as possible, cope with threats

Figure 3.9 The SWOT (TOWS) matrix

Source: Adapted from Weihrich, Heinz, 'The TOWS Matrix—A Tool for Situation Analysis', *Long Range Planning* (1982), Vol. 15, No. 2, pp. 54–66.

Another criticism has been raised by Fifield and Gilligan (1998), who claim that the use of SWOT has generally become of no real value in practice. They list several reasons which have contributed to this, the most common being that managers simply list strengths and weaknesses and then opportunities and threats without paying sufficient attention to their real significance; the result is what they call 'a balance sheet approach'.

Finally, whatever analytical tool is chosen for its strategic analysis, an organization needs to review the inputs on a regular or ongoing basis in order to identify how they are changing and the implications of these changes for the future direction of its marketing strategy development.

Conclusion

The formulation of marketing strategy is the development of long-range plans for the effective management of the major factors and key trends in an organization's marketing environment. Therefore, development of a marketing strategy should be based on a thorough understanding and effective use of environmental opportunities and threats while taking into account the organization's strengths and weaknesses. Increasing environmental uncertainty coupled with increasing pressure on organizations to create and sustain a distinctive competency means that scanning and analysis of the internal and external environment will become an important part of every marketer's job. For companies to remain competitive, they will need to develop better methods of gathering, evaluating, and disseminating intelligence to those who need it. The availability of such market information and competitive intelligence is essential for the development and success of any marketing strategy in today's business environment.

Summary

This chapter has discussed in greater detail the first part (or stage) of the strategic marketing management process, namely strategic analysis. Strategic analysis is concerned with understanding the strategic position of the organization in terms of its external environment, its internal resources and competencies, and the expectations and influence of stakeholders. Strategic analysis is central for any development of marketing strategy. Without it strategic managers could be wrongly guided and the strategy formulated might not be in tune with the key trends in the organization's marketing environment. For proper conduct of strategic analysis different sets of market information and competitive intelligence should be gathered. The relevant variables and forces in the organization's marketing environment should also be scanned and analysed. Such an analysis aims not only to identify the possible opportunities and threats in the external environment but also the organization's internal strengths and weaknesses. Many analytical models and frameworks are available to support such an analysis and strategic managers should make their choice based on their understanding of how to operationalize the selected model. To conclude their strategic analysis and to inform the subsequent strategic choices, strategic managers should attempt to find a strategic fit between external opportunities and internal strengths while working around external threats and internal weaknesses.

KEY TERMS

Strategic analysis Concerned with understanding the strategic position of the organization in terms of its external environment, internal resources and competencies, and the expectations and influence of stakeholders.

Environmental scanning The process of collecting information about the forces in the environment. Scanning involves observation, perusal of secondary sources, such as business, trade, government, and general interest publications, and marketing research.

Environmental analysis The process of assessing and interpreting the information gathered through market intelligence and environmental scanning.

Strategic group approach An analytical device designed to aid in industry structural analysis. It is an intermediate frame of reference between looking at the industry as a whole and considering each firm separately.

Strategic choice Involves understanding the underlying bases guiding future strategy, and generating strategic options for evaluation and selecting from among them.

Strategy implementation The translation of strategy into organizational action through organizational structure and design, resource planning, and the management of strategic change.

DISCUSSION QUESTIONS

1 Market information and competitive intelligence are essential for the development of effective marketing strategy. What are the relevant types of information you would recommend to a company of your choice for conducting a meaningful strategic analysis?

2 Competitor analysis is central for the development of marketing strategy. Advise your company on a systematic way of undertaking an effective competitor analysis.

3 How can a decision-maker identify and analyse strategic factors/forces in the organization's external environment? What analytical models could s/he use to support the analysis?

4 Making reference to a company of your choice, undertake an internal analysis to assess the company's resources and capabilities.

5 Describe the three components of the strategic marketing management process: strategic analysis, strategic choice, and strategy implementation.

6 To what extent do you agree/disagree that SWOT analysis is of real value to an organization and what would you suggest to improve the outcome of the analysis?

ONLINE RESOURCE CENTRE

Visit the Online Resource Centre for this book for lots of interesting additional material at: **www.oxfordtextbooks.co.uk/orc/west/**

REFERENCES AND FURTHER READING

Aaker, David A. (2001), *Strategic Market Management* (New York: John Wiley & Sons, Inc.).

Ansoff, Igor H. (1991), 'Critique of Henry Mintzberg's The Design School: Reconsidering the Basic Premises of Strategic Management', *Strategic Management Journal*, Vol. 12, No.6, pp. 449–61.

Ansoff, Igor H. (1994), 'Comment on Henry Mintzberg's Rethinking Strategic Planning', *Long Range Planning*, Vol. 27, No.3, pp. 31–2.

Buzzell, Robert D., and Bradley T. Gale (1987), *The PIMS Principles* (New York: The Free Press).

Buzzell, Robert D., and Frederik D. Wiersema (1981), 'Successful Share-Building Strategies', *Harvard Business Review*, Vol. 59 (January–February), pp. 135–44.

Chussil, M. J. (1991), 'Does Market Share Really Matter?', *Planning Review*, Vol. 19 (September–October), pp. 31–7.

Cool, Karel, and Ingemar Dierickx (1993), 'Rivalry, Strategic Groups and Firm Profitability', *Strategic Management Journal*, Vol. 14, No.1, pp. 47–59.

Cravens, David W. (1994), *Strategic Marketing* (New York: Richard D. Irwin).

Cvitkovic, Emilio (1989), 'Profiling Your Competitors', *Planning Review*, Vol. 17 (May–June), pp. 28–31.

Daft, Richard L., Juhani Sormunen, and Don Parks (1988), 'Chief Executive Scanning, Environmental Characteristics, and Company Performance: An Empirical Study', *Strategic Management Journal*, Vol. 9, No.2, pp. 123–39.

De Castro, Julio O., and James J. Chrisman (1995), 'Order of Market Entry, Competitive Strategy, and Financial Performance', *Journal of Business Research*, Vol. 33, pp. 165–77.

Dibb, Sally, Lyndon Simkin, William M. Pride, and O. C. Ferrell (2001), *Marketing: Concepts and Strategies* (Boston: Houghton Mifflin Company).

Diffenbach, John (1983), 'Corporate Environmental Analysis in Large US Corporations', *Long Range Planning*, Vol. 16, No.3, pp. 107–16.

Drew, Stephen A. W. (1997), 'From Knowledge to Action: the Impact of Benchmarking on Organizational Performance', *Long Range Planning*, Vol. 30, No.3, pp. 427–41.

Fiegenbaum, Avi, and Howard Thomas (1990), 'Strategic Groups and Performance: The US Insurance Industry, 1970–84', *Strategic Management Journal*, Vol. 11, No.3, pp. 197–215.

Fifield, Paul, and Colin Gilligan (1998), *Strategic Marketing Management: Planning and Control, Analysis and Decision* (Oxford: Butterworth-Heinemann).

Freeman, Edward R. (1984), *Strategic Management: A Stakeholder Approach*, (New York: Pitman Publishing, Inc.).

Gale, B. T. (1992), 'Quality Comes First When Hatching Power Brands', *Planning Review*, Vol. 20 (July–August), pp. 48–9.

Gatignon, Hubert, Erin Anderson, and Kristiaan Helsen (1989), 'Competitive Reactions to Market Entry: Explaining Interfirm Differences', *Journal of Marketing Research*, Vol. 26 (February), pp. 44–55.

Grant, Robert M. (1991), 'The Resource-Based Theory of Competitive Advantage: Implications for Strategy Formulation', *California Management Review*, Vol. 33, No.3, pp. 114–35.

Haverty, John L., and Myroslaw J. Kyj (1991), 'What Happens When New Competitors Enter an Industry', *Industrial Marketing Management*, Vol. 20, No.1, pp. 73–80.

Hooley, Graham J., John Saunders, and Nigel F. Piercy (1998), *Competitive Positioning: The Key to Market Success* (Harlow: Prentice-Hall International Ltd.).

Jennings, Daniel F., and James R. Lumpkin (1992), 'Insights between Environmental Scanning Activities and Porter's Generic Strategies: An Empirical Analysis', *Journal of Management*, Vol. 18, No.4, pp. 791–803.

Johnson, Gerry, and Kevan Scholes (1999), *Exploring Corporate Strategy* (Harlow: Prentice-Hall Europe Ltd.).

Kaplan, Robert S., and David P. Norton (1992), 'The Balanced Scorecard—Measures That Drive Performance', *Harvard Business Review*, Vol. 70 (January–February), pp. 71–90.

Kaplan, Robert S., and David P. Norton (1996), 'Using the Balanced Scorecard as a Strategic Management System', *Harvard Business Review*, Vol. 74 (January–February), pp. 75–85.

Kerin, Roger A., V. Mahajan, and Rajan P. Varadarajan (1990), *Contemporary Perspectives on Strategic Market Planning*, (Englewood Cliffs: Prentice-Hall, Inc.).

Kotler, Philip (1994), *Marketing Management: Analysis, Planning, Implementation and Control*, (Englewood Cliffs: Prentice-Hall, Inc.).

Kotler, Philip (2000), *Marketing Management* (Englewood Cliffs: Prentice-Hall, Inc.).

Kotler, Philip, and Gary Armstrong (2000), *Principles of Marketing* (Englewood Cliffs: Prentice-Hall, Inc.).

Lambkin, Mary (1988), 'Order of Entry and Performance in New Markets', *Strategic Management Journal*, Vol. 9 (Special Issue), pp. 127–40.

Miles, Raymond E., and Charles Snow (1978), *Organisational Strategy, Structure and Process* (New York: McGraw-Hill, Inc.).

Mintzberg, Henry (1990), 'The Design School: Reconsidering the Basic Premises of Strategic Management', *Strategic Management Journal*, Vol. 11, No.3, pp. 171–95.

Mintzberg, Henry (1994), 'Rethinking Strategic Planning Part I: Pitfalls and Fallacies', *Long Range Planning*, Vol. 27, No.3, pp. 12–21.

O'Shaughnessy, John (1995) *Competitive Marketing: A Strategic Approach*, (London: Routledge).

Porter, Michael E. (1979), 'How Competitive Forces Shape Strategy', *Harvard Business Review*, Vol. 57 (March–April), pp. 137–45.

Porter, Michael E. (1980), *Competitive Strategy: Techniques for Analyzing Industries and Competitors* (New York: The Free Press).

Porter, Michael E. (1985), *Competitive Advantage: Creating and Sustaining Superior Performance* (New York: The Free Press).

Reger, Rhonda K., and Anne Sigismund Huff (1993), 'Strategic Groups: A Cognitive Perspective', *Strategic Management Journal*, Vol. 14, No.2, pp. 103–24.

Schwalbach, Joachim (1991), 'Profitability and Market Share: A Reflection on the Functional Relationship', *Strategic Management Journal*, Vol. 12, No.4, pp. 299–306.

Shetty, Y. K. (1993), 'Aiming High: Competitive Benchmarking for Superior Performance', *Long Range Planning*, Vol. 26, No.1, pp. 39–44.

Smith, Daniel C., and John E. Prescott (1987), 'Demystifying Competitive Analysis', *Planning Review*, Vol. 15 (September–October), pp. 8–13.

Smith, Ken G., Curtis M. Grimm, Martin J. Gannon, and Ming-Jer Chen (1991), 'Organizational Information Processing, Competitive Responses, and Performance in the US Domestic Airline Industry', *Academy of Management Journal*, Vol. 34, No.1, pp. 60–85.

Speed, Richard J. (1989), 'Oh Mr Porter! A Re-Appraisal of Competitive Strategy', *Marketing Intelligence and Planning*, Vol. 6, No.5, pp. 8–11.

Taylor, James W. (1992), 'Competitive Intelligence: a Status Report on US Business Practices', *Journal of Marketing Management*, Vol. 8, No.2, pp. 117–25.

Thomas, James B., Shawn M. Clark, and Dennis A. Gioia (1993), 'Strategic Sensemaking and Organizational Performance: Linkages Among Scanning, Interpretation, Action, and Outcomes', *Academy of Management Journal*, Vol. 36, No.2, pp. 239–70.

Utterback, James M., and W. J. Abernathy (1975), 'A Dynamic Model of Product and Process Innovation', *Omega*, Vol. 3, No.6, pp. 639–56.

Weihrich, Heinz (1982), 'The TOWS Matrix—A Tool for Situation Analysis', *Long Range Planning*, Vol. 15, No.2, pp. 54–66.

Wheelen, Thomas L., and David J. Hunger (2000), *Strategic Management and Business Policy* (New York: Addison-Wesley Publishing Company, Inc.).

Williams, Jeffrey R. (1992), 'How Sustainable Is Your Competitive Advantage?', *California Management Review*, Vol. 34 (Spring), pp. 29–51.

Wilson, Richard M. S., and Colin Gilligan (1997), *Strategic Marketing Management: Planning, Implementation and Control* (Oxford: Butterworth-Heinemann).

KEY ARTICLE ABSTRACTS

Kangis, Peter and M. Dolores O'Reilly (2003), **'Strategies in a dynamic marketplace: A case study in the airline industry'**, *Journal of Business Research*, 56 (2), pp. 105–12.

This article has used two case-study companies from the airline niche market, namely Ryanair and Aer Lingus, to find out how they responded to different environmental stimuli when they formulated and implemented their marketing strategies.

Abstract: In the wake of deregulation of air travel in Europe, an examination of how Ryanair and Aer Lingus have responded to this external stimulus has revealed significant differences of importance to strategists. Information was collected from published sources and through interviews with senior management of the two airlines. The niche market and seamless service of Aer Lingus, the established airline, has exposed this provider to the full might of international competition and has resulted in higher costs and lower financial returns. In contrast, the no-frills approach of Ryanair, a recent entrant, has allowed low prices to be supported and helped to draw new passengers to routes hitherto restricted to other forms of transport. An assessment of the outcomes of these contrasting responses highlights the need for managers to question the suitability of theory and received wisdom to guide action.

Ghobadian, Abby, Howard Viney, Philip James, and Jonathan Liu (1995), **'The Influence of Environmental Issues in Strategic Analysis and Choice: A Review of Environmental Strategy Among Top UK Corporations'**, *Management Decision*, 33 (10), pp. 46–58. © Emerald Group Publishing Limited. **http://www.emeraldinsight.com**

This paper examines the business environment in the UK and how the large corporations appreciate and recognize the effect of this environment when planning their businesses.

Abstract: Corporations across the world are experiencing growing pressure to incorporate environmental issues into their strategic decision-making process. This pressure characterizes the increased global significance of the environment. This study examines the extent to which the issue is recognized by UK corporations, and how the environment affects corporate business planning. The research also reflects on the key motivational factors leading to the adoption of environmental policies, and comments on the nature of those influences. Key findings show that UK companies recognize the environment is an issue, but that the degree of importance attached is based on a variety of factors, resulting from unique corporate perceptions of opportunity and threat. Companies are generally concerned with meeting legal compliance levels of investment. However, some companies are seeking to become 'environmental managers', having identified the existence of opportunities for achieving competitive advantage.

Camelo-Ordaz, Carmen, Fernando Martin-Alcazar, and Ramon Valle-Cabrera (2003), 'Intangible Resources and Strategic Orientation of Companies: An Analysis in the Spanish Context', *Journal of Business Research*, 56 (2), pp. 95–104.

This paper aimed to analyse the linkage between the resources and capabilities possessed by companies and their strategic orientation, and at determining the influence exercised by competitive market factors on the choice of a particular strategy. The survey was distributed to 130 companies in Spain and factor analysis was used to analyse the data.

Abstract: To obtain a sustainable competitive advantage, companies must analyse the resources and capacities they possess in order to select strategies likely to offer the best returns. Therefore, the fit that exists between a company's set of resources and capacities and its strategic orientation has constituted a fundamental subject of study in strategic management. Three hypotheses that aim to analyse the linkage between the resources and capabilities possessed by companies and their strategic orientation are defined, and the influence exercised by competitive market factors on the choice of a particular strategy is determined. For the empirical testing of these hypotheses, a sample of 130 out of the 500 largest Spanish companies was taken, subjecting the data obtained to various techniques of multi-variant analysis.

Amaravadi, Chandra S, Subhashish Samaddar, and Siddhartha Dutta (1995), 'Intelligent Marketing Information Systems: Computerized Intelligence for Marketing Decision Making', *Marketing Intelligence and Planning*, 13 (2), pp. 4–13. © Emerald Group Publishing Limited. **http://www.emeraldinsight.com**

The development of a competitor intelligence system is essential for marketing managers to support strategic marketing decisions. Such an intelligence system will enable them to share knowledge and expertise about their rivals in the marketplace. This article supports what has been highlighted in Figure 3.6 and discusses a framework that illustrates information exchanges among various subgroups of an organization.

Abstract: Marketing knowledge and expertise are a critical corporate resource for carrying out strategic decision-making that supports marketing functions. Intelligent marketing information systems (IMkIS) can offer a way for marketing managers to share knowledge and expertise. Such sharing could help improve the economics and effectiveness of the marketing function. Traditional marketing information systems (MkIS) are limited in their managerial support capabilities. Unlike MkIS, an IMkIS incorporates, among other features, the use of a knowledge base of marketing strategies. The shortcomings of MkIS are discussed, and a framework of IMkIS relationships is offered which illustrates information exchanges among various subgroups of the organization. Furthermore, a design of an IMkIS based on this framework is offered. The creation of a knowledge base is demonstrated by capturing the strategic marketing moves of a corporation for the case of PepsiCo, by using published information sources.

END OF CHAPTER 3 CASE STUDY

A World-Class Financial Institution: A Corporate Analysis

Introduction

The HSBC Group, its name derived from its founding institution (the Hong Kong and Shanghai Banking Corporation Limited established in 1865 by Thomas Sutherland,

who saw the need for a locally based bank to finance the growing trade between China and Europe). Today, headquartered in London, HSBC's international network comprises of 7,000 offices in 81 countries, with a local presence in Europe, the Asia-Pacific region, the Americas, the Middle East, and Africa. HSBC has approximately 170,000 employees worldwide and a customer base of 32 million, of which 4 million represent their growing e-commerce base. In 2001, HSBC was ranked 27th by market capitalization in the Financial Times Global 500, but in comparison to similar banking institutions it was ranked second behind the enormous multinational corporation, Citigroup. HSBC has been awarded numerous awards including 'Most Admired Financial Company' by *Management Today*, 'Best Company in Asia' by *Finance International Asia*, and 'Best Global Bank' by *The Banker*.

HSBC aims to become the world's leading financial services organization while balancing earnings from more stable, mature economies and those in more volatile emerging markets.

Target customers and market segments

HSBC has always been keen to ensure that whilst it improves economies of scale and makes better use of resources throughout the group, it still maintains the value of local decision-making and local accountability. Its organizational structure is a matrix that has crossing lines of responsibility between attractive customers and market segments.

The HSBC group is divided into five divisions that are based on customer-defined sections (see Figure C3.1). The services offered within each segment are: Personal Financial Services (PFS), Commercial Banking, Corporate Investment Banking and Markets (CIBM) and Private Banking. The Other category encompasses activities such as income and expenses of wholesale insurance operations, central operations, and the results of central operations and investment portfolios. From 1999 to 2001, net interest income has been consistently around 56%–57% of revenues, whilst other income has been around 43%–44%.

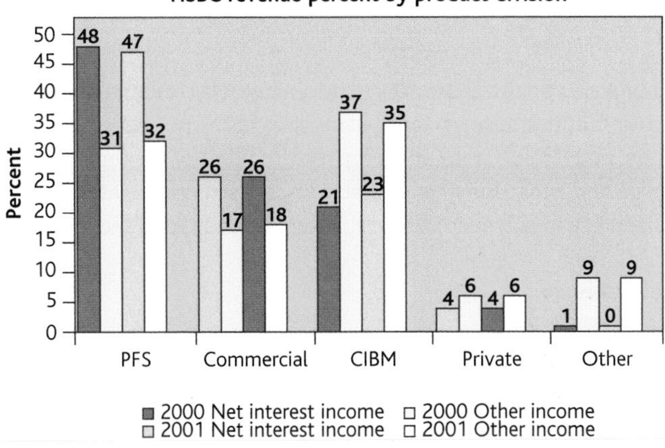

Figure C3.1 HSBC revenue percent by product division

Personal financial services

The Personal Financial Services (PFS) division targets individual customers including those who are self employed. HSBC provides a variety of products and services for their 29 million worldwide customers. This includes current cheque and savings accounts, loans and home finance, credit cards, insurance and investment services (primarily through telephone and the Internet), and financial planning. HSBC has introduced many new specialized services within this area in order to attract new customers and/or expand existing ones. This includes Premier, an international service for their most valuable personal customers, Individual Solutions, HomeStart, and Smart Mortgage. They have also signed an agreement with American Express to supply their travellers' cheques through HSBC branches worldwide.

Commercial banking

Commercial banking covers middle markets and smaller commercial relationships. Like PFS, commercial banking extends its services with traditional documentary credit and insured export finance, leasing finance and factoring, payments and cash services, and insurance. With 1.8 million customers worldwide, this segment is one of HSBC's traditional strengths. The bank believes it has the largest international franchise in this sector of any financial services company.

Corporate investment banking and markets

This segment encompasses a huge variety of businesses and offerings. With a small customer base of 12,000 international corporations, HSBC is still developing its capabilities here. This division includes all general banking products as well as trade banking products such as securities, debt and equity issuer services, and trustee and stock lending facilities. Complex insurance services tailored for businesses, investment banking, treasury and capital markets services including foreign exchange, currency and interest rate bonds, and other special derivatives are also offered. HSBC has ambitious plans for this segment in support of its strategy for the development of wealth management across the group.

Private banking

This segment provides financial services to internationally-orientated high net worth individuals and their families through four businesses: HSBC Republic, HSBC Guyzeller, CCF Private Banking, and HSBC Trinkhaus & Burkhardt. Some of the services that they provide include deposits and fund transfers, tax and trustee structures, asset and trust management, mutual funds and currency, lending, letters of credit, and securities transactions.

Geographical presence

HSBC also defines its market segments by geographic location. It introduces new products on a country basis to satisfy customer need and depending upon the success it will then roll it out across the globe. HSBC identifies five geographic segments: Hong Kong; Europe; North America; Rest of Asia Pacific; and Latin America. Figure C3.2 illustrates HSBC's revenue from six regional areas (with the USA and Canada shown separately).

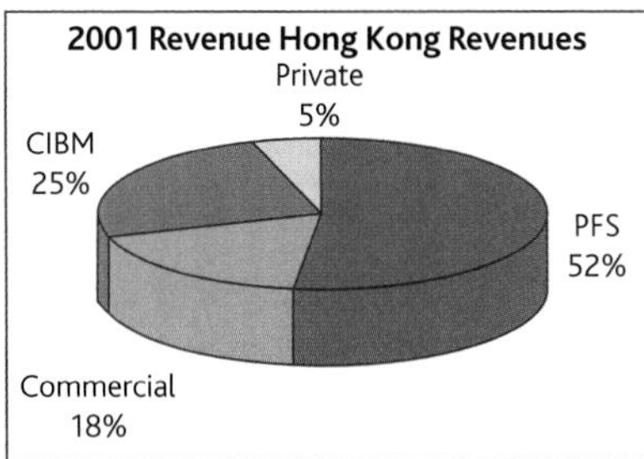

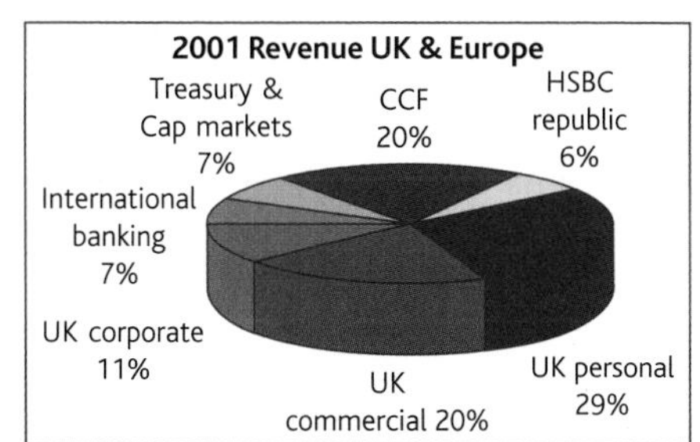

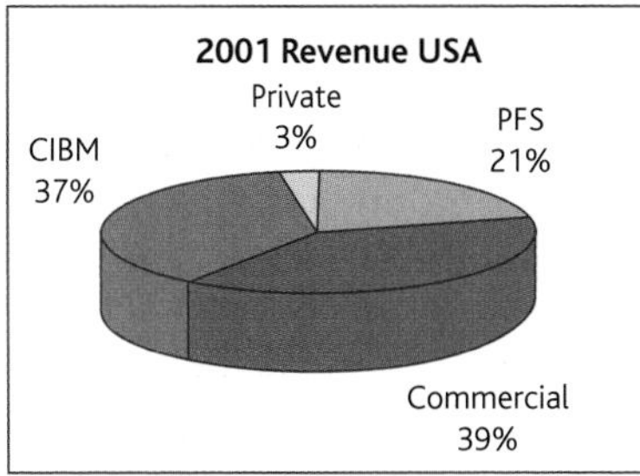

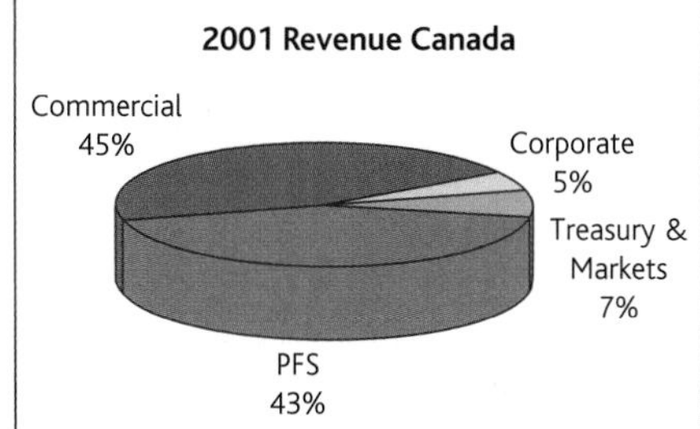

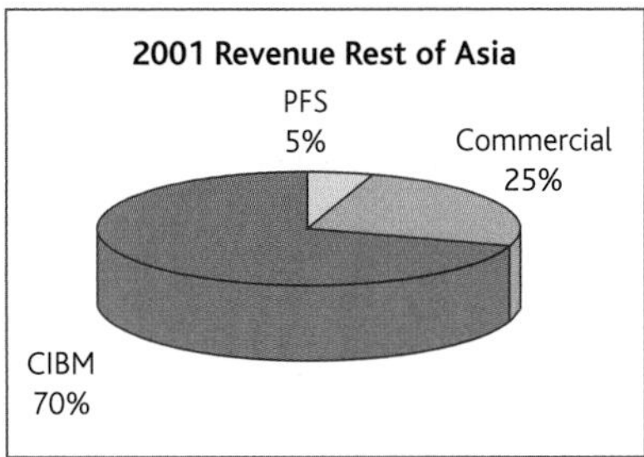

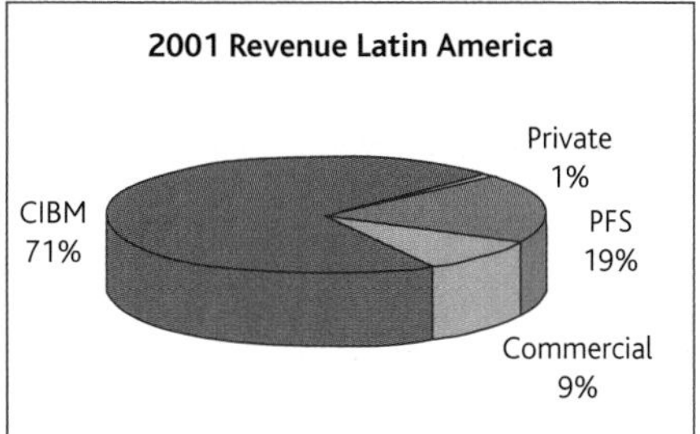

Figure C3.2 HSBC revenue in six regional areas

Current business portfolio

HSBC has a strong capability in Commercial Banking, PFS, and certain parts of CIBM. Currently it struggles in the area of Private Banking. HSBC has a large market share in Hong Kong but growth opportunities here are beginning to slow down. HSBC has room for more growth in Europe outside the UK. Key opportunities lie in Rest of Asia, specifically China and the Middle East. Once the political economy begins to stabilize in parts of Latin America, this will be another area for HSBC to grow in. Figure C3.3 plots the portfolio on the BGC matrix.

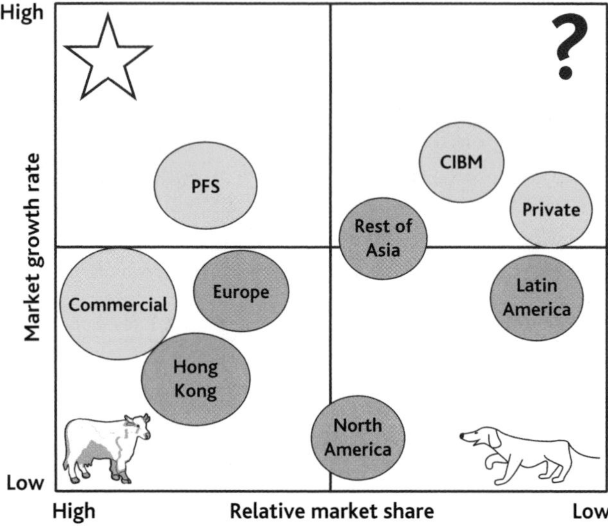

Figure C3.3 HSBC business portfolio on BGC matrix

Core competencies and competitive advantage

Within the HSBC Group there are three main areas for synergy: revenues, costs, and capital.

- **Revenues:** with economies of scale across virtually all financial services product lines, the opportunities to cross-sell are enormous.
- **Costs:** the ability exists to implement a single technology platform across the businesses, to benefit from global purchasing agreements, and to centralize a large portion of administration functions.
- **Capital:** a pool of capital is maintained at Group level to meet unforeseen events around the world.

Current strategic direction

HSBC aims to become the world's leading financial services organization while balancing earnings from more stable, mature economies and those in more volatile, emerging markets. To achieve this, HSBC has developed a strategy called 'Managing for Value'. This strategy has four components:

1. Development of global wealth management—to deepen relationships with personal customers and provide them with a full range of financial services
2. Growing its commercial business—by building on its historic strength in trade-related banking

3. Integration of corporate and investment banking for larger customers—a major effort to align traditional corporate banking and credit services
4. Establishing the HSBC hexagon as a global brand with local identity—'The world's local bank'.

HSBC plans to use a combination of organic growth and acquisition to achieve its strategic objectives. The integration of Republic Safra with Trinkhaus, Guyerzellar, and CCF, together with the willingness to buy in expertise (joint venture with Merrill Lynch), demonstrates the management's commitment to its objectives. The purchase of major new subsidiaries in South America in 1997 extended the group's reach in emerging market, whilst the acquisition in 1999 of Republic of New York Corporation and Safra Republic Holdings, reinforced HSBC's presence in highly developed markets: the USA, Switzerland, and Luxembourg. HSBC is a long-term investor in businesses and markets and currently is focused on improving and expanding its e-business offerings.

Conclusions

HSBC has successfully integrated various businesses and geographic regions. As HSBC continues to focus on becoming customer driven, increasing its network, and providing product innovation, it is clear that it aims to strengthen its core competencies and improve its competitive position. Through improved economies of scale, increased brand recognition, and effective use of resources, HSBC can create and build upon its strong international presence. HSBC dominance in selected regions, market segments, and products and functions increases its capacity to diversify. However, there may be risks to performance from:

- fast pace of consolidation among peers, using acquisitions to enter new regions and business
- non-banks building their advisory services to affluent/corporate sectors, core segment
- service providers hijacking payments systems/e-systems.

The emerging opportunities for future investment must also take into account:

- a switch to fee-driven value exchange away from balance sheet intermediation
- capex strength to leapfrog rivals in technology, time to market
- balance sheet enables both organic/inorganic investment opportunities for growth

Source: This case was prepared by Dr Essam Ibrahim (2003) for class discussion and not to illustrate either effective or ineffective handling of an administrative situation.

QUESTIONS

1. Using the models illustrated in the chapter, analyse the external (macro) environment of HSBC and identify the emerging opportunities and threats that will affect the future investment of HSBC in the UK financial market.
2. Critically evaluate the current business portfolio of HSBC and advise the company on ways to expand its financial service offerings to serve other market segments.

3. The current strategic direction of HSBC is to become the world's leading financial services organization while balancing earnings from more stable, mature economies and those in more volatile emerging markets. Comment on the organization's 'Managing for Value' strategy and its components as a strategic initiative for achieving the above goal.

Part III Where do we want to be?

I. Introduction
1. Overview
2. Marketing strategy: analysis and perspectives

II. Where are we now?
3. Environmental and internal analysis: market information and intelligence

III. Where do we want to be?
4. Strategic marketing decisions and choices
5. Segmentation, targeting, and positioning strategies
6. Relationship strategies

IV. How will we get there?
7. Product innovation and development strategies
8. Branding strategies
9. Service marketing strategies
10. Pricing and distribution strategies
11. Marketing communications strategies
12. E-marketing strategies

V. Did we get there?
13. Strategy implementation and control

VI. Conclusion
14. Social marketing and CSR

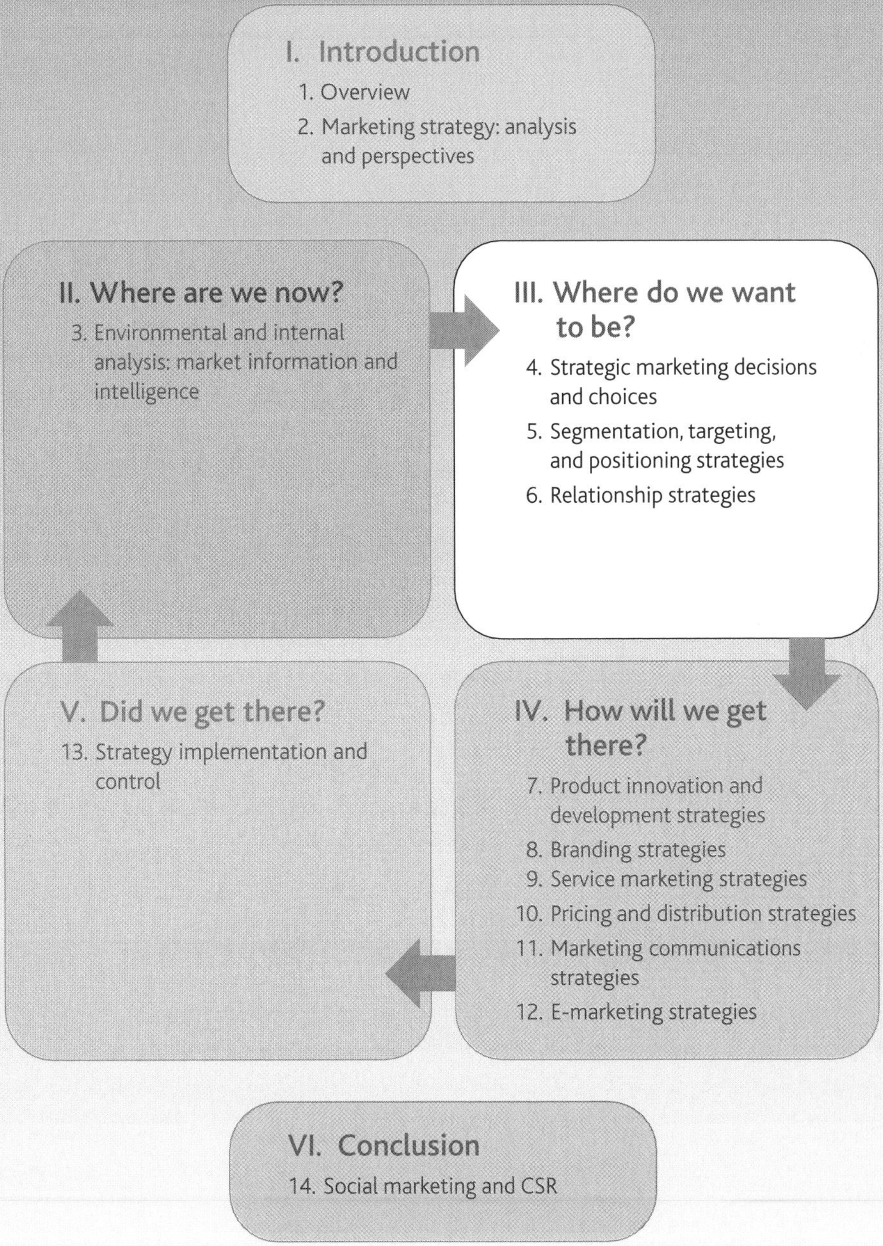

4

Strategic marketing decisions and choices

LEARNING OBJECTIVES

- Outline the outcome of the strategic marketing analysis discussed in Chapter 3 and explain how to translate such outcome into a justified set of strategic choices and decisions for the future
- Discuss strategic decisions taken at the corporate and SBU levels such as selection of directional strategy, allocation of resources, and choice of generic strategy
- Discuss in more detail the strategic marketing decisions, including products to offer, markets to target, and competitive position strategies
- Review the analytical models and frameworks that can be used to help in the strategic choice and decisions stage

CHAPTER AT A GLANCE

Introduction

The primary thrust of this chapter is to discuss in more detail the second stage/area of the Strategic Marketing Management process (SMM), that is, strategic choice and decisions. *Strategic choice* involves understanding the underlying bases guiding future strategy, and generating strategic options for evaluation and selecting from among them (Johnson and Scholes, 1999). Drawing upon the strategic analysis undertaken previously, managers will have to identify and assess the alternative ways in which their organization can use its specific strengths to capitalize on opportunities or minimize threats, and invest in available opportunities to overcome its weaknesses. The key task is to generate a well-justified set of strategic alternatives and choose the ones that will contribute to the achievement of the corporate overall goals and objectives. Figure 4.1 shows the hierarchy of strategic choice and decisions that should be taken at the three organizational levels: corporate, SBU (Strategic Business Unit), and functional levels. The key strategic marketing decisions that are expected at this stage are: creation of a mission statement, selection of a directional strategy, allocation of resources between SBUs, identification of strategic orientation, development of marketing objectives and strategy including products to offer, markets to target, and

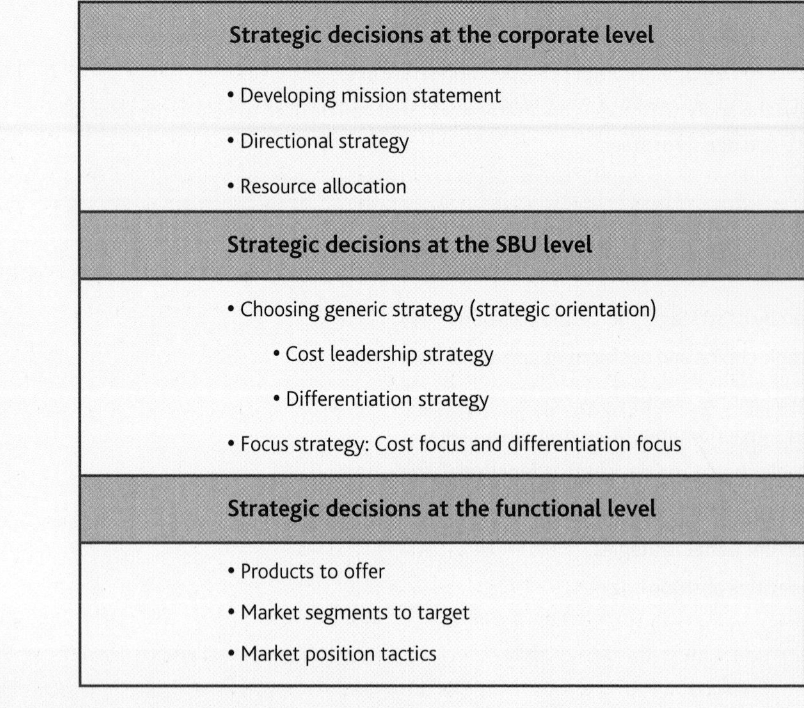

Strategic decisions at the corporate level
• Developing mission statement
• Directional strategy
• Resource allocation
Strategic decisions at the SBU level
• Choosing generic strategy (strategic orientation)
• Cost leadership strategy
• Differentiation strategy
• Focus strategy: Cost focus and differentiation focus
Strategic decisions at the functional level
• Products to offer
• Market segments to target
• Market position tactics

Figure 4.1 Hierarchy of strategic choice and decisions

market position strategies. This chapter will look at each of these strategic decisions and review key models and frameworks that are frequently used to inform and assist in making such decisions.

Hierarchy of strategic choice and decisions

Having analysed the organization's marketing environment (see Chapter 3) and identified the emerging opportunities and threats and internal strengths and weaknesses, strategic managers at different organizational levels are required to translate the outcome of such analysis into a number of alternatives and choose the most appropriate options. Strategic decisions at the corporate level involve developing a mission statement, deciding on a directional strategy, and allocating resources. Another set of strategic decisions are taken at the SBU level. Strategic managers at the SBU level have to choose a generic strategic orientation (cost leadership, differentiation, focus) for the firm based on the unique competitive advantages it has. Strategic choice and decisions taken at the functional level are related to the various functional areas within the organization (i.e., marketing, finance, R&D, production, etc.). Within the marketing area, strategists should consider such decisions as products to offer, market segment(s) to target, and market position strategies.

Strategic choice and decisions at corporate level

Defining the corporate mission

Drummond and Ensor (1999) define the mission of an organization as the unique purpose that distinguishes it from other companies and defines the boundaries of its operations. It defines the primary direction of the organization and forms the key foundations upon which objectives and strategies are based. The development of a mission statement is a vital point in strategy development since it represents a vision of what the organization is or should attempt to become. The mission statement is important from both an internal and an external point of view. Inside the company, it serves as a focal point for individuals to identify the organization's direction and ensure unanimity of purpose within the firm, thereby facilitating the emergence of a firm culture. Outside the company, the mission statement contributes to the creation of firm identity, i.e., how the company wants to be perceived in the marketplace by its customers, competitors, and the general public (Wilson and Gilligan, 2005).

To investigate how companies define and develop their mission statements, David (1989) conducted a survey of 181 US companies. The results of this survey identified nine main components included in mission statements, namely: customers, products or services, location, technology, concern with survival, philosophy, self-concept, concern with public image, and concern with employees. It has also been suggested that the company's mission is shaped by five elements: the company's history; the preferences of the management; the market environment; the organization's resources; and the organization's distinctive competencies. While management defines the corporate mission in the early stage of strategy development process, this mission should be reviewed and updated as shifts in the strategic direction occur over time.

A good mission statement is one that can be seen to exhibit certain characteristics, short on numbers and long on rhetoric while still remaining succinct (Wilson and Gilligan, 1997). Below is an example of a mission statement which has been framed with a very narrow view:

> We shall build good ships—at a profit if we can—at a loss if we must—but always good ships
> *Newport News Shipbuilding* [since 1886].

Another example of a mission statement, which gives a much broader frame of reference, has been developed by Scottish Power: 'To be recognised as a highly rated utility-based company trading in electricity, other utility and related markets, providing excellent quality and service to customers and above average returns to investors'.

Choosing the directional strategy

Every corporation must decide its intention and orientation towards growth by asking three fundamental questions.

1. Should we expand, cut back, or continue our businesses unchanged?
2. Should we concentrate our activities within our industry boundaries or should we diversify into other lines of business?
3. If we want to grow and expand nationally or internationally, should we do so via self-development or through external acquisition, mergers, or strategic alliances?

Wheelen and Hunger (2004) noted that a corporation's directional strategy is composed of THREE general directional orientations, called grand strategies (see Table 4.1).

- growth strategies expand the corporation's activities
- stability strategies make no change to the corporation's existing activities
- retrenchment strategies reduce the corporation's level of activities

For an example, see Mini Case Study 4.1.

TABLE 4.1 The directional (Grand) strategies

Growth strategies	Stability strategies	Retrenchment strategies
Concentration	Pause/Proceed with caution	Turnaround
• Vertical growth	No change	Captive company
• Horizontal growth	Profit	Sell-out/Divestment
		Bankruptcy/Liquidation
Diversification		
• Concentric		
• Conglomerate		

Source: Wheelen, Tom, and Hunger, J. David, *Strategic Management and Business Policy* (9th edn, 2004), pp. 10, 14, 138. Redrawn by permission of Pearson Education, Inc, Upper Saddle River, NJ.

MINI CASE STUDY 4.1

'Something In The Air: European Airline Consolidations Is Edging Forward'

The agreement under which Lufthansa will take over Swiss International Air Lines is the second such step in the slow restructuring of Europe's airline industry. As with the 2004 acquisition of KLM of Netherlands by Air France, the German-Swiss deal is structured gradually, to preserve national flying rights. But further consolidation of European airlines is likely to follow, as competitive pressures mount on the legacy carriers.

In the initial stages, Germany's national carrier will offer to buy the 15 per cent of stock held by small shareholders. After clearance by the competition authorities, it will increase its stake to just 49 per cent so it does not forfeit the flying rights owned by Switzerland's flag-carrier. Once those rights are secured, Lufthansa will take control of 100 per cent of the Swiss airline.

A similar solution might have been possible after Swissair collapsed in late 2001, but Switzerland was not at that stage prepared to surrender control over its national airline. After three years of losses totalling SFr1.8bn ($1.54bn), the Swiss have realised its resuscitated successor cannot survive as an independent carrier.

They have also recognised that worries about losing their own airline were exaggerated. While restructuring and cost-cutting will continue as planned, there will be some expansion of profitable long-haul routes. Lufthansa also promises to maintain Zurich as a hub—although direct links between Switzerland's business capital and other global centres would almost certainly have been provided by other airlines so long as there was the demand.

Further European consolidation is likely to follow, with SN Brussels Airlines close to taking over Virgin Blue, and speculation continuing over BMI, the British carrier in which Lufthansa has a 30 per cent stake. British Airways and Spain's Iberia are building stronger links, and Alitalia of Italy is in intensive care. All are under pressure from the growth of budget (low-cost) carriers such as easyJet and company cost-cutting that has reduced the number of business travellers paying premium fares. Many legacy carriers still face high costs in maintaining national networks, bloated staffing and expensive pension commitments. Record fuel prices have added to the burden.

Consolidation would be easier if negotiation between the European Union and the US to create an open aviation area could be concluded. This would help avoid problems over flying rights that now dog cross-border mergers. It would also ease ownership restrictions, making it easier for transatlantic deals between airlines.

Source: *Financial Times*, 24 March 2005, p. 18.

Having identified the general directional orientation of the corporation (growth, for example), strategic managers can then choose one or more specific sub-strategies such as concentration or diversification. They might decide to concentrate their efforts on one product line or one industry, or diversify into other market segments or even different industries. Ford made a strategic decision in the mid-1990s to take over Jaguar and Aston Martin Lagonda, the two British car companies, in order to achieve quick growth/expansion. This decision enabled Ford to serve new segments and has been seen as one that gave Ford a wider presence in the passenger car market by serving almost every segment in the market. Today, the company claims it sells a variety of car models within a price range of £8000+ (Ford Fiesta) to £250000+ (Aston Martin).

Corporate managers may select stability rather than growth as a directional strategy by making no changes to the corporation's current activities. This strategy is generally more popular in small businesses where owners find a profitable niche and enjoy their success in serving customers within this segment. While useful for small businesses in the short run, the stability strategy can be risky in the long term. For example Tesco, the UK's largest superstore, with its wider presence and intense competition not only in the high street but also in small towns, has threatened smaller retailers such as bakers and butchers.

The corporate manager may choose to pursue a retrenchment strategy if the organization has a weak competitive position in one or more of its markets resulting in less acceptable profits. This situation puts more pressure on the company to improve its performance by eliminating those product lines or SBUs that are dragging down the overall performance of the company. This strategy was adopted by BMW in 2000 after six years of owning Rover, the British car manufacturer. BMW had invested \$3.4 billion in Rover over six years but failed to turn it into a profitable business. Eventually, BMW decided to sell Land Rover to Ford and the rest of the company to a British venture capital firm (MG Car Company).

Allocating resources between the SBUs

Large corporations with multiple products and/or strategic business units must decide how these SBUs should be managed to enhance the overall corporate performance. How much money, time, and other resources should be given to each SBU to ensure overall success? One of the most frequently used techniques for allocating resources between SBUs is portfolio analysis. Portfolio analysis, which has had a colourful history in the business literature since the late 1960s, is a key tool for assessing the strength of SBUs' position in the market and allocating resources between them. Market attractiveness is largely determined by forces outside a firm's control, while a business unit's competitiveness can be shaped by the firm's strategic choices. Portfolio analysis relates attractiveness and competitiveness indicators to inform strategic decisions by suggesting a balanced mix of products and businesses that will ensure growth and profit performance in the long term. Portfolio analysis takes two forms: (a) product portfolio analysis and (b) business portfolio analysis. The following are some models strategic managers can use when conducting portfolio analysis:

- the Boston Consulting Group (BCG) matrix (see Figure 4.2), which focuses on market share and market growth
- General Electric's business screen which places the SBUs in the nine cells matrix using the attractiveness of the industry and the position of business
- the Shell directional policy matrix, which classifies the prospects for section profitability and the firm's competitive capabilities
- Hofer's analysis, which is an expansion of the BCG matrix and GE model, assesses businesses in terms of their competitive position and stage of industry evolution

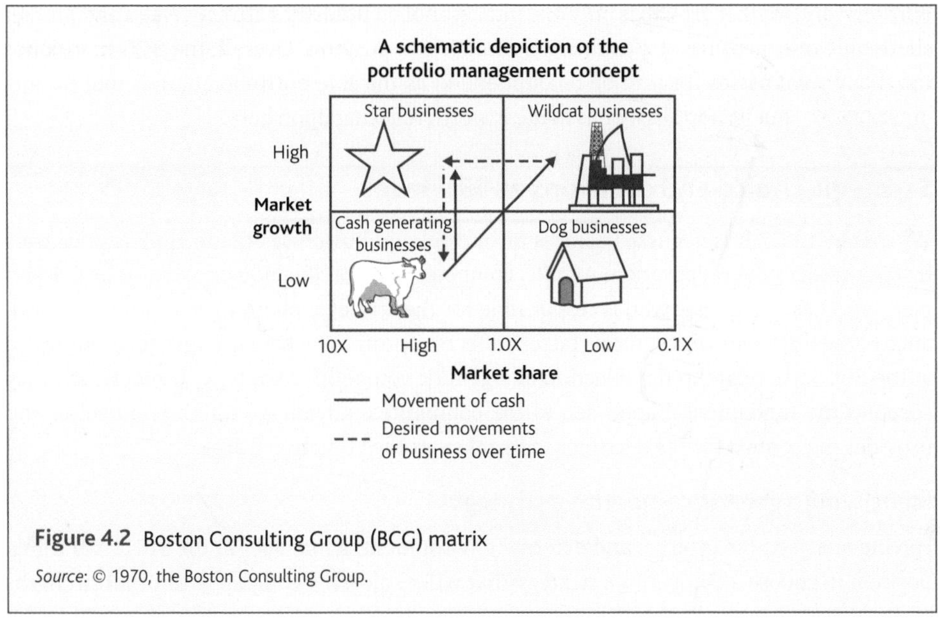

Figure 4.2 Boston Consulting Group (BCG) matrix

Source: © 1970, the Boston Consulting Group.

The BCG matrix is the most popular model used by strategists to guide discussions about allocating resources between SBUs and so is the focus of our attention here. In many respects it is inferior to more discursive portfolios such as the GE business screen, but for many businesses it is seen as the simplest way to portray the corporation's portfolio of investments. The BCG matrix can be used with the product life cycle concept to provide a useful strategic framework for resources allocation. Figure 4.2 illustrates four positions a business unit (SBU) can attain in a market/segment based on the market share it has and the growth rate of the market/segment. Figure 4.2 also illustrates the movement of cash between different SBUs and desired movements of businesses over time. SBUs are expected to change their positions in the market (matrix) over time. They generally start as 'problem children—wildcat' and with successful management they move into the 'stars' category. Eventually they become 'cash cows' as the growth of the market starts to slow down. Finally they become 'dogs' when they begin to lose their market shares. It has been suggested that each SBU should set up its strategic objectives based on its position in the BCG matrix. Build/Growth will be, arguably, an appropriate strategic objective for the 'stars', while Hold/Harvest will be appropriate for the 'cash cows'. Investment can be selected for the 'problem children', while divestment will be appropriate for the 'dogs' who are seen as having no potential.

The BCG matrix is a well-known portfolio analysis tool with many advantages. It helps organizations planning the desired movement of business over time, as well as the movement of funds from SBUs where there is less need for it to other SBUs where it is desperately needed. However, researchers have identified several limitations. The use of *high* and *low* to define the rate of market growth and level of market share is too simplistic and of course only one product or service can appear on the left-hand side as having the highest relative market share. In addition the cut-off point of 10% growth is far too high for most businesses.

Furthermore, market growth is only one indicator of an industry's attractiveness and market share only one measure of a company's competitive position. Overall, the BCG matrix has too many weaknesses for it to be recommended as the sole portfolio analysis tool for any organization, but its popularity has made it worth focusing upon here.

Strategic choice and decisions at SBU level

What is an SBU? It is a single business or interrelated businesses that can plan separately from the rest of the corporation. An SBU competes in a specific industrial sector or marketplace and has a manager who is responsible for the strategic planning and profit performance of the SBU, and who controls factors affecting profit. The key strategic decisions taken at the SBU level relate to the selection of a generic competitive strategy. A generic strategy specifies the fundamental approach to the competitive advantage a firm is pursuing and provides the context for the decisions to be taken in each functional area.

Identifying a generic competitive strategy

Having analysed the internal and external environment, a manager at the SBU level is in a position to choose a competitive strategy that will exploit the company's internal strengths and external opportunities and to utilize its competitive advantage over its competitors. An appropriate selection and formulation of a generic competitive strategy will best position the company's offerings against competitors' offerings and give the company the strongest possible competitive advantage within its industry (Kotler and Armstrong, 1996).

In the strategy literature, different types of generic strategy have been suggested (Utterback and Abernathy, 1975; Miles and Snow, 1978; Porter, 1980). For instance, Utterback and Abernathy (1975) proposed cost-minimizing and performance-maximizing business strategies that may be positioned at opposite ends of the spectrum. Miles and Snow (1978) proposed four types of competitive strategy, which are 'reactor,' 'defender,' 'analyser', and 'prospector.' Porter (1980) pulled all the types of strategy together and suggested three generic types of competitive strategy: cost leadership, differentiation, and focus.

While Porter (1980) originally proposed focus as a third generic strategy, he introduced differentiation focus and cost focus as two variants of focus strategy in his subsequent book *Competitive Advantage* (1985) (see Figure 4.3). In his later book *The Competitive Advantage of Nations* (1990), Porter dropped focus as a separate strategy and began viewing it instead as competitive scope.

Porter's generic competitive strategies

Cost leadership is a low-cost competitive strategy that aims at the broad mass market and requires aggressive construction of efficient-scale facilities, vigorous pursuit of cost reduction from experience, tight costs, and overhead control, avoidance of marginal customer accounts, and cost minimization in areas like R&D, service, salesforce, and advertising. Because of its lower cost, the cost leader is able to charge a lower price for its products than its competitors and still make a satisfactory profit. Having a low-cost position also gives a company a defence against rivals. Its lower costs allow it to continue to earn profits during times of heavy competition. Its high market share gives great bargaining power with its

Cost leadership strategy	Differentiation strategy
Cost focus strategy	Focused differentiation strategy

Figure 4.3 Porter's generic strategy

Source: Porter, Michael E., *Competitive Advantage: Creating and Sustaining Superior Performance* (1985). Redrawn with the permission of the Free Press, a division of Simon & Schuster Adult Publishing Group. © 1985, 1998 by Michael E. Porter. All rights reserved.

suppliers because it buys in larger quantities. Its low costs serve as a barrier to entry, as few new entrants will be able to match the leader's cost advantage. As a result, cost leaders are likely to earn above average return on investment (Porter, 1980). Note that sometimes cost leadership is confused with setting low prices. Certainly cost leaders are more able to make a profit at lower prices than rivals, but it is not necessarily part of the strategy. For example Dell has a cost advantage with its direct business model. However, its prices are by no means the lowest.

Differentiation is a generic strategy that involves the creation of a slightly or significantly differentiated offering, for which the company may charge a premium. This speciality can be associated with design or brand image, technology feature, dealer network, or customer service. Differentiation is a viable strategy for earning above average returns in a specific business because the resulting brand loyalty lowers customers' sensitivity to price. Buyers' loyalty also serves as an entry barrier—new firms must develop their own distinctive competence to differentiate their products in order to compete successfully (Porter, 1980).

What to choose? Differentiation strategy is more likely to generate higher profit than is low-cost strategy because differentiation creates a better entry barrier. However, low-cost strategy is more likely to generate increases in market share (Caves and Ghemawat, 1992).

Cost focus is a low-cost strategy that focuses on a particular buyer group or geographic market and attempts to serve only this niche, to the exclusion of others. In using a cost focus strategy, the company seeks a cost advantage in its target segment. This strategy is based on the belief that a company that focuses its efforts can serve its narrow strategic target *more efficiently* than can its competitors. However, a focus strategy does necessitate a trade-off between profitability and overall market share (Wheelen and Hunger, 2004).

Focused differentiation, like cost focus, concentrates on a particular buyer group, product line segment, or geographic market. Either the target segments must have buyers with unusual needs or else the production and delivery system that best serves the target segment must differ from that of other industry segments. In using a differentiation focus strategy, the company seeks differentiation in its target segment. This strategy is valued because of the belief that a company that focuses its efforts can serve its narrow strategic target *more effectively* than can its competitors (Wheelen and Hunger, 2004).

Focused differentiation and cost focus are not the same. Whilst cost focus exploits differences in cost behaviour in some segments, differentiation focus exploits the special needs of buyers in certain segments (Porter, 1985a). Another comparison can be made between overall differentiation and differentiation focus. These two are perhaps the most often confused strategies in practice. While the overall differentiator bases his strategy on widely valued attributes, the differentiation focuser looks for segments with special needs and meets them better.

Stuck in the middle. Porter (1980) suggested that for a company to be successful over time, it must pursue just one of the generic competitive strategies, otherwise the company will become 'stuck in the middle' with no competitive advantage because the cost leader, differentiators, or focusers will be better positioned to compete in every segment. Dess and Davis (1984) supported Porter's contention that a firm that fails to pursue a generic strategy will suffer. Their empirical research showed that commitment to just one of the three generic strategies would result in higher performance than if a company fails to stick to a single strategy. However, other studies have pointed out that some businesses with both low cost and high differentiation can be very successful (Miller, 1992; Cappel et al., 1992). The results of these studies suggested that companies which compete with both a low-cost and a differentiation strategy will perform better than those businesses primarily competing with either a low-cost or a differentiation strategy. The case of the Japanese car producers of Toyota, Nissan, and Honda is the best example of companies that have managed to pursue both a low-cost and a high-quality position. It can be argued that improving product quality may result indirectly in a lowering of costs. However, this is often temporary and requires strict conditions because differentiation is usually costly.

Criticism of Porter's generic strategies

Although generally acknowledged by academics and practitioners, Porter's typology has been widely criticized as a concept and in its application. Coyne (1986), for example, argued that, while Porter's generic strategies are conceptually appealing, they have practical limitations. It has also been argued that Porter's presentation of the three generic strategies give the impression that it is up to the firm to choose among them, though the appropriate selection of a generic strategy will be highly dependent on the firm's key resources and capabilities, the industry life cycle, and the state of competition in the market (Wright, 1987). Table 4.2 illustrates the commonly required skills and resources and the common organizational requirements for each of Porter's generic strategies.

From a marketing perspective, Baker (1992) argued that Porter's three generic strategies are typical marketing strategies that have been implemented by marketers for the past thirty years. Porter had just re-branded such marketing strategies using different names. Cost leadership invariably depends upon standardization and so is equivalent to an undifferentiated marketing strategy. Differentiation is identical in both models. Cost focus and focus differentiation are both variants of a concentrated marketing strategy and involve niche marketing.

TABLE 4.2 Requirements for generic competitive strategies

Generic strategy	Commonly required skills and resources	Common organizational requirements
Overall cost leadership	• Sustained capital investment and access to capital • Process engineering skills • Intense supervision of labour • Products designed for ease of manufacture • Low-cost distribution system	• Tight cost control • Frequent, detailed control reports • Structured organization and responsibilities • Incentives based on meeting strict quantitative targets
Differentiation	• Strong marketing abilities • Product engineering • Creative flair • Strong capability in basic research • Corporate reputation for quality of technological leadership • Long tradition in the industry or unique combination of skills drawn from other businesses • Strong co-operation from channels	• Strong co-ordination among functions in R&D, product development, and marketing • Subjective measurement and incentives instead of quantitative measures • Amenities to attract highly skilled labour, scientists, or creative people
Focus	• Combination of the above policies directed at the particular strategic target	• Combination of the above policies directed at the particular strategic target

Source: Reprinted with the permission of the Free Press, a division of Simon & Schuster Adult Publishing Group, from 'Competitive Strategy: Techniques for Analyzing Industries and Competitors' by Michael E. Porter.

Support for Porter's generic strategies

Despite the above criticisms, other scholars have defended the concept and its application. Herbert and Deresky (1987), for example, emphasized that the generic strategies form a simplified system and offer several important advantages for guiding strategy selection.

- They highlight the essential features of separate, situation-specific strategies, capturing their major commonalities so that they facilitate the understanding of a broad strategic pattern.
- They provide guidance at the corporate level on decisions concerning business portfolio management and resource allocation.
- They assist business-level strategy development by suggesting priorities and providing broad guidelines for action.

From the preceding arguments, it is fair to say that although Porter's generic strategies have been subject to general criticism, the concept itself describes the generic strategic approaches available to companies. It goes beyond competitive analysis to show exactly what the different types of competitive strategies are, how a competitive strategy can be selected, what its effects on the competitive forces are, and, finally, the advantage and disadvantages of each strategy.

Strategic choice and decisions at functional level

Strategic decisions taken at this level are related to the various functional areas within the organization (e.g., marketing, finance, R&D, production, etc.). The development of the functional strategies and the coordination between them play a major role in creating and sustaining a firm's competitive advantage. In this section, more details will be provided on the key strategic decisions taken within the marketing department. These decisions include marketing objectives to support corporate strategy, products to offer, market segment(s) to target, and market position strategies. This section will also outline various strategic decisions taken in other functional areas (e.g., production, finance, R&D, etc.) within the organization.

Setting the marketing objectives

From analysis of its external and internal marketing environment, a company can develop its specific marketing objectives for the planning period. While a few businesses may decide to pursue a single objective, most companies will have a mixture of marketing objectives including sales growth, market share, innovativeness, customer satisfaction, reputation, and brand loyalty. It is the pursuit of these marketing objectives which should provide the framework for both planning and control processes. Although marketing objectives are primarily designed to guide overall marketing activities, they will also be used for evaluation purposes to judge whether the chosen strategy has accomplished its purpose in the market. Without objectives, strategic marketing decisions and all that follow will take place in a vacuum (McDonald, 1996a). Key characteristics and guidelines for developing an appropriate set of objectives are:

- **hierarchical:** objectives should go from most important to least important
- **quantitative:** in order to avoid ambiguity, marketing managers must turn objectives into measurable targets with respect to size and time
- **realistic:** objectives should be developed based on the result of detailed analysis of the firm's capability, its competitive strengths, and external opportunities
- **consistent:** to avoid confusion, marketing managers have to pursue compatible marketing objectives. It is obviously unrealistic to aim for substantial gains in both market share and profitability at the same time

If a company's strategic objectives are inaccurately developed, either focusing too much on short-term goals or being so general that they provide little real guidance, there might be a planning gap between planned and achieved objectives. When such a gap occurs, strategic managers have to change their strategies to improve performance or adjust objectives downward to be more realistic.

Marketing strategy

Although marketing was recognized in Chapter 2 as an orientation that guides an organization's overall activities, this does not deny that marketing is a distinct function. At the functional level, the major task of marketing managers is to influence the level, timing, and character of demand in a way that will help the company achieve its objectives. The marketing manager is the company's primary link to the customer and the competition and must, therefore, be especially concerned with the development of the company's positioning strategy and marketing mix programmes.

The development of marketing strategy has been discussed extensively in the marketing literature (Baker, 1992; Hooley et al., 1993; Cravens, 1994; Dibb et al., 1997; Kotler, 2000). For example, Hooley et al. (1993) pointed out that the development of marketing strategy can be seen at three main levels. At the first level, the core strategy of the company will be selected, where the marketing objectives and the broad focus for achieving them will be identified. At the next level, market segments and targets (both customers and competitors) are selected and the company's differential advantage in serving the customer targets better than the competition is identified. Taken together the identification of targets and definition of differential advantage constitute the creation of the competitive positioning of the company and its offerings. At the third level, a marketing organization capable of putting the strategy into practice must be created. The marketing department, at this stage, is concerned with establishing the marketing mix programmes that can convey both the positioning and the products/services themselves to the target market.

Another approach to marketing strategy development is suggested by Cravens (1994). This approach is shown in Table 4.3, which illustrates the sequential steps to developing a marketing strategy, a summary of the important issues to be considered at each step, and the major actions/decisions that are required.

Table 4.3 illustrates the role marketing can play in **creating competitive advantage** and considers that role as a fundamental step in developing a marketing strategy. This role has been widely discussed in the marketing literature since the end of the 1970s, and covering different areas and different applications (Cook, 1983, 1985; Chattopadhyay et al., 1985; Parasuraman and Varadarajan, 1985; Weinrauch et al., 1991; Dholakia and Dominguez, 1995). For example, Cook (1983) introduced the concept of strategic marketing ambition and related this concept to the marketing mix as a new paradigm of marketing strategy. In the same research, an operational measure of differential marketing advantage and methods of analysis were introduced in an illustration of competitive investments, marketing strategy, and differential advantage. Comments on Cook's new paradigm of marketing strategy were found in Chattopadhyay et al. (1985) and Parasuraman and Varadarajan (1985). These two studies, in particular, identified a number of limitations of Cook's framework and suggested alternative formulations to overcome these limitations. In response to these criticisms, Cook (1985) made it clear that marketing strategy should be formulated with reference to market demand and competitive conditions. Thus a marketing strategy, in Cook's view, is the manner in which company resources are used in the search for a differential advantage.

TABLE 4.3 Selecting and developing marketing strategies for different market and competitive situations

	Important issues	Major actions/decisions
Product-market definition and analysis	• Evaluating the complexity of the product-market structure • Establishing product-market boundaries	• Defining product-market structure • Customer profiles • Industry/distribution/competitor analysis • Market size estimation
Market segmentation	• Deciding which level of the product market to segment • Determining how to segment the market	• Select the basis of segmentation • Form segments • Analyse segments
Define and analyse industry structure	• Defining the competitive area • Understanding competitive structure • Anticipating changes in industry structure	• Sources of competition • Industry structure • Strategic group analysis
Competitive advantage	• Deciding when, where, and how to compete	• Finding opportunity gaps • Cost/differentiation strategy/focus • Good/better/best brand positioning strategy
Market targeting and positioning strategies	• Deciding market scope • Good/better/best brand positioning strategy	• Selecting targets • Positioning for each target • Positioning concept • Marketing mix integration

Source: Cravens, David W., *Strategic Marketing*. © 1994. Reproduced by permission of McGraw-Hill Education, Inc.

To investigate the role that marketing strategy can play in creating a competitive advantage, Weinrauch et al. (1991) conducted an empirical study to examine the perceptions and attitudes of smaller manufacturers in finding and using affordable marketing techniques to create a low-cost advantage. The results of this research indicated that many small manufacturers could develop a low-cost marketing strategy and compete effectively in the marketplace by finding a small niche and offering distinct products.

Another study, by Quinn and Humble (1993), examined how marketing techniques can be used in the service industry to create a competitive advantage. The research suggested an approach called **PROMPT** to gain a competitive edge in this industry. This approach contains six elements: **P**rioritizing customer needs, **R**eliability, **O**rganizing for customers, **M**easuring customer satisfaction, **P**ersonal training, and **T**echnology focusing.

Other functional strategies

Financial strategy

The primary job of the financial manager is to manage funds. The financial manager ascertains the best sources and uses of funds and controls their use. From a strategic point of view, the financial area should be analysed using a number of sophisticated analytical techniques to see how well it manages funds. In addition, the best mix of externally generated short- and long-term funds in relation to the amount and timing of internally generated funds should be identified and should be appropriate to the company's objectives, strategies, and policies. Any financial manager must be knowledgeable about all these functions in order to formulate and implement an effective financial strategy (Wheelen and Hunger, 2000).

An early study by Clarke (1988) explored the meaning and nature of financial strategy and how such a strategy can be used to create a competitive advantage for an organization. In Clarke's view, the goal of financial strategy is to provide the firm with an appropriate financial structure and funds to achieve its overall objective. In addition, it examines the financial implications of a firm's strategic options and identifies the best financial course of action. It can also provide competitive advantage through a lower cost of funds and a flexible ability to raise capital to support a competitive strategy.

In the same context, Wheelen and Hunger (2000) supported the role of financial strategy in creating a competitive advantage for a firm. They pointed out that a financial strategy usually attempts to maximize the financial value of the firm by establishing the trade-off between achieving the desired debt-to-equity ratio and relying on internal long-term financing via cash flow. Such a trade-off, in Wheelen and Hunger's view, is a key issue in any financial strategy development, which would lead to the creation of competitive advantage for the firm.

Manufacturing strategy

Manufacturing strategy has been defined as the management principles dictating how a product is manufactured, how resources are deployed in production, and how the infrastructure necessary to support manufacturing should be organized (Zahra and Das, 1993). Manufacturing strategy, in Zahra and Das's view, creates and adds value by helping a firm to establish and sustain a defensible competitive advantage, which is the unique position an organization develops vis-à-vis its competitors. The primary task of the manufacturing manager is to develop and operate a production system which will produce the required number of products or services with a certain quality, at a given cost, and within an allocated time. Several studies have been conducted to discuss how the manufacturing facilities can play a significant role in creating competitive advantage to organizations (Langowitz, 1991; Sisodia, 1992; Honeycutt et al., 1993; Zahra and Das, 1993).

Langowitz (1991) pointed out that design for manufacturing (DFM) contributes to the creation of competitive advantage by serving as the basis for a differentiation or low-cost position in the marketplace. DFM, in Langowitz's view, can provide differentiation through speed of delivery, quality, and variety in combination with the former two. On the other hand, DFM can contribute to a low-cost position by reducing scrap and rework, by creating efficiencies in purchasing, assembly, and inventory, and by allowing a firm to move up the learning curve faster. Zahra and Das (1993) also described how a firm can create competitive advantage from its manufacturing resources in two principal ways: either by gaining a first mover advantage, or by erecting mobility barriers. Either method, in their view, requires a firm to attain a distinctive competence by the appropriate use of its manufacturing resources.

Honeycutt et al. (1993) indicated that the ability to rapidly alter the production of diverse products can provide firms with a distinct competitive advantage. They concluded that companies adopting flexible manufacturing technology can react more quickly to market change, enhance customer satisfaction, and increase profitability. Thus competitive strategy based on flexible manufacturing technology enables firms to be better positioned in the marketplace.

Recently, Wheelen and Hunger (2004) supported the need to adopt a flexible manufacturing strategy as a way to react quickly against a competitor's moves in the marketplace. These authors justified this need using the concept of the product life cycle. As the product moves up its life cycle curve, there will be a need to increase production volume and modify product features. Increasing competitive intensity in many industries has forced companies to switch from adopting a traditional mass production strategy to a continuous improvement strategy. Because a continuous improvement strategy enables firms to adopt the same low-cost approach as does a mass production strategy, albeit at a significantly higher level of quality, it is rapidly replacing mass production as 'the' manufacturing strategy.

Research and development (R&D) strategy

A company's technology helps define the strategic group(s) within which it competes and the type of competition it faces. The R&D manager is responsible for suggesting and implementing a company's technology strategy in the light of its overall objectives, strategies, and policies. The job of the R&D manager, therefore, involves (1) choosing among alternative new technologies to use within the company, (2) developing methods of embodying the new technology in new products and processes, and (3) deploying resources so that the new technology can be successfully implemented. Wheelen and Hunger (2000) pointed out that R&D strategy deals with three ingredients: basic R&D, which focuses on theoretical problem areas; product R&D, which concentrates on marketing and is concerned with product improvements; and process R&D, which concentrates on quality control and the improvement of production equipment. Companies that depend on either product or process technology for their success are becoming increasingly concerned with the development of R&D strategies that complement business-level strategies.

Earlier research by Shetty (1987) investigated the relationship between product quality and profitability. The results of this research suggested that a strategic focus on quality improvement through an effective R&D strategy is one of the best ways to improve market position and profitability and to gain a sustainable competitive advantage. Thus, the R&D strategy concerned with improving product quality must be recognized as a significant part of a company's competitive strategy.

Human resources management and other functional strategies

Strategies related to human resource management, information systems technology, and other areas within a firm are likely to play a significant role in creating and enhancing competitive advantage. Human resources management, for example, is seen as a strategic tool to achieve the match between individuals and jobs available. This match will enhance job performance and employees' satisfaction and will properly equip employees to carry out the company's strategic objectives. Osbaldeston and Barham (1992) pointed out that management development is a major strategic tool and should be integrated with competitive strategy to enhance organizational ability to compete in a complex and changing environment. Putting management development strategy at the heart of competitive strategy also enables the company to build its collective competence and to create the learning organization essential for future competition. In the same context, Ingram (1995) highlighted the role of human resources in generating competitive advantage. This role, in Ingram's view, has hitherto remained relatively neglected in business strategy and economics.

The role of information technology in creating and improving competitive advantage has been discussed by many authors (Turner, 1991; Powell and Dent-Micallef, 1997; Wheelen and Hunger, 2000; Porter, 2001). Turner (1991), for example, pointed out that if a firm is to succeed in its business environment, it will need to access information which adds value to strategic decision-makers and which, when analysed, enhances competitive advantage. Information technology will be necessary to ascertain what the company's competitive advantage is and how able it is to convert advantage into strategic positions.

Examining the role of information technology in producing competitive advantage, Powell and Dent-Micallef (1997) conducted empirical research in the retail sector. They found that information technologies (IT) alone have not produced sustainable competitive advantage but a number of firms have gained advantages by integrating IT with the firm's infrastructure of human and business complementary resources such as flexible culture, partnerships, integration of strategic planning and IT, and supplier relationships. For example Dell integrated supply chain management with customer-driven order processing, complete control over the build process, logistics, delivery, a strong relationship management system, disintermediation, and mass customization, etc. This led to a significant competitive advantage (none of its rivals has grown as fast). Dell has capitalized on its first mover status and has managed to stay ahead of the competition by employing IT as a strategy and seeking to develop strategic alliances with others such as Microsoft.

The recent development of Internet-based strategy is the best example of how IT can be used to create competitive advantage. (See Chapter 12, 'E-marketing', for more detailed arguments for and against the use of IT and the Internet as sources of competitive advantage.) Porter (2001), for example, stated that the Internet per se does not lead to competitive advantage. His premise was, however, that the Internet can be used as part of the business strategy and the business strategy itself is the driver for the creation of competitive advantage.

It is true that many companies do not grasp the strategic importance of IT, but those that do can capitalize on the benefits that employing a coherent IT strategy can give. Wheelen and Hunger (2000) highlighted the significant role of IT for an organization's business strategy. They gave several examples to illustrate how companies are increasingly adopting information systems strategies to provide business units with competitive advantage. Many companies are also attempting to use information technology to build closer relationships with their customers and suppliers through sophisticated systems. (See Mini Case Study 4.2.)

MINI CASE STUDY 4.2
'UK Banks Lag Behind Rest Of The World In Reporting Their Customers'

UK banks are falling behind their peers in the rest of the world when it comes to protecting customers from internet fraud, according to a survey, writes Maija Pesola.

A security audit of the UK online banking sector by Information Risk Management (IRM), the IT security consultancy, found that very few banks have sufficiently sophisticated mechanisms for authenticating online customers and preventing their details from being stolen. Out of 18 banks surveyed by IRM, 11 used simple password and username details, which are repeated each time an online customer wants to access his/her account.

Only a handful of banks use more sophisticated authentication systems that ask for slightly different information each time—for example, users might be asked to provide three letters from a memorable word. It takes time for a hacker to discover the whole of the memorable word, as this is never spelt out in full. However, if a hacker has installed spy-software on a user's computer to monitor everything that is typed in, the word can be discovered over time.

None of the top UK banks use external security mechanisms—such as smartcards, random password generators or fingerprint scanners to authenticate their customers. 'The UK has fallen behind other countries on this', said Phil Robinson, chief technology officer at IRM. 'Smartcards, for example, are popular in places like Germany, Switzerland and Hong Kong'.

In fact, the Hong Kong Monetary Authority has mandated that all banks in its territory must have two-factor authentication systems in place by this summer. 'I am surprised the Financial Services Authority is not requiring the same here', Mr Robinson said, 'certainly minimum standards need to be set'.

On the positive side, Mr Robinson noted that UK banks were doing relatively well in solving other technical problems that could lead to identity theft—for example, ensuring that account details were not inadvertently being stored in the computer's memory, and that banking programs would automatically log users out if the computer was unused for a long time. Many banks are also very vocal in educating customers about the risks of identity fraud.

Source: *Financial Times*, 14 April 2005, p. 6

Deciding on products to offer and markets to target

Having analysed the organization's marketing environment and formulated its overall objectives, marketing managers are in a position to consider a number of strategic options and to take the relevant marketing decisions to help in achieving these objectives. Fundamental marketing decisions that should be considered at this stage are product/s to offer and market/s to target. While the topic of segmentation, targeting, and positioning is discussed in more detail in Chapter 5, this section will present some possible options. Ansoff 's 2X2 matrix (shown in Figure 4.4) is a useful and convenient analytical framework that is usually used to guide marketing managers in making such strategic decisions.

The Ansoff matrix illustrates the four possible options available to any organization in relation to product/market strategy. **Market penetration** as a strategic option involves

	Present product	New product
Present market	Market penetration strategy	Product development strategy
New market	Market development strategy	Diversification strategy

Figure 4.4 Ansoff's product/market matrix

Source: Ansoff, H. I., 'Strategies for Diversification', *Harvard Business Review*, Sept–Oct, 1957, pp. 113–24. Reprinted by permission of *Harvard Business Review*.

selling more of the organization's existing products in its existing marketplace, which means increasing the level of penetration in these market segments. Adopting this option will depend on competitor activity and the likely development of existing market segments over the next two to three years. Market penetration is the least risky option of the four alternatives since the organization will be targeting market segments it already understands using products or services it knows. Consumer product manufacturers such as Procter & Gamble and Unilever are expert in using their promotional activities to implement the market penetration strategy to gain the dominant market share in a product category.

Product development involves developing additional or new products to serve existing market segments. The aim here is to expand the product range in the present marketplace in order to increase the level of sales. This strategic option is more risky than market penetration as it entails developing a new product where there is uncertainty as to how it will be perceived by existing customers. The development of a new product may also create a degree of cannibalization that might affect the net growth in the marketplace and issues of product rollover.

Market development takes place when the organization keeps its focus on the present product range, but searches for new market segments and looks at ways of marketing its existing products in these new segments. The degree of risk associated with this option is probably higher than with the above two options. It is not very likely that the existing products, without modification, will satisfy customer requirements in different market segments. Also entering a new market will obviously require the organization to undertake an environmental analysis in order to understand the new market.

Diversification is probably the riskiest of the four alternatives as it involves the marketing of new products into new markets, though the potential return can be high. Producing new products will definitely require an increase in resources used, and reasonable

TABLE 4.4 Critical success factors in action

Critical success factors	Strategies	Performance indicators
Ability to achieve critical mass volumes through existing brokers and agents	• Develop closer ties with agents • Telemarket to brokers • Realign agents' compensation	• Policies in force • New business written • Per cent of business with existing brokers
Be able to introduce new products within six months of industry leaders	• Underwrite strategic joint ventures • Copy leader's products • Improve underwriting skills	• Elapsed time to introduce • Per cent of products introduced within six months • Per cent underwriters having additional certification
Be able to manage product and product line profitability	• Segment investment portfolio • Improve cost accounting • Closely manage loss ratio	• Return on portfolio segments • Actual product cost/revenue versus plan • Loss ratio relative to competitors

Source: Wilson, R.M.S. and Gilligan, C., *Strategic Marketing Management: Planning, Implementation and Control* (1997), with permission from Elsevier.

investment. Serving new market segments will also need further analysis of the micro marketing environment, including customers and competitors.

It should be mentioned here that the choice between the four strategic options will be influenced by a number of external and internal factors. External factors include the state of competition in the market and the critical success factors in the industry. Internal factors, on the other hand, include the product life cycle and the shape of the company's product range. For example, it might be more risky for a firm in a fast-changing marketplace to stay with the penetration strategy than to follow market development. Table 4.4 sets out the critical success factors in action.

Deciding on competitive tactics to implement strategy

A tactic is a specific operating action specifying 'how', 'when', and 'where' a strategy is to be implemented. Compared to strategies, tactics are narrower in scope and shorter in time horizon. Tactics may therefore be viewed (like policies) as a bridge between strategy formulation and implementation. Some of the tactics available to implement competitive marketing strategies are those dealing with timing ('when') and competitive position ('how') (Wheelen and Hunger, 2000).

Timing tactics

A company that moves earlier than its competitors to manufacture and sell a new product, new design, or new model is called the *first mover*. A company that moves after the first mover is called a *late mover*. Others may be classed as *early followers*. The three categories represent the timing tactics that a company has to compare and select from in order

Goal	Move before competition	Move with competition	Move away from competition
Market share protection (hold defend)	i. Mix adjustments ii. Deterrent action	i. Imitate ii. Compensate	i. Merger ii. Acquisition iii. Collusion
Market share advancement (growth)	i. New areas ii. New segments iii. Additional channels iv. Penetration pricing	i. Capitalize ii. Leapfrog	i. New offerings ii. Reciprocal agreements

Figure 4.5 Competitive timing/direction matrix

Source: O'Shaughnessy, J., *Competitive Marketing: A Strategic Approach* (1995), p. 243. Redrawn by permission of Routledge.

to act or react against its competitors. The comparison and selection, as with any other strategic posture, depends on the company's resources, capabilities, and competencies. Furthermore, a company that has previously moved first does not necessarily have to be constantly proactive.

O'Shaughnessy (1995) identified competitive timing movement depending on market share as a goal of the firm. In O'Shaughnessy's view, using market share as the goal, a firm seeks either market share protection or market share advancement. In the light of the chosen goal, the firm has to decide whether to *move before* the competition, *move with* competition, or *move away from* competition. When the chosen goal and the selected action are combined in a matrix, a set of strategic options are available to a firm. (See Figure 4.5.)

While Figure 4.5 illustrates several tactics, these options are not exhaustive nor are they mutually exclusive, since some of them may be adopted simultaneously (O'Shaughnessy, 1995). Two issues need to be clarified in this approach. The first is to redefine the traditional typology of *hold, build, harvest*, and *acquire* as tactics rather than competitive strategies. Build, hold, and harvest are the results of a generic strategy and, similarly, acquisition and vertical integration are not strategies, but means of achieving them.

The second issue is the view of market share as an ultimate goal for the firm's competitive strategy. Some firms might go so far as to set the goal that all their business units should have the highest market share in their industries. This approach to strategy is dangerous. Market share is certainly relevant to competitive position; however, it is per se not important competitively; competitive advantage is. Pursuit of the higher market share for its own sake may guarantee that a firm never achieves a competitive advantage or that it loses the one it has. Such a goal also embroils managers in endless debates over how an industry should be defined to calculate shares, obscuring the search for competitive advantage, which is at the heart of strategy.

A number of studies have been conducted to identify sources of advantage for the market pioneers and/or to assess the impact on a firm's performance of being first mover (Robinson and Fornell, 1985; Robinson, 1988; Lambkin, 1988; Moore et al., 1991; Mascarenhas, 1992). Robinson and Fornell (1985), for example, examined the relationship between the order of market entry and market share in the consumer goods market and the factors that lead to an order-of-entry advantage. The evidence indicates that both consumer-based and firm-based factors result in long-term market share advantages for pioneers relative to late movers. They also suggest that order of entry is a major determinant of market share. Robinson (1988) found that market pioneers have substantially higher average market share than late movers, and these share advantages are influenced by both business and industry characteristics.

Additional research by Lambkin (1988), Mascarenhas (1992), and De Castro and Chrisman (1995) examined the relationship between the order of entry and a firm's financial performance. These studies suggest that first movers tend to enjoy a long-term profit advantage over their rivals. This high return is generally necessary to compensate the pioneer for its heavy investment in designing the new product and developing the market. Other advantages of being a first mover have been identified. The company can build its reputation as a leader in the industry, move down the experience curve to assume the cost leader position, and earn temporarily high profits from buyers who value the product or service very highly. Research by De Castro and Chrisman (1995) suggests that pioneering firms will usually choose a differentiation strategy, whilst a greater proportion of late movers will choose a low-cost strategy.

Being first mover does, however, have some disadvantages which, conversely, are the advantages enjoyed by late movers. These disadvantages are: pioneering costs; demand uncertainty; changes in buyer needs; technological discontinuities; and, finally, imitation risk.

Competitive position

According to its competitive position a company can implement its competitive marketing strategy by pursuing offensive or defensive tactics. Wheelen and Hunger (2000) pointed out that an offensive tactic usually takes place away from a company's position in the marketplace, whereas a defensive tactic usually takes place within.

While a number of writers have defined the terms 'offensive' and 'defensive' as two types of competitive strategy (Kotler and Armstrong, 1996; Lambin, 1997; Wilson and Gilligan, 1997), other writers have explicitly looked at it as a competitive tactic (Porter, 1985a; Wheelen and Hunger, 1998). This is for two reasons. First, strategy by definition should be formulated and implemented for a long period of time, but for a firm to be defensive or offensive this will depend on the state of competition in the marketplace at any given point of time. The state of competition, by its nature, is dynamic rather than static and, therefore, it is not required/needed for a firm to be offensive or defensive at all times. For this reason, offensive and defensive actions are strategic tactics that are implemented by firms to meet the changing state of competition.

Secondly, generic strategy is a way by which the entire firm's activities are engaged to achieve and sustain competitive advantage. Therefore, a firm's generic strategy (low cost or differentiation) should be oriented by the goal of competitive advantage within its industry rather than being done to defend or take offensive action in relation to market share in a market segment or geographical area. In other words, a firm can act offensively in one segment or geographical area and defensively in another. Adopting this view, a discussion of competitive tactics (those of leading, challenging, following, or niching) becomes necessary.

1. **Market leader:** the firm with the largest market share and, by virtue of its pricing, advertising intensity, distribution coverage, technological advance, and rate of new product introduction, it determines the nature, pace, and bases of competition. To remain number one leading firms may implement both offensive and defensive tactics.
2. **Market challenger:** a runner-up firm that is fighting hard to increase its market share. It may choose to adopt an aggressive stance and attack other firms, including the market leader. To do this it will implement offensive tactics.
3. **Market follower:** another runner-up firm that wants to hold its share without 'rocking the boat'. It may adopt a less aggressive stance and a defensive tactic in order to maintain the status quo, but at the same time follow the leader.
4. **Market nichers:** firms that serve smaller segments not being pursued by other firms. By concentrating their efforts in this way, market nichers are able to build up specialist market knowledge and avoid expensive head-on fights with larger companies. Speed (1989) discriminates between segmenters and nichers. A segmenter, in Speed's view, selects a group of customers within the market whose needs can be met by a smaller section of the industry, whereas a nicher selects a group within a market whose needs may be met economically by only one company.

According to this classification, Figure 4.6 illustrates an overview of how market leaders might defend their current position, how challengers might attempt to seize share offensively, and how followers and nichers will act accordingly. The competitive tactics illustrated in Figure 4.6 are explained and discussed below in the light of the four market positions classification.

Competitive tactics for market leader

If a company is to remain the dominant company in a market, it needs to defend its position constantly. To do so, three major competitive tactics should be considered.

Expanding the total market

The market leader needs to search for *new users, new uses, and more usage*. Search for *new users* by attracting buyers who are still unaware of the product, or who are resisting it because of its price or its lack of certain features. Search for *new uses* by discovering and

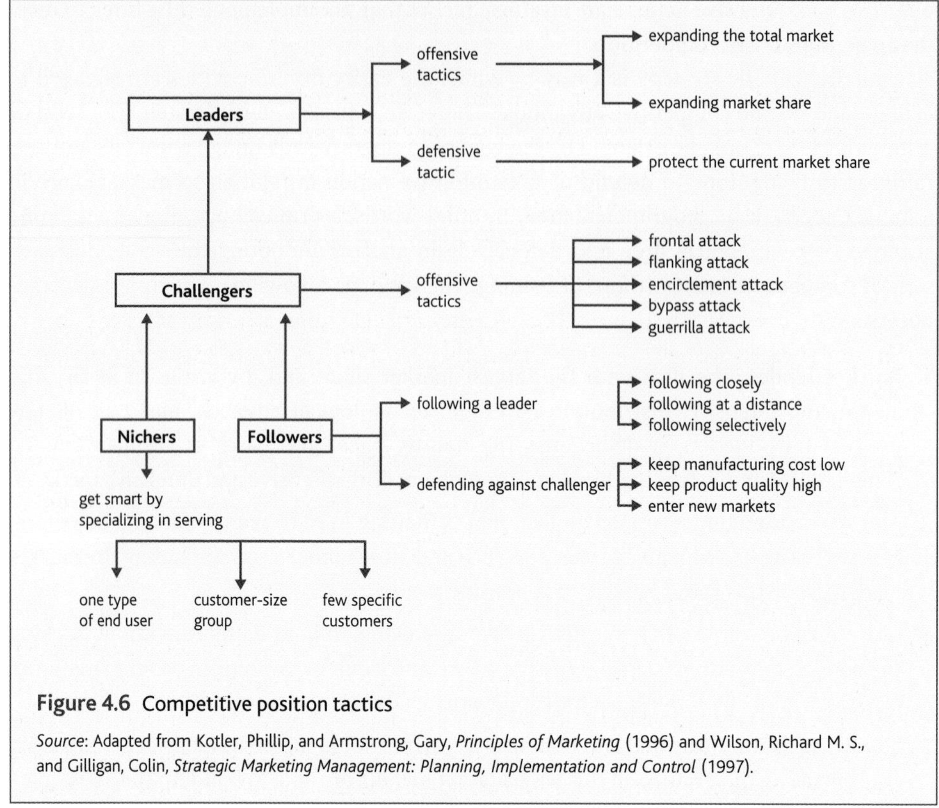

Figure 4.6 Competitive position tactics

Source: Adapted from Kotler, Phillip, and Armstrong, Gary, *Principles of Marketing* (1996) and Wilson, Richard M. S., and Gilligan, Colin, *Strategic Marketing Management: Planning, Implementation and Control* (1997).

promoting new ways for the use of the firm's product. Search for *more usage* by encouraging existing users of the product to increase their usage rates (Kotler and Armstrong, 1996).

Expanding market share

At the same time as trying to expand the total market, the market leader should not lose sight of the need to defend its market share. According to the saying 'the best defence is a good offence', the market leader may adopt an offensive tactic to increase its market share over other competitors. This can typically be done in a variety of ways including heavier advertising, improved distribution, price incentives, and new products (Wilson and Gilligan, 1997). By doing this, the market leader increases its market share on the expense of its competitors and reaps the benefits of this increase in the form of higher profitability.

Protect the current market share

It has long been recognized that leaders are often vulnerable to attack. Therefore, a market leader has to adopt defensive tactics to protect its position. Porter (1985b) pointed out that defensive tactics aim to lower the probability of attack, or reduce the threat of attack to an acceptable level. Porter suggests just three types of defensive tactic, such as raising structural barriers, increasing expected retaliation, and lowering the inducement for attack. Kotler and Armstrong (1996) use military analogies to suggest six types of defensive tactic:

- **Position defence,** in which a company builds fortifications around its current position, but simply defending a current position or product rarely works.

- **Flanking defence,** in which the company carefully checks its flanks and attempts to protect the weaker ones.
- **Pre-emptive defence,** where, in contrast to a flanking defence, the leader firm can be more aggressive, striking competitors before they can move against it.
- **Counter-offensive defence,** despite its flanking or pre-emptive efforts, a market leader company can be attacked, so it needs to respond to minimize the threat. Counter-attack is particularly important in those markets that are crucial to the leader. Therefore, the leader must act decisively and swiftly (Chen and MacMillan, 1992).
- **Mobile defence,** involves more than aggressively defending a current market position; the leader extends itself to new markets that can serve as future bases for defence or offence.
- **Contraction defence,** if a firm finds that its resources are spread too thinly and competitors are nibbling away on several fronts, it opts to withdraw from those segments in which it is most vulnerable or in which it feels there is the least potential. It then concentrates its resources in other segments to be less vulnerable.

Competitive tactics for market challenger

Wilson and Gilligan (1997) pointed out that the challenger can attack the market leader, avoid the leader, and, instead, challenge firms of its own size or smaller. The choice of who to challenge is thus fundamental and is a major determinant not just of the likelihood of success, but also of the cost and risk involved. Attacking a strong leader requires the challenger to meet three conditions. First, the assailant must have a sustainable competitive advantage (in cost or differentiation). Secondly, the challenger must be able to partly or wholly neutralize the leader's other advantages. Finally, there must be some impediment to the leader's retaliating (Porter, 1985b). A number of possible attack tactics have been suggested by Wheelen and Hunger (1995), Kotler and Armstrong (1996), and Lambin (1997):

- **Frontal attack:** consists of opposing the competitor directly by using its own weapons, and without trying to use its weak point.
- **Flanking attack:** as an alternative to a costly and generally risky frontal attack, the challenger can concentrate its strength against the competitor's weaker flanks or on gaps in the competitor's market coverage.
- **Encirclement attack:** involves attacking from the front and sides. A challenger encircles the competitor's position in terms of products or markets or both.
- **Bypass attack:** the challenger chooses to change the rules of the game. It might diversify into unrelated products, move into new geographic markets, or leapfrog into new technologies to replace existing products.
- **Guerrilla attack:** the fifth tactic open to a challenger is in many ways best suited to smaller companies with a relatively limited resource base. The challenger might use selective price cuts, executive raids, intense promotional outbursts, or assorted legal actions.

Competitive tactics for market follower

As an alternative to challenging for leadership, many companies are content to adopt a far less proactive posture and simply follow what others do. The market follower can learn from the leader's experience and copy or improve on the leader's products and programmes, usually with much less investment. Wilson and Gilligan (1997) identified three distinct postures for market followers, depending on how closely they emulate the leader.

- **following closely,** with a similar marketing mix and marketing segmentation
- **following at a distance,** so that the follower can flag up some areas of differentiation, and diminish the obvious similarities with the leader
- **following selectively,** both in product and market terms so that the likelihood of direct competition is minimized

Competitive tactics for market nicher

A nicher is interested in one or two niches, but not in the whole market. The objective is to be a large fish in a small pond rather than a small fish in a large pond (Lambin, 1997). The key idea in nichemanship is specialization. A market nicher can specialize in serving one type of end-user, specialize in serving a given customer-size group, or focus on one or a few specific customers. Although there are many advantages of niching, specialization can prove risky if the market changes in a fundamental way as the result of either greater competition or an economic downturn, leaving the nicher exposed. For this reason, there is a strong argument for multiple niching rather than single-sector niching (Crainer, 1990).

Conclusion

Drawing upon the strategic analysis of the organization's internal and external environment, managers will have to evaluate several strategic alternatives available to them and make strategic decisions that will define the future direction of their organization. The key task is to generate a well-justified set of strategic choices and select from them the ones that will strengthen the future position of the organization in the market(s) in which it has elected to compete. Figure 4.1 shows the hierarchy of strategic decisions taken at the three organizational levels: corporate, SBU, and functional. Strategic decisions that are expected at the corporate level are the creation of a mission statement, the selection of a directional strategy, and the allocation of resources between SBUs. The key strategic decision that should be taken at the SBU level is identifying the organization's strategic orientation for the future, that is, one of the three generic strategies (cost leadership, differentiation, focus). Strategic decisions, within the marketing area at the functional level, include products to offer, markets to target, and market position strategies. In this chapter, we have presented and discussed each of these strategic decisions and reviewed what is available in the extant literature to support our discussion.

Summary

This chapter has discussed in more detail the second stage/area of the Strategic Marketing Management process (SMM), namely strategic choice and decisions. Strategic managers, at this stage, aim to understand the underlying bases guiding future strategy, generating strategic options and selecting from among them. They will have to use the organization's strengths to capitalize on external opportunities and/or minimize threats, and invest in available opportunities to overcome the organization's major weaknesses. A number of strategic choices and decisions should be taken to contribute to the achievement of the overall corporate goals and objectives. The first set of these strategic decisions will be taken at the corporate level, the next set will be taken at SBU level, and the final set will be taken at the functional level. The chapter has discussed the various sets of strategic decisions at each level and reviewed key analytical models that have frequently been used to inform decision-making at each level.

KEY TERMS

Strategic choice Involves understanding the underlying bases guiding future strategy, and generating strategic options for evaluation and selecting from among them.

Mission statement A generalized statement that serves as a focal point for employees to identify the organization's direction and to ensure unanimity of purpose within the firm. It also contributes to the creation of organization identity and how the organization wants to be perceived in the marketplace by customers, competitors, and the general public.

Directional strategies The corporate directional strategies are those designed to achieve growth and stability or a reduction in the corporation's level of activities.

Low-cost strategy A generic strategy pursued by organizations which aims at the broad mass market and requires aggressive construction of efficient-scale facilities, vigorous pursuit of cost reduction from experience, tight costs, and overhead control, avoidance of marginal customer accounts, and cost minimization in areas like R&D, service, salesforce, advertising.

Differentiation strategy Another generic strategy which involves the creation of a unique product or service for which the company may charge a premium. This speciality can be associated with design, brand image, a technology feature, dealer network, or customer service.

Focus strategy A generic strategy which involves concentrating the marketing effort on a particular segment and competing in this segment using cost factors or a differentiation approach.

DISCUSSION QUESTIONS

1 Discuss the differences between strategic decisions taken at the corporate level and those taken at the SBU level.

2 It has been suggested that growth as a grand strategy is more suitable for large corporations, while a stability strategy is the one that should be adopted by small firms. Discuss this proposition.

3 To what extent do you agree that Porter's typology of generic strategy is the most appealing strategic framework for both academics and practitioners?

4 Making reference to a market of your choice, identify with justifications who you would consider the market leader(s), market challenger(s), and market follower(s) in this market. Support your answer with examples.

5 Discuss the major advantages that the first mover might gain by manufacturing and selling a new product, new design, or new model to the market before competitors.

ONLINE RESOURCE CENTRE

Visit the Online Resource Centre for this book for lots of interesting additional material at: **www.oxfordtextbooks.co.uk/orc/west/**

REFERENCES AND FURTHER READING

Aaker, David A. (2001), *Strategic Market Management* (New York: John Wiley & Sons, Inc.).

Ansoff, H. I. (1957), 'Strategy for Diversification', *Harvard Business Review*, Vol. 25, No.5, September–October, pp. 113–24.

Baker, Michael J. (1992), *Marketing Strategy and Management* (London: The Macmillan Press Ltd.).

Cappel, Sam, Peter Wright, Mark Kroll, and David Wyld (1992), 'Competitive Strategies and Business Performance: An Empirical Study of Select Service Businesses', *International Journal of Management*, Vol. 9, No.1, pp. 1–11.

Caves, Richard E., and Pankaj Ghemawat (1992), 'Identifying Mobility Barriers', *Strategic Management Journal*, Vol. 13, No.1, pp. 1–12.

Chattopadhyay, Amitava, Prakash Nedungadi, and Dipankar Chakravarti (1985), 'Marketing Strategy and Differential Advantage: A Comment', *Journal of Marketing*, Vol. 49 (Spring), pp. 129–36.

Chen, Ming-Jer, and Ian C. MacMillan (1992), 'Nonresponse and Delayed Response to Competitive Moves: The Roles of Competitor Dependence and Action Irreversibility', *Academy of Management Journal*, Vol. 35, No.3, pp. 539–70.

Clarke Christopher J. (1988), 'Using Finance for Competitive Advantage', *Long Range Planning*, Vol. 21, No.2, pp. 63–9.

Cook Victor J. (Jr.) (1985), 'Understanding Marketing Strategy and Differential Advantage', *Journal of Marketing*, Vol. 49 (Spring), pp. 137–42.

Cook, Victor J. (Jr.) (1983), 'Marketing Strategy and Differential Advantage', *Journal of Marketing*, Vol. 47 (Spring), pp. 68–75.

Coyne, Kevin P. (1986), 'Sustainable Competitive Advantage—What It Is, What It Isn't', *Business Horizons*, Vol. 29, No.1, pp. 54–61.

Crainer, Stuart (1990), 'A Niche for High Performance', *Marketing Business*, Part 13 (October), pp. 14–15.

Cravens, David W. (1994), *Strategic Marketing* (New York: Richard D. Irwin).

David, Fred R. (1989), 'How Companies Define Their Mission', *Long Range Planning*, Vol. 22, No.1, pp. 90–7.

De Castro, Julio O., and James J. Chrisman (1995), 'Order of Market Entry, Competitive Strategy, and Financial Performance', *Journal of Business Research*, Vol. 33, pp. 165–77.

Dess, Gregory G., and Peter S. Davis (1984), 'Porter's (1980) Generic Strategies as Determinants of Strategic Group Membership and Organizational Performance', *Academy of Management Journal*, Vol. 27, No.3, pp. 467–88.

Dholakia, Ruby Roy, and Luis V. Dominguez (1995), 'Introduction: Special Section on Marketing Strategies and the Development Process', *Journal of Business Research*, Vol. 32, No.2, pp. 113–14.

Dibb, Sally, Lyndon Simkin, William M. Pride, and O. C. Ferrell (1997, 2001), *Marketing: Concepts and Strategies* (Boston: Houghton Mifflin Company).

Drummond, G., and John Ensor (1999), *Strategic Marketing Planning and Control* (Oxford: Butterworth Heinemann).

Herbert, Theodore T., and Helen Deresky (1987), 'Generic Strategies: An Empirical Investigation of Typology Validity and Strategy Content', *Strategic Management Journal*, Vol. 8, No.2, pp. 135–47.

Honeycutt, Earl D., Judy A. Siguaw, and Stephen C. Harper (1993), 'The Impact of Flexible Manufacturing on Competitive Strategy', *Industrial Management*, Vol. 35, No.6, pp. 2–4.

Hooley, Graham J., John Saunders, and Nigel F. Piercy (1993), *'Competitive Positioning: The Key to Market Success* (Harlow: Prentice-Hall International Ltd).

Ingram, Peter (1995), 'Employment and Competitive Advantage', *Business Economist*, Vol. 26, No.1, pp. 23–35.

Johnson, Gerry, and Kevan Scholes (1999), *Exploring Corporate Strategy* (Harlow: Prentice-Hall Europe Ltd.).

Kotler, Philip (2000), *Marketing Management* (Englewood Cliffs: Prentice-Hall, Inc.).

Kotler, Philip, and Gary Armstrong (1996), *Principles of Marketing* (Englewood Cliffs: Prentice-Hall, Inc.).

Lambin, Jean-Jacques (1997), *Strategic Marketing Management* (Maidenhead: McGraw-Hill International Ltd).

Lambkin, Mary (1988), 'Order of Entry and Performance in New Markets', *Strategic Management Journal*, Vol. 9 (Special Issue), pp. 127–40.

Langowitz, Nan (1991), 'Becoming Competitive Through Design for Manufacturing', *Industrial Management*, Vol. 33, No.4, pp. 29–31.

Mascarenhas, Briance (1992), 'Order of Entry and Performance in International Markets', *Strategic Management Journal*, Vol. 13, No.7, pp. 499–510.

McDonald, Malcolm (1996a), *Strategic Marketing Planning* (London: Kogan Page, Ltd).

McDonald, Malcolm (1996b), 'Strategic Marketing Planning: Theory, Practice and Research Agendas', *Journal of Marketing Management*, Vol. 12, No.1–2, pp. 5–27.

Miller, Danny (1992), 'The Generic Strategy Trap', *The Journal of Business Strategy*, Vol. 13 (January–February), pp. 37–41.

Miles, Raymond E., and Charles Snow (1978), *Organisational Strategy, Structure and Process* (New York: McGraw-Hill, Inc.).

Moore, Michael J., William Boulding, and Ronald C. Goodstein (1991), 'Pioneering and Market Share: Is Entry Time Endogenous and Does It Matter?', *Journal of Marketing Research*, Vol. 28 (February), pp. 97–104.

Osbaldeston, Michael, and Kevin Barham (1992), 'Using Management Development for Competitive Advantage', *Long Range Planning*, Vol. 25, No.6, pp. 18–24.

O'Shaughnessy, John (1995), *Competitive Marketing: A Strategic Approach* (London: Routledge).

Parasuraman, A., and P. Varadarajan (1985), 'More on Marketing Strategy and Differential Advantage', *Journal of Marketing*, Vol. 49 (Spring), pp. 124–8.

Porter Michael E. (1980), *Competitive Strategy: Techniques for Analyzing Industries and Competitors* (New York: The Free Press).

Porter, Michael E. (1985a), *Competitive Advantage: Creating and Sustaining Superior Performance* (New York: The Free Press).

Porter, Michael E. (1985b), 'How To Attack The Industry Leader', *Fortune*, Vol. 111, No.9 (29 April), pp. 153–66.

Porter, Michael E. (1990), *The Competitive Advantage of Nations* (New York: The Free Press).

Porter, Michael E. (2001), 'Strategy and the Internet', *Harvard Business Review*, 79 (3), pp. 63–78.

Powell, Thomas C., and Anne Dent-Micallef (1997), 'Information Technology As Competitive Advantage: The Role of Human, Business, and Technology Resources', *Strategic Management Journal*, Vol. 18, No.5, pp. 375–405.

Quinn, Michael, and John Humble (1993), 'Using Service to Gain a Competitive Edge—The PROMPT Approach', *Long Range Planning*, Vol. 26, No.2, pp. 31–40.

Robinson, William T., and Claes Fornell (1985), 'Sources of Market Pioneer Advantages in Consumer Goods Industries', *Journal of Marketing Research*, Vol. 22 (August), pp. 305–17.

Robinson, William T. (1988), 'Sources of Market Pioneer Advantages: The Case of Industrial Goods Industries', *Journal of Marketing Research*, Vol. 25 (February), pp. 87–94.

Shetty, Y. K. (1987), 'Product Quality and Competitive Strategy', *Business Horizons*, Vol. 30, No.3, pp. 46–52.

Shetty, Y. K. (1993), 'Aiming High: Competitive Benchmarking for Superior Performance', *Long Range Planning*, Vol. 26, No.1, pp. 39–44.

Sisodia, Rajendra S. (1992), 'Competitive Advantage Through Design', *The Journal of Business Strategy*, Vol. 13, No.6, pp. 33–40.

Speed, Richard J. (1989), 'Oh Mr Porter! A Re-Appraisal of Competitive Strategy', *Marketing Intelligence and Planning*, Vol. 6, No.5, pp. 8–11.

Turner, Paul (1991), 'Using Information to Enhance Competitive Advantage—The Marketing Options', *European Journal of Marketing*, Vol. 25, No.6, pp. 55–64.

Utterback, James M., and W. J. Abernathy (1975), 'A Dynamic Model of Product and Process Innovation', *Omega*, Vol. 3, No.6, pp. 639–56.

Weinrauch, Donald J., O. Karl Mann, Julie M. Pharr, and Patricia A. Robinson (1991), 'Marketing Strategies of Small Industrial Manufacturers', *Industrial Marketing Management*, Vol. 20, No.3, pp. 251–9.

Wheelen, Thomas L., and David J. Hunger (1995, 1998, 2000, 2004), *Strategic Management and Business Policy* (New York: Addison-Wesley Publishing Company, Inc.).

Wilson, Richard M. S., and Colin Gilligan (1997), *Strategic Marketing Management: Planning, Implementation and Control* (Oxford: Butterworth-Heinemann).

Wilson, Richard M. S., and Colin Gilligan (2005), *Strategic Marketing Management: Planning, Implementation and Control* (Oxford: Butterworth-Heinemann).

Wright, Peter (1987), 'A Refinement of Porter's Strategies', *Strategic Management Journal*, Vol. 8, No.1, pp. 93–101.

Zahra, Shaker A., and Sidhartha R. Das (1993), 'Building Competitive Advantage on Manufacturing Resources', *Long Range Planning*, Vol. 26, No.2, pp. 90–100.

KEY ARTICLE ABSTRACTS

Varadarajan, Rajan, Satish Jayachandran, and J. Chris White (2001), 'Strategic Interdependence in Organizations: Deconglomeration and Marketing Strategy', *Journal of Marketing*, 65 (1), pp. 15–28.

There is a wide range of publications in the marketing literature that look at different strategies adopted at the three organizational levels: corporate, SBU, and functional. This is a useful article, which doubts the benefits of dependency between strategies at these three levels. The paper suggests that a deconglomerate firm can be more competitive and more innovative.

Abstract: Although strategy exists at multiple levels in a firm (corporate, business, and functional), there is a dearth of research in the marketing literature that focuses on the dependency between strategies at different levels. This study addresses this issue by examining the relationship between deconglomeration and marketing strategy. Deconglomeration refers to the divestiture behaviour of a conglomerate firm and the transformation of its business portfolio from one that is largely composed of several unrelated businesses to one composed of fewer, related businesses. Drawing on multiple theoretical perspectives, the authors propose a conceptual model delineating the environmental and organizational drivers of deconglomeration and its outcomes for marketing. The study suggests that after deconglomeration, (1) a firm can be expected to be more competitor and customer oriented, (2) multimarket contact with competing firms and seller concentration will increase, (3) businesses retained by the firm will be more innovative and place greater emphasis on advertising than on sales promotion, and (4) the firm's culture may become more externally oriented.

Shoham, Aviv, and Avi Fiegenbaum (1999), 'Extending The Competitive Marketing Strategy Paradigm: The Role of Strategic Reference Points Theory', *Journal of Academy of Marketing Science*, 27 (4), pp. 442–54.

This paper describes the use of Strategic Reference Points (SRP) for strategic choice in marketing and the consequences of this theory for business performance.

Abstract: The purpose of this article is to extend and integrate the new strategic reference points (SRP) theory, developed in the strategic management area, into the discipline of strategic marketing management. The major new tenet of the theory is the inclusion of cognitive, organizational processes and benchmarking simultaneously. First, the authors describe the impact of the marketing SRP on marketing strategic choice behaviour captured in the trade-off between risk and return (risk averse vs risk lover) as was proposed by prospect theory. Then they explore the performance consequences of integrating the newly formed stages while considering organizational process and implementation issues of reference points such as content, configuration, consensus, and change.

Horton, Keith S. (2003), 'Strategy, Practice, and The Dynamics of Power', *Journal of Business Research*, 56 (2), pp. 121–6.

The following two papers are included because they correspond quite well to the section on information technology in Chapter 4. The first paper attempts to conceptualize a link between strategy, power, and the management of the information system (IS). The second paper has developed a conceptual (mathematical) model of the IS development process and suggests the model should be improved and tested in an empirical study.

Abstract: The notion of strategy in general, and information system strategy (ISS) in particular, can be viewed as being fundamentally concerned with mechanisms of power. This study suggests that an underlying problem in relation to information systems (IS) and strategy has been the generally unacknowledged political nature of such activity, of which power relations are an implicit part. In order to address perceived deficiencies in the understanding of IS strategy formation, theoretical work is discussed that reflects some of the developments in thinking about concepts of power in organizational settings. It is argued that ISS formation is an inherently social activity that occurs within organizational settings, and that the very notion of strategy embodies mechanisms of power.

To improve both theory and practice in relation to ISS formation, this carries with it an implicit acknowledgement that some means of thinking through the varied dynamics of power is valuable.

Wainwright, Charles E. R., Katherine A. Reynolds, and Lisa J. Argument (2003), 'Optimising strategic information system development', *Journal of Business Research*, 56 (2), pp. 127–34.

Abstract: The last decade has witnessed major change within the information systems (IS) environment with a corresponding emphasis on the importance of specifying timely and accurate information strategies. This study responds to this emphasis via the development of an optimization model to aid the formulation of IS strategy. The model is suitable for all organizations which seek to plan long-term investment strategies; however, it is particularly applicable to small- to medium-sized enterprises which need to balance long-term investment against the risk of short-term expenditure. The study initially describes the modular nature of the model prior to a disclosure of the optimization process at the centre of the approach. The optimization method uses a linear goal programming mathematical approach to analyse IS investment projects through the multivariate optimization of business goals. The study concludes with a discussion of the validation of the model via an industrial case study.

END OF CHAPTER 4 CASE STUDY

Glaxosmithkline (GSK): Strategic Evaluation and Future Directions

GSK is one of the world's largest and most influential pharmaceutical firms. Over 90% of its sales are generated outside the UK; with around 50% in the USA, the largest pharmaceutical market in the world. As such, the USA is central to GSK's success and profitability. Created by the merger in 2000 between GlaxoWellcome and SmithKline Beecham, the British based company has successfully integrated its business and consolidated its position as a market leader. GSK operates in three primary sectors: vaccines, pharmaceuticals, and consumer healthcare, dealing with three main therapeutic groups: infections, the central nervous system, and metabolic and gastric conditions. GSK faces challenges from generic competition, regulators, and investor demands for growth and improved governance. Provided that GSK can manage these issues, it has the capability to become the leading global pharmaceutical company.

Company history

First established in 1715, GSK has been the product of mergers throughout its long history, the first of which can be traced back to 1792 with the sale of a single pharmacy in London. The need to merge became apparent by the mid-1970s, with unsuccessful bids by Beecham for Glaxo, and Glaxo for the Boots pharmacy chain. However, as shown in Figure C4.1, it is only in the last 15 years that the mergers that shape the company as it is today have taken place. Unusually, GSK today is the product of not two, but four distinct companies. The 1989 merger of Smith Kline Beckman and Beecham, and the 1995 merger of Glaxo and Wellcome were designed to produce two companies that could both be dominant global players in the pharmaceutical market. However, the pace of globalization, increasing pressure from generic medicine, and the necessity for ever increasing research budgets meant that by 2000 SmithKline Beechman and GlaxoWellcome had

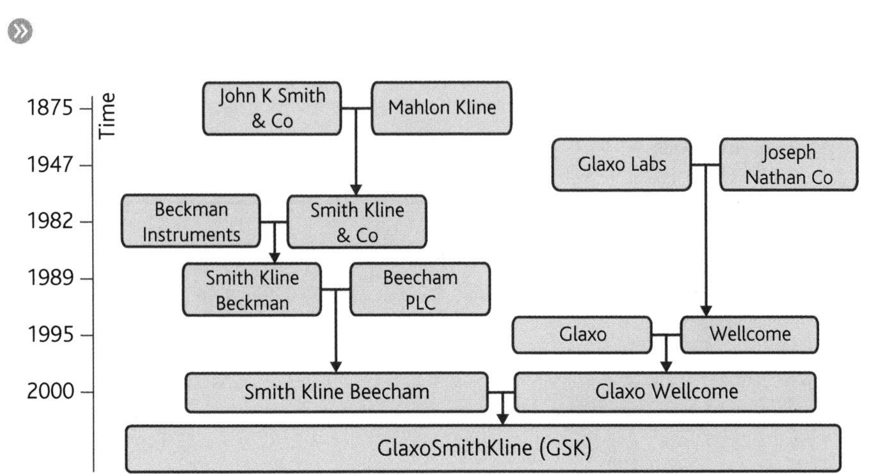

Figure C4.1 Formation of GSK

no choice but to merge or face being taken over. As two British based companies, they faced the additional hurdle of not having the same level of access to US stock market funds as their main American competitors. By merging, they could at least counter this through increasing their share of funds available to FTSE 100 members. The £130bn merger briefly formed the UK's largest company, as well as the world's largest pharmaceutical firm.

Due to the hybrid nature of GSK's business development heritage of acquisitions and mergers, global entry strategies are difficult to trace, particularly as the new organization now operates in 118 countries (GSK Annual Review 2002) across North and South America, Europe, Asia, Africa, and the Middle East. GSK has also formed strategic alliances with several other companies, one of the largest of which is with Shionogi & Co., Ltd in Japan to develop and market several drugs in clinical trials, including new agents to fight against HIV and neurological disorders. Commenting on the plan to form the joint venture, Dr Tadataka Yamada, Chairman, Research and Development of GlaxoSmithKline said, 'We are delighted with this ground-breaking alliance. Through this type of creative joint venture, we are able to provide GlaxoSmithKline with access to a promising portfolio of compounds already in clinical development while Shionogi has the opportunity to increase its global market presence. This type of innovative agreement is a signal of how we wish to partner with companies in Japan and around the world.'

Company structure and sales

GSK is a truly global firm with more than 100,000 employees, manufacturing facilities in 38 countries, and sales capability in more than 150 countries. Despite its British heritage, headquarters, and stock market listing, it maintains the bulk of its operations base in the USA—its largest market. Again, despite its UK origin, GSK enjoys an unusually large share of the US market. This can be seen as a reflection of the strength of its 40,000-employee sales operation and the quality of its product lines. Figure C4.2 illustrates the global sales of GSK by region. It is no surprise that 80% of sales occur in North America and Europe.

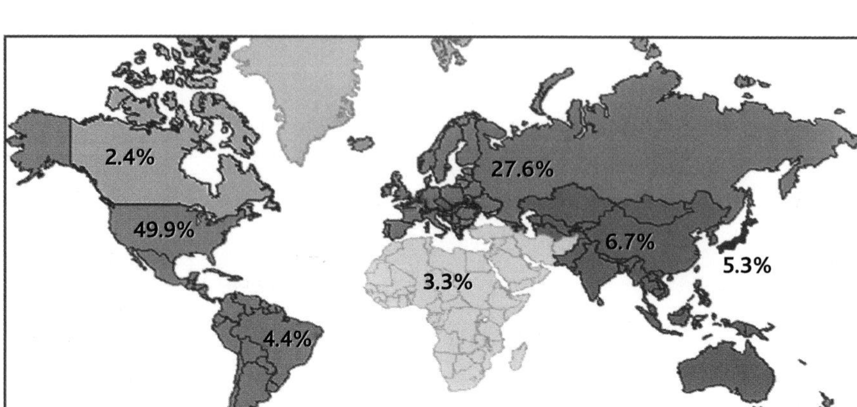

Figure C4.2 GSK sales by region 2002

One differentiating factor for GSK is that it has, by non-Japanese standards, a significant presence in the notoriously difficult Japanese market. Again, this demonstrates that the strong R&D capability of GSK, and the high-quality drugs it produces, enable it to overcome the difficulties of entering the hyper-regulated Japanese market.

GSK is a well-capitalised company, with low debt and access to key financial markets. With a market capitalization of $135bn at the close of business on 19 December 2003, debt of a little over $9bn, and a strong balance sheet GSK has a sound financial footing on which to invest in its future growth. GSK has invested heavily in R&D and can afford to take an opportunistic approach to drug development. With two out of three new R&D sites already furnished with High, and Ultra High Throughput Chemistry technologies and automation, GSK has found its position as one of the leading companies involved in genome and DNA technologies. Additionally, as the only company currently investing in all three of the WHO priority disease areas, GSK is a leading firm in producing medicines for developing countries.

Key competitors

GSK is one of the top ten pharmaceutical companies. Besides competing with other branded pharmaceutical companies, GSK is also competing with companies manufacturing generic products that are now recording rapidly increasing sales. On an individual market level, GSK's competitors could be defined as any company with a competing product. However, on a global level GSK's main competitors are classified by analysts as being Novartis, Pfizer, and Schering-Plough (See Table C4.1).

Besides competition from the above, GSK is also faced with competition from generic drugs. During 2002, GSK suffered a decrease in some of its major products due to the 

TABLE C4.5 Direct competitor comparison

	GSK	Novartis	Pfizer	Schering-Plough	Industry average
Market cap	135.55bn	108.16bn	261.53bn	24.58bn	185.71m
Employees	106,166	72,877	98,000	30,500	161
Rev. growth	—	21.40%	0.40%	3.90%	16.40%
Revenue	34.03bn	23.15bn	32.37bn	10.18bn	44.66m
Gross margin	79.02%	76.50%	81.08%	69.39%	58.40%
EBITDA	11.53bn	7.83bn	5.83bn	1.01bn	836,000
Oper. margins	30.39%	24.33%	14.31%	6.48%	5.34%
Net income	8.08bn	4.67bn	3.73bn	402.00m	−706,000
EPS	2.762	1.886	0.63	0.274	0.00

Source: Yahoo Finance.

loss of patents and the subsequent increased use of generic drugs. Products affected were Augmentin and Ceftin with a substantial decrease in the USA, Europe, and internationally. The Arthritis therapeutic area was also affected resulting in an 84% decrease in sales. The Central Nervous System (CNS) therapeutic area also encountered competition for Paxil and Wellbutrin. GSK is also suffering from an increase in global sales of generic analgesics.

Key product areas

Whilst the success of any pharmaceutical company in any particular area is tied to the fortunes of the blockbuster drug in that sector, GSK has a sufficiently broad range of products to be able to look across the whole product spectrum. The key product areas that shape GSK's production portfolio are summarized below (GSK Annual Review 2002).

1. Central nervous system

Central nervous system (CNS) therapy has been GSK's core sales area, amounting to £4.5bn (25% of total sales) in 2002. However, 2004 sales are predicted at £3.7bn, with the key product Paxil down by a one-third, and a steady decline in sales is expected in future years. CNS's leading products for depression and anxiety disorders (Seroxat/Paxil and Wellbutrin) showed the highest sales in 2002, £2.1bn and £882 million respectively. Lamictal, for epilepsy, continued to grow across all regions with total sales of £438 million. In January 2003, the US Food and Drug Administration (FDA) approved the use of Lamictal for the treatment of partial seizures in paediatric patients aged two years or above, improving the sales prospects for Lamictal.

2. Respiratory area

Respiratory is GSK's second biggest product area, accounting for 22% of total sales. Its three key products, Seretide/Advair, Flixotide, and Serevent, reached total sales of £2.4bn in 2002. Sales of Seretide/Advair grew 96% (sales in 2001 £850 million) and Advair is today the market leader in new prescriptions in the US asthma market after less than two years on the market. The Group expects European marketing authorization within the next few months for the use of Seretide as a new treatment for chronic obstructive pulmonary disease.

3. Anti-viral area

Anti-viral sales are growing across all regions and totalled £2.3bn. Sales of Trizivir, GSK's new triple combination therapy for HIV, grew 95% from 2001 to £315 million (and are expected to increase to £535 million in 2004). Valtrex for herpes achieved strong sales growth of 26% worldwide with sales amounting to £425 million in 2002. In September 2002, Valtrex was approved by the FDA for the treatment of cold sores in healthy adults and in October 2002, GSK filed a further application for Valtrex, seeking the first ever indication to reduce the risk of transmission of genital herpes.

4. Anti-bacterial area

Anti-bacterial sales declined worldwide by 12% from 2001 and by 22% in the USA, resulting in sales of £2.2bn in 2002. This decrease was the result of generic competition for Augmentin and Ceftin. In the USA GSK's two new antibiotics, Augmentin ES (for children) and Augmentin XR (for adults) are performing well.

5. Metabolic and Gastro-intestinal area

In the metabolic and gastro-intestinal area the Avandia franchise, Avandia and Avandamet, grew 19% for the year with sales totalling £809 million. Avandia is now approved in 81 countries. Avandamet, launched in the fourth quarter of 2002, is the first treatment for type 2 diabetes that targets insulin resistance and decreases glucose production in one convenient pill. Meanwhile, Zantac had a decrease of 21% in 2002, with sales totalling £382 million in 2002.

6. Vaccines

Within vaccines, the hepatitis franchise grew 12%, with total sales growing to £483 million and European sales growing 10%. Vaccine sales in the USA were up 16% and reached £290 million, benefiting from the launch of Twinrix and continued strong growth in Havrix, driven by new state mandates requiring Hepatitis-A vaccination for schoolchildren. In the USA, GSK's new Pediarix vaccine was launched in January 2003.

7. Oncology

In oncology, Zofran sales grew 22% to £708 million, driven by a strong US performance, up 28% to £525 million. Total sales within the oncology and emesis therapeutic area accounted to £977 million, a total of 5% from the group's global sales.

8. Cardiovascular area

Cardiovascular sales grew 14%, with total sales reaching £655 million, benefiting from a strong performance in the USA, up 16% to £430 million.

9. Arthritis

In the Arthritis area, sales faced an 84% decrease to only £23 million. This loss was made up of a decrease of sales of 93% in the USA, 38% in Europe, and 21% internationally due to increased competition from generic products.

10. Consumer healthcare

Consumer Healthcare (Over the counter medicines, Oral care, and Nutritional healthcare) sales grew by 2%, to £3.2bn. This was due to an increase in OTC pharmaceuticals sales of 4% and a Nutritional healthcare increase of 3% partly offset by a decline in Oral care sales of 2%. Sales of nicotine replacement pharmaceuticals (i.e., Patches,

Inhalers, and Gum, etc.) grew by 4%, driven by a strong performance from Nicoderm/Niquitin/Nicabate. In the USA and the UK, growth was strong thanks to increasing awareness and changes in government legislation.

In analgesics, Panadol recorded growth of 5%, partly offset by declines in a number of other brands. Abreva in the USA and Zovirax in Europe (used in the treatment of cold sores) drove dermatological sales growth of 5%. In gastro-intestinal medicines, sales of Citrucel rose by 19% but this was offset by declines in Tums and Tagamet. Oral care sales grew marginally in Europe but declined in the highly competitive US market. Overall, Oral care sales declined by 2%, reaching sales of £1.1bn. This decline was principally a result of reduced sales of the Aquafresh Brand, although this was offset by an increase in sales of the Sensodyne, Polident, and Poligrip brands. In Nutritional healthcare, Lucozade and Ribena reported strong growth in Europe, driven by increased availability and promotion. Horlicks sales declined primarily in international markets (GSK Annual Review & Annual Report 2002).

Figure C4.3 illustrates the actual and predicted sales by sector for 2003–2005. **Figure C4.4** presents a BCG matrix of GSK's product area to illustrate the point that the challenges facing GSK vary by sector.

Product portfolio: key products

Five key products account for around 20% of GSK's turnover: **Paxil**, **Wellbutrin**, **Advair**, **Avandia**, and **Augmentin. Figure C4.5** shows the actual and predicted sales for these five products for the period 2000–2009. As this graph shows, there is some imbalance between the sales volumes of the various products. Currently Paxil (an antidepressant) and Augmetin (for respiratory infections) are GSK's biggest sellers, between them accounting for around 15% of GSK's pharmaceutical sales. However, both are facing challenges from generic competition leaving GSK with a damage limitation exercise to make the inevitable decline in sales as low as possible. Avandia, a diabetes drug, is performing well and is expected to continue steady growth to achieve blockbuster status. In addition, Wellbutrin is likely to show growth in the future, though it will suffer a short-term drop in growth due to the expiry of the patent on the original version of the drug. The star product is Advair (for asthma), which has the potential to dominate the US market for asthma treatments. However, Advair does demonstrate that dependence on one product for future growth has a high element of risk. Recent fears that regulatory changes would damage sales of Advair turned out to be unfounded; however given the nature of R&D in the pharmaceutical industry, it only needs one discovery by another firm for GSK to lose this franchise. GSK therefore desperately needs some of the new blockbusters in its product pipeline to be a success.

Product pipeline

GSK is currently facing a dilemma: whilst its past results have been strong, and the merger is now behind the firm, it faces declining sales of its current key products, and over-dependence on Advair for future profits. At a December 2003 R&D meeting, GSK unveiled 147 new products under development, including 20 that have the potential to become blockbusters with sales of over $1bn per annum. However, whilst GSK's product pipeline is one of the best, if not the best in the industry, there are substantial concerns amongst investors over GSK's track record of actually getting drugs

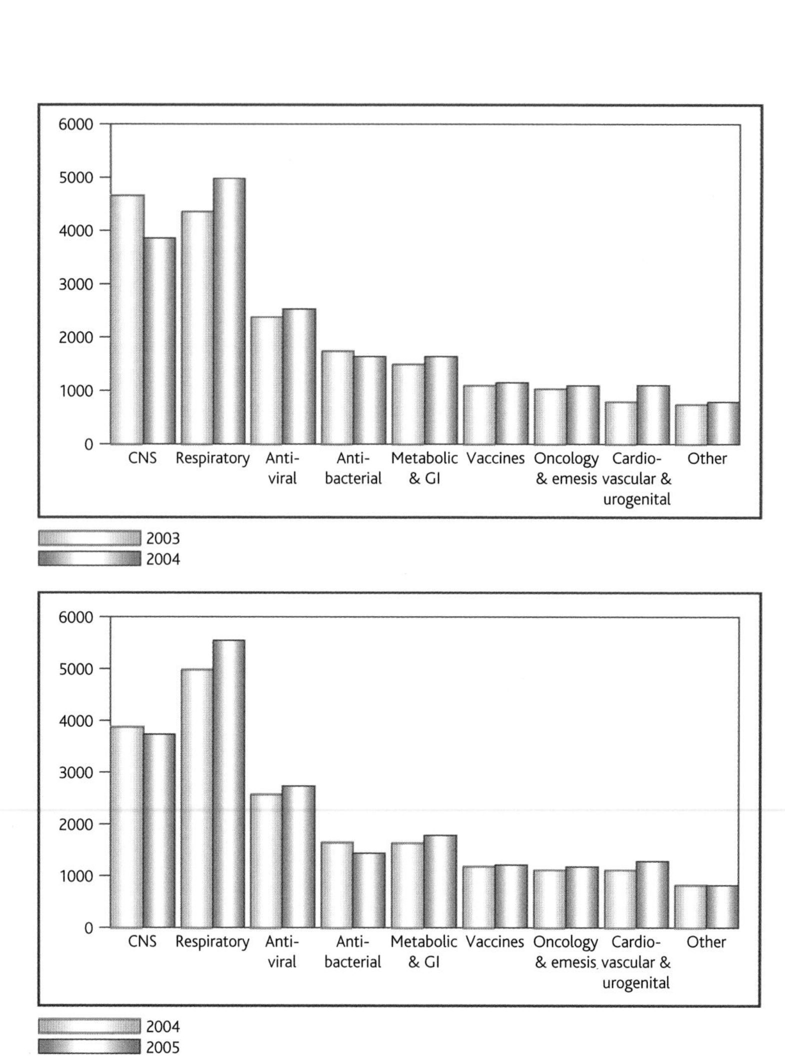

Figure C4.3 Actual/projected sales figures for pharmaceuticals by category for the years 2003/2004 and 2004/2005 (in £m)

Source: Morgan Stanley, 2003.

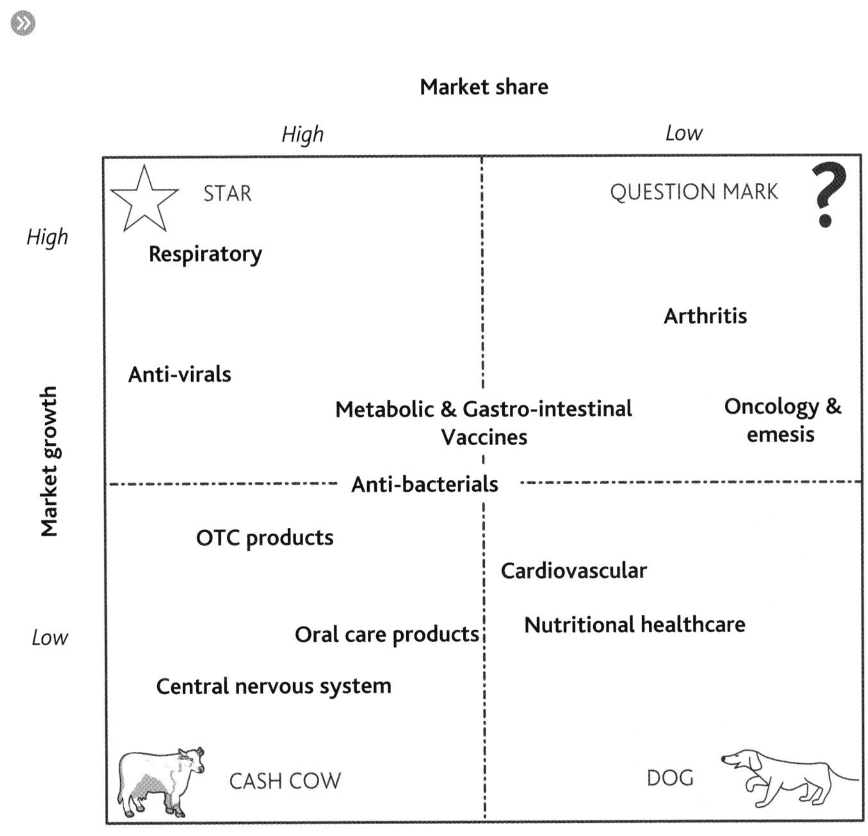

Figure C4.4 BCG matrix for GSK's product areas

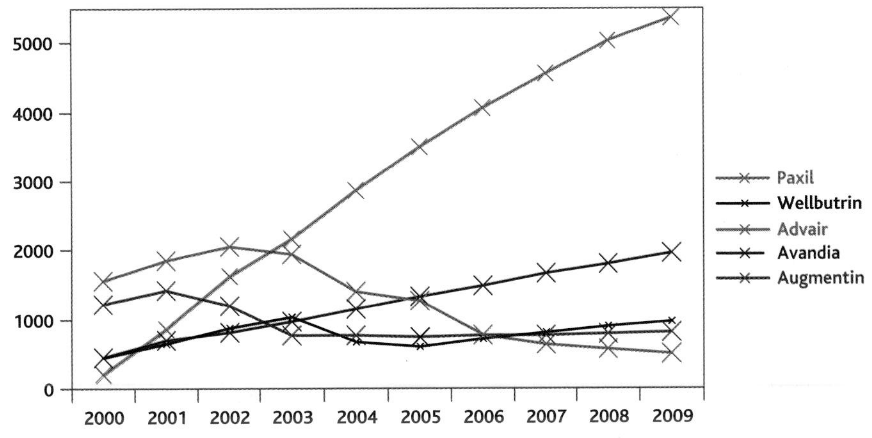

Figure C4.5 Sales of key products 2000–2002 (actual) and 2003–2009 (predicted) in £million per annum

Source: Morgan Stanley, 2003.

» into development. Whilst there is significant potential for GSK to be the world's fastest growing pharmaceutical company after 2006, the costs of launching drugs are spiralling and, even at a late stage, the US FDA can refuse to give authority for a drug to be sold. For example, in August 2003 approval for Ariflo (a drug for life-threatening breathing difficulties) was denied. The cost of clinical studies required before a drug can be launched has doubled in the last few years to $860 million for each drug launched between 2000 and 2002. Despite these risks, if GSK can successfully implement even a proportion of its potential drug launches then it is likely to meet the aggressive growth targets it is setting itself. GSK's key pipeline blockbuster products fall into five categories as follows (adapted from *The Guardian*, 2003):

- **Cancer:** Glaxo's new drug compound blocks two biological switches in the growth of tumours, whereas its main competitors only block one each.
- **Heart disease:** Glaxo's drug attacks the enzyme that inflames arterial walls.
- **Pain:** Glaxo's inhibitor could treat osteoarthritis, rheumatoid arthritis, back and neuropathic pain, a much wider range than existing drugs.
- **Diabetes/Obesity:** Glaxo's inhibitor promotes glucose elimination. Designed for diabetes, particularly the increasing market for obesity related Type II diabetes. Could also have application in obesity treatment as a chemical Atkins diet.
- **Cervical cancer:** Glaxo's vaccine appears to be 100% effective in preventing infection by the papilloma viruses with the highest risk of cervical cancer.

Conclusion

Despite the competitiveness of the international pharmaceutical market, the above analysis has shown that GSK's long-term strategy is broadly sound. In the short term, GSK faces several challenges from generic competition, pressure from regulators and government, and investor demands for growth and improved governance. Provided GSK can deal with these issues it has the capability to meet its goals. Through the merger that formed GSK, the company now has the scale and international clout required. With an effective global presence it is a major player in the key North American and European markets. The fact that more than 50% of sales come from North America is impressive considering that GSK is essentially a British company.

Source: This case was produced by the author for class discussion, October 2003.

QUESTIONS

1. Critically evaluate the GSK's product/market strategy and comment on the corporation's growth strategy in the global pharmaceutical market.
2. Analyse the competitive environment in which GSK operates. Based on your analysis advise the company on the most appropriate of Porter's generic strategies (low-cost, differentiation, focus) to pursue.
3. Although GSK's long-term strategy is sound, the company faces several challenges from generic competition, pressure from regulators and government, and investor demands for growth and improved governance. To what extent do you think that the company has the capability to meet its strategic goals in the pharmaceutical industry?

5

Segmentation, targeting, and positioning strategies

LEARNING OBJECTIVES

- Examine the ways in which companies can segment markets
- Discuss ways in which marketers can measure the effectiveness of identified target segments
- Identify the various ways in which marketers can reach the identified market segments
- Provide an explanation of the importance of positioning the product in the head of the target consumer
- Present several important tools for perceptual mapping so that the reader can understand how to achieve a powerful position within the mind of the target consumer

CHAPTER AT A GLANCE

Introduction

Market segmentation is vital for company success. Without a clear idea of the nature of the target segments, the firm is forced to use a scatter-shot approach to marketing strategic decision-making, with little chance for success. Dividing the market up into reasonable segments is only a starting point. The firm then must develop a series of strategic goals and strategies for effectively reaching those identified segments. Targeting requires the firm not only to aim at but hopefully to hit its target segments. The final important aspect involves the establishment of an important perceptual position in the mind of the consumer. The company whose brand comes immediately to mind when a need arises in a particular product/service class has a distinct advantage over its competitors. This chapter will present a series of possible foundations for effective segmentation and mechanisms for developing action plans for reaching those segments, and will discuss ways in which the marketing strategist can enhance their product/service position inside the mind of the targeted consumer.

Foundations for effective segmentation

With the vast array of different wants and needs that exists for any product or service class, it is unlikely that any company can have the luxury of appealing to an entire market. The buying requirements for this wide array of consumers would be widely varied. This might be possible in the early stages of a product or service form life cycle; however, as competition builds, the company is forced to give consumers a reason to prefer its product offerings to those of the competitors through differentiation. For this to be successful, it is necessary for the company to identify target segments of consumers and tailor its offerings to best meet the wants and needs of that particular group of consumers. Market segmentation therefore involves the analysis of mass markets to identify subgroups of consumers with similar wants and buying requirements. The point is to maximize between-segment differences while minimizing within-segment differences using a variety of grouping variables. The firm is then in a position to tailor its offerings to best meet the desires of the consumers belonging to that segment. The point is for the firm to identify clusters of similar consumers that will allow for more efficient uses of resources and improve firm performance. The identification of a segment allows the firm to identify a profile of its typical desired customer, which in turn would allow the firm to develop a product configuration, pricing scheme, promotional campaign, and distribution coverage plan to best meet the needs of that identified typical consumer.

Criteria for identifying segments

The most important variables for identifying segments are as follows:

Geography

- Global
- Global regional

- National
- National regional
- City/State
- Neighbourhood/Local
- Topography
- Climate

Demography

- Gender
- Age
- Education
- Income
- Occupation
- Religion
- Ethnicity
- Family size
- Stage of family life cycle
- Social status/Class

Psychography

- Personality
- Lifestyle
- Values

Behaviour

- Usage rate
- Loyalty level
- Event creation
- Key benefits

Each of these will now be discussed with illustrative examples.

Geographic bases for segmentation

Geography focuses on the 'where' issues. It ranges from local/neighbourhood to global, and it could encompass any variation between the two extremes. Here the main mechanism for segmentation is the nature of the geographic market being covered. Local segmentation, often used by small firms getting their start, keeps the market confined to a manageable area of coverage until a far greater understanding of possible niches is gathered. Since these firms often are not sure who their direct competitors are or will be, they opt for a group of nearby customers to reach. Picture the small restaurant getting its first connection to potential area customers with the placing of windscreen flyers or door-to-door leaflets to tell people that they are open for business.

Global segmentation would assume that the company sees the entire world as its appropriate playing field. This would indicate that the firm sees the broadest array of customers as its potential market. The danger of this approach normally entails the potential for cultural inappropriateness without some modification for different regions or nations. The other options are all variations limited by the amount of geographic coverage. Often companies will use geographic mapping programs (like SPSS Maps) to address geographic segmentation by measuring potential trading area coverage. There are often assumptions made that if their best customers are located in a particular area, there may be important opportunities to build other strong customers in that coverage area. Kotler (2003) mentions the use by many companies of customer cloning whereby the densest geographic areas are mapped and the company assumes that if the majority of customers are located in a particular area, then the best potential customers will come from that area.

Another aspect of geographic segmentation, which often is overlooked, is topography. The contour of the land within a geographic area may have a bearing on effective segmentation. Topography includes such elements as rivers, mountains, lakes, and valleys, which may affect population movement. The costs of overcoming physical obstacles may make a significant argument for effective segmentation. This might also apply to climatic conditions. Arid desert conditions as opposed to humid rainforest conditions can also be an appropriate mechanism for segmentation.

In practice, larger firms undoubtedly utilize a variety of different segmentation approaches given different types of products. Campbell's soup had great success in the Upper Midwest of the United States with its cheddar cheese soup, but this product had little relevance for the US southwest so the company added jalapeno peppers to spice it up and found great acceptance for the product as a coating for tortilla chips.

Demographic bases for segmentation

Here the overall market is subdivided using a series of demographic variables. One of the most obvious ways to segment demographically is by gender, but this is a complex term. **Gender** does not just address physical sexual makeup. It also contains a psychological component. How the individual sees him/herself in terms of their sexual makeup and orientation is becoming less distinct in a variety of developed countries. Sex segmentation involves choosing males or females as the target audience. Certainly there are a variety of products that have attempted this form of segmentation, from cosmetic companies to alcoholic beverages; however, it is more difficult now as one's feelings of masculinity/femininity affiliation may be a more appropriate segmentation tool (see Mini Case Study 5.1). In the United States, Virginia Slims cigarettes were oriented to women, but it was not clear that they did not have appeal to those males who felt a particular affinity for things of a feminine nature.

Age is another basis for demographic segmentation. This can be clearly seen in the segmentation being done by Sony and Microsoft for their popular computer gaming systems and hand-held systems (Sony's PlayStation and PSP and Microsoft's X-Box). The aim is to reach the computer-savvy youth with considerable discretionary income to spend on

MINI CASE STUDY 5.1 'The changing faces of man'

The metrosexual designation is now upon us. This apparently valid social trend has created a group of male consumers who are concerned about personal grooming and body image. With both gay men and such heterosexual representatives as David Beckham, the metrosexual represents a growing cohort of young men, primarily urban cosmopolitans. The brand agency Dragon has conducted research among both men and women and has found strong evidence for the metrosexual in the UK. Apparently young men in the UK are becoming more focused on grooming and have concerns for the appearance of their bodies and their overall health. Dragon has also learned that there are boundaries for metrosexuals in the UK at this point. Only 8 percent of their respondents said that they were willing to carry some kind of manbag (a male handbag). So the extreme is not yet the reality.

Dragon's research found that when men were asked who they would most like to be for a day, the answers most often given were David Beckham or Brad Pitt who are known for their style and looks as opposed to their personalities or intellects. For 52 per cent of the respondents, the gym was the most important mechanism for staying fit and healthy while cycling and jogging came in second at 38 per cent. The old mainstay for keeping fit had been football, but in this research only 28 per cent made that choice. They found that one man in every ten spends an inordinate amount of time and money on his appearance, while one in three claim that they do the basics.

A research firm known as Key Note estimates that the grooming market for men will grow from £500 m in 2004 to £632 m in 2007. A company known as Mintel has also found that there is a strong bias to those under 24 years of age in the use of skincare products.

Boots has begun to address what it sees as an important segment through the creation of a male grooming zone in its larger stores. Boots will be staffing these male zones with trained experts who can answer customer questions. Boots has seen a rise in male purchases of skincare products from 25 percent in 2002 to roughly 40 percent in 2004. Men as consumers of these products are becoming better informed and more demanding, which has forced Boots to add additional products to its mix for male grooming. Simon McCandlish is the commercial manager of suncare, skincare and men's products at Boots, and he believes that poor grooming is quickly becoming unacceptable today. It is also only a matter of time before anti-ageing products become available for men. McCandlish is quick to provide a warning concerning the metrosexual, however, since he is not certain that metrosexuals should be too closely covered since they are only one part of a larger male population that appears to be taking greater interest in grooming. The courting of metrosexuals might alienate a larger group of male consumers. Boots wants to appeal to as many consumers as possible.

Source: Robert Gray (2003), *Marketing*, 27 March, pp. 28–30.

computer games, music CDs, and DVDs. Youth can clearly be seen in the segmentation of toys, music, cereals, clothing, electronics, and mobile telephones.

With globalization forces at work, there is an increasing opportunity for similarity of youth segments, in terms of wants and needs driven strongly by the world entertainment media (cinema, music, television). This primarily applies to developed countries as income levels in developing countries would not support these types of products and services.

Elderly consumers provide another promising avenue for product/service segmentation. With life expectancies significantly increasing in many developed countries, the elderly have become increasingly lucrative as a segmentation vehicle. (See Mini Case Study 5.2.) The United States has seen a considerable increase in the segmenting of older consumers by fast food franchisers both as consumers looking for places to socialize with others and as potential employees. A wide range of health-related products are being aimed at increasingly older consumers with travel and leisure products/services and low-fat and low-carbohydrate food/beverage products.

MINI CASE STUDY 5.2 'Marketing: Smoking out Images of Pipes And Slippers'

Skateboarding, bottom-pinching, crowd-surfing. Hardly activities that are associated with older people, at least in the minds of the advertising industry. More traditionally, the elderly have been depicted as kindly, slightly doddery souls.

But this image is increasingly off the mark. It not only misrepresents the current older generation, it positively alienates them. That can hit sales, which is bad news for business as this ever-increasing group—in the developed world, at least—has unprecedented spending power. No wonder brand owners from Germany to Japan are so jumpy about getting it wrong.

Some brands have realized that they are missing a trick and are doing something about it. An example is Complan's reinvention from a caring, sickbed 'meal replacement' drink to a proactive brand with a sense of humour.

This is where the bottom-pinching comes in. The new packs are covered with cartoon-style illustrations depicting all sorts of lively activities.

'Complan effectively gives you a "helping hand". So we created a series of tongue-in-cheek vignettes of stereotypical "old people" doing stereotypical "young people's" things such as skateboarding, bungee jumping, and bottom-pinching', explains Richard Murray of brand design agency Williams Murray Hamm.

'We didn't want to compound a sense of Complan being for the ageing, the toothless, and the infirm, hence the overall cheery look.'

It is too early to say whether the new look is successful as packs are only just starting to appear in stores. But, according to all the recent research into this age group, it seems to be speaking the right language.

From Age Concern in the UK, to Focalyst in the US, the message is that the pipe-and-slippers connotations may have been appropriate for the old folk of yesteryear, but things have changed.

Traditionally, marketers have divided up their target markets by age, and marketing for the old has been serious and problem-related, pandering to their perceived fears and needs.

'Clearly, the classic "I've fallen down and can't get up!" imagery just won't work any more', says Heather Stern, director of marketing and client development at Focalyst, a joint venture between AARP Services and research firm The Kantar Group, focusing on understanding baby boomers and 50-plus consumers.

The difference is that in the 1950s, today's 50- and 60-year-olds were the 'first' teenagers, and as such are no carbon copies of their own ageing parents.

In January, Focalyst will reveal research which identifies the segments or niches within this age group. These are not about age but about different life events, such as becoming a grandparent, finding new love, retirement, getting a new job, or coping with bereavement.

Research from international design consultancy Ideo into this age group backs these findings up. 'Targeting older people alienates older people, too. Talk to their interests and aspirations, not their age', says Gretchen Addi, human factors specialist at Ideo.

Age, she says, is increasingly an irrelevance. 'Many 50- and 60-year-old people that I have interviewed are healthier than some 30-year-olds, so again, age is not the card to play.'

So advertising and marketing that instead highlights these life events is becoming more popular. Saatchi & Saatchi's campaign for Ameriprise Financial in the US focuses on the idea that the baby boomer generation will approach retirement very differently to previous generations. Instead of using actors, Saatchi & Saatchi featured true stories of people from that generation, in an attempt to demonstrate their individuality.

Using real people in advertising can also avoid bland stereotypes. This has worked for Unilever's Dove skincare brand, with its Real Beauty campaign by Ogilvy & Mather featuring some women with grey hair.

Older celebrities, too, are not living up to the ageing stereotypes, and that makes them ideal spokespeople for this generation. US-based Fidelity Investments, for example, has appointed Paul McCartney as spokesperson. This may strike some consumers as a bizarre move for the ex-Beatle, but with his second wife and new baby, Mr McCartney is seen as a realistic example of a 20th century man in his 60s.

Complan has also gone for the older spokespeople. Three former members of the 1970s dance troupe Pan's People, now in their 50s, have been signed up as the face of Complan's funkier sub-brand, Complan Active.

High-profile examples are few and far between, however. According to Age Concern's report, *How Ageist is Britain,* half of those surveyed thought that those responsible for advertising and sales literature took no notice of older people.

But not all the blame for older people being ignored and patronized can be laid at the feet of the advertising and marketing industries. They may have a lot of money—they represent 50 per cent of total consumer spending in the US—but they are not always in a rush to spend it.

As Simon Silvester, executive planning director at Young & Rubicam Emea, says: 'When it comes to innovations, people over 35 are slower to get into them. It pays to put money into people when they're young and reap the brand benefits through brand loyalty.'

He sees this as a particular problem in Germany, where the emergence of an ageing population has happened very quickly and people over 35 have become very conservative. 'They want the same things for less money,' he says, while in Japan, 'people over 35 don't get into new technology and their focus is about getting more for less.'

» But the biggest change for the ad industry to embrace is that the so-called 'grey market' is no minority group. By 2041, more than 20 m people in the UK will be over 60—or 37 per cent of the population.

'It used to be that the grey market was the niche market,' says Mr Silvester, 'but now it's more mainstream, and the upshot is that youth has become the niche.'

Source: Claire Dowdy (2005), *Financial Times*, 7 November.

An interesting shift in focus was seen for Red Bull energy drinks in the UK, which had built a credible position with targeting to what was considered the 'edgy youth' interested in nightclubs and extreme sports. The company shifted its segmentation target in 2004 to older consumers interested in golf, which would move the product into the mainstream. The company has plans to distribute Red Bull in UK golf clubs and will align itself with the European Professional Golfers Association Tour (Sweeney, 2004). Another attempt to shift focus can be readily seen in the recent re-launching of Burton Food's Viscount brand of biscuits. The new product is called Viscount Minis, and the new target is the younger woman who buys biscuits and confectionery to share. This is a distinct departure from the more mature female consumers who were previously seen as the key segment for the company's biscuits.

An important approach to age segmentation involves the concept of a **cohort of society** moving through the ageing process together. While birth age is relatively easy to use as a basis for grouping potential consumers, it actually has little to do with consumer motivations. Defining moments and events in late adolescence/early adulthood (17–23 years of age) provide a set of fairly stable values that stay with members of the same generational cohort throughout their lives. This has been used successfully in the United States (Schuman and Scott, 1989). *Advertising Age* (15 January 2001) presented six main generational cohorts in the US market: (1) the **GI Generation** (those born between 1901 and 1924) who are conservative and civic-concerned; (2) the **Silent Generation** (those born between 1925 and 1945) who are interested in conforming and raised families at an early age and are concerned with youthfulness and vitality; (3) the **Baby Boomers** (those born between 1946 and 1964) who believe that personal acquisitions are important, have high levels of disposable income, and who are concerned with value and do not want to be perceived as older; (4) **Generation X** (those born between 1961 and 1981) who are considered to be somewhat cynical, have great economic power, and feel somewhat lost or alienated; (5) **Generation Y** (those born between 1976 and 1981) who are a subset of generation X, interested in an urban style, like outdoor activities, and enjoy retro-style products; and lastly (6) the **Millennials** (those born between 1982 and 2002) who are multicultural, interested in high-tech products, are well educated, and are more used to violence and sex as a part of life.

It was noted by Jacqueline Scott and Lilian Zac (1993) that there have been many similarities in life experiences shared by Americans and British, which would suggest that similar cohorts could be effectively used for segmentation in the UK. This, however, may not work globally. An interesting recent study by Schewe and Meredith (2004) examined generational cohorts in a global setting, and found that there are a number of countries which may not have the kinds of cohorts that have been found in the USA. They argue that for cohorts to be formed, there are three requirements: (1) a telecommunications infrastructure that facilitates mass communications, (2) a population which is reasonably literate, and (3) the events involved must have significant social impact. Schewe and Meredith (2004) propose that these conditions can be met in all developed countries as well as India, Eastern Europe, Lebanon, and China. They urge that underdeveloped nations are not fertile ground for cohort segmentation. They found through extensive research that there are distinctly different generational cohorts in Brazil and in Russia. These cohorts provide a valuable opportunity for segmentation.

The **level of education** can also be an effective basis for segmentation. The complexity of certain products makes them more appropriate for proper evaluation and usage by individuals with higher levels of education. There are certain products which are actually targeted to different levels of students from primary school (with such products as crayons, books, games, and snack products) to higher levels of education such as secondary school and university (with products like calculators, computers, apparel, music, and DVDs). The USA has seen the advent of the SKIPPies acronym as descriptive of an important buying group (School Kids with Income and Purchasing Power). Firms like Coca-Cola, Nike, and Nabisco have all turned to in-school promotions to attract the teenage student segment.

Cort et al. (2004) report that one particularly successful in-school marketing programme used in the United States is offered by Channel One. This in-school television network broadcasts a 12-minute daily programme with two minutes of commercials to over 12,000 schools throughout the country and carries news and programming of interest to students. In return for allowing the programming during classes, the school receives television sets and receiving equipment. It is hoped that the advertiser utilization of the system will begin to build the seeds of brand awareness and loyalty in a unique environment with long-term consumer relationship potential.

A logical basis for segmentation is **level of income**, but in many countries, the larger concern is the individual's level of purchasing power. The important distinction in income is found in the difference between disposable income and discretionary income. For basic necessity types of products (food, clothing, and shelter), the starting point would be to examine disposable income, which is the income that is left over after taxes and creditors are paid. Discretionary income is what is left over from disposable income after basic necessities have been acquired. The remainder is then used to buy such products/services as fashion items/jewellery, cosmetics and fragrances, and a variety of leisure time products/services like holidays, and gym memberships.

Occupation can also serve as an appropriate basis for segmentation. There are a series of products/services that are aimed at homemakers as opposed to professionals, students, 'white collar' workers (managers, executives, professionals) as opposed to 'blue collar' workers (labourers, tradespeople), the retired/pensioners, and the unemployed.

Religion is an important basis for segmentation particularly when religious teachings or doctrine make the consumption of certain products mandatory or prohibited. Some products may never be allowed (beef for Hindus, alcoholic beverages for Muslims) while others may depend on the time of year or even day of the week. Acceptable articles and types of clothing may be dictated by religion (coverings to be worn by women in the Middle East). In the USA, Manischewitz Company sells products which meet Jewish Kosher standards.

Ethnicity equates to national country/culture of origin. In the United States, McDonald's has been particularly focused on race and ethnic heritage as a segmentation tool. Ads are run with Asian-American, African-American, and Hispanic-American settings, which include appropriately representative models, locales, music, and language. This also can apply just as easily to any national origin and cultural extraction. The key element would involve the use of effective representations of those cultures. In many developed countries, there are significant ethnic communities with considerable purchase power which are effective targets for segmentation strategies. In Great Britain there are considered to be 17 different ethnic groups according to the *Labour Force Survey* published in 2003 (Marketing Pocket Book 2004). The breakdown in thousands of individuals is shown in Table 5.1.

What these statistics clearly indicate is that there are a series of large ethnic groupings in Great Britain that may prove to be desirable bases for product/service segmentation. Palumbo and Teich (2004) suggest that minority and ethnic group segmentation must also consider the impact of acculturation since the amount of time that the individual has spent in the society will impact their outlook. Parallel strategies should be developed for targeting both acculturated ethnic groups and those not yet acculturated. The authors suggest that this is just as applicable in the USA as in Western Europe, given the heavy influx of immigrants into these countries/cultures.

TABLE 5.1 UK population by ethnic group 1995 and 2001 (in 000s)

	1995	2001
White—British	NA	51,312
White—Other	NA	1,690
Indian	866	956
Pakistani	548	728
Black—Caribbean	486	618
Black—African	292	506
White & Black—Caribbean	NA	271
Bangladeshi	184	261
Other—Asian	173	250
Chinese	123	180
White & Asian	NA	145
White & Black—African	NA	65
Black—Other	232	72
Other mixed	NA	30
Totals:		
White	52,894	53,002
Ethnic minorities	3,237	4,364
Other	333	282
Total population	**56,144**	**59,139**

Family size is another segmentation variable worth considering. The existence of the extended family in many developing countries is an important consideration since there are various members of the family unit who can play a variety of roles in the product/service choice process. Kellogg's had seen problems in its advertisements aimed at Brazil when it showed the father and the child in a breakfast setting. It was seen as not representative of real life, since the father would not be the one normally getting the child his or her breakfast. In Brazil the individual would be the grandparent. The ads were changed and were received much more favourably as a result.

Family life cycle stage reflects a variety of life conditions that have a potential impact on product/service purchase decisions. If the target segment is single as opposed to married, there may be a series of preferences linked to that life state. Examples can be found in food packaging of meals for one person as opposed to two or more, dating services, and fashion and hygiene products to help the individual find a date/partner. Later life stages include young marrieds, marrieds with no children, married with young children, married with older children, empty nesters (those marrieds whose children have left home and who are now on their own), and older marrieds or those who are older but single again. These types of segmentation mechanisms are particularly useful in terms of leisure time activity choices as one's leisure time usage is heavily influenced by the nature of one's home family situation. Automobile companies use life-cycle stage segmentation quite heavily. Vans are often chosen by families with young children since they have more space for carrying several children at a time to a sports or school activity, while small sports cars with only two seats are aimed at singles or young marrieds.

In Great Britain, the 2003 National Readership Survey (NRS, Ltd) in its SAGACITY Life Cycle Groupings utilizes four distinct life cycle stages: dependent (mainly under the age of 24 and either living at home or a full-time student), pre-family (under the age of 35 and having established their own household but without children), family (under the age of 65 with one or more children in the household representing as a group the main shoppers and primary income earners), and late (all adults whose children have left the home or those adults older than 35 without any children). For SAGACITY, these categories are then further divided into categories based upon previously discussed criteria (income and occupation). Here life cycle stages are then divided into the white group (where the primary income earner works in the ABC1 occupation group) and the blue group (where the primary income earner works in the C2DE occupation group). Finally, in terms of the family and late categories, each is subdivided into two sub-categories in terms of income: better off and worse off. This combination approach leads to the identification of 12 separate and distinct categorizations for segmentation purposes. The theory here is that each subdivision reflects a group with different aspirations and behaviours.

Finally, social class/status can also be utilized as an effective basis for segmentation. There are six accepted grade definitions used in the UK reflecting social class (National Readership Survey, 2003): (1) A, **upper middle class** (3.5% of the population), which reflects higher administrative, professional, and managerial occupations, (2) B, **middle class** (21.6% of the population), which includes intermediate levels of each of the occupations mentioned above, (3) C1, **lower middle class** (28.5% of the population), which includes junior levels of each of the above-mentioned occupations along with supervisory and clerical positions, (4) C2, **skilled working class** (20.7% of the population), including skilled manual labourers, (5) D, **working class** (16.5% of the population), incorporating semi-skilled as well as unskilled workers, and (6) E, **those at the lowest level of subsistence** (9.2% of the population), including state pensioners, widows (with no other earners), casual workers, and the lowest-grade workers (WARC, 2004). Each of these groups has different wants, needs, expectations, and preferences. Demographic bases are the most frequently used of all segmentation bases since they are the easiest to actually measure. Often they can be determined from readily available secondary data sources. When focusing on perceptual issues, segmentation mechanisms become a bit more complex.

Psychographic bases for segmentation

Psychographic bases for segmentation centre on perceptual issues. These segments are determined by combining individuals who are psychologically similar in their orientations. These distinctions are based upon similarity of lifestyles, personalities, and values. Psychographics are often associated with the acronym AIO, which stands for activities, interests, and opinions, and segments which are exactly the same in terms of demographics may be significantly different in terms of their psychological makeup. This is an extremely important segmentation base due to its excellent potential for effective targeting of the segment due to an understanding of how the segment members live their daily lives and the opportunity to tie products and services to their particular values and aspirations.

Lifestyle reflects the ways in which the individual chooses to live his/her life. What types of activities people enjoy, what life settings they desire, and who they surround themselves with are all components of lifestyle. A British company which has built its segmentation on lifestyles is the clothier, Ben Sherman, which has found a distinctive niche with a return to the look and styles of the 1960s (O'Loughlin, 2005). Two recent themes have been utilized: (1) the **Park Life** campaign (connecting their mod fashions to classic British icons like Big Ben and Hyde Park) and (2) the **Mods in the Mansion** campaign (tying affluent rock stars to country homes). In the United States, there are three main lifestyle groupings that are often chosen for segmentation: (1) the arts and culturally oriented consumer, (2) the sports enthusiast, and (3) the outdoor adventurer. The arts consumer is one who enjoys attending cultural events (e.g., symphony concerts, opera, ballet), which assumes a more educated, higher social grade, and a quieter type of individual, who needs cultural infusion to be happy. The sports enthusiast is seen as a younger, less educated individual, who is more outgoing and loud in voice and mannerisms. Finally, the outdoors person is one who enjoys the great outdoors. This individual enjoys a variety of ways to commune with nature, and is more apt to enjoy camping, hiking, jogging, and biking.

A recent study by Orth et al. (2004) attempted to use lifestyle patterns to segment beer consumers in the United States. Using cluster analysis with lifestyle survey respondents, the authors identified eight different segments: (1) **TV-opposing moderates** (11% of respondents, who do things in moderation), (2) **Unromantic thrill seekers** (9% of the respondents, who look for thrills but are not interested in social or romantic activities—predominantly male and younger), (3) **Unexcited romantics** (9% of the respondents, who prefer quiet, leisurely and romantic activities to thrills—predominantly females), (4) **Lazy**

opportunists (15% of the respondents, who prefer not to be active—predominantly older), (5) **Interactive party animals** (15% of the respondents, who prefer activities which involve social interactions and shy away from activities which are done on one's own or are quiet—predominantly male and younger), (6) **Introvert individualists** (14% of the respondents, who prefer to do things on their own), (7) **Outgoing socializers** (12% of the respondents, who prefer social activities), and (8) **Rushing adrenaline addicts** (16% of the respondents, who prefer activities involving excitement and motion).

Personality is another mechanism for segmentation. Kotler (2003) lists the four main variations of personality as: compulsive, gregarious, authoritarian, and ambitious. Here the idea is to group people into roughly similar personality types with the underlying assumption that people will be more favourably disposed toward those of a similar personality profile. Personality has also been applied to products and services in the work of Jennifer Aaker (1997), who found that brands can be imbued with personality traits. Her research identified five different personality traits for brands: sincerity, ruggedness, sophisticated, competence, and excitement. The idea is to match the brand personality with the consumer segment personality profile to establish a strong connection.

Another approach to psychographic segmentation involves the use of **core values**. The company tries to match its core values with those of its customer segments, building positive associations. The company stresses values in its products/services as well as in its corporate environment and culture, and the hope is that the segment will become loyal to the company because it embodies the core values that are of importance to the consumer. Core values are deepset in the individual by life experiences and teachings, and it is not easy to change them. The Body Shop, Ben and Jerry's Ice Cream, and Starbucks are all companies that try to resonate with the consumer by stressing concern for the environment, the use of natural materials, and human welfare. They hire people who embody these concerns, they infuse their store atmospheres and marketing communications with these values, and they back appropriate social causes, all indicating that not only do their products fit with these values, but everything that they do as an organization is based on these values. This creates a powerful connection with the consumer, and creates strong consumer loyalty. The work of Shalom Schwartz (1994) focuses on the identification of basic cultural core values. Schwartz identified seven cultural value types: (1) **conservatism** (where the stress is placed on maintaining the status quo and system order), (2) **intellectual autonomy** (freedom of thought, curious, creative, innovative), (3) **affective autonomy** (freedom of action, adventurous, free spirited), (4) **hierarchy** (roles in society, social power, authority), (5) **mastery** (successful, ambitious, competent, confidence), (6) **egalitarian commitment** (loyalty, social justice, honesty, equality, responsibility), and (7) **harmony** (harmony of human beings and their natural surroundings along with social harmony, peace, helpfulness). When a more global view of segmentation is taken by large corporations, there may be effective bases for global segmentation found in these basic cultural values.

A multi-based approach to segmentation incorporating both individual psychological values and demographics, known as the VALS typology, was developed by a company called SRI International. The organization, which at present oversees the VALS system, is SRI Consulting Business Intelligence (**www.sric-bi.com/VALS/**). For the US market, SRI identified eight separate groups for segmentation purposes: (1) **actualizers** (10% of the population), who are successful individuals with high self-esteem and significant financial resources, and who are very cognizant of their personal image as a representation of their character, (2) **fulfilleds** (11% of the population), highly educated, older individuals, concerned with maintaining order, satisfied with their life circumstances, and who make practical purchase decisions, (3) **experiencers** (13% of the population), who are impulsive, variety-seeking, younger, looking for more excitement, concerned with buying the latest fashions and electronics, (4) **achievers** (14% of the population), who are career-oriented, hard working, family-focused, buyers of prestige goods and services, (5) **believers** (17% of the population), who are nationalistic, patriotic, conservative, religious, community-oriented, interested in buying national products, (6) **strivers** (12% of the population), who are financial under-performers, concerned with betterment of their lives and living conditions and without self-esteem problems, (7) **makers** (12% of the population), who are do-it-yourselfers, with manual skills and who like to be independent and self-sufficient, and like conservative governments that do not infringe upon individual rights, and (8) **strugglers** (12% of the population) are elderly who are poor, lack skills, are relatively uneducated, are primarily focused on safety and security issues, and are wary consumers. The VALS system was a breakthrough in that it built on demographic variables and lifestyles and personal aspirations, and the eight categories provided marketers with new opportunities to build relationships with key consumer segments.

A similar approach has been taken in the UK with the Social Value Group typology as developed by Consumer Insight Ltd from its 2003 Survey. This survey is the largest survey of social changes that has been attempted in the UK, and the segments identified are based upon values, beliefs, and motivations and are linked to the various stages of Maslow's hierarchy of needs. The following are the segments which resulted from the 2003 Survey: (1) **self actualizers** (15.9% of the population), who are individualists, creative, people-oriented, relationship-oriented, looking for change without being judgmental, (2) **innovators** (9.1% of the population), who are risk takers, self-confident, want new and different products and services, and have clear goals in mind to achieve, (3) **esteem seekers** (22.3% of the population), who are materialistic, looking to surround themselves with the kinds of trappings and having the kinds of experiences that would provide them with social status, (4) **strivers** (15.1% of the population), who are also concerned with personal image and status, but their concern is to gain status only in the eyes of their particular peer groups, and they tend to keep traditional values, (5) **contented conformers** (14.3% of the population), who are concerned with being a part of the norm, so that they go along with the crowd, which provides the security that they seek, (6) **traditionalists** (18.6% of the population), who are conservative and do not like to take risks, who feel that traditional values and behaviours are safe and comfortable, and who are quiet and reserved, and (7) **disconnected** (4.7% of the population), who live in the here and now, who are unhappy with their situations, and are somewhat apathetic. It is possible to see many similarities between the American VALS segments and the Social Value Group segments. The values and beliefs upon which these segments are built change very slowly, and they are significant drivers of consumer purchase behaviour. These segments would seem to have important implications across Europe and the United States for those companies looking at identifying homogeneous segments on a global front.

Behaviouristic bases for segmentation

These bases are built around groups in which consumers have similar understandings of, uses for, and responses to particular products or services. **Usage rate** involves the amount that is normally consumed by the individual, and the normal categorizations are: light, moderate, and heavy users. The wants and needs of each group may be somewhat different from each other. Heavy users are far more important for most companies than others because they consume such high volumes and because they may be more likely to be loyal to a particular brand than moderate or light users. Rewards systems like frequent flyer miles are aimed at the frequent travellers to keep them coming back to the same airlines. Many hotels and motels aim at frequent business travellers by offering them a wide variety of business services (in-room Internet access, business desks with fax/printer capabilities, free newspapers, free continental breakfasts, etc.). One interesting attempt to segment on usage rate can be seen by Interbrew UK, which launched its half-pint can of Stella Artois in 2005 to reach those who drink primarily on special occasions rather than on a daily basis. Another example can be seen in their 2004 introduction of a draught beer dispenser for the home aficionado, which was created in a partnership with Philips Electronics.

Loyalty level is another effective base for segmentation. There are five different levels of loyalty: brand insistence, brand loyalty, split loyalty, shifting loyalty, and no loyalty (the switchers). **Brand insistence** is the highest level of loyalty, and it reflects the consumer who when faced with the favourite brand not being available, will not buy any alternative brand. **Brand loyalty** reflects the consumer who will buy the favourite brand if it is available, but in the event that it is not available, may purchase another brand instead. **Split loyalty** reflects having loyalty to more than one brand. Here the consumer may want only two of the brands available in the product/service class, but either might be acceptable on any given occasion. This consumer does not care whether the diet cola that he/she drinks is Diet Pepsi or Diet Coke, but will not accept any other cola drink. **Shifting loyals** are those who are loyal to one brand for a period of time and then shift to another brand for a period of time. Finally, **switchers** are those who have no loyalty to any brand in that product or service class. These consumers are primarily deal and variety-focused. Studying these different groups tells you quite a bit about your strengths as well as your weaknesses. Studying the brand insistent only tells you what you are doing right for that particular group of individuals. This will not provide any helpful insight on what you failed to do to attract others. Studying the brand loyal and the shifting loyals provides insight into who the brand's direct competitors are in the eyes of those consumers, studying the switchers tells you about what it takes to potentially attract consumers with deals and special promotions.

A 2002 study was published in *McKinsey Quarterly* by Stephanie Coyles and Timothy Gokey which cautioned that companies must be far more cognizant of changes in buying patterns because active management of migration patterns allows companies to stop potential customer defections and to shift consumers to higher levels of loyalty and consumption. The authors recognize six important loyalty profiles: (1) **Emotive loyalists** (emotionally attached to the company and its products), (2) **Deliberate loyalists** (who rationally choose the company and its products as the best possible choice), (3) **Inertial loyalists** (who see the costs of switching away as too high), (4) **Lifestyle downward migrators** (who may have experienced life changes and their needs are no longer being met), (5) **Deliberately downward migrators** (who are prone to frequent reassessment of their needs and have found a better solution in some other company and its products), and (6) **Dissatisfied downward migrators** (who are actively dissatisfied due to one or more bad experiences). The authors suggest that if one only studies the defectors, this misses more subtle buying changes which can lead ultimately to defection, when it may be too late to get them back (Coyles and Gokey, 2002).

Another type of behaviouristic segmentation involves the **creation of special events**. The US florists, greetings card companies, and confectionery companies have long focused on special occasions. The creation of such special days of recognition as Sweethearts' Day, Bosses' Day, Secretaries' Day, and even Mother-in-Laws' Day are all examples of segmentation on the basis of a special event as opposed to everyday occurrences. Some companies have chosen the opposite approach in focusing on those types of products and services that are used every day without the need for a special occasion. Usually this type of approach is used by the company that has nurtured a connection with a particular occasion but which wants to branch out into other use occasions. Another segmentation approach using events is to focus on critical events in the consumer's life. This is the type of segmentation used by jewellery companies to promote diamond engagement rings or anniversary gifts.

Benefit segmentation is based on the assumption that consumers can be grouped in terms of the key benefits that they seek from the use of certain products or services. There can be two or more different segments who buy the same products or services but seek different key benefits from the use of the products or services. For example, McDonald's may appeal to one group because its offerings are inexpensive, to another because of the taste of its food items, to another because it offers convenience, and to another because it offers an opportunity for socialization with peer group members. Some elderly consumers have become an important constituency for McDonald's because they like to have a chance to regularly meet with friends in a social setting and a breakfast or lunch meeting at McDonald's provides this opportunity. Other elderly consumers like McDonald's for meals because of the value menu items given their limited income levels. Pomegranate growers have found that pomegranate juice contains high levels of anti-oxidants, which have been found to help the body ward off cancer. The key health benefits from the use of the product then provide an excellent special basis for segmentation. This anti-oxidant health benefit segmentation has also been successfully used by the growers/processors of blueberries and concord grapes and the growers/bottlers of red wines. Whenever there is a new medical finding that shows how the use of a particular product can add years to one's life, a new segmentation mechanism will be created. This has been seen surrounding the cholesterol-reducing capabilities of oat bran, the heart attack preventative use of aspirin, and the cold-preventative power of Echinacea.

A recent study that appeared in the *British Food Journal* examined two important trends that affect British food consumption: convenience and health concerns. This study found that these are really not overlapping trends as convenience food items and health-oriented food items are most effectively segmented using distinctly different segmentation variables. The authors found that household size and region of residence were the most important segmentation variables for convenience-oriented food items, and they also found that gender and age were the most important segmentation variables for health-oriented food products (Shiu et al. 2004).

Since the point of segmentation is to identify a homogeneous group of consumers with a high probability of interest in the product/service offered, new and creative combinations of different segmentation schemes are being attempted every day. A variety of tools to help the strategic marketer with segment identification will now be discussed.

Segmentation tools

The main tools used for segmentation are cluster analysis, conjoint analysis, discriminant analysis, and perceptual mapping. **Cluster analysis** is a group of multivariate techniques whose main purpose is to classify objects in such a way that within-group differences are minimized and between-group differences are maximized according to some grouping variable. These objects can be products or survey respondents. The goal is to create clusters that are similar within and distinctly different from one another, which are clearly the goals for consumer segmentation. The best starting point for clustering is to define clear and distinct customer needs. Often this can be preceded by qualitative mechanisms such as focus groups or in-depth interviews to examine a variety of different constituent groups to determine their needs and motivations. Once these needs are identified, then survey research instruments can be created and cluster analysis can be used to examine the nature of the respondents involved and the possibilities of grouping into meaningful and effective consumer segments.

Conjoint analysis on the other hand involves the use of a series of possible product/service attribute combinations to see which ones are actually preferred by survey respondents. In this case the company chooses a series of possible variations of product attributes (e.g., three types of scent, four colours, three package sizes, three different prices), and a series of attribute combinations are generated in a partial factorial design (so that consumers only respond to a subset of all possible attribute combinations making the process considerably more manageable for the respondent). The consumer can rank or rate the offerings in terms of preference, and from the various choices made, decomposition is utilized to develop a series of scores (utility part worths) for each variation of each attribute. From this analysis the company can see what the optimal product configuration would be for each relevant consumer target segment. Coca-Cola often uses this type of analysis to assess the possibility of new can colours (e.g., colours in addition to the normal red, white, and silver) or new product flavours (e.g., coke with lime, vanilla coke, cherry coke, coke with lemon). The company can gain a good idea of potential consumer reactions to product changes or new product offerings using this kind of tool.

The third approach to segmenting is **discriminant analysis**, which involves identifying a series of variables that help to discriminate the members of one or more groups from others in the dataset. The basic idea is to examine a series of possible differentiating variables that would explain and hopefully allow prediction of different possible group memberships. One way to use this approach would involve including in the analysis a variety of product/service attributes and demographic data which when combined could explain what makes buyers different from non-buyers of a particular product or service. It might also be used to examine non-users as opposed to light users, moderate users, and heavy users. The technique produces formulae that can be used to explain and predict group membership. In order to test the effectiveness of the models generated, all respondents are then classified according to the discriminating functions generated, and the predicted group membership is compared to the actual group membership as a check for accuracy. If there were four categories involved (non-users, light users, moderate users, and heavy users), the prior probabilities would be 0.25 (1 in 4), so any classification scheme that does better than 0.25 would be an improvement on pure chance.

The fourth tool is **multidimensional scaling**, which involves a variety of different techniques that can visually demonstrate how particular consumers view the various offerings in a particular product or service class. These techniques are also often referred to as perceptual mapping because the goal is to spatially differentiate the perceptions of consumers relative to their preferences for or the similarities among a set of objects (e.g., companies, products, services) in terms of distances in multidimensional space. These techniques allow the researcher to determine what types of attributes are most distinctively associated with their products or services. Certainly it is important for the consumer to have a clear idea of what the product stands for, and it allows the researcher to determine whether consumer perceptions match company management perceptions. The use of multidimensional scaling also provides important strategic direction if the company finds that a competitor is associated in the minds of the target market with attributes that are more appropriately associated with its own product. In this case the company can try to communicate in advertisements to its target audience to educate them on the relevance of those important attributes to its products or services. As an example, if the company found that its competitor was seen as more environmentally friendly, the company could mount an advertising campaign to show how it is working to protect and maintain the environment.

Latest thinking

A promising new approach to global segmentation was suggested by Keillor and Hult in 1999. The authors suggested a framework which they named the NATID approach to segmentation, which was comprised of the following components: (1) National Heritage, (2) Cultural Homogeneity, (3) Belief System, and (4) Consumer Ethnocentrism. Ian Phou and Kor-Weai Chan (2003) validated this framework using a sample of respondents from six different Asian nations. The authors set up a useful matrix in which they utilized consumer ethnocentrism scores (low and high) on one axis and NATID scores (low to high) on the other axis. The five cells of the matrix and the segmentation strategic implications were as follows: (1) **High NATID—High Consumer Ethnocentrism** (e.g., Thailand and Korea) segment, in which customized products with high local content present opportunities for competitive advantage, (2) **Low NATID—High Consumer Ethnocentrism** (e.g., Hong Kong) segment, in which standardized products have the potential for success but the economic threat of foreign products has to be downplayed, with a strong emphasis placed on benefits to the nation from these products in any promotional campaigns, (3) **High NATID—Low Consumer Ethnocentrism** segment, in which the goal must be to assess what the other key dimensions of national identity are that would help in segmentation (e.g., religious philosophy, historical heritage) since standardized products have great potential when combined with an adjusted marketing mix strategy, (4) **Low NATID—Low Consumer Ethnocentrism** (e.g., Singapore and Japan) segment, in which standardized products have potential when the country market is highly homogeneous, but when the market is heterogeneous, then segmentation should focus on such differentiators as psychographic variables, and (5) **Middle Ground** (e.g., Taiwan) segment, in which there is a challenge to find the single best dimension for country differentiation, but in this case it may be that customized or standardized products might have potential depending on the nature of the country market. The use of this framework as a part of a multivariable segmentation mechanism would seem to offer a great deal of potential for identifying viable global segments.

Targeting

Once the firm has identified a series of potential market segments for consideration, the next step is targeting. This involves deciding on the number of different segments to select and serve and the best action plans to reach the identified segments. The first consideration from a strategic standpoint is to decide on the type of pattern of coverage that the firm will utilize. According to one of the great marketing strategists, Derek F. Abell (1980), the firm faces the following choices: (1) **single-segment concentration** (where one product is geared towards one market segment in a niche strategy), (2) **selective specialization** (where the firm aims different product variants at different segments with the idea of one product per segment), (3) **product specialization** (where the firm aims a particular product variant to a variety of different segments), (4) **market specialization** (where the firm aims a variety of product variants at one particular market segment), and (5) **full market coverage** (where the firm uses undifferentiated marketing aiming a variety of product variants across a variety of segments).

Measuring effectiveness of target segments

Once the segments have been chosen, then how do we know whether they are viable or not? Kotler (2003) presents the most recognizable series of requirements for segments to be appropriate. He suggests that they must be: (1) **measurable** (e.g., size of segment, income and purchasing power, and characteristics of the segment), (2) **accessible** (reachable by the firm and able to effectively serve the segment), (3) **substantial** (large enough and capable of generating sufficient profits), (4) **differentiable** (truly distinct from other segments in terms of composition and response to marketing stimuli), and (5) **actionable** (marketing programmes can be developed to effectively identify, attract, and serve the segment).

Marketing segmentation vs product differentiation

There is a trade-off within most organizations that must be considered when segmenting markets, which involves production and marketing. In one case unrestrained marketing might identify a wide range of distinct market segments, but while there may be demand for these segments, there may be no cost-effective way to develop the necessary product variations to address the needs of all the identified segments. On the other hand, unrestrained product differentiation might identify a wide variety of product variations that could be produced by the firm, but there may be no demand for some or all of the identified segments. This mandates that marketing and production work together to find the most cost-effective product variants to serve the most promising consumer market segments. Take for instance the situation in the United States in 1985 involving the Ford Motor Company Thunderbird and the imported Honda Accord. In an attempt to convince the consumer that he or she could have any type of Thunderbird that they could want (mass customization), they offered as many as 19,000 different possible product variations. However it became clear that problems would arise when the Ford service departments tried to deal with all of the possible variations when handling servicing problems on all of the different possible product variants. What kinds of inventories of parts would be required for all of these possible segments? There is no way that there were 19,000 different viable segments for this product. It would have been surprising if more than 50 distinct offerings were in demand. The Honda Accord being shipped in from Japan provided only 34 different product variations, which would suggest that they had clearly thought through the issue of viability of each of the identified consumer segments. This balancing of segmentation with differentiation is an effective integrated strategic approach to finding viable segments with cost-effective product/service variants.

Targeting improvement

There is concern that segmentation can produce a wide variety of segments which cannot effectively be reached with a targeting strategy. There is also the possibility that some market segments may be very difficult (in terms of time and money) to effectively measure. A 1999 article in *McKinsey Quarterly* presented some interesting suggestions for how marketing strategists can attempt to create segmentation strategies that can work even if it is hard to determine who exactly is included in the segment (Forsyth et al., 1999). The authors suggest that before attempting to identify and reach target customers, a viable alternative approach could be to consider whether certain collective segment traits may be associated with profitable strategies. They provide three options for these profitable strategies: (1) **self-selection**, which concentrates on enabling the customer to find and select the best product as opposed to finding the appropriate customers (examples provided include different sizes of washing-up liquid bottles and cereal packets) and which is best suited for large customer bases with such small individual sales that mass customization is not viable, (2) **scoring models**, which involve the development of a series of questions to allow quantitative scoring that would place customers into different categories depending on what is most important for those customers (e.g., credit card companies that distinguish good risk customers from bad risk customers) to allow appropriate targeting strategies to best reach those particular categorized groups of customers, and (3) **dual-objective segmentation**, which attempts to convert unreachable segments into actionable segments through a series of reclassification approaches which attempt to reclassify outliers into different categories and then follow-up profitability analyses are run. The idea is to try to place those who do not cleanly fall into consumer target segments into other possible segments. It may be that the outliers become a separate segment themselves rather than becoming squeezed into inappropriate segmentation schemes, or that the outliers do not make sense for targeting at all. The idea is to sometimes step back from the comfortable segmentation approaches and look at things from a different angle to see if there are new possibilities that may work better than old ways.

Positioning

Positioning refers to the placing of the product or service in a particular perceptual position within the mind of the consumer. This would follow the processes described in segmentation and targeting. The idea here is that there is a specific consumer segment in mind and a specific plan to reach it, and now the idea is to ensure that the target consumer has a clear and distinctive image in mind regarding the product/service offerings being aimed at them that is consistent and positive. Al Ries and Jack Trout, advertising executives with over 50 years of experience between them, made a strong statement in their landmark book, *Positioning: The Battle for Your Mind* (2001), that the real battle does not take place at the cash register when the consumer goes to the shop to make a purchase, but in the mind of the consumer before he/she ever even goes to the shop. They argued that it is positioning that is the strategic key. If the consumer has a particular product or service name that automatically comes to mind when a need arises in that particular product or service category, that is the product or service that the consumer is most likely to buy. The point is to keep your product brand name automatically at the top of the choice possibilities (the favourite brand). As Ries and Trout explain, there is a ladder inside every consumer's head for each and every product and service class. All of the brands that compete that are known to the consumer are therefore placed on different rungs of that ladder. The strategic goal is to get to the top rung where the consumer has chosen a particular brand as the best or their favourite. Once the need arises in that class, the top rung brand is what will normally come to mind and will more than likely be purchased by the consumer. For Ries and Trout, the key was to understand the ladder and develop strategies according to where on the ladder the particular brand was placed by the consumer. Being on the top rung of the ladder allows the firm to enjoy consumer franchise.

Consumer franchise

This is a term that is reported to have been coined by Dr Peter Sealey, then Global Marketing Director for Coca-Cola Corporation, who has since left the company to become a consultant in California. **Consumer franchise** is the ability of the firm to keep its product, brand, or company name foremost in the mind of the target consumer. It is considered to be a bankable asset since there is a psychological buffering built in for the firm that is on the top rung of the product/service class ladder. When bad news appears regarding a particular company, if the product or brand in question is on the top rung of the ladder (the favourite or preferred brand), the psychological process known as denial can buffer the company because the consumer is put in a mental situation where they think it could not possibly be their favourite brand that could have done something wrong. We tend to assume that our judgement is infallible, and when something happens that questions that judgement, we step back and refuse to believe that we have made a mistake. This denial is a powerful protectant for the company. No company saw more benefit from this denial and the power of consumer franchise than the Coca-Cola Corporation when New Coke was introduced with a completely different product formulation than had been used for the previous Coke product. As the groundswell built against Coke, with loyal consumers asking why the formula had been changed, Coke sensed a problem and implemented a contingency plan, introducing Classic Coke. New Coke did not fare well in the marketplace, but Coke was not hurt because it did take corrective action, and it was protected by its consumer franchise and never felt the negative effects financially or in lost market share. To illustrate how powerful consumer franchise is as a buffer, one colleague to this day claims that everything was part of a carefully designed strategic plan to offer an additional brand product, but the delay between introduction of New Coke and the introduction of Classic Coke would argue that this was not a carefully designed plan from the beginning but a mistake with little negative backlash. Coke had to take corrective action, but it was able to fare well, demonstrating the power of its consumer franchise. Of course my colleague was born and raised in Atlanta, Georgia, the home of Coca-Cola, which might explain the perceptual basis for his argument!!

Consumer franchise has two major components, a behavioural component and an attitudinal component. How does a company measure whether it is the favoured or preferred brand behaviourally? By examining its market share figures and sales, it can be seen if the brand is the favoured brand or not. Attitudinally, the only way to know is to do consumer surveys. In this case consumers can be asked to indicate their favoured brand among a series of choices, or consumers can be asked, if a need arose in a particular product category, what brand would they choose? The key strategic aspect to remember here is that a downturn in brand image might not immediately affect brand sales. There is usually a lag. As a result, it is important for companies to track both their results in the marketplace and their brand images so that any brand image problem can be corrected before it has a negative impact on corporate performance. If only the behavioural side is tracked, then the company may be caught in a situation where it is not sure what is actually causing the problem in the first place. If bad press is caught and corrected before it has a chance to affect consumer perceptions, any future performance problems may be eliminated before they manifest themselves.

The next step will be to examine ways in which the company can assess its perceptual position inside the heads of its target audience. This involves the use of perceptual mapping.

Perceptual mapping

Perceptual mapping is the visual representation of the different competitive brand offerings/objects of interest in perceptual space. In other words, it represents a map of the various offerings within the minds of the target consumers. This is where 'perception equals reality' comes home to marketing strategists. The only thing that is important is what the consumer believes—not what management believes to be the case. This can only be determined via survey instruments. As was previously mentioned, the attitudinal component of consumer franchise is the often-neglected side, as behaviour is the representation of what has already been done. The problem is that past behaviour is no guarantee of future purchase behaviour.

Two of the most useful approaches to perceptual mapping are factor mapping and multidimensional preference mapping (MDPREF). Factor mapping combines factor analysis with two and three-dimensional mapping which allows the viewer to see how a placement according to a multiple, variable grouping appears as opposed to a series of individual variables being used for mapping as is done using MDPREF. The best way to explain this is to present an illustrative example and compare the maps produced by the different techniques.

Factor analysis is a data-reduction technique which attempts to take a series of items that are seen as the tangible representations (i.e., a series of attributes) of a particular object (i.e., a form of product/service) and comparing the responses across all of the attributes, indicating where these attributes were perceived to be similar in some ways for certain groups of variables and different from other groups of variables. The basic idea is that factor analysis seeks to determine which attributes were seen by respondents as similar (or related in some way) to other variables and which attributes (or groups) were distinctly different from each other. **Factor mapping** then uses factor groupings as mapping axes to see how various competitors are perceived by target consumers in relation to each other. A number of years ago, the author conducted a study of the perceptions of a sample of target consumers in relation to the various hospitals in a large metropolitan area of the southeastern United States. The variables that were identified as having a role in the choice of a hospital at the time were as follows:

- friendliness of the nurses
- hospital atmosphere
- quality of the food
- ability of the staff
- family orientation
- staff attitude
- quality of the nursing care
- friendliness of the doctors
- hospital reputation
- condition of the equipment
- compassion of the staff
- hospital cleanliness
- size of the hospital
- quality of the doctor care
- paediatric services availability

- community involvement
- range of services provided
- VIP services available
- hospital progressiveness

These were assessed through factor analysis to examine whether the respondents tended to see some of these as related to each other and which as not. It was not expected that these attributes would be seen as completely separate and distinct, and the factor analysis solution indicated the following factor subgroupings:

Factor 1

- friendliness of nurses
- hospital atmosphere
- quality of the food
- family orientation
- quality of nursing care
- friendliness of the doctors
- hospital cleanliness
- quality of doctor care

Factor 2

- condition of equipment
- size of hospital
- hospital reputation
- paediatric services available
- community involvement
- range of services provided
- VIP services available
- hospital progressiveness

Factor 3

- ability of the staff
- staff attitude
- compassion of the staff

As factor analysis did not label these factors in the analysis, it is up to the researcher to examine the related items and determine what the items share in common to come up with a meaningful name for each factor. In this case, Factor 1 is connected to a series of attributes which all have a bearing on the hospital atmosphere or ambience, and this was the name given to that factor. Factor 2 included items which seemed to relate to the status of the hospital, and as a result, this was the name given to that factor. Finally, Factor 3

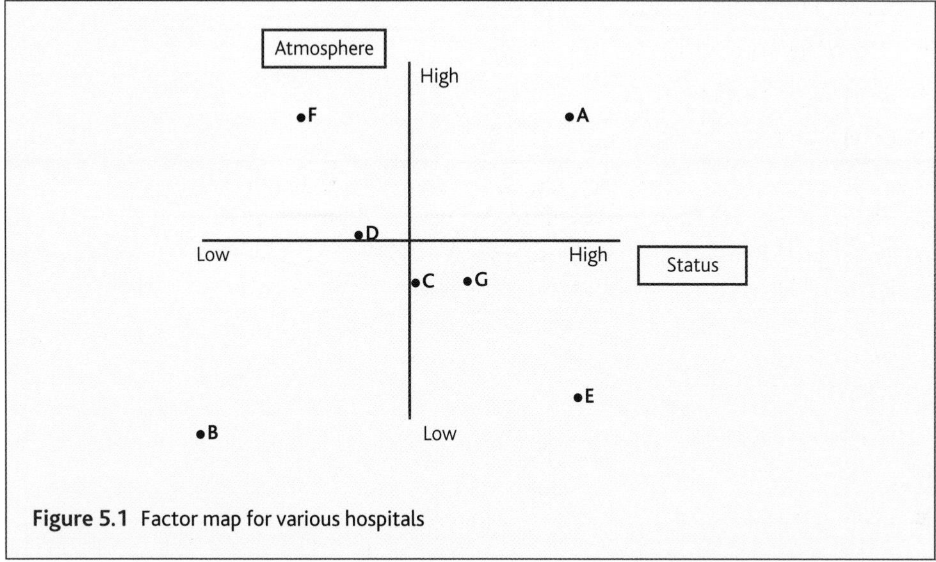

Figure 5.1 Factor map for various hospitals

focused on aspects of the staff (as opposed to the doctors and the nurses), and was labelled accordingly. Of these three factors, 1 and 2 were significantly more important for explaining the variances in the data; therefore, Factors 1 and 2, rather than Factor 3, were used to map the various hospitals. The resulting factor map therefore represents a two-dimensional perceptual map with atmosphere and status being the axes. The factor map for the various hospitals is shown in Figure 5.1.

When using this kind of perceptual mapping, the placement of the various competitor institutions is placed on the composite scores for each of the two factors using the factor results; therefore, it provides a good overview of the various hospitals and the perceptions of their images and offerings as indicated by the sample of area consumers. In this case Hospital A is clearly in the best position having a good atmosphere and being perceived to be high in status. At the other end, hospital B is a disaster. Hospitals C, D, and G all indicate confusion on the part of the respondents since there is no clear distinguishing factor for any of them. That leaves Hospital F, which has a good atmosphere but is seen as low in status and Hospital E, which is seen as high in status but low in atmosphere. This type of perceptual map provides the strategic marketer with possibilities for strategic positional improvement. Strategic marketing promotional campaigns can be utilized to attempt to change the perceptions of the respondents by educating them as to how the various institutions are better than they were perceived to be. Advertisements, for example, can focus on a variety of attributes associated with either atmosphere or ambience which will help get the point across to the target audience that reality is different from perception and this will hopefully change perceptions.

MDPREF approaches the data in a different way. It assumes that each and every attribute is important on its own and utilizes the scores for each of the attributes across all of the respondents to determine which attributes differentiate which hospital in perceptual space. For this hospital data, the MDPREF map was as Shown in Figure 5.2.

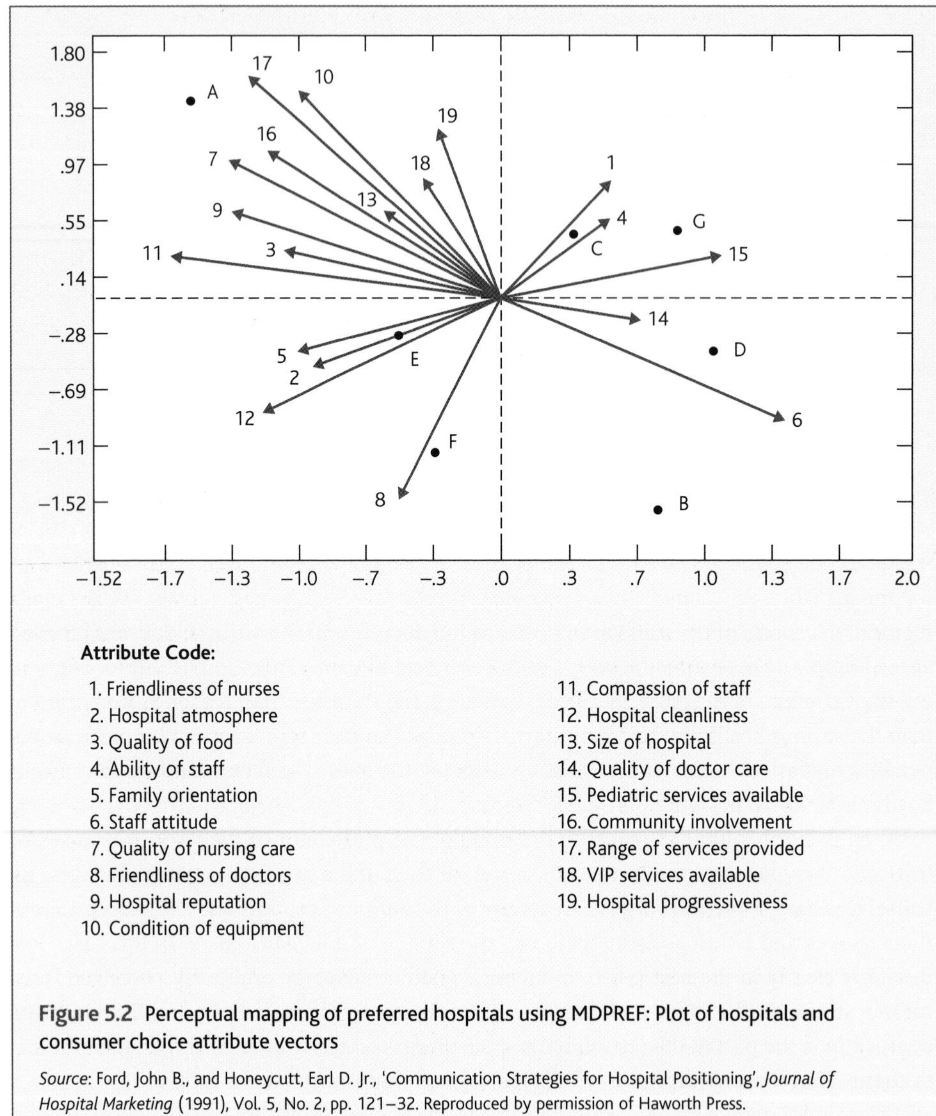

Figure 5.2 Perceptual mapping of preferred hospitals using MDPREF: Plot of hospitals and consumer choice attribute vectors

Source: Ford, John B., and Honeycutt, Earl D. Jr., 'Communication Strategies for Hospital Positioning', *Journal of Hospital Marketing* (1991), Vol. 5, No. 2, pp. 121–32. Reproduced by permission of Haworth Press.

In this case the individual attribute drivers can be assessed and used in a positioning strategy. As with the factor mapping, Hospital A has the best position in the minds of the target market as 10 of the 19 attributes are clearly associated with that hospital. With perceptual mapping of this type, the vectors from the origin out are the attributes driving this perceptual placement. Hospital B is not associated with any in a positive manner. If the vector is followed through the origin backwards, then B would be seen as associated with the negative side of all of the vectors driving A's position. Again, this is a disastrous position. All of the other hospitals have particular attributes associated with them, and these become the bases for niching strategies. The other options involve re-educating the target audience if the perceptions of the marketplace are not backed by hard evidence.

What becomes clear when one views these two different approaches to perceptual mapping is that each has its own strengths and weaknesses, but both offer valuable strategic insight. Factor mapping is easy to use, but it becomes more difficult to interpret when there are three or more critical factors involved, as the researcher has to compare a series of two- or three- dimensional maps to interpret the data. Multidimensional scaling is more difficult to use, but it shows the various individual attribute drivers of perceptual differentiation, which can provide more exacting strategic direction. The point, however, is that the only way to accurately assess positioning is to get into the heads of the target consumers and see how they perceive the various competitors.

Positioning and the importance of consistency

As positioning reflects the position that the brand or product has achieved on the product or service class ladder, the key strategic issue associated with positioning is to present a clear and consistent message to the target audience. The company that constantly tinkers with its image stands the chance of confusing its target market. If strategic decisions are made which are inconsistent from time to time, the consumer is left with potentially mixed messages which become confusing and create cognitive dissonance. The often-seen use of brand extension creates a potential problem for strategic marketers as their company, which may have been clearly positioned in the past, begins to put its name on inconsistent products which set off alarm bells inside the heads of loyal customers. Look at the recent movement by Mercedes and Volvo to lower-priced product lines as a strong example. Can the company offer products at the top end and in the middle at the same time? The problems faced by Calvin Klein when selling jeans through Sears and at the same time selling extravagantly priced designer gowns should still resonate with the marketplace today. How can a company undermine its own distinctive perceptual niche? This leads potentially to strategic suicide. Harking back to the consumer franchise discussion reminds us that there is an attitudinal side which must be periodically tracked along with the behavioural side. Inconsistencies might not be reflected in a downturn in sales until much later, and then the problem becomes image reinstatement for the brand.

Sage positioning wisdom

Jack Trout revisited the issue of Positioning in 1996 with Steve Rivkin in the book, *The New Positioning: The Latest on the World's #1 Business Strategy*. The critical message of the book was to report that many companies had run into positioning problems and needed to take corrective perception action. The authors suggested that this had occurred as a result of two major problems: (1) companies losing their focus in the mind of their target markets (through line extension and diversification), and (2) companies not noticing that their markets were changing underneath them. The answer to these problems is to reposition the product. This often means going back to basics and determining what it was that made the company successful in the first place and returning to these foundations. It also may mean determining how to make a passé product more relevant. All of this requires keeping in tune with the expectations and perceptions of the target market. Trout and Rivkin (1996) present six positioning pitfalls that companies must be aware of and avoid: (1) the obvious factor (positioning is the search for what is obvious, and when the marketer feels that things need to be more complex or creative and clever, obvious is replaced by complex and confusing), (2) the future factor (constantly changing and modernizing strategy to deal with the future and its possible changes), (3) the cutesy factor (instead of telling things in a straightforward way, many companies like to get cute and creative), (4) the would-be-hero factor (the second-guessing of hard chargers in the company who, in trying to get the CEO's attention, play around with the positioning of the product), (5) the numbers factor (endless line extensions to maintain a healthy increase in sales to generate larger numbers), and (6) the tinkering factor (what are seen as improvements internally can often be seen as confusing by the target market). What becomes obvious when examining these is that the real problem ultimately is that the company does not take a distinctive position in the mind of the consumer and then maintain it consistently.

Conclusion

When companies approach the process of segmentation, processing, and positioning as a series of logical steps in a process, they enhance their chances of success. Only in the rarest of circumstances is a company in the luxurious position of being all things to all customers, and as a result, the company must find appropriate target consumers, understand them, effectively reach them, and grab a position of importance on the product/service class ladder inside their heads. The company then has to avoid the lure of change for the sake of change and focus on consistency. This requires keeping up with the perceptions of consumers and continuing to build and maintain consumer franchise.

Summary

Segmentation involves the identification of a distinct subset of consumers within the overall marketplace that have a desire for the products/services that the company produces. There are a variety of tools and techniques that can be used for segmentation across a variety of segmentation criteria. The firm must carefully assess the different segments and choose those that have the greatest potential for success. Once the firm has identified the various segment possibilities, the next step involves the assessment of the potential for each segment so that only those with the highest chances for success are chosen. Once the particular segments are chosen, the company must decide on how it will use the various pieces of the marketing mix to reach those segments. Targeting focuses on how to most effectively reach the various market segments. The last step involves the assessment of the particular perceptual space that the product achieves within the heads of the target segment consumers to ensure that the product is on the top rung of the product class ladder. The power of this position is found in the fact that when a need arises in the mind of the consumer, the product that commands the top rung of the mental ladder of competing products is the one most likely to be chosen for purchase.

KEY TERMS

Market segment A homogeneous subset of all consumers in a particular market.

Mass market All consumers are treated the same way, with a single product configuration.

Mass customization Each individual consumer is treated separately, with a product configuration to suit the needs of each consumer.

Market segmentation The process of identifying appropriate separate subsets of consumers for targeting purposes out of all the consumers in that market.

Topography Land contours that can affect the geographic grouping of appropriate target segments of consumers.

Cohort A group of consumers that go through life together and share common experiences.

Acculturation The exposure of a foreign visitor to a local culture and the impact that exposure will have on the visitor and their cultural makeup.

Psychographic segmentation Segmentation predicated upon the activities, interests, and opinions of a particular group of people. This will normally involve such variables as lifestyle and personality for segmentation purposes.

Targeting The use of the marketing mix elements to reach the consumers identified in the market segmentation process.

Product differentiation Production-based orientation which examines the various forms and variants of the product which the company can cost-effectively produce.

Positioning The process involved in placing the product into the mind of the consumer in terms of a position on the product/service class ladder.

Consumer franchise A term coined at Coca-Cola that refers to the ability to keep the company brand, product, or company name foremost in the mind of the consumer. It is comprised of a behavioural component and an attitudinal component.

Perceptual mapping The use of a variety of tools to examine the various competing products and the positions that they command in perceptual space within the minds of the target market.

DISCUSSION QUESTIONS

1 Why is market segmentation vital for company success?
2 What is psychographic segmentation, and why is it so important for marketing strategists?
3 What are the seven cultural values that were identified by Schwartz, and why are they important for marketing strategists?
4 What are the various levels of loyalty that were discussed in the chapter, and how can they be used for segmentation purposes?
5 What are the four different tools that were discussed for segmentation? How are they different from each other?
6 What is the difference between market segmentation and product differentiation?
7 What are the five different patterns of target market coverage that were discussed in the chapter?

8 What are the five criteria that were presented by Kotler to assess the viability of various target market segments under consideration?

9 How does consumer franchise relate to the concept of positioning, and why is this relevant for marketing strategists?

10 What are the differences between factor mapping and multidimensional scaling, and why is perceptual mapping so important?

11 Why is there a need for repositioning?

ONLINE RESOURCE CENTRE

Visit the Online Resource Centre for this book for lots of interesting additional material at: **www.oxfordtextbooks.co.uk/orc/west/**

REFERENCES AND FURTHER READING

Aaker, Jennifer (1997), 'Dimensions of Brand Personality', *Journal of Marketing Research*, Vol. 34, No. 3 (August), pp. 347–56.

Abell, Derek F. (1980), *Defining the Business: The Starting Point of Strategic Planning* (Upper Saddle River: Prentice-Hall).

Churchill, Gilbert A., Jr. (1979), 'A Paradigm for Developing Better Measures of Marketing Constructs', *Journal of Marketing Research*, Vol. XVI (February), pp. 64–73.

Cort, Kathryn T., Judith H. Pairan, and John K. Ryans, Jr. (2004), 'The In-School Marketing Controversy: Reaching the Teenage Segment', *Business Horizons*, Vol. 47, No. 1, pp. 81–5.

Coyles, Stephanie, and Timothy C. Gokey (2002), 'Customer Retention is not Enough', *McKinsey Quarterly*, No. 2, pp. 81–9.

Ford, John B., and Earl D. Honeycutt, Jr. (1991), 'Communication Strategies for Hospital Positioning', *Journal of Hospital Marketing*, Vol. 5, No. 2, pp. 121–32.

Forsyth, John, Sunil Gupta, Sudeep Haldar, Anil Kaul, and Keith Kettle (1999), 'A Segmentation You Can Act Upon', *McKinsey Quarterly*, No. 3, pp. 7–15.

Gerbing, David W., and James C. Anderson (1988), 'An Updated Paradigm for Scale Development Incorporating Unidimensionality and Its Assessment', *Journal of Marketing Research*, Vol. XXV (May), pp. 186–92.

Keillor, B. D., and G. Tomas M. Hult (1999), 'The Development and Application of a National Identity Measure for Use in International Marketing', *Journal of International Marketing*, Vol. 4, No. 2, pp. 57–73.

Kotler, Philip (2003), *Marketing Management*, 11th edn (Upper Saddle River: Prentice-Hall).

O'Loughlin, Sandra (2005), 'Ben Sherman Brings U.K. Lifestyle to Spring', *Brandweek*, Vol. 46, No. 2 (10 January), p. 9.

Orth, Ulrich R., Mina McDaniel, Tom Shellhammer, and Kannapon Lopetcharat (2004), 'Promoting Brand Benefits: The Role of Consumer Psychographics and Lifestyle', *Journal of Consumer Marketing*, Vol. 21, No. 2/3, pp. 97–108.

Palumbo, Frederick A., and Ira Teich (2004), 'Market Segmentation Based on Level of Acculturation', *Marketing Intelligence & Planning*, Vol. 22, No. 4, pp. 472–80.

Phou, Ian, and Kor-Weai Chan (2003), 'Targeting East Asian Markets: A Comparative Study on National Identity', *Journal of Targeting, Measurement and Analysis for Marketing*, Vol. 12, No. 2, pp. 157–68.

Ries, Al, and Jack Trout (2001), *Positioning: The Battle for Your Mind*, 20th Anniversary Edition (New York: McGraw-Hill).

Schewe, Charles D., and Geoffrey Meredith (2004), 'Segmenting Global Markets by Generational Cohorts: Determining Motivations by Age', *Journal of Consumer Behaviour*, Vol. 4, No. 1, pp. 51–64.

Schuman, H., and Jacqueline Scott (1989), 'Generations and Collective Memories', *American Sociological Review*, Vol. 54, No. 3, pp. 359–381.

Schwartz, Shalom (1994), 'Beyond Individualism/Collectivism', in *Individualism and Collectivism: Theory, Method, and Applications*, Vol. 18, *Cross-Cultural Research and Methodology Series*, Uichol Kim, Harry C. Triandis, et al. (Thousand Oaks: Sage Publications), pp. 85–119.

Scott, Jacqueline, and Lilian Zac (1993), 'Collective Memories in Britain and the United States', *Public Opinion Quarterly*, Vol. 57, No. 3, pp. 315–31.

Shiu, Eric C. C., John A. Dawson, and David W. Marshall (2004), 'Segmenting the Convenience and Health Trends in the British Food Market', *British Food Journal*, Vol. 106, No. 2/3, pp. 106–18.

Sweeney, Mark (2004), 'Red Bull Targets Golfers in Shift to Mainstream', *Marketing* (26 May), p. 1.

Trout, Jack, and Steve Rivkin (1996), *The New Positioning: The Latest on the World's #1 Business Strategy* (New York: McGraw-Hill, Inc.).

KEY ARTICLE ABSTRACTS

Keillor, B. D., and G. Tomas M. Hult (1999), 'The Developments and Application of a National Identity Measure for Use in International Marketing', *Journal of International Marketing*, 4 (2), pp. 57–73.

This paper presents a promising new approach to global segmentation using the concept of national identity. The authors propose the use of the NATID approach to segmentation, which is comprised of the following components: (1) National Heritage, (2) Cultural Homogeneity, (3) Belief System, and (4) Consumer Ethnocentrism.

Abstract: This study develops a measurement instrument designed to explicate the degree to which national identity can be specified and the differences between that national identity and that of other nations. Utilizing Churchill's (1979) and Gerbing and Anderson's (1988) guidelines for scale construction and application, the study develops an instrument to measure national identity and establishes norms for its usage, using samples from the USA, Japan, and Sweden. The overall objective is: (1) to develop an empirically sound instrument for measuring national identity, (2) to explore the importance placed on a unique national identity in the three nations comprising the samples, and (3) to consider differences in the underlying dimensions comprising these countries' national identity and their impact on marketing strategy. The development of such a measurement instrument should provide a means by which the results of cross-cultural and cross-national research can be empirically tested and on which more rigorous theory building can be based.

Schewe, Charles D., and Geoffrey Meredith (2004), 'Segmenting Global Markets by Generational Cohorts: Determining Motivations by Age', *Journal of Consumer Behaviour*, 4 (1), pp. 51–64.

Generational cohorts have been successfully identified and utilized in segmentation in American markets. This relevant article examines generational cohorts in a global setting, and the authors caution that while generational cohorts can be effectively identified in different country settings, they should not be approached as the same as those found in the United States.

Abstract: Marketing has long rested on the use of market segmentation. While birth age has been a useful way to create groups, it describes segments but in itself does not help to understand segment motivations. Environmental events experienced during one's coming-of-age years, however, create values that remain relatively unchanged throughout one's life. Such values provide a common bond for those in that age group, or cohort. Segmenting by 'coming-of-age' age provides a richer segmentation approach than birth age. This approach, known to work in America, is used in this paper to create generational cohorts in Russia and in Brazil.

Orth, Ulrich R., Mina McDaniel, Tom Shellhammer, and Kannapon Lopetcharat (2004), 'Promoting Brand Benefits: The Role of Consumer Psychographics and Lifestyle', *Journal of Consumer Marketing*, 21 (2/3), pp. 97–108. Reprinted with permission, Emerald Group Publishing Limited.
http://www.emeraldinsight.com/jbs.htm

This paper presents a unique approach to the use of lifestyle patterns to segment beer consumers in the USA. Using cluster analysis with lifestyle survey respondents, the authors identify eight different consumer segments.

Abstract: Because consumers can vary greatly in their value composition, they may seek a range of different benefits from products and brands and hence will react differently to marketing communications emphasizing selected brand benefits. The present study adapts a scale for measuring benefits that drive consumer preferences for craft beer. As part of this process, five dimensions of utility are identified, such as functional, value for money, social, positive, and negative emotional benefit. In order to support decisions on market segmentation and brand positioning, those dimensions of benefit are profiled against consumer brand preferences, lifestyle segments, demographic, and behavioural variables. Based on the results, guidelines for communication strategies are offered that address the benefits sought by specific segments more holistically.

END OF CHAPTER 5 CASE STUDY 'Rich, but not fortune's fools'

Jim Taylor, a veteran US market researcher, has some strong views on how to market to America's wealthiest people. 'Don't use adjectives, they hate adjectives. And don't use the word luxury, because luxury offends against their notion of who they are.'

Mr Taylor, whose career has included working as chief executive of Yankelovich, the market research company, feels he is speaking with authority—after co-directing what he believes is an unprecedented wide-ranging survey of the attitudes of 500 of the US's wealthiest families.

'These are not people who you can get sitting together in a room, give them \$100 and a slice of pizza, and get them to tell you what they think,' he says of the subjects of the research behind the Worth-Harrison Taylor Study on the Status of Wealth in America.

Mr Taylor and Doug Harrison, who co-directed the survey, collected data from 500 households with non-real estate liquid assets of at least \$5 m (£2.8 m)—an entry level that represents the highest segment of the annual mail-based Affluent Market Research Programme by TNS, the leading market information company. In addition, 20 per cent of the group had assets of more than \$20 m.

'It is white men, who are married and have been to college, although it is not necessarily the Harvards of this world,' says Mr. Harrison. The research also indicates that luxury marketers are misjudging their target, he says.

'The marketing world that targets them tends to think of this as a homogeneous class, and tends to break it by degrees of wealth, as opposed to experience. But the experience factor is critical.'

The project, conducted this summer, evolved from Mr Taylor's marketing work for Lyle Anderson, a Seattle-born property developer who has developed luxury gated communities and private golf resorts in the US, Mexico and at Loch Lomond in Scotland. Mr Anderson's company was considering building a luxury community on the Sea of Cortez in Mexico that would include state-of-the-art medical facilities. 'He asked me to prove that the demand for something like that really existed,' says Mr Taylor.

With support from Bill Curtis, publisher of *Worth* magazine, which became a sponsor of the research along with US Trust, the private bank, Mr Taylor and Mr Harrison set out to find 200 wealthy people who they knew would be prepared to talk to them. They then asked those interviewees to recommend others, in a variation of the 'snowball' technique developed by McKinsey in his work on sexual attitudes in America. The surveys involved in-depth two-hour interviews, mostly at the individuals' homes, conducted by young married women who were 'of the class'; and a half-hour, self-administered questionnaire.

Extrapolating from the group, the two estimate that their results reflect the attitudes of 750,000 households across the US, with average net assets of $28 m, giving a total of $21,000bn. The estimated annual average consumption of each family, they argue, is about $850,000, giving a total of $650bn.

The results, says Mr Taylor, provide fascinating insights into what he calls the latest generation of American wealth: only 19 per cent of those surveyed had been wealthy for longer than 15 years, and of that only 16 per cent had inherited the money. The others had built fortunes in the 1980s and 1990s, often through the development of venture capital financing that gave individuals with a big idea the opportunity to develop it outside the large corporations that dominated post-second world war America.

'Here's the number one finding: they almost all come from the middle class,' says Mr Taylor. He and Mr Harrison were also surprised by the low representation of people who had made their money on Wall Street. 'By far, it is someone who had a really good idea, believed in their idea and persisted in making it happen. Someone who went broke a couple of times, got hosed a couple of times, but didn't give up.'

Mr Taylor and Mr Harrison argue that luxury marketers forget that the way wealthy people feel about their money reflects the degree of distance from their predominantly middle class backgrounds.

'They come from the middle class, they don't know anything about luxury brands except what they see on TV; they don't know how to spend money, they don't know how to go on vacation. And suddenly they find themselves with money to spend,' he says. 'Being wealthy is a learnt process, and it doesn't happen overnight, it takes almost 15 years to get it right . . . What most marketers don't realise is that the most important thing they can do is education.'

In an effort to understand how attitudes change over time, the two divided their results into three stages of wealth—which they dubbed apprentice, journeyman and master. Asked whether 'luxury items such as watches, jewellery and cars' are a waste of money, 59 per cent of the apprentices—wealthy for less than five years—said they were. The figure dropped to 40 per cent for the masters, who had been wealthy for more than

15 years. Ninety-two per cent of the apprentices agreed that they 'still felt middle class at heart', compared with 68 per cent of the masters.

The survey results suggested, however, that certain attitudes born from their early experiences remain, in particular a deep conservatism about spending money—despite some signs of more 'indulgent' spending in the journeyman phase.

'In purchasing, they look for quality, they look for taste and aesthetics and they look for brand (90 per cent said shopping decisions were influenced by "a brand I can trust"). And after they've found it, they go online—every dollar saved is a dollar of principle,' says Mr Taylor, who notes that the survey's respondents spent an average 13.7 hours a week surfing the Internet.

The consciousness of price produces some interesting anecdotes; Mr Taylor cites one respondent who carefully justified the purchase of a company jet because his company saved $40,000 for every hour he did not have to spend waiting in airports.

'The advice they give to marketers, is "don't tell me what I need, I know what I need". The second thing is "don't use adjectives" . . . they don't want it to be suggested that they can't judge quality. Educate them to the rudiments of quality.'

A separate survey of 40 top luxury-marketing executives, conducted this summer by the Harrison Group and AgencySacks for *BrandWeek*, also reflected sharp differences in the way they perceive their clients.

The marketers estimated that about a quarter of the wealthy were divorced or widowed; the survey found that 83 per cent were married, and only 9.8 per cent were divorced or widowed. Fifty-five per cent of the marketers believed the wealthy wanted others to know they were wealthy—against only 11 per cent of the Harrison Taylor survey. 'The marketers tend to think of the wealthy based on the fantasies of these corporate wealthy people,' says Mr Taylor. He adds that the wealthy are also concerned about the way they are portrayed in the media. Sixty-nine per cent of respondents said they believed the wealthy were portrayed negatively, while 62 per cent believed that they were 'under assault'.

'They perceive the media to be dominated by images of indulgent and criminal wealth—from Donald Trump and Paris Hilton to Bernie Ebbers. But they themselves are very sober; they are very careful. Not spending is what rich people do. Because spending is bad.'

Source: Jonathan Birchall (2005), *Financial Times*, 13 December.

QUESTIONS

1. What challenges do marketers face when trying to segment the wealthy?
2. How can marketers utilize the finding that there are different stages of wealth?
3. Are the wealthy in the United States primarily from old-money families?
4. Do you think that the UK wealthy are similar? Why or why not?
5. How would this information change marketers' approaches to targeting?
6. What types of products do you believe are best suited to the wealthier Americans?

6 Relationship strategies

LEARNING OBJECTIVES

- Examine the importance of developing relationships with customers
- Discuss ways in which marketers can assess customer desirability and rank customers in terms of customer value to the firm
- Identify the various ways in which marketers can build loyalty with customers
- Provide an explanation of the importance of customer relationship management systems
- Present various approaches to the building of customer databases with which to strategically address customer relationship building strategies while also explaining the potential pitfalls inherent in ill-designed and ill-conceived data mining approaches and relationship management systems

CHAPTER AT A GLANCE

Introduction

Marketing has gone through a rather pronounced paradigm shift over the past decade as business to customer (B2C) companies have changed their focus from transaction based to relationship centred. This has occurred as companies have slowly recognized that one-time purchases do not single-handedly keep companies in business. It is repeat purchases that are the key to success. The United Kingdom and the United States saw a number of industries during the 1960s and 1970s add significantly to their new business development capabilities, but what they did not realize was that the focus on new business development neglected the real lifeblood of the company, its loyal customers. Important accounts that are assumed to be a given are often taken for granted, and if all efforts are placed on the more fickle customers (who are also less profitable), then how much time is there left to spend paying attention to the needs of the loyal customers?

As companies like O_2 and AT&T analysed their marketing activities and assessed their customer makeup, they realized that a good portion of their marketing efforts and expenditures were aimed at the smaller and more problematic accounts. They were among the earlier companies that realized that **the 80–20 rule** did have merit. This rule states that on average an industry can expect that 80% of its revenues will come from 20% of its customer base. If one takes the time to carefully consider this ratio, the reciprocal suggests that 20% of revenues then come from 80% of the customer base. A more appropriate goal might be to spend 80% of the time nurturing the relationships with that important 20% of the customer base and leaving only the remaining 20% of the time and effort devoted to the less profitable accounts. Support was empirically provided for this relationship by Frederick Reichheld in his 1996 book, *The Loyalty Effect*, in which he reported that it is five times more costly to bring in a new customer than it is to keep an existing customer as will be explained in the next section.

Customer lifetime value (CLTV) has recently become a vital consideration for many companies as they recognize that happy customers are loyal customers who not only spread their satisfaction by word of mouth to friends, colleagues, and relatives, but also spend increasing amounts on the purchase of particular products/services over time. CLTV is the present value of the future profits that will accrue from the customer's lifetime purchases. The company must attempt to measure future earnings from the customer as well as be able to subtract from those earnings the cost of acquiring and maintaining the relationship with the customer. The key issue is to determine CLTV for each individual customer or group of customers so that each group can be assessed to determine the proper investments that will be necessary to make in each customer to build meaningful relationships and retain customers. This sets up an important future revenue stream that cannot be overlooked. General Motors Cadillac division has analysed CLTV, and has determined that a Cadillac customer will spend approximately US $350,000 over their lifetime (Best, 2005). This would include both the purchase of automobiles and maintenance. One can see what a loss it would be to lose that customer early in their product purchase life cycle. Such lost customers represent potentially hundreds of thousands of dollars of lost revenue. Best (2005) also illustrates CLTV in a description of credit card customers over a five-year period. Research has shown in the USA that a new credit card customer will generate an average company profit in the first year of $30, this escalates to $42 in the second year, and this will grow to $55 by the fifth year. The obvious goal should be to retain the customer since the loss of that customer in the first year would lose the company a considerable amount by the fifth year.

The focus on customer retention and the implementation of customer relationship management (CRM) programmes and strategies is seen as a very hot topic within the B2C world of competition, but what is so puzzling is that business to business (B2B) companies have been practising CRM strategies for over fifty years! This is nothing new for them. Business-to-business marketers have always known that building relationships with their customers is vital for long-term success. The salesforce has long been an important tool for industrial marketers to manage their customers and keep them happy. The dyadic relationship between the supplier and corporate buyer has been studied for many years, and intelligence gathering by the salesperson, the tiering of customers, the monitoring of key accounts, the demonstration of interest in the customer and the importance of solving customer problems are all accepted parts of effective B2B strategies. The point is that there is nothing new or groundbreaking in what is being touted as 'hot' by B2C marketers.

The early adoption of these techniques by industrial marketers was predicated upon their dealing with relatively smaller groups of possible customers who had significantly greater purchasing power than B2C consumer counterparts. A lost account can be devastating to the B2B marketer; whereas, losing individual consumers probably will not even be noticed or tracked by many consumer goods companies. However, intense competition for an ever-diminishing resource base (the target consumer audience) has forced B2C marketers to change their mindsets, and they are now looking at ways to accomplish this. The purpose of this chapter is to present the various ways in which companies can build and maintain strong and profitable relationships with their customers. (See Mini Case Study 6.1.)

Relationship marketing

What is **relationship marketing**? It is the development of long-term and intimate relationships between buyers and sellers. It involves open communications and the ability to know the customer so well that changes in wants and needs can be anticipated before they become critical. This means that companies really have to communicate effectively and often with their customers. The problem is that all customers are not equal. One of the best frameworks in which to discuss the nature of different customers is the loyalty ladder as envisioned by Payne (2000) as an expansion upon the innovative work of Raphel and Raphel (1995). Payne's ladder (see Figure 6.1) includes the following designations from least to most desirable: suspects, prospects, customers, clients (hostages/mercenaries/terrorists), supporters, advocates, and partners. This framework presents an effective mechanism for discussing relevant costs and communications strategies.

Suspects

Suspects are individuals who are not yet even mildly warm leads for the selling company. They are possibly prospects, but they are not yet interested in your products or services. These are probably not the kinds of individuals that companies should spend much time

MINI CASE STUDY 6.1

'BT signs licensing deals for pay-per-view television service'

BT Group will announce today that it has signed licensing agreements with Paramount, the Hollywood studio, the BBC, and Warner Music, to provide content for its new pay-per-view broadband television service.

The telecommunications group is planning to launch the service in autumn next year [2006]. The move will signal BT's entry into the media and entertainment arena, and will pitch the group against television groups including British Sky Broadcasting, the satellite company, and the unified national cable group being formed through the merger of NTL and Telewest, which has made a bid for Virgin Mobile.

There will be intense competition to capture television viewers who have yet to sign up to a digital television service. Media groups are also keen to lure consumers, who may have a digital service for their first television set, to switch their second and third televisions to digital services.

With 2.9 television sets a household, there were 70 m television sets in the UK, said Dan Marks, head of television at BT. Of this about half had yet to switch to digital.

BT's service will be broadband based, attached to a Freeview box, which will have a personal video recorder capable of storing up to 80 hours of programming. Users will also have a 'catch-up TV' service, where they can buy programmes missed in the past seven days.

Andrew Burke, head of entertainment at BT, said that the service's strength was that customers would not have to pay a subscription. They would have to buy a set-top box, and then pay only for what they watched.

That would make BT the first to offer video-on-demand to UK viewers without a subscription, although the cable companies are already offering video-on-demand to subscribers.

BSkyB has announced the purchase of Easynet, a telecommunications and broadband company, for £211 m, with the intention of offering more video-on-demand.

Because the market is still in its infancy, however, it is unclear how much viewers will be prepared to pay for single programmes. BT will offer users films, popular BBC programmes as well as music videos and other music programmes from Warner Music.

BT is understood to be negotiating content deals with ITV and other music and film studios. The broadband service will enable owners to use the set-top box for instant messaging, chat and video telephony on television, while online games and community services are expected to be made available.

The group's announcement comes as it is set to take the wraps off more of its futuristic retail offerings based around its broadband services and give City analysts an insight into planned new sources of revenue.

BT is expected to give more detail on plans to market its voice-over broadband service, commonly known as voice-over internet protocol or Voip. Voip has so far been a niche product at BT, but has caught the imagination because of companies such as Skype, which offer much cheaper calls than traditional telecom operators.

Source: Emiko Terazono and Mark Odell (2005), *Financial Times*, 8 December.

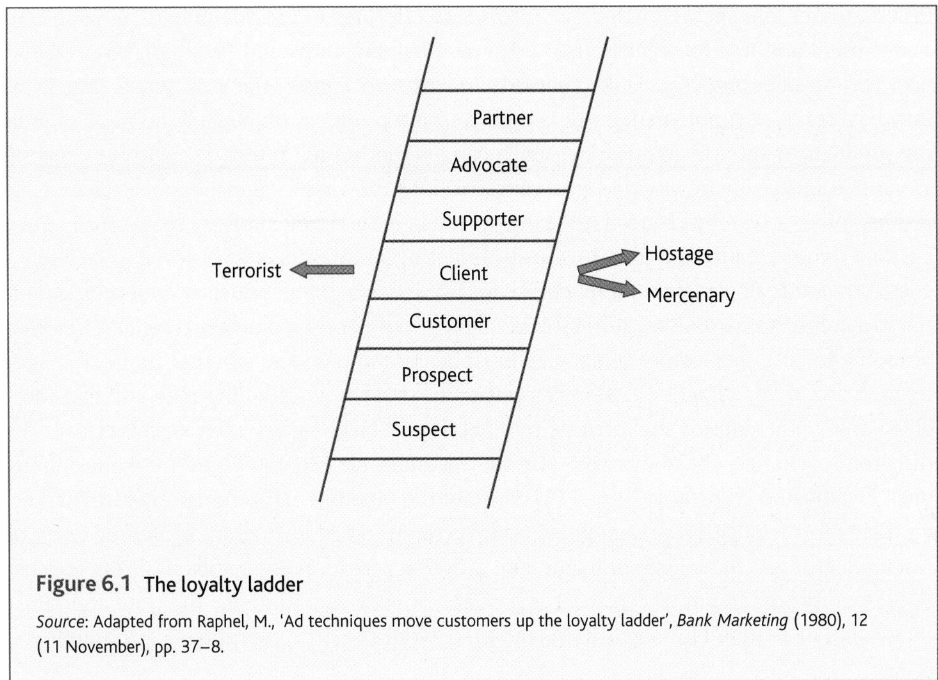

Figure 6.1 The loyalty ladder

Source: Adapted from Raphel, M., 'Ad techniques move customers up the loyalty ladder', *Bank Marketing* (1980), 12 (11 November), pp. 37–8.

or effort upon to develop relationships. There are some industries that simply do not lend themselves to customer relationships and retention. In the used-car industry, the fickle nature of these customers would argue against spending time and effort building rapport and friendship since they are likely to go where they get the lowest price in future transactions. The cost would most certainly outweigh the benefits. The firm must develop some kind of mechanism to determine whether the suspect is worth spending time with. One promising approach to this kind of assessment is **customer equity** as posited by Blattberg and Deighton (1996).

Customer equity

From a financial standpoint marketing budget setting becomes the job of balancing what is spent on customer acquisition with what is spent on retention. Blattberg and Deighton (1996) refer to this as the **customer equity test**, and in order to estimate this amount, the authors suggest that the firm first measures each customer's expected contribution to offsetting the company's fixed costs over their expected lifetime. Then, expected contributions to net present value are discounted at the rate set by the company as its target rate of return for any marketing investments, and finally the company adds together all of the discounted expected contributions across all of the company's current customers. The authors suggest that it is quite similar to assessing the value of a property portfolio. They caution that the balance between acquisition and retention spending is always changing. They provide the following guidelines for managers: (1) invest in the highest-value customers first (airline frequent flyer miles are a good example of how this can be done—the more they fly, the greater the rewards that accrue); (2) transform product management into customer management (the idea is to shape offerings to provide maximum benefit to heavy users and less for light users—Lego membership clubs and benefits); (3) consider how add-on sales and cross-selling can add to customer equity (the idea here is that there may be a series of supplementary or complementary products which go hand in hand with the products or services in question which can add additional future value to the revenue stream generated by the retained customer); (4) look for ways to reduce acquisition costs (if acquisition costs can be reduced, the long-term payout is significantly increased); (5) track customer equity gains and losses against marketing programmes (the firm can develop a customer equity flow statement much like a cash flow statement which will identify potential problems that would not normally be highlighted in an income statement); (6) relate branding to customer equity (managers must be careful to assess whether brand management is negatively affecting customer management since cross-selling may add considerable value); (7) monitor the intrinsic retainability of customers (when customer uses for the product change, the ability to retain the customer also changes, and marketing funds must be adjusted accordingly); and (8) consider the possibility of writing separate marketing plans for acquisition of customers and for retention of customers (different types of research, different management teams, and different measures are involved). From the customer equity standpoint, the suspect is probably a poor candidate for the time and effort that would be required for acquisition, and there would be little guarantee of profitability.

Prospects

A better candidate would be found in the prospect. This is a warm lead, who has interest in your product but who has not yet made a purchase. Customer equity would probably be higher for the prospect than for the suspect; however, interest is not a guarantee of purchase, and the other question that should be asked is what is the probability of purchase. This is not a regular buyer of your products or services, and the problem is that the costs of acquiring and retaining the prospect may far outweigh their potential lifetime value. The old methods of adding product selection and/or cutting prices to attract prospects may be difficult as adding new products/services may add to excessive inventory and cutting price will reduce margins and intensify competition across sellers (Raphel and Raphel, 1995). This argues for greater focus or expertise to increase the likelihood of attraction of interested prospects. If prospects are a major focal point for the company, direct marketing can help to reach prospects where they live or work. It also helps to have salespeople interact with prospects and get known and recognized. The reason for this is that relationships are based upon familiarity and trust. However, too much time should not be spent focusing on prospects as there is little assurance that acquiring them will lead to a lifetime of loyalty, especially in the case of lower-level consumer products where customers may be more deal and variety prone. Again, the need is to clearly identify the various levels of customers served by the firm and concentrate efforts depending upon the value of those different customers.

Customers

A customer, of course, is someone who has actually bought your product or service. The game is to try to enhance that individual or company's purchase frequency and volume over time, so that the customer becomes increasingly profitable and valuable to the company. The important question is whether all customers are 'good' customers. Service organizations are finding that it is necessary to manage the service experience carefully to ensure that it meets the expectations of key customers. This requires that important customers do not interact with customers who might negatively affect customer value perceptions. Imagine the situation for a restaurant where an affluent couple are having a romantic evening when the waiter brings a loud and hard-drinking group to a nearby table. Loud voices and interactions could certainly affect the ambience for the romantic setting. The restaurant must understand who the important customers are and prevent others from harming the service quality perceptions of these key customers. This might mean turning some customers away. In the example above, however, it is not immediately clear who are the most important customers. The restaurant would have clearly understood and would handle relationships accordingly. If the loud and obnoxious group are regulars and spend £500 per month dining at that restaurant, they would be seen as potentially far more important than the romantic couple who come once a year and spend only £80.

This raises the question of how to deal with different and potentially incompatible consumers. Compatibility management is a concept from the services literature that is quickly gaining support for use in dealing with the mixing of different types of customers.

Compatibility management

Much depends on a thorough understanding of the target customers and spending patterns. This is referred to in the services literature as **compatibility management** and is an important consideration for service businesses where customer interactions can significantly affect the service experience. Some companies can adjust for different customers by using different pricing and different venues to keep incompatible customers from interacting with each other. Sporting events and concerts provide opportunities for wealthier patrons to separate themselves from others through differential pricing. Paying top prices allows closer access to the sports pitch or to the acts on the stage. The idea, of course, is to provide the best experiences for those who are desirable.

What becomes particularly meaningful once the company has a viable customer base is to examine the variety of customers served and decide on a tiering of those customers. Especially in the B2C world of myriad customers, relationships with all customers might not be efficient or effective. If customer lifetime value (CLTV) can be calculated for each relevant customer group, then the profitability of each customer group can be assessed. As a result, one particularly relevant approach to ranking or prioritizing customers is based upon the impact that that group of customers specifically has on firm profitability. Zeithaml, Rust, and Lemon's (2001) customer profitability pyramid is also gaining wide acceptability (see Figure 6.2).

Customer profitability pyramid

Zeithaml et al. (2001) proposed the creation of a customer pyramid based upon profitability for firms trying to improve long-term firm performance. The authors argue that tiering based upon profitability has become a high priority especially for service firms, like FedEx, Bank of America, The Limited, Hallmark, and GE Capital Corporation. This would also have

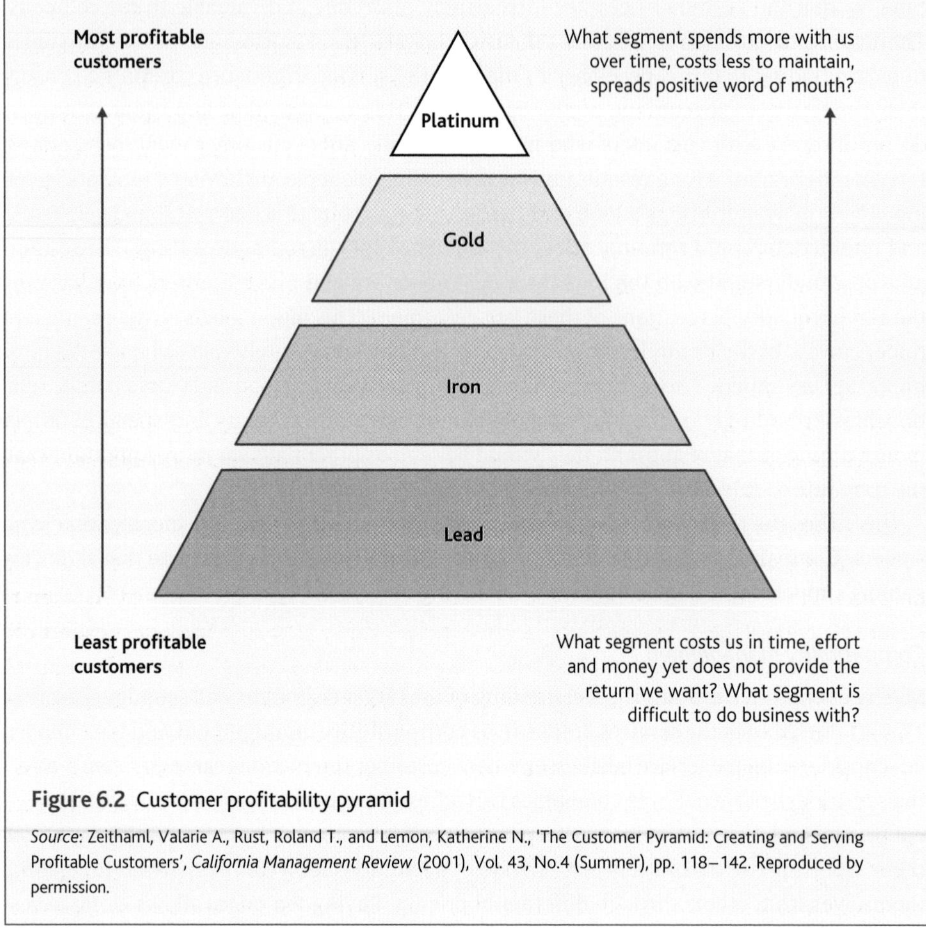

Figure 6.2 Customer profitability pyramid

Source: Zeithaml, Valarie A., Rust, Roland T., and Lemon, Katherine N., 'The Customer Pyramid: Creating and Serving Profitable Customers', *California Management Review* (2001), Vol. 43, No.4 (Summer), pp. 118–142. Reproduced by permission.

value for consumer and industrial products companies. This is a natural extension beyond segmentation that was covered in the previous chapter. The authors suggest that profitability tiering allows the company to manage the customer mix for maximum profitability. The firm can build stronger associations between service quality and profitability as well as provide an effective tool for optimal resource allocation. The point is to match customized services and products to customer utility, ultimately producing greater customer value, which in turn would lead to higher profits. The authors suggest that there are four necessary conditions that must be met to allow the use of customer tiers. First of all, profitability tiers must vary and have identifiable profiles. Profile descriptions will lead marketers to identify optimal marketing activities to reach different tiers. Secondly, customers in different tiers must view service quality differently. Different customer expectations of service quality allow the company to develop optimal bundles of attributes to offer the various tiers. Thirdly, different factors must drive customer acquisition and increases in purchase volume. As a result, the company can acquire new customers and stay with them as they move to higher profit tiers over time. They can meet perceptual service quality expectations in different ways as the customer moves to subsequently higher tiers. The point is to get the customer early and stay with them as they move up. Lastly, improvements in service quality should have different profit impacts for different customer tiers. Theoretically, higher tiers should see greater customer responses from improvements in perceived service quality in terms of new customer development, business volume, and the average profit level for each customer.

Using empirical data, Zeithaml et al. (2001) proposed the use of a customer pyramid with four different tiers based upon the gradation in metal values. These four tiers are as follows (from the least profitable level to the highest): (1) the Lead Tier (the bottom of the pyramid—includes those customers who are costing the company money rather than bringing in any profits); (2) the Iron Tier (second tier from the bottom—they provide volume for the company but do not buy enough to warrant any special treatment); (3) the Gold Tier (second tier from the top—there is high volume but profits may be limited due to desire for price discounts); and (4) the Platinum Tier (top of the pyramid—customers who are heavy users, loyal, profitable, and not price sensitive).

The authors suggest that the use of the profitability pyramid is particularly useful if the following conditions are met: (1) when service resources are limited (obviously the firm only has limited resources to put to use servicing their customers, so care must be taken to ensure that profitable customers are not 'short changed'); (2) when customers expect different kinds and levels of services (different customers have different needs, and serving all customers in the same way is inefficient as well as ineffective); (3) when customers will pay for different levels of service (different customers will pay for desired delivery and speed); (4) when customers define value in different ways (customers may consider other things than price as a basis for value like time, effort, or convenience, and if there are different value definitions, then different tiers can be arranged so that customer expectations can be matched to value); (5) when customers can be physically separated from one another (customers in lower tiers should not be aware that they are getting less service handling than those above them, so separation helps to keep them from finding out); (6) when they can be reached either in a group or individually (either may be needed depending on the strategies utilized per tier, since different tiers will require different strategies).

Using the alchemy analogy, the authors suggest that strategic relationship building can move customers into higher and more desirable tiers of the pyramid. So the authors suggest that to turn gold customers into platinum customers, the following strategies are recommended:

- become a full-service provider (if the customer can get everything they need from the firm, they will become better customers)
- provide outsourcing (taking on something that the customer used to have to do themselves)
- increase brand impact through line extensions (tying additional complementary offerings in with the company's umbrella of offerings)
- create structural bonds (providing customized services that utilize technology and can help the customer be more productive), and offer service guarantees (making sure that the customer is always satisfied by making it right)

In order to turn iron customers into gold customers, the following strategies are recommended:

- reduce the customer's non-monetary costs (reduction of search costs)
- add meaningful brand names (adding brands to the offering lines that are perceived to be better quality than the others normally carried)
- become knowledgeable about the customer using technology (building databases that can add customer knowledge and pinpoint recommendations)
- become knowledgeable about the customer by leveraging intermediaries (using dealers to gather information about local needs of customers)
- develop frequency programmes (the higher the use, the more accrued benefits for the customer), and
- create strong recovery programmes (finding out when customers are disappointed and correcting the problem before the customer is lost)

Finally, in terms of lead customers, the authors suggest that a firm should only attempt to move customers up from lead to iron if there is good future potential. Otherwise, it might be best to send these customers on their way looking for a different provider. If there is strong potential, the authors suggest the following strategies:

- Raise prices (adding prices for services that customers previously had received for free) and
- Reduce costs (find less expensive ways to deal with these customers—like remote automated sites)

One problem is that more research is needed to connect the profitability pyramid to CLTV. While there is usually strong support for the argument that higher levels of loyalty will be associated with greater customer lifetime value, there are still a few gaps in the research. In particular, it is not yet clear whether the advocate is any more profitable than the mercenary (client). More work is clearly needed.

Clients

Clients are regular customers. Customers become clients when they have some level of trust in the seller and believe that the seller's offerings will be beneficial to them. This is the first actual development of a relationship between the buyer and seller; however, it is not necessarily a relationship that will last forever, and it may not be a relationship that remains mutually beneficial for both of the parties involved. Payne (2000) raises the issue of clients who are potentially difficult or problematic for the seller. Some clients might begin to feel as though they are hostages to the seller due to some leverage that the seller utilizes over them. The loss of a feeling of mutual benefit raises questions about the life expectancy of that relationship, and the client may look for any opportunity to jump to another seller if one appears. For a relationship to properly exist, there should be mutual benefits that are achieved by the parties to the relationship.

Another type of problematic client is the mercenary. This type of client is one that only appears to have loyalty to the relationship, but may hold the tenuousness of that relationship over the seller's head to maintain some kind of leverage over the seller. The idea is that this kind of client is not involved in a meaningful relationship, and again, one-sidedness in a relationship creates instability. The mercenary can easily be attracted by a 'better deal' from someone else in the industry.

The other type of client that becomes a serious problem for the seller is the terrorist. Now the client is in a position to hold the company as a hostage rather than the reverse situation. What kind of client becomes a terrorist? A dissatisfied client! Raphel and Raphel (1995) talked about the fact that when companies can make unhappy customers happy, they can raise their loyalty level significantly above what it was before the complaint. In the services literature this is known as the 'recovery paradox'. The customer who has a problem, but is handled successfully by the company to alleviate that problem, becomes even more committed to the relationship than before the problem occurred. The point to be made here is that even your best customers might at one time become unhappy with you for some reason. The key is to open the doors of true communication with your good customers to ensure that they remain satisfied with the relationship. A client who has a problem which is not immediately rectified stands the chance of becoming a terrorist. One unhappy client can tell from seven to eleven others about his/her dissatisfaction, which can not only negatively affect other existing clients, but also discourage others from becoming new clients (Pruden, 1995). Ritson (2003) found in a study of disgruntled US consumers that dissatisfied customers took steps to undermine the company involved by creating 'symbols of defiance' out of company logos. Examples include Shell's logo being changed to Hell, and Greenpeace's modification which changed Esso to 'E$$O'. These active detractors can wreak a certain amount of havoc on target companies.

Monitoring of client satisfaction becomes an important barometer to measure the potential for changes in relationships so that proper corrective action can be taken to 'shore up' the relationship. Of course the use of marketing for its own sake is not necessarily a good way to handle this. As Pruden (1995) puts it, relationship strategists must be careful not to let 'frequency marketing' take the place of 'aftermarketing'. Both of these can be considered as relationship marketing.

Pruden (1995) defines **frequency marketing** as a strategy aimed at identifying the best customers, keeping them, and increasing their expenditures through the development of intimate long-term relationships. On the surface this would appear to mirror relationship marketing; however, Pruden suggests that there is an important difference in that relationship marketing should be more like 'aftermarketing', which focuses on the retention of more than just a small percentage of the best customers. **Aftermarketing** involves long-term relationship building in which the firm actively attempts to move customers up the loyalty ladder and tries to minimize the outflow of 'unhappy' buyers. Pruden suggests that this may not be practicable for all businesses. While direct merchants can effectively utilize frequency marketing, he suggests that aftermarketing is preferable for manufacturers of products and services who depend upon mass distribution.

A relevant question to raise here is whether the company should rush to coddle all clients who appear to have a problem. It is always possible that a client's needs may have changed over time, and that the company is not able to cost effectively cater to that client's new needs. In such cases it may be preferable for the company to look at outsourcing that customer rather than cater to them in a way that might prove detrimental to other more profitable clients. The key is to continuously monitor the relationships to see what is happening. Some customers can effectively be re-energized, while others cannot. The company is best served by realizing that some clients may no longer be as profitable and beneficial as they once were and in a positive way move them to another provider (with the hope of keeping them from becoming a terrorist). The idea is to help the customer remain satisfied while being moved to another supplier. The point is to make the transition as smooth and painless as possible.

Supporters

Supporters are those who buy everything you produce that they can use. They are supportive of your company and its products and services, and while they may spread good word-of-mouth for you, they will not necessarily be motivated to the level of an advocate. They will not go out of their way to recruit others to your company. You convert a client to a supporter through the provision of great service. The idea here is to start to find ways to reward clients for their purchases and loyalty so as to move them to supporters, that is, to find ways to provide extra value and benefits for the buyer. In terms of communications at this point, the job of the marketer is to avoid the danger of over-promising. Customers must have their expectations met and surpassed, if possible. Over-promising sets up the potential for unconfirmed expectations. Strategically, however, the cost of providing the extra value that motivates supporters to become more than clients must not exceed the profitability of the supporters.

Advocates

Advocates are valuable commodities. Here are the consumers who buy your products and services and actively recruit others to do the same. These are the individuals that you want to keep happy. One way to do that is with the kinds of incentives that loyalty schemes carry with them. However, advocates are not necessarily big spenders and the loyalty ladder must not be confused with the customer pyramid.

Loyalty schemes

Loyalty schemes are programmes that are established by companies to provide added value to the regular purchaser as opposed to the irregular customer. They provide increasing benefits for higher levels of company loyalty. In the UK two particular loyalty schemes that have been particularly successful are the one for the Tesco Clubcard, and the other is that created by Nectar (which is believed to have the largest number of cardholders in the UK). The basis of these and similar schemes is to build up points or credits for purchases, which allow the consumer to get rewards like discounts off a series of special products or announcements about new offerings that no others receive. Frequent flyer miles programmes for airlines are also examples of loyalty programmes, whereby travellers build up miles that can be used to upgrade classes of service or even to obtain free airline tickets.

A number of airlines and other organizations offer their own credit cards which can build reward points that can be used every time a purchase is made using that credit card. These programmes are all designed to keep the customer satisfied and loyal and to entice them to increase their use of the company's products and services.

Are such schemes really about loyalty? Is this the same thing as the kind of loyalty that one feels for a football team or a friend? No, loyalty here means keeping the customer coming back to purchase the products or services of the company. So the use of a loyalty scheme is aimed at keeping and hopefully intensifying the support of the consumer and moving the consumer from being a supporter to being an advocate.

Loyalty schemes have their downsides as well. Dowling and Uncles (1997) raised some serious questions about loyalty schemes. The authors suggested that loyalty may not offer better returns than price cuts, a movement to the use of everyday low prices, expanded advertising programmes, or expanding of distribution outlets. They argue that this may be due to the fact that most loyal customers are 'polygamous'. In other words, they tend to have two or three favourite brands and rarely focus on one single brand. Dowling and Uncles challenge some of the norms that have been accepted regarding the use of loyalty schemes and raise questions about whether repeat-purchase loyal customers are any less expensive to sell to, whether they buy more than others, whether loyal customers are any less price sensitive, and whether loyalty scheme members are willing to recommend certain sellers any more than other satisfied customers. People at the consumer goods level tend to look mostly for variety, special deals, and availability as, for example with breakfast cereals, car rentals, and fast food. In higher-level programmes like airline frequent flyer programmes, customers on average belong to three different schemes.

Most loyalty schemes appear to be focused on either big or small brands. Big brands generally have more buyers and they buy more frequently, but small brands have fewer buyers who also buy less at any one time. For these brands the only way to grow market share is to get a greater number of buyers through a better distribution system, as opposed to getting current customers to buy more. The authors' conclusion is that only those loyalty schemes that build presence and encourage stocking are appropriate for the consumer marketplace. As a result, the best candidates for loyalty programmes are high-involvement products where the actual scheme enhances the value proposition of the product (e.g. a Northwest Airlines Visa card to build Northwest Airlines frequent flyer miles). Indirect benefits, like a bank offering frequent flyer miles, are ineffective. For loyalty programmes to be effective, they should be fully costed and the incentive to motivate the next consumer purchase should be maximized (the more spent, the higher the reward). Done correctly, loyalty schemes can neutralize competitor programmes, broaden brand distribution, enhance brand image, and increase value, but they should not be attempted when low-involvement goods are involved, other than to counter a competitor's offering.

The aim is to convert the supporter to an outright advocate. As supporters are important to the company, they need to be communicated with even more than the lower-level consumers on the ladder. These individuals need to feel as though they belong to the company (Raphel and Raphel, 1995). They need to be treated in a special way. If things are done correctly, the supporters will want to become advocates as they see that there are additional benefits associated with reaching that higher status on the ladder. These are also the individuals who are effective spokespeople to reach others who want to be like them. Peers can significantly affect the opinions of others like themselves. Lindstrom (2005) explains that these individuals need to be fully engaged by the company in almost every aspect of the business from R&D to website design. This creates that personal sense of ownership which helps to make a person a true advocate for the company. The power of word-of-mouth at this level can be seen in the results of NOP World's 2004 Global Brand Advocacy Survey, which surveyed 30,000 consumers worldwide and found that the highest levels of brand advocacy in the world were for Mercedes Benz with 59% of those surveyed considering themselves 'active brand advocates' ('Brand Advocacy Survey', 2004). Other brands with high levels of advocates were BMW (53%), Toyota (51%), Nokia (50%), and Sony (46%). Word-of-mouth is believed by many consumers to be the best mechanism for recommendation for a company.

Partners

For B2B customers, partnership exists where the buyer and seller enter into a joint position of commitment and the buyer often has to modify the ways in which he/she works to accommodate the seller. For example, a company buying new payroll software may need to retrain finance staff, pay staff on a different day of the month than previously, and format the information communicated differently. Obviously this will produce the highest level of commitment to the relationship. The B2C setting does not lend itself as well to this kind of relationship but such partnerships do occur in cases where buyers have to change how they behave. For example, if you buy a camera from Canon and organize your photographs using Canon brand software you may well be reluctant to buy another camera and learn how to use a new package and potentially change how you organize your photographs.

In a partnership both parties (B2B or B2C) have a vested interest in the partnership owing to trust and commitment. The seller needs to continually solidify relationships. A good example of this can be seen in the way that Boeing Aircraft Corporation builds its partnerships with the major airlines of a variety of countries. If your best customers are asked what your new products need to be able to do for them, they will feel a greater need to buy them once they are built. Thus, a Boeing partner, 'China' (a consortium of state-led airlines), recently ordered a large number of newly developed Boeing 787 Dreamliners to stock its national airline fleet.

Customer relationship management

After examining the nature of relationship marketing, the loyalty ladder, and customer valuation, the next logical step is to look at the mechanics of relationship management. Customer retention is obviously an important goal for any company, especially in light of the costs necessary to acquire a new customer as opposed to keeping an old one. Kotler (2003) explains that there are two ways to strengthen customer retention: (1) to create high switching barriers (the price of looking for another supplier, evaluating them, switching to them, and the potential loss of customer discounts which are loyalty based), or (2) to deliver ever-increasing levels of customer satisfaction. Kotler suggests that the latter is preferred since switching barriers are difficult and costly to erect. So how does the company deliver appropriate levels of customer satisfaction? The corporate solution is the creation of a customer relationship management (or CRM) system. CRM is a process by which a firm gathers information about the wants and needs of its customers to enable it to adjust its offerings to better fit those wants and needs. It involves data gathering, storage, and dissemination to those who need it. Often this involves the acquisition of relationship management software and data mining techniques, which promise to effectively track customers and build large customer storehouses of data, for use by the company in building long-term relationships. The foundation of this system is the database of information, often referred to as the customer information file (CIF). Winer (2004) suggests that there are five major areas of content that make up the customer information file: (1) basic descriptions of the customers (usually in terms of demographics and customer names and addresses), (2) customer purchase histories (records of all purchases made by the customer, showing price paid, purchase location, and product variant purchased), (3) customer contact histories (records of all customer contacts with company personnel), (4) customer response information (records of customer reactions and responses to various marketing promotions and activities), and (5) customer value (an estimate of the monetary value of the customer). The customer information file then serves as the basis for analysing customers to find out how to build better relationships and increase their profitability.

Emmy Favilla (2004) studied a series of successful companies and found that they were carefully monitoring all customer 'touch points' and finding ways to offer superior service to continuously impress their customers. Favilla (2004) provided a series of examples of companies and what they were doing to improve service levels. One example presented was Starwood Resort Hotels which had to handle over 14 million calls each year using 900 call centre agents across various cultures. Starwood implemented an automated customer interaction recording and performance evaluation mechanism that created a consistent customer experience, improved reservation sales volume, helped supervisors improve call centre productivity, and improved customer service quality ratings. Another example involved Hewlett-Packard (HP), which was trying to use 10–12 different methods of handling common service processes. This complexity created enormous employee frustration levels and customers became confused from receiving a variety of inconsistent responses. HP corrected the situation through the development of a single, global help desk mechanism to improve service delivery, which reduced overall cost per employee and improved tracking and trend analysis. Another excellent example was the South African Revenue Service which had to deal with taxpayer information kept in eight different systems. Different IT systems were used based upon a series of taxpayer subcategories. To correct the situation the company created an integrated multiple-taxpayer system through a team of companies including Accenture, IBM, and Siebel Systems. The result was savings of almost $12 million per week and significantly improved response time to answer taxpayers' questions.

One can easily see the benefit inherent in obtaining customer information in a B2B marketing situation, since industrial marketers have fewer customers to deal with on a regular basis than B2C companies. It gets more complex for companies aiming at large groups of customers, especially when there are many competitors with what appear to be very similar offerings. Fournier et al. (1998) raised the important question of how B2C companies can build meaningful intimate relationships with 'hordes' of individual consumers. Part of the problem that they acknowledged was that many B2C customers get 'bombarded' with surveys which ask for information to help the company build a database of customer information. The biggest difficulty for the consumers is that they keep giving out information, but do not see anything coming back to them for their efforts. They are tired of filling out surveys and hearing nothing in return. They feel disconnected rather than part of an intimate relationship. The authors caution that developing customer intimacy requires the company to take a holistic view to create 'life satisfaction' for the customer rather than merely customer satisfaction. They suggest that this would require in-house controls of free customer helplines, regular Internet monitoring, trend analyses to understand consumer lifestyle trends, and the tracking of customer perceptions to avoid negative customer backlash.

It is important to set up appropriate mechanisms for data collection which allow the firm to understand its consumers more effectively and to keep them trusting and committed. Davenport and Klahr (1998) discuss the importance of managing customer support knowledge and ensuring that front-line personnel get the knowledge whenever needed to help customize the offering to the needs of the most profitable customers. This kind of support knowledge would include such information as known customer problems and solutions, questions frequently asked by customers (and their answers), and customer product/service questions and a series of recommendations. Davenport and Klahr (1998) suggest that this customer knowledge not only improves the solutions for customers, but also ensures more consistent solutions. Further, it improves the quality of the customer handling on the very first call, and also reduces the costs per customer call. It would also reduce the number of calls to the customer support desk, thus reducing the need for front-line personnel with technical expertise, and allowing more front-line people to be hired for their people skills. Other benefits would include reductions in the cost of field service calls, faster and better on-the-job training, and increased satisfaction for front-line staff. Ultimately the most important improvement would be in the overall satisfaction of the customer.

The following knowledge-oriented technologies have been found to be effective for use in the management of customer support knowledge: (1) rule-based expert systems (systems like the computer building system at the Dell website); (2) probability networks (relating symptoms to underlying causes and solutions in a network of probabilities); (3) rule induction (where examples are provided and rules are generated which are used to test situations and provide possible recommendations, which works best when example cases are complete and comprehensive); (4) decision trees (some products allow decision trees to be created to cover all possible symptoms and solutions, which helps novices more effectively than experts); and (5) case-based reasoning (a method which holds details of past situations or cases and reviews these in an attempt to retrieve a series of similar cases when a new problem is identified; this helps the user to develop a solution based upon the facts and previous solutions; this new case is then added to the case-base).

Managements have voiced concerns regarding the proper management of customer support knowledge. One difficulty is that customer support knowledge is cross-functional and requires all the relevant functional areas to be included—which may be quite a challenge. Another managerial concern is that employees may worry that technology may give rise to their elimination and replacement by the new system, raising serious morale issues. It is also possible that the new system may need smaller numbers of technical and product experts. Ultimately management has expressed concern that customer support systems may end up taking the burden away from support personnel and placing it directly on the consumer, which may not be appropriate.

Data mining has become an important tool in customer relationship management. This is the analysis of consumer databases to look for possible new relationships that can provide direction for innovative customer relationship strategies. Since the early findings of synergies in reservations among airlines, hotels, and car hire in the SABRE reservation system utilized by American Airlines, customer data have been analysed to look for possible relationships that researchers never before knew existed. The trouble is that it is not enough just to gather data just for the sake of having data to add to the customer knowledge system. Davenport et al. (2001) report that many companies have been investing in customer transaction tracking systems which have built very large databases, but with few helpful insights into who their customers are. The problem is that many companies rely on raw data rather than observing and getting to know their customers. The problems mentioned previously by Fournier et al. (1998) suggested that just asking customers for information isn't really enough, and this is what Davenport et al. (2001) are suggesting. They interviewed personnel from 24 leading companies in the field of customer relationship management and found that the best companies went out of their way to combine transaction data with human data (information about how customers function). The authors found that these 24 leading firms had certain practices in common which should provide help for other companies looking to improve their CRM programme. They found that the best firms tend to focus on their most valued customers. Of course the company has to know which customers are worth the cost. The authors also found that these better firms made every effort to prioritize objectives. They would first set customer relationship objectives and then prioritize them according to their business strategies. Successful companies aim for the optimal knowledge mix by combining transaction-focused data with consumer-qualitative data to better understand not only what consumers do but why they do it. One pitfall that these companies have avoided is the development of one repository for all data. Firms are best served by pursuing many different kinds of customer information since they often have significantly different types and groupings of customers. Successful firms are those that can think creatively about human knowledge. This requires unconventional thinking since the most successful companies use creative solutions combining both explicit (documented and retrievable from storage) and tacit (observed, understood, but not stored for easy access) information by having executives interact in meaningful ways with customers. What else do these successful companies do? They look at the broader context, which means that they must shift their cultures from being product oriented to customer focused. This requires both cultural and structural changes, and there is also a pressing need to avoid focusing on only one customer type since the organization must balance generalized response systems with distinct customer types and groups. Finally, the authors found that successful companies establish a process and tools. They found that many firms stop after developing a management strategy, but successful firms know what they want to accomplish, create a plan, get the proper tools, and get results. The main point here is that data collected for the sake of collecting data will do very little to help the company build strong relationships with customers. These relationships must be carefully nurtured with different types of information being collected and managed to allow the firm to best address different customer types and needs. (See Mini Case Study 6.2.)

MINI CASE STUDY 6.2
'Faulty customer data and the faux-royal slipper syndrome'

Opening a stack of circulars and credit card solicitations this weekend, my thoughts turned to the late Edgar F Codd. The British mathematician, who died two years ago, was the father of 'relational' databases, today used by government agencies looking for signs of terrorist activity, retailers analysing weekly sales figures and credit card companies deciding whose mailboxes to stuff.

It is hardly an exaggeration to say that Ted Codd's invention changed the world. Until the early 1980s, when his ideas were widely adopted, data was mostly stored in 'hierarchical' databases that were both inflexible and difficult to interrogate without a PhD in computer science. The relational model, based on an easy-to-analyse system of rows and columns, made it possible to identify quickly, say, customers in California with two children and size 11 feet.

This led not only to the development of the direct marketing industry but also to many of the information technology tools we take for granted. Relational databases underpin enterprise resource planning systems, customer relationship management systems, supply chain management systems, executive dashboards and other faddish tools of the executive trade.

Judging by the contents of my mailbox, however, very few companies are exploiting the real potential of relational databases. Most of the direct mail I receive is based on information that is inaccurate (I am not, and never have been, a supporter of the Oakland Raiders), out of date (my Honda Accord was written off more than a year ago) or incomplete (since when did British citizenship imply an interest in faux-royal carpet slippers?).

It seems unlikely that lack of investment is to blame. Companies spend billions of dollars each year on the hardware and software required to store, retrieve and analyse customer data. They collect names, addresses, transactions, telephone calls, website clicks and more besides. The world's largest commercial database (belonging to an unnamed corporation) now includes close to 3,000bn records, a fivefold increase in two years, according to Winter Associates, a US consulting company that tracks these things.

Data integrity—or, rather, lack of integrity—is a problem that even the biggest IT budget cannot overcome. In a world where people move house, change car and swap spouse every few years, much of the information stored in corporate databases is unreliable. There are also human errors to contend with. Oh, for a quiet word with the hotel clerk who once tapped me into a reservation system as 'Mrs'—thereby triggering an avalanche of offers for cut-price pedicures.

Even if the information they hold is correct, few organizations seem to know how to use it. Most big corporations employ statistics savants whose job it is to glean 'insight' from mountains of raw data. But they are, for the most part, distanced from the real centres of corporate power. It is rare indeed to find a company that has made data analysis a source of genuine competitive advantage.

A few do exist. Capital One, the financial services group, was founded with the explicit intention of using analytics to market first credit cards and now a wider range of banking products. You may disparage the group's prodigious output of junk mail, but the record of shareholder wealth creation demands respect. Harrah's, the casino group headed by Gary Loveman, the colourful former Harvard Business School professor, has also established itself as a market leader by putting analytics front and centre. The group's loyalty scheme has turned customer retention from a game of roulette into something approaching marketing science.

A small handful of retailers also seem to have taken analytics to a high level. In the UK, Tesco has used its customer loyalty scheme to establish market leadership over rival grocers such as J. Sainsbury and Asda. In the US, Wal-Mart commands hushed reverence among data mining aficionados, although the world's largest retailer remains notably discreet about what data it collects and how it uses it.

Tom Davenport, professor of information technology and management at Babson College, Massachusetts, points to a number of common traits between these companies. First, data analysis is a corporate priority rather than a job left to business units. The chief cheerleader in most cases is none other than the CEO.

Second, a substantial investment has been made in not only hardware and software but also hiring business analysts with a profound grasp of statistical methods. Capital One and Harrah's each employ a legion of pointy-headed statisticians. Data analysis is not delegated to amateurs with Excel spreadsheets.

Third, while these companies are not afraid to attempt sophisticated predictions and modelling, they focus on just one or two aspects of the business where analytics might deliver real advantage. Thus Harrah's has concentrated on its loyalty scheme, with the aim of substantially increasing occupancy rates at its casino hotels. Wal-Mart seems to have focused less on customer data than on merchandizing—getting the right goods on the shelves for any given day and location.

These companies also know that analytics will not compensate for shortcomings in other aspects of the business. Witness the dismal financial performance of the US airline industry despite its massive collective investment in yield management and customer loyalty schemes. Similarly, knowing that fatigued dads tend to buy beer along with nappies—a triumph of what retailers call 'market basket analysis'—is fruitless if they prefer to visit the store next door. Codd, father of four children as well as an epoch-making advance in information technology, would surely have concurred.

Source: Simon London (2005), *Financial Times*, 7 December.

The authors present a series of helpful general rules for gathering and managing data from a series of customer encounters. They suggest that every customer be given a unique identifier. This allows knowledge to be shared about particular individuals. They also suggest that an internal champion be found. This means that individuals must be brought into the process who will get value out of the results, and they should be encouraged to become strong advocates and champions. Companies should do their homework by finding out what their target customers value so that any efforts to gather information from them will be enhanced. The authors warn companies not to overwhelm everyone with useless knowledge. It is imperative to get at the most useful pieces of information through the use of appropriate filtering techniques. Finally, the authors suggest that companies start simply by first approaching those in close proximity who serve the same customer, to gain economies and efficiencies in information gathering, then branching out from there.

CRM pitfalls to avoid

Companies can easily get caught up in spending enormous amounts of money on a variety of customer relationship management schemes, but many of these will fail. Rigby et al. (2002) suggest several strategies to avoid significant CRM pitfalls. The first of these pitfalls is the implementation of CRM before a customer strategy has been developed. The first step to CRM must be for the company to develop a customer strategy. This will require a clear identification of the customers that the firm wants to build relationships with. These identified customers must then be categorized into different groups ranging from the most profitable down to the least profitable, which will allow a clear delineation of actions and responses and efforts for the various segments. The authors suggest that the customer strategy must involve debates involving the following five questions:

1. How must our present value proposition change to gain greater customer loyalty?
2. How much customization is appropriate and profitable?
3. What is the value to be gained from increasing customer loyalty, and would this vary by customer segment?
4. How much time and money can we invest in CRM at the present time?
5. If customer relationships are important to us, why aren't we already building a CRM programme, and what might we be able to do in building customer relationships without investing in technology?

The authors warn that CRM may not be the answer if the company concludes that cost reductions or the handling of all customers in a standardized way makes more sense.

The second CRM pitfall is the implementation of a CRM programme before the organization has become a customer-focused entity. The danger here is that the company says that it wants a CRM programme but has not restructured its processes to better meet customer needs. Often company executives do not see the need for internal system and structure changes since they assume that CRM affects only processes that involve face-to-face interactions with the customer. The authors claim that successful companies work for years to modify their structures and processes before ever attempting CRM initiatives.

The third peril is the assumption that more CRM technology is always to be preferred. Often executives will assume that CRM must be technologically intensive. But this may not be the case. It may make sense to provide incentives to motivate company employees to better track customer needs as opposed to investing enormous sums of money in buying the latest and most complex technology. The authors suggest that excellent CRM programmes are comprised of a variety of technologies from low to high. They suggest that managers really need to ask themselves where their CRM needs fit on the technology spectrum. The best way to deal with the complexity issue is to start with low-tech alternatives and then assess whether more is needed.

The fourth and final peril is that you may stalk your customers rather than woo them. Managers often end up trying to build relationships with the wrong customers or with the right customers but in the wrong way, if they forget that the types of relationships will depend on what their company stands for and what types of relationships it wants to build with its customers. As the authors describe the situation, relationships involve two sides. A company may want to build stronger ties with affluent customers, but those customers may not want closer relationships with the company. It may also be that the company does not build a relationship with customers who value relationships, and these customers will undoubtedly be lost to competitors. Another challenge is building relationships with those customers who do not want them, and by whom the company will be seen as an irritant. The use of loyalty programmes can often fall into this pattern. Having the ability to contact customers does not mean that the company should contact them. It depends on the customer strategy mentioned earlier, rather than the CRM programme.

Latest thinking on customer relationships

Two recent developments in customer relationship management are worth reporting. One deals with taking relationships with customers to a higher plane, to engender emotional ties with customers, and the other focuses on the radical premise that companies have been focusing on incomplete data in their approaches to customer relationship databases, and that what would be better would be to let customers build their own databases of their transactions. These new databases are referred to as personal knowledge banks. Each of these will now be discussed in turn.

Building customer love

Bell (2002) suggests that it is no longer sufficient to just have a relationship with your customer, you need to develop the 'love' of your customer. Bell claims that this is what has made Starbucks, Ritz Carlton Hotels, and Harley-Davidson such successful companies. The author suggests that there are seven important steps in building customer love (the 7 Es—see Figure 6.3): (1) enlistment: customers care when they share (the key is knowing exactly when and how to include customers, since bringing them in as co-producers of a service makes them more loyal); (2) engagement: the power of straight talk (since customers who have a problem and complain spend twice as much as customers who have a problem and do not complain, the company must find a way to listen to and talk straight with customers in such a way that customers believe that their input made a difference); (3) enlightenment: growing customer love (educating and keeping customers up to date helps to build their loyalty and commitment); (4) entrustment: affirming the covenant (reliability is vital for trust, so to convince customers that you can be trusted, you must be seen as caring for them to get them to care for you); (5) empowerment: customer control through consistency (customers feel in control when they have an offering that is consistent—keep the core offering intact); (6) enchantment: making the process magical (service which surprises adds the sizzle, and not showing how keeps the mystery and builds devotion); and (7) endearment: giving without a **toll** or price (showing generosity to customers if backed by authenticity says that you really care about them and are not just concerned with profit).

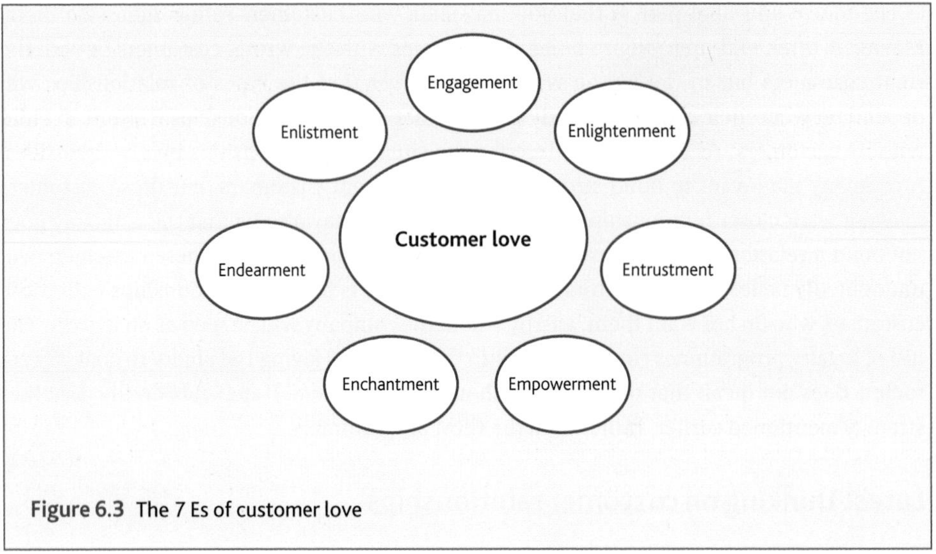

Figure 6.3 The 7 Es of customer love

Bell offers the following key benefits from the achievement of customer love: (1) customers who love you go out of their way to take care of you; (2) customers do not just recommend the company to their friends, they insist on their friends using the company; (3) they both forgive you for mistakes (once you have earned their love) and try to back you up to others who have had bad experiences; (4) they will give helpful, candid, and forthright feedback when they see a problem; (5) they do not take legal action against you; and (6) they will pay more for what you offer because they feel that your offering is worth it. These are powerful benefits, and the analogy of social/human relationships applied to buyers and sellers is a helpful strategic perspective. With the bar being ever raised on customer expectations, keeping up with the customer and keeping him/her happy in their devotion is a key to long-term viability and success.

Developing personal knowledge banks

Watson's 2004 article in *Harvard Business Review* suggested that companies, which have been building databases to focus on the customer's transactions with their products and services, are missing important information. They are missing the customer's interactions with the particular industry as a whole. This then leads to an inference gap. Watson argues that the only mechanism that can provide the magic information that is needed is the customer him- or herself since they are the only ones who know all about their interactions with all companies in the industry. The only thing that makes sense, therefore, is to have the customer control and manage his or her own database of information that could be given to companies for use if it could add value. Watson refers to this as the customer managed interaction (CMI), which has also been referred to as the personal knowledge bank. These knowledge banks could be utilized to attract proposals from sellers to meet certain buying needs expressed by the customer. Watson argues that these personal knowledge banks could serve as the ultimate interface between the customer and a variety of companies for an ever-increasing range of goods and services. The problem for companies is to let the control stay with the consumer, so they would need to earn the right to get access to consumer data. There are a variety of issues that would have to be dealt with before this use of personal knowledge banks could become practical (e.g., privacy and security as well as rules governing access, etc.), but this new way of looking at things could be far bigger than CRM.

Conclusion

Once companies have gone through the process of segmentation, processing, and positioning, they must look to the creation of meaningful relationships with those customers. Customer acquisition is far more costly than customer retention, and the building of intimate relationships with key customers allows the firm to keep in step with changes in customers' wants and needs and enables them to take corrective action in refining product and service offerings to retain those customers. Some customers may cost far more to retain than they are worth. All organizations must carefully assess which customers to build relationships with, and work to keep those valued relationships. The use of customer relationship management systems is an important approach to managing customer relationships, but committing to a CRM system requires careful preplanning, and a commitment throughout the organization to being customer oriented. Putting a system in place for the sake of having a system usually leads to serious problems over time as the system may not fit with the company outlook and environment.

Summary

Relationship marketing is important for company success. Normally a company will not be successful trying to focus on single transactions since companies depend on repeat purchases for long-term success. Taking care of important customers is vital, especially in light of the 80–20 rule that states that in most industries 80% of the revenues come from 20% of the customer base. Spending an inordinate amount of time and effort to bring in problematic customers is both inefficient and ineffective especially since there is less time remaining to take care of the mainstay customers. The issue is that key customers must be nurtured to remain loyal to the company and continue to buy the products of the company. While B2B marketers have known this for decades, B2C marketers have only recently been acknowledging the importance of customer relationship management systems. Relationship building requires the acquisition of relevant customer information, the storage of that information in databases, and the use of that information to adjust company offerings to build ever stronger and more profitable customer relationships.

KEY TERMS

80–20 rule The rule which is built on the understanding that 80% of the company's revenues come from only 20% of its customers.

Customer lifetime value (CLTV) The present value of the future profits that will accrue from the customer's lifetime purchases. The company must attempt to measure future earnings from the customer as well be able to subtract from those earnings the cost of acquiring and maintaining the relationship with the customer.

Relationship marketing The development of long-term and intimate relationships between buyers and sellers. It involves open communications and the ability to know the customer so well that changes in wants and needs can be anticipated before they actually become critical.

Customer equity test Where the firm first measures each customer's expected contribution to offsetting the company's fixed costs over their expected lifetime. Then expected contributions to net present value are discounted at the rate set by the company as its target rate of return for any marketing investments, and finally the company adds together all of the discounted expected contributions across all of the company's current customers.

Compatibility management The management of different groups of customers to ensure that there is no interaction that could devalue the service for important customers.

Customer profitability pyramid A ranking of customers in a pyramidal design with customer groups positioned on the pyramid by profitability for the firm. The top of the pyramid contains the Platinum customers, the second tier the Gold customers, the third tier the Iron customers, and the base of the pyramid is made up of the least profitable customers, the Lead customers.

Frequency marketing A strategy aimed at identifying the best customers, keeping them, and increasing their expenditures through the development of intimate long-term relationships.

Aftermarketing Long-term relationships being built in which the firm actively attempts to move customers up the loyalty ladder and tries to minimize the outflow of unhappy buyers.

Loyalty schemes Programmes that are established by companies to provide added value to the regular purchaser as opposed to the irregular customer. They provide increasing benefits for increasing levels of company loyalty.

Customer relationship management (CRM) A process by which a firm gathers information about the wants and needs of its customers to enable it to adjust its offerings to better fit those wants and needs. It involves data gathering, storage, and dissemination to those who need it.

Customer information file (CIF) Another name for the customer database built by the firm to better understand customer wants and needs so that stronger ties can be built with the customer. The CIF contains such information as descriptions of the customer, his/her purchase histories, the various contacts the customer has had with company personnel, information on how customers have reacted to marketing activities, and measures of customer value.

Data mining The analysis of consumer databases to look for new possible relationships that can provide direction for innovative customer relationship strategies.

Customer love Where the firm goes beyond building a relationship with its customers to the point where there is a stronger emotional bond between the company and the customer. This is where customers believe that the firm actually cares about their well-being.

Personal knowledge banks Databases of customer information that are built, managed and owned by the consumer. These could be made available to companies if the consumer chose to do so. These databases would include all transactions that the consumer had with all companies in a variety of industries.

DISCUSSION QUESTIONS

1 Are repeat purchases important for company success?

2 What are the two important mechanisms used for determining customer desirability, and how do they differ?

3 How is customer lifetime value measured?

4 Why have loyalty schemes been criticized by strategic marketers?

5 Is data mining important for building customer relationships?

6 Should human data be incorporated into a customer relationship management programme?

7 How do personal knowledge banks help in the development of better and stronger customer relationships?

ONLINE RESOURCE CENTRE

Visit the Online Resource Centre for this book for lots of interesting additional material at: **www.oxfordtextbooks.co.uk/orc/west/**

REFERENCES AND FURTHER READING

Bell, Chip R. (2002), 'In Pursuit of Obnoxiously Devoted Customers', *Business Horizon*, (March–April), pp. 13–16.

Best, Roger J. (2005), *Market-Based Management: Strategies for Growing Customer Value and Profitability*, 4th edn (Upper Saddle River: Prentice-Hall).

Blattberg, Robert C., and John Deighton (1996), 'Manage Marketing by the Customer Equity Test', *Harvard Business Review*, Vol. 76 (July–August), pp. 136–44.

Bold, Ben (2004), 'John Lewis Backs Card with Rewards Scheme', *Marketing*, 1 April, p. 8.

'Brand Advocacy Strategy' (2004), *Brand Strategy* (6 October), p. 7.

'Brand Strategy Briefing: Land Rover Case Study—Customers at the Wheel' (2004), *Brand Strategy* (3 November), p. 54.

Davenport, Thomas H., and Philip Klahr (1998), 'Managing Customer Support Knowledge', *California Management Review*, Vol. 40, No. 3 (Spring), pp. 195–208.

Davenport, Thomas H., Jeanne G. Harris, and Ajay K. Kohli (2001), 'How Do They Know Their Customers So Well?', *MIT Sloan Management Review* (Winter), pp. 63–73.

Dowling, Grahame R., and Mark Uncles (1997), 'Do Customer Loyalty Programs Really Work?' *Sloan Management Review* (Summer), pp. 71–82.

Favilla, Emmy (2004), '10 Strategies for Customer Service Success', *Customer Relationship Management*, Vol. 8, No. 6 (June), pp. 38–45.

Fournier, Susan, Susan Dobscha, and David Glen Mick (1998), 'Preventing the Premature Death of Relationship Marketing', *Harvard Business Review*, Vol. 78, No. 2 (January–February), pp. 42–51.

Kotler, Philip (2003), *Marketing Management*, 11th edn (Upper Saddle River: Prentice-Hall).

Lindstrom, Martin (2005), 'Extreme Loyalty: Show Off Your Brand Tattoos', *Media* (25 February), p. 24.

McKelvey, Charlie (2005), 'Leader: Can Data Ease Boots' Headache?', *Precision Marketing* (11 February), p. 13.

'Online Retail: Customer Retention' (2004), *New Media Age* (25 March), pp. P.S.5–P.S.6.

Payne, Adrian (2000), 'Relationship Marketing: The UK Perspective', in J. Sheth and A. Pravatiyar (eds), *Handbook of Relationship Marketing* (Thousand Oaks: Sage), pp. 39–68.

Pruden, Doug R. (1995), 'There's a Difference Between Frequency Marketing and Relationship Marketing', *Direct Marketing*, Vol. 58, No. 2, pp. 30–1.

Raphel, Murray, and Neil Raphel (1995), *Up the Loyalty Ladder* (New York: Harper Collins).

Reichheld, Frederick F. (1996), *The Loyalty Effect* (Boston: Harvard Business School Press).

Rigby, Darrell K., Frederick F. Reichheld, and Phil Schefter (2002), 'Avoid the four Perils of CRM', *Harvard Business Review*, Vol. 80, No. 2 (February), pp. 101–10.

Ritson, Mark (2003), 'Brand Terrorists Offer an Insight into How the Public Interpret Ads', *Marketing* (27 November), p. 18.

Watson, Richard T. (2004), 'I Am My Own Database', *Harvard Business Review*, Vol. 84 (November), pp. 1–2.

Winer, Russell S. (2004), *Marketing Management*, 2nd edn (Upper Saddle River: Prentice-Hall).

Zeithaml, Valarie A., Roland T. Rust, and Katherine N. Lemon (2001), 'The Customer Pyramid: Creating and Serving Profitable Customers', *California Management Review*, Vol. 43, No. 4 (Summer), pp. 118–42.

KEY ARTICLE ABSTRACTS

Blattberg, Robert C., and John Deighton (1996), 'Manage Marketing by the Customer Equity Test', *Harvard Business Review*, 76 (July–August), pp. 136–44.

From a financial standpoint marketing budget setting becomes the job of balancing what is spent on customer acquisition with what is spent on retention. This article presents a useful mechanism for aiding in this balancing, which the authors refer to as the customer equity test.

Abstract: Decision calculus is used to help managers determine the optimal balance between spending on acquisition and spending on retention. The ultimate goal is to grow the company's customer equity to its fullest potential. A series of guidelines and suggestions is provided to help frame the issues that affect acquisition, retention, and customer equity. When managers strive to grow customer equity rather than a brand's sales or profits, they put a primary indicator of the health of the business at the forefront of their strategic thinking, the quality of customer relationships.

Davenport, Thomas H., Jeanne G. Harris, and Ajay K. Kohli (2001), 'How Do They Know Their Customers So Well?', *MIT Sloan Management Review*, (Winter), pp. 63–73.

There is a problem in customer relationship management when customer data is being gathered simply for the sake of having data to add to the customer knowledge system. The helpful article reports that many companies, which have been investing in customer transaction tracking systems, have built very large databases, but have few helpful insights into who their customers really are. The problem is that many companies rely on raw data rather than really observing and getting to know their customers.

Abstract: Many firms know about their customers, but few know the customers themselves or how to get new ones. Leaders in customer knowledge management go beyond transaction data, using a mix of techniques, and they are not afraid to tackle difficult problems. Guidelines are presented: (1) Focus on the most valued customers. (2) Prioritize objectives. (3) Aim for the optimal knowledge mix. (4) Do not use one repository for all data. (5) Think creatively about human knowledge. (6) Look at the broader context. (7) Establish a process and tools.

Zeithaml, Valarie A., Roland T. Rust, and Katherine N. Lemon (2001), 'The Customer Pyramid: Creating and Serving Profitable Customers', *California Management Review*, 43 (4), pp. 118–42.

This paper discusses the strategic uses of a customer pyramid based upon profitability for those firms trying to improve long-term firm performance. The authors argue that this is useful for both consumer and industrial products companies.

Abstract: Customer profitability can be increased and managed. By sorting customers into profitability tiers (a customer pyramid), service can be tailored to achieve even higher profitability levels. Highly profitable customers can be pampered appropriately, customers of average profitability can be cultivated to yield higher profitability, and unprofitable customers can be either made more profitable or weeded out. Tailoring service to the customer's profitability level can make a company's customer base more profitable, increasing its chances for success in the marketplace.

END OF CHAPTER 6 CASE STUDY
Relentless competition in car industry—what carmakers are doing to counter

The cost of fragmentation

For the past 20 years, carmakers round the world have been trying to emulate Japanese companies' success in lean manufacturing, seen as the benchmark for ensuring quality and efficiency, especially as practised by Toyota. Most car factories have now been revamped more or less along Japanese lines, so the gap between Japanese and Western producers has become much smaller. The main thrust of competition at the moment is in product development. Each company is trying to compete in every segment of the market, with a plethora of niche models designed to attract particular groups of consumers, and to renew them rapidly enough to keep interest fresh.

This is causing the market to fragment. The days are over, says Richard Parry-Jones, boss of product development at Ford, when you could get 30% of the European mid-sized market (which means 10% of the total market) with just one bestselling model. 'Nowadays you would need five or six derivative, including a five-door, a station wagon, an MPV and an SUV'.

In Europe and Japan, the main difference between cars has traditionally been size. Small cars were usually basic; medium-sized cars, epitomized by the ubiquitous Ford Cortina, a little less so. Now even the small cars have fancy fittings such as electric windows and air conditioning, and there are whole new categories of niche vehicles, such as Fiat's cheap-and-cheerful new Panda and the ultra-cheap new Renault Logan. Given the huge range of models that car companies must offer now, they have found they need factories that are completely flexible, able to switch from making one model to another to meet fluctuating demand.

»

» For some years now, manufacturers have used common platforms to serve as the basis for a whole range of models, aiming to widen their range without wholesale redesigning, engineering and tooling-up. Models that share the same basic architecture can be welded and assembled on the same lines by the same robots. Platform-sharing was carried furthest by Volkswagen under its former chief executive, Ferdinand Piech. But his successor, Mr Pischetsrieder, quickly concluded that the process had gone too far.

So what else can car companies do to make themselves even more competitive?

The magic answer to this, some say, is 'build to order' (BTO). Various working groups in the industry have been studying the feasibility of what is often called the 'three-day car', quickly assembled to the customer's actual orders, rather than to the forecasts made by the sales department.

A low cost entrant

One interesting idea has recently surfaced from a team led by Steve Young at A. T. Kearney, a consulting firm, working with Martin Leach, a former president of Ford Europe and the product-development wizard behind the revival of Ford's Mazda associate. The team set out to design a 'new generation' car company, a bit like the new low-cost budget airlines now spreading everywhere.

What they came up with was a 'virtual' company that would outsource just about everything, from organizing networks of suppliers to manufacturing, some design and delivery, and service. Manufacturing would be done in small plants within each national market, to ensure that it was close to the customers. Parts would be made in a network of factories in low-wage countries, a rigorous extension of what is already happening in the industry today.

Such a company, the team found, would have an operating margin of about 22%, roughly double that achieved by Nissan, the best of the conventional volume carmakers in 2002. That would make its returns nearly three times better that Toyota and BMW; four times better than Peugeot and DaimlerChrysler; and more than 20 times better than GM and Ford.

The secret behind this high return is that such a company would be offering services throughout the whole automotive supply chain. It would sell mobility, not cars. At the moment, explains Mr Young, the car companies win revenues (and profits) only from the start of the life of a car. But if they leased the car and retained ownership throughout its entire life on the road, typically eight years, they could tie in revenues from such things as insurance, servicing and repairs.

Their putative company, which they dubbed Indego, would make four models and aim to sell a quarter of a million of each. But because the company would be leasing the cars several times over as used vehicles and providing associated services, such as insurance, 250,000 vehicles going through several transactions over eight years could generate the same sort of revenue as a conventional car company making 2 m vehicles a year. Moreover, the product-development costs would have been written off against eight times the volume of eventual revenues. Mr Young says that the exercise has been well received by many manufacturers, particularly component firms, which are trying to introduce elements of his model into their operations. »

» If distributed manufacturing and the virtual car company sound somewhat familiar, it is because elements of them have been mooted before. About six years ago, Peter Wells and Paul Nieuwenhuis of Cardiff Business School launched the idea of micro-factories assembling low volumes of cars within local markets; their micro-factories would also act as retail distribution points.

Indego seems to have been inspired by other pioneers too. In 2002 Jacques Nasser, then boss of Ford, tried to turn his company into an all-singing, all-dancing consumer outfit providing automotive services. In many ways he was ahead of his time. But Ford, and Mr Nasser's career, came to grief because his grand strategy involved too many initiatives and too much expensive diversification downstream. When the company had to replace millions of defective Firestone tyres fitted to its SUVs, the audacious experiment suddenly stopped. That may have set back much-needed changes in the way the car industry is organized by a generation.

Source: *The Economist*, 4 September 2004. Copyright the Economist Newspaper Ltd, London 2004.

QUESTIONS

1. How do car companies build relationships with customers?
2. Can loyalty schemes help car companies?
3. What kinds of B2B relationships does this case suggest for car companies to improve their competitiveness?
4. How can relationships be built in the framework of a virtual company?
5. What kinds of consumer database would help car companies build stronger relationships with consumers?
6. Can a car company 'mass customize' its products?

Part IV How will we get there?

I. Introduction
1. Overview
2. Marketing strategy: analysis and perspectives

II. Where are we now?
3. Environmental and internal analysis: market information and intelligence

III. Where do we want to be?
4. Strategic marketing decisions and choices
5. Segmentation, targeting, and positioning strategies
6. Relationship strategies

V. Did we get there?
13. Strategy implementation and control

IV. How will we get there?
7. Product innovation and development strategies
8. Branding strategies
9. Service marketing strategies
10. Pricing and distribution strategies
11. Marketing communications strategies
12. E-marketing strategies

VI. Conclusion
14. Social marketing and CSR

7

Product innovation and development strategies

LEARNING OBJECTIVES

- Examine the role of innovation and product development in marketing strategy
- Review the range of innovation and product development objectives
- Assess the two main adoption theories and their implications for marketing strategy
- Examine the main options for market and innovation strategies

CHAPTER AT A GLANCE

Introduction

Product innovation and development offer all organizations an important means to gain a competitive advantage. From a strategic perspective, innovation is based upon technological superiority and posits that buyers will seek goods and services that provide the greatest interest, performance, features, quality, and/or value for money. Innovation can be an integral part of marketing strategy owing to its ability to reduce costs and/or differentiate. The 'and' part of the sentence has provided one of the biggest challenges to Porter's cost-differentiation framework in that in many markets the name of the game is to both reduce costs AND differentiate. Buyers have become increasingly demanding and no longer see a contradiction between product innovation and development and falling prices. For example, mobile phone manufacturers such as Nokia and Sony-Ericsson offer superior products every year at similar or below previous prices.

Another strategic element of innovation is that it often brings previously unrelated companies into competition—competitive boundaries have blurred. Take the case of telecommunications. Previously separate sectors such as computing, entertainment, telephony, and utilities are now locked in fierce competition. Thus, in the UK, BT has developed alliances with content providers to provide a variety of services over broadband. Similarly Siemens, Sony, and Panasonic have entered the photographic marketplace using digital technology and Dyson displaced the top-selling Hoover vacuum cleaner with its 'cyclone' bag-less technology.

Innovation can be used to find 'comfort zones' in the marketplace. The best strategic place for any organization is to occupy a space that rivals have no interest in or cannot easily emulate. Patek Philippe uses established technology to build classic watches while Seiko uses innovation to produce digital watches with advances such as kinetic energy. Innovation and development only have strategic value if positioned appropriately. Rolex has no interest in advances in Velcro strap technology! Finally, consider BMW's 'The Ultimate Driving Machine' pitch to the market. Here is a company saying it will not use technology that makes driving a car like sitting on a sofa.

Innovation and development are strategic issues. This chapter is divided into three sections. The first looks at setting objectives for innovation and development. This is followed by one looking at targeting issues. Finally, overall product innovation and development positioning are examined. However, the first task is to examine how to define innovation.

What is product innovation?

Innovation is a noun with a definition along the lines of 'the introduction of something new' or 'a new idea, method or device' as with Pepsi Max and Persil Tablets. This is not entirely satisfactory given such definitions do not appear to provide any distance between innovation and invention (which involves designing or creating something which has never been made before such as the Sony Walkman or Bluetooth Wireless Technology).

Strictly speaking, the difference between the innovation and invention is that invention applies to things that are 'new-to-the-world' whereas innovation refers to subsequent changes and adaptations. An obvious example would be Alexander Graham Bell's 'electrical speech machine' of 1876. Looking back we can see that the telephone was the precursor to the Internet, but it would be stretching the truth to say Bell invented the Web. So we recognize that both the telephone and the Web were new-to-the-world despite the myriad of innovations that can be traced back to the telephone.

To a large extent the invention/innovation discussion is a subjective one as hindsight and perspective show that inventions are rarely completely new. Therefore, in marketing, the talk is mainly of innovation rather than invention. 'Innovation' has grown to cover invention and relates to any significant changes to a product or service, as perceived by the market. See Mini Case Study 7.1.

MINI CASE STUDY 7.1

'Taiwan research team learns how to be genuinely creative'

As Huang Kuo-ping speaks, a toy monkey the size of a mouse starts to jump and quiver in his chest pocket. 'Oh, I'm shouting again,' he says, toning down his voice. The cheerful mechanical engineer is hard of hearing and has invented the monkey as a device to let him know when to speak more softly. Such an invention is exceptional enough but what is even more surprising is that Mr Huang is being paid to solve such problems. Together with 18 colleagues from fields as varied as electronic engineering, music, industrial design and cartoon drawing, Mr Huang works at the Creativity Lab at Taiwan's Industrial Technology Research Institute.

ITRI established the lab last year in an attempt to foster genuine innovation to help Taiwanese companies create completely new products—not just excel at making existing products better and cheaper. The facility is the first step on a path several Asian countries have pledged to follow. Yet few have so far succeeded in doing so.

Taiwan built up an electronics industry in the 1980s that has become a world market leader in products such as notebook computers and cellphones. The island continually ranks among the top three or four countries in terms of the number of patents granted in the US.

But very rarely, if ever, does Taiwan come up with ideas that can change the world. 'How can we innovate in leaps, like Sony did with the Walkman or Apple did with the iPod?' asks Hsueh Wen-Jean, the creativity lab's director.

Lin Hsin-yi, ITRI chairman and chief economic adviser to Chen Shui-bian, Taiwan's president, says: 'The thousands of patents we get in the US every year do not mean anything. Most are process patents which result in cost reductions but not in revolutionary new things.'

ITRI, incubator for what have become some of the world's largest technology companies, acknowledges that this lack of innovation will change only if Taiwan's research landscape evolves.

'At our lab, innovation is being targeted from the basis of people's needs, not from the perspective of what technology can do next,' says Ms Hsueh. »

» Eight local companies, including chip design house Via, motorcycle maker Sanyang, and Liuli Gongfang, a designer of traditional Chinese glass art objects, are working with the lab on projects with intriguing titles such as 'Robotic Life' and 'Smart Cities'.

So far not one commercially viable product has been invented. But ITRI president Johnsee Lee considers that a good sign. 'In Taiwan, we have been taught to answer questions rather than finding the right questions to ask,' he says.

The researchers are being allowed to spend most of their time learning how to be creative, indulging in brainstorming sessions, developing theories on idea generation, drawing pictures and building objects.

'It is about your way of life,' says Nicholas Negroponte, chairman of the Media Lab at the Massachusetts Institute of Technology, which co-operates with Taiwan's creativity lab. 'The heterogeneity of American society helps in sparking creativity. Living in a homogenous society like Taiwan, you are at a disadvantage.'

The lab's industrial partners are patient. Frank Lin, Sanyang vice-president, says his company has been developing concept vehicles since the early 1990s in an attempt to drive innovation but has not been able to get beyond incremental improvements. Despite having a flat screen with a global positioning system instead of traditional instruments, Sanyang's latest concept product is still no more than a motorbike.

Source: Kathrin Hille (2005), *Financial Times*, 2 December, p. 2.

Establishing innovation objectives

Launching innovative products and services is a risky business, especially if the technology is discontinuous (i.e., requires a significant change in behaviour and/or in complementary technology, e.g. DVD recorders cannot play VHS tapes). If it goes wrong, as it often does, the costs can be enormous. Shortening the new product development (NPD) process can be a formidable competitive weapon. Xerox is a case in point, when it recaptured its lead in the copier market by reducing its seven-year NPD process to only two.

The following marketing strategies form the 'umbrella' of innovation activities pursued by organizations. They are activities conducted by market leaders, challengers, and niche players who use innovation as a competitive tool in the marketplace (followers tend to introduce innovation once the risk has reduced).

New-to-the-world: Motorola invented the first 'mobile' phone in 1973, but it was not until 1985 that phones first came to market in a format that would be recognized as mobile. New-to-the-world products make up about 10% of all innovations and can provide significant market advantages in the intervening space before rivals can introduce their own versions.

Additions to existing lines: for example when Heinz added 'Green' to its range of ketchups. Studies show additions to be about 25% of all marketing innovations and to be valuable in offering new choices to loyal as well as new customers and thereby increasing overall sales.

Improvements/revisions: for example when Kellogg's introduced a foil wrap for its cereals to improve freshness. Improvements and revisions tend to account for about 25% of all marketing innovations and to be particularly useful at maintaining loyalty and distancing from rival and often me-too products. Thus, in the case of Kellogg's Cornflakes, the foil wrap distinguishes the brand from supermarket own labels.

New product lines: for example when the engineering and transport company Atkins added management and project services to its range of design and engineering solutions or when Sony added laptops to its audio-visual products. Indications are that new product lines account for about 20% of all innovations and can be successful in increasing the spend of loyal customers and enhancing loyalty.

Cost reductions: as with the introduction of cheaper flights in Europe by easyJet and Ryanair and SouthWest Airlines in the United States, these account for slightly above 10% of all innovations. Such airlines have introduced new processes and ways of doing business to fill a gap in the marketplace for cheap foreign travel. Cost reductions can open up new markets for companies and provide relatively safe spaces to operate within as long as established rivals are unable to change their processes sufficiently to match.

Repositions: in its widest form a reposition includes any kind of reposition, even just a change in advertising. However, in the specific context of innovation and development, it involves significant changes in at least one element of the mix, that is, product, price, place, promotion, or people. For example, Lucozade was repositioned in 1985 from an energy drink for the sick to energy replacement for sports people. The advertising used the athlete Daley Thompson with the claim: 'Lucozade Replaces Lost Energy'. Tablets and cans were introduced to introduce portability, but no change was made to the formula of the drink. Studies indicate that repositions account for slightly less than 10% of marketing innovations a year and are especially used to revitalize a brand by companies faced with ageing markets and/or declining sales (e.g., Brylcreem).

Aside from repositioning, all of the above innovation strategies need some new product or service to be developed. Accordingly, the following sections will examine the early stages of the innovations strategy: the NPD process, market preparation, and product rollovers.

NPD process

Process

New ideas have been traditionally developed by a three-stage process:

1. **Idea generation.** Involves activities like problem analysis, listing attributes and changing combinations, suggestion boxes, brainstorming, and customer requests. Ideas are then screened by their market attractiveness and market competitiveness.
2. **Business screening analysis.** Involves identifying positioning, creating a concept, and attempting to predict market behaviour.
3. **Development and test marketing.** Sales forecasting, product development, market tests, possible marketing mix, and break-even analysis.

Once a company has established the qualitative and quantitative nature of its objectives it has to ensure that there is a process in place to enable innovation to happen and to transplant innovative ideas into manageable projects. It may help to break the process into stages.

From an organizational perspective the whole process might be driven **functionally**: the new product passes sequentially between departments and ends with marketing. Alternatively, a **parallel** approach might be adopted where all the elements are developed in tandem so that marketing has involvement from the generation of the idea onwards. It is also important to foster an innovation climate inside the firm compatible with the overall vision of the organization which might affect how to motivate and reward individuals and groups. One big question in many organizations is how to make the most of the inevitable failures. Innovation is a multi-level activity involving market understanding, finance, and complex product or service delivery. Senior managers will play a vital role in innovation strategy and a champion such as Jack Welch at GE might play a pivotal role.

Toolkit strategy

The toolkit strategy enables customers of NPD companies to undertake their own innovation and is an important example of the direction in which the NPD process is moving. At its core the basic problem of NPD is that the 'need information' side of the equation resides with the customer while the 'solution information' resides with the manufacturer. Take the case of BBA, which develops speciality flavours to bolster and enhance the taste of processed foods. A traditional project might start with a client requesting a single sample of a 'meaty flavour' for a soy product. The shipment is then made within six days. After three weeks the client might respond with: 'It's good, but we need it less smoky and more gutsy' (Thomke and von Hippel, 2002). BBA then attempts to modify the flavour in two days. Several more iterations may occur before they get it right. BBA bears most of the development risks with R&D costing from around £600 for a minor tweak to £160,000 for an entirely new flavour. Furthermore, on average, most clients only accept about 15% of new flavours after full market evaluation, with 5 to 10% eventually making their way to the marketplace.

In response BBA have shifted more innovation activities to their customers. They have developed an Internet-based tool containing a data set of flavour profiles. Customers are able to select information and manipulate it on-screen and send the new flavour design directly to an automated machine (often located at the client's site) and the product in made within minutes. After tasting, if needed, the flavour can be manipulated and tweaked again.

Take another case—the custom computer chip industry. Traditionally manufacturers were only able to undertake projects for companies wanting high volumes, given the high cost of developing bespoke chips for such uses as robotic circuitry. Companies such as LSI Logic have transformed the process by providing both large and small customers with DIY tools to design their own chips. Such developments are based on companies taking their knowledge, developed over decades, and incorporating it into sophisticated CAD/CAM (computer aided design/computer aided manufacturing) programs that contain libraries of design options to solve numerous problems using graphical interfaces. They also enable testing through computer simulations to build virtual prototypes easily and quickly. By standardizing transistor design and adding LSI's solution information, the customer toolkit can function.

When to develop such toolkits? Customer innovation and toolkits make sense when you are faced with shrinking markets and customers seeking customized products. They are also useful when you need to go through many iterations to develop a product. Another pointer is if an organization uses high quality computer-based simulations to develop new products and it has computer-adjustable production processes.

Systematic inventive thinking

Product developers are constantly striving for the 'innovation sweet spot'. This is the point where a new product idea is different enough from the existing product to attract customer interest and at the same time close enough to the company's existing position and capabilities for it to make sense to customers and for it to be delivered by operations. 'Systematic Inventive Thinking' (SIT) provides a highly disciplined approach to new product idea generation that represents the interests of both customers and the company (Goldenberg, Horowitz, Levav, and Mazursky, 2003) and is worth a particular mention.

The starting point for SIT is to list all the main elements of a product in terms of physical components and attributes such as colour and expected useful life. The next stage is to identify the immediate environment, again in terms of physical components and attributes (e.g., ambient temperature and type of user). Finally, five innovation patterns (based on the work of a Russian engineer, Genrich Altshuller) may be manipulated to develop a new product idea.

The five patterns of innovation are subtraction, multiplication, division, task unification, and attribute dependency change.

- **Subtraction** is about removing components or attributes.
- **Multiplication** involves adding elements like developing a double waste bin unit that can be used for rubbish and recycling or a double-bladed razor that lifts whiskers when shaving. (Note the need for qualitative change rather just straight multiplication.)
- **Division** is the breaking down of an existing product into its component parts as when the integrated hi-fi is divided into modular systems involving speakers, amplifier, tuner, tape player, and CD player.
- **Task unification** concerns assigning a new task to a product such as when Rubbermaid placed assembly instructions for storage cabinets on the packaging rather than on a separate enclosed sheet.
- **Attribute dependency change** involves the relationship between the attributes of a product and the attributes of the immediate environment, as with the development of male and female razors.

One case cited (by Goldenberg, Horowitz, Levav, and Mazursky, 2003) was the development of a new business card for a company. Having examined conventional business cards it was decided to choose the pattern of 'subtraction'. A business card was developed without a job title and instead a hole cut in the place where the job title would normally be placed. It demonstrated clearly that the company was non-hierarchical, but it presented several challenges. It undermined the primary function of a business card, it might make junior employees insecure if they had no title, it might seem an inadvertent error, and the meaning of the hole was not obvious. The next stage was 'task unification', which involved the assignment of a new task to the product. One idea was to use the hole as a window to frame additional information such as different job titles, trade association memberships, weekend activities, and intellectual interests. This demonstrated a lack of hierarchy while appearing to be innovative and offered a multifaceted view of an employee. It left a problem of how to provide a variety of role definitions. The final solution was to shrink the card to accommodate a standard rotating 'wheel' made of card that could be turned to show the multifaceted job functions, roles, relationships, and interests of the card bearer. A new product!

Market preparation

Once a new product is developed, market preparation is about 'warming up' the marketplace for the innovation. In the case of high-tech products cooperative strategies with rivals are becoming the norm (Easingwood and Koustelos, 2000). This is because alliances and licensing help signal to consumers that this new technology will not leave them marginalized, as happened when Betamax tape recorders were overtaken by VHS despite being of superior quality. Many lessons have been learnt and standard operating agreements enabling planning and stability have mushroomed. For example, Psion, Motorola, Ericsson, and Nokia agreed to adopt Psion's operating system (EPOC) as the platform for WAP. Psion's rivals knew that if they did not abandon their own systems Microsoft Windows CE was likely to dominate. Being prepared to supply to original equipment manufacturers (OEMs) is another strand of market preparation, as for example IBM supplying leading edge hard drives to rivals such as Acer and Dell.

From a communications stance, PR on a forthcoming release is crucial. Intel always releases details of all its new chips, such as Celeron, which helps develop anticipation and excitement in the market. Crucially the PR appears late enough in the process so prevent rivals from reacting with copy-cat products in time to damage Intel's market share (Intel does not seek alliances). PR can also be used by companies to 'educate' the market about the new technology, but this is often a more long-term process.

Product rollovers

Short product life cycles increase the frequency of 'product rollovers', the displacement of old products by innovations (Billington, Lee, and Tang, 1998). Ideally, existing innovations would be sold out just when a new product was introduced, but this rarely happens. The Osborne II replacement for the Osborne I, the first successful portable computer, is a classic example. Adam Osborne announced the forthcoming Osborne II in late 1982. The market response was to cancel orders for the Osborne I and wait. Slow sales of the Osborne I were not alleviated by the arrival of the replacement as, owing to technical problems, the introduction of the Osborne II slipped. The company eventually had to file for bankruptcy in late 1983. Certainly this is an extreme case, but it demonstrates the point.

Should the old product be sold out before the new is introduced or should they be sold simultaneously? If so, should they be sold at different prices, in different geographic regions, or by different channels? The two strategic options are: **solo-product roll** and **dual-product roll** (Billington, Lee, and Tang, 1998).

Solo-product roll aims to have all the old product sold out at the planned introduction date (e.g., HP's Deskjet 510 replacing the Deskjet 500). This is a high-risk and high return strategy. It can prove to be expensive if the old product is sold out too early or there are high inventory levels in place as potential sales may be lost.

Dual-product roll is where both old and new products sell simultaneously for a period (e.g., the Pentium III and IV). It is less risky than the solo option, but requires the marketing of both old and new products with the consequent risk of confusing the marketplace. Geographic rolls can reduce confusion (e.g., Mercedes first introduced the 190C in Europe and then in North America). Another angle is to differentiate by channels, (e.g., Nike introducing new models at premium retailers while selling older models through discounters). Dual pricing may also be utilized, as with the aggressive pricing of older computer chips. A fourth strategy is the so-called 'silent' approach, which is to quietly introduce a new rollover without any fanfare (Sony and new hi-fi models). The point is to manage new products and the process of displacement of old products *jointly* rather than separately.

Targeting

When it comes to targeting it is vital to consider adoption patterns. The following section will examine the two frameworks suggested by Rogers (1983) and Moore (1999, 2004a).

Rogers: The B2C perspective

Innovation strategy without any idea of buyer behaviour is a non-starter. Everett M. Rogers' (1983) seminal work on the adoption of innovation was the first to compellingly categorize consumers' readiness to adopt new products. Rogers identified five adopter types: innovators, early adopters, early majority, late majority, and laggards.

- **Innovators:** risk-taker and willing to try new ideas
- **Early adopters:** respected opinion leaders in the product field who are more cautious
- **Early majority:** do not seek leadership but are more likely to adopt than the average buyer
- **Late majority:** more risk-averse and will adopt an innovation after there has been a sizeable take-up already
- **Laggards:** highly risk-averse and traditional. Once an innovation has reached 'traditional status' they will come into the market

There are various implications arising from Rogers' typology. In order for an innovation to enter from the left of the market and move to the right it will need to have a relative market advantage. This might involve quality or convenience or anything that avoids the 'bad bits' of what it aims to supersede. For example, Recaro introduced a leading edge child seat for Porsche and Aston-Martin drivers.

Strategically it will also help if an innovation maximizes compatibility with the existing marketplace in terms of physical space (e.g., a relatively large home computer would no longer be a viable option for most customers), is able to hook into the current inventory of alternatives, links to other similar products, and needs no or few behavioural changes. For example, attempts to introduce non-QWERTY keyboards have met with universal failure. As noted above, convergent standards are key issues. Companies introducing new digital phones increasingly make them compatible with US, Asian, and European standards. One interesting variation on this theme used by Luz Engineering installs industrial solar heaters costing from £1 million to £3 million at no initial cost to buyers. Instead, they are required to take out a 20-year contract at a discount rate to buy steam at 350°F with the local power company.

It also helps if the innovation is not too complex, can be communicated readily, and can be tried and tested. Finally, Rogers argued that perceived risk needs to be as low as possible—in particular uncertainty of performance, consequences of failure, financial cost, physical health concerns, and effects on self-image.

Moore: The B2B perspective

Rogers' view of adoption largely held sway until the late 1990s when Geoffrey A. Moore introduced his ideas of 'chasm strategy' (1999, 2004a and see 2004b). Moore pointed out that innovative products do not normally slide in from the left-hand side and work their way steadily across to the right. Instead, they often meet with failure, which he categorized as falling into 'the chasm' (see Figure 7.1). Studies indicate that only about 10–12% of new products make it to market. Before going any further we must make the point that most disappear because of internal rather than external market processes:

- about 40% disappear after **business screening**
- a further 20% of innovations evaporate in **development**
- around 10% are dropped after **test marketing**

Once introduced to the marketplace around 30–50% of all new products fail to meet with commercial success, and for high-tech products the position may be considerably worse.

Crossing the chasm

Moore has argued that the fundamental issue for success in crossing the chasm is to understand the difference between the early and late markets. His perspective is B2B rather than

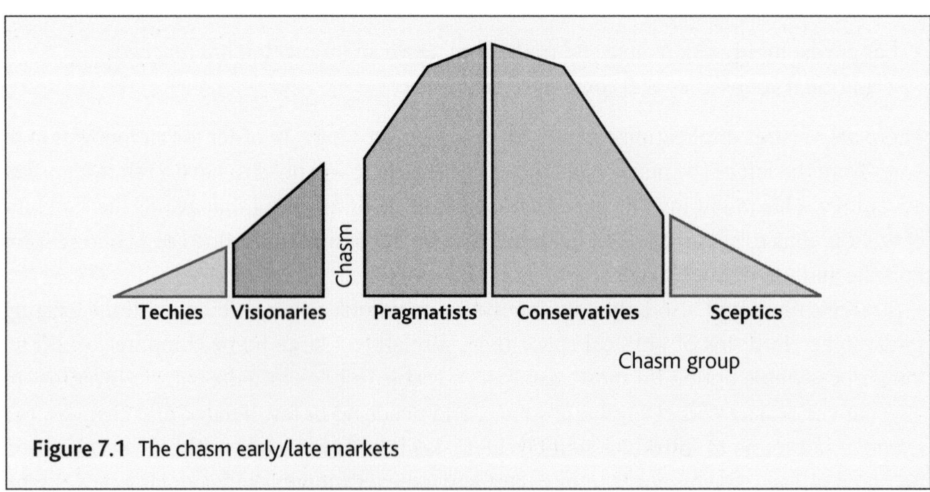

Figure 7.1 The chasm early/late markets

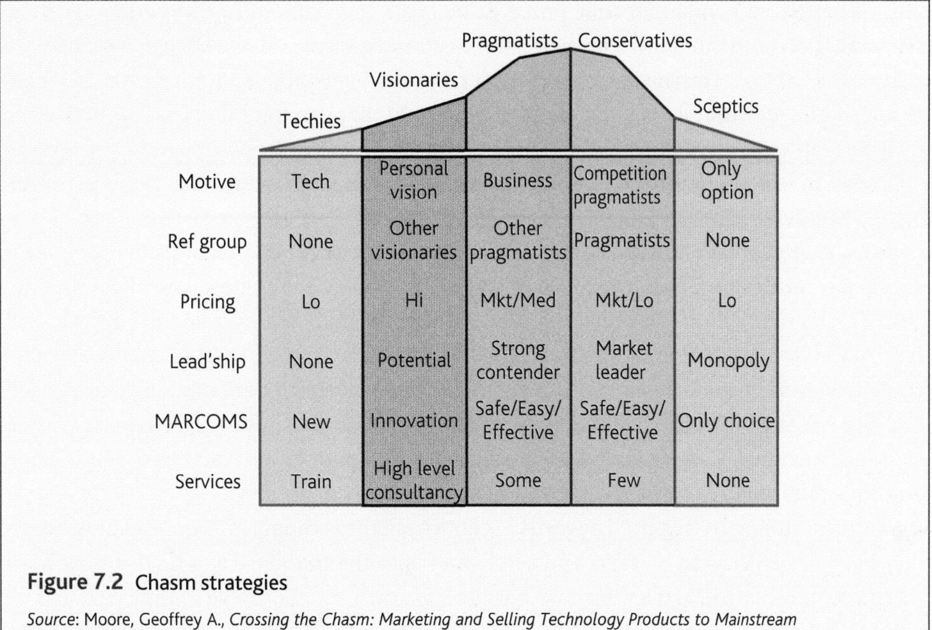

Figure 7.2 Chasm strategies

Source: Moore, Geoffrey A., *Crossing the Chasm: Marketing and Selling Technology Products to Mainstream Customers* (1999).

Rogers' B2C view although the implications of chasm marketing may be equally applicable to B2C markets (see Figure 7.2).

Techies: companies that are largely motivated by technology. They do not particularly reference the behaviour of other companies and are willing to purchase high-tech products at a relatively low price and assume the risk of debugging any problems. They are not bothered if the supplier is a market leader but will need considerable training especially with a discontinuous technology. Communications to this group should stress 'newness'.

Visionaries: companies that are looking to get ahead of rivals. They are not interested in technology for its own sake, rather they see new technology as a way of getting ahead. They reference other visionaries, will accept relatively high pricing, and will need high levels of consulting training. Communications to this group should stress innovation rather than newness and they are likely to respond better to companies that exhibit signs of potential leadership in using the new technology. If a company is unable to establish a business value for its innovation with visionaries, it is unlikely to cross the chasm.

Pragmatists: on the other side of the chasm sit the pragmatists. The failure of most high-tech products rests on their inability to resonate with the pragmatic company. Pragmatists are looking to fix a 'broken business process'. Essentially the problem posed by pragmatic companies is that if the innovation fails to fix something that they perceive as 'broken' they simply will not purchase the technology. They reference other pragmatic companies (not Techies or Visionaries), are prepared to pay a market price, and may need some training services. However, pragmatists are looking to buy from companies that they see as strong contenders for market leadership in the technology. They do not want to be left holding innovations from companies that prove to be 'also-rans' and will need communications stressing that the technology is proven, safe, easy, and effective. If you have it, a particularly safe execution is to emphasize market leadership. The new high-tech product is launched in an 'all out' way that leaves customers in no doubt that you intend to push your product into the marketplace. Microsoft's launch of Windows XP was a classic case of a concentrated approach to execution with a massive coordinated campaign across the globe with little expense spared.

Conservatives: behind the Pragmatists sit the conservative companies that, as you can guess, are much more risk-averse than Pragmatists. They see themselves in competition with Pragmatists, whom they also reference. However, their risk-aversion means that they tend to wait to see whether or not the technology 'stays the course', what standards develop, and which market leaders emerge. Pricing to this group needs to be at market price or lower and the communications required are broadly similar to those for the Pragmatists: safe, easy, and effective. Case studies work particularly well with Conservatives. Given the penetration of the technology by this point, Conservatives need few services.

Sceptics: similar to Rogers' 'Laggards', Sceptics are the companies at the end of the curve that have to be dragged 'kicking and screaming' into the market. They tend to buy when there is no alternative. What they have has broken down and they have to replace it and the new technology is the only alternative. For example a small firm of solicitors may be running their business with 5–10-year-old computers. They do the job and there is no reason to replace them except when they are uneconomic to replace. They do not reference other companies, need low prices, will tend to buy from the leading company in the market and are unlikely to need much in the way of communications or training services.

Two marketing campaigns

Moore suggests that the best strategy for crossing the chasm is to conduct two marketing campaigns.

The early market involves Techies and Visionaries. Techies can be used to make sure the innovation works and to 'iron out any bugs'. Visionaries should then be targeted and used to develop the whole product (see Figure 7.3) including pre- and post-sales issues, software, and peripherals. Visionaries will enable the company to find the competitive advantage within the technology and establish the basis of the appeal to the Pragmatists.

Moore argues that as Pragmatists reference each other a 'bowling alley strategy' is required to make headway with this segment. The idea is to target and dominate a specific market that has influence over other markets—hence the bowling alley analogy—one pin goes down and also (it is hoped) knocks down several other pins too. Thus when USDC developed an active-matrix flat panel screen, with each pixel linked to its own transistor, it targeted the world's leading air forces which it knew had a pressing need to adopt paper quality screens (Easingwood and Koustelos, 2000) and would influence outside commercial markets. Another example of targeting was NTT's Digital Photo System. The system enabled the transmission of digital pictures via mobile phones and was targeted at newspapers and insurance companies and later migrated out to other industries. Once the Pragmatic market has been penetrated and the chasm has been crossed, the Conservatives will then enter the

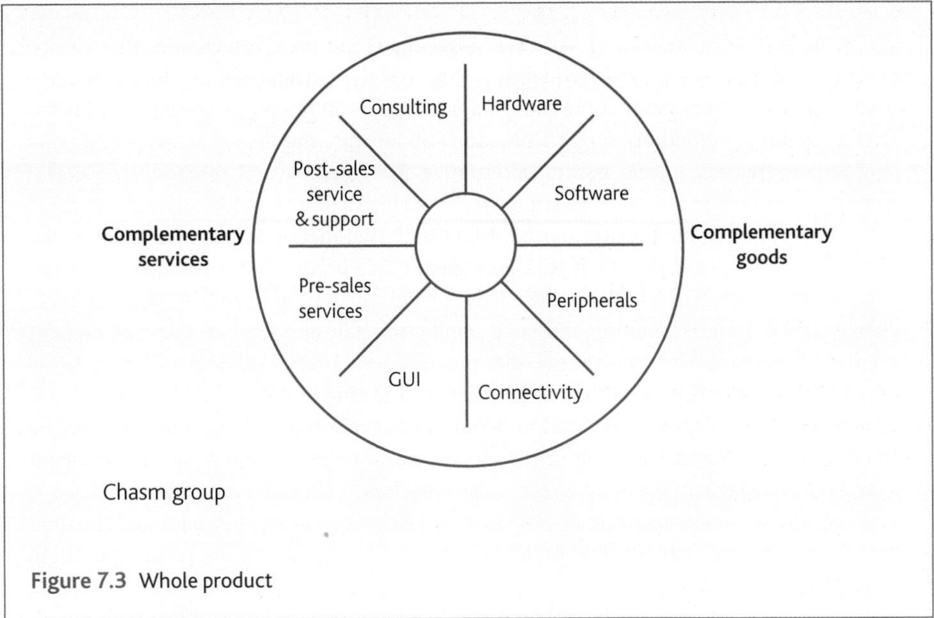

Figure 7.3 Whole product

market, buying from market leaders. Thus, industry opinion leaders have been successfully used by Compaq and NEC. Doctors are commonly used by pharmaceutical companies to influence general practitioners.

If you aren't the market leader

Innovation strategies that stress market dominance are all very well for the leading players in such markets, but what do you do if you are the smaller player in the marketplace? (See for example Mini Case Study 7.2.) Yoffie and Kwak (2002) have identified what they call a 'judo' strategy—an approach particularly well suited to small players in innovative markets.

MINI CASE STUDY 7.2 Innovation by a small player in the market: Wild Child

Like most mothers, Leanne Preston was horrified when she found that one of her three children, after complaining of an itchy scalp, had head lice. She knew that she insisted on regular hair washing and personal hygiene, yet the condition seemed so 'dirty'. A few days later the children brought home a note from their school, proclaiming that head lice were a problem at present, and advising that parents please check their children for the condition regularly and treat it when necessary.

Much to Leanne's dismay, she discovered that the chemical insecticide treatments recommended to her by both friends and pharmacists contained either Pyrethrins, Synthetic Pyrethroids (permethrin and bioallethrin), or Organophosphates (in the form

» of malathion or maldison). All these ingredients are toxic insecticides that can be potentially dangerous if used frequently or incorrectly, particularly for babies under 6 months of age, asthmatics, people suffering from scalp conditions, or pregnant or breast-feeding women. Something ought to be done about this, she thought. Leanne began a year-long search for a safe, natural alternative. Her reading and research in libraries throughout her home state of Western Australia led her to traditional Aboriginal medicine.

In early 1998 Leanne Preston started Wild Child Therapeutic Products. She called the first product she developed 'Quit Nits Treatment'. This product is a combination of natural oils and Australian wildflower essences that rids the hair of head lice (without harsh chemicals), as well as soothing and conditioning the hair and scalp. A short while later she developed Quit Nits Preventative that prevents a re-infestation of head lice. It is the only product of this nature in the marketplace. Her testing of the product, and the distribution of free samples to friends and to parents at her children's school demonstrated the treatment to be effective. Evidence from clinical trials suggested that a natural treatment such as Quit Nits is actually more effective at killing lice, highly efficient against their eggs, and also shows no adverse side effects. Late in 1998, Leanne Preston patented the Quit Nits Treatment and Quit Nits Preventative in Australia, and patents are pending for both products.

The human head louse, *Pediculus humanus*, is one of several kinds of lice with mouth parts specialized for sucking blood. The small, wingless insect has a flattened body about 3 mm long (1/8 in), with a claw on the end of each leg that helps it cling to the hair of its host. Females lay whitish eggs, called nits, once a day, attaching them to the hair with a sticky substance until they hatch in about a week. Head lice are unpleasant and undiscriminating guests. They infest people who bathe often as well as those who do not, leaving itchy red spots on their hosts' scalps.

Contrary to conventional belief, head lice are not the result of poor hygiene. No amount of washing with ordinary shampoo rids a child's hair of lice, or more especially, the nits. Indeed, lice actually thrive on clean hair, as hair that is free of the oils present in greasier, dirtier hair, allows the nits to attach more easily and permanently. Head lice are especially prevalent among young children, and move between young heads with ease, particularly as young children tend to play in close proximity. They often hug each other in play, or pore over a book or game together, and the lice jump easily from one head to another.

Leanne Preston worked hard to establish a distribution network through pharmacies, chemists, and health stores. Indeed, the Wild Child products captured a 15% share of the Australian market within the first 12 months of the firm's operation. Observers saw this as a spectacular result for a 'cottage industry' which was still based out of Leanne Preston's home in the Western Australian tourist town of Margaret River. In June 1999, Leanne Preston was a finalist in the Challenge Bank Female Business Owner Award, recognition of her achievements so far.

The reaction of the larger Australian pharmaceutical companies was not unexpected. Pfizer quickly developed and launched an alternative product called Neutra-lice in early 1999. However, Leanne Preston is unconcerned, and believes that the product has only cannibalized existing insecticidal head lice treatments. Quit Nits continued to steadily gain market share throughout 1999. »

» Consumer response to the Wild Child's head lice product range exceeded Leanne Preston's expectations. Many parents tracked Leanne Preston down personally to congratulate her on developing a natural alternative for head lice treatments, and to encourage her to develop other healthcare products for children.

A range of baby care products has been developed, again embracing Wild Child's company philosophy of utilizing natural remedies to treat healthcare problems. These products were scheduled for release in early 2000, again to be distributed through the pharmaceutical network. Early negotiations indicate that supermarket chain Coles Myer is also interested in carrying the products.

In addition to the Australian market, Wild Child has received numerous letters, e-mail and telephone calls from around the world (in particular, the United Kingdom and New Zealand), all requesting further information and many wishing to purchase the Quit Nits product.

However, Preston remarks: 'Whilst the response and support from Australia and potential distributors has been overwhelming, unfortunately the investment required for the cost of entry into these markets is at present prohibitive for Wild Child. This is not to say that a physical presence within these markets is not possible in the future, and I would dearly love it to occur. Ideally, I would like Wild Child products to be available in overseas markets because I really believe in them. Also I would like to be there before a competitor is able to undermine the products' unique advantages and benefits.'

Currently, Wild Child's promotional efforts tend to be very restricted. As Leanne Preston explains: 'First, demand for our products currently exceeds supply. Second, we still have limited resources, so an extensive promotional campaign is beyond our means. Third, we simply don't have the time to devote lots of attention to promotion—I would rather put that effort into the development of new products and the improvement of our existing range.' The company does have a promotional brochure which is distributed through retail outlets and in response to mailed requests, and there has been limited advertising in certain specialized outlets. Wild Child has also gained a lot of favourable press coverage.

Source: Caroline Stewart prepared this case under the supervision of Professor Leyland Pitt, Faculty of Business Administration, Simon Fraser University as the basis for analysis and class discussion and not to illustrate either effective or ineffective handling of an administrative situation. Reproduced with permission.

Yoffie and Kwak focus upon the case of Palm Inc. which they argue provides a powerful example of judo strategy at work. Judo strategy relies on speed, agility, and creative thinking, and makes it difficult for stronger rivals to compete. Judo strategy is an approach to competition based on skill rather than size or strength and uses the three principles of 'movement', 'defining space', and 'speed'.

Movement

One of the key tactics in movement is the 'puppy dog play'. In essence keep a low profile until you are strong enough to fight. Palm's first handheld organizer was introduced at a low key and exclusive industry trade show in early 1996. It sold moderately well with 10,000 units per month for about five months but, and this was key, it sold primarily to self-rated computer experts earning $100,000 plus per annum. When they then bought it for their friends and colleagues for Christmas, sales began to take off. All the while Palm management downplayed its success: 'a little organiser that happens to connect to your PC'. By positioning it as a companion to the PC they hoped to keep out of Microsoft's sights. Instead of a platform, the Palm was a device. According to Microsoft's CEO, Steve Ballmer, Palm didn't catch the company's attention for at least two years.

Define the competitive space

The next judo tactic is to define the competitive space. A race that pitched the PDA as the digital equivalent of a Swiss Army Knife would have given ground to bigger and stronger competitors. Instead, Palm kept it simple with a concept based on a calendar and an address book. No wireless communications or spreadsheets that would have favoured the big players were emphasized. To keep it simple Palm integrated its software and hardware design, whereas Microsoft developed the software and then 'threw it over the fence to the hardware manufacturers'.

Follow through fast

The next tactic is to follow through fast. As Microsoft began to enter the market and refine its product with Windows CE in late 1997, Palm realized that it had to maintain and, if possible, increase its lead over its rivals. It did this by fairly moderate innovation but with a strong focus on design, functionality, and low prices. Typical Windows CE devices retailed for about twice the price of Palm's and offered lots of features that consumers were not too bothered about and had less attractive designs. Meanwhile Palm introduced the Professional, the Personal, and the III, IIIx, V, and VII between 1997 and 1999. Critically, by building market share Palm encouraged developers to create a multitude of applications for the Palm operating system and few others. This process was aided by the quiet introduction of a Palm software developer kit in 1996, making the code open.

Palm is still the main player in the market and has recently merged with Treo. This is a perfect match given Palm's marketing expertise and Treo's product competency. However, the Windows CE operating system and merging of mobile/PDA technology has left Palm slightly on the back foot compared to rivals such as HP. It will be interesting to see how Palm's judo strategy finally plays out.

Innovation 'modes'

Despite strong contentions to the contrary by such companies as Sony, very little technological innovation is developed without some sense of a strategy. Once a new innovation or development has reached the market, people's perceptions and expectations are often changed (as with flat screen televisions or photocopying), and the innovations often re-shape how people live or work. Market success normally requires an overall strategic framework.

Overall, companies learn from markets, and the customers learn from new technologies. For any organization the degree of focus on either innovation and/or the customer can vary. There are, therefore, as shown in Figure 7.4, four strategic options of low/high market

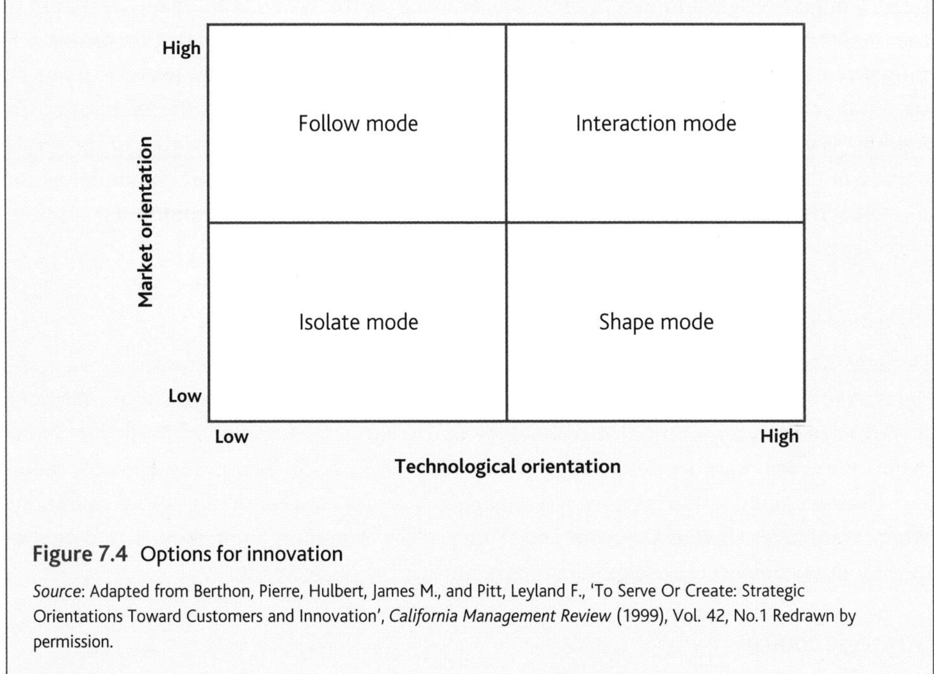

Figure 7.4 Options for innovation

Source: Adapted from Berthon, Pierre, Hulbert, James M., and Pitt, Leyland F., 'To Serve Or Create: Strategic Orientations Toward Customers and Innovation', *California Management Review* (1999), Vol. 42, No.1 Redrawn by permission.

orientation matched with low/high innovation orientation (the framework in Figure 7.4 is modified from the work of Berthon, Hulbert, and Pitt, 1999).

Isolate mode

The so-called 'isolate' mode (bottom left of the quadrant) is where an organization has both a low innovation orientation and a low market orientation. The flows between customer and technology are almost non-existent and technology either stagnates or is developed for its own sake. Stagnation or evolution occurs separately from the market. Such organizations are introverted and may be exemplified by the British automobile and motorcycle industry of the late 1960s and throughout the 1970s. British Leyland introduced innovations, but these were often tangential to market needs and preferences.

Follow mode

The low innovation but high market orientation organization is in the 'follow' mode (top left) of the quadrant. Here technology is used in response to the needs and wants of the customer and may be seen with the development of the BMW 1 Series or the Courtyard concept by Marriott Hotels. All are examples of companies designing products based on what customers want.

Shape mode

Organizations in the high innovation but low market orientation mode are in the 'shape' (bottom right) part of the quadrant. Shaping is where a company applies a technology that defines human needs and determines the nature of customer demand. A recent shaper in the market would be the Apple iPod—a technological entrant that has disproportionately influenced the criteria by which later entrants, such as the Creative Zen, have been judged by. Berthon, Hulbert, and Pitt suggest two distinct forms of shaping. 'Definers' lead the market, as with Chrysler's minivan of the early 1980s, and Compaq's forging of the server market in the 1990s. 'Influencers', on the other hand, shape markets but do not define the market or dominate it. For example the Apple Macintosh shaped expectations of computers without leading the market.

Interaction mode

Organizations that achieve a high market orientation married to high innovation are in the 'interaction' mode (top right) of the quadrant. This is where a true dialogue occurs between an organization's application of technology and what customers want. Such interaction occurred before mass markets arose of course, such as with men's and women's tailoring. However, interaction is being applied apace with the concept of one-to-one marketing where companies such as Dell.com and iTunes allow customers to prepare their own specifications of computers and compilations of music CDs, respectively.

Strategic choice

Which mode to choose? It is difficult to be prescriptive as each has its good points—even isolation might have its proponents in some circumstances! A 'shaping' strategy would suit a rapidly evolving technology such as genetics, but given the power of large supermarkets, suppliers of fast-moving consumer goods (FMCG) might be best to 'follow'. Overall, it is likely that interaction would be most popular. In particular, of the four, interaction is the most likely to maximize prices and profitability. Organizations that use technology in an interactive way and develop customized offerings reduce customer price pressures. For example, with customization car dealers are likely to reduce the need to offer discounts to close a sale. The next section will focus on this strategy, and will explore the factors that affect an organization's ability to offer customization.

Customization

Mass customization is similar to mass production in terms of its basic structure, but there are significant differences. Instead of selecting one variety of product, the consumer provides unique information so that the product can be tailored to varying degrees. This means that the production process has to be flexible in order to tailor the product or service in the required way. Take the car industry. Only about 7% of cars in the USA are 'customized' or, as it is known in the car industry, 'built to order' (BTO). By contrast, BTO cars in Europe account for 20% of all cars sold. This is partly a reflection of the smaller size of dealers in Europe (given land prices) and the higher proportion of premium sales.

One major benefit of following a customized innovation strategy is that there are no finished goods inventories for producers. On the other hand customers inevitably have to wait longer than they might otherwise. Technologically the differences between mass customization and mass production are only matters of degree. The key differences are the requirements for richer information flows and added process flexibility. Unfortunately these provide significant barriers to the growth of mass customization as a primary innovation strategy for most organizations. There are essentially four key capabilities in mass customization (Agrawal, Kumaresh, and Mercer, 2001; Swaminathan, 2001; see also Duray et al., 2000), namely 'elicitation', 'process flexibility', 'logistics', and 'inventory', which form the boundaries to any organization's strategy to mass customize.

Elicitation

Elicitation requires some means of interacting with customers in order to find out their requirements. This is a difficult process. In order to elicit information, companies are presented with the problem of enabling customers to decide what they want. Sometimes customers are certain about what they want, but often they are not. People make selections from menus. However, depending upon the nature of the product concerned they might find the process frustrating and give up without buying anything. This is particularly likely with low-priced and standardized everyday products. Physical measurement makes elicitation more difficult. For example, when Levi Strauss experimented with mass customization of women's jeans, their sales staff had to take measurements in stores as body-scanning equipment is still some way off. There is some experimentation with prototypes but the technology remains fraught with difficulties. Nevertheless, such things as 3-D views of sofas and 3-D body images that enable people to 'try on' clothes online from catalogues have been developed (see **www.myvirtualmodel.com**).

Process flexibility

Process flexibility involves the use of production technology so that the product can be tailored according to the customer's information. This presents another challenge. One-dimensional processes are relatively straightforward. For example, a bicycle frame can be customized by size and easily cut as required. Two-dimensional printing and printing-like technology are also relatively easy to undertake as printing and patterns involves zero dimension dots, one-dimensional lines, and two-dimensional patterns. However, three-dimensional processes are much less flexible. Robots are slow and expensive, so three-dimensional mass customization, such as for car parts, is a long way off.

Logistics

Logistics involves the processing and distribution stages so that the identity of each customer is maintained right through to delivery of the customized product. Logistics can present a considerable constraint to customization. Thus, Levi Strauss took several years to develop washable bar codes to enable them to customize jeans and sew and wash them in bulk while tagging each order.

Inventory

Customization raises the question of how much inventory to carry to guarantee required service levels? How will the equipment cope with capacity? What levels of components will be needed? How do you manage the large number of suppliers required? With the shorter product life cycles in customization, how do you manage inventory phasing, marketing, and bringing on suppliers?

On the demand side, the key implication for inventory relates to sales forecasting. Establishing aggregate demand for product A (e.g., a Toyota Corolla) is one thing, but establishing accurate forecasts for sub-set configurations of product A (e.g., an LX Model with air-conditioning) is another. Problems mount when there are several products (B, C, D . . .) with their own possible configurations, and especially when each product's sales could have an effect on the sales of others.

Car industry

The car industry presents an interesting case for customization and demonstrates the pros and cons of a marketing strategy for such an innovation strategy, rather than headline cases such as computers or the music business. A car company using customization as its main innovation strategy would have to leave plants idle during troughs of demand and operational changes would also be required. For example paint shops currently run batch operations to reduce costs and to minimize emissions and waste. Such economies and environmental benefits would be lost if colours were customized. Additionally, customization would also require delivering a mix of components according to individual orders rather than thousands of components as one batch.

US dealers might also resist BTO changes as they mainly feel that large numbers of cars on display at a showroom demonstrate that they are 'healthy' and open for business. BTO would also require radical changes to labour organization and IT systems that might be painful to implement. Finally, from a customer perspective, it remains unclear how far they are willing to trade off delivery times of up to six months against customization.

Implementation

There are five primary approaches to implementing mass customization involving the degree of standardization.

Partial customization is the most common approach. However, it can lead to a degree of cannibalization if noticeable. For example, two cars might share the same wire harnesses for their audio systems without consumers being aware of this, whereas consumers would easily notice if the dashboards were the same.

Process customization requires firms to store inventory in a semi-finished form to be customized to the specific order. For example, Honda redesigned its cars so that saloons, 4 × 4 s and sports models all come from the same production line.

Product customization involves offering a large variety of products while stocking relatively few and thus being prepared to substitute higher-specification products. For example, Avis and other car-hire companies substitute more expensive models when less expensive ones are out of supply.

Procurement customization occurs where there is commonality in part and equipment purchasing across a wide variety of products. For example, PC manufacturers can aggregate their demand across a wide variety of products.

Finally, an ingenious alternative is to offer '**virtual customization**' (see Swaminathan, 2001; Papathanassiou, 2004). This involves setting up a network via the Internet or channel. For example, in the case of the car industry if customers can be offered access to dealers' cars, cars in transit, cars on the assembly line, or cars scheduled for production, the chances are that they will find the one with the right colour and options for them. Thus, customization or BTO, as coined by Forrester Research (Agrawal et al., 2001), is replaced by the ability to 'locate to order'. Customers do not care whether the product was especially built for them or not or where it was found in the supply chain as long it has the features that they want. Virtual customization via shops or the Internet may be a strategy with considerable appeal not restricted to the car industry.

Conclusion

Innovation can be a winning component of any marketing strategy. The vast majority of today's brand leaders have introduced breakthrough innovations at some point in their histories. This chapter has focused on the use of innovation and product development, but the reality is that the vast majority of companies do not see these as the panacea in the marketplace. To be fair, unplanned and untargeted innovation simply leads to what has become known as 'innoflation'—a position where new products and services are launched into the marketplace at a frenzied pace with very little impact. Consumers just get confused, company supply chains overheat, and the end result is a poor return on investment. Study after study has shown that at heart most consumers are loyal to a core of products and services in most markets and so if there is to be any innovation it needs to be focused upon existing brands. Today too many organizations take a risk-averse stance and would rather stay with the tried and tested and buy out any competitors who appear to have hit upon 'blockbuster' innovations in the marketplace. As Airbus, Dell, Dyson, e-Bay, easyJet, and Tesco have shown (to name but a few) challenging or reinventing what you offer through innovation can hold the key to market success. This chapter has shown that what is required is a measured and planned approach to innovation and its potential impact on costs and/or differentiation in the marketplace. It is to be hoped that more companies will reduce their concentration on immediate competitors and consider wider lateral innovation, based upon new definitions of market needs and wants. For many companies, the wisest strategy would be to include innovation in their marketing strategy rather than to focus on best value alone. At the bare minimum all companies should regularly review their innovation strategy against current and anticipated market needs and wants.

Summary

Product innovation and development can play a pivotal role in marketing strategy. Central is the concept of new product development (NPD), a creative activity towards which there are many different approaches, such as systematic invention thinking. Particular strategic issues to consider are market preparation and product rollovers, which can have a dramatic impact on product innovation and development. Strategic frameworks that can provide considerable insight include Rogers' product adoption curve and Moore's concept of 'crossing the chasm'. Smaller players in the market should consider a judo strategy. An organization's overall innovation mode is worth careful thought. Customization is becoming an increasingly important area of marketing strategy.

KEY TERMS

New-to-the-world Significantly new product or service market introductions that are often discontinuous.

Innovation Subsequent changes and adaptations to 'new-to-the-world' introduction. 'Innovare' is the Latin verb meaning to change or to alter.

NPD New product development.

Toolkit strategy Enabling customers to take significant control over the NPD process.

Systematic inventive thinking An NPD system based on the work of Genrich Altshuller to manipulate idea generation and stimulate relevant creativity.

Market preparation Market strategies to ensure that new-to-the-world products do not shock consumers.

Product rollovers Displacement of existing products by new.

Adoption patterns Differences in the propensity of customer types to adopt innovations.

Judo strategy An innovation strategy used by relatively smaller companies to outwit larger rivals based upon skill rather than size or strength.

Customization Tailoring products and services to suit individual needs and wants.

DISCUSSION QUESTIONS

1. Briefly outline and describe the umbrella of activities included in product innovation and development.
2. Are there any particular kinds of innovation that are more important than others or does it depend upon market conditions?
3. Toolkit strategy is a growing trend amongst B2B product developers. Do you think such an approach to innovation might work in any particular B2C markets?
4. Apply the five patterns of systematic inventive thinking (subtraction, multiplication, division, task unification, and attribute dependency change) to the iPod. Can you create what you regard to be a viable new product that adds value?
5. Can you name two or three products that have recently failed to cross the chasm? To what extent do you think lack of interest from pragmatists was the problem?
6. What are the major advantages and disadvantages of customization?

ONLINE RESOURCE CENTRE

Visit the Online Resource Centre for this book for lots of interesting additional material at: **www.oxfordtextbooks.co.uk/orc/west/**

REFERENCES AND FURTHER READING

Agrawal, Mani, T. V. Kumaresh, and Glenn A. Mercer (2001), 'The False Promise of Mass Customization', *The McKinsey Quarterly*, 3, pp. 62–71.

Berthon, Pierre, James M. Hulbert, and Leyland F. Pitt (1999), 'To Serve Or Create: Strategic Orientations Toward Customers And Innovation', *California Management Review*, 42 (1), pp. 37–58.

Billington, Corey, Hau L. Lee, and Christopher S. Tang (1998), 'Successful Strategies For Product Rollovers', *Sloan Management Review*, Spring.

Duray R., P. T. Ward, G. W. Milligan, and W. L. Berry (2000), 'Approaches to Mass Customization: Configurations and Empirical Validation', *Journal of Operations Management*, 18 (6), pp. 605–25.

Easingwood, Chris, and Anthony Koustelos (2000), 'Marketing High Technology: Preparation, Targeting, Positioning, Execution', *Business Horizons*, 43 (3), pp. 27–34.

Goldenberg, Jacob, Roni Horowitz, Amnon Levav, and David Mazursky (2003), 'Finding Your Innovation Sweet Spot', *Harvard Business Review*, March, pp. 120–9.

Moore, Geoffrey, A. (1999), *Crossing the Chasm: Marketing and Selling Technology Products to Mainstream Customers* (New York: Capstone Publishing).

Moore, Geoffrey, A. (2004a), *Inside the Tornado: Strategies for Developing, Leveraging, and Surviving Hypergrowth Markets* (New York: Harper Business).

Moore, Geoffrey, A. (2004b), 'Darwin and the Demon: Innovating within Established Enterprises,' *Harvard Business Review*. July–August, pp. 86–93.

Papathanassiou, E. A. (2004), 'Mass Customisation: Management Approaches and Internet Opportunities in the Financial Sector in the UK', *International Journal of Information Management*, 24 (5), pp. 387–99.

Rogers, Everett M. (1983), *Diffusion of Innovations*, 3rd edn (New York: Free Press).

Thomke, Stefan, and Eric von Hippel (2002), 'Customers as Innovators: A New Way to Create Value', *Harvard Business Review*, April, pp. 74–81.

Swaminathan, Jayashankar M. (2001), 'Enabling Customization Using Standardized Operations', *California Management Review*, 43 (3), Spring, pp. 25–35.

Yoffie, David B., and Mary Kwak (2002), 'Mastering Strategic Movement at Palm', *Mit Sloan Management Review*, January 2002, pp. 47–53.

Zipkin, Paul (2001), 'The Limits of Mass Customization', *MIT Sloan Management Review*, 42, Spring, pp. 81–7.

KEY ARTICLE ABSTRACTS

Vorhies, Douglas W., and Michael Harker (1999), 'Capabilities and Performance Advantages of Market-Driven Firms', *European Journal of Marketing*, 33 (11/12), pp. 1171–1202. © Emerald Group Publishing Limited. **http://www.emeraldinsight.com**

This is a useful paper. It places NPD and innovation within the context of the marketing mix and assesses the relationship to marketing orientation.

Abstract: Although progress has been made in understanding market-driven businesses from a theoretical perspective, relatively few empirical studies have addressed the capabilities needed to become market driven and the performance advantages accruing to firms possessing these capabilities. One of the barriers faced has been in defining what is meant by the term 'market driven'. This paper develops a multidimensional measure useful for assessing the degree to which a firm is market driven. The paper presents evidence that market-driven business units developed higher levels of six vital marketing capabilities (in the areas of market research, pricing, product development, channels, promotion, and market management) than their less market-driven rivals and significantly outperformed these rival business units on four measures of organizational performance.

Nijssen, Ed J., and Karin F. M. Lieshout (1995), 'Awareness, Use and Effectiveness of Models and Methods for New Product Development', *European Journal of Marketing*, 29 (10), pp. 27–45.

The following article points out that awareness of methods and models of NPD and innovation (e.g., brainstorming, concept testing, and conjoint analysis) differ greatly. The authors found an overall penetration level of only 30% for NPD methods and models.

Abstract: The article focuses on awareness, use and effectiveness of models, and methods for new product development. The strategic importance of new product development (NPD) and new product models and methods. A large number of models and methods have been introduced to improve a company's performance in NPD. These models and methods include brainstorming focus groups, in-home use tests, limited roll-outs. As NPD has become a strategic necessity for companies and the commercial success rate of new products is still low, high adoption and diffusion of new product models and methods may be expected. Even though the use of new product models and methods in themselves will not guarantee success, their use may complement a company's NPD efforts and may assist them to become more successful. New product models and methods may help to identify problems at an early stage and assist in directing the NPD effort in the right direction. Despite the positive influences these models and methods may have on companies' efforts, major potential users are unaware of the existence of these models and methods, they experience an unsupportive organizational culture for their use, or they have used them for a (short) period but have then decided to abandon their use.

Hart, Susan (1993), 'Dimensions of Success in New Product Development: an Exploratory Investigation', *Journal of Marketing Management*, 9 (1), pp. 23–41.

This paper indicates that there is not much evidence that NPD success or failure is measured financially.

Abstract: As a key element in survival and sustaining growth, the constant development and re-development of products has been the subject of many academic and consulting group studies. The specific focus of these studies has often been to identify and describe the critical success factors which determine the outcome of new product developments. In order to fulfil their objectives, the studies have focused on many aspects of the management of NPD programmes in companies, and attempted to relate them to a number of alternative outcomes. This has called for the measurement of 'success' itself. Unfortunately, there is very little consensus amongst the studies regarding how best to operationalize 'success', and researchers have employed a variety of measures, focused on different levels of analysis, sought data from different sources, and used different data collection methods. This paper examines the performance measures used in several major NPD studies and shows how success 'measures' have been treated as financial and non-financial. In addition, attention is drawn to the problems inherent in the different definitions of success. Finally, using data from an empirical survey, the relationship between financial and non-financial outcomes is examined.

END OF CHAPTER 7 CASE STUDY

'The 1997 Asian Crisis forced Samsung to switch its focus from cheap consumer electronics to the top end of the market'

When the Industrial Design Society of America gathered in June for its annual award ceremony—the Oscars of the industrial design world—one company won more prizes than any other.

Samsung Electronics, the South Korean manufacturer, received gold medals for a 'revolutionary' portable printer and an 'elegant' flat- screen monitor. Two Samsung flat-screen TVs and a microwave oven won silvers. Only Apple, the US technology company renowned for its hip designs, has won more IDSA awards than Samsung over the past five years.

With a market capitalisation of $57bn (€47bn, £32bn) and net profits last year of $5.2bn, Samsung has emerged over the past few years as one of the world's most powerful and fastest-growing technology companies. The design accolades show how its consumer electronics, once dismissed as cheap imitations of more sophisticated Japanese products, have come to be among the most innovative and desirable on the market. But the company is more than a maker of sought-after high-street goods: it is also the world's largest producer of two of the main components used in digital devices—liquid crystal displays (LCDs) and memory chips.

Analysts expect Samsung to double its profits this year, putting it alongside the likes of Citigroup, General Electric and Exxon Mobil as one of the handful of global companies that generate more than $10bn of annual net profits. Samsung is forecast to overtake Motorola this year as the world's second-largest maker of mobile phones after Nokia, and is challenging Japanese groups for leadership in flat-screen TVs and computer equipment.

Executives at Samsung's headquarters overlooking 600-year-old Namdaemun Gate—once the main entrance to central Seoul—believe the group's combination of businesses will allow it to benefit as the world shifts away from analogue technology—which was dominated by Japanese and western companies—and embraces digital products. 'There is no company better positioned than Samsung to benefit from the convergence of digital technologies,' trumpets Chu Woosik, head of the company's investor relations.

Samsung's earnings have allowed it to invest more in its production facilities than most rivals, fuelling rapid growth in capacity and efficiency. The company has made Won15,680bn ($13.6bn, €11.3bn, £7.7bn) of capital expenditure in the past two years and plans a further Won8,940bn this year. But Samsung's expansion is not without risks. Competition is intensifying, with Japanese and western technology companies fighting back, Taiwanese and other Korean companies racing to catch up and rivals emerging in China.

'Samsung's earnings momentum is slowing,' says a western fund manager. 'The period of double- or triple-digit earnings growth is coming to an end.'

Samsung's success stems from a radical restructuring in the late 1990s, when the company was a struggling maker of cheap consumer electronics. Lee Kun-hee, Samsung's »

» chairman, recognized there was no future for price-led, volume manufacturing in South Korea as the country's cost base increased and competition intensified from China.

The 1997 Asian financial crisis, when South Korea was forced to accept a $58bn bailout from the International Monetary Fund, exposed the weaknesses in the country's corporate sector. In response, Samsung cut its workforce by one-third, sold off unviable businesses and slashed debts.

'Our history was based on manufacturing volume and market share, not profitability and technology,' says Eric Kim, executive vice-president of marketing. 'Left to our own devices we would not have made such a fundamental shift but the IMF crisis forced our hand. We realised we could no longer compete on price at the low end of the market. We had to improve our brand, design and technology.'

Mr Kim recalls the scepticism inside and outside the company about Samsung's ability to execute such a transformation. But today the company sits near the top end of every market in which it competes, with its reputation for technical innovation and trend-setting design.

David Steel, vice-president of marketing for the company's digital media business, says much of Samsung's creativity has come from its four design centres in London, Tokyo, San Francisco and one elsewhere in Seoul. 'That's where you find the guys with green hair and pony tails,' he says. 'We've given our designers a lot of influence within the company.'

Samsung has become the second-most valuable corporate brand in Asia, worth $12.6bn, just $200 m less than Sony, according to Interbrand, the brand consultancy. Mr Kim says the timing of Samsung's restructuring was crucial. It came as the technology industry was expanding rapidly in the late 1990s. At the time, Samsung seemed to be missing the party. In fact, it was busy making the aggressive cost cuts and difficult strategic choices its competitors would face a couple of years later when the technology sector crashed. This helps explain why Samsung has grown so rapidly over the past four years while many of its rivals have, until recently, been retrenching.

Samsung's turnround also came as digital technology started to replace analogue. This opened the way for a range of new consumer goods, such as MP3 players and DVDs, and more sophisticated versions of existing goods, such as TVs and mobile phones. In addition, it promised huge markets for components such as memory chips and LCDs. Samsung had relied on second-hand technology from Japan. But the switch to the faster more versatile digital provided an opportunity to become more innovative.

'It would have been impossible for a newcomer to catch up in analogue because the incumbents had so much experience,' says Mr Kim. 'But digital technology was a blank canvas.'

Samsung was also helped by strong domestic demand for digital products. South Koreans were among the earliest, most enthusiastic adopters of digital technology, boasting the world's highest usage of broadband internet and wireless data services.

White goods and other low-end products that had once been Samsung's mainstay were shunted to the periphery while investment was focused on memory chips, LCDs, mobile phones and other digital consumer goods. Samsung's diversification across four main product fields set it apart from competitors. Some analysts, used to criticizing South Korean companies for excessive diversification, questioned whether Samsung could match more specialist companies. Gradually, however, critics have been won over. 'Samsung has proved me wrong,' says Dan Heyler, an analyst at Merrill Lynch in Hong »

» Kong. 'They have done a great job of reducing earnings volatility from their cyclical business through diversification.'

Another advantage of Samsung's business model is the reliable supply of chips and LCDs it guarantees to the company's consumer goods businesses. Motorola, which spun off its semiconductor division in July, suffered shortages of chips last year, while Japanese TV-makers are fretting about their reliance on Korean and Taiwanese manufacturers for LCDs. Mr Steel says Samsung's structure makes sense in an era when different technologies are converging. 'People ask why we have all these different businesses. But these are the core building blocks of digital products: chips, wireless technology and displays. Each division complements the other,' he says.

Jae Lee, analyst at Daiwa Securities, says that for all the talk of innovative technology and branding, Samsung's biggest advantage is more prosaic: low costs.

This has little to do with the company's home base. South Korea is no longer a cheap place to do business. But heavy investment in capacity and technology has made Samsung's production lines among the most efficient in the industry. In semiconductors, Samsung is rapidly increasing the size of its silicon wafers from 200 mm to 300 mm, reducing production costs by one-third as each can be used to produce more microchips. In LCD, Samsung has formed a joint-venture with Sony to build the industry's first so-called seventh-generation production line, allowing more screens to be cut from each piece of glass. 'They have invested a lot of money to make sure they are always ahead of their competitors,' says Mr Lee. 'The strategy is to be the lowest-cost producer in each of its markets. When the markets turn bad, Samsung is still making money.'

Samsung has positioned itself at the top end of its markets where margins are highest. In mobile phones, it specializes in internet-enabled, colour-screen camera phones, with an average selling price of $176, compared with Nokia's $135 in the second quarter. In LCD, it is aiming for leadership in large-sized TV screens, leaving Taiwanese manufacturers to make the bulk of lower-value computer monitors. In semiconductors, it has diversified from its core dynamic random-access memory production into more sophisticated chips such as NAND flash, used in many digital devices. However, Samsung's margins are under pressure. After more than doubling to 27.8 per cent in the first quarter of this year, operating profit margins shrank in the second quarter to 24.9 per cent. This was largely caused by falling prices of mobile phones as Samsung seeks more sales in the highly competitive US market. Margins are expected to remain tight as Nokia seeks to protect its eroding market leadership, while the Japanese-Swedish Sony Ericsson, South Korea's LG Electronics and other Asian rivals become more powerful.

In LCDs, Samsung expects prices to fall by up to one-third in the second half because of increasing supplies. Multi-billion-dollar LCD plants are springing up across East Asia, but sluggish uptake of flat-screen TVs has so far failed to justify the investments.

Capacity is also growing fast in the memory industry as rival manufacturers race to build 300 mm wafer fabrication plants and jump on the NAND flash bandwagon. Much of the competition is coming from resurgent Japan, whose electronics industry is seeking to reassert its superiority over Korea and Taiwan in technology and quality.

Meanwhile, Chinese manufacturers are moving aggressively into the sector—although Samsung, which has opened several production plants in China, sees the country's low-cost manufacturing base and domestic market as an opportunity rather than a threat. »

Mr Steel says price volatility is inevitable in cyclical technology markets but urges investors to keep their eye on the long term. Taking LCDs as an example, he says lower prices are necessary to trigger demand for flat-screen TVs, which now cost thousands of dollars each. 'There's a lot of analyst talk about supply gluts and slow demand but we're at a very early stage of the game,' he says. 'It's going to be bumpy but these are long-term investments.'

There are bound to be casualties in the race for leadership of volatile and unproven markets for digital technology. Samsung is calculating that by investing big and moving quickly it will be one of the survivors. But the company is not taking success for granted. 'If we begin to coast or relax, everyone is going to come back at us,' says Mr Steel. 'You can think of a lot of companies that have had their time and let it slip. The message from our top management is: we're not going to let that happen to us.'

The family ties that trouble shareholders

Samsung is best known around the world as a consumer electronics brand. But technology is just part of its sprawling business empire that ranges from shipbuilding, engineering and chemicals to financial services, hotels and a theme park.

The group is the biggest of the family-controlled conglomerates, known as chaebol, that dominate the South Korean economy. Samsung is nearly four times larger than its nearest rivals, LG and SK, and accounts for about one-third of the country's stock market capitalisation.

At the head of Samsung's controlling family is 62-year-old Lee Kun-hee, one of the most powerful men in South Korea, who controls the group through a complicated web of shareholdings that tie together its 27 subsidiaries.

This opaque structure worries minority shareholders, who have seen their returns eroded from the widespread chaebol practice of using profitable businesses to subsidise weaker affiliates and fund risky expansion.

Samsung has largely avoided the recent financial crises that have engulfed other chaebol, such as Daewoo and Hyundai. But the group's flagship electronics company was forced to help bail out Samsung Card, its troubled credit card affiliate, last year and suffered heavy losses from a failed expansion into carmaking in the 1990s.

Concern about corporate governance partly explains why shares in Samsung Electronics, by far the biggest part of the group, trade on a price to earnings ratio of about 6, compared with Intel's 19 and Nokia's 13. At such a discount to the sector they are very cheap.

'Samsung's corporate governance has improved a lot. But it still isn't good enough for a company of its size and global stature,' says Jang Hasung, professor of finance at Korea university. '[Samsung Electronics] plays a big brother role in the group. People see it as a cash cow. When there is a problem elsewhere in the group, people think [Samsung Electronics] will sort it out.'

Mr Lee directly owns only 1.66 per cent of Samsung Electronics but indirectly controls a further 10 per cent through affiliates. Meanwhile, the chairman's son, Jae-yong, is being groomed to replace his father.

However, Jae Lee, an analyst at Daiwa Securities, says the Lee family's power is checked by the growing influence of foreign investors. 'When [Samsung Electronics] invested in the motor business there was still a foreign ownership limit of 20 per cent. Now the

» company is 58 per cent foreign-owned. Management knows they can no longer make investments that go against shareholders' interests.'

Chu Woosik, head of investor relations for Samsung Electronics, says day-to-day running of the company is left to professional managers, while Mr Lee sets long-term strategy. The role of outside directors has been strengthened to increase accountability and the company has become more focused on shareholder value.

A New York listing has long been mooted for Samsung Electronics. Mr Chu says the company already meets the standards of accounting and transparency required by US regulators but its affiliates, which must also comply, do not. The electronics company has promised gradually to dispose of its shareholdings in unrelated businesses, such as Samsung Card, but Mr Chu warns this will take time. 'These are the legacies of the past. It cannot be fixed overnight,' he says.

Source: Andrew Ward (2004), *Financial Times*, 6 September, p. 15.

QUESTIONS

1. Is the replacement of analogue by digital an example of new-to-the-world or innovation?
2. What market preparation strategies would have best suited the introduction of digital technologies in any of Samsung's markets?
3. To what extent might Moore's concept of 'crossing the chasm' aid the new digital marketing strategy, as compared with Rogers' adoption curve concept?
4. What mode quadrant would you place Samsung in?
5. Choosing one of Samsung's digital products, such as cameras or mobile phones, do you think it would be possible for the company to implement a full customization strategy?

8

Branding strategies

LEARNING OBJECTIVES

- Provide an overview of the complex nature of branding
- Examine the ways in which consumers attach meaning to brands and the impact on company performance
- Discuss ways in which brand managers can streamline brand costs and improve brand profitability
- Identify the various ways in which brand managers can strategically create relationships between their brands and consumers and realize competitive advantages
- Present several strategic assessment tools that will aid the brand manager in assessing the nature of brand meaning and value and help in brand reinforcement and revitalization

CHAPTER AT A GLANCE

Introduction

Branding is a major component of product strategy. The ability to develop and nurture effective brands is probably the single most important skill set within the marketer's professional toolkit. Brands communicate valuable information to the customer, and a thorough understanding of what the brand signifies to the customer is an essential part of brand management. Whatever the company does can have an impact on customer perceptions of the brand, and the potential impact of corporate strategic decisions must be assessed, particularly in terms of consistency with the understanding and expectations of the customer. Daryl Travis (2000), the author of *Emotional Branding*, argues that a company's brand and its image become integrally linked. What the brand signifies to consumers becomes inextricably linked to their perceptions of the company. The values inherent in the brand often merge with the company's values. The important thing to remember is that to the customer, perception is reality, and as a result, the firm must be careful to regularly assess the nature of its brand image and ensure that possible strategic actions will enhance and not potentially undermine its brands and ultimately its own corporate image. This chapter will examine the complex nature of brands and present a series of strategic suggestions to help the brand strategist to create, maintain, and enhance this valuable company asset. The final section will provide a brief overview of the latest thinking regarding brands, the lovemark.

The complex nature of brands

A brand is a complex entity with multiple facets. Brands have concrete as well as intangible attributes that must be considered holistically. This section will attempt to shed light on this complex subject by defining what a brand is, examining the various functions performed by brands, discussing the nature of brand identity and brand equity, and finally by examining the various branding hierarchical choices. Branding represents one of the most important assets that the company can acquire, but it must be carefully managed. It is not just a logo or a name. A brand represents different things to different constituencies, and the key to effectively managing brand equity is to understand what goes on inside the heads of customers. The management of an array of products for multiple target groups of consumers raises difficult questions for brand managers without a sophisticated set of brand assessment tools and techniques.

Branding and functionality

So what exactly is a brand? The American Marketing Association provides a basic starting point. It defines a brand as a name, symbol, word, sign, design or combination that differentiates one or more offerings of a seller or group of sellers from the competition. So at a base level, a brand is what identifies the company selling goods and/or services. It is information laden and helps the consumer make the choice to fill a particular need among a series of similar offerings. However, as Berthon et al. (1999) explain, brands perform a series of functions for both the buyer and the seller. For the buyer, brands help:

(1) with product identification, which reduces search costs, (2) signal particular quality levels, which reduces perceived risk, and (3) provide social status, which reduces social and psychological risks. They suggest that there are also a series of benefits for the selling company in the form of: (1) the facilitation of customer identification and purchase, which improves financial performance, (2) the breeding of customer familiarity, which aids in the introduction of new product offerings, (3) the ability to identify specific product offerings clearly, which aids promotional efforts, (4) the differentiation of company offerings from those of competitors, which enables the use of premium pricing, (5) the distinctiveness of the product offering, which allows for the identification of appropriate target segments and tailored communications/promotions, and (6) the enhancement of brand loyalty, which promotes repeat purchases. A brand is much more than just a signifier.

Brand identity

As David Aaker (1996a) explains in his best-selling book, *Building Strong Brands*, each person's identity provides them with direction, purpose, and meaning, and the identity of a brand provides it with direction, purpose, and meaning. He explains that at its most basic level, the brand has a core identity, which is its essence and which remains constant, and an extended identity, which focuses on a series of psychological and physical aspects that give it nuance and texture. Aaker, one of the best-known branding strategists in the world, suggests that brand identity (see Figure 8.1) is comprised of 12 dimensions that are grouped around four distinct brand perspectives (brand as product, brand as organization, brand as person, and brand as symbol). The first of these perspectives, brand as product, involves the following dimensions: (1) product scope (what are the brand's associations with a particular product or a series of products?), (2) product-related attributes (one or more distinctive attributes that have strong associations with the brand and provide the bases for value propositions), (3) quality/value associations with the brand, (4) uses or applications

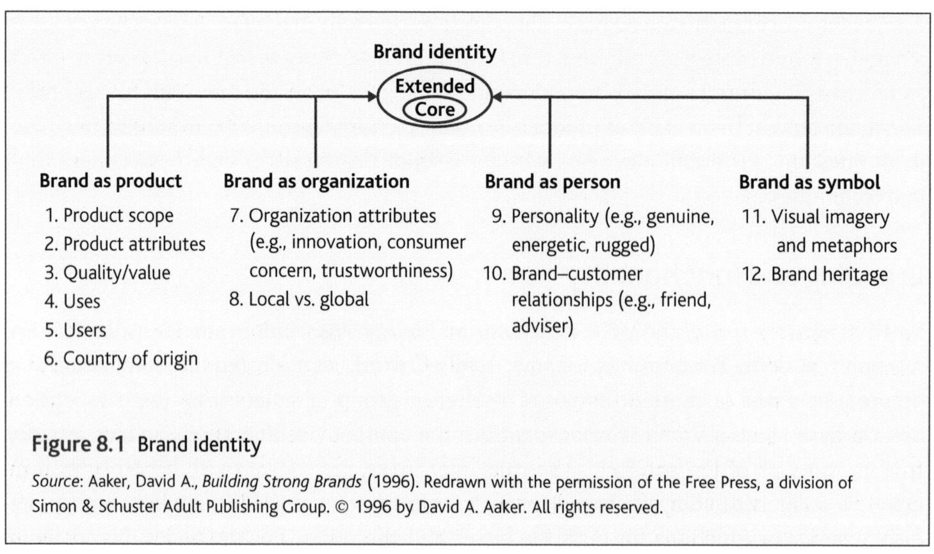

Figure 8.1 Brand identity

Source: Aaker, David A., *Building Strong Brands* (1996). Redrawn with the permission of the Free Press, a division of Simon & Schuster Adult Publishing Group.

(strong associations between occasions for use and the brand), (5) users (brand associations with particular types or groups of consumers), and (6) country of origin (associations between the brand and a country or geographic region). The question to examine here concerns the nature of the brand as the embodiment of the products associated with it. Is the brand immediately thought of as a product or group of products?

The second perspective involves the following associations between the brand and a particular organization: (1) organizational attributes (one or more distinctive company-related attributes that have strong associations with the brand, e.g., innovative, young, socially responsible, etc.) and (2) local vs global (is the brand a local brand for a local company or is it a global brand?). Is the brand the embodiment of the company and/or its reach? Does the brand bring a particular company to mind?

The third perspective involves the brand as a person and has two major dimensions: (1) personality (infusing a brand with particular personal traits, e.g., compassionate, responsible, athletic, etc.) and (2) relationships with customers (the development of personal relationships between the brand and customers, e.g., a friend, a mentor, etc.). The brand here can be seen as a person with a distinct and identifiable personality that may provide the basis for a more intriguing and lasting relationship than a brand whose identity is based primarily on product attributes. Is the brand a friend that you can count on?

Finally, the fourth perspective involves the brand as a symbol comprised of two dimensions: (1) visual imagery (the associations between the brand and particular images, e.g., the McDonald's golden arches, the Nike swoosh, etc.) and (2) heritage (associations built upon the history associated with the brand).

Clearly, a brand is a complex entity that potentially means different things to different segments, and a better understanding of brand identity is an integral part of a successful brand management program. The key is to understand the perceptions of the consumers relative to the array of company brands. Aaker (1996a) emphasizes that successful brand companies have a clear idea of their brand identity, and strategically brand identity serves as the basis for the development of a meaningful brand value proposition (based on functional and/or emotional benefits) which when combined with the building of credibility in the eyes of the customer help lead to a lasting and meaningful relationship between the brand and the customer that will, when effectively managed, lead to profitability. Aaker (1996a) presents Nestlé as an example of a company that truly understands the importance and essence of branding. Nestlé utilizes the term brand constitution, and brand importance is reflected throughout the organization.

Brand equity

While brand identity addresses the components of the brand and the associations and relationships involved, brand equity focuses on the measurement of brand value. Aaker coined the term in his 1991 book, *Managing Brand Value*, and defined it as a set of assets (as well as liabilities) connected to the name and symbols of the brand that adds to (or detracts from) the value of the product or service to a company and/or that company's customers. The point is to compare brand assets to brand liabilities and maintain a strong and viable brand equity valuation. Brand equity (see Figure 8.2) is comprised of five different

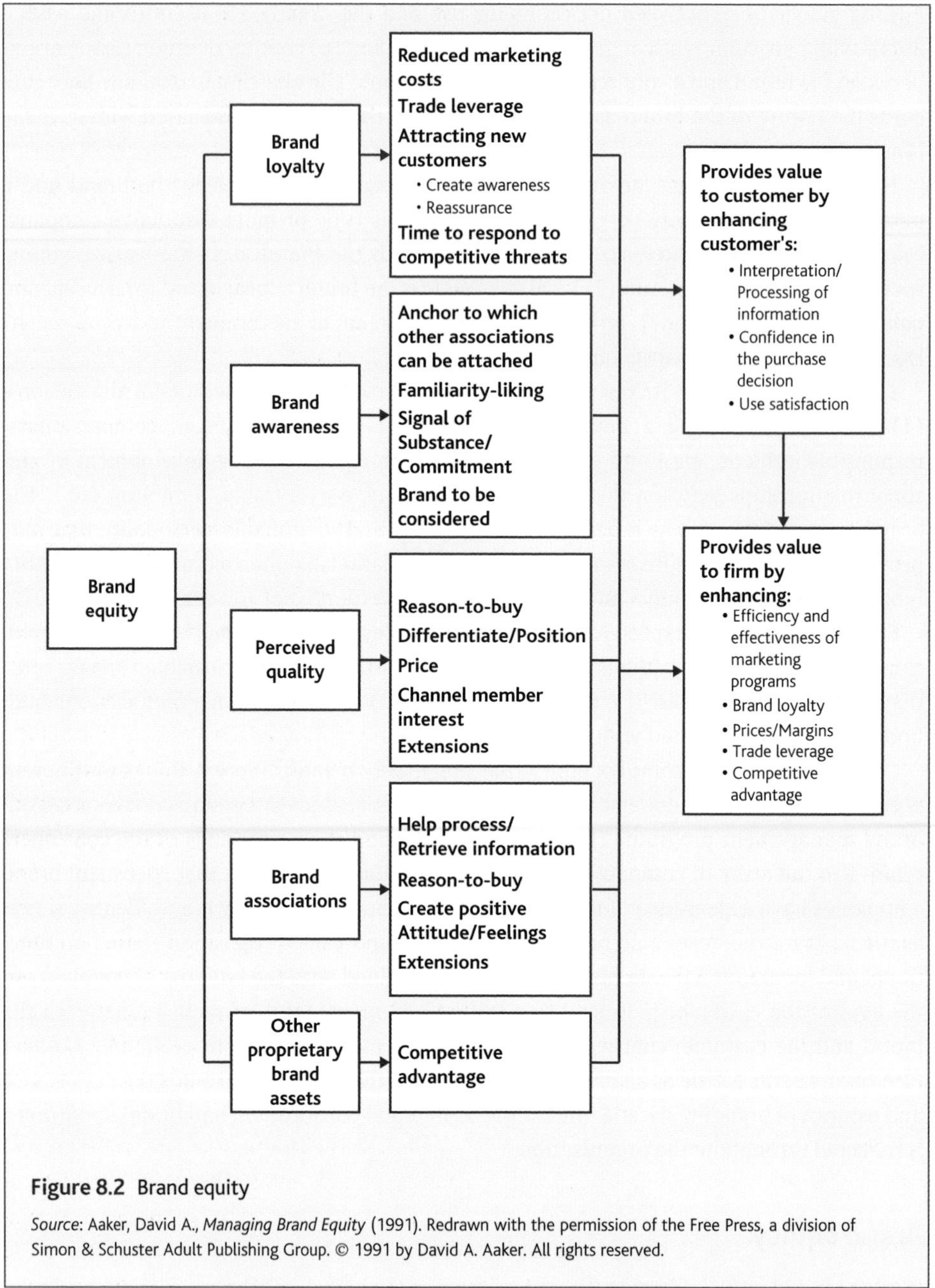

Figure 8.2 Brand equity

Source: Aaker, David A., *Managing Brand Equity* (1991). Redrawn with the permission of the Free Press, a division of Simon & Schuster Adult Publishing Group.

categories of assets: (1) brand name awareness, (2) brand loyalty, (3) perceived quality, (4) brand associations, and (5) other assets (i.e., patents and trade marks).

Brand awareness is the lowest level of brand equity. If the consumer is aware of the brand, then it will more likely be a candidate for his/her choice set, and familiarity certainly has the potential to generate positive feelings. A brand that is top-of-mind will have a greater likelihood of selection.

Brand loyalty is the strongest measure of the value of a brand. Loyal customers are ones who will come back time and again to purchase the brand. Loyal customers will spread positive word-of-mouth and help attract a new set of customers. Loyal customers allow greater potential for the use of price premiums, and they represent a significant barrier to new competitor entry.

Perceived quality is an important category of assets for three reasons: (1) perceived quality has been shown to be the only brand association that is able to drive firm profitability, (2) perceived quality is often the major focal point for strategic positioning, and (3) perceived quality has the ability to affect many other brand perceptions (Aaker 1996b).

A strong foundation for brand equity involves the various **brand associations** that customers will develop (Aaker, 1996a). Brand identity, which was discussed in the previous section, is the driving force behind the development of brand associations and focuses on what the brand is expected to signify inside the head of the customer.

Finally, the last set of assets involves **proprietary assets** like trade marks and patents that can add to the value of a brand.

How does a company measure brand equity? Aaker (1996b) suggests that brand equity can effectively be assessed utilizing 10 sets of brand measures that involve a series of measures related to customer brand perceptions and market behaviour. There are two measures which address brand loyalty: (1) three items which assess the price premium that the brand can command over other competing brands, and (2) four items which address the customer's level of satisfaction with and loyalty to the brand. There are also two measures which examine perceived quality/leadership: (1) three items which address perceived quality relative to competing brands, and (2) three items which measure the nature of brand leadership and innovativeness as compared with alternative brands. There are three measures which assess brand associations/differentiation: (1) two items which examine the perceived value of the brand, (2) three items which address brand personality, and (3) three items which focus on the perceptions of the company which owns and manages the brand. There is a single measure for brand awareness, which contains four items, which reflect knowledge of and familiarity with the brand. Finally, the last two measures involve brand performance in the market: (1) brand market share and (2) three items connected to price and distribution indices.

These measures allow the brand manager to effectively measure the value of the brand as a firm asset, and examination of brand value at regular intervals allows the brand manager to maintain a steady brand course and to take specific corrective action when downward trends are identified. Aaker (1996b) suggests that these measures can effectively be applied across a variety of products and markets. A more detailed discussion of brand equity and its measures will be presented in the explanation of brand revitalization in the strategic brand management section of this chapter.

An understanding of the complexity of brands is an essential starting point to the development of an effective brand management system. Brand management involves a variety of different strategic brand choices and an assessment of the perceptual impact of those choices on various customer groups. Before we turn to the nature of strategic choices for the maximization of profitability and the achievement of sustainable competitive advantage, the nature of the various brand choices must be addressed. For a small company with a single product or service offering, the branding decision is somewhat simpler than it would be for a company with a vast array of different product lines and product variants within each line. The first main decision is whether to tie the company name to the product or to create a distinct identity for the product that is separate from that of the company. Most companies have more than one brand that they are managing, and the options they face are far more complex than those facing the startup business. Brands can be thought of as having layers like those of an onion, and the brand manager must understand the complexity of the brand hierarchy that they oversee.

Brand architecture

So what are the various options for branding that are available for brand managers? A brand portfolio can contain a variety of different types of brand roles and relationships, and this complex structure of brands can be seen as analogous to the complex structures designed by an architect (see Petromilli et al., 2002; and Devlin, 2003). Thus a new discipline has emerged which is referred to as brand architecture (Aaker and Joachimsthaler, 2000b). These authors (2000b) created the brand relationship spectrum to help with brand architectural analysis (see Figure 8.3). They show a range of different branding relationships that extend from the **house of brands** at one extreme to the **branded house** at the other. The house of brands involves a company that manages a disparate group of brands that stand on their own. Procter & Gamble and Colgate Palmolive represent houses of brands. Each has the potential to own a particular niche market on its own merits and build strong brand relationships with specific target segments. There is a focused value proposition that is created for each niche, and the brand can connect directly with the niche consumer. Aaker and Joachimsthaler (2000b) suggest that the creation of a house of brands allows the company to potentially:

- avoid brand associations that would be perceived as incompatible
- signal breakthrough advantages for new offerings
- own a new product class association by using a powerful name that reflects a key benefit
- avoid or minimize channel conflict

The authors suggest that there are two possible options for the makeup of a house of brands: (1) no connection being made across the brands (e.g., RCA to General Electric), and (2) shadow endorsement (here the link is not actively identified, but many customers understand the connection, which can add credibility to the brand and lessen possible detrimental effects on the endorsing brand, e.g., Old Navy and Gap).

Moving from the extreme of the house of brands position, the authors then suggest a second category, which they call **endorsed brands**. These brands are independent but they are also given credibility by being officially endorsed by another brand. Here product-specific brands are combined with company brands. Three options are presented for this category: (1) token endorsement (where the endorser brand is the main focus, not the token endorser, e.g., GE light bulbs, where the GE logo is included on the bulb), (2) linked

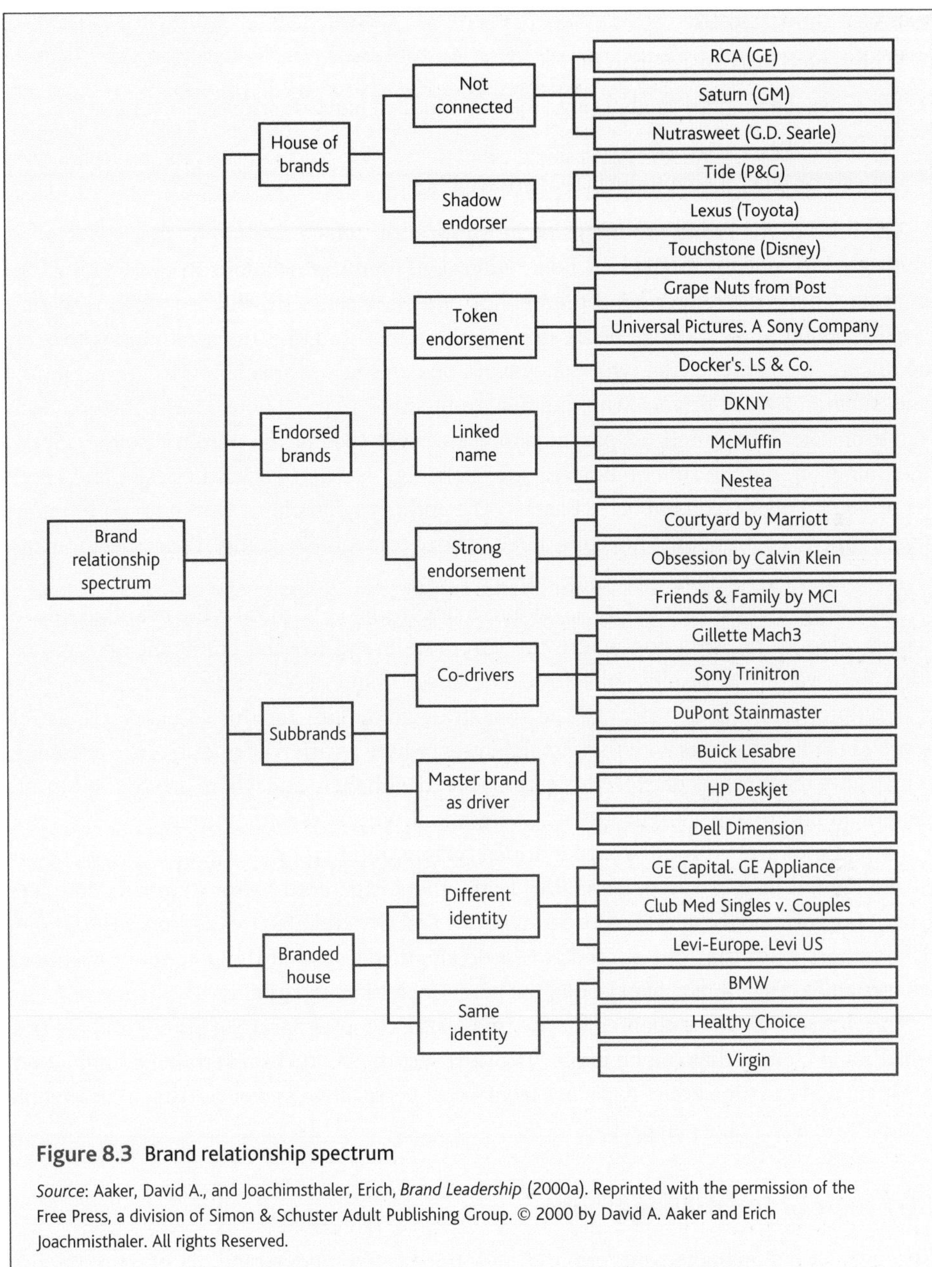

Figure 8.3 Brand relationship spectrum

Source: Aaker, David A., and Joachimsthaler, Erich, *Brand Leadership* (2000a). Reprinted with the permission of the Free Press, a division of Simon & Schuster Adult Publishing Group. © 2000 by David A. Aaker and Erich Joachmisthaler. All rights Reserved.

names (where a name with common components creates an entire family of brands, e.g., McDonald's and Chicken McNuggets, Egg or Sausage McMuffin, etc.), and (3) strong endorsements (where the endorser brand is not necessarily the main focus, e.g., Courtyard by Marriott, Holiday Inn Express). Aaker and Joachimsthaler (2000b) suggest that token endorsement is a viable option when the endorser:

- is well known already
- is presented in a consistent manner
- has a visual metaphor symbol (e.g., the outstretched hands for Allstate Insurance Corporation)
- appears on a family of products that are credible

The third of the brand groupings is the **subbrands**, which are brands that are strongly connected to a parent brand and build additional brand associations in to the combined offering. This is a stronger bond than endorsement. Because the link is stronger, there is greater potential for damage being done to the parent brand if the associations that are added are inconsistent. The two strategic options presented for subbrands are: (1) parent and subbrand as co-drivers with neither dominating (e.g., Gillete Mach3 razors, Sony Trinitron televisions) and (2) parent brand as driver (where the parent brand is clearly the dominant and the subbrand is an extension, e.g., Hewlett-Packard Deskjet and Laserjet printers, Volkswagen Rabbit or Passat). The authors again offer a caveat for co-branding that if the two co-brands are not considered to be of comparable quality, the association may hurt the image of the more highly regarded brand.

The last grouping presented by Aaker and Joachimsthaler (2000b) is the **branded house**, which refers to the situation where the corporate brand has the dominant driving position for a variety of product offerings. The lesser brand in this situation acts merely as a descriptor and not as a driver. The two strategic options for this category are as follows: (1) brand offerings with the same identity (where a variety of offerings are presented which have the same set of expectations associated with them and where the descriptors are generic in nature, e.g., Virgin Airways, Virgin Rail, Virgin Records, Virgin Cola, etc.) and (2) brand offerings with different identities (where different brand groupings are seen to have different images and personalities from others, e.g., Ford Motor Company and Ford Credit Corporation, General Electric Appliances and General Electric Capital Corporation). The authors warn that this approach is problematic because of the potentially disparate images and associations that exist and the potential for incompatibility.

This first section of the chapter has focused on the complex nature of brands and the possible brand choices that can be made. The next section will focus on strategic brand management and examine brand decisions from a cost perspective as well as from a sustainable competitive advantage perspective.

Strategic brand management

Strategic brand management requires a sophisticated understanding of two important issues: (1) industry cost structure, brand efficiency, and brand profitability, and (2) consumer perceptions of brand and the potential for sustainable competitive advantage. Both are important considerations and will be addressed in turn.

Industry cost structure, brand efficiency, and brand profitability

A brand is a difficult thing to measure. Strategic brand decisions will have an impact on a firm's financial performance, and there are a number of strategic possibilities that can be considered for ways in which brand managers can improve brand performance from a cost and profitability perspective. Operational efficiencies can be achieved from such mechanisms as brand leveraging, brand consolidation, premium branding, co-branding, the use of non-traditional communication/promotional channels, and the use of new brand valuation mechanisms (advertising turnover and brand ROI). Each of these will be discussed in turn.

Brand leveraging

Strong brands often produce above-average returns for shareholders, and there is great pressure on brand managers to use the name recognition that accompanies a strong brand to increase potential sales and profits by attaching the name to other company offerings (Court et al., 1999). These authors identified three factors which appear to be driving diversified brand leveraging: (1) leveraging causes a spreading out of the support costs associated with brand management, (2) convergence is causing the merging of many separate industries, opening up many new market opportunities, and (3) relationship building appears to mean more to customers than functional benefits. While leveraging can produce economic benefits, there is also a downside to aggressive leveraging, as was found in the unsuccessful strategies employed by both BIC and Gucci. The authors found that a number of successful brands were leveraged and still had strong leveraging possibilities, such as Sony and Disney. What do these companies do that makes them successful? First of all, they identify a 'golden thread' which can tie together a diversified group of businesses. One example they give is Disney and its focus on 'wholesome fun' and another is Sony and its elegance of design. These companies were also found to invest in the creation of a high-credibility brand personality that can be leveraged. The examples they provide are General Electric with its slogan of 'bringing good things to life' and IBM's 'solutions for a small planet'. The last thing that these companies do is aggressively leverage via cross-selling of products.

One issue that the study uncovered was that it may be possible for a focused branded company to diversify and leverage its brand, but it must be careful in doing so due to the fact that: (1) consumers can be confused by moves into inconsistent areas for a previously focused brand and (2) companies must make every effort to cover all of the opportunities in their home area of focus before venturing out. Focused brands with leveraging potential are those that have slowly and continuously broadened their category definitions and resulting brand identities. This McKinsey study indicated that there is a significant relationship between company success and four organizational requirements: (1) they must build brand stewardship (brand should be considered a 'treasured asset'); (2) brand leveraging must be explicitly built into corporate planning; (3) they must nurture and develop a variety of supporting capabilities (like new business development and cross-selling); and (4) they must develop and utilize appropriate performance metrics.

Brand consolidation

In this era of convergence, as mentioned in the previous section, there are a number of mergers/acquisitions taking place that present challenges for brand managers. Consolidation of brands certainly appears economically sound on paper, but the reality according to a 1997 McKinsey study by Knudsen et al. is that only one of every five consolidations is successful.

They discuss the forces at work which have facilitated brand consolidation: (1) the enormous growth in mergers and acquisitions and the resulting large and awkward brand portfolios with little strategic synergy and (2) the fact that most of the value of mergers and acquisitions is tied to intangible assets (e.g., 70% in the UK in the early 1990s, significantly up from only 18% in 1980) and brands comprise a large proportion of those assets. Knudsen et al. (1997) also describe the pressure to consolidate which comes from globalization forces and lifestyle convergence, the ever-increasing reach of media vehicles, and international scale economies. This is compounded by the strong financial showings of dominant brands in return on sales and the pressure that builds to increase returns.

Can brand consolidation be successful? The authors believe that it can. They state that consolidation correctly pursued can lead to: (1) the creation of a synergistic mixture which results in greater sales than the individual brands produced by themselves before the consolidation due to the reduction in cost of goods sold (with narrowing of the product range and greater focus for promotional efforts) and resulting improvements in operating margins (e.g., Procter & Gamble which shortened its variety of brands by nearly one-third during the 1990s in the United States and improved share and profit margins at the same time) and (2) a 'makeover' for the previously stodgy brands that are now being fused together (e.g., Philips and Whirlpool).

If a company decides to consolidate its brands, these authors believe that there are three choices that can be made: (1) to phase out a brand, (2) to quickly change to a single brand name, or (3) to combine brands using co-branding or putting brands under a single umbrella brand. The first of these choices appears to be appropriate for the company that has an alternative brand which has a large, loyal following. The second option is more challenging, and these authors report few successes from their studies. This choice would appear to be appropriate when companies must act quickly in the face of (a) aggressive global expansion by competitors and (b) escalating promotional expenditures in order to maintain their brand positions as costs are skyrocketing. The authors mention that one success for this choice can be seen in the ability of Procter & Gamble to consolidate two toilet paper brands White Cloud and Charmin into the Charmin brand. The authors also point out that Procter & Gamble may have succeeded because of their controls over the distribution channels while also utilizing heavy trade and consumer promotions during the transition. Finally, co-branding appears to be the most common transition strategy with both brands being kept for a period of time to allow the consumers as well as the distribution channel members to adjust to the changes. Knudsen et al. (1997) suggest that there are essentially three important steps to be followed in brand consolidation that can be followed either sequentially or simultaneously. The first step involves the streamlining of the brand portfolio with a harmonization of the products involved. They caution that hurried streamlining may create confusing or diluted value propositions. The second step involves the harmonization of package designs and logos, and the final step involves a merging of the brands' perceptual positioning.

Premium branding and relative market share

A new approach to profitability, market share, and the use of premium branding was suggested in 1997 by Vijay Vishwanath and Jonathan Mark. The authors studied many premium branded goods and found that market share by itself does not appear to drive profitability. They found that brand profitability is driven both by market share and by the nature of market or category in which the brand competes. Greater profits can be achieved if a category or market is dominated by a series of premium brands as opposed to a category dominated by value-oriented or private-label brands. Their analysis showed that brands with high relative market shares achieve approximately 10% return on sales, while those with low relative market share achieve results of less than 5% return on sales. The finding suggests that brand managers must answer two questions when planning brand strategy: (1) Is the category 'premium' or 'value'? and (2) Is the brand's relative market share high or low? The authors developed a four-cell matrix using these two dimensions, and came up with four types of brand situation: (1) the **high-road brand** (premium brand category and high relative market share with an average return on sales of greater than 20%), (2) the **hitchhiker brand** (premium brand category and low relative market share with an average return on sales of 15 to 20%), (3) the **low-road brand** (value brand category and high relative market share with an average return on sales of 5 to 10%), and (4) the **dead-end brand** (value brand category and low relative market share with an average return on sales of less than 5%).

Vishwanath and Mark (1997) provide a series of strategic suggestions for brand managers, in line with their brand positions on the matrix. Hitchhiker brands should follow the pricing choices of the leader. They should also focus on innovating to stay ahead in their niche. The high-road brand should also innovate but ensure that prices do not get too much higher than those of other brands since consumers will trade up, but not if the gap is too large. The low-road brand must streamline wherever possible to lower costs to free up resources for brand equity building. Costs can be cut by: (1) reducing stock-keeping units, (2) closing unnecessary facilities, (3) consolidating suppliers, and (4) standardizing components. Finally, the options for the dead-end brand are: (1) to slash prices to build share from the leader, (2) to outsource where size does not allow sufficient economies of scale, (3) to bring together several smaller brands to build economies of scale, or (4) to introduce a super-premium brand that completely changes consumers' expectations.

Co-branding

One important way in which brand managers can reduce costs is through the pursuit of an appropriate co-branding arrangement. Prince and Davies (2002) discuss co-branding as the bringing together of two separate company brands to be marketed together to create a new joint offering with additional value for the customer. Examples include such successful pairings as British Airways and Hertz, Adidas and the New Zealand Rugby Union, Starbucks Coffee and Barnes & Noble Bookstores, and Kellogg's cereals and Walt Disney. A number of operational benefits can accrue to co-branding partners. Prince and Davies (2002) suggest that co-branding can make transactions more efficient through sharing of retail sites (e.g., Starbucks and Barnes & Noble). The authors suggest that Starbucks gets use of space in the bookstore and gets revenues from the high traffic of shoppers as a result. Barnes & Noble gets the benefit of lower expenses for overhead and up-front investments, which are being shared with Starbucks. Another example which they provide involves the site-sharing arrangement between Dunkin' Donuts and Baskin-Robbins. In this arrangement, they share the same space and share the expenses while offering what are considered to be complementary products but with different peak activity times (doughnuts in the morning and ice cream in the afternoon and evening). Co-branding may be a viable strategic option, but it requires a careful assessment of the potential candidates for partnering. Prince and Davies (2002) suggest that a strong co-branding relationship will depend on the product and brand fit between the two co-brands. They suggest that the following questions must be answered when searching for the right co-branding partner:

1. Is there a compatible fit, based on what each brand stands for?
2. What if there is market volatility?
3. How is the co-branding to be financed?
4. Can we rely on commitments?

The authors also suggest that a co-branding courtship period occurs, which includes a series of stages: (1) the assessment of opportunities, (2) the setting of objectives, (3) the development of strategies, (4) the initiation of the relationships, and finally, (5) the negotiation of the partnership agreement.

Abratt and Motlana (2002) suggest that co-branding is an effective mechanism for global brands to be successful in local markets. The local brands bring high local brand equity to a global brand that may not have high local brand equity. Co-branding then becomes a great tool for introducing new consumer products. The synergies that are created can often create an impression of greater value and reduce the financial risk associated with a normal new product introduction. They suggest that co-branding makes sense for acquisitions because the acquiring company develops a brand portfolio with a heritage that can help weak products (see Mini Case Study 8.1).

Non-traditional communication/promotional channels

Joachimsthaler and Aaker (1997) studied successful European brands and found that European brand managers had discovered some interesting ways to streamline promotional expenses that had not been utilized effectively by their US counterparts. The authors found that European brand managers utilized a variety of efficient and effective promotional channels to build brand awareness as opposed to the normal mass-media, cost-inefficient mechanisms. They cite such examples as use of publicity (e.g., Body Shop's connection to environmental causes and firm actions to promote these causes—see Mini Case Study 8.2), event sponsorship (e.g., Swatch's sponsoring of fashion, social, and sporting events, Virgin's participation in Compuserve's UK Virtual Shopping Centre), membership club development and maintenance (e.g., Nestlé and the Casa Buitoni Club), and theme park development (e.g., Cadbury World and Legoland). Aaker and Joachimsthaler (2000b) found that these companies were successful not only in discovering more efficient ways to promote their brands, but also in being able to enhance the relationships between their brands and consumers, further solidifying their brand image and engendering loyalty as well as profitability.

MINI CASE STUDY 8.1
Local market success through co-branding: Danone in South Africa

Local brands are well known in their local markets and have high levels of brand equity, but often, global brands do not have high equity positions in local markets. This can create difficulties when entering new markets. The use of co-branding (e.g., brand partnering, brand alliances, joint branding) is an excellent method for global brands to build on the name recognition of local brands while synergistically providing financial and technological support for the smaller local brand company.

Danone, the French yogurt maker, was faced with a challenge when attempting to enter the potentially lucrative South African market. Danone was virtually unknown in South Africa, but it had considerable international brand recognition. Company management realized that some kind of an alliance with a respected local company could help them build a strong position in South Africa.

When studying the market, Danone management found that the leading brand of yogurt in South Africa, Clover, enjoyed a 48 percent share in their home market (with the nearest competitor far behind at only 15 percent market share). Local market research indicated that South Africans associated the name Clover with quality for a range of dairy products. Danone saw the potential for a lucrative relationship and began to court Clover with a purchase of a share of the company in December of 1995, and in 1997 they signed an agreement with Clover to start a company called Danone Clover. In this arrangement the majority position was held by Danone with a 55 percent share.

In March of 1998 Danone introduced Danone Corner yogurt in South Africa, and research showed that it was seen as a very innovative product and created awareness and brand recognition for Danone. The introduction was heavily promoted using television, newspapers and magazines. Danone then looked to build on this success with the incorporation of the Danone brand name into Clover's line of fruit yogurts. Danone realized that solely using the Danone brand was not feasible since: (1) they were relatively unknown in South Africa, (2) it had not gained a significant share of the market with the Danone Corner brand, and (3) Clover was a strong brand that could be further leveraged.

As a result of extensive market research, they decided to go with a co-branding arrangement, Clover Danone, and this required the redesign of all Clover's yogurt packaging. The new design incorporated the Danone logo with the Clover seal. The co-branding arrangement was found to be synergistic as Clover was able to benefit from Danone's international experience, global brand exposure, innovative capabilities and quality associations. Danone also gained by leveraging the enormous brand equity Clover had built in South Africa and by tapping into Clover's quality reputation for dairy products.

The co-branding relationship proved to be successful as Clover Danone's share of the yogurt market increased from 48 percent in 1997 to 57 percent in 2000. The next biggest competitors, Dairy Belle and Parmalat, had shares of 12 and 11 percent respectively. This brand alliance provided strong synergistic benefits that allowed both partners to benefit in ways that could not have been achieved individually.

Source: Russell Abratt and Patience Motlana (2002), 'Managing co-branding strategies: global brands into local markets', *Business Horizons*, September–October, pp. 43–50.

MINI CASE STUDY 8.2 Core brand identity: The Body Shop

Brand identity (the brand concept from the standpoint of the brand owner) is the foundation of any brand-building strategy. A clear and effective brand identity, which is accepted and practised by everyone within the firm, should be clearly linked to the company's vision, culture and values. This identity should guide strategic decisions since all programs and communications must reinforce rather than confuse and undermine the brand. No company lives this out better than The Body Shop.

The core identity of The Body Shop is 'profits with a principle'. The idea is to make the company name synonymous with corporate social responsibility. The message that is sent to employees and customers alike is that the company is constantly focused on bettering society. The company officially opposes animal experimentation, actively supports women's issues, promotes recycling efforts, makes contributions to rainforest preservation projects, and participates in awareness raising for the protection of endangered animals and alternative energy sources. An example of this orientation can be seen in their children's bath products where they include entertaining and informative storybooks about a variety of endangered animals. One recent summer employees and supporters of The Body Shop sent over 500,000 signatures to the President of Brazil to request the stoppage of tree burning in the rainforests.

These efforts are not seen as merely tangential to the brand but integral to the brand. Every time a customer comes into one of the company's retail outlets they are greeted by a store employee wearing a t-shirt with the company name on it and a social message prominently displayed. Company employees reflect the interests of the company in their own personal philosophies. It is part of the interview process and a requirement for employment that the individual believes in and supports social causes. Store atmospherics also reflect this orientation with a series of strategically placed posters and a variety of bright and colourful handouts (printed on recycled paper) which provide the customer with information about products carried in the store, particular social causes which the company supports, and about how to join social cause advocacy organizations and participate in rallies.

The Body Shop has effectively built a solid identity for its brand that is the embodiment of everything that the company stands for, which has helped them financially by building them a strong market position. It has also proven to be an effective forum for differentiation from all of its competitors, which tend to fall into a melting pot of perceptual confusion. Most skin care and cosmetic companies choose to promote how their products will transform the user rather than how the user can better the world around them. If the Body Shop's customers feel that it fits with their personalities and interests, they are much more likely to embrace a long-term relationship with the company and its products.

Source: Erich Joachimsthaler and David A. Aaker (1997), 'Building brands without mass media', *Harvard Business Review*, January–February, pp. 39–50.

New brand valuation mechanisms

Two recent approaches to asset valuation from a financial resource perspective may aid brand managers to achieve greater efficiencies. One of these involves the measurement of advertising turnover and was suggested by Herremans et al. (2000). The authors suggest two ratios for analysis to tie brand asset valuation to the efficiency and effectiveness of marketing expenditures: **advertising turnover** and **brand ROI**. The earlier discussion of brand equity provides mechanisms for overall brand valuation, but there are few mechanisms that allow the brand manager to evaluate marketing spending as it relates to the brand. The authors state that most brand valuation has been done for the purposes of external reporting, but little has really focused on valuations for internal strategic purposes. They argue that marketing investment and advertising investment are one and the same for brand valuation purposes since advertising makes up such a large part in brand building compared to any other marketing promotional mechanisms, and as a result they suggest a ratio, **advertising turnover**, which examines the relationship between advertising expenditures and brand value. This measure would therefore reflect how effectively the firm has converted advertising expenditures into brand value. Advertising turnover is calculated by dividing brand value by advertising expenditures on a year-by-year basis and examining trends. Herremans et al. (2000) then went back and analysed advertising turnover for 12 brand companies over a five-year period using brand values and advertising expenditures reported in annual reports, Securities and Exchange Commission reports, and *Advertising Age*. Based on the relationships that they uncovered, they classified the companies into five categories: (1) **high-efficiency brand enhancers** (where both are increasing, but brand values are rising at a faster rate than advertising expenditures), (2) **low-efficiency brand enhancers** (where both are increasing, but advertising expenditures are rising faster than brand values), (3) **brand future unknown** (where brand values are rising but advertising expenditures are decreasing and sustainability is in serious question), (4) **brand deterioration** (where brand values are decreasing but advertising expenditures are increasing with dangerous implications), and (5) **brand neglect** (where both advertising expenditures and brand values are decreasing with serious negative ramifications).

Herremans et al. (2000) also suggest an additional measure for effective brand assessment, the **brand ROI**. They posit substitutions in the normal calculations for ROI to convert the focus to the brand. They assume the following formula for calculating ROI (sales/investment × net income/sales), and they substitute brand sales for sales, brand value for investment, and brand sales for sales. Thus, the formula becomes:

$$\text{Brand ROI} = \frac{\text{Brand sales}}{\text{Brand value}} \times \frac{\text{Net income}}{\text{Brand sales}}$$

The first part of the formula reflects the brand turnover (brand sales/brand value), which shows the effectiveness of brand value conversion into sales, while the second part is the brand return on sales (net income/brand sales), which indicates how well brand sales convert into operating income. These financial assessment tools can be a valuable enhancer of strategic perspective.

This section has focused on the cost side of brand management, but there is also the need to examine brand management from the perceptual side. The perceptions of brand, brand personality, and brand value are key strategic considerations that significantly improve brand strategic planning perspective in the pursuit of sustainable competitive advantage.

Consumer perceptions of brand and sustainable competitive advantage

Brand management cannot focus on financial assessment alone. There is also an enormously important perceptual aspect, which was discussed earlier in the chapter. Companies are finding that brand management has an image and personality management component, which must also be carefully assessed and tracked over time. This section will focus on such image-oriented strategic issues as: (1) the balance between consumer familiarity and brand regard, (2) brand personality, (3) customer involvement with the brand, and (4) brand perceptual reinforcement and revitalization.

Customer familiarity and brand regard

Brand image and meaning are important for brand success. As discussed earlier in this chapter, there are powerful forces urging brand managers to extend brand name and leverage the power of the brand. Vicki Lane (1998) addresses the critical issue of maintaining perceptual brand balance in the face of extension/leveraging. She discusses the importance of assessing consumer familiarity with the brand as well as consumers' regard for the brand. She posits that both dimensions must be carefully examined and kept in balance for brand success. Lane (1998) argues that consumer familiarity results from: (1) brand awareness, (2) the ease with which it is brought to mind, and (3) brand usage. Brand regard results from: (1) product quality perceptions, (2) user satisfaction, and (3) prestige. Certainly there is a correlation between brand familiarity and likeability, and when balance is maintained, brand success is enhanced. There is, however, the possibility that brand familiarity will not coincide with brand regard, as was found for such brands as Spam and Yugo. Lane (1998) argues that brands that are balanced in terms of familiarity and regard are better candidates for extension/leveraging than those that are out of synch.

A study of a variety of brands indicated five categories of brands in terms of familiarity and appeal. Those that were in balance were: (1) **diamonds** (which are very high on familiarity and appeal, have exceptional brand equity, and serve as powerful bases for brand extension, e.g., Coke, Kraft, Campbell's Soup), (2) **troopers** (which are high in familiarity and appeal, geared toward a broad market and good for extensions that fit with brand image and quality perceptions, e.g., Tropicana juices and drinks), and (3) **developers** (which are low in familiarity and appeal, with little problem of cannibalization and where extensions can build awareness and regard if product quality is high, e.g., Healthy Choice). The other two categories identified in this study were: (1) **tarnished treasures** (with low consumer regard relative to familiarity, where price competition has hampered high regard, and the risk of cannibalization is high, e.g., Spam and Marlboro cigarettes), and (2) **coveted icons** (with high consumer appeal relative to familiarity, reflective of a prestige image for a somewhat exclusive product, where extension has a high potential for undermining perceptions of brand quality and exclusivity (e.g., Lamborghini, Bang & Olufsen, Bose). Balanced brands have greater potential for leverage than those that are unbalanced, and brand managers must approach extension armed with a clear understanding of how the brand is perceived by the marketplace. The tendency for coveted icons to want more and risk jeopardizing their exclusive niches can be seen clearly in the difficulties now being confronted by Mercedes, which is facing the difficulty inherent in managing a range of products to a variety of customers after expanding into lower-price categories with its C-class product line. Perceptual inconsistencies accompany too wide a range of quality levels and commensurate prices. This is what forced Honda, Nissan, and Toyota to develop separate premium brands (e.g., Accura, Infiniti, and Lexus respectively). It is important that financial/economic considerations do not take precedence over the perceptual aspects of the brand.

Brand personality

An important aspect to brand and brand image is the nature of a brand personality, which facilitates the attraction of individuals who feel an affinity for products that embody attributes that reflect their own personalities. A good example of an effective personality development and brand success can be found in the recent resurgence in performance of a fading retail brand, Abercrombie & Fitch (Henderson and Mihas, 2000). These authors suggest that retailers can develop successful brands by: (1) establishing a precise definition of the target segment of consumers and their particular needs and expectations, (2) deciding which benefits they can provide to those customers that will lead to the creation of a distinctive market positioning, and (3) creating a brand image that not only fits with those benefits to be provided, but at the same time offers both satisfaction as well as energy and excitement. To accomplish this, Abercrombie & Fitch (A&F) reinvented itself from an old and tired sporting-goods retailer to a vibrant and relevant retailer with a new and powerful personality. Henderson and Mihas (2000) attribute A&F's successful turnaround to a personality that emphasized such consumer attributes as independent, fun loving, and sexually 'uninhibited'. These traits aligned them effectively with teenagers and college students, the company's target audience. But just developing a personality does not allow you to keep it relevant. A&F is committed to keeping its personality in tune with its target audience and maintains the valuable associations it has created through such mechanisms as: (1) sending staff members to college campuses on a monthly basis to talk to students about their lifestyles and fashion desires, (2) designing stores for better retail experiences for its target audience by providing meeting places for communication and socialization with large and comfortable armchairs, and by employing vibrant salespeople who are actively recruited from area college campuses and dress in A&F clothing, and (3) the use of sexually uninhibited models and settings in pictures on the walls, on the merchandise bags, and in the catalogues sent to target consumers.

Another company, which has been able to build on this kind of personality connection with its target audience, is Victoria's Secret lingerie and intimate apparel. The company utilizes salon settings with sexually charged images and promotional tie-ins like lingerie models, fashion events, and television spectaculars as means to building connections to its target audience. The store colours, music, salespeople, and layout all support the personality of youth, vitality, and sexual excitement. Clearly any connections that can be built with target customers help to ensure the success of the brand, and a particularly promising avenue for relationship building involves the concept of brand personality.

Customer brand involvement and perceptual connections

Companies have found that the key to brand success is to build strong relationships with customers by enhancing customer experiences with the brand, its personality, and its heritage (Joachimsthaler and Aaker, 1997). This involvement and relationship building can clearly be seen in innovative attempts to enhance customer experiences with the brand. Cadbury's theme park, Cadbury World, in Bournville, England, allows the customer to experience the brand in multiple ways, creating a link between brand, brand attributes, brand personality, and the customer. What was once just a factory tour has now become an entire theme park with emphasis on the Cadbury brand heritage via a chocolate museum, a restaurant, a tour of the plant, and a big chocolate sales store. Visitors learn about the history of chocolate (with characters portraying historic figures like Cortez, Montezuma, and King Charles II) as well as the history of John Cadbury and his company. This idea was so successful that it encouraged Hershey Chocolate to open its own version of this experience in New York City.

Another example can clearly be seen in the development of the HOG clubs by Harley-Davidson motorcycles. These *H*arley *O*wners *G*roups regularly get together to rise and celebrate the history and heritage of the motorcycles. Nestlé has also worked to develop customer groups with its Buitoni pasta products by creating Casa Buitoni Club, which involves customers in the history of Buitoni and of pasta through visits to the Buitoni family home in Tuscany and a series of mailings of newsletters, Italian lifestyle literature, recipes, and discount coupons. Customers get continual positive brand reinforcement while the company hopes to build ever-increasing involvement with the customer.

Brand perceptual reinforcement and revitalization

Kevin Lane Keller (1999), another respected brand expert, suggests that brand management must always take a long-term perspective with respect to brand equity and valuation. Any strategic decisions made in the short term can affect the future potential of the brand by impacting brand awareness and image. Keller suggests that effective brand management requires a long-term perspective with continuous reinforcement of brand meaning and, when necessary, brand revitalization.

Reinforcement of brand equity occurs when marketing tactical decisions convey consistent meanings to consumers. A series of important questions raised by Keller (1999) in this regard are:

1. What products are represented by the brand?
2. What benefits are supplied by the brand?
3. What specific needs are satisfied by the brand?
4. How does the brand make those products associated with it superior?
5. What distinct and favourable brand associations are made by consumers with the brand?

Keller (1999) warns that the most important consideration in brand reinforcement is the consistency of the support (in terms of both the type and amount) provided by the company to the brand. He emphasizes that price increases with inadequate marketing support are potentially disastrous. This is not meant to suggest that brand management should not make any changes to its marketing efforts for the brand, but that any changes made must keep the image integrity of the brand. Some companies have been forced to come back to old themes for advertising when new creative ideas did not register well with consumers from a perceptual standpoint. Kentucky Fried Chicken was forced to return to using Colonel Sanders to promote the product after eliminating his likeliness in favour of modernizing the company image. Change for the sake of change has the potential to undermine the brand's position in the head of the consumer. The reinforcement of brand meaning depends on the types of brand associations in the heads of brand consumers. Keller (1999) posits that these associations can be based upon either product-related associations (e.g., product design or production innovations which lead to an improved product which is not significantly different from what consumers expect) or non-product-related types of associations (e.g., new advertising approaches and creative ideas that create a position for the brand that is perceived to be better while remaining consistent with brand image).

Keller (1999) notes that there may be times over the brand's lifetime when strategic chances will be taken that may not be successful and potentially undermine the vitality of the brand. In these instances, brand managers should consider revitalizing the brand. Revitalization requires a careful assessment of brand meaning and associations so that meaningful repositioning decisions can be made. This requires the implementation of a thorough **brand audit**. The brand audit is a comprehensive examination of the various sources of brand equity from the perspective of the company as well as the consumer. Keller (2000) introduced his own tool for effective brand auditing, the Brand Report Card, which involves ratings from 1 (extremely poor) to 10 (extremely good) for honest answers to the following brand equity questions (Keller 2000):

1. How well does the brand excel at delivering the benefits customers truly desire?
2. How well does the brand remain relevant?
3. How well does the pricing strategy reflect consumers' perceptions of value?
4. How well is the brand positioned in the minds of consumers as compared with competing brands?
5. How consistent are the brand's marketing programmes and the messages sent to the consumer?
6. Do the brand portfolio and hierarchy actually make sense?
7. How well does the brand utilize and coordinate a full range of marketing activities to build brand equity?
8. How well do the brand's managers understand what the brand means to consumers?
9. How well does the company give proper support to the brand, and how well has this support been sustained over the long run?
10. How well does the company monitor the sources of brand equity?

Keller (1999) suggests that once a brand audit has been done, the important brand associations will be better understood, and the firm will be able to take one or more of the following paths: (1) expanding brand awareness (e.g., finding additional or new usage opportunities for the brand, as Arm & Hammer Baking Soda did), (2) improving brand image (e.g., strengthening positive associations and/or eliminating negative associations using such mechanisms as brand heritage/history, (3) balancing both old and new target segments (e.g., bringing in a younger customer and keeping relationships with loyal older customers at the same time), and (4) retiring and/or consolidating brands (that no longer fit or would be too costly to revitalize, e.g., Procter & Gamble's merging of the White Cloud and Charmin toilet paper brands and the Solo and Bold detergent brands). The brand audit is a vital assessment tool for effective brand management.

Lovemarks, the latest brand thinking

One of the most interesting new views on branding is presented by Kevin Roberts, CEO for Worldwide Operations for Saatchi & Saatchi, in his 2004 book, *Lovemarks: The Future Beyond Brands*. It is Roberts' premise that branding itself is flawed since brands are not actually making strong emotional connections with people. He claims that there are six reasons for this: (1) brands are worn out from overuse, (2) brands are no longer mysterious, (3) brands can't understand the new consumer, (4) brands struggle with good old-fashioned competition, (5) brands have been captured by formula, and (6) brands have been smothered by creeping conservatism. What is needed is to build an emotional bond with the consumer to such an extent that the consumer actually feels a love for the product. Roberts believes that love goes beyond reason, and a love bond is an emotional attachment that transcends logic and reason.

According to Roberts: (1) while a brand stands for information, a lovemark focuses on relationship, (2) while a brand is recognized by consumers, a lovemark is loved by people, (3) while a brand is generic, a lovemark is personal, (4) while a brand presents a narrative, a lovemark creates a love story, (5) while a brand promises quality, a lovemark presents a touch of sensuality, (6) while a brand is symbolic, a lovemark is iconic, (7) while a brand is defined, a lovemark is infused, (8) while a brand is a statement, a lovemark is a story, (9) while a brand is a set of defined attributes, a lovemark is wrapped in mystery, (10) while a brand is a set of values, a lovemark is a spirit, (11) while a brand is professional, a lovemark is passionately creative, and finally (12) while a brand needs an advertising agency, a lovemark needs an ideas company (p. 70). Roberts presents a series of brands that he believes have been elevated to lovemarks. Among them are IKEA, Singapore Airlines, Twinings, BBC, Snaidero, and Campbell's Soup. The movement from brand to lovemark will not be an easy journey, but the strategic possibilities are infinite. Only time will tell.

Conclusion

Strategic brand management requires an understanding of not only brand costs and profitability, but also consumer perceptions of brand meaning, image, and value. Tactical brand decisions predicated upon cost savings and increased efficiencies must never be attempted without a clear understanding of the perceptual implications of those decisions, as brand perceptual inconsistencies may seriously undermine brand value and long-term brand equity. The company that regularly reassesses its brand equity will be in a better position to maintain its relevance with its target markets and ensure not only its long-term brand survival, but also its profitability and market leadership.

Summary

A brand is a complex entity that serves as a product and/or company identifier and provides utility for both buyers and sellers. A brand establishes important associations in the minds of target consumers, and these associations facilitate the building of a brand identity, meaning, and value. Customer perceptions of brand are an integral part of brand management and must be carefully examined and brand refinements undertaken to maintain relevance to the consumer. Brand managers must be able to undertake thorough brand audits to understand what the brand truly means and how it is valued by, not only the target customer, but firm management as well. Brand managers must constantly look for ways to improve brand efficiency and effectiveness but must also guard against making decisions that can confuse their loyal customers and undermine the brand relationships that have been built. Successful brand managers treat brands as valuable firm assets that require constant nurturing.

KEY TERMS

Brand A name, symbol, word, sign, design, or combination that differentiates one or more offerings of a seller or group of sellers from the competition.

Brand identity At its most basic level, the brand has a core identity, which is its essence and which remains constant, and an extended identity, which focuses on a series of psychological and physical aspects that give it nuance and texture.

Brand equity A set of assets (as well as liabilities) connected to the name and symbols of the brand that adds to (or detracts from) the value of the product or service to a company and/or that company's customers.

Brand architecture A complex structure of brands in a brand portfolio with a variety of different types of brand roles and relationships. The idea is that this structure is analogous to the complex structures designed by an architect.

Co-branding The bringing together of two separate company brands to be marketed together to create a new joint offering with additional value for the customer.

Brand leveraging Where the company uses the name recognition that accompanies a strong brand to increase potential sales and profits by attaching the name to other company offerings.

Advertising turnover A measure of the relationship between advertising expenditures and brand value. This measure would reflect how effectively the firm has converted advertising expenditures into brand value. Advertising turnover is calculated by dividing brand value by advertising expenditures on a year-by-year basis and examining trends.

Brand ROI An ROI calculation that focuses on the brand where the normal formula (sales/investment × net income/sales) is modified, with brand sales substituted for sales, brand value for investment, and brand sales for sales.

Brand personality The embodiment of the personality traits of the consumer in the brand itself.

Brand audit A comprehensive examination of the various sources of brand equity from the perspective of the company as well as the consumer.

Lovemark A move beyond branding to where the name becomes a symbol of love to the consumer. The key is that the name triggers an emotional attachment that transcends reason.

DISCUSSION QUESTIONS

1 What are the various benefits provided for both buyers and sellers through the use of branding?

2 What is brand identity, and why is it so important for effective strategic brand management?

3 How does the brand manager assess brand value?

4 What is brand leveraging, and what are the forces driving its use?

5 What benefits can be achieved through brand consolidation?

6 What are advertising turnover and brand ROI, and how are they helpful for strategic brand managers?

7 What is a brand audit, and why is it vital for brand revitalization?

8 How would a brand manager attempt to develop a brand personality, and how can this lead to the creation of a competitive advantage?

ONLINE RESOURCE CENTRE

Visit the Online Resource Centre for this book for lots of interesting additional material at: **www.oxfordtextbooks.co.uk/orc/west/**

REFERENCES AND FURTHER READING

Aaker, David A. (1991), *Managing Brand Equity* (New York: The Free Press).

Aaker, David A. (1996a), *Building Strong Brands* (New York: The Free Press).

Aaker, David A. (1996b), 'Measuring Brand Equity Across Products and Markets', *California Management Review*, 38, No. 3 (Spring), pp. 102–20.

Aaker, David A. (1997), 'Should You Take Your Brand to Where the Action Is?' *Harvard Business Review*, 75 (September/October), pp. 135–43.

Aaker, David A. and Erich Joachimsthaler (2000a), *Brand Leadership* (New York: The Free Press).

Aaker, David A., and Erich Joachimsthaler (2000b), 'The Brand Relationship Spectrum: The Key to the Brand Architecture Challenge', *California Management Review*, 42, No. 4 (Summer), pp. 8–23.

Abratt, Russell, and Patience Motlana (2002), 'Managing Co-Branding Strategies: Global Brands into Local Markets', *Business Horizons*, (September/October), pp. 43–50.

Berthon, Pierre, James M. Hulbert, and Leyland Pitt (1999), 'Brand Management Prognostications', *Sloan Management Review*, 40 (Winter), pp. 53–65.

Court, David C., Mark G. Leiter, and Mark A. Loch (1999), 'Brand Leverage: Developing a Strong Company Brand', *McKinsey Quarterly*, No. 2 (Spring), pp. 100–7.

Devlin, James (2003), 'Brand Architecture in Services: The Example of Retail Financial Services', *Journal of Marketing Management*, 19 (9/10), pp. 1043–66.

Edmundson, Gail, Paulo Prada, and Karen Nickel Anhalt (2003), 'Lexus: Still Looking for Traction in Europe', *Business Week* (17 November), p. 122.

Henderson, Terilyn A., and Elizabeth A. Mihas (2000), 'Building Retail Brands', *McKinsey Quarterly*, No. 3, pp. 110–17.

Herremans, Irene M., John K. Ryans, Jr., and Raj Aggarwal (2000), 'Linking Advertising and Brand Value', *Business Horizons*, (May/June), pp. 19–26.

Joachimsthaler, Erich, and David A. Aaker (1997), 'Building Brands Without Mass Media', *Harvard Business Review*, 75 (January/February), p. 50.

Keller, Kevin Lane (1999), 'Managing Brands for the Long Run', *California Management Review*, 41, No. 3 (Spring), pp. 102–24.

Keller, Kevin Lane (2000), 'The Brand Report Card', *Harvard Business Review*, 78 (January/February), pp. 3–10.

Knudsen, Trond Riiber, Lars Finskud, Richard Tornblom, and Egil Hogna (1997), 'Brand Consolidation Makes a Lot of Economic Sense: But only One in Five Attempts Succeeds', *McKinsey Quarterly*, No. 4 (Autumn), pp. 189–94.

Lane, Vicki R. (1998), 'Brand Leverage Power: The Critical Role of Brand Balance', *Business Horizons*, (January/February), pp. 75–84.

McWilliam, Gil (2000), 'Building Stronger Brands through Online Communities', *Sloan Management Review*, (Spring), pp. 43–54.

Petromilli, Michael, Dan Morrison, and Michael Million (2002), 'Brand Architecture: Building Brand Portfolio Value', *Strategy & Leadership*, 30 (5), pp. 22–9.

Prince, Melvin, and Mark Davies (2002), 'Co-Branding Partners: What Do They See in Each Other?' *Business Horizons*, (September/October), pp. 51–5.

Rao, Akshay R., and Robert W. Ruekert (1994), 'Brand Alliances as Signals of Product Quality', *Sloan Management Review*, (Fall), pp. 87–97.

Roberts, Kevin (2004), *Lovemarks: The Future Beyond Brands* (New York: Powerhouse Books).

Rogers, Daniel (2003), 'Brand Britain Goes Regional', *Marketing* (27 March), pp. 24–5.

Travis, Daryl (2000), *Emotional Branding* (Roseville, CA: Prima Venture Publishing).

Vishwanath, Vijay, and Jonathan Mark (1997), 'Your Brand's Best Strategy', *Harvard Business Review*, 75 (May/June), pp. 123–9.

KEY ARTICLE ABSTRACTS

Aaker, David A., and Erich Joachimsthaler (2000), 'The Brand Relationship Spectrum: The Key to the Brand Architecture Challenge', *California Management Review*, 42 (4), pp. 8–23.

A brand portfolio can contain a variety of different types of brand roles and relationships, and this complex structure of brands can be seen as analogous to the complex structures designed by an architect. This article presents a discussion of brand architecture, and the authors present their brand relationship spectrum to help companies manage a variety of brands and subbrands.

Abstract: This paper introduces a powerful brand architecture tool—the brand relationship spectrum. It is intended to help architecture strategists employ insight and subtlety to subbrands, endorsed brands, and their alternatives. Subbrands and endorsed brands can play a key role in creating a coherent and effective brand architecture.

Herremans, Irene M., John K. Ryans, Jr., and Raj Aggarwal (2000), 'Linking Advertising and Brand Value', *Business Horizons*, (May/June), pp. 19–26.

This paper is particularly useful in that it argues that most brand valuation has been done for the purposes of external reporting, but little has really focused on valuations for internal strategic purposes. The authors suggest that marketing investment and advertising investment are one and the same for brand valuation purposes, and they propose a new ratio, advertising turnover, which examines the relationship between advertising expenditures and brand value.

Abstract: Regardless of whether it explicitly appears on the balance sheet, most top executives would agree that the value of a company's brands—its brand equity—is one of its most important assets. This is especially true for major consumer goods companies. While all intangible assets can be of considerable importance in today's competitive environment, this article focuses on brand equity, particularly on developing performance measures of various marketing and advertising activities as they relate to brand equity.

Keller, Kevin Lane (2000), 'The Brand Report Card', *Harvard Business Review*, 78 (January/February), pp. 3–10.

The brand audit is a comprehensive examination of the various sources of brand equity from the perspective of the company as well as the consumer. This article presents a helpful tool for effective brand auditing, the Brand Report Card, which involves ratings from 1 (extremely poor) to 10 (extremely good) for honest answers to a series of key brand equity questions.

Abstract: Building and properly managing brand equity has become a priority for companies of all sizes, in all types of industries, in all types of markets. After all, from strong brand equity flow customer loyalty and profits. The rewards of having a strong brand equity are clear. The problem is that few managers are able to step back and assess their brands' particular strengths and weaknesses objectively. The 10 characteristics that the world's strongest brands have in common are identified and a Brand Report Card is constructed. The Brand Report Card is a systematic way for managers to think about how to grade their brand's performance for each of the 10 characteristics. It helps to identify areas that need improvement, recognize areas in which the brand is strong, and learn more about how the brand is configured.

END OF CHAPTER 8 CASE STUDY

Brand Britain: the shift from London to Regional cities

In late March of 2003, a new branding campaign for Britain was unveiled by the British Tourist Authority (BTA) soon to be merged with the English Tourism Council (ETC). The new branding campaign was presented to 3,000 tourism chiefs, opinion leaders and operators at the British Travel Trade Fair. This event was held in Birmingham, and it was felt that this was symbolic of the shift away from mainstay London as the focus for tourism campaigns to other regional cities as attractive travel destinations within Britain. In fact, the biggest promotional campaign for Britain in 2003 from BTA/ETC is the £6m campaign to encourage European travellers to make short visits in Britain's regional cities.

All of this is part of a plan by BTA to bring back travellers to Britain after the serious setbacks in 2001 in the concerns surrounding foot and mouth disease and the September 11 terrorist attacks. Economic frustrations and the fear of terrorist acts have exacerbated the problem. Tom Wright, chief executive of the BTA reports that 'research shows short breaks made by Europeans are the fastest growing segment in the market, comprising 25 percent of the nine million visits made to Britain last year (2002)'. He adds that the 'problem is that visitors often don't make it beyond London. Citybreak spending in London is worth £808m a year, but the most popular cities, such as Manchester and Edinburgh, generate just £8m to £12m. We want to redress the balance.'

It would appear that there is a sense that London's attraction capability has slipped in recent times. A hotel chain marketer recently remarked that hotel 'occupancy has been devastated by fears of terrorism, hardly helped by footage of tanks at Heathrow'. He went on to say that the 'transport system has also come in for a lot of bad coverage. All of this makes provincial cities seem a relatively exciting tourism prospect.'

As a result, the BTA is concentrating on regions, energized over the past five years by billions of pounds of National Lottery funding, which has produced urban regeneration, cultural development in the form of new museums and art galleries, and innovative architectural designs. Particular cities that have experienced this resurgence include Birmingham, Bristol, Cardiff, Liverpool, Newcastle/Gateshead, and Oxford. These cities have all been chosen as candidates for the European Capital of Culture in 2008.

Tom Wright had joined BTA recently, and he stresses that he will not be 'rebranding Britain'. He is doing his best to disassociate himself from a previous publicity outcry over the attempts of his predecessor to rebrand Britain through the 'Cool Britannia' campaign of the mid-1990s. Seren Welch, who is BTA's head of branding, explains that they 'are building on the existing brand—with its distinctive cultural heritage, stability and continuity—and using the emerging cities to convey Britain's diversity'.

The strategy for marketing Birmingham and Liverpool will have three core messages: accessibility, affordability, and a series of offers. Their approach has been fashioned to a certain extent from the tourism successes seen in such cities as Barcelona, Bilboa and Milan. What has particularly aided this growth in tourism has been the availability of low-cost airfares. As Wright explains it: 'People have talked about outbound no-frills flights from Britain's regional cities, but they forget this conversely means Europeans can visit Britain's regions more easily. Low-cost carriers now fly from 86 start points in Europe to 16 British destinations. With 11 key European markets providing 60 percent of inbound visitors, we can focus on the connectivity of those countries with our own cities.' Affordability as a message will challenge the normal perception of Britain as an expensive place to visit. The rates of hotels in regional cities are significantly lower than those of London. When this is considered along with low-cost airfares and free entry into many museums, inclusive packages become price competitive.

Lastly, there are local events that can be built in to the offerings. As Seren Welch explains, there 'is a pattern in the wider tourism market for later and later bookings. In this context, an event and a good package deal to that event can be a trigger to making the trip.' The BTA keeps in close touch with regional city marketers so that attractive local events can be noted and incorporated into integrated marketing efforts.

Rebranding of other countries has taught valuable lessons for Britain. Creenagh Lodge is the Chairman of Corporate Edge, a brand consultancy which has been involved with rebranding efforts for New Zealand among other nations. Lodge believes that it is imperative to stay up with the latest trends in holiday bookings. She explains that growth

» 'in modular holiday packages as opposed to fully inclusive tour programmes creates a growing need for niche and tailor-made products, hence the focus on city breaks. By highlighting the regional diversity of the destination brands, it ultimately builds the core values for Britain.'

The task facing BTA is sizeable. Britain currently is behind the U.S., France, Spain and Italy as favourite tourist destinations and will have to compete for business with emerging Eastern European destinations, which have been quick to incorporate tourism marketing schemes. The BTA reported in its annual report for 2002 that the 'UK's position in some core markets is not as strong as some of its rivals, and the global tourism market is changing'.

Source: Daniel Rogers (2003), 'Brand Britain Goes Regional', *Marketing* (27 March), pp. 24–5.

QUESTIONS

1. What are the branding challenges and opportunities here?
2. What are the downsides to lessening the focus on London as a destination?
3. What are the downsides to the regional focus?
4. What types of marketing research should be done to allow for better decision-making?
5. What would you recommend be done given the strengths and weaknesses of the different approaches?

9

Service marketing strategies

LEARNING OBJECTIVES

- Provide an overview of the nature of services and how they differ from manufactured goods
- Discuss ways in which services can streamline operations and improve productivity and profitability
- Examine the nature of the customer service experience
- Establish the relationship between customer value and sustainable competitive advantage
- Present several strategic tools for fine assessment of the service process and the delivery of customer value

CHAPTER AT A GLANCE

Introduction

There is little doubt that the service sector is the fastest growing sector of the world economy. In the OECD countries (Organisation for Economic Co-Operation and Development), services now account for almost 70% of GDP (Gross Domestic Product), and service jobs make up the largest category of all employment opportunities, with nearly 65% of all OECD country workers employed in activities related to services (OECD, 2001). Even in the emerging economies services are rapidly growing and often comprise more than 50% of GDP (World Bank, 2003).

Services are by nature intangible, heterogeneous, inseparable, and perishable, and they create unique strategic challenges. While an understanding of industry structure can aid the service strategist to streamline service delivery and improve profitability, it is also vital to achieve sustainable competitive advantage (SCA) through customer satisfaction and the creation of perceived value (Naumann and Jackson, 1999). Services cannot be protected in the same way as manufactured goods with property rights such as patents, so they are easily copied, unless the company has built a perceptual bond with its customers. To beat competitors, the service firm must continually meet and/or exceed customer expectations (Ford et al., 2001). This forces the firm to continually monitor the wants and needs of its target customers and to strategically refine its offerings to enhance customer value.

The focus on customer value is relevant not just for service firms. Many global industries are now being forced toward standardization of offerings as life cycles mature. The road to parity creates enormous strategic turbulence as firms attempt to differentiate their offerings from those of competitors. Manufacturers can differentiate through the development of value-laden complementary services (much as Saturn, a division of General Motors in the USA, has done through its innovative approach to supply chain management), but the key is to ensure that these complementary services are perceived by target customers as adding real value to the overall offering (Cohen et al., 2000).

The challenge for service firms is to create a position of perceptual value and power that cannot be easily copied by competitors. This requires a constant balancing of operational efficiency and customer relationship building. This chapter will focus on the distinctive nature of services, operational efficiency and profitability, the nature of the service experience, and the creation of customer value.

The distinctive nature of services

Service strategists gain helpful planning insight when they examine the ways in which services are significantly different from manufactured goods. Too often it is easier to assume that what works for goods will work for services, but this is not a valid assumption. There are four readily accepted distinguishing characteristics of services that create unique strategic challenges, and which are displayed in Figure 9.1. With an understanding of these characteristics, strategists are in a better position to understand the importance of customer satisfaction to profitability and sustainable competitive advantage. Each of these characteristics will now be discussed and strategic implications presented.

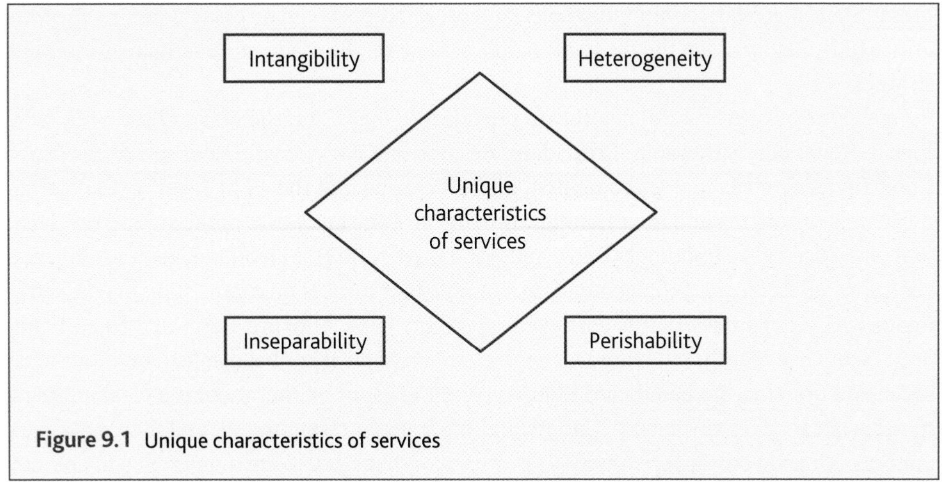

Figure 9.1 Unique characteristics of services

Intangibility

Since services cannot be held in the hand, felt, and touched, they present a challenge for strategic marketing decision-making as competitive differentiation has to be experienced by users and there really are no strategies for disposal of unsold stock. Intangibility intensifies any perceived risk on the part of the consumer, and it becomes necessary to find ways to reduce uncertainty wherever possible. Ted Leavitt noted in 1981 that consumers of a service will find a way to infer some degree of tangibility by observing the evidence of the service and thereby making assumptions about quality from the evidence at hand. Service providers are forced, as a result, to strategically manage physical evidence to provide surrogate tangibility to what is intangible. The challenge for the services marketer is to find images as well as physical evidence that enhance perceptions of service quality. Healthcare providers can readily display diplomas to enhance credibility, restaurants can provide potential customers with copies of recent reviews from food critics or by displaying awards from food ratings services (e.g., Michelin), holiday resorts can provide high-quality photographs of their facilities in their promotional materials as well as testimonials from creditable sources to reduce uncertainty, and some service providers can actually offer limited trial memberships to give consumers a chance to experience the service on a risk-free basis (e.g., AOL). A number of service providers over the years have found ways to build tangibility into their offerings through the attachment of mental imagery that enhances consumer perceptions of service quality. A good example can be seen in Travel Inn's slogan, 'Everything you need for a good night's sleep'. In the United States Allstate Insurance Company has utilized the catchphrase, 'You are in good hands with Allstate'.

A key strategic issue is that even the most intangible services (pure services like consulting projects or executive seminars) have certain tangible aspects to them that can be used to convey perceptions of service quality. Consulting personnel can dress in a suitable manner to convey professionalism, the consulting offices where meetings with the client take place can be managed to convey success and professionalism through various atmospheric components (e.g., furniture, floors, walls, lighting, colour, music), and the various promotional materials, communications, and project reports can be presented in such a way as to exude quality. Even the most intangible service can be made more tangible in creative strategic ways.

One of the most successful healthcare providers in the USA is the Mayo Clinic, with facilities in Rochester, Minnesota, Scottsdale, Arizona and Jacksonville, Florida. At the Mayo Clinic the patient really does come first, and every aspect of the clinic is set up to communicate this to patients and their families from the attitude and attire of the staff to the decor and ambience of the buildings (Berry and Bendapudi, 2003). Mayo management utilizes a sophisticated 'evidence management' programme that focuses on a consistent and effective image and set of values that is conveyed on a daily basis. Leonard Berry and Neeli Bendapudi spent five months studying Mayo to understand how it has been able to build the most successful brand in the healthcare industry, and they suggest that there is a clear strategic message for services marketers: 'Understand the story you want to tell, and then make sure your people and your facilities provide evidence of that story to customers, day in and day out' (p. 101).

Heterogeneity

Heterogeneity means that it is difficult to be a low-cost provider or to differentiate for positioning purposes. Each time there is an interaction between service personnel and the consumer, the service is being provided, and impressions are built in the mind of the consumer regarding the quality of that service offering. One difficulty in setting up quality control systems in service firms is that you can certainly require that personnel meet certain standards of education and certification, but you cannot control the 'human factor'. The inconsistencies brought on by changes in mood states and emotions can cause differences in interactions between service provider personnel and consumers. Of course service personnel and their inconsistencies are not the only problems. The consumers themselves are different, and their physical and emotional makeup will affect interactions.

The key for the services marketer, in light of the heterogeneity of service interactions, is to ensure as much consistency as possible. While total consistency is impossible, there are mechanisms that can be utilized to reduce inconsistencies. One involves the design of the service in such a way as to make it as uniform as possible. This might be accomplished via automation where possible or by training service personnel to follow strictly controlled guidelines. Hand in hand with this approach would go the need for an effective employee selection, motivation, and retention process. No matter how sophisticated the service is, there is no substitute for hiring the right people, training them effectively, and putting them into an environment that nurtures their success. The challenge for the marketer is to standardize as much as possible while allowing enough flexibility for the service personnel to be able to address the distinct differences that may be found across a wide variety of customers. Many service providers have found that another strategic approach is also necessary to eliminate the problems inherent in heterogeneity: the use of money-back guarantees. If the firm expects that, even with tight controls, there may be the chance of a disgruntled customer, the offering of a money-back guarantee may alleviate any post-production dissonance that might arise from poor service provider-customer interactions.

Berry and Bendapudi (2003) found that employee selection is a vital link to the consistent message being sent to the customer by service firms. They describe the process utilized by the Mayo Clinic and the care put into the selection process and training programme. One of the keys to success for Mayo has been the consistency with which they select individuals based upon their abilities and knowledge as well as their emotional connection to the core values of the service. If service personnel embody the principles and values of the organization, they can be given more power to tailor the service experience to the specific needs of each and every customer. This empowerment has certainly made a difference at other successful service organizations like Southwest Airlines (Barrett, 1998) and American Express Company (Grant, 1998).

Inseparability

Inseparability means that customers are co-producers/designers of the service and therefore can experience the strategy directly (i.e., low cost or differentiation). In co-production it is hard to reduce costs and maintain a quality image; whereas with products, cost-cutting need not necessarily lead to a change in quality image as it can be hidden more easily. If the customer is actively engaged in participating, they may feel a closer affinity and potential loyalty. Think how difficult it would be for a doctor to treat a patient if the patient is not willing to discuss his/her physical condition in detail. Companies can foster a more proactive involvement on the part of the customer.

Another way to deal with this issue is to look at the location issue. The production must be brought to the customer, so providing additional locations for the service provision and training personnel to effectively handle greater demand for the service should help. This argues for greater decentralization and employee empowerment to ensure the highest service quality level. This has helped build loyal followings for easyJet, Virgin, and Apple Computers. Another strategic approach that could help involves training service personnel how to deal with problematic customers to reduce the potential for customer dissonance. Vocal, problematic customers can negatively affect other customers who are present, and moving them quickly into a manager's office where their difficulties can be addressed by a manager can greatly enhance the experience for all concerned.

Paul Hemp, a senior editor of *Harvard Business Review*, spent a week as a room-service waiter for the newest Ritz-Carlton hotel in Boston, Massachusetts, and he found that it is vital for managers to see what things are like at the interaction level between customers and service personnel to develop proper strategic insight. Ritz has exceptional standards for excellence in dealing with its clientele (called appropriately the Gold Standards), has proven training programmes for personnel (the Ritz-Carlton Learning Institute), and an effective communication mechanism from the customer to the service employee to management which allows for the service to be customized to the needs of clients (Hemp, 2002).

Perishability

Perishability means that it is essential to get cost and/or differentiation strategies right, as if you are unsuccessful, the opportunity is lost; whereas product companies can hold stock and reposition on price. Almost thirty years ago Earl Sasser presented a series of strategic alternatives for effectively synchronizing supply and demand. He suggested that if there are problems in demand, then service firms can: (1) use differential pricing to shift demand from peak to off-peak periods, (2) provide new offerings that stimulate off-peak demand, (3) develop complementary services to help customers while they wait, and (4) make use of reservations systems to manage demand. From the capacity side, Sasser suggested the use of: (1) part-time employees to help out during peak hours, (2) increased participation on the part of the customer, (3) routines during peak hours which allow personnel to deal with demand more efficiently, (4) services which could be shared with other service providers, and (5) facilities for future expansion when and if necessary (Sasser, 1976).

These defining characteristics of services are helpful in the development of service strategy, but it is imperative to understand both the nature of industry structure and the expectations of customers in order to gain sustainable competitive advantage.

Operational efficiency and profitability

Since services are basically intangible, difficult to protect legally, and have relatively low barriers to entry, they are easy to copy. Operational excellence is one way in which service firms can achieve strategic success. Operational excellence can be garnered in a number of different ways: streamlining and cost cutting, creative strategic alliances, and internal employee culture creation and enhancement. Strategic successes provide excellent opportunities for service firms to improve operations and raise profit margins. A series of effective mechanisms for operational improvement will now be discussed and illustrated with company examples.

Streamlining and cost-cutting

Many service providers have found the need to improve operations to eliminate inefficiencies and improve profit margins. To a certain extent customer value is enhanced when the firm's cost-cutting can be passed along, with visible savings for the customer (Mendonca and McCallum, 1995). Four major trends have forced service providers to focus on cost-cutting: (1) ever-intensifying competition as industry regulations open competition to new and varied types of competitors (e.g., deregulation and the sanctioning of new and creative strategic alliances), (2) slowing industry growth projections, (3) increasing levels of parity across providers, and (4) increasing levels of customer expectations. Service firms must satisfy customers at ever decreasing cost levels (Arnold et al., 1998). Service providers have recently embraced some of the cost-cutting benefits that were experienced by western manufacturers attempting to remain competitive with the Japanese during the 1990s (Swank, 2003). This recent use of 'lean service management' focuses on re-engineering operations to improve profitability. Swank (2003) warns service providers to always measure any improvements in performance and productivity from the customer's perspective. Whatever is attempted should not detract in any way from perceptions of customer value. Otherwise competitiveness would be severely eroded. So in what specific ways can services improve their productivity? Friedman (1998) makes the following suggestions:

- Operate with fewer workers by providing supporting equipment and systems or helping employees do more (e.g., automation for efficiencies like scanners for supermarkets and ATMs for banks).
- Eliminate certain elements of a process (e.g., check-in and check-out processes for hotels and car hire companies).
- De-skill certain jobs to allow the use of a broader pool of workers (e.g., point-of-sale machines that do not require skilled employees to oversee).
- Take non-customer work requirements from frontline service personnel and delegate them to others within the organization (e.g., moving international currency exchange capabilities out of neighbourhood bank branches to special regional offices).
- Determine those tasks that must be performed close to the customer as opposed to those which can be done far away (e.g., regional customer service centres as opposed to local).
- Offload certain work requirements to suppliers (e.g., hospitals and prepackaged surgery kits).
- Change customer expectations in terms of their involvement in the process (e.g., self-service petrol stations and customers filling their own soft drink cups at fast-food restaurants).

Friedman warns against the elimination of any aspects of the service that would be valued by customers. He also strongly warns against simply reducing the number of employees (since frontline personnel are critical and doing more may make them cut back on each part of the process) or asking the same number of employees to take on a greater array of tasks.

Swank (2003) provides an excellent example of service streamlining. Jefferson Pilot Financial was extremely successful in transforming itself into a lean service management enterprise by re-engineering its New Business operations. The company implemented a number of changes that improved efficiency while reducing costs. Process employees were moved closer to one another, having been previously located according to functional area of work. Customer files were then more efficiently moved along from group to group. Procedures were also standardized, with all files being stored alphabetically and process employees were housed in similar settings to ensure consistency and to allow substitute employees to work efficiently when needed. It was also found that previously there had been feedback loop-backs whereby applications might go back to previous processing stages and cause delays. These were eliminated. Another improvement involved setting common work tempos for employees so that higher hourly goals for completing applications could be set. This type of process re-engineering proved to be extremely beneficial for Jefferson Pilot Financial as this allowed the company to charge lower premiums and handle applications more quickly.

Metters and Vargas (2000) argue that for services to streamline and improve efficiency, they must redesign the jobs of the personnel involved in the service delivery process. They suggest that sometimes technologies become available that allow cost-cutting across the entire service while improving the level of the quality of the service provided. When these technologies exist, they should be adopted immediately. When these technologies are not available, they suggest that management should consider ‘decoupling’ service tasks to gain

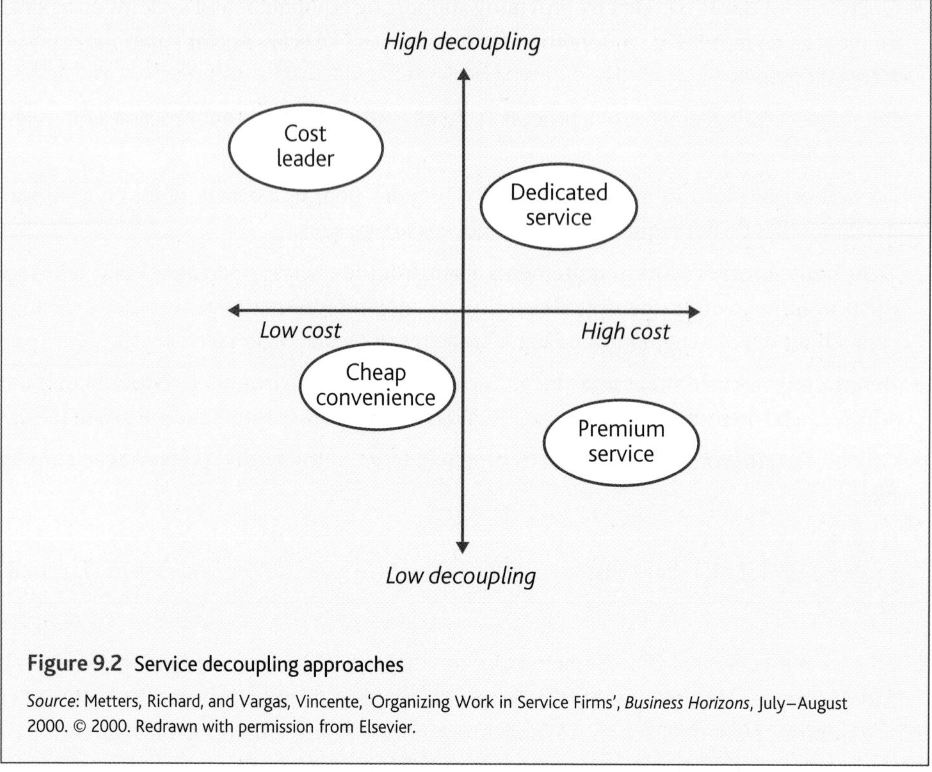

Figure 9.2 Service decoupling approaches

Source: Metters, Richard, and Vargas, Vincente, 'Organizing Work in Service Firms', *Business Horizons*, July–August 2000. © 2000. Redrawn with permission from Elsevier.

efficiencies. Decoupling involves removing certain tasks involving little customer contact from frontline or front office personnel, standardizing them, and moving them into remote back office locations. They present four different competitive approaches to decoupling (see Figure 9.2) and provide illustrative examples for each. The first category presented is the **Cost leaders** (companies that compete on price and decouple for the main purpose of lowering costs. The focus here is to take complex jobs with multiple tasks and make them simpler through standardization with the use of specialized labour and new technologies to achieve economies of scale. The decoupling of complex jobs allows for the reduction of work variance. This reflects Michael Porter's (1980) overall cost leadership strategy. Vargas and Metters (2000) use the discount stockbroker Charles Schwab & Co. and the insurance company GEICO as examples of Cost Leaders. These firms eliminated localized personnel who had high customer contact and were paid by commissions, which was the standard of their industries. The standardization of certain basic components of the customer delivery process significantly streamlined operations and improved profitability.

The second type of company is the **Cheap convenience** company which attempts to make their service offering more convenient while maintaining a relatively low cost structure. Metters and Vargas (2000) refer to this as a 'kiosk' strategy, where the firm utilizes multiple service units in different locations to provide easy customer access but offering only a limited range of services. This equates to Porter's (1980) differentiation strategy. For these firms fewer, cross-trained employees are utilized doing both back office and front office work. Examples of successful competitors in this category include Dollar General, 7–11 (Southland Corporation), and Edward D. Jones stock brokerage services. These firms compete against the Cost Leaders by offering many convenient smaller product-line outlets. The key to success for these firms is the development of easy-to-use software and the use of tightly scripted service encounters between customers and service personnel.

The third category is the **Dedicated service** firm that decouples to support front office personnel, with cost reduction as a secondary concern. Here tasks are separated by personality type and ability. Decoupling here allows more variety and flexibility to enhance employee morale and customer service experiences. The driving concept here is worker suitability, with matching of service work to personality type. Back office tasks are centralized by region, or particular back office contacts are specified for each group of front office workers. Long-term relationships are built between back office and front office to help the service delivery process flow smoothly. This approach requires more staff and potentially higher costs. Many traditional hospitals and insurance companies follow this kind of service strategy. The key here is to set up proper reward structures based on how well the back office personnel support the front office workers.

The final decoupling approach is the **Premium service** firm where less decoupling is used in order to maximize responsiveness and customization. Again, this reflects a differentiation strategy (Porter, 1980), but the strategic goal is to provide personalized service at premium prices. Intimate relationships are built between customers and service personnel. Frontline personnel are given power to customize a variety of offerings to meet the specific needs of each customer while back office personnel are minimally decoupled. Metters and Vargas (2000) provide the example of the US firm Krispy Kreme doughnuts as a Premium Service firm in comparison to Cost Leader Dunkin' Donuts. A sound, differentiating device for hospitals can involve the development of specialized maternity (e.g., the Tennessee Birthing Center) or paediatric orientations (the Children's Hospital of Philadelphia).

Creative strategic alliances

A creative strategic way to improve service profitability involves strategic partnering between different service providers (Ernst and French, 1996). Alliances can effectively be used to strengthen brands and cut costs. These alliances can take the form of co-branding, co-marketing, outsourcing, licensing, or distribution agreements, to name but a few. Examples can readily be seen in the strategic partnerings of airlines like the Star Alliance, Northwest Airline, and KLM, and United Airlines and Lufthansa as well as in the offering of T-Mobile WiFi hotspots at Texaco service stations, Starbucks coffee on United Airlines flights, and the UK mobile operator 3 offering Sony BMG music videos for download to its customers with mobile phones. These alliances offer another approach to differentiation of service offerings by allowing partners to retain their own independent brands and financial control while cutting costs and improving profits. Savings are facilitated through sharing of assets and/or business processes or through the outsourcing of components of the offering.

Ernst and French (1996) caution that any partnerings must ensure that there is no eroding of each partner's core service concept. There are two main types of strategic alliance for services: brand-sharing alliances and asset-sharing alliances. Brand-sharing alliances increase customer benefits through joint offerings with minimal system integration. The idea is to create greater value for the consumer by offering complementary services rather than to achieve enormous cost savings. Citibank developed a relationship with American Airlines to offer its credit card users benefits in the form of frequent flyer miles. This required only a minimum of coordination and integration, but both brands enjoyed brand enhancement. Asset-sharing alliances look to business system integration for the purpose of significant cost savings. These alliances can involve the sharing of retail floor space, computer systems, equipment, and technology. 7–11 (Southland) has asset-sharing relationships with Citgo petrol stations to share the cost of floor space. Similarly, Little Caesar's Pizza has sales outlets in K-Mart stores and McDonald's has food outlets in Wal-Mart stores. Some of these alliances can become more like mergers than strategic partnerings as the partners become integrally linked with one another. This can be seen in the airline industry with such pairings as UsAir and British Airways which have common hubs, maintenance, and ticketing facilities. It has been estimated that this alliance has resulted in cost savings and increased revenues for the partners of over $100 million per year (Ernst and French, 1996).

Instrumental to any partnering is the need to ensure the best fit between partners in terms of customer demographics and brand image. Customers must readily see the benefit in the pairing of services. Ernst and French (1996) provide the following suggestions for managing alliances:

- Prepare for an alliance as you would for a merger.
- Mechanisms must be established for strategy development, organizational decision-making, and assignment of financial accountability in the new alliance culture.
- Both partners must move quickly and effectively to manage the transition.
- Budget sufficient time for alliance work.
- Monitor progress on a weekly basis, at least at the beginning.
- Build in mechanisms for conflict resolution and decision-making.
- Consider exit options.

Another approach to alliances that can have synergies for service firms and aid in the cost-cutting process is outsourcing. Allen and Chandrashekar (2000) report that more than 90% of all US service firms have outsourced some of their service offerings. Doing so potentially allows firms to get goods and services at a lower cost and with a higher quality by relying on firms that specialize in certain components of service delivery. Anything that the firm believes is not part of its core competency becomes a candidate for outsourcing. This enormous trend toward outsourcing began with IT as a functional area with providers like Andersen Consulting, but it has spread to all kinds of service businesses. Hotels outsource concierge services, restaurant services, and cleaning services. Airlines outsource cleaning and maintenance and reservations services. Almost anything can be outsourced, provided that it does not potentially erode firm core competencies and confuse the customer. A good overview of outsourcing possibilities based on the levels of service provided by the service contractor can be found in Figure 9.3.

Level of contractor contribution

	Labour contracting	*Mixed outsourcing*	*Complete outsourcing*
Contractor provides...	• Some employees	Some or all of the following: • Employees • Materials • Process and systems • Technology and equipment • Facilities • Management/supervision	• Employees • Process and systems • Technology and equipment • Materials • Facilities • Supervision
Host firm provides...	• Some employees • Process and systems • Technology and equipment • Materials • Facilities • Management/supervision	Some or all of the following: • Employees • Materials • Process and systems • Technology and equipment • Facilities • Management/supervision	• Program management

Figure 9.3 Categories of service outsourcing

Source: Allen, Sandy, and Chandrashekar, Ashok, 'Outsourcing Services: The Contract is Just the Beginning', *Business Horizons*, March–April 2000. © 2000. Redrawn with permission from Elsevier.

Outsourcing must be carefully managed. Allen and Chandrashekar (2000) provide a series of strategic suggestions for the proper care and handling of outsourcing. First of all they suggest that the management of outsourcing requires a shift for managers from the management of people to the management of contracts. The wording of the contracts becomes the focal point rather than the governing of personnel. An important first step in the process should be to clearly define the expectations for the use of outsourcing. A key point that the authors make is that outsourcing should not be used as a method for eliminating a problem area for the firm if the real problem stems from something that is systematic within the firm itself. Outsourcing often involves the combination of contract workers with regular service personnel, and there is always the challenge of dealing with divided loyalties and employee role conflict. Outsourcing managers must deal with potential conflicts between these two different types of workers. While cohesiveness of the workforce is challenging, with proper open communications and thoughtful strategic planning, outsourcing can be a powerful mechanism for service streamlining.

Internal employee culture creation and enhancement

The challenges inherent in streamlining through outsourcing highlight the importance of employees in the service mix. The front office and back office personnel are instrumental to the provision of the service and ultimately influence the customer's perceptions of quality and value. Service firms are constantly faced with employee turnover, and many of the problems experienced have to do with the lack of care and nurturing of these important facilitators. Hays (1996) suggests that poor service from internal service units within the service firm have forced a number of services to consider outsourcing when a far more productive approach would involve paying more attention to these internal units and providing them with better training and support. Setting up a supportive internal culture could keep employees in these internal service units happier and more productive. Hays (1996) posits that internal service improvements can lead to dramatically increased internal service productivity (gains of 20–60% are possible), an elevation of overall quality ceilings, and the development of new sources of competitive advantage.

Another challenge that faces service firms is the availability of service personnel. Friedman (1998) warns that service strategy is dependent upon the availability of appropriate employees, and that service firms must change their way of thinking about service employees as the phenomenal growth of the service sector has led to a labour shortage, with the number of employees having been outpaced by new job creation. Friedman (1998) proposes that service firms create effective value propositions for employees, tap new employee segments (e.g., older adults and the disabled), and change work structures so that they will keep good employees and be seen as the preferred employer in a particular service area. One of the most important ways in which a company can keep good employees and attract qualified candidates is to create an environment in which the employees are treated in the same way as they would treat customers. This 'golden rule' has worked exceptionally well for such service success stories as Southwest Airlines, Ritz-Carlton Hotels, Walt Disney Corporation, and Nordstrom's Department Stores.

Streamlining service operations and improving productivity and employee morale are all excellent strategies for improving profitability, but the other side of the equation which is equally important is to ensure that the customer experience is the best that it can be. In order to continually meet or exceed customer expectations it is imperative that service strategists understand exactly what the consumer expects to be delivered by the service. This next section will focus on the nature of customer service expectations and the achievement of sustainable competitive advantage.

The service experience

In order to be successful, service strategists have to understand exactly what the consumer is looking for when they 'experience' the service in question. Each customer will have a set of expectations regarding the service experience that must be met to ensure customer satisfaction. How is customer satisfaction ensured? Research has consistently shown that the key to service firms' success is keeping the customer happy. Fulfilment appears to be the key ingredient in the concept of customer satisfaction (Oliver, 1997). If a service meets or exceeds the expectations of the customer, he/she will enjoy a sense of fulfilment and will be satisfied with the service consumption experience. The key for the service strategist therefore is to determine how to measure service quality. Zeithaml et al. (1990) have done extensive work examining the concept of service quality, and they found that service quality is a multi-faceted construct with five distinctive dimensions: reliability (dependability and accuracy), responsiveness (helpfulness and promptness), empathy (customer understanding and individualized attention), assurance (employee competence, courtesy, and trustworthiness), and tangibles (condition of physical evidence). The authors created a survey instrument to assess customer perceptions of service quality along these five dimensional lines that they named SERVQUAL (Parasuraman et al., 1988). SERVQUAL has been used in many settings to compare the expected service delivery with the actual customer perceptions of service delivery to provide an excellent service process evaluative tool.

Why is this set of relationships so important? Because perceptions of service quality lead to customer satisfaction, which in turn leads to positive purchase intentions, which leads to sales and profits (Heskett et al., 1997). Satisfied customers are likely to come back and spend more in the future while also passing the word to others. Reichheld and Sasser (1990) found that the longer a service company is able to retain its customers, the more they will spend on the services offered by the company. Mini Case Study 9.1 looks at the experience of UK banks in improving their image with their customers.

MINI CASE STUDY 9.1 Image makeovers: the case of UK banks

UK banks have recently realized that they need to forge better connections to customers, and they have begun a rapid series of rebrandings. These image makeovers are not without serious risks. The poor showing of the Post Office as it re-emerged as Consignia indicates the potential for disaster in tinkering with company image. Barclays recently followed image relaunches in 2003 for NatWest and Abbey National, but Abbey National endured a variety of criticisms after its radical makeover.

Barclays decided to soften the company eagle icon and the lettering associated with the name. Sara Deeks, the Barclays brand strategy director, suggests that the image reshaping is focused on creating international brand image consistency. She explains that they 'wanted the look and feel of a global player. Our rebrand isn't about being friendly. The question we ask is whether people would entrust their salary to a mate or to an expert in the field.' The company believes that its rebranding is more of an evolutionary change for the brand. What is most important for them is whether the rebranding makes any significant difference to the bank's customers. They are not interested in merely making cosmetic changes.

NatWest feels that its recent revamping actually focused on addressing customer needs. Besides a series of redesigns for its fascias, it has undertaken a four-year renovation of its branch office interiors to allow customers greater ease of access to its various services. In particular, the branch reconfiguration involves creating more interview space and lower-level service desks.

Abbey National has been the recipient of a fair amount of criticism for its efforts. The claims that accompanied its image makeover stated that the company would be 'turning banking on its head', but the problem was that customers didn't seem to believe the claim, and the company admitted that it had missed its first-quarter profit expectations. Small shareholders at a recent meeting stated that they believed that the rebranding was a » large 'waste of money'. The key is that whatever rebranding is attempted, the effects must positively resonate with customers.

One problem that banks as service organizations face is that they are large enterprises, and any attempted overhauls are expensive and time-consuming. While Barclays has not announced the figures for its rebranding, it is believed to have spent £400,000 for the hiring of Williams Murray Hamm, a brand consultancy. As part of its rebranding efforts, Abbey National spent £11 million for the redesign and renovation of its branch offices.

Abbey National reported a £1 billion loss, and it took little time to make additional changes in its brand image by dropping National from its name, introducing a pastel-coloured, lower-case logo, and made the promise to customers to revolutionize personal banking. Abbey's director of customer propositions, Angus Porter, believes that the rebranding was an important component to its three-year business repositioning that will improve communications to customers. He states that in order to 'signal to staff and customers that we are different, it's important to have a physical change. The overhaul of the branches was overdue and the "umbrella couple" logo was stuck in the 70s. Research showed that people had a fondness for Abbey, but saw National as having institutional connotations.'

Criticisms have been aimed at banks that stress that changes in identity are a poor strategic alternative to fixing internal problems. Angus Porter argues that banks 'operate in a hard-nosed business world. We have three years to achieve the results the City wants. Doing it quietly is not viable.' One who believes that image changes for banks is a necessity is Rita Clifton, Chairman of Interbrand, who states that the problem is that banks 'have not been the most consumer-oriented businesses'. She proposes that banks can 'either tell people you are going to do it and have a clear path to what you want to achieve, or you rebuild the business from the bottom up before you change the visual identity.' If you follow the former pathway, Clifton explains that the 'danger is that you feed people's prejudices. On the other hand, lower-key changes are less likely to make an impact. Bank revamps need to be interesting enough to make people break out of the inertia that characterizes the sector.'

One success story that experts point to is the work done by HSBC to Midland following its acquisition. Paul Gordon, managing director of financial services agency CCHM explains that what made it success was that HSBC 'did it quickly, clearly and with conviction, but left very strong niche brands, such as first direct alone'. Other banks have mistakenly ignored important issues in the minds of customers in order to implement expensive and poorly-timed campaigns such as Barclays' 'Big Bank' ads during a time of branch closures. Sara Deeks explains that Barclays learned a valuable lesson from that failure and has now established a brand reputation group, which meets to discuss various image issues.

One important question is whether a bank is able to tell if a rebranding is enhancing customer loyalty. Abbey implemented a customer-tracking programme involving the interview of 600 individuals per month. Angus Porter says that attitudes are changing. He states that people 'are becoming more open to dealing with Abbey. There have been important shifts in terms of it being a brand for everyone.'

If the bank cannot deliver on promises that it makes, there is the risk that whatever is done to remake the image will be reacted to as wasteful. Richard Murray from

» Williams Murray Hamm explains that if 'you are changing for the sake of being different, the cracks will always show'.

Source: Alexandra Jardine (2004), 'Banks Suffer Identity Crisis', *Marketing*, 6 May, p. 17.

Service firms are quickly realizing that service delivery involves a performance on their part. This performance must be the best that it can be; therefore, service firms are realizing the relevance of the 'service as drama' metaphor.

Service as drama

A unique perspective-enhancing approach to understanding the service experience was suggested in 1983 by Grove and Fisk. They proposed the value of the strategic use of dramaturgy whereby a service is thought of as a drama with three important components: a stage, actors, and an audience (see Figure 9.4). Each of these will now be discussed in turn and strategic insights provided.

The stage

The stage refers to the physical setting for the delivery of the service. In a performance there are two areas of the stage, one that is clearly visible (the front stage) and one that is not visible (the backstage). There is a great deal of preparation that takes place behind the scenes before the play is performed, and while there are actors directly in front of the audience

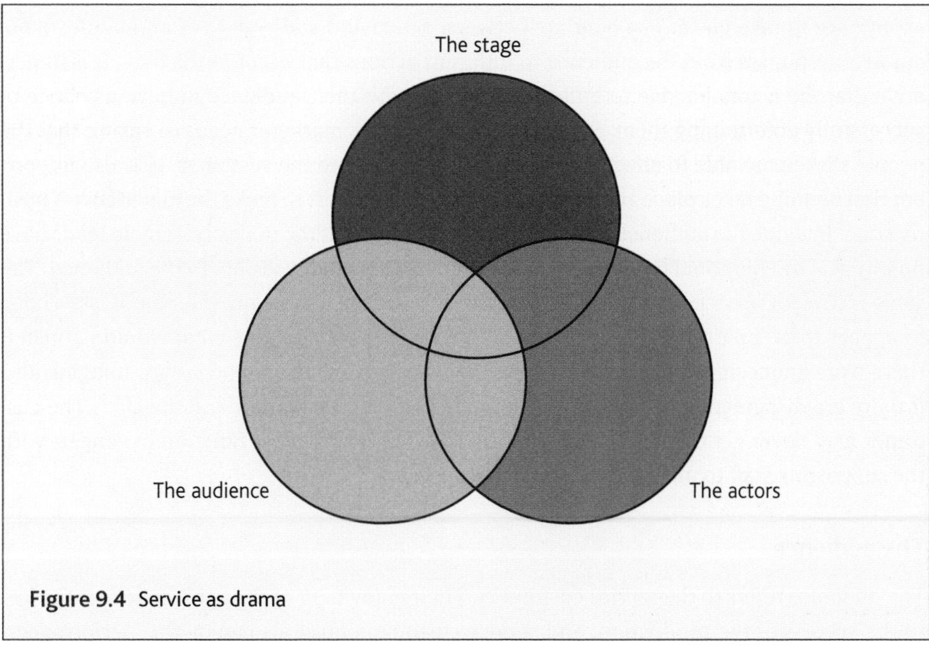

Figure 9.4 Service as drama

performing, there are others behind the scenes participating in a variety of ways to make the production work effectively. There are many other supporting individuals who help to make the play successful (e.g., lighting crew, sound crew, makeup people, stage crew, etc.), and this is certainly the case when considering the operation of a service firm. Think of all of the unseen individuals who help to make the airline trip successful (reservations, food preparation, cleaning services, aircraft maintenance, baggage handling, etc.). The front stage personnel interact in a face-to-face setting with the customer; however, there are those who are basically invisible to the customer but are integrally involved and necessary for the effective performance of the service. The appearance and mannerisms of the front stage personnel are important to the customer because they are readily visible, so the actors' appearance is certainly a part of physical evidence. The appearance of the backstage personnel is not as important (unless they are visible to the audience). Of course, the stage appearance is also important (physical evidence) as well as other atmospheric variables (lighting, music, etc.) that are all part of the service setting. Again, however, the front stage is more relevant to this discussion as the backstage area is normally not visible to the customer. In service firms, it may be important to actually show what goes on backstage as part of the uniqueness of the service offering. Of course errant noises from backstage would not help the delivery of the play, so all must be carefully coordinated. The services marketer should look at all aspects of the delivery setting and attempt to conform to customer expectations.

The actors

A play has a series of actors who perform for the audience. The performers are the frontline service personnel who interact and offer the service to the customer. What is important for a stage play to be successful is the bond that builds between the actors and the audience. If the audience do not feel any affinity for the actors, there is little chance for a meaningful experience to take place. The bonding between actors and audience is often manifested in emotive responses from the audience to different actions that occur in the play. It is imperative that the actors be able to build these bonds with their audience to have a chance of successfully entertaining them. Strategically the services marketer needs to ensure that the people chosen are able to effectively interact and bond with the customer. It is also important that bonding takes place among the various cast members to make the experience a positive one. Imagine the audience reaction in a romantic play if the male and female leads have no physical or emotional bonding between them that is readily visible to the audience. The same is true for service personnel. The various interfacing service provider employees need to appear to be a part of a team with bonds between them. Imagine what would happen if there were animosities between the actors and the lighting and sound crews. Imagine also if there are disagreements between the waiting staff at a restaurant and the chef. The customer may never get the meal he or she ordered. The actors must function in concert with the supporting staff to make the production a success.

The audience

The audience refers to the service customers. Their enjoyment of the performance is the key to the success of the production, and service customers must also enjoy the 'performance' during the service experience or they will not come back again. As many marketers have painfully learned, one-time purchasers will never keep a company in business. Repeat purchase is what makes a company successful, and service firms must ensure that their customers enjoy the experience and want to repeat it. Valuable insight is provided through the use of the drama metaphor particularly as it relates to the nature of the audience in that the makeup of the audience must be carefully managed. What is important to consider is that all customers do not necessarily interact well together. The patrons who are spending a large amount of money to attend the opening night of a new opera production in New York, Rome, or London and wearing formal evening dress would not want to be seated next to customers wearing jeans and T-shirts with screaming babies on their laps. These two groups of potential customers are not compatible with each other, and this is something that service providers must approach carefully. If there is a clear target audience in mind for the service, then the strategic goal should be to offer that constituency the best experience that they can receive. Everything that is done should be geared to that customer and his or her service experience expectations.

This use of the drama metaphor (dramaturgy) provides a new perspective for service strategists in that it is easy to understand while also bringing out the subtleties of the nature of the service experience and the 'moment of truth'. In a very real way, the service experience is indeed a theatrical performance, and the enjoyment of the customer is vital for firm survival.

The Walt Disney Company provides an excellent example of service provision as drama in its theme park operations in that its employees are carefully selected and trained to be members of the 'cast', the stage both in the foreground and behind the scenes is kept neat and clean at all times, and members of the audience are engaged on a regular basis as co-producers of the service with cast members as well as with each other (Grove et al., 1992).

The key to success for service firms involves meeting or exceeding customer expectations, and it is this perceptual position in the head of the customer that serves as the basis for sustainable competitive advantage.

Customer value as sustainable competitive advantage

Since service firms do not have the benefit of patents and other high barriers to entry, competitive advantage for service firms lies in continually exceeding customer expectations (Ford et al., 2001). If the customer believes that the quality he or she is receiving is the best that it can be, there is no reason to switch to the offerings of another provider. So how does the service firm ensure that it can provide value to the customer and achieve sustainable competitive advantage? One consideration is the definition of the target customer in question. Many service firm failures point to the impossible nature of being 'all things to all customers' (Arnold et al., 1999). Successful segmentation is a necessity for service success. These authors found that global wireless communications companies were suffering from this 'all things to all people' malaise, and they found that the few successes that existed were based upon clear segmentation strategies. They found that firm success was facilitated by a four-pronged approach to segmentation: (1) identify the most attractive customers to serve, (2) restructure business systems to cater to these customers as efficiently as possible,

(3) create a basis for sustainable perceptual differentiation, and (4) establish an organizational entity that stays focused on the appropriate customer segments and applies metrics to ensure that the proper segments remain satisfied. Of course, the authors stress the importance of not differentiating for the sake of differentiating, but to base differentiation on specific sets of viable customer needs. Mini Case Study 9.2 examines the case of Wanadoo as it seeks to become broadband market leader in the UK.

Service strategists are quickly accepting the importance of relationship building with customers, which can be facilitated through effective segmentation. Zeithaml et al. (2001) found that a number of successful service firms have actually created customer pyramids which differentiate customers by profit potential and recognize that different groups of customers have different sets of expectations. These firms (like Fedex and Bank of America) cater to the more profitable customers and downplay the strategic efforts to reach the less

MINI CASE STUDY 9.2 Wanadoo takes on British Telecom

Wanadoo is a French broadband supplier that plans to go head-to-head with BT to become the broadband market leader in the UK. This is a major undertaking. In order for this to be successful, Wanadoo must literally become a household name throughout the UK. This is a tall task for the company once known as Freeserve. A major rebranding that was reported to have cost £30 million has relaunched the company as Wanadoo, and the hope is for it to take the market leadership position away from British Telecom. This is a daunting goal given the fact that BT has 80 per cent of the digital subscriber lines in the UK and wields an advertising budget of £100 million. Peter Turner, the marketing and communication director for Wanadoo UK, has been challenged by company CEO, Eric Abensur, with establishing Wanadoo as the most famous Internet brand in the UK.

Turner had worked for Freeserve from its inception, but the company was focused on providing free access to the Internet. As Turner explains, 'now the future is broadband and we knew we had to change to play a part in that'. Wanadoo is well recognized throughout the Continent, but it is not well known in the UK. A two-stage advertising campaign began in April of 2004 through M&C Saatchi with a three-week burst with the message that 'Freeserve is changing' which was followed up with a longer campaign to build the Freeserve brand. Turner indicates that awareness of Wanadoo 'has increased—it's at 90% now—and it has been more than just a marketing rebrand. We had to tell the population, because we didn't want to lose the history of Freeserve, which has played a major role in the internet's development.'

Obviously, industry wisdom would argue that now that this service provider is making inroads into consumer consciousness, the next step would be to mount an expensive marketing campaign to allow the company to effectively compete in an all-out price war, but Turner wants to find more creative and less costly ways to compete. He suggests that companies like Orange have been successful using such creative approaches as two-for-one cinema marketing initiatives. Turner understands that services must differentiate themselves from the competition, and he believes that the combination of innovation with superior customer service will work to help Wanadoo become the UK market leader.

Source: Ben Carter (2004), 'Freedom Fighter', *Marketing*, 19 May, p. 26.

profitable segments. The authors make the following suggestions regarding when firms should utilize this customer pyramid:

- when service resources, including employee time, are limited
- when customers want different services or service levels
- when customers are willing to pay for different levels of service
- when customers define value in different ways
- when customers can be separated from each other
- when service differentials can lead to upgrading customers to another level
- when they can be accessed either as a group or individually

Probably the most useful lessons come from observations of the most successful service providers. Companies like Walt Disney, Southwest Airlines, Marriott International, and Ritz-Carlton are all known for their service excellence in handling both sides of the service equation. They constantly refine and improve operational performance while continuously monitoring and providing customer value. Ford et al., (2001) studied these successful companies and identified 10 lessons that can help any service firm to maximize customer value perceptions and ensure a strong perceptual position in the head of their customers:

- base decisions on what the customer wants and expects
- think and act in terms of the entire customer experience
- continuously improve all parts of the customer experience
- hire and reward people who can effectively build relationships with customers
- train employees in how to cope with emotional labour costs
- create and sustain a strong service culture
- avoid failing your customer twice
- empower customers to co-produce their own experience
- get managers to lead from the front, not the top
- treat all customers as if they were guests

Successful service firms must understand the nature of the service experience and set up operating systems that continuously ensure that customer expectations are being not only met, but exceeded. The good news is that services of any size can gain sustainable competitive advantage if they set up effective service cultures that give the appropriate customers what they want while creating an internal environment that ensures employee satisfaction and loyalty.

Can customer service be a viable basis for service differentiation? The latest thinking

When a service company uses customer service as its sole focus for differentiation from its competition, it may face perceptual difficulties. If everyone stands for service, then there is no distinction in focusing on customer service as the main foundation for differentiation. The question is whether such companies as BT, British Gas, and British Airways can build strong brands by focusing on customer service in their advertising campaigns. These companies all stressed customer service in their advertisements in 2003, and Lloyds TSB is preparing to do the same thing by emphasizing relationships with its customers as the 'heart of its brand'. Most services build from the standpoint that offering great service is a foundation for creating loyal customers. If people are treated well, they should not want to go anywhere else. So an important question is why these kinds of major corporations would stress customer service in their advertisements. Craig Smith (2004) and Robert Gray (2004) raise some interesting questions. Gray (2004) suggests that BT, British Gas, and British Airways have built differentiating positions in very competitive markets by honing their delivery of customer service. But he questions whether customer service should be the main message in all company communications. Some of the criticisms raised by industry experts include the fact that customer service is not actually a strategy in and of itself, customer service as a sole focus for differentiation may miss key elements that helped to build the company credibility and success in the first place, and the fact that research has indicated that consumers don't see customer service as particularly interesting—it is perceived to be boring and lacking in imagination. Gray (2004) provides direct comments from key personnel at BT, British Gas, and British Airways who believe that stressing customer service is the only viable way to differentiate their services. This may not be the case. As Fred Wiersema notes in his study of 5,000 companies, companies need to continually exceed their past offerings and set new standards in their offerings of customer service to stay ahead of the competition (Wiersema, 2001). Merely offering customer service is not enough, offering incomparable service is the key to success. Gray (2004) suggests that the company that stresses service must be able to deliver on its promise. Smith (2004) suggests that such catchphrases as 'the way to fly,' 'more power to you', and 'do the right thing' are too nebulous to mean very much to customers. Good customer service may be a necessary requirement for a company to be a serious competitor in a service industry, but the company would do better to focus on other differentiators when building its image. As Smith (2204) suggests, service should be improved to compete against strong rivals; however, service is a weak platform for true differentiation. If everyone is for excellent customer service, then no one is really differentiated perceptually. Other bases will have to be developed.

Conclusion

Services are distinctly different from manufactured goods, and, as a result, pose unique challenges for service strategists. Service consumption involves an experience that must be understood by the service strategist so that the service that is offered meets or exceeds the expectations of the customer. Customer satisfaction from a fulfilling service experience will lead to loyalty and profitability, but it is imperative for the service strategist to monitor changes in the expectations of consumers so that continuous service quality improvements can be facilitated. It is also important to streamline where possible to build on company strengths and minimize weaknesses. The firm that keeps offering the most enjoyable service experience for its customers while eliminating inefficiencies will stay ahead of the competition. It is also worth remembering that customer service as a means for service firm differentiation may not be a viable strategy and that other defining characteristics may be more viable.

Summary

Service strategy is totally dependent upon the customer receiving the service experience that he/she expects. Market research examining the expectations of customers provides a necessary foundation for service design and implementation. Successful services have managers who understand the wants and needs of customers and have the courage to empower their employees to be able to adapt service offerings to the special situations faced by customers. Being customer focused becomes the key strategic consideration for all service employees, and it helps when there is a supportive service culture that puts the customer first, with profits following. This is a difficult stand for management to take as profitability is such an important driver, but those willing to be bold will potentially reap the kinds of rewards that service pioneers like Virgin, BSkyB, Southwest Airlines, and Marriott International have come to enjoy.

KEY TERMS

Intangibility The fact that services cannot be held in the hand, felt, and touched means that they present a challenge for strategic marketing decision-making as competitive differentiation has to be experienced by users and there really are no strategies for disposal of unsold stock.

Heterogeneity The aspect of services that focuses on inconsistencies brought on by changes in mood states and emotions that can cause differences in interactions between service provider personnel and consumers.

Inseparability The service interaction takes place in a meeting of the customer and service provider personnel. The interaction creates the service experience. This means that customers are co-producers/designers of the service

Perishability The fleeting life of a service offering. Once the service is provided, it is consumed at that time. Since a service cannot be stored, there is a need to synchronize supply and demand.

Decoupling Where the service provider removes certain low-customer contact tasks from frontline or front office personnel, standardizing them and moving them into remote back office locations. The decoupling of complex jobs allows for the reduction of work variance.

Streamlining Where the service provider looks to improve operations through the elimination of service inefficiencies and to improve profit margins.

Outsourcing Where the service provider looks to contract out service components to outside suppliers. Anything that the firm believes is not part of its core competency becomes a candidate for outsourcing. It potentially allows firms to get goods and services at a lower cost and with a higher quality by relying on firms that specialize in certain components of service delivery.

SERVQUAL A survey instrument developed by Berry et al. (1988) to measure service quality, which compares customer perceptions of ideal service provision to actual service delivery perceptions for a range of service process characteristics.

Dramaturgy A helpful strategic analytical device in which a service is thought of as a drama with three important components: a stage, actors, and an audience. The service experience can then be examined from all relevant facets.

DISCUSSION QUESTIONS

1 What are the four distinguishing characteristics of services and what challenges do they create for the services strategist?

2 Describe ways in which services can streamline and improve operational efficiency and profitability?

3 What is the service experience and why is it so important for services strategists?

4 Why is the drama metaphor beneficial for services strategists?

5 Why is customer segmentation important? What is needed for successful segmentation?

6 What is the customer pyramid, and how do you know if a service firm should make use of it?

7 What are the 10 strategic lessons learnt from the most successful service providers?

ONLINE RESOURCE CENTRE

Visit the Online Resource Centre for this book for lots of interesting additional material at: **www.oxfordtextbooks.co.uk/orc/west/**

REFERENCES AND FURTHER READING

Allen, Sandy, and Ashok Chandrashekar (2000), 'Outsourcing Services: The Contract is Just the Beginning', *Business Horizons*, (March–April), pp. 25–34.

Arnold, Scott, Greg A. Reed, and Paul J. Roche (1999), 'Wireless, not Profitless', *The McKinsey Quarterly*, No. 4 (Fall), pp. 112–21.

Arnold, Scott, Byron G. Auguste, Mark Knickrehm, and Paul J. Roche (1998), 'Winning in Wireless', *The McKinsey Quarterly*, No. 2 (Spring), pp. 18–32.

Barrett, Colleen (1998), 'Southwest Airlines Company: Luv Your Customer', in *Customer Service: Extraordinary Results at Southwest Airlines, Charles Sachwab, Land's End, American Express, Staples and USAA*, Fred Wiersema, ed. (New York: Harper Business).

Berry, Leonard L., and Neeli Bendapudi (2003), 'Clueing in Customers', *Harvard Business Review*, 81 (February), pp. 100–6.

Berry, Leonard L., and A. Parasuraman (1991) *Marketing Services: Competing Through Quality* (New York: The Free Press).

Booms, Bernard H., and Mary Jo Bitner (1981), 'Marketing Strategies and Organizational Structures for Service Firms', in *Marketing of Services*, James H. Donnelly and William R. George, eds. (Chicago: American Marketing Association), pp. 47–51.

Cohen, Morris A., Carl Cull, Hau L. Lee, and Don Willen (2000), 'Saturn's Supply-Chain Innovation: High Value in After-Sales Service', *Sloan Management Review*, (Summer), pp. 93–101.

Ernst, David, and Thomas D. French (1996), 'Coffee and One Way to Boston', *The McKinsey Quarterly*, No. 1 (Winter), pp. 165–76.

Ford, Robert C., Cherrill P. Heaton, and Stephen W. Brown (2001), 'Delivering Excellent Service: Lessons from the Best Firms', *California Management Review*, 44, No. 1 (Fall), pp. 39–56.

Friedman, David S. (1998), 'Help Wanted', *The McKinsey Quarterly*, No. 1 (Winter), pp. 34–45.

Grant, Stephen (1998), 'American Express Company: Make Membership a Privilege', in *Customer Service: Extraordinary Results at Southwest Airlines, Charles Sachwab, Land's End, American Express, Staples and USAA*, Fred Wiersema, ed. (New York: Harper Business).

Gray, Robert (2004), 'Customer Service is not a Strategy', *Marketing*, (July 21), pp. 32–4.

Grove, Stephen J., and Raymond P. Fisk (1983), 'The Dramaturgy of Service Exchange: An Analytical Framework for Services Marketing', in *Emerging Perspectives on Services Marketing*, Leonard L. Berry,

Lynn G. Shostack, and Gregory D. Upah, eds. (New York: American Marketing Association), pp. 45–9.

Grove, Stephen J., Raymond P. Fisk, and Mary Jo Bitner (1992), 'Dramatizing the Service Experience: A Managerial Approach', in *Advances in Services Marketing and Management: Research and Practice*, Vol. 1, Teresa A. Swartz, David E. Bowen, and Stephen W. Brown, eds. (Greenwich, CT: JAI Press, Inc.), pp. 91–121.

Gummesson, E., and J. Kingman-Brundage (1991), 'Service Design and Quality: Applying Service Blueprinting and Service Mapping to Railroad Services', in *Quality Management in Services*, P. Kunst and J. Lemmink, eds. (Assen/Maastricht: Van Gorcum).

Hays, Richard D. (1996), 'The Strategic Power of Internal Service Excellence', *Business Horizons*, (July–August), p. 20.

Hemp, Paul (2002), 'My Week as a Room-Service Waiter at the Ritz', *Harvard Business Review*, 80 (June), pp. 50–62.

Heskett, J. L., W. E. Sasser, Jr., and L. A. Schlesinger (1997), *The Service Profit Chain* (New York: The Free Press).

Leavitt, Theodore (1981), 'Marketing Intangible Products and Product Intangibles', *Harvard Business Review*, 59 (May/June), pp. 94–102.

Martilla, John A., and John C. James (1977), 'Importance-Performance Analysis', *Journal of Marketing*, 41 (January), pp. 70–9.

Metters, Richard, and Vincente Vargas (2000), 'Organizing Work in Service Firms', *Business Horizons*, July–August, pp. 23–32.

Mendonca, Lenny, and Gordon D. McCallum (1995), 'Battling for the Wallet', *The McKinsey Quarterly*, No. 2, pp. 76–92.

Naumann, Earl, and Donald W. Jackson, Jr. (1999), 'One More Time: How Do You Satisfy Customers?' *Business Horizons*, (May–June), pp. 71–6.

Oliver, R. L. (1997), *Satisfaction: A Behavioral Perspective on the Consumer* (New York: McGraw-Hill).

Organisation for Economic Co-Operation and Development (2001), *Innovation and Productivity in Services* (Paris: OECD).

Parasuraman, A., Leonard L. Berry, and Valarie A. Zeithaml (1988), 'SERVQUAL: A Multiple-Item Scale for Measuring Consumer Perceptions of Service Quality', *Journal of Retailing*, 64 (Spring), pp. 12–37.

Parasuraman, A., Leonard L. Berry, and Valarie A. Zeithaml (1991), 'Understanding Customer Expectations of Service', *Sloan Management Review*, 32, No. 3 (Spring): pp. 38–49.

Porter, Michael E (1980), *Competitive Strategy: Techniques for Analyzing Industries and Competitors* (New York: The Free Press).

Pottruck, David S. (1998), 'Charles Schwab & Company, Inc.: Invest in Trust', in *Customer Service: Extraordinary Results at Southwest Airlines, Charles Sachwab, Land's End, American Express, Staples and USAA*, Fred Wiersema, ed. (New York: Harper Business).

Quinn, James Brian, Thomas L. Doorley, and Penny C. Pacquette (1990), 'Beyond Products: Service-Based Strategy', *Harvard Business Review*, 68 (March/April), pp. 58–68.

Reicheld, Frederick, and Earl Sasser (1990), 'Zero Defections: Quality Comes to Services', *Harvard Business Review*, 68 (September/October), pp. 105–11.

Sasser, Earl (1976), 'Match Supply and Demand in Service Industries', *Harvard Business Review*, 54 (November/December), pp. 133–40.

Shostack, G. Lynn (1984), 'Designing Services that Deliver', *Harvard Business Review*, 62 (January/February), pp. 133–9.

Smith, Craig (2004), 'Customer Service is no Basis for a Brand', *Marketing*, (July 21), p. 30.

Swank, Cynthia Karen (2003), *Harvard Business Review*, (October), pp. 123–9.

Wiersema, Fred (2001), *The New Market Leaders* (New York: The Free Press).

World Bank (2003), *World Development Indicators 2003* (Washington, DC: The World Bank).

Zeithaml, Valarie A., and Mary Jo Bitner (2003), *Services Marketing: Integrating Customer Focus Across the Firm*, 3rd edn (Boston: McGraw-Hill Irwin).

Zeithaml, Valarie A., Roland T. Rust, and Katherine N. Lemon (2001), 'The Customer Pyramid: Creating and Serving Profitable Customers', *California Management Review*, Vol. 43, No. 4 (Summer), pp. 118–42.

Zeithaml, Valarie A., A. Parasuraman, and Leonard L. Berry (1990), *Delivering Quality Service: Balancing Customer Perceptions and Expectations* (New York: The Free Press).

KEY ARTICLE ABSTRACTS

Berry, Leonard L., and Neeli Bendapudi (2003), 'Clueing in Customers', *Harvard Business Review*, 81 (February), pp. 100–6.

One of the most successful healthcare providers in the United States is the Mayo Clinic which has facilities in Rochester, Minnesota, Scottsdale, Arizona, and Jacksonville, Florida. At the Mayo Clinic the patient really does come first, and every aspect of the clinic is set up to communicate this to patients and their families from the attitude and attire of the staff to the decor and ambience of the buildings. This insightful article addresses the effective use of evidence management to ensure that a service organization presents a consistent and effective image and set of values that is conveyed on a daily basis.

Abstract: When customers lack the expertise to judge a company's offerings, they naturally turn detective, scrutinizing people, facilities, and processes for evidence of quality. The Mayo Clinic understands this and carefully manages that evidence to convey a simple, consistent message: the needs of the patient come first. From the way it hires and trains employees to the way it designs its facilities and approaches its care, the Mayo Clinic provides patients and their families with concrete evidence of its strengths and values, an approach that has allowed it to build what is arguably the most powerful brand in healthcare. A five-month study of evidence management at the Mayo Clinic was conducted. This led to the identification of best practices applicable to just about any company, in particular those that sell intangible or technically complex products. Essentially, companies need to determine what story they want to tell, then ensure that their employees and facilities consistently show customers evidence of that story.

Ford, Robert C., Cherrill P. Heaton, and Stephen W. Brown (2001), 'Delivering Excellent Service: Lessons from the Best Firms', *California Management Review*, 44 (1), pp. 39–56.

Companies like Walt Disney, Southwest Airlines, Marriott International, and Ritz-Carlton are all known for their service excellence in handling both sides of the service equation. These firms constantly refine and improve operational performance while continuously monitoring and providing customer value. This article represents a study of the best service providers to determine what makes them successful. The authors present 10 lessons that can help any service firm to maximize customer value perceptions and ensure a strong perceptual position in the head of their customers.

Abstract: Delivering excellent service is a challenge for most organizations. While many aspire to it, the evidence from customer satisfaction surveys indicates that too few firms are able to deliver service excellence. On the other hand, some organizations consistently deliver excellent service. This article reviews 10 lessons these benchmark service organizations have learnt and shows how these organizations use them to meet and exceed the ever-rising expectations of their customers. These lessons can be emulated by any organization seeking such excellence.

Swank, Cynthia Karen (2003), 'The Lean Service Machine', *Harvard Business Review*, 81 (October), pp. 123–9.

Service providers have recently embraced some of the cost-cutting benefits that were experienced by western manufacturers attempting to remain competitive with the Japanese during the 1990s. This article discusses 'lean service management' through re-engineering operations to improve profitability; however, service providers must be careful to always measure any improvements in performance and productivity from the customer's perspective. Whatever is attempted should not detract in any way from perceptions of customer value.

Abstract: To establish itself as the independent life-insurance advisers' preferred partner, Jefferson Pilot Financial set out to reduce the turnaround time on policy applications, simplify the submission process, and reduce errors. The firm's managers looked to the 'lean production' practices that US manufacturers adopted in response to competition from Japanese companies. The firm appointed a 'lean team' to re-engineer its New Business unit's operations, beginning with the creation of a 'model cell'—a fully functioning microcosm of Jefferson Pilot Financial's entire process. Customer-focused metrics helped erode the employees' 'My work is all that matters' mindset. The results were so impressive that the firm is rolling out similar systems across many of its operations. To convince employees of the value of lean production, the lean team introduced a simulation in which teams compete to build the best paper aeroplane based on invented customer specifications.

END OF CHAPTER 9 CASE STUDY
KLM Royal Dutch Airlines: strategic evaluation and future direction

Introduction

KLM Royal Dutch Airlines (KLM), whose home base is Amsterdam Airport (Schiphol), is an international airline operating worldwide. The company forms the core of the KLM Group, which includes KLM Cityhopper and Transavia, is Europe's number four airline as measured in revenue terms, and has four key airline activities: passenger transport, cargo transport, engineering, and maintenance, and the operation of charters and low-cost/low-fare scheduled flights (see Figure C9.1).

In merging with the French carrier Air France, KLM has at least guaranteed its short-term survival in a very competitive industry. KLM and its partners serve more than 350 cities, around 73 countries in six continents. In fiscal year 2002/2003 (the year ended 31 March 2003), KLM carried more than 23.4 million passengers and 489,000 tons of cargo and provided engineering and maintenance services to more than 20 airlines. KLM operates a modern fleet of 219 aircraft, many configured for combined passenger/cargo flights. The airline needs to identify a clear strategic direction in order to ensure appropriate and effective international development with its French partner, given that as a combined unit they will become the largest operator in the European airline industry.

KLM's goal is to become the first choice passenger and cargo airline and provider of maintenance services, while consistently enhancing shareholder value, providing a stimulating and dynamic working environment, and participating in mutually beneficial relationships with its partners. By striving to attain excellence as an airline and by participating in the world's most successful airline alliance, KLM intends to generate value for its customers, employees, and shareholders. They aim to execute this mission by developing their own stand-alone position as well as participating in global alliances. KLM

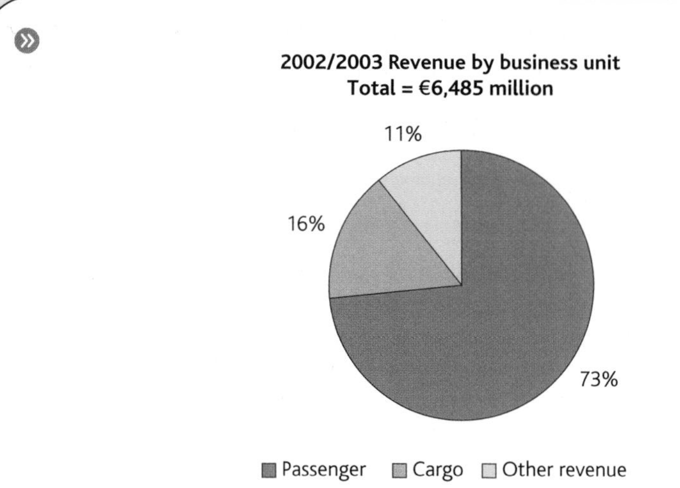

Figure C9.1 Revenue by business unit

announced a restructuring plan in April 2003 to deliver €650 million improvements in operating income by April 2005, which will require a 10% reduction in unit costs.

KLM has a very diverse employee base, encompassing 65 nationalities, the majority of which are located in the Netherlands. Despite having a predominantly unionized workforce, KLM has managed to reach agreement on the need to downsize, resulting in 3,000 being unemployed. One of the strengths of KLM is its approach to partnering, a key component of this being its joint venture with Northwest Airline. This joint venture relates to both passenger and cargo traffic. Each partner contributes to the joint venture the difference between its traffic revenues and operating expenses, and shares on a 50:50 basis in the total contribution generated. Other strengths of KLM are in the areas of operations management, engineering, and maintenance[1] (in that they sell this service to other players in the industry), and their ability to profitably manage the Transavia holiday business.[2] The latter in particular appears successful due to leveraging the country of origin effect.

It has been claimed that KLM may have to reconsider its resource competencies and organizational capabilities to develop an effective strategy that will result in sustaining a solid competitive advantage. This can be completed independently or via the collaboration with Air France. For example KLM can leverage its capacity and operations management expertise to provide a more efficient service to time-conscious travellers or can take the cost advantages of this competence and translate them into a service for the value-conscious consumer. This will provide an aspiration to leadership in one or two key areas. KLM also needs to ensure that it meets its competitors' average performance in other areas.

KLM, however, is less successful in financial performance and developing a foundation for sustainable competitive advantage. Key pressures in the external environment coupled with ineffective early measures to offset have resulted in questionable financial performance (a record net loss of €416 million was posted for the financial year to 31 March 2003). Unlike some competitors, KLM has not actively sought a route to differentiation, e.g. product innovation (BA with its flatbed addition), or been aggressive with technology (American Airlines with the SABRE reservation system), to create a strategic advantage that would position it to make above average profits. It therefore has not used distinctive organizational capabilities to contribute to superior customer value due to its focus on cost management and survival; its resources/threshold competencies are predominantly the same as those of its competitors or are easy to imitate.

Key trends in the European airline industry

Deregulation

The global airline industry is such a sophisticated environment in which to operate. Distorted as it is by a maze of international cartels, complicated subsidies, and government regulations, it is not surprising that airlines have not offered a real rate of return to shareholders over the last sixty years. Recent developments suggest that rapid change is afoot within the industry and a period of accelerated change—prompted by government talks regarding the deregulation of transatlantic aviation—will drive a period of industry-wide consolidation over the next five years.[3] If governments in the EU and USA can reach an agreement, we will see further deregulation in both markets.

Competitive landscape

The major macro-environmental change will undoubtedly be government deregulation. It is important to note that deregulation of the airline industry has only been undertaken in the USA and Europe, and in an incomplete fashion. The industry is swamped with far too many operators, offering too many flights, and is distinguished by a large number of flag-waving national carriers that disappeared in other industries, such as the car industry many years ago. The world's biggest carrier, American Airlines, has barely 7% of the global market, whereas the world's biggest carmaker, General Motors, has (with its associated firms) about a quarter of the world's automobile market.[4]

The leading airline players and many others companies have lobbied hard to promote deregulation. United Airlines and BA, for example, have been lobbying their respective domestic governments for many years, hoping that a deregulated transatlantic aviation market will emerge providing the impetus for total deregulation. In terms of government legislation, the most significant change of late is the EU assuming responsibility for brokering air traffic agreements, allowing more focus, especially for Europe to negotiate as a single entity. Indeed, the EU and USA have recently held the first set of talks aiming to liberalize transatlantic aviation.[5] If an agreement comes into existence, there will be direct negotiations between the giant European and American markets over full liberalization, including mutually unrestricted access for operators within the EU, the USA, and the territorial waters over which they fly.

Intense competition

The European airline industry is second to that of the USA in terms of airline traffic transport, having 29.58% of world passengers, 31.63% of world passenger kilometres (RPKs)

1. KLM's Engineering & Maintenance Business is one of the three largest aircraft maintenance companies affiliated to an airline in the world.
2. The largest Dutch holiday transporter to destinations in and around the Mediteranean.
3. 'Open Skies and Flights of Fancy—Airlines', *The Economist* (London), 4 October 2003.
4. 'A way out of the wilderness. Airlines: The problems of the airline industry (Industry Overview)', *The Economist* (USA), 3 May 2003.
5. 'Open Skies and Flights of Fancy—Airlines', *The Economist* (London), 4 October 2003.

TABLE C9.1 European airline traffic, June 2003

Airline	European airline traffic June 2003 RPKs (billions)	% change −2002	ASKs (billions)	% change −2002	Load factor %	+/− 2002
AF Group	**8.53**	**−0.1**	**10.99**	**0.8**	**77.6**	**−0.7**
AUA Group	1.16	−6	1.61	−3.4	71.9	−1.9
BA Group	**9.05**	**5.8**	**11.79**	**3.1**	**76.8**	**2**
Finnair	0.96	−11.7	1.35	−3.8	71.4	−64
Iberia	3.47	2	4.53	−0.5	76.7	1.9
KLM	**4.54**	**−9.2**	**5.7**	**−8.5**	**79.7**	**−0.6**
LH Group	**7.77**	**−3.7**	**10.2**	**−3.1**	**76.2**	**−0.5**
SAS	2.86	−1.2	4.12	2.9	69.3	−2.8

Source: *Air Transport World* (Cleveland), Aug. 2003, Vol. 40, No. 8, p. 10.

and 27.77% of world freight traffic kilometres (FTKs), and owning 29.73% of the world's aircraft.[6] These indicators and others are presented in Table C9.1.

The performance indicators reveal much about KLM's position in comparison with other players in the market. First, at 10.7%, KLM's relative market share is considerably lower than that of British Airways, Air France, and Lufthansa who have at least 5% more than the Dutch carrier. Moreover, in terms of revenue generation, KLM also comes out well below Air France, British Airways, and Lufthansa, generating less than half the revenue of Lufthansa. In addition, KLM's geographical coverage looks impressive, given that this figure includes the routes of its American partner, Northwest Airlines. This picture is further corroborated when passenger figures are taken into account: KLM carries considerably fewer passengers than the three other leading airlines and, interestingly, only carries double the number of passengers of the much-smaller niche player Ryanair. This environment compelled KLM to seek a partner and instigate consolidation, in line with industry trends. A brief analysis of the leading European carriers is given below.

British Airways, Europe's number one carrier BA has been ranked first as it has the largest market share of all the European carriers; generates the largest market share with smaller employee and passenger numbers than comparators (the company has instigated a policy of shrinking to profitability); and offers a visibly differentiated product through a well-known brand.

Lufthansa, Europe's second carrier Lufthansa has been ranked second. Despite offering a slightly-lower market share than Air France, it turned in an operating profit in 2002 and also paid a shareholder dividend. It offers a highly differentiated product, is market leader in terms of technological investment, and has instigated serious cost-cutting measures which should leave Lufthansa in a stronger position.

Air France, Europe's number three carrier Air France has been ranked third, despite polling a larger market share than Lufthansa due to a number of underlying restructuring issues that need to be addressed over the next five years. First, the French government still

6. 'A year not soon forgotten; ATW's World Airline Report', *Air Transport World*, July 2002, Vol. 39, No. 7, p. 28(4).

owns a sizeable share in the carrier and privatization will need to take place if the airline is to compete in the long term. Secondly, the merger will be complex and will therefore affect the merged airline's performance.

KLM, Europe's number four carrier KLM, when judged by a number of criteria, clearly emerges as Europe's fourth airline. The carrier's fortunes should be improved through the merger with Air France.

Low-cost carriers Ryanair and easyJet have been ranked fifth and sixth respectively. Although these low-cost carriers have relatively miniscule market share and turnover levels compared to the established network carriers, their ability to operate at lower cost and to take market share from both the network and charter carriers suggests they could be more formidable opponents in five years' time.

See Table C9.2 for an analysis of the competitors in the European airline industry.

Consolidation and alliances

During the last year, Alitalia and Swiss International Air Lines have announced that they need to be taken over by more robust players to ensure survival. In addition, Virgin Airlines and the low-cost carrier BMI/British Midland have also considered closer links which could eventually lead to merger.[7] Without doubt the biggest merger was the recent announcement of a deal between Air France and KLM.

The merger gave an indication of how the airline industry might change beyond all recognition over the next few years. As one commentator has noted, 'although the Air France and KLM brands are to remain separate, the partnership between the two promises to become more intimate than any other deal in the industry. Most airline alliances are little more than joint-marketing exercises, but the Franco-Dutch group plans to integrate its operations more fully'.[8] Moreover, Alitalia has also announced that it would be interested in joining this new alliance, the Franco-Dutch group, subject to the Italian carrier restructuring. However, the merger will have a profound effect on the structure and composition of airline alliances, and offers an insight into the form industry consolidation will take in the future. Significantly, the alliance will give the new company a combined market share of over 28% and it will therefore be Europe's largest carrier in terms of market share, employee level, geographical coverage, and passenger numbers.

Post-merger, KLM will become part of the SkyTeam alliance, as will KLM's current partner Northwest (also bringing its US ally Continental Airlines into the fold). This could bring the SkyTeam alliance into rivalry with Star, the biggest of the international alliances along with the OneWorld group. A summary of these key alliances is included in Table C9.3. It has been suggested that 'the three alliances could, in a fully liberalized world, be the kernel of three global mega-carriers'.[9] To date, deregulation has been limited to bilateral deals. Deregulation, therefore, combined with a consolidation of carriers in the marketplace, could result in a handful of carriers, bonded in effective, meaningful alliances that operate on vast economies of scale, operating global air travel. Europe currently has 23 flag carriers, yet the next five years suggests it will have many fewer.

7. Flottau, J., 'Europeans Mull Consolidation', *Aviation and Space Technology* (New York), 16 June 2003, pp. 112–14.
8. 'Open Skies and Flights of Fancy—Airlines', *The Economist* (London), 4 October 2003.
9. Ibid.

TABLE C9.2 Analysis of Competitors in the European airline industry

Measurements	Global				Regional	
	Air France	British Airways	KLM	Lufthansa	Ryanair	easyJet
Market share	**17.6%**	**18.1%**	**10.7%**	**16.1%**	**1.31%**	**1.38%**
Revenue (2002) (in US $m)	13,695.60	12,150.00	7,066.00	17,787.70	918.00	861.50
Employees	71,525	57,014	33,038	94,135	1,897	2,045
Coverage	199 destinations	270 destinations	350 destinations	330 destinations	75 destinations	30 destinations
	85 countries	99 countries	75 countries (with Northwest)	90 countries		
Routes	France Europe North Africa Africa/Middle East Americas Asia Pacific Indian Ocean	UK Europe North America Africa Middle East South Asia Far East Australasia	Netherlands Europe Asia Pacific North Atlantic Central and South America Middle East South Asia Far East Australasia	Germany Europe Asia Pacific North Atlantic Central and South America Middle East South Asia Far East Australasia	Europe	Europe
Passenger numbers	38045	34445	19380	43949	11091	9235
RPK (passenger traffic—in millions)	96,802	99,710	58,894	88,570	7,251	7,642
Load factor	77.2%	72.8%	80.2%	73.9%	74.1%	80.4%
Operating profit (in USD)	174,960	465,000	−143,600	1,509.000	284,552	123,008
Generic strategy (subjective)	Focus	Differentiation	Survival	Focus	Cost leadership	Cost leadership
Alliances	SkyTeam	OneWorld	SkyTeam (pending)	Star	None	None

TABLE C9.2 *(continued)*

Measurements	Global				Regional	
	Air France	British Airways	KLM	Lufthansa	Ryanair	easyJet
Advantages (strengths)	• Advantages of scale: the KLM merger will give the Franco-Dutch alliance a market share larger than British Airways. • Good hub at Paris CDG (which is expanding)	• Excellent brand • Highly differentiated product • Has already implemented serious cost-cutting measures	• Cost leadership • Good European spokes • Attractive loyalty scheme • Expertise in operations management • Expertise in engineering and maintenance	• Differentiated product: Implemented €30m customer service improvement programme (first airline to commit to equipping all long-haul aircraft with broadband internet access)	• Good logistics • Lower operating costs than network carriers • Lower operating costs than easyJet • Enjoys protection from business cycles (decline in premium demand when economy is poor)	• Good logistics • Lower operating costs than network carriers • Enjoys protection from business cycles (decline in premium demand when economy is poor)
Disadvantages (weaknesses)	• Privatization: AF needs to privatize so it can operate more efficiently in an increasingly competitive environment. This, combined with need to merge efficiently with KLM, is AF's biggest challenge	• Personnel issues (recently adversely affected by wildcat strikes)	• Questionable financial performance • Lack of product differentiation	• Needs to radically cut operating costs • Needs to slim down workforce (which will be difficult in unionized Germany)	• Scarcity of available new routes may be damaging to market growth objectives in short term	• Higher operating costs than Ryanair • Scarcity of available new routes may be damaging to market growth objectives in short term
Target customers	Business and Leisure	Business and Leisure	Business and Leisure	Business and Leisure	Leisure and short-haul business	Leisure and short-haul business
Future direction	Re-positioning to be Europe's largest airline (after taking over KLM)	Shrinking to profitability	Junior partner in alliance with AF	Cost-cutting to improve competitive position	Wants to dominate European air transport by 2010	Wants to dominate European air transport by 2010
RANKING	**3RD**	**1ST**	**4TH**	**2ND**	**5TH**	**6TH**

Current picture and challenges

The current picture of the competitive environment is relatively straightforward. The established network carriers are facing formidable challenges—driven by legislation and economic downturn—which will result in more consolidation within the industry

TABLE C9.3 The transformation of strategic airline alliances

Airline alliance	Members	Comments
SkyTeam	Aero Mexico	*KLM, Northwest Airlines, and Continental set to join subject to approval of KLM/AF merger*
	Air France	
	Alitalia	
	CSA Czech Airlines	
	Delta Airlines	
	Korean Airlines	
	KLM	
	Northwest Airline	
	Continental Airlines	
Star	Lufthansa (including Eurowings)	
	Air Canada	
	All Nippon Airways	
	Austrian Airlines	
	LOT Polish Airlines	
	Mexicana	
	Singapore Airlines	
	Thai Airways	
	VARIG	
	Air New Zealand	
	Asiana Airlines	
	BMI/British Midland	
	SAS	
	SpanAir	
	United Airlines	
OneWorld	British Airways	
	Alaska Airlines	
	America West Airlines	
	Emirates	
	JAL	
	SN Brussels Airlines	
	Air Lingus	
	American Airlines	
	Cathay Pacific	
	Finnair	
	Iberia	
	LanChile	
	Qantas	

over the next five years. In addition to these external challenges, there are challenges from within the European airline industry itself. This comes from the new low-cost carriers. These carriers, most notably Ryanair and easyJet, have ambitious strategies and market share targets. The low-cost airlines have made money even in the most difficult period for the airlines. In 2001, while most traditional players reported losses and some succumbed to the competition, Europe's leading low-cost carriers were more than merely profitable: 'Ryanair and easyJet boasted operating margins of 26% and 9.5% respectively—results that traditional airlines only dream about. In June 2002, Ryanair had a market capitalization of €4.9 billion ($4.82 billion), 45% more than that of British Airways, which has revenues that are 20 times larger'.[10] It is therefore evident that, in the medium and long term, Europe's low-cost carriers can mount a challenge to the established carriers in Europe and Ryanair and easyJet warrant inclusion in the top six European airlines.

Strategic orientation, branding, and organizational structure

Strategic orientation

KLM's strategic choice differs by business unit and is far more evident in two of the four units. The Transavia business has executed a cost focus strategy to a particular customer segment, i.e., the regional leisure traveller, whilst the service and maintenance business has adopted an almost industry-wide differentiation strategy (high quality service for all airlines routing via Schiphol). The passenger and cargo traffic businesses, on the other hand, appear to be 'stuck in the middle'. They have neither been a low cost airline nor pursued innovative ways of differentiating their service to customers. They have focused on operations and aimed to be more efficient than their counterparts. Choice of KLM's generic strategy should take into consideration the corporation's capabilities and resources.

KLM has a strong resource position in terms of its operations management and service, and its maintenance capabilities. Its market position and knowledge of customers is strong in the current markets served by Transavia, but looks weak in regard to the international market. This situation leads KLM to develop a strategy that leverages its resource competence and knowledge of local markets whilst identifying the need to leverage the Air France merger in the other areas. This translates into a cost focus position for the Transavia business, and industry-wide differentiation for its service and maintenance business (specifically targeting all airlines with routes via its maintenance hubs).

The trends and nature of competition within the airline industry indicate an opportunity for KLM to use its superior resource position (operations and process management for air passengers/cargo) to deliver a higher level of value (product and service quality) to customers at a comparable cost to the competition, i.e., a non-premium position recognizing the difficulty in demanding more for a perceived commodity service. This approach would signify a geographically centred preference for a differentiation strategy, the global positioning being delayed until the merger with Air France is established.

Direction of long-term development

The KLM/Air France combined venture needs to be able to produce a global offer that appeals to global customers, demonstrating sustainable added value through inevitable competition. KLM having merged with Air France, the combined organization needs to decide which combined businesses need more investments to build, which should stay put, which should be harvested, and which should be liquidated. KLM's business units are categorized using the BCG matrix as shown in Figure C9.2.

Organizational structure

A key post-merger challenge for KLM is to remodel its organizational structure to be able to compete effectively in the market and to accommodate its new partnership with Air France. The pre-merger structure concentrates the decision-making process at the board level rather than devolving it to the business unit level. Emphasis on a survival strategy

10. Bingeli, U., and Pompeo L. (2002), 'Hyped Hopes for Europe's Low-Cost Airlines', *The McKinsey Quarterly*, No. 4.

		High	Low
Market growth rate	High	**Star** Transavia **Hold**	**Question mark** Service/Maintenance **Build**
	Low	**Cash cow** Cargo **Harvest**	**Dog** Passenger traffic **Divest**

Figure C9.2 KLM business units position using the BCG matrix

has led to a focus on reducing costs from the infrastructure, resulting in a flat organizational structure. This structure reflects KLM's cautious, conservative ethos but the merger with Air France signals a commitment to remodelling its organizational structure, operations management, and company strategy to ensure a smooth and successful transition to its post-merger status as the joint leading operator in Europe.

Branding

The KLM brand is utilized for three out of four of KLM's business units: passenger traffic, cargo, and service/maintenance. Their fourth business unit, regional travel business, utilizes its own unique brand, i.e., Transavia. Within their alliance structure, KLM and NorthWest have retained two separate local brands;[11] KLM is more widely recognized in the European market and NorthWest within the North American market.

KLM's aim is to convey reliability, safety, and freedom, and a message of being at home in the sky via its corporate branding. Its use of the Swan symbol to convey these attributes has the advantage of being neutral and independent across cultural boundaries. The KLM brand and the Transavia subbrand are also widely recognized as symbols of Dutch heritage and, as such, aim to leverage the country of origin effect in creating brand value in local markets.

11. Local versus International Brands as outlined by H. Muhlbacher, L. Dahringer, and H. Leihs (1999), *International Marketing: a Global perspective*, 2nd edn (London: Thomson Business Press).

Power

The merger with Air France presents new challenges in that it expands the spectrum of stakeholders with whom KLM must engage successfully. The key relationships which KLM must successfully manage include those with Air France, political heavyweights, Northwest airlines, the SkyTeam Alliance, and loyal KLM 'frequent flyers'. In its relationships with these groups, KLM must seek to protect its own business interest while fostering new partnerships and ensuring it maximizes benefits from new arrangements. In political terms, it must lobby all key political players (e.g., the EU, the French and Dutch governments, etc.) to ensure its voice is heard in the debate over liberalization and related issues of concern. Other key challenges facing KLM at present are:

- Financial performance issues need to be resolved before it can develop a solid foundation for sustainable competitive advantage.
- It needs to meet the average performance indicators of comparators.
- It must ensure that implementation of the merger with Air France is well managed and that both partners fully integrate their operations to optimum effect, facilitating delivery of sustainable competitive advantage over their key competitors.
- It must ensure that the collaboration with Air France provides value for the consumer and does not damage the existing customer base.
- It must leverage the full benefits of the SkyTeam multilateral alliance.

Conclusion

In conclusion, it is evident that KLM is at a defining moment in the continuing process of internationalization, and its strategic decisions at this juncture will largely determine the success or failure of the new merger with Air France and KLM's industry position thereafter. The industry is highly competitive, a trend which will continue for the foreseeable future, and the key challenge for KLM is to embrace the opportunities offered by merger to shake off past strategic reticence and emerge as a stronger player in a partnership which should position it as joint leading player in the European airline industry.

In order to build and sustain competitive advantage, KLM must ensure that it fully capitalizes upon its core resources and competencies, an area in which it has previously been found less efficient. It is recommended that KLM and Air France both should review their value adding organization and activities in order to achieve their target in the European airline industry.

Source: This case was prepared by Dr Essam Ibrahim (2004) for class discussion and not to illustrate either effective or ineffective handling of an administrative situation.

QUESTIONS

1. How can an airline as a service find ways to build competitive advantage over its competitors?
2. Why is this strategic alliance with Air France so important for KLM's future?
3. Will this make a difference to KLM's customers? Why?
4. What is the downside to this kind of strategic alliance for KLM?

10

Pricing and distribution strategies

LEARNING OBJECTIVES

- Examine the separate and complementary roles of pricing and distribution in marketing strategy
- Assess pricing mindsets and strategic options
- Evaluate the buyer's perspective of distribution and its implications for strategy
- Review the role of pricing and distribution amidst the drive towards the commoditization of products and services

CHAPTER AT A GLANCE

Introduction

Pricing and distribution are distinct yet complementary elements in marketing. Strategically they are difficult to separate. A premium-priced watch cannot be sold at a discount jewellers. A tractor producer that wants a specific mark-up is going to find it difficult to control margin if it sells through intermediaries. Setting pricing and distribution strategies are separate, but complementary decisions. This chapter will review the options individually and then examine the issues where decisions meet head-on.

Traditional marketing strategies (cost or differentiation strategies) do not provide any intrinsic logic on pricing or distribution. Note: Porter was talking about 'cost' and not 'price'. He argued that if you had lower costs, you could charge lower prices and opt for low cost distribution networks, and that relatively low costs provide a potential advantage over rivals in terms of profitability. That is, you could also charge the same price as rivals and make more money. The price of anything and the route by which it is distributed simply reflect its value. Certainly a low cost producer is positioned to offer lower prices or discounts, but it is far from certain that it would do so. For example, Dell has attained cost leadership in the industry with its direct-to-customer distribution process. Nothing is built that hasn't been ordered, so inventories are reduced and with direct sales there are no intermediaries to take a share of the profit. Yet Dell's prices are not the lowest. What it has been able to do in a hyper-competitive market is to combine cost leadership with customized one-to-one products (the ultimate differentiation) and direct-to-customer distribution which is a powerful value-added offering. By contrast Sony offers greater design differentiation at similar prices but distributes its computers via authorized dealers and its own (largely franchised) network of retail Sony Centres.

The moral is that customers look for value when they buy rather than absolute price. Value is a perceptual concept as, for example, with Sainsbury's. Sainsbury's have tried to meet intensifying price competition from the likes of Tesco and Asda, but no matter what else it does to get itself into shape, there is a widespread consumer perception that its prices are slightly high. However, most companies approach price setting from the basis of covering their costs plus a profit mark-up and there is no denying the general logic of covering costs (at least in the longer term—however defined!). For many computer buyers a computer customized directly to their requirements provides more value than one off the shelf from a retailer. The strength of Dell's customization strategy and Sony's focus on aesthetic design will be tested as computer technology and standards converge. When all computers have Internet access, large flat screens, fast processors, big hard drives, CDRWs, and DVDs, etc., product differentiation will become less achievable and servicing and styling more important, so Sony may win out. But nothing is clear. In this market environment, price and distribution provide a means of strategic differentiation. This chapter will review these and other issues in pricing and distribution. It begins with an assessment of pricing strategy.

Pricing

Definition

Pricing has generally been seen as tactical rather than strategic and is considered to be much easier than creating the product in the first place. Essentially it has been the 'Cinderella' of marketing. In essence, a price is just a number. Given that prices affect sales, all things being equal, a small increase or decrease can have a disproportionate impact on profitability compared to any other marketing decision. For illustration see Table 10.1 which shows how a 10% increase in price outweighs reductions in costs in terms of effect on profitability.

Pricing strategy involves deciding more than this: how much, where, when, and how a buyer will pay are the key decisions. This is what holds together individual pricing decisions based upon an organization's objectives and how it wants to set its 'numbers' within the market. Most companies face enormous pressures on prices with inflation running at around 2% overall. Companies that have tried to raise prices have often been forced to drop them, sometimes below their original price, in order to recapture lost share. Thus, pricing has become ever more important in recent years as customers have shifted to lower-price alternatives or substituted one kind of good or service for another rather than accept higher prices. There are several elements in pricing strategy to consider (see Schindehutte and Morris, 2001).

Value: price is fundamentally about value. Customers place prices within the context of perceived value. For example, when people pay more for sitting in the front row of a theatre they still see the same play as everyone else, but get the benefits of being closer to the actors. Perception is all, as with the UK positioning of Stella as an expensive lager although it is not premium-priced (see Figure 10.1).

TABLE 10.1 Effect of price changes

XYZ Products		**Effect of a price increase of 10%***	
Sales	£m 200		£m 20
Costs:		Costs:	
Materials	50	Materials −10%	5
Labour	50	Labour −10%	5
Mkt & Adv	10	Mkt & Adv −10%	1
R&D	10	R&D −10%	1
Other variable	20		
Total variable	140	Total variable −10%	14
Total fixed	*40*	Fixed −10%	4
Net profit	20		

* This assumes no volume change. A fall in volume (so long as sales do not drop by more than 20% as a result of the price increase) will also lead to higher profits.

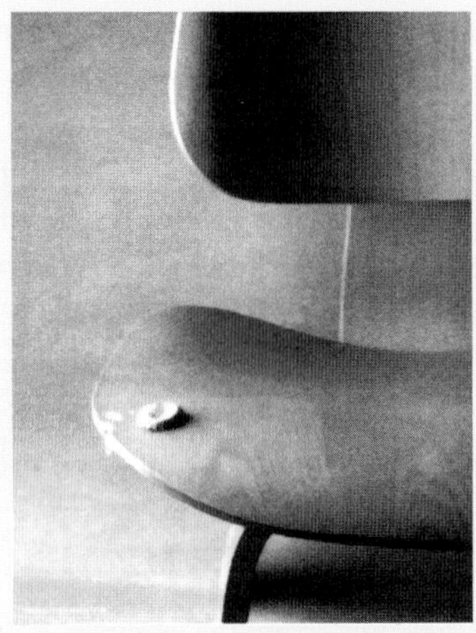

Figure 10.1 Communicating a price position—Stella Lager

Source: By permission of Lowe Worldwide.

Variable: prices can be changed in a number of ways apart from the absolute level, such as by time form or terms of payment.

Variety: prices can be set at different levels across multiple products and services to achieve different objectives for positioning and contribution as with bundling or unbundling items.

Visible/Invisible: prices may be open and visible or hidden and confusing for customers. In the USA Sprint demonstrated invisible pricing when it offered 4,000 call minutes for $39.99 a month—which appears to be a cent a minute (Ayres and Nalebuff, 2003). Unfortunately only 350 of these minutes were 'anytime' with the rest (3,650) being restricted to evenings and weekends. Go over your 350 limit and you pay 35c a minute.

Virtual: of all the decisions marketers make, a price change is arguably the easiest and quickest to make. It might not prove to be successful but the decision to raise or lower a price can be made quite straightforwardly in most organizations.

Strategic mindset

Pricing can be a mindset issue for many companies and the consequences of the wrong decision can be dire. This has been demonstrated in an experiment involving 60 managers by Joel Urbany (2001). He gave these managers a straightforward choice: you sell sunglasses for $10 with a unit cost of $7 and you are thinking of cutting the price by 50c. According to the best sales estimate, (a) if you hold the price you will have a 100% chance of selling 1,000 units, and (b) if you cut the price to $9.50 you have an 80% chance of selling 1,250 units and a 20% chance of selling only 1,000. Statistically both options are identical as each produces a $3,000 profit. However, option (a) is risk free and so might seem to be the logical choice. Despite that, most of the 60 managers opted to reduce the price. Even when they were told competitors would match the cut, they still chose to do it. Furthermore, most continued to want to reduce the price in the face of new evidence that the cut would lead to lower profits!

The case of Polaroid demonstrates (Shantanu et al., 2002) another kind of problematic pricing mindset. Polaroid was the first company to develop digital-imaging technology, but decided not to run with it. The reason was that Polaroid had relied on the 'razors-and-blade' approach to business in that it sold cameras cheaply and made money on the film. Digital imaging did not fit into this paradigm and so it gave up its lead with the technology. While this is an extreme case, it does demonstrate how an innovative company lost out because it lacked the appropriate pricing strategy.

Strategic options

Successful pricing means that the prices set have to complement the company's overall marketing strategy and the whole process has to be holistic, i.e., prices need to be coordinated across the business. For example, if a list price is agreed within marketing and accounts it needs to be established whether this price is fixed or open to debate with customers. If list prices are then reduced by sales in negotiations with buyers this can lead to confusion. To implement a holistic approach it might be necessary to change the internal incentives. Dolan (1995) suggests eight stages to pricing strategy.

Reverse cost-plus

The first stage is to reverse the traditional cost-plus based pricing approach. This can be achieved by assessing the value that buyers place on a product or service. This is an 'outside-in' rather than an 'inside-out' approach and requires considerable intelligence gathering either formally (e.g. market research) or informally (e.g. comments from the salesforce).

Variations in value

Having considered this, it is then best to look for variations in how buyers value products. Wherever possible try and separate markets (e.g. both companies and individuals use Post-it notes and may be prepared to pay different prices) and segments (e.g. heavy, medium, and light users) and charge accordingly. Performance will have different values to different buyers—pest control to a restaurant chain is more valuable than it might be to an exhaust fitting centre.

Price sensitivity

Beneath the value that buyers place on product or service performance is price sensitivity. Buyers can differ greatly in their price sensitivity based upon their overall elasticity. Much will depend on who bears the cost, e.g. an individual or his/her employer might purchase a flight. Also, what percentage of total expenditure does the product represent? Obviously people and organizations tend to be less price sensitive when the percentage is lower. Another factor is the buyers' ability to judge quality, as with a watch or a lawyer. To what extent can buyers compare prices and how time critical is the purchase? Are there switching costs? A bank might increase its charges for a current account, but regular customers are unlikely to move owing to perceived high switching costs. Thus, Napster charged its UK users nearly twice the amount it charged US citizens. Napster argued that its pricing reflected the cost of the content, and VAT was included in the UK package, unlike in the USA.

Individual or bundled?

The next stage in the strategy is to identify the formal pricing structure. Should prices be individual or bundled? Figure 10.2 shows a position where the optimal price for a product is £70. Buyer A will not buy again unless the prices drops to £20 but Buyer B will purchase again at £50. If the seller sticks to a £70 price it will make two sales for a total of £140. However, knowing Buyer B's price preferences for further units the seller could sell both buyers two units at £140 plus a further four units to B totalling £155, making total sales of £295. Assuming the seller can still make a profit with a £30 price, bundling prices in this instance would make sense.

Competitor reaction

The key issue now is to consider how competitors will react to any price changes. If the company puts up the price by 5% would competitors do nothing, match the increase, reduce their prices, or change some other element of their mix? Thus, after Asda's announcement that it was to drop petrol prices by around 2p a litre in 2004, BP slashed its prices by the same amount. At the same time fierce rivals Sainsbury's and Tesco reduced their own petrol prices at forecourts following Asda's move. Tesco also added a promotion where, for every £50 spent on shopping, customers would get five pence a litre off the price of petrol. Sometimes regulation is required: in 2004 the European Commission fined Wanadoo (the parent company of UK ISP Freeserve) £6.9 m for predatory pricing, following complaints that rival ISPs were being forced out of the market.

Units	Buyer A	Buyer B
1	£70	£70
2	£20	£50
3	£20	£40
4	£20	£35
5	£20	£30

Optimal Price:
£70

Quantity Discount:
Buy 1st = £70
Buy 2nd = £50
Buy 3rd = £40
Buy 4th = £35
Buy 5th = £30

Figure 10.2 Effect of quantity discounts (Producer's cost = $20)

Source: Dolan, Robert J., 'How do you know when the Price is Right?' *Harvard Business Review* (1995), Vol. 73 No.5.

POS

Towards the end of the process it is now important to monitor what prices are realized at the point of sale. If you are distributing through an intermediary there may be discounts given for early payments, rebates on volume, negotiated discounts, etc. A company may also need to consider margins in line with product returns, service guarantees, damage claims, and so on. These should all be taken into account with the price. For example, UK coach operator National Express launched a low fare scheme offering tickets from £1 for a single journey from a variety of UK cities to London. The fares were available on the Internet only and were modelled on e-ticket technology employed by airlines such as easyJet and Ryanair.

Emotion

Research may be needed to assess buyers' emotional response to a price. Buyers develop price points that they see as fair. For example a rise in price for advertising space by the *Evening Standard* in 2003 led to a considerable fall in bookings as advertisers did not think the rise was justified by market circumstances. On the other hand good deals may reduce margins but produce fantastic word-of-mouth in the marketplace.

Customer costs

Finally, wherever possible a company needs to decide whether the returns justify the costs of serving buyers. In relationship marketing this has led many companies to focus on who they regard as their most profitable customers. This can be a socially and politically charged issue as when banks have been found to occasionally send out directives to their branches on who to encourage or discourage from opening an account. In a recent case one bank advised its branches to discourage anyone aged over 40 from opening a current account as by this stage of life most people had made their key financial decisions and would be less likely to provide much profit. (See Mini Case Study 10.1.)

MINI CASE STUDY 10.1

'Pricing reflections on the wonder and woes of a new inkjet printer'

I experienced an apotheosis recently when I bought a new Hewlett-Packard inkjet printer. It scanned! It photocopied! It even printed! And all for £50! I felt as if the roof of the store had lifted off and the god of retail, who I'd guess resembles Philip Green in a white robe, was bathing me in radiance.

But as the poet Keats remarked, Joy's hand is ever at its lips bidding adieu. I left the shop gripped by the impotent fury us middle-aged guys do so well, having paid £52 for a couple of print cartridges to go with my 'bargain' printer. What precious elixir could they contain, I had asked the bored teenager at the till. Pearls dissolved in vintage Krug?

Then anger gave way to admiration. I surmised that manufacturers such as HP lure buyers with cheap printers, clawing back the discounts later with expensive cartridges. That got me thinking about pricing strategies. Setting prices can be pretty » nerve-wracking. Pitch them too low, and you could forfeit margins. Pitch them too high, and turnover could disappoint. How do you reach a profitable compromise?

Michael Pollitt of Judge Business School told me that about 35 per cent of businesses simply set prices in line with the market, while 25 per cent aim to undercut it. Another 35 per cent add a mark-up to costs. A final 5 per cent 'let their customers set their prices'—and presumably end up weaving baskets under the supervision of strong, patient men in white jackets.

Naufel Vilcassim of London Business School added that most products and services are also set relative to a 'reference price', which is what customers expect to pay for average quality. This may reflect the experience of the customer rather than the real costs to the supplier. For example, some internet users remain aggrieved that data businesses no longer dish out scads of free content via the web as they once did.

The latitude you have in setting prices depends on how obscure or obvious the value of your product or service is. There are huge opportunities for profit in 'credence goods' where, according to Jaideep Prabhu of Imperial College's Tanaka Business School, 'The customer cannot tell the value even after consumption.' A good example, he chuckled, would be management consultancy.

Margins are less malleable in 'experience goods', such as food and drink, where quality can be gauged through consumption. The worst pricing squeezes occur in 'search goods', where customers can find out what a given outlay will buy them. PCs belong to this category because computing power is easily compared.

The political correctness in business is that competition is bracingly healthy. So is cod liver oil, which is equally horrid for recipients. If transparency depresses margins, then a pricing strategy that increases opacity may raise them. Selling cheap printers and costly cartridges has this result, even if that is not what manufacturers such as HP intend. Customers, especially retail ones, tend to focus on initial rather than subsequent costs. Prof Prabhu calls it the 'razors and blades' strategy. Mobile phone companies, opticians and insurers all deploy it.

A weakness of the razors and blades strategy is that a rival may start selling cheap blades to fit the low-cost razor you hoped would lock customers into your brand. In printers, this competition comes from makers of cheap generic cartridges and from cartridge recyclers, such as the Cartridge World chain.

Reputational risk is another problem. I am not the only person to fume about the high cost of printer cartridges. Both the Office of Fair Trading and the Consumers' Association have criticized manufacturers in the past. Thomas Zackor of Hewlett-Packard told me wearily: 'It is enticing to look at cartridge costs on a price per millilitre of ink basis, but it does not make much sense.' Developing a new cartridge type can cost as much as $1bn (£563m), he said.

Mr Zackor added HP was helping to set up a new standard for comparing the output of different cartridges, which should improve price transparency. However, he declined to say whether margins were significantly lower for printers than for cartridges. 'We look at it from the perspective of the whole system,' he said firmly.

HP's imaging and printers division generated decent rather than disproportionate earnings of $2.8bn on net revenue of $18.4bn in the nine months to July 31. Those figures dispelled any lingering resentment I felt about pricey ink cartridges. They make HP's pricing structure look like a sensible way of protecting margins, rather than a rip-off.

» Perhaps HP can learn from the insouciance of businesses that represent price opacity as a badge of exclusivity, such as management consultants. I called a McKinsey official, hoping he might twitch aside the customary veil of secrecy. Did the company, for example, copy plumbers by charging according to the swankiness of clients' cars and houses?

'I couldn't possibly comment,' he said, sounding gratifyingly appalled. 'Come on,' I wheedled, 'I'm only asking for a flash of your ankles.' 'Our heritage means we tend not to discuss internal processes,' he said. 'Some girls do and some don't?' 'You might say that,' he purred.

Later, Fiona Czerniawska of the Management Consultancies Association told me 60 per cent of its members worked for a fixed charge, 30 per cent for costs plus a margin and 10 per cent for contingency fees. But I could not help feeling she was ruining the magic for me.

Source: Jonathan Guthrie (2005), *Financial Times*, 26 October, p. 14.

Maintenance and Loyalty

Every B2B or B2C consumer knows that the price paid for a good or service can vary at any time or place. A price variation might be the result of promotions such as bonus packs, temporary price cuts, coupons, circulars, on-pack coupons, or end-of-aisle displays (Davey, Childs, and Carlotti, 1998). Furthermore, some policies can mask price while others highlight it. A £10 cash transaction feels quite different from a £100 one, yet the same transactions by credit card feel identical as both involve signing the same slip of paper. Not surprisingly, theatres find that pre-booking cash-paying customers are much more likely to turn up for shows than credit card ones!

How does such a myriad of pricing policies come about and what is the best policy overall? Potter (2000) suggests several strategies for maintaining price points in a hyper-competitive environment where many buyers have relatively easy access to prices on the Web. One way of holding price in a market that is falling involves 'bundling' benefits. As the price of the standard product falls, the price may be maintained by including previous options as standard. For example, Chrysler responded to price falls in the sports utility market by offering air conditioning and power steering as standard on the Jeep Cherokee. Another approach is to mount joint promotions, such as a grocery chain offering discounted airline tickets to customers who have spent £50. Rebate programmes play a similar role where, after purchasing a product, consumers send off proof of purchase and claim a rebate. Bundling, in whatever format, is only a viable policy as long as the bundled benefits cost less than the amount by which the price would have dropped.

Unbundling benefits takes the opposite approach: where a good or service that was a standard feature is removed and becomes an option. For example, Nissan reduced the price of one its sports cars by 4.5% but at the same time changed the T-bar roof from 'standard' to an option. Buying the T-bar increased the base price of the car by more than the price reduction!

Alternative service levels can also be offered at different price points. Lower prices can be offered without substantial service provision and may include demands for advance payments in order to obtain savings, as Marriott has done in selling rooms. Similarly, when a car hire company had to reduce its prices owing to market pressures, it introduced cancellation fees on bargain offers. At the other end of the scale it introduced a new premium price point with enhanced services as there is always a segment of the market willing to pay more.

Linking future purchases to current transactions is another strategy to explore. For example, car manufacturers often sell to car hire companies with an agreement to repurchase the cars after a set period. The car hire companies get new cars at a keen price and the car manufacturers are in a favourable position to re-negotiate new contracts when the hire companies rotate the cars.

Changing the price effectiveness period involves maintaining the price over time. The aim is to lock-in potentially volatile customer volume or to obtain a higher price when it is expected that prices will fall. For example, many credit card companies have lengthened the time during which new customers can benefit from low levels of interest on debt. Similarly, mobile phone companies offer discounts on long-term contracts in view of the likelihood of future price falls.

An important factor in the degree of consumption of any product or service is cost, so in the long run strategies to maintain or raise prices may cause considerable upset and disloyalty. It has been found that consumption increases the chances of loyalty and that the more customers appreciate prices the more likely they are to consume. Higher consumption helps develop long-term relationships as customers are more likely to repeat the same patterns in the future. In a field study health club members who worked out four times a week were much more likely to renew their memberships than those who worked out once a week (Gourville and Soman, 2002). This is the phenomenon of sunk cost.

Timing of payment has been found to be important as well. For example, people who pay 'up front' large sums for memberships of health clubs tend to use the facilities regularly in the first few weeks after payment. However, as the sunk cost effects dissipate, they tend to treat their memberships as if they were free and work out less and less. Members who pay on a monthly basis are much more likely to attend regularly. Thus the bundling of prices mentioned above may operate in a similar way. For example, people who buy tickets for a series of plays at a festival are much less likely to attend each play than people who buy tickets separately for each performance. When prices are bundled, consumers lose sight of the cost of each ticket. When loyalty is a factor, the advice would be to introduce itemized billing as much as possible so that customers get a better sense of price and, therefore, commitment.

New product target pricing

Target pricing has become an increasingly important component in the marketing pricing strategy of new products. The idea is to develop products and services from the design stage and onwards with a final target price objective for a particular market (Cooper et al., 1996). The strategy was pioneered by leading Japanese electronics and car manufacturers and has since spread to Germany, the UK, and the USA and beyond. Part of its benefit is that low-margin products are normally eliminated from the new product development process. However, the main benefit is that target pricing is a disciplined approach to pricing that brings the reality of the marketplace in consideration throughout the entire process from idea conception to eventual output of the product or service. The process starts with mapping attractive segments in the market and targeting the most attractive ones. Next, the level of quality and functionality for success is determined given a particular price. The organization finally designs the sourcing, production, and delivery process for the product or service that will enable it to achieve the desired profit level with this target market. The whole process has been developed in response to the demands of buyers in both B2B and B2C markets for not only low prices but differentiation as well.

Camera manufacturers provide a good example of the approach. The new Canon Rebel SLR camera incorporates a host of cost-saving technologies to produce a camera that is around half the price of rivals but similar in features. Olympus is another company that has followed the practice. The company has produced a strategic plan that identifies the future mix of businesses by product line, the desired levels of profitability, and the contribution of each product to brand equity. As part of the process Olympus undertakes continual proprietary and external technological reviews as well as mapping of the general business environment (factors like exchange rates and changing income levels). A great deal of market research is undertaken one-to-one, in focus groups, fashion centres, and interviews with professional photographers to identify trends.

Target pricing is more difficult to achieve when a company does not have much control over the design and supply of components. However, Komatsu demonstrated a viable approach in cooperation with its suppliers. In order to implement target pricing Komatsu had to provide its suppliers with the parameters required to meet its required margins from early sub-assembly of its heavy equipment. Thus, the company subcontracts the target pricing objectives to its suppliers to fit the overall targeted price. The idea is not to compromise the quality of the product, but rather to balance the value equation between what is produced and what buyers demand. Engineering is pressed to the limit to meet the targeted price.

Implementing pricing strategy

To implement pricing strategy three 'capitals' are required: human, systems, and social. Companies need to invest in all three capitals for pricing strategy to work.

Human

Human capital means training and hiring people who understand pricing across a range of products or services, customers, suppliers, and competitors. For example Roche has an internal university to increase knowledge among its employees about pricing (Shantanu et al., 2002).

Systems

Systems capital relates to the hardware and software to process and implement pricing decisions. Large grocery chains have led the field by using price-sensitive tools and category management systems to efficiently manage prices. Sophisticated systems are also used by many manufacturers in B2B markets in a variety of ways such as helping sales representatives to understand the profitability of a deal. By using such systems the sales reps can quote prices almost immediately to customers instead of having to go back to the office to calculate the price, which means that deals can be reached much more quickly.

Yield Management Systems (YMS) are becoming increasingly common in the service sector (Desiraju and Shugan, 1999) to profitably fill capacity using complex pricing systems administered by computer. YMS employ such systems as discounting early purchases, limiting early sales at those discounted prices, and overbooking capacity. Such systems were first developed in the mid-1980s in the airline industry and have migrated out into other areas such as hotels, car hire, and all kinds of events. Marketers have developed complex YMS based on sophisticated mathematical computer programs. The basic objective of YMS is to adjust price over time to fill all the available capacity at a profit. In practice it generally boils down to partitioning prices by time periods with discounts early on so that a hotel might charge £80 for bookings six months ahead but as the hotel fills up on these dates and the space becomes more scarce the YMS automatically raises the price. This is a further example of the impact of technology on marketing strategy, which now increasingly turns on a set of rules of behaviour rather than being based on strategic insight.

Social

Social capital is the glue that coordinates and holds together the many participants in a pricing decision. Internally it may involve, for example, persuading divisions to accept pricing policies. In one case, according to (Shantanu et al., 2002), it took two years for the manufacturer concerned to replace divisional managers with ones who were willing to accept the pricing strategy. Sometimes social capital is needed externally to implement pricing policy. For example, several retail chains felt that Procter & Gamble was trying to dictate to them and set about undermining the then new EDLP (everyday low pricing strategy). Wholesalers were also upset and several added their own surcharge on P&G brands or stopped stocking them.

Distribution

Definition

Distribution strategy is a vital element in creating value and has a direct bearing on marketing (pricing, promotion, packaging, salesforce logistics) and delivery, installation, repair and servicing, as well as outbound logistics (order processing, warehousing, and inventory). Distribution is about making a supply of something available to people—be they buyers or users. It can be physical (supplying hard copy of an accounting software package for a customer in a box), a service (supplying a training session for an accounting package), or virtual (downloading an accounting package via the Internet). It is intrinsically linked to pricing for most companies, as the mark-up of distributors can account for a significant amount of the price and is normally at least 50%.

Buyer's perspective

The strategic marketing perspective on distribution is to ask the central question: what do buyers want? Of course what buyers want will vary, but some core wants are:

- availability
- speedy delivery
- reliable supply
- range of choice
- empathy when supply is interrupted
- convenience
- service and support
- a good price

However, people are increasingly leisure 'time poor' in both B2C and B2B markets and keen to trade-off shopping time against leisure so, of all the items on the list, convenience is the primary concern of most buyers (Seiders et al., 2000). As a consequence, convenience has driven just about every innovation in retailing such as supermarkets, department stores, shopping malls, the Web, and self-scanning in the pursuit of providing what customers want. Despite this, few managers define convenience from the customers' point of view or have a systematic convenience strategy. Instead, 'convenience' has become a generic term for a bundle of attributes such as product assortment, salesperson expertise, speed of check-outs, hours of business, service levels, layout, and parking.

From the customers' point of view, convenience means 'speed and ease'. Speed and ease consists of four elements—'access', 'search', 'possession', and 'transaction'. Access is about being easy to reach; search is about enabling customers to speedily identify what they want; possession relates to the ease of obtaining products; and transaction is about the ease of purchase and return of products. What is clear is that convenience is a dynamic construct: 24-hour photo processing is no longer fast and renting a video is now seen by many as a task.

As with all aspects of convenience, access is relevant to both store and non-store shopping. Accessibility factors include parking, location, availability, hours of opening, proximity to other outlets, as well as telephone, mail, and Internet. Convenience simply does not exist without access. Electrical retailer Comet struck a deal with energy giant Npower to offer its customers across the UK the chance to sign up for electricity and gas supplies. Comet customers will be able to obtain savings on Npower's gas and electricity dual-fuel offer. Energy companies hope such deals will reduce the cost of acquiring customers. They also see them as an alternative to the pushy door-to-door selling tactics which have given the industry a bad name.

Access only gives distributors a good start in the process, it is nothing more than that. Customers, be they B2C or B2B, increasingly want access to products and services to be as fast and direct as possible with very little hassle. This appears to be a global trend, as for example in Japan which has seen double-digit sales growth in convenience stores offering everything from afternoon tea, evening meals, faxing, and paying utility bills to buying magazines. Thus, direct shopping via catalogues and the Internet is largely being driven by time- and place-related convenience.

Search convenience, identifying and selecting the products you want, is connected to product focus, intelligent outlet design and layout, knowledgeable staff, interactive systems and product displays, packaging, and signage, be they physical or virtual. Specialist distributors are particularly good for search convenience in that they provide product concentrations in such areas as telephones, bicycles, ties, or office supplies. Shoppers can be confident of a good choice. Nevertheless, even the most highly specialized outlets could fall short if they have poor design and layout or staff with little knowledge. Solutions can be provided in a number of ways such as in-store kiosks, clearly posted prices, and mobile phones for sales staff linked to 'knowledge centres'. One example of good practice is the German discount chain, Adler Modemarkte GmbH, which uses colour-coded tags to help customers quickly spot their sizes. Sound training can prepare sales staff to act more like personal shoppers by anticipating choices and matching the merchandise to the shopper. Demonstrations can also work well, as with Dixons' displays of car audio systems in its larger stores which enable customers to test out every one on display.

Possession convenience is about having merchandise in stock and available on a timely basis. For example, the Nordstrom clothing store guarantees that advertised products will be in stock and the spectacles retailer Lens Crafters prepares glasses on the same day, generally in one hour. But while there are numerous examples of good practice, possession convenience has its limitations. In particular while the Internet scores highly in search convenience, it is generally low when it comes to possession convenience. Shoppers might save a trip to the store but invariably they have to wait for their purchases.

Transaction convenience is the speed and ease with which consumers can effect or amend transactions before and after the purchase. There have been a variety of innovative approaches in recent years, such as robot selection of items to self-scanning in outlets like Waitrose (the latter being a process which is perceived by shoppers as faster despite the time it takes to scan each item). Well-designed service systems can mitigate the peaks and troughs in store traffic as with Sainsbury's use of electronic sensors to track customer traffic to predict checkout requirements. Single queues used by banks and post offices can be effective but cannot be replicated by supermarkets owing to lack of space. Some stores empower employees to take a customer's word on the price of an unmarked item (within reason) to keep queues moving. Transaction convenience is a significant issue on the Internet. Many Internet shoppers drop out when completing the first page of the billing form. Internet sites often require too much personal information, often designed to increase their advertising revenues. Furthermore, customers are not properly prepared for shipping and handling costs. Pure Internet retailers also have problems with returns compared to their bricks and mortar counterparts. It generally is not as easy to return items via the post and often shoppers have to pay the (non-refunded) postage. Unconditional guarantees go a long way, but Internet retailers are generally at a disadvantage when it comes to returns.

Distribution options, principal channels: buyer's perspective

Having discerned what buyers want, any distribution system must have an efficient strategy enabling it to satisfy these wants in the most effective manner. There are a number of options for a seller to reach a buyer (the choice is more limited for services) but these can be broadly broken down into three avenues: direct, salesforce, or intermediary as shown in Figure 10.3 and in more detail in Figure 10.4.

Direct	Salesforce	Intermediary
• Internet	• Own	• Franchise
• Telephone	• Another firm's	• Wholesaler
• Mail	• Contract	• Agent/Merchant
• Catalogue		• Distributor
• Own channel		• Partner

Figure 10.3 Distribution options*

*More limited for services.

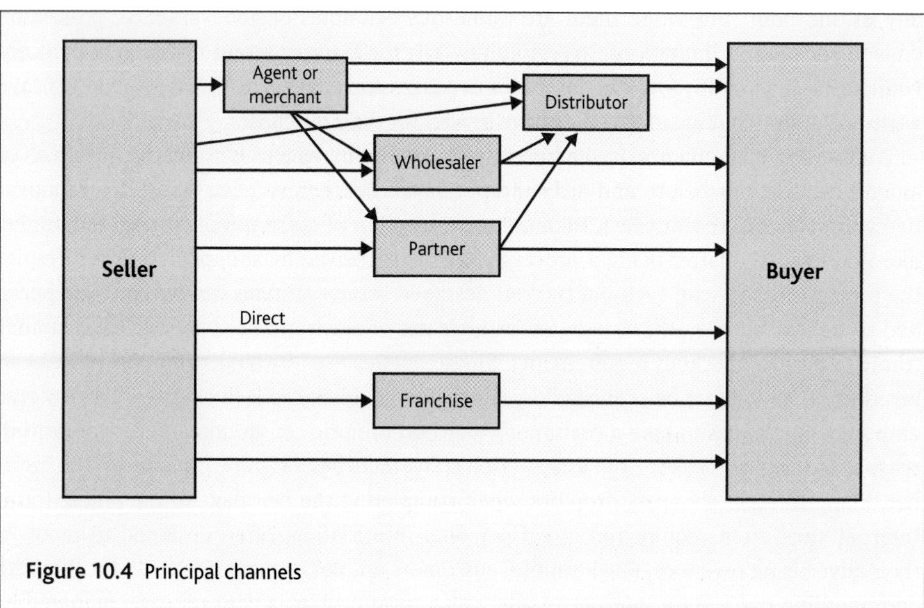

Figure 10.4 Principal channels

Direct

Going direct to a buyer can be achieved by using the Internet, telephone, mail, catalogue, some form of direct advertising (press, DRTV, or radio), or own distribution network. Direct channels can provide a reliable supply and a good price, and can be extremely convenient by saving the physical requirement to shop. However, they are prone to problems of availability, speedy supply (no instant purchases can be made aside from digital products), range of choice (e.g. companies like Lands' End only offer their own branded clothes), empathy when supply is interrupted, and service and support (especially if items have to be returned).

It is a gross simplification, but on the whole direct channels are best when the strategy is cost focus for niche or mass markets. Buyers are often prepared to sacrifice negatives like speedy delivery against the benefits of a lower price. Strategically such channels may also work with highly differentiated items that cannot be obtained elsewhere. For example, when Royal Doulton offers its commemorative plates through direct response advertising in the *Radio Times*, it enables the company to reach a large number of potential buyers cost efficiently compared to the alternatives.

From the suppliers' perspective, this option provides considerable control over the mechanics of distribution and revenues, reliability of supply is directly linked to production, and there is no need to motivate a channel. However, it requires logistical expertise even if many of the supply chain relationships are contracted out (e.g. delivery) and so the investment required may be relatively high.

The main question with direct distribution is why would an organization choose any other way? The reason is largely down to discrepancy of assortment—most suppliers have a small number of products and services whereas consumers desire variety of choice and ease of purchase, especially in B2C markets. Few people would buy their groceries from individual suppliers as it would be too time consuming (it is more manageable through intermediaries like Tesco). Thus direct distribution, which has many advantages for suppliers, is largely confined to specialist single item purchases and B2B markets where consumers are willing to trade off any disadvantages for cheaper prices or highly differentiated (or often unique) products or services. The Internet has accelerated the process by driving down transaction costs and made direct supply a lot easier for both seller and buyer.

Salesforce

An alternative to going direct is to use a salesforce, and the choices are to: (1) set up your own; (2) use another organization's; or (3) hire on a contractual basis. The use of a salesforce in the B2C marketplace is largely no longer viable and very few companies have continued to use one. That is not to suggest that the use of a salesforce in B2C markets was ever very common: since the 1950s it has been largely confined to a relatively small group of industries and companies such as vacuum cleaners and financial products. There are small niche companies using salesforces in particular regions in the UK, but few large ones (the Co-Operative Society still uses agents for its financial products for the home) as even the Prudential, famous for its 'Man from the Pru' campaign, has disbanded its operation. The one major exception in recent years has been the use of salesforces by competing gas suppliers (e.g. British Gas and Southern Electric) in the newly deregulated gas market. After all, gas is an industry that is used to managing large numbers of staff to read meters. It has occasionally been highly controversial as some heavy-handed tactics have been used by a small group of unscrupulous salespeople.

The problems of using a salesforce strategy in most B2C markets have been that the fragmentation of households, the rise of overall employment, and the increase in car ownership and alternative means of shopping mean that door-to-door selling just does not have much appeal in B2C markets. There are simply too few people at home in the day. Added to this, few people are receptive to calls in the evening and society as a the whole is more suspicious of strangers 'at the door'. All this, combined with the rise in buyers' access to information, has meant that very few people will ever buy a product or service from a salesperson at the door other than for domestic services like window cleaning.

The B2B marketplace is quite different and operates with an active salesforce in just about all markets. Sustaining a longer-term customer relationship requires developing a close personal bond between the parties involved. Salespeople tend to liaise regularly with a distinct and small group of senior managers, whatever the size of the company. However, the decision to select, continue, or terminate a purchase or contract at larger corporations has long been known to be the product of joint decision-making processes, involving a large number of decision-makers and influencers. Furthermore, with increasingly decentralized management structures in companies many salespeople find that they are increasingly isolated from key decision-makers.

Individuals within the client company may assume one or more roles (Webster and Wind, 1972) that have a direct or indirect influence on the salesforce relationship. **Users** are the most easily identified by a salesperson. **Buyers**, senior managers, may be easily identified, but can often be more conspicuous than their 'real' importance to the decision. **Influencers** may include a wide group of people such as finance directors, production managers, and lawyers who may help establish relationship criteria and direction. The **decider** may be the 'buyer', but in many organizations that person may be someone removed from day-to-day activities. Their criteria are likely to be less well informed and far more subjective than those of specialist personnel, or they may involve issues of prestige. Alternatively, the decision-maker may make judgements based on those of a supplier client: exhibiting dissonance, reducing behaviour to seeking 'reassurance' or 'safety'. **Gatekeepers**, who control the access of information to the buying centre (either positively or negatively), may include such people as marketers, PR, sales, PAs/secretaries, and receptionists. Senior and top managers may also channel information on rival suppliers that they have gathered.

Furthermore, Webster and Wind's (1972) industrial-buying tasks of 'new buy,' 'modified re-buy', and 'straight re-buy' provide a helpful typology for appreciating the strategic issues for salespeople. Customers involved in **new tasks** will perceive a high risk so a salesperson can be effectively utilized to provide advice. With such decisions a salesperson offers a convenient way to assess the market offering and much can be learnt from discussing proposed purchases with different salespeople. However, at this stage a salesperson can be used to provide a lot of information but may not win the business. At the new task stage with large capital purchases the customer is generally obliged to visit the salesperson's site to see the equipment in operation (or possibly to visit one of their customers' premises). Service and support are also important and these can be discussed directly with a salesperson along with availability and speed of delivery. However, any individual supplier will offer a narrow range of choice which is generally 'pieced' together by potential buyers in discussions with several competing salespeople. **Modifying** a familiar purchase is often done in cooperation with a salesperson. The importance of availability and range of choice diminishes along with service and support because at this stage the buyer is likely to have a greater knowledge of these aspects from previous experience. What is important is reliability, the empathy of the salespeople, and convenience of buying.

With the **straight re-buy** perceived client risk is minimal because the task is characterized by repetitive actions. Here the salesforce's role is largely to take the order rather than to give advice and it may be more marginal strategically. Convenience is pre-eminent in continued purchasing and in most mature markets the re-buy is the mainstay business of most salespeople.

Having your own salesforce clearly provides optimum control and ability to motivate. But it might be more cost effective to use the services of another organization (normally not a competitor but with the rise of global alliances it might be) or to contract the salesforce out. In either case there will be loss of control and questions over loyalty and motivation other than for monetary rewards so generally this is not as attractive an option except in the short term.

Salesforce decisions are often determined by the margins at stake. For example, it is not uncommon in some markets, such as the aerospace industry, for a company like British Aerospace to employ a salesperson for 5–15 years without making a single sale. It might take this long for a salesperson to develop relationships with government agencies and other buyers and there is no prospect of contracting this role outside the business. If a sale is made it might be worth several billion pounds to British Aerospace and, therefore, ultimately worth the effort. Strategically there is no substitute for a salesperson(s) in such markets.

Intermediaries

An intermediary channel has to be used when it is difficult or impossible for a supplier to 'meet' its customers. In one development TNT Mail linked up with Express Dairies in June 2004 to launch a B2C letter and parcel distribution service in competition with Royal Mail. The move is the latest development in the deregulation of UK postal services, which will see Royal Mail lose the monopoly it has enjoyed for hundreds of years.

There is an ownership issue here. If you own a shop and sell your products through it, that shop would not be classified as an intermediary. However, if you sell your products through an identical shop that you do not own, that shop would be classified as an intermediary. There are several different types of intermediary: agent, distributor, franchiser, merchant, and wholesaler. An agent acts as principal intermediary between the seller of a product or service and finds buyers without taking ownership. A merchant performs the same but does take ownership. Wholesalers stock products (not services) before the next level of distribution. Distributors do just that—they distribute the product within a market. Franchising occurs where a company offers a complete brand concept, supplies, and logistics to a franchisee who invests an initial lump sum and thereafter pays regular fees to continue the relationship (e.g. KFC).

Strategically, intermediaries enable firms to offer just about everything buyers want: availability, speed of delivery, reliable supply, range of choice, empathy when supply is interrupted, convenience, and service and support. From a customer's perspective there are few, if any, downsides except for the kind of B2B customer identified in the previous section who is involved in a measured choice and needs to deal with a salesperson.

If intermediaries can satisfy just about all the needs of customers the question is, why do many organizations choose to go direct? What are the trade-offs and disadvantages of intermediaries? One obvious problem is the lack of control, which is the opposite of the advantages of the direct channel. Suppliers are often at the mercy of intermediaries in terms of such matters as where their products are placed on shelves and how they are finally priced, and the consequent effect on sales and margins. Competitors may offer all kinds of inducements to intermediary channels (if allowed by the channel owners) to pre-empt rivals' products, in terms of shelf space, stocking, and advice. Thus a company might run an effective advertising campaign for its lipstick only to find that when consumers go into shops to buy the product they are advised to buy another brand which is available at a special price or a company might launch a new shampoo only to find a rival has usurped demand by offering bonus packs in the week of the launch and diminishing the available shelf space for the new product.

In short, for many suppliers, intermediaries are a market in their own right and require considerable resources to support and develop relationships with—hence the issue of 'push' and 'pull' and the importance of branding. Take a brand like Sony. Despite product parity in many electronic markets, Sony remains the premium electronics brand in the B2C marketplace. Any electrical retailer without Sony products is going to be less of a destination for most shoppers as they will expect to see the brand. Sony has supplier power and can negotiate higher margins and better shelf positioning and stocking for its products than its rivals.

Channel conflict

An additional problem for many suppliers is channel conflict, especially for premium and high-priced products and services. Conflicts can arise vertically, that is between sequential members in a distribution network such as agents and distributor over such matters as carrying a particular range or price increases. Horizontal conflicts may arise between members of a channel such as between agents or between distributors where competition may be deemed to be unfair. Within any channel there are often collisions of interests given all channel members naturally seek to maximize their profits and resources. For the most part, major channel conflicts are rare. However, one particular area has seen a significant amount of channel conflict in recent years: grey marketing (see Mini Case Study 10.2).

Grey marketing occurs when distributors purchase goods in one market, such as fluid pumps or drill bits, either from an authorized dealer or directly from the manufacturer, and resell the same goods in another market at a higher price. They undercut the prices of the authorized dealers in a market and still make a healthy profit. Such activity is not necessarily illegal, but can fall foul of licence agreements or be counter to trade regulations. For example, Tesco recently lost a dispute with Levi's to sell jeans sourced in the grey marker in its supermarkets.

Companies that find their goods being distributed by grey marketers face a mix of problems aside from lost profits. For a start, price discounting can affect their image and relationships with authorized dealers can become strained as they watch their markets being eroded. Furthermore, they might face legal challenges as unauthorized imports might not meet local safety or import regulations. Moreover, forward planning becomes difficult

MINI CASE STUDY 10.2
'Black, White and Grey are the Three Colours of a Free Market'

Free markets tend to evolve and mutate in quite remarkable ways. The more marketers attempt to restrict distribution, the more markets develop alternative channels.

Perfume is perhaps the best illustration of how manufacturers attempt to limit distribution to particular retailers. This is partly motivated by the need for a consistent price and also because perfume brands are uniquely vulnerable to being presented in the wrong kinds of retail settings. As a result, however, the three shades of the market have emerged in perfume distribution: white, grey and black.

The white market is the approved market. For the manufacturer, this is the ideal distributor and hopefully the sole source of the product for consumers. For perfume, Selfridges is a white market. It has a tremendous retail brand that co-brands the perfumes. It rarely runs price promotions and when it does it is usually with the distributor's consent. Best of all, Selfridges has the space and setting to present each perfume in its ideal context: on its own island within the store populated by highly trained and motivated sales staff. Selfridges, like all white markets, is awarded a host of manufacturer-bestowed benefits such as in-store ad displays and exclusive promotional items such as towels or make-up bags.

Walk out of Selfridges onto Oxford Street and take a left turn. The Perfume Shop is a grey market because it does not usually get its perfume from the manufacturer but rather from the white markets who are able to sell on the product for a small margin or to clear stocks. The grey market has a very different market offering. The brands are sold at a steep discount, often up to 75%, and rather than being presented in exclusive manufacturer islands they are stacked up shoulder to shoulder against each other. There are no product service personnel and, devoid of manufacturer-supplied promotional material, the grey market stores usually use framed magazine ads to present the illusion of manufacturer sponsorship.

Exiting the Perfume Shop you walk down Oxford Street. At some point on your walk you will spot the black market in action. A lone trader will be selling three or four perfume brands from a sheet of cardboard placed precariously on top of a rubbish bin. As a black marketer he must have broken the law, and not just a manufacturer agreement, in order to get his stock, so the perfumes are likely to be either stolen or counterfeit. His only promotional aid is his verbal sales pitch and his only market intelligence comes in the form of his partner, the spotter, who remains out of sight watching out for any policemen on patrol. Rather than shun the white and grey markets, the black marketer actively seeks them out and attempts to market his products in close proximity to his more expensive competitors.

These three markets, black, white and grey, operate literally within a stone's throw of each other. Each offering apparently the same brand, and yet each representing a completely different form of distribution channel. Sometimes the beauty and complexity of markets can be literally right in front of us.

Source: Mark Ritson (2002), *Marketing*, 13 June.

as they no longer have full knowledge of sales patterns and their reputation may be further damaged if grey marketers fail to provide a decent level of service.

In a survey of over 400 US-based exporters (Myers and Griffith, 1999), 20% felt that their exports were severely affected by grey exports. Regions particularly badly affected by grey markets are Western Europe and the Pacific Rim, followed by Latin America. Areas such as the former Soviet Union were less prominent, though this might reflect lower levels of trade activity. Within Western Europe, Germany and the UK were identified as the worst markets in terms of grey activity. In the UK, hot-spot items were: welding alloys, hand cleansers, dental care products, electronic ignition systems, and conveyor belts. If equalizing prices is not an option, and if the alternative of seeking a legal solution is preferred, what strategies should companies adopt to challenge grey marketers?

One worthwhile strategy is to coordinate distribution channels horizontally. What this means in practice is the sharing of information with distributors such as sales databases. If one distributor notices unfamiliar sales activities it can alert both the manufacturer and distributors in nearby markets and thereby 'flag' potential problems. Distributors should also be encouraged to update and input data on changing regulations in their markets. This will help manufacturers and other distributors to forecast potential grey market activity. For example, the EU might significantly change tax arrangements for a particular good between members and non-members of the community, and there may be consequences for grey markets.

Grey marketers often take advantage of differentials between goods such as colours and size or chemical compositions and emission control systems. When restrictions occur in some markets, grey marketers often seize opportunities to supply from another region where such restrictions do not apply. In such cases evidence needs to be gathered on specific product attributes to lobby local governments to amend their legislation.

Another consideration is to restrict the power of salespeople and lower-level managers to set different prices for particular customers. Wide price margins within markets encourage buyers to seek lower prices if they cannot access the 'deals' they see on offer. Finally, it is advisable for companies to 'stay in touch' with their distributors. Web-based databases offer the opportunity to replace the annual or bi-annual meeting with constant discussion.

Price and distribution strategies meet

Appropriate strategies for price and distribution will depend on a variety of factors, but should be synchronized. Clearly it would be a mismatch to distribute high-priced luxury handbags in discount stores and would only confuse potential buyers. The inherent brand position and direction must be taken into account. Market position is another factor. A follower brand with a relatively small market share is likely to follow the price and distribution patterns of leaders and generally be sold at a lower price and be placed in slightly less favourable positions by distributors. The product life cycle (PLC) is also a consideration. The PLC is a tool in widespread managerial use (despite its problems) given its ability to provide some strategic insights. Depending on where an organization is on the PLC, the kinds of price and distribution decisions may vary considerably. Bearing these three points in mind a number of observations can be made on price and distribution.

Market leader

Just about every market has an acknowledged market leader—a firm with a dominant market share that sets the standards or rules in the marketplace. Obvious examples are Sony and televisions, Tesco and supermarkets, and BT and broadband. Market leaders have a lot going for them, but have to remain ever vigilant to the activities of rivals trying to usurp their position by exploiting some weakness in the marketplace. Leading brand names in the consumer, business, and not-for-profit marketplace have retained their leadership surprisingly well over the past 30–50 years and have been the subject of much academic research studying their viability and longevity.

Dominant market leaders need to expand the total market as much as possible as they are the ones most likely to benefit, given their leadership position. They can achieve this by means of strategies for market usage and new applications as well as by considering developing niche markets that may have been previously neglected. Their distribution networks are usually fully in place, which leaves price as the main weapon in their armoury. They might directly attack challengers by price reductions as BT has recently done in the landline phone marketplace and Esso has with its 'Price Promise'. If attacked by a challenger dropping its price a leader is generally advised to 'take stock of the situation' before deciding on the best form of counterattack. Normally market leaders have enough strength to wait and decide on the best response, which might be to delay matching such decreases. For example, Sony has generally been able to maintain its premier price differential in the marketplace despite the challenges of rivals like Samsung.

Market leaders have several attacking or defensive options in declining markets. As leaders, they have the greatest visibility in the market and by reducing their prices they can encourage rivals to rapidly exit from the marketplace. Alternatively they may decide to milk their position, maintain their prices, and steadily withdraw and reallocate their resources to other markets where they consider they have better prospects.

Market challenger

The market challenger is the main reason for the nervousness of the market leader. Unlike market followers, market challengers are substantial firms or institutions in their own right, with sufficient resources and skills to occupy the market leader spot. Any marketplace is dynamic and firms' fortunes can go up or down. Colgate's market leadership of toothpaste has been eclipsed by Crest, Hoover's dominance of vacuum cleaners rocked by Dyson, and Sainsbury's lost its market leadership to Tesco. Market challengers normally do not wipe out the business of the market leader, but they can edge their way towards equality or gradually overtake the market leader. Market challengers have little alternative but to attack leaders either directly or indirectly. They need to make better use of pricing and distribution to attack the leader's weaker spots (flanks). A concentrated all-out attack on a leader may be the best way forward to enable the challenger to take the high ground with lower prices. Attacking other challengers, followers, or smaller niche players in the marketplace rather than the leader can launch indirect price attacks on the leader. The challenger can discreetly build market share without going head-to-head on price with the leader, by picking off weaker geographic markets or segments in so-called 'bypass' attacks. In this way Swatch managed to outmanoeuvre Seiko in the fashion watch segment. Relatively smaller challengers may adopt 'guerrilla' tactics by picking off smaller markets intermittently. But unless backed up by some wider and deeper campaign at some later point, small-scale price tactics will never dismount a leader.

Market follower

Market followers, as their name implies, make a conscious decision to chase and emulate the market decisions of leaders and/or challengers. They may clone prices and distribution and trade successfully upon the 'leftovers' of other companies. Generally they build distribution behind leaders and challengers and set their prices somewhat lower. Their profitability emanates from their decision to forgo investing in either uncertain new product development or educating consumers to new ways of thinking, in favour of simply following the actions of leaders or challengers in the marketplace. Followers, by their nature, do not seek leadership or to overtly challenge a leader. They can make good profits simply by providing imitations of leader or challenger products, the only deterrent being legal, such as from patents in the drug industry. Service sectors, like banking and hotels, are particularly prone to followers, as it is impossible to copyright a service provision, as are capital-intensive sectors in the business marketplace like fibre optic cables and steel. Typical examples of followers are Virgin Cola, Marks & Spencer jeans, Acer laptops, Holiday Inns, and the Orange mobile phone service. By definition, market followers need to stick to their title. They need to follow leaders and challengers and not launch price or distribution attacks. If they launch attacks, they will become challengers and will need the requisite resources and skills to survive such combat.

Market niche

The application of the market niche brings the discussion of pricing and distribution full circle. The reason is simple: a market niche is the application of market leadership to a small and/or distinct part of the marketplace. The micro policy is based upon the macro one. Success with a niche policy is based upon the reality that market leaders or challengers have little or no interest in niches. Thus, Bang & Olufsen can survive extremely well in its high-priced, selectively distributed, and upmarket, style-conscious (but not expert) hi-fi marketplace, knowing that the likes of Sony or Marantz would have great difficulty in stretching their image to challenge them. Similarly, in the brewing, fashion, and cosmetics markets a host of small players continue to make good profits exploiting niche market opportunities that neither leaders nor challengers or followers would want to occupy. Thus, most major breweries are just not interested in developing products to rival micro breweries with their wheat, herbal, and chocolate beers (to name but a few!). The secret of successful sole niching is to operate within a niche that has very little appeal for major players in the wider marketplace. The basis of the market niche strategy, be it a sole strategy or one adopted by leaders or challengers, is to specialize. Market niche strategies may be based upon goods or services, segments, channels, or promotional images. Best practice for sole nichers is to develop more than one market niche so that the company or institution is less vulnerable to attack from a rival. It is essential that a sole nicher be not seen as a potential rival to a leader or challenger, which might lead to a direct attack. An ideal position for a sole nicher would be one where just about everyone else in the marketplace regards their niche as too much effort to bother with. That way they can charge premium prices and develop selective and discreet distribution channels. A company marketing high-priced organic non-dairy chocolate products only through delicatessens and healthfood shops is unlikely to have much trouble from the likes of Cadbury's! Leaders or challengers can use niches either to entrench their positions or as a form of attack. As discussed above, in the hands of leaders or challengers a niche can provide a basis for market growth or to indirectly attack a rival's market position.

Conclusion

The reality for most marketers is that the pricing and distribution 'dice' have been 'thrown' by their companies. L'Oreal's dermatological skincare range Vichy was delisted by Boots in 2003, because Boots preferred to stock the brand on shelves, but Vichy would rather position the brand closer to behind-the-counter products. Vichy was reluctant to compromise on its international distribution strategy, which positions the brand as a specialist pharmacy product rather than a mass-market or premium skincare range. Thus, for the most part, strategies have to be developed in line with historic price points and distribution structures. In many markets pricing and distribution strategies meet positioning and customer wants. Take the case of the petrol companies and supermarkets. The supermarkets moved into the retailing of petrol in the early 1990s, undercutting the prices of petrol companies and offering volume discounts based on how much people spent on their groceries. In response the petrol companies transformed their garage operations into convenience stores offering many of the same staple products as the supermarkets but with much longer opening hours. In response several supermarkets, in particular Tesco, have extended their opening hours (selected stores being open for 24 hours).

Overall, intensive distribution is largely found for low-priced convenience or impulse products or services where the opportunity to buy is important. Exclusive distribution is generally used for high-priced luxury items in order to achieve superior brand image, product support, better sales effort, and control over price. Selective distribution tends to work well for speciality producers (e.g. sewing machines) where knowledgeable dealers are needed and buyers are prepared to seek out dealers.

Undoubtedly the Internet has provided the biggest challenge to suppliers and bricks and mortar channel members. For example, Dixons was initially reluctant to fully develop its website as the company feared cannibalization of its high street operation. Strategically it might make sense, but there is conflict with the established paradigm of on-street and out-of-town shopping outlets. What to do? In cases like this the prevailing positioning mindset might prove to be a drawback and the Web opportunity might be taken by a pure Internet start-up like Dabs.com.

The problems faced by marketers are that so many individual and combined methods for pricing and distribution are possible and that the Internet has had a major (negative) impact on many traditional intermediaries. The key challenge for marketers in this environment is how to price and distribute in a way that supports a chosen position and fends off the drive to commoditization. This is especially, though not exclusively, what is happening in many B2B markets. Take the case of handling and storage products (e.g., hand trucks, stackers, pallet trucks) made by companies like Caterpillar, BT Rolatruc, Komatsu, and Jungheinrich. They are used to stack and manoeuvre products in warehouses and for deliveries, etc. Such products are fast approaching commodity status and are traded on the Web with increasingly small margins as a result, which in turn leaves the companies with fewer resources to invest in R&D for future differentiation. There is no easy solution to the problem. Given that it is less easy to evaluate a service than a product, commoditization of services is less of a problem. However, it has happened with reasonably transparent and highly competitive services such as house conveyancing, where solicitors all charge similar standard prices.

Summary

Value holds the key to both pricing and distribution. Buyers are savvy and smart, most markets are mature with products and services near (or at) parity, and distribution channels are varied and largely accessible physically and/or virtually. Any strategies attempting to 'rip off' or over-charge will fail and longer-term trust will evaporate. As a consequence of these challenges, price and distribution are likely to remain key issues in marketing strategy in the immediate future.

KEY TERMS

Elasticity A measure of the relationship between the percentage change in demand for a good or service and the percentage change in price. For example, if the price of a brand of coffee rises by 10% and demand falls below 10%, the brand would be inelastic. However, if the price were to rise by 10% and demand fall by more than 10%, the brand would be elastic.

Bundling Grouping together features or goods or services to form a single price.

Price at POS The price realized at the final transaction between seller and buyer.

Target pricing The development of goods and services with a specific price at POS at mind.

Yield management systems (YMS) Pricing based on complex computer programs to maximize profitability. Generally prices are discounted for early purchasers.

Intermediary Any distributor operating between seller and buyer who may or may not take ownership of the good or service.

Channel conflict Potential or existing disputes between different forms of distribution, for example BA airline ticket sales via its website and its travel agent network.

Grey marketing Distributors purchasing goods or services in one market and reselling them in another at a higher price.

DISCUSSION QUESTIONS

1 In what ways might an organization's pricing 'mindset' act negatively on its pricing strategy?

2 If you could only follow two of Dolan's eight pricing strategy stages, which ones would you choose and why?

3 What is the role of price in loyalty? What pricing strategies can be used to enhance loyalty and repeat purchases?

4 To what extent do you think systems-based rules will take over pricing strategy decisions?

5 Convenience has come to the fore as the key element on which to base distribution. Assess the arguments for and against focusing on convenience over other core wants such as range of choice.

6 Why is the salesforce so important to B2B marketing strategy and so unimportant to B2C?

7 What strategies would you recommend for an organization faced with intense grey marketing distribution in one of its markets?

ONLINE RESOURCE CENTRE

Visit the Online Resource Centre for this book for lots of interesting additional material at: **www.oxfordtextbooks.co.uk/orc/west/**

REFERENCES AND FURTHER READING

Ayres, Ian, and Barry Nalebuff (2003), 'In Praise of Honest Pricing', *MIT Sloan Management Review*, 45 (1), pp. 24–8.

Cooper, Robin, Bruce W. Chew, and Bernard Avishai (1996), 'Control Tomorrow's Costs Through Today's Designs', *Harvard Business Review*, 74 (1), pp. 88–99.

Davey, K. K. S., Andy Childs, and Stephen J. Carlotti (1998), 'Why Your Price Band is Wider than it Should be', *McKinsey Quarterly*, 3, pp. 116–27.

Desiraju, Ramarao, and Steven M. Shugan (1999), 'Strategic Service Pricing and Yield Management', *Journal of Marketing*, 63 (1), pp. 44–57.

Dolan, Robert J. (1995), 'How Do You Know When the Price is Right?', *Harvard Business Review*, 73 (5), pp. 174–9.

Gourville, John, and Dilip Soman (2002), 'Pricing and the Psychology of Consumption', *Harvard Business Review*, September, pp. 91–6.

Myers, Mathew B., and David A. Griffith (1999), 'Strategies For Combating Gray Market Activity', *Business Horizons*, 42 (6), pp. 71–5.

Potter, Donald V. (2000), 'Discovering Hidden Pricing Power', *Business Horizons*, 43 (6), November–December, pp. 41–8.

Schindehutte, Miner, and Michael Morris (2001), 'Pricing as Entrepreneurial Behavior', *Business Horizons*, 44 (4), pp. 41–9.

Seiders, Kathleen, Leonard L. Berry, and Larry G. Gresham (2000), 'Attention, Retailers! How Convenient is Your Convenience Strategy?', *Sloan Management Review*, Spring, pp. 79–89.

Shantanu, Dutta, Mark Bergen, Daniel Levy, Mark Ritson, and Mark Zbaracki (2002), 'Pricing as a Strategic Capability', *MIT Sloan Management Review*, Spring, pp. 61–6.

Urbany, Joel E. (2001), 'Are Your Prices Too Low?', *Harvard Business Review*, 79 (9), pp. 26–8.

Webster, Frederick, and Yoram Wind (1972), *Organizational Buying Behavior* (Englewood Cliffs: Prentice-Hall).

KEY ARTICLE ABSTRACTS

Avlonitis, George J., Kostis A. Indounas, and Spiros P. Gounaris (2005), 'Pricing Objectives Over The Service Life Cycle: Some Empirical Evidence', *European Journal of Marketing*, 39 (5/6), pp. 696–714.

The service sector tends to be somewhat neglected in the pricing literature. This paper redresses the balance by assessing pricing objectives at different stages of the services life cycle and provides empirical evidence on practice.

Abstract: The purpose of this paper is to explore the pricing objectives that service companies pursue along with the extent to which these objectives are influenced by the stage of the services' life cycle. The paper reviews the existing literature and analyses data from 170 companies operating in six different services sectors in Greece in order to achieve the research objectives. The literature on the pricing of services reveals the complete lack of any previous work endeavouring to examine empirically this potential influence. The study concludes that the objectives are mainly customer oriented and aimed at improving the companies' financial performance in the market. Furthermore, the stage of these services' life cycle, along with the sector of operation, seems to have an influence on the pricing objectives pursued. The context of the study (Greece) limits the wider applicability of the research findings, suggesting the need for replication of the current study in different national contexts. The practical implications of the findings are that managers might have much to gain by adopting a 'situation-specific approach' when setting prices. Thus, different pricing objectives should be set as a service passes from one stage of its life cycle to another, while different services necessitate a different pricing approach.

Narus, James A., and James C. Anderson (1996), 'Rethinking Distribution: Adaptive Channels', *Harvard Business Review*, Jul–Aug, pp. 112–21.

This paper examines how many companies have rationalized their channels and moved from multiple to fewer distributors in an attempt to raise quality. Examples are cited for different types of company and countries. It is argued that the successful use of distribution in marketing is, to a large extent, based upon some degree of experimentation.

Abstract: To solve distribution problems, a handful of forward-looking companies are experimenting with their distribution channels to make them more flexible and responsive. Although the scope of the experiments and the specifics vary widely, each embraces a concept the authors call adaptive channels. The potential benefits of these new arrangements come from the opportunity to leverage resources and share capabilities within the channel. To learn more about innovative distribution practices, the authors conducted an extensive research study in 1994 and 1995 of 27 US, European, and Japanese organizations that are considered to be leaders in distribution. These companies' initiatives can be divided into three broad categories. In the first, the distribution channel is designed to ensure that the members are routinely able to cope with unexpected or unusual demands for products and services. In the second, the new arrangements focus on meeting customers' growing demands for broader market offers. In the third, the objective is to improve the quality of service throughout the distribution channel by substituting the superior capabilities of one member for the inferior capabilities of another.

Ross, Elliot B. (1984), 'Making Money with Proactive Pricing', *Harvard Business Review*, Nov–Dec, pp. 145–56.

This paper examines the concept of 'proactive pricing': taking advantage of pricing opportunities in the marketplace. Topics covered include pricing strategy and tactics, developing a pricing framework, the influence of decision-makers in pricing, changing and setting prices, and the importance of timing.

Abstract: Although the roots of capitalism stretch back many centuries, setting prices remains an inexact science. The pricing decision, one of the most important in business, is also one of the least understood. Many industrial companies, according to the author, habitually set prices reflexively on the basis of simple criteria: to recover costs, to maintain or gain market share, to match competitors. As the author shows, however, some companies have discovered the benefits of thinking more shrewdly about pricing. The rewards of a better understanding of pricing strategy and tactics can be substantial. By carefully studying pertinent information about customers, competitors, and industry economics, and by selectively applying appropriate techniques, proactive pricers can earn millions of dollars that might otherwise be lost. Across a spectrum of industries ranging from lighting equipment to computer software, customers are gaining power at the expense of suppliers. Competitive intensity is increasing, causing speciality products to evolve into near-commodities. Computerized information systems enable the purchaser to compare price and performance factors with unprecedented ease and accuracy. Improved communications and increased use of telemarketing and computer-aided selling have opened up many markets to additional competitors.

END OF CHAPTER 10 CASE STUDY

'We Can Build A Juggernaut'—P&G and Gillette lead the way through a new retail landscape

At mid-afternoon in Dominick's supermarket just west of the Loop, Chicago's business district, shoppers are browsing the store's 15 aisles. Beth Pedroso, a member of the floor staff, explains how its business is doing in personal and healthcare, where a toothbrush and toothpaste section stretches for 24 feet (7 metres). Gillette razor blades are selling so well that 'there isn't really a lot of competition', she says. To the left of the razor display, the shelf where Crest teeth-whitening strips should be is empty. That premium Procter & Gamble product has become a 'high theft' item, available on request and although $36.59 a packet, very popular.

It is consumer demand such as this that enables Jim Kilts, the Gillette chief executive who initiated the $57bn acquisition of his company by P&G, to say of the deal: 'We believe we can build a juggernaut.'

Combined, P&G and Gillette can go to retailers boasting that the group offers no fewer than 21 brands that each have about $1bn in annual sales. They include Ariel and Tide laundry detergents, Head & Shoulders and Pantene shampoos, Crest toothpaste and Pringles snacks at P&G, plus Oral-B toothbrushes, Mach3 razors and Braun shavers at Gillette.

The group, boasting annual sales of $60bn, will have unprecedented global reach, leapfrogging rival Unilever in sales and moving closer to challenging the Anglo-Dutch company's dominance in emerging markets such as Asia. The move not only means P&G's rivals will come under pressure to respond. It also prompts questions about whether some of the largest consumer goods companies are moving ***defensively*** to strengthen their bargaining power against powerful retailers such as Wal-Mart, which has 8% of US consumer spending pass through its tills and has been expanding substantially in foreign markets.

»

A combined P&G/Gillette will be able further to build its market share in basic oral care and shaving products, while its scale will also increase the cost of doing business for rivals in emerging markets, says Morgan Stanley. P&G/Gillette's ability to accelerate the growth it can generate at the top 10 global retailers may prompt rivals—such as Colgate-Palmolive and Kimberly-Clark—to merge.

The P&G/Gillette marriage holds out the prospect of bringing them an even greater share of the fastest-growing, high-margin segments of the consumer business: personal health and beauty care. This encompasses products such as Crest's sought-after tooth whitener, Spinbrush electric toothbrushes and men's grooming products.

A.G. Lafley, P&G's chief executive, says the 'women hair removal' businesses alone is a $10bn market that is growing at 8% annually. The health and personal care business as a whole will now represent half of P&G's portfolio, he says. The rest includes everything from Duracell batteries to Folgers coffee. Much of the growth will come from emerging markets. Bill Pecoriello, households and personal care analyst at Morgan Stanley, says emerging markets account for 20% of Gillette's sales but contribute 60% of growth and that these markets are growing at 20%.

Most importantly, the deal takes advantage of profound structural changes in the consumer goods and retailing industry. Channels of distribution have widened, meaning that a loaf of bread that once could be found mainly in supermarkets is now being offered by large pharmacies, while pharmacy departments have sprung up in supermarkets.

Sherif Mityas, vice president of the retail practice at the consultancy A.T. Kearney, estimates that traditional US grocery stores such as Dominick's, owned by Safeway, have in the past year boosted by 30% in the amount of space they devote to grooming, health and personal care products.

Sanjay Dhar, professor of marketing at the Graduate School of Business at the University of Chicago says: 'The conventional channels of distribution are blurring. With both of them together—Gillette having a lot of knowledge of drugstores and P&G having more knowledge of supermarkets—I think they bring together something that's not been seen before, backed by fantastic brands. The number of brands being stocked by retailers has fallen as retailers focus on carrying the number one and two selling branded items and offer a private label alternative made by a third party. That means it is increasingly important for a consumer to win aisle space at stores.'

Pradeep Chintagunta, another marketing professor at the University of Chicago, adds: 'By increasing the basket of items you offer the retailers, you can also improve your relationship with them, because you are now dealing with more categories. The merger means, even more than before, that no retailer can completely ignore them'.

'You could do without one or two of these products, but not without all of them or the consumer will likely take their business elsewhere', says Allan Adamson of the brand consultancy Landor.

Anne Coughlan, associate professor of marketing at the Kellogg School of Management at Northwestern University says the two companies share a 'common method of selling'. 'P&G already has a good relationship with Wal-Mart, so it has the leverage to apply this to the Gillette line,' she says.

While some suggest that the combined company will also have greater purchasing power with Wal-Mart, there are many who disagree, citing the relative strength of consumer goods companies. A recent study of the 50 largest publicly listed retailers by

Insead, the Paris-based business school, says that while retailers have delivered superior sales growth between 1993 and 2002, manufacturers' margins have been consistently higher.

Bear Stearns estimates that 16% of the combined company's sales will be to Wal-Mart's 5,100 stores, while it represents about 5% of Wal-Mart's sales. At A.T. Kearney, Mr Mityas says: 'Wal-Mart will push the combined P&G/Gillette entity just as hard on prices as ever. This ***acquisition*** is not a position against Wal-Mart, it's a position against their competitors.' The proliferation of private label goods at retailers such as Wal-Mart means that P&G/Gillette, as well as rivals, will have to remain vigilant over threats to their lower-priced products.

Prof Dhar points out that large retailers in Europe, where supermarkets' own private-label lines are more widespread than in the US, are acquiring US retailers and instilling these businesses with their knowledge of private label practices. However, P&G/Gillette is partially insulated from the private label threat because about half of total sales will be in the faster growth health and beauty sectors. It can also draw on 'a larger pool of marketing dollars to strategically invest in their brands', says Mr Mityas.

Christine Augustine, analyst at Bear Stearns, argues that large retailers will in any case continue to seek the right balance between their private brand offering and national brands. 'After all, national brands help validate the private brand assortment,' she says. By combining, P&G/Gillette will be able to deliver their products more efficiently to those channels by unifying their supply chains. For example, P&G trucks that would have delivered detergents to one outlet can now deliver razors as will. Both companies have in recent years installed 'back room' software systems from Germany's SAP on a global basis, which can be integrated relatively easily to help track inventories, shipments and sales.

Financially, both are also operating from positions of strength, after a period of drift. According to Clayton Daley, P&G chief financial officer, that meant there was no urgency to marry the two consumer goods giants. 'We'd [P&G] been meeting or beating our [sales and earnings] targets so clearly this was not a deal that we needed to deliver. This simply was an option that came along and we thought had the potential to be explored,' he says.

Gillette's Mr Kilts, who will oversee the integration, maintains there 'isn't a weakness in this combination'. He adds: 'Both companies have come from turnaround periods and have great potential. I'm a firm believer that the consumer products industry needs to consolidate and I'd rather lead that consolidation than get stuck with the leftovers at the end.'

While most observers expect the minimal product overlap will allow the deal to be cleared by US and European regulators—though P&G's Old Spice and Gillette's Right Guard deodorants may be a focus of scrutiny—it will require all of Mr Kilts' skills to meld the two corporate cultures. Employees at P&G's Cincinnati headquarters are nicknamed 'Proctoids' for their conservative culture. Gillette knew too little about globalization and marketing, says Bill Schmitz, a Deutsche Bank analyst. While Mr Kilts has done much to change that, the company 'hides a lot of complacency'.

Culture will be crucial when it comes to innovation. Half a century ago, consumer goods companies' success came from devising a single product that had a lasting impact on people's daily lives, such as disposable baby nappies, making the companies a lot of money in the process.

Today, there are few signs that such innovations are on the horizon. The Energizer-owned Schick-Wilkinson Sword, Gillette's rival in the razor business, recently introduced a razor with four blades, trumping Gillette's Mach3 with three blades. Ms Coughlan of Northwestern University asks: 'How many more blades can you put in a razor and how much more incremental benefit can you get?' The two companies are looking at the possibilities that might come from combining P&G's knowledge of skincare for women—through its Olay brand of creams—with Gillette's presence in the men's grooming sector.

David Harding, a partner at Bain & Company's consumer products business, says innovation is crucial because of retailers' focus on the top two branded items in a category. This creates an incentive for consumer goods companies to keep pushing out new products. 'The reason why there is so much talk about innovation is that you always want to give the consumer an excuse to pay more for products,' he says.

That explains why P&G has undergone a profound culture change in its innovation process since 2000, from being closed to ideas from the outside to actively seeking them. Mr Lafley says: 'Fundamentally you have to ask yourself whether you are inherently a commodity business or an innovation business. What we've tried to do is accelerate innovation from within.' It was difficult for P&G by itself to generate enough big ideas internally to fuel significant growth, he says. Absorbing Gillette into the group will be 'about commercialising more of your innovation'.

Gary Stibel, chief executive of the New England Consultancy, points out that P&G's Tide detergent has seen some 70 technical improvements since its debut 50 years ago and says: 'There are not mature brands, only mature brand managers. Gillette and Procter are only limited by their imaginations.'

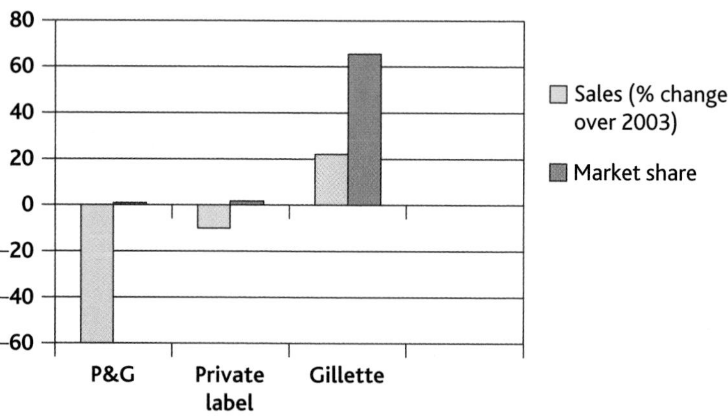

Figure C10.1 Share of US razors market 2004 (total market size $199m*)

*excluding Wal-Mart.

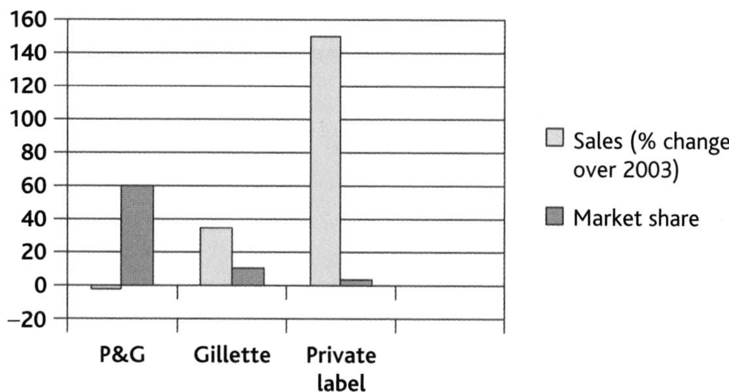

Figure C10.2 Share of US tooth bleaching market 2004 (total market size $274m*)

*excluding Wal-Mart.

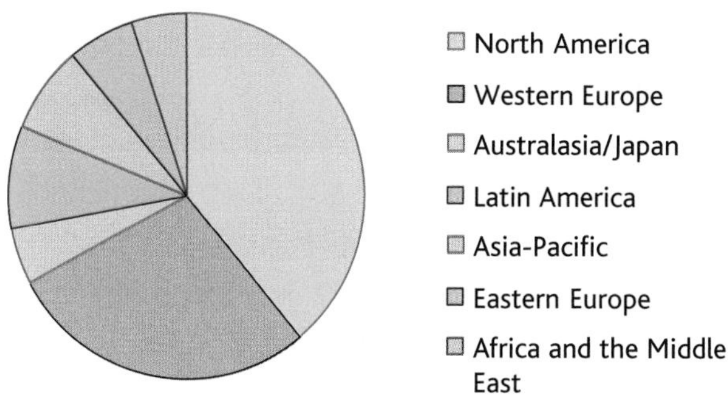

Figure C10.3 Geographic sales distribution Pro-forma P&G/Gillette group (%)

Source: Jeremy Grant (2005), *Financial Times*, 4 February, p. 15

QUESTIONS

1. Using Schindehutte and Morris's typology, where would you place P&G/Gillette's strategy? Is it value, variable, variety, visible/invisible, or virtual (or a combination)?
2. Is this appropriate given market conditions? If not, argue a case for a different choice (or combination).

3. To what extent does P&G/Gillette have scope to:
   a. Bundle its prices?
   b. Apply target pricing?
4. How would you assess P&G/Gillette's customer convenience in terms of:
   a. Access?
   b. Search?
   c. Possession?
   d. Transaction?
5. In light of your answer to question 4, what are the strategic implications for P&G/Gillette?
6. Might any of your P&G/Gillette's strategic choices create channel conflict?

Marketing communications strategies

LEARNING OBJECTIVES

- Assess where marketing communications (MARCOMS) sit within overall marketing strategy
- Examine the key elements in the MARCOMS process
- Provide a strategic view of MARCOMS with a focus on the creative brief
- Assess the key issues in media choice and use
- Review the operational issues in implementing a MARCOMS strategy

CHAPTER AT A GLANCE

Introduction

MARCOMS are central to Porter's generic cost-differentiation focus strategies framework and refer to four central types of media: advertising, direct marketing, PR, and sales promotions. There are two layers to explore in using these four media in a MARCOMS strategy. They relate to what the client wants to 'say' as opposed to execution, which relates to 'how' you say it. For example, the strategy for a recent campaign for Captain Birds Eye Ready Meals has been to communicate that the products contain no artificial colours, flavourings, or preservatives, a message that has considerable resonance in their core target market given the concerns over children's diets in the UK. The execution of the campaign shows children in a school going through the first few letters of the alphabet for the names of colours, flavourings, and preservatives. In an emphatic and unambiguous delivery of the intended message, the commercial finishes at 'the letter *N*', at which point the Captain Birds Eye character explains that the letter stands for 'not in my food'. If a marketing campaign is being devised by an agency for a client, the strategy needs to be clearly agreed between the client and agency at the beginning of the campaign process. The interpretation of the strategy by the agency becomes the executional layer. The message often has to entertain, or be creative in some way, to stand out from the clutter of communications that people are exposed to.

Can MARCOMS be used to reduce **costs**? The answer is largely 'no' for the short term, but 'yes' when a longer perspective is taken. The basic profit formula is:

$$\text{Profit} = (\text{price} - \text{cost}) \times \text{volume}$$

How do MARCOMS fit in terms of cost in the formula? In the short run a client can spend money on MARCOMS to help justify a price increase or increase volume, but this will only add to costs. In the medium to long term MARCOMS can support price through brand preference and provide some competitive protection for a brand. Furthermore, increased volume can be encouraged by pointing out new uses for the brand or by targeting new markets. Successful MARCOMS can lead to higher sales and in turn economies of scale. MARCOMS can also directly reduce costs in the medium to long term through replacing (or increasing the efficiency of) an organization's routes to markets and in reducing market research costs. A company with a large salesforce and/or call centre may find that MARCOMS can create an environment in which it can reduce the number of staff hired. For example customers can manage their own accounts and track orders (customer-managed relationships), fill out surveys, customize products, and find answers to their questions via advertising and direct marketing and the Web. Additionally, successful PR may reduce legal costs when related to crisis management and generally enhance goodwill. Even sales promotions, which largely increase costs when they involve price discounting and bonus offerings, can sometimes reduce costs. For example if a sales promotion involving free samples directly induces a customer to try a product, the adoption cycle can be fast-tracked.

Differentiation is central to spending on MARCOMS. Despite the conventional wisdom that a great many products and services are equal, there are probably more differences in offerings today than ever before. If you take any consumer or business market, the amount of choice is substantial, and often impossible for buyers to cognitively process. MARCOMS gives organizations the opportunity to establish their position in the market and assert their distinctiveness. While there are a great many 'me-too' communications, at heart all organizations, be they for or not-for profit, seek to establish a point of difference. This chapter will review and assess the primary issues in MARCOMS strategy. It begins with a look at IMC.

IMC

The American Association of Advertising Agencies defines IMC (Integrated Marketing Communications) as:

> a concept of marketing communications planning that recognizes the added value of a comprehensive plan that evaluates the strategic roles of a variety of communications disciplines, e.g., general advertising, direct response, sales promotion and public relations—and combines these disciplines to provide clarity, consistency and maximum communications impact.

The idea is to combine all four primary media to provide a holistic and integrative approach. Unfortunately surveys have found differences in how organizations embrace IMC as a philosophy.

There are clearly considerable benefits to integrating communications to ensure that an organization's messages appear more consistent. For example, if a petrol company...

- ran advertising extolling its environmental activities...
- which was linked to direct marketing for a credit that donated a percentage of spending to an environmental NGO...
- and a sales promotion to win an eco-tourist holiday...
- with a marketing PR campaign featuring members of staff working on environmental projects in their spare time...

then the message would be consistent in all media. One particularly important aspect of IMC is that it elevates the status of internal marketing, an oft-neglected aspect of MARCOMS. Employees, especially those interacting with customers, need to be kept informed and therefore able to contribute to an organization's communications. If service quality is about reducing the gap between a customer's expectations and his/her perceptions of service, it is vital to show staff previews of forthcoming campaigns as well as involve them in development whenever possible and appropriate. Appropriate media include intranets, e-mail, voicemail, newsletters, staff seminars, and sometimes creative placements within monthly salary statements. There are numerous cases in marketing history where campaigns have failed because no one thought to tell the staff what was happening such as when Clerical Medical Investments decided to reposition the brand in the early 1980s.

IMC presents a number of logistical barriers and requires considerable resources to place advertising, direct marketing, sales promotions, and PR or MPR (i.e., marketing PR—a more proactive form of PR rather than one based on reactions to events) into one unit. Take the case of General Motors (GM) which has been one of the pioneers of IMC. As reported by Prescott (1991), GM demonstrates the administrative strain of implementing IMC:

> At General Motors, which received a lot of publicity four years ago when it combined a portion of its PR with marketing at the corporate level, a two-tiered organizational structure was set up to direct IMC. A Communication Council, made up of 41 communicators and directors from throughout the corporation, meets once a month and prioritizes IMC tasks. Once a task is agreed upon, the process for its execution is to appoint a Stakeholder Communication Team composed of a 'champion,' a 'lead coordinator,' and appropriate GM departmental representatives.

Also, the risk, as Mark Twain aptly put it, is that if you put all your eggs in one basket—'watch that basket'. If the central message does not resonate with the audience or appears not to be genuine, then the whole communications campaign, not just one part of it, will flop. Running separate communications in different media may present a less consistent image, but does spread risk. For this reason IMC has yet to be widely adopted and so this chapter will not look solely at the integrated (IMC) perspective of marketing communications. Mini Case Study 11.1 looks at the pros and cons.

MARCOMS strategic process

Audit

The MARCOMS strategic process can be seen in Figure 11.1. The process starts with an audit of the marketplace such as can be obtained with the **PESTLE** (political, economic, social, technological, legal, and environmental) assessment. The aim is to establish the key overall trends in the market, their importance and likelihood, and what aspects to focus upon for the MARCOMS plan.

The next stage is to examine the **competitors** in the marketplace. Four questions need to be answered:

1. How many competitors are there and what share does each have?
2. What positions do they take up? Why?
3. Are any doing well or badly? Why?
4. How important is their presence in this market?

A **SWOT** then needs to be carried out detailing the strengths, weaknesses, opportunities, and threats. The key issues identified need to be related to communications. Examples are how well or poorly first-name and prompted mentions of the brand are, the brand's share of category spending, and attitudes towards the brand. Strengths and opportunities need to be leveraged and weaknesses and threats addressed.

The implications for the brand then need to be addressed. A useful tool to use is the **Brand wheel**. The brand wheel (see Figure 11.2) views a brand as an onion with different layers that can be 'pealed' (see the work of Ward et al., 1999 for a similar analysis).

Features: This layer describes how the brand delivers its promise. For example an insurance company has assets, expert and trained staff, call centres, Web contact, a variety of policies, guarantees, and a geographic spread of offices.

MINI CASE STUDY 11.1
In Search of Integration: Campaigns Must Combine All Marketing Options

One of the hottest issues in adland is how to co-ordinate and integrate all the marketing options available. Loyalty schemes, sponsorship, public relations, database marketing, event marketing, sales promotion, websites and interactive media—not to mention good old-fashioned advertising—offer clients a bewildering variety of options. These demand decision. What is the right way to carve up a total marketing appropriation between, say, advertising, sponsorship and public relations—and how can they all be made to work together?

Several new agencies promise to answer these questions with a gamut of 'integrated marketing' skills in-house. In the past few years new shops have combined traditional media advertising with database marketing. But the latest agencies have combined advertising with public relations, consultancy, corporate design and, most frequently, a promise of 'the right marketing solution, whatever that may be'.

No longer do new agencies just offer the best creativity in the world, because everyone believes integrated marketing is the name of today's game.

Clients have always required their communications to be coherent and complementary. But there appears to have been a radical shift of emphasis for several reasons.

First, during the recession clients sought marketing inputs that might be cheaper than traditional advertising. In those gloomy days of plummeting advertising budgets, clients experimented with different marketing approaches. That impetus continues.

Second, when the consolidation and profitability of advertising agencies peaked in the late 1980s, they began to hunt for other sources of income. Because they are restricted from taking on competitive accounts, once they reach a certain size agencies find it almost impossible to outperform the advertising market. But they can develop other marketing skills, and then sell total packages to clients. The trend towards integration has emanated as much from the needs of agencies as from clients.

Third, some of the options available, such as loyalty cards and the internet, are genuinely new and use innovative technology. Clients have been feeling their way forward gingerly so it has been important for them to be integrated with well-established methods.

But fourth, and most important, like every other aspect of business, marketing techniques grow more specialist every year. It is difficult for anybody to be competent in all of them.

But pulling together all the options is only the first stage. What criteria should be used in apportioning the total marketing budget between them? Can their relative cost efficiencies be compared? Whose is the responsibility? Should it be somebody in the client company or the agency? Or will another kind of specialist have to be invented?

Finding the right answers will not be easy. Marshall McLuhan's famous aphorism, 'the medium is the message', is coming home to roost.

Source: Winston Fletcher (1998), *Financial Times*, 23 February, p. 11.

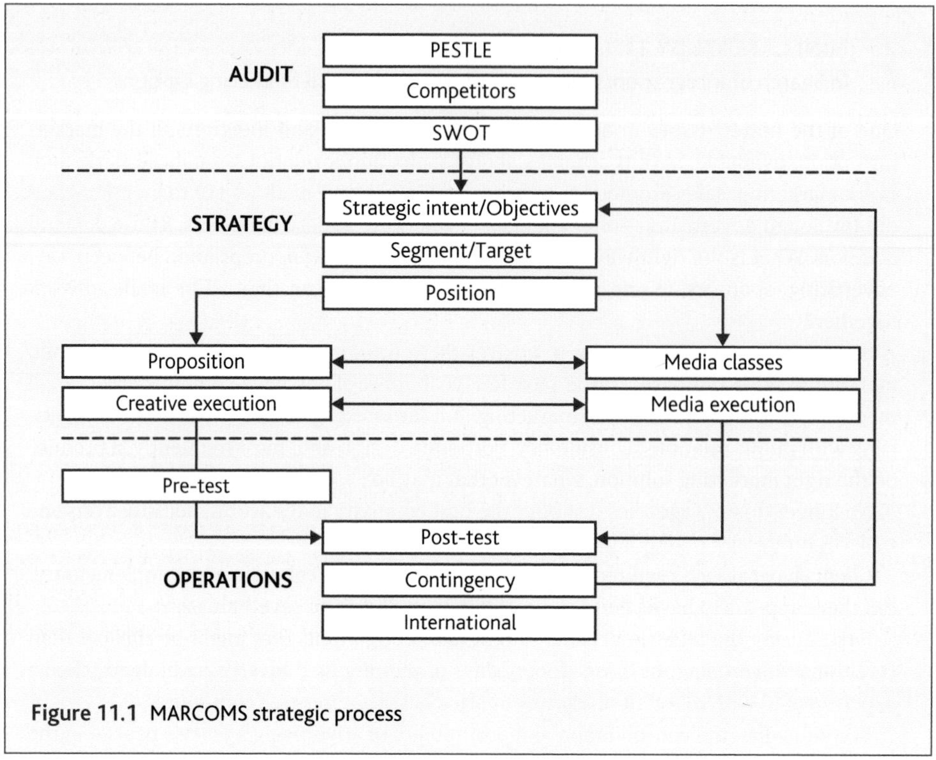

Figure 11.1 MARCOMS strategic process

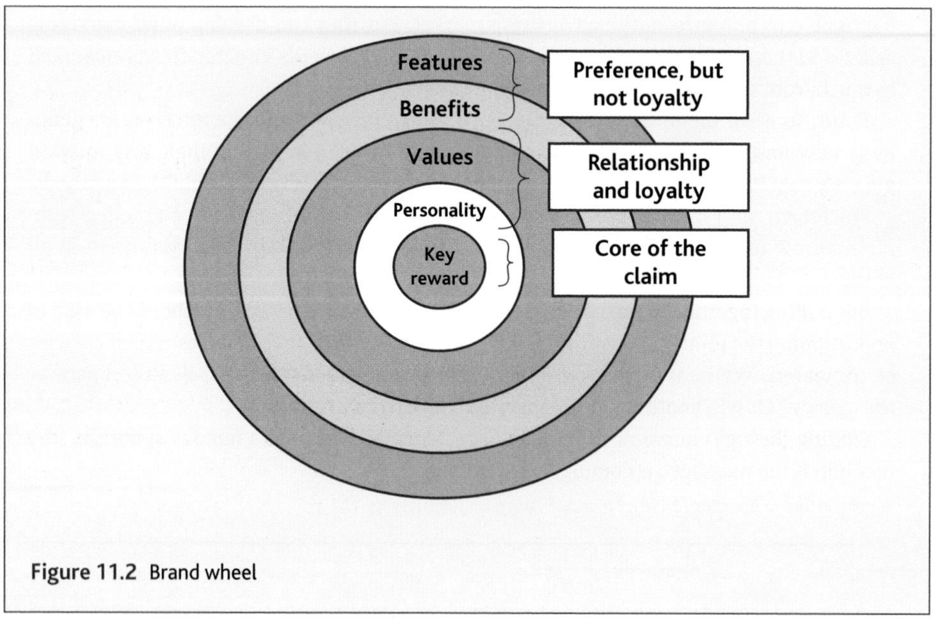

Figure 11.2 Brand wheel

Benefits: The next layer explains how these features are translated into benefits for the target audience. In the case of an insurance company these features provide informed choice, security, convenience, and service.

Values: Increasingly since the 1990s all organizations need to consider their place in society. Buyers are concerned with product quality and price, etc. but as society's wealth has grown there is an increasing interest in the wider societal effects of organizations. For example, many people are prepared to pay more for environmentally friendly products—those where a fair price has been paid to developing countries for the materials used—and to be loyal to companies that treat their workforce well. To continue the case of our insurance company, what values does it have? Does it contribute to charities? Does it treat its staff fairly? Does it operate in an environmentally friendly way? Do people know what it stands for?

Personality: Whether or not an organization addresses the issue formally, it will be viewed as having some kind of personality in the marketplace. Thus for many IBM still has an image of the blue-suited businessman despite years of attempting to relax its image and Apple continues to be seen as a group of creative types. Organizations exude a certain emotional feeling that is communicated in many ways and not just through MARCOMS. However, it is difficult to ask an audience, 'What personality does organisation X have?' So in order to reach this element of the brand wheel researchers generally use analogies. They ask questions such as:

- 'If brand X were a car, what would it be?'
- 'If brand X were an animal, what would it be?'
- 'If brand X were a person, who would it be?'
- 'If brand X were a lunch, what would it be?'

The intention is to establish the kind of personality of the brand without directly posing the question. Going back to the insurance company, it might be seen as like a Mercedes E-Class, a tiger, Gordon Brown (the UK Chancellor), and a meal at an up-market restaurant. In short, a classy, powerful, and aggressive organization. In reality such research would not yield such a neat set of results as lots of cars, animals, etc. would be named. Furthermore, buyers are extremely marketing literate and so often the results are of dubious value as they fully appreciate the context of the questions. Insight is provided by *why* people made their choices rather than the *choices* concerned.

Key reward: The key reward is the central reason that people buy and/or use the brand based upon the four preceding elements on the brand wheel. This is the identification of the key element(s) on the brand wheel. It might be something based upon one of the layers, such as the benefit of security or the classy personality. Or it might be a cumulative reason formed by a clustering of factors—our insurance company might offer the best customer service.

Most MARCOMS tends to focus upon one of different levels of the wheel. Figure 11.3 shows Omega's position on the brand wheel is literally about personality with the key reward of having 'arrived'.

CINDY
CRAWFORD'S CHOICE

CONSTELLATION
The Omega Constellation is a rare blend of style and elegance, a superb example of the watchmaker's art. This is no wonder, since Cindy Crawford assisted Omega in its design, creating the only watch she is proud to wear.

Ω
OMEGA
www.omegawatches.com

Figure 11.3 Example of brand wheel focus

Occasionally a great communication will successfully combine the outer layers of the wheel with the inner. For example in 1981 the first ad in Harley-Davidson's makeover in the United States featured several rows of mean-looking Hell's Angels staring at you with the headline: 'Would you sell an unreliable motorcycle to these guys?' The campaign brilliantly integrated the outer wheel preference for the bike (reliability) with the inner wheel of emotional loyalty (heritage and styling).

As shown in Figure 11.2, features and benefits will provide preference, but not necessarily loyalty. Values and personality are the character of the brand and offer the potential for loyalty. For example, you might find cheaper insurance than your current policy; however, you like the values and personality of your chosen organization and so prefer to stay with them. For example, in the mobile phone marketplace in the UK there is an operator that is currently offering some extremely attractive deals yet there are indications that customers are wary of its apparently poor service and coverage.

Establishing the strategy

The next phase of the MARCOMS strategy process is to identify the strategy (see Figure 11.1). Most of the topics in the rest of this chapter feature in what agencies call the 'Creative Brief': a written summation of the MARCOMS task that will manage and stimulate the development of creative work to address that task.

The brief generally starts with agencies isolating in a few simple sentences what the aim of the communications is—the strategic intent. Bear in mind that the creative team in most agencies (the copywriter and the art director) are not business strategists. There might be hundreds of pages of research defining and explaining the task, which they will never read or even want to read. What they want is something succinct and to the point. Tasks should be focused, measurable, and capable of inspiring the creative team to do good work. Broad examples of tasks include:

- Announce/launch
- Build/re-build corporate reputation
- Generate leads
- Increase sales
- Increase/maintain share
- Justify a price or price increase
- Stop a decline

However, tasks can be articulated and a stronger direction indicated. Examples of specific tasks would be:

- Pepsi wants to be the badge of a generation
- Coca-Cola wants to be the classic choice

Both tasks are easy to comprehend and distinct and do not need to be complicated by further elaboration. If you think about it, all the documentation and briefing in the world can be given before a major sports event, but the task for all the players is to simply win the game. In the same vein, with the Apollo programme NASA's objective was to get a man on the moon. Strategic intent broadly falls into five areas, starting with product superiority.

Product superiority could be the central strategy of the campaign. The intention of the strategy is to communicate that a product or service can fix a problem or better fulfil a desire. There is an adage in the communications business that if you throw 10 balls at someone he/she will not catch a single one. If you throw just one it has a much greater chance of being caught. The implication is that objectives should be single-minded and focused, as suggested by the unique selling point (USP) (Reeves, 1961):

> To gain a purchase, an advertiser must persuade the potential buyer that there is a unique benefit from the product.

Thus a recent campaign for the Volkswagen Passat only featured the revised braking system of the new model—a significant benefit to focus upon.

Tangible performance benefits such as those involving technology or design can often give an edge, but can be short-lived if easily copied. This has led to the variation of the 'ESP' which stands for '**emotional selling proposition**'. ESP takes the concept away from Reeve's tangible benefits to the intangible rewards that products and services can provide. Emotional strategies are about making the product, service, or organization matter to the customer, using the same single-minded approach as the USP. Thus, the Co-Op with its banks and supermarkets adopts an ethical stance in the marketplace and communicates this through its MARCOMS. You might not get a better deal, product, or service; you feel good because your money is part of an ethically aware organization.

The **cultural identification** strategy is about making the product, service, or organization part of the consumer's world. For example, HP Sauce ran a campaign featuring the use of the sauce by various 'tribes' in the UK such as 'white van' drivers and women out on a hen night. In a similar attempt at cultural identification Knorr's Pot Noodles caused considerable controversy over a campaign promoting the brand (whose main target audience is young men) as the 'Slag of all Snacks' and associating the brand with infidelity.

Salience is the main concern of the **product definition** strategy. How can new products or services be made salient? Or, how can a product that has lost its salience, regain it? This strategy is about finding something to say that will rekindle a brand that has lost its tarnish and esteem in the market. Perhaps one of the most high profile cases in the UK would be Marks & Spencer. While the food part of the business continues to prosper, the clothing has lost market share to cheaper supermarket alternatives such Asda's George range and also to more design-oriented labels such as Liz Claiborne, Hobbs, Monsoon, and Jill Saunders. In an attempt to re-establish salience M&S embarked on a bold TV campaign in 2002 featuring a naked, size 14 woman, which unfortunately did not work (according to the *Observer*, 9 January 2005, no one wanted the woman's wobbly bottom), and the company has since focused communications on design, style, and new ranges. Establishing salience is rarely solely achieved by communications and often requires changes associated with the rest of the marketing mix. Without making other changes, communications will be unable on its own to turn around the M&S clothing brand to its pre-1990 place in the market, but it can play a role.

Possibly the most difficult of all strategies to engage in is the **paradigm shift**. Here the aim is to alter the consumer's definition of a brand and/or category. One of the most successful UK attempts at a paradigm shift in recent years has been Volkswagen's campaign for the Skoda. The campaign has shown, in a variety of amusing executions, disbelief amongst the public and motor trade that the car concerned is a Skoda. The Skoda heritage may mitigate against the car being seen as the equivalent of a Volkswagen in the immediate future, yet the campaign has undoubtedly contributed towards the repositioning of the car as a sensible purchase rather than a joke. An example from the United States is Cadillac, which has successfully reinvented itself with new models accompanied by creative MARCOMS that have begun to turn around the image of an overly flashy and dated car. Ironically, once a paradigm shift has been achieved, an even greater communication challenge can be what to do next. As with the Skoda, the strategy of, 'I can't believe it's a Skoda' can be pursued for only so long before it loses its impact. Skoda changed its strategy to focus upon the kinds of people who owned the car. The campaign featured people being asked for advice on personal matters in their homes by strangers who were passing by. The reason? The passers-by had seen that they had bought a Skoda which implied that they were people whose opinion was worth having.

Setting objectives

The next stage is to translate the strategic intent into objectives. MARCOMS objectives are normally only applied to communications activities. Examples would be:

- 'Exposure message to...'
- 'Create 40% awareness amongst...'
- 'Create attitude/opinion that...'
- 'Increase preference amongst...'
- 'Encourage trial amongst...'
- 'Reinforce loyalty amongst...'

There are three levels to MARCOMS objectives: 'exposure', 'awareness', and 'attitudes/relationships'.

Exposure represents the lowest level of objective. David Ogilvy once famously noted that: 'you cannot save souls in an empty church' (Ogilvy, 1980). Thus, exposure is simply an objective related to the desired level of opportunity to see (OTS) (all MARCOMS are only ever opportunities to see as you cannot force an audience to listen and/or read your communications) and coverage to achieve the MARCOMS objectives. Most agencies seek an average of two to three OTSs amongst the target market in order to give the MARCOMS a chance to work, given that some repetition is needed for full comprehension and remembering. The level of coverage required will vary depending upon the strategic objectives of the campaign and size and location of audience. An example might be to cover 40% of the target audience with an OTS of four.

Exposure is a useful objective to help decide upon the weight of MARCOMS required and also helps to disentangle reasons for failure. Unfortunately exposure is not illuminating about response. A campaign might effectively cover its chosen audience with the hoped-for

OTS and still have little impact if people do not respond. A higher-level objective involves 'awareness'.

Awareness can be measured at two levels: 'spontaneous' and 'prompted'. Spontaneous awareness often involves open-ended questions such as:

- 'Tell me of all the major supermarkets that you have heard of...'
- 'Any more?'
- 'Is that all?'

Prompted awareness, as the name implies, provides the prompts:

- 'Which one or ones of the following supermarket chains have you heard of': Asda, Jeffrey's, Marks & Spencer, Morrisons, Sainsbury's, Tesco, Waitrose?'

Note that there is in the list a little-known supermarket chain called Jeffrey's. In fact, Jeffrey's does not exist! Quite often a fictitious prompt is provided to gain an understanding of how seriously the questions have been answered. If 5% of the sample say, 'Yes, I have heard of Jeffery's', you can broadly discount all the responses by about 5% as the chances are these people would say 'Yes' to any name.

Large to medium-sized clients (not SMEs) often undertake bespoke research or buy panel data to find out their unprompted and prompted awareness. They then evaluate their MARCOMS spending by the impact on the figures. Maybe they had 25% unprompted awareness before the campaign, set objectives to raise it to 30%, and subsequently achieved 35%. In this case the campaign would be deemed a success. People rarely buy brands that they have never heard of and so improving unprompted and prompted awareness is an extremely important objective for MARCOMS.

Nevertheless you could have extremely high awareness and yet your brand might still be performing badly. High awareness does not of itself mean that people want to buy your products or services. A classic from advertising history is the Strand cigarette. The Strand tobacco company launched a TV campaign in the late 1950s showing Terence Brooks, a Frank Sinatra lookalike, lighting up on a lonely street corner. The accompanying caption said, 'You're never alone with a Strand', with Cliff Adams' haunting instrumental playing in the background. The ads were hugely popular, Terence Brooks became a teenage pin-up, and the 'Lonely Man Theme' was a huge hit. Despite the enormous awareness, Strand became associated with loneliness and unsociability, and the brand soon disappeared from the market. Awareness has its limitations.

The highest level of MARCOMS objectives relates to **attitudes/relationships**. Attitudes are positive or negative views of an object such as an organization, product, service, or idea that led to the formation of relationships. Generally marketers recognize the difference between 'opinions' and 'attitudes' before and after purchase. People hold opinions about products and services pre-purchase but once they have tried them they hold attitudes. Research shows this to be a complex construct as people can be 'ambivalent' in their attitudes as they can simultaneously possess a positive and a negative attitude towards an object. 'Explicit' attitudes towards an object are ones held at a cognitive level. It has been found that attitudes can be held at a deeper 'implicit' level—revealed through experiments based upon how quickly people make judgements about stimuli. Both explicit and implicit attitudes seem to affect people's behaviour. However, there are lots of intervening variables that operate between attitudes and behaviour. Thus, you might feel that the Mercedes S-Class is a great car but not buy one because either you do not have the resources or it simply is not a priority. However, if you did not think that the S-Class is a great car, then you would be very unlikely to buy one even if you did have the resources and it was a priority.

Given the closeness of fit between attitudes and behaviour, the highest level of MARCOMS objective relates to reinforcing positive attitudes or attempting to change negative ones to positive. Clients are concerned by whether the target audience likes the MARCOMS as such liking is generally associated with liking the brand. Certainly there are cases where for a variety of reasons (price, inertia, or convenience, in particular) people buy or use products or services that they hold negative views about but this does not generally hold. As a final point, there are considerable difficulties in measuring attitudes towards MARCOMS. Not only are few clients prepared to pay for the research but, even if they did, the link between MARCOMS and behaviour is often unclear.

Segment/target

The next stage is to describe the **segment or target** that the communication is aimed at. Given the lack of a business strategic background among most creative teams in agencies, this is not normally a technical description. ACORN groups, precise demographics, and psychographics are not required. What is required is a description of a person or a group that goes beyond report format and is based upon what is, or is not, important. For example, a segment or target description for a campaign aimed at frequent international flyers or organizational travel buyers would not point out all the details. Instead, the brief would mention such things as frequent flyers needing a good rest or sleep en route before business meetings while travel buyers are looking for deals with leading airlines and the need to justify costs. What kind of cars might such people drive? What kind of papers or magazines do they read? What do they do in their spare time? Any pointers that help build a profile and picture of the target audience should be included.

Position

The next thing to consider is how you might want to **position** the client (see Ries and Trout, 1981). A position refers to how potential buyers see the product and is expressed relative to competitors. This is what you want to achieve and should be measurable and achievable, otherwise it is not worth stating. Generally it tends to relate to rational or emotional aspects. For an MP3 player it might be to position the product as having the capacity for the number of songs you want to carry and that it is 'cool'. The issue here is how MARCOMS might help position the player. MARCOMS might also address **repositioning**, which involves changing the identity of a product, relative to the identity of competing products. There is also the potential for **de-positioning**: attempting to change the identity of competing brands relative to the identity of your own brand in the minds of the target market. Bear in mind that positioning is not something you can 'do' to people. People position brands using their own judgements—their minds are not wax tablets to be written on. Overall, the most successful positions are those that resonate best with the audience and are rooted in a brand's sustainable competitive advantage.

Proposition

Having decided upon the position required, you need to decide what communications **proposition** will enable you to achieve this. The proposition spells out what you want to say. At this stage agencies look for what they call 'big ideas'. The term, originating with the advertising business, has been co-opted by politicians in recent years. Communications big ideas require collaboration and hard work, and often the making of difficult choices and judgements and the exclusion of product facts. They have to be sold and defended and may change (a lot) in execution, but they are central to the strategy. Some key questions to ask of a proposition to judge whether it stands up as a big idea or not are:

1. Does it have staying power?
2. Does it spark dramatic creative ideas?
3. Is it credible?
4. Is it distinctive?
5. Is it focused and single-minded?
6. Is the promise meaningful?

Some potential sources of a proposition are:

- Brand image characteristics
- Direct comparisons with rivals
- Disadvantages of non-use
- Generic benefits
- How product/service is made
- Newsworthiness
- Price characteristics
- Product/service characteristics
- Product/service comparisons
- Product/service heritage
- Satisfying psychological/physiological needs
- Surprising points about the product/service
- User characteristics
- Ways of using the product/service

The key issue to consider is: is the proposition relevant? Does it relate to the target audience's problems or desires? Strategically, is it competitively different? Can it be expressed in a single-minded execution?

You know if you have a good proposition if it gives the creatives an 'angle' or 'way in' to develop some good creative work. It does not need to be liberating as restricted propositions can lead to exceptionally creative work (see Mini Case Study 11.2). It should also force a strategic choice or direction in the marketplace by being single-minded rather than all-encompassing. It goes without saying that any chosen proposition should be based on truth (rational or emotional). Thus a recent B2B campaign by IBM extolling the benefits of on-demand processes in business used a variety of scenarios that while fictitious in themselves (e.g. the demand for pink or white dresses being instantly fed back through the supply chain from the moment of sale at the cash register) effectively demonstrated the nature of IBM's proposition. Propositions to avoid are ones that communicate very little to the creative team such as:

- 'A wide range and good value.'
- 'Stylish and modern.'
- 'The best car on the market.'
- 'The right food for your dog.'

None of the above would give a creative team much of a clue as to what was required. However, to say that a particular mayonnaise 'takes the humdrum out of everyday food' or that a particular washing machine is 'the family workhorse', gives the team a much better idea of what is required. See Mini Case 11.2 for a discussion of the role of the creative brief.

MINI CASE STUDY 11.2

'The Art of the Brief'. It may sound like a double oxymoron, but a good creative brief is key to getting the ads you really want

The basic trouble with creative briefs is that they're often neither creative nor brief.

But before we wade into this quagmire, there's an old story from The Great War that goes something like this. The commander of a regiment is planning an attack. He needs to inform headquarters, but his lines of communication are cut. Forced to rely on word of mouth, he composes what he believes is a simple, foolproof message, 'Send reinforcements, we're going to advance'. The message is relayed from soldier to soldier all the way down the line until it reaches headquarters. But the message they receive is, 'Send four and sixpence, we're going to a dance'.

It's the same today with creative briefs. We have more lines of communication—phone, fax, e-mail, post—but still, often enough, the message is somehow garbled in transit. Using the creative to figure out what the brief should have said in the first place often compounds the problem. The creative goes back and forth, back and forth, back and forth, until at some point, usually the last possible moment, it's deemed close enough. Without a doubt, a lot of time and money is lost in this shuffling back and forth. Even worse, arguably, is the aggravation factor. What's going on here?

Business communicators, paradoxically, have no time to communicate. What they have is just enough time to issue an order or make a request.

Consequently, briefs tend to get short shrift. Out of necessity, they are often written hastily based on verbal exchanges or scribbled notes. This starts the ball rolling. 'Send reinforcements, we're going to advance' becomes 'Send free breath mints, we're going to a plant'. Someone at the agency receives the message and hears, 'Send foreign six pens, we're going free lance'. Someone in the creative department, in turn, receives this, scratches their heads, and thinks, 'Sounds like I'm out of a job'. But they mull it over anyway and decide, because, after all, they're supposed to be creative, that the message must actually be, 'Send four and six pence, we're going to a dance'. And so they produce all sorts of concepts featuring British coins and dance halls and, after minor modifications, present it to the client. Much gnashing of teeth ensues. Back and forth it goes until eventually, through the production of many false start pieces of creative, everyone understands that reinforcements are needed due to the impending advance.

Writing, unfortunately, seems to have lost some of its former connection with thinking and vice versa. Writing, like thinking, entails separating the important from the trivial, and that means making decisions about what to include and what not to include.

In a creative brief, a lot of information is a hindrance. After all, it's a brief, it's supposed to be short and to the point. As a friend of mine, a marketing executive, said, 'The creative has to be brief, so the brief should be creative'. He meant that no one should be expected to plow through a long, badly written document any more than someone reading a newspaper should be expected to comb carefully through an ad. The document should be brief because, typically, the person who has to read it only has a few brief moments.

It follows, therefore, that the person writing the brief exercise some 'creativity' in getting to the point as quickly and clearly as possible. As any professional writer knows, good writing is the result of much rewriting. After writing, smart writers read critically what they have written. If it doesn't read well, it wasn't well thought out. That's where rewriting comes in. Our old high school English teachers were right, if you can't get the sentence to flow, scrap it entirely and rethink the whole thing.

On the whole, briefs tend to be addressed to a general audience rather than to the specific audience for whom the brief is intended. Creative briefs tend to be a hodgepodge of brand truisms, marketing-speak, and primary, secondary and tertiary 'objectives'. Basically, they're laundry lists. Typically, agency creative people have to be briefed on the meaning of the brief! As an exasperated art director once said to me, 'It's a creative brief, for crying out loud, a brief for the creative team, but it couldn't have been written for me, because I can't understand it.'

The irony is that creative briefs are seldom brief and almost never creative. But isn't creativity the job of the creative person? At an agency, it should be everyone's job. In the ideal creative brief, someone, an account planner, a creative director or an account supervisor, will have narrowed the entire brief to less than a page and have rendered the objective in a single sentence. The ideal brief is just one step away from being an ad.

The retired president of a large New York ad agency once said that a creative brief should be 'as hard and brilliant as a diamond, and as tight and confining as a pair of handcuffs'. For example, the original brief for what became the famous Absolut vodka campaign was, 'You can do anything you want creatively, but you must always show the product and no headline can be longer than two words and one of those words must be Absolut'. A brilliant pair of handcuffs!

Building better briefs

With all that in mind, here are six ways to better briefs:

1. The goal of a brief is to strip away subjectivity

The personal likes and dislikes of marketers and agencies should not come into play. Objectivity and clarity are what matter most.

2. Vocabulary, spelling and grammar still count

The pace of modern life, changing cultural values and new technology have conspired against old technology such as vocabulary, spelling and grammar. But these old tools are still what matter most when it comes to communication.

3. A format is not a substitute for thinking

The typical brief is formatted with headings such as background, objective, insight, brand positioning and so on. This encourages a 'fill in the blanks' approach to writing. Rather than thinking through every brief, the writer simply relies on cutting and pasting material from past briefs. The brief gets slapped together and this leads to confusion. Briefs don't need formats; they need thinking and writing.

4. The creative must be brief; therefore, the brief must be creative

The more creative the brief, that is, the more thoughtful, imaginative and concise, the less time consumed, the less confusion caused and the more creative the communication. Blaise Pascal, the 17th-century French mathematician, inventor and writer, once wrote, 'I have only made this letter rather long because I have not had time to make it shorter'.

5. A brief should be a pair of handcuffs

Room for interpretation in a brief is a recipe for failure. Slap on the cuffs! One cuff on the client, the other on the agency.

6. Briefs should be taken seriously

Briefs should almost be contractual, in the sense that client and agency have agreed to abide by the document. Briefs should be written in stone.

A creative brief should be 'as hard . . . as a diamond, and as tight . . . as a pair of handcuffs'.

Source: W. Bruce MacDonald (2003), *Marketing*, 27 October.

Having decided upon the proposition, it remains to consider if the claim can be **supported**. If you cannot support the proposition you cannot have it. Why should anyone believe such a message if it cannot be supported? What are the key facts or figures that provide the evidence? None of this has to appear in the execution, but it must appear in the creative brief otherwise the proposition will be simple puffery. Thus, if the proposition states that a tyre will continue to perform even when punctured, what is the evidence? Has it been tested and is it true? The evidence does not need to appear in the ad, however, the claim cannot be made without it.

Some potential **problems** that can arise at this stage of strategy development are:

- confusing client's problem with the prospect's problem
- lack of focus
- lack of meaningful target audience
- lack of positioning
- treating support as the proposition
- re-stating objectives as the proposition

The next creative strategic issue is how to reflect the **brand's character**. This is a key strategic issue for any brand as the wrong character may at best add little value and at worst severely damage its market standing. In the broadest sense brand character reflects how the brand is positioned in its communications. Does the brand's character exude fun or it is serious? Does it set out to shock or reassure? Is it modern or traditional? Take the case of the highly acclaimed Walkers crisps campaign that uses Gary Lineker in a mischievous role in contrast to his 'Mr Nice Guy' image. However, many of the banks, such as NatWest and Barclays, understandably produce campaigns with more serious appeals. Significant changes in brand character need to be conscious and well-thought through strategically. Oliviero Toscani first started working on Benetton's advertising in 1982 and increasingly produced work that focused upon the company's values rather than its products. The communications of the brand's character became its values.

Creative execution

The creative execution stage is where the chosen strategy is translated into a piece of communication. If the strategy was to be based on user characteristics, perhaps a chocolate eaten by 'macho men', it would be stated as the proposition. For example, Yorkie ran a successful campaign for many years showing rugged-looking lorry drivers biting into Yorkie bars. Nothing was said in any of the ads. They did not run headlines in the press saying 'Macho Men Eat chunky chocolate!' The art of execution is to translate the stated proposition in a highly relevant and creative way without literally restating the proposition.

A variety of techniques may be used such as the 'associative' which involves providing easy links to the proposition (e.g. a laptop side by side with an ant, suggesting the strength of the product), the use of celebrities (see Erdogan et al., 2001), e.g. Linda Barker and Currys, or simply 'show and tell' (explaining the proposition clearly and rationally).

Finally, before the execution can be finalized **what *must* be included** has to be agreed. These elements rarely have any impact on strategy as for most companies what must be included simply means a logo, phone numbers, and website addresses. However, MARCOMS strategies are constrained by the law and the Advertising Standards Authority's legal, decent, honest, and truthful code. The vast majority of clients, agencies, and media support the use of the law and codes of practice as they recognize that such frameworks benefit the industry. For example when advertising alcoholic drinks on broadcast media the ASA code states that advertisers 'must not suggest that regular solitary drinking is acceptable or that drinking is a means of resolving personal problems. Nor must they imply that drinking is an essential part of daily routine or can bring about a change in mood.' Any strategies attempting to communicate such messages would not be allowed to air. There are specific codes for a number of industries, not just alcohol, including financial services, solicitors, charities, medicines, and food and beverages, to name but a few. Clients and their agencies need to ensure that their executions do not transgress any of the codes or their ads will not be shown. However, the client may also impose particular constraints. For example, some advertisers will not allow direct comparison with rivals in their communications whereas others, particularly car companies in their local advertising, regularly compare their products with those of their competitors.

Media strategy

Tangential to, and often parallel with, the development of the creative strategy is the development of the media strategy (see Table 11.1 for an overview of MARCOMS media options). Three questions need to be answered:

1. Where is the communication(s) going to appear?
2. How frequently?
3. How much is to be spent?

The answers to these questions can vary greatly depending upon the strategy. Media strategy is about attempting to ensure that a client's message is seen or heard by the right people, in the right place, in the right environment, with the right frequency and weight, and at the right price, and remembering that each problem is different. British Airways chose to wrap a building to publicize its flat beds for Club Class passengers. Channel No. 5 featured Nicole Kidman and produced a 180-second commercial to reposition the brand towards a younger audience. The impact of the commercial was considerable: the frequency of the schedule raised awareness and influenced attitudes towards the brand on a scale that a smaller spend could never have matched.

Spend has to be targeted by buyer characteristics, geography, and season. After gathering information the classic approach is the four Ws:

- **Who:** Define the exact audience (e.g. '34–45 year old women').
- **Where:** Determine geographic area (e.g. 'every major urban market').
- **When:** Decide upon the time of purchase (e.g. 'prior to most house moves').
- **What:** Establish creative material (e.g. 'describe the time-saving characteristics of a new washing machine').

In a case such as this the most efficient choice might be a selective choice of newspapers, TV, or posters. However, the solution is rarely as simple as this. Normally a mix of media is used and media planners/buyers normally use past experience along with research.

A choice needs to be made in media strategy between media **classes** and media **vehicles**.

TABLE 11.1 Marcoms overview

Medium	Definition	Horizon	Form	Scope
Advertising	A paid for communication by an identified sponsor with the aim of informing and influencing one or more people.	Mainly long term	TV, press, posters, radio, web, cinema, digital, SMS.	Awareness, attitudes.
Direct marketing	The recording, analysis, and tracking of customers' direct responses in order to develop loyalty.	Short and long term	Direct mail, DRTV & radio, telemarketing, press, inserts, leaflets, web, digital, SMS.	Mainly retention but also acquisition.
PR	The formulation, execution, and sustained effort to establish and maintain goodwill and mutual understanding and reciprocal goodwill between an organization and its stakeholders.	Short and long term	Community relations/CSR, corporate advertising, crisis management, events, internal communications, investor relations, media relations, public affairs, lobbying, sponsorship, web, digital.	Credibility, visibility, and reputation.
Sales promotions	An incentive for the customer, salesforce, or distributor to make an immediate purchase.	Mainly short term	*Consumer*: Coupons, contests, trial, mail-in offers/refunds, group promotions, self-liquidations, instore promotions, point-of-sale, web, digital, SMS.	*Consumer*: Trial, re-trial, extended trial, build database.
			Trade: Dealer merchandise, contest advertising, allowances, trade allowances/staff incentives, web.	*Trade*: Gain a listing, increase distribution, increase inventory, improve shelving space/position.

Media class

Media class refers to the vertical decision involving media type, e.g. press or TV. The primary choices are:

- cinema
- direct mail
- posters/billboards
- press
- public relations
- radio
- sales promotion

- sponsorship
- TV
- Web

An important factor in choosing between classes is how well the chosen medium **reaches** the chosen audience. Most media classes have a good reach of the population. In the case of television, only a tiny percentage of households do not have a television set. However, the number of readers of newspapers and magazines is slowly but steadily falling each year; the cinema audience is much more likely to be made up of teenagers than adults; posters tend to reach urban audiences more than rural; commercial radio tends to be more downmarket than its BBC (non-commercial) counterparts.

Creative scope is another consideration. How does the chosen medium use audio and/or visual communications and in what context? The first issue is simply whether the strategy needs sound, movement, or a still picture or printed word for impact. Different media can offer these forms of communication either singularly or in combination. Context refers to the primary location of the receiver and the time allocated. For example, most people watch television in their homes with family or friends, newspapers are often read while commuting or at work alone, and posters are seen singly or in groups in the community at large. Such issues can affect choices. For example, car companies normally use posters to 'announce' new cars to the community. A further issue is timing. Some media classes set the time for the message to be decoded by the receiver whereas others allow the receiver to decide upon the time allocated. Thus if a full-page ad is placed in the *Daily Mail* the reader can flick over it or give it full attention. A TV commercial by contrast sets the time, whatever the requirements of the receiver. The conventional strategy is to place ads for 'boring' products in media where the advertiser can determine the time.

Media history is a straightforward issue. The questions to be asked are what has been used before and what worked? Risk-averse advertisers in particular are inclined to use familiar classes of media. Occasionally a risk is taken and it can pay off spectacularly well, as when Whiskas switched much of its budget away from broadcast media to direct marketing, but such success from a risky action is rare.

The **location** of the audience located also needs to be considered. Thus, if you are targeting a specific district within London or Glasgow local media will be more cost effective than national. National/pan-regional campaigns require media with larger coverage.

Distribution channels may play an important role in choice too. If there is a channel in the distribution chain, how will it react to your choice of media class? Try telling a major supermarket chain that you want a significant amount of shelf space for a new shampoo and that you are going to spend a lot of money on advertising the product on hot air balloons. Don't wait for a positive reaction! The chain is likely to expect to see a heavyweight TV campaign.

Finally the size of the **budget** will affect the strategy. How big is your budget? What is the threshold for the effective use of the chosen medium? If you have just about enough money to produce a TV commercial or a large poster, but little left over to buy the needed frequency, it might be better to consider a cheaper medium.

Overall, the key strategic aspect of media class choice is what **competitors** are using. Maybe they have made the right choice or maybe not. The recommended strategy is to use similar classes to those used by competitors if you can match their budgets, but target different ones if not. For example, Go-Cat, the first dried cat food, launched the product using the *Radio Times*. It was close to TV where the major rivals were, but fitted their budget a lot better.

Media vehicles

Media vehicle choice concerns the choice within the chosen class, e.g. if the press is chosen will it be *The Times* or the *Sun*? Or if TV is chosen what programmes will be targeted? The choice of media vehicles will depend on a number of quantitative and qualitative issues. Media planners and buyers will seek the most effective vehicles for their clients within the chosen medium. Decisions cannot be left to numbers. Thus the numbers might suggest a particular tabloid 'red top' newspaper for a luxury car advertiser. However, qualitatively the car company's brand might not benefit from the association with the 'red-top' and a quality daily (with a less cost-effective audience than the red-top) will be the preferred choice. Also, editorial content and positioning count with media vehicles.

Once the choice of vehicle has been made, the key decisions involve frequency and impact, and each issue will affect the other. With limited resources agencies and their clients are forced to trade off one against the other. If you double the frequency, without the commensurate doubling of the budget, the spaces purchased will inevitably have to be halved and the impact consequently reduced. The key strategic issue here is the advertisers' decay rate.

The concept of the decay rate refers to the implication of stopping all advertising activity. If you stop MARCOMS tomorrow, what happens to the brand's awareness and positive attitudes? What would it look like in a week, a month, or six months' time? Powerful brands like IBM and Max Factor would have extremely slow decay rates and would probably still be well known after years of no MARCOMS. However, lesser brands, those that are not top-of-mind in their product categories, may soon be forgotten. If awareness and positive attitudes play a major role in their sales they will be in considerable trouble if they stop the campaign. Such brands get 'hit' twice in the marketplace. They have to maintain some presence, but the need to maintain this may mean that they have to take smaller spaces and are probably going to be less visible. Bigger brands can use MARCOMS between intervals of non-activity and so not only have more resources to devote to MARCOMS, but can purchase bigger/higher impact spaces as a consequence. Strategically all that smaller advertisers can do is to attempt to maximize their creativity so that their smaller budgets can have a higher impact than the often bland communications of market leaders.

Frequency

MARCOMS exposures can take some time to 'wear in', but they also eventually 'wear out' (Ray and Webb, 1986). Conventional wisdom dictates that the response function to MARCOMS tends to be concave, that is, with each subsequent impression the response is reduced (Broadbent, 1999). The idea is that most impact is made with the first impression and thereafter the impact diminishes. The implication is that 'wear in' is fast and 'wear out' is continuous. It is certainly commonsense that once you have paid attention to a piece of MARCOMS you are unlikely to give the same degree of attention subsequently. For example, if you read an ad in a newspaper giving details about a new camera you would be unlikely to bother to read it again in its entirety. Strategically it means that clients, all things being equal, need to produce a piece of MARCOMS that is so creative and entertaining that it can be seen again and again and still be enjoyed (as with the Guinness surfing commercial). Or they must produce a variety of cheaper executions that support the same strategy, but provide sufficient interest so that 'wear out' is reduced.

At a macro level, clients with high awareness can afford to use high-impact bursts of MARCOMS expenditure as they will not be forgotten in the intervening periods. On the other hand clients with low awareness may need a more continuous ('drip') spend to maintain their presence. Timing of purchase may also play a role. Car companies face seasonality of purchases, but also know that a new car is a considered purchase so that they need a continual presence in the marketplace as there is a long gestation period in decision-making. Micro-level considerations involve timings during the week or month. For example, most household goods are purchased on Fridays and over the weekend so a lot of clients aim to reach their audiences on Wednesday and Thursday just prior to consumer spending.

How much to spend?

Setting the MARCOMS budget is crucial for two reasons: if too much is spent, short-term finances are stretched (Hung and West, 1991). However, if the budget is too small, longer-term opportunities may be lost and competitiveness eroded. A variety of methods are used to set budgets and most firms use multiple methods (about two or three). Here is a list of the leading methods being used.

Judgemental methods

Arbitrary: Solely determined on the basis of what is 'felt' to be necessary.

Affordable: The company determines what it can spend on areas such as production and operations and then decides how much it can then afford for advertising.

Objective and task

Spending is in accordance with what is required to meet the advertising objective(s). Ranked by importance objectives are set, tasks agreed to meet these objectives, and then costs estimated. If the campaign cannot be afforded, objective(s) of lower importance are eliminated until the budget can be afforded.

Measurement

ROI: Advertising is considered an investment, and money is spent to the point where the ROI is diminishing.

Incremental: The budget is allocated in an incremental series of tests, mainly using direct and interactive media such as direct mail and the Internet and tools like barcode data. Spending is increased or decreased in line with the results achieved.

Quantitative models: Computer simulation models are used, involving statistical techniques such as multiple regression analysis.

Percentage of sales

% last year's sales: Set percentage of previous financial year's sales.

% anticipated sales: Set percentage of the firm's anticipated sales.

Unit sales: The company allocates a fixed percentage of unit price for advertising and then multiplies this amount by projected sales volume (e.g. 5% unit price × 200, 000 units forecast).

Share of voice

Competitive absolute: The budget is set in line with that of the closest rival.

Competitive relative: All the competitors in the market tend to spend in line with their market share.

In terms of the methods used, indications for the USA and UK are broadly that:

- about 30% of budgets use judgemental methods
- about 30% of budgets use objective and task
- 20% use measurement
- approximately 15% use percentage of sales
- about 5% use competitive methods

Researchers have investigated whether consumer (B2C) advertisers use more sophisticated methods than those advertising to businesses (B2B) and found that on the whole they do. In a similar vein they have investigated whether larger advertisers have a greater vested interest in good practice than smaller ones, and again found that they do.

From a strategic perspective, there are some puzzling aspects to these findings. Organizations setting a budget based upon a percentage of anticipated sales must see MARCOMS as a function of sales rather than vice versa. For example if you set your budget at 10% of sales, and predict your sales to be £10 million for the next financial year, you will allocate £1 million towards MARCOMS. Furthermore, if you hold it at 10% the allocation of resources will spiral upwards when business is good and downwards when bad despite regardless of what the appropriate allocation might be.

It has been a matter of concern to researchers over the years to understand why organizations continue to use somewhat naïve methods like percentage of sales, arbitrary judgement, and competitive share instead of, or without combining with, the objective and task method and measurement (see, for example, Piercy, 1987a, 1987b; West and Hung, 1993). From an organizational perspective, it has been suggested that MARCOMS budgeting can be categorized into five types of decision processes.

1. **Bottom-Up:** Decided purely by the marketing department.
2. **Bottom-Up/Top-Down:** Initiated by the marketing department, modified by the CEO/directors, and finally decided upon by the marketers taking the final decision.
3. **Top-Down:** Decided purely by the CEO/directors.
4. **Top-Down/Bottom-Up:** Initiated by CEO/directors, modified by the marketing department, and finally decided by the CEO/directors.
5. **Committee:** Decided on by a committee representing all.

Surveys suggest that about 65% of firms use bottom-up processes, about 30% top-down, and less than 5% committees. Naïve methods for setting the MARCOMS budget have been correlated with top-down processes. This is because senior managers know that they will not lose their positions if they get the budget wrong (Piercy, 1986). Therefore, they do not need to justify their resource allocation strategies or do their homework. By contrast, when the process is bottom-up, marketers feel the need to justify their decision and are less likely to base it upon naïve methods such as arbitrary judgement or what is affordable.

It might be asked why any organization would use one of the competitive or percentage of sales methods. On the face of it these methods have little to recommend them for there is only a very general logic to setting a budget in line with that of your competitors or with a competitive position or at a fixed percentage each year. To a large extent the reason is that such methods are 'process harmonious'. They do not put a strain on decision-making. An organization that always sets its budget roughly in line with that of a major competitor or always at a fixed percentage avoids a lot of haggling over the distribution of resources and everyone has a sense of what the norm is and to some extent what is fair. By contrast methods such as the objective and task method can be highly contentious and discordant. The objectives set by the marketing department might bear little relation to those held by R&D or production or sales and so conflict will occur. In this light, there is an essential logic to using such methods as they enable an organization to avoid dysfunctional behaviour and to move forwards regardless of whether the optimal allocation of resources has been made, and this is the essential compromise. Unfortunately the ideal marginal utility method, whereby organizations spend on MARCOMS to the point when an extra £1 of spending results in a £1 return but a further spend of £1 results in a return of only 99p, is, of course, completely impossible to implement!

Operations

The final stage of MARCOMS strategy is the operational. This involves measurement, monitoring and contingency, and international.

Measurement

The use of measurement directly relates the strategy to behaviour, using aggregate data like sales, market share, and profits, or individual purchasing behaviour (see Vakratsas and Ambler, 1999). There are several problems in focusing on behaviour, since the effects of MARCOMS are dependent on other factors in the marketing mix and it is therefore difficult to know the impact of MARCOMS alone. Also, quite a large part of the effect of advertising in particular is long term, which makes it difficult to evaluate.

Another approach for measuring effectiveness is to use intermediate measures. These are measures of mental effects, which MARCOMS create, that is, what happens to the minds of people following exposure. According to the traditional hierarchy of effect models on how MARCOMS work, these mental effects, cognitive or affective, are assumed to precede behavioural outcomes such as purchase (see Vakratsas and Ambler, 1999).

Aside from neurological research using brain-scanning techniques, there have been few radical changes in intermediate MARCOMS effectiveness measures used in the last thirty years. The leading intermediate effectiveness measures can be categorized into three groups: attention, processing, and communication.

Attention measures involve memory (recall) tests to indicate whether people paid attention to a communication and if they remember it. Recall requires the remembering of an ad without any external aid, while recognition requires identification of a previously seen ad. Recall can be category prompted or brand prompted, which are sometimes referred to as unaided (spontaneous recall) or aided recall (as mentioned above). Both measures can be used in pre-tests and post-tests. Measures of physiological reactions also only measure attention. Tests are done by using EEGs, brainwaves, or eye movements. Measures of eye movement have been shown to exhibit some relationship with brand recognition, but not with brand recall or brand attitude. Qualitative testing methods (focus groups, in-depth interviews, and such) give an insight into purchasing behaviour and generate ideas in the development of MARCOMS, but they are not appropriate when testing brands' strength or evaluating effects.

Processing measures are immediate responses to a campaign and involve learning, attention, emotional responses, and acceptance. These are focused on the MARCOMS rather than the brand and should be conducted directly after exposure, which means that they are more suitable for pre-tests than post-tests as such responses are transient. An acceptance measure is one where a person agrees with the benefit or claim being made in the MARCOMS or the brand. The two main measures of acceptance are cognitive response measurements and adjective checklist measures. The Adjective Checklist List (ACL) is made up of a list of descriptions from which the respondent can check which they disagree or agree with. It has been found that ACLs can be used as diagnostic tools to predict performance either in pre-tests or post-tests. The cognitive response measurement (CRM) also measures attention but uses open-ended questions, in which respondents are asked orally or in writing about their thoughts immediately after exposure; these are widely used by practitioners.

Communication effects are relatively enduring mental associations connected to a brand and can be used in both pre-tests and post- tests. There are five effects that can be measured according to Rossiter and Percy (1997): category need, brand awareness, brand attitude, brand purchase intention, purchase facilitation. The **category need** is when the buyer sees the category as a solution to a need, wherefore it requires a perceived connection between product and buyer motivation. **Brand awareness** is when a buyer is aware of a brand within a purchase category and it is a prerequisite for purchase and for formation of brand attitude. **Brand attitude** is an overall positive or negative evaluation of the brand relative to other brands. **Brand purchase intention** is measured by asking whether respondents have an intention of purchasing a product in a category within a certain period of time.**Brand purchase facilitation** identifies if there are any hindrances to purchasing the brand in the marketplace (e.g. poor distribution).

Monitoring

Monitoring involves tracking MARCOMS effectiveness in the market over time. It generally involves measuring the brand, competitor brands, promotions, media spending, and trade activity. Monitoring is commonly done on an ad hoc basis. Usually measures are used before and after a campaign runs. However, there is a risk that this could lead to an over- or under-estimate of the effects depending on when the tests are performed. Continuous monitoring is preferable and involves weekly, bi-weekly, or monthly interviews with small samples of buyers over the campaign period and after. This enables a relatively continuous and more sensitive measure of effect. Unfortunately relatively few firms are prepared to devote sufficient resources to undertake such monitoring and receive the feedback loop to feed into the development of the next campaign (see Figure 11.1).

Contingency

The MARCOMS contingency stage relates to monitoring. In essence it is a scenario based upon ineffectiveness. If the campaign is deemed to be a failure, the contingency plan should be undertaken. This might involve stopping the MARCOMS in progress and replacing them with an alternative campaign or, more likely, making some kind of adaptation to the creative activity or modifying the media schedule and spend. A contingency is basically a plan for coping with failure and it needs to be agreed before the campaign runs who will be responsible and what key measures will be used to make the decision over failure or success.

International

This section is essentially concerned with advertising as few clients treat direct marketing, sales promotions, or PR from a global perspective given the logistical problems involved (e.g. rules and regulations surrounding sales promotions make it virtually impossible to have standardization).

The key perspective is the choice between the 'glocal' approach of thinking global but acting local (coined by Akio Morita, the founder of Sony) in contrast to Levitt's (1983) view that the world is one global marketplace where consumers have similar needs and where companies should standardize their mix. Either way, one important issue facing international clients is whether to standardize or customize their MARCOMS. Most international marketing strategies have elements of both approaches.

The main argument for a localized strategy of advertising is effectiveness. Advertising may need to be localized because of powerful forces in the environment such as culture, education, and marketing elements such as the product life cycle. The main arguments for standardization of global advertising are centred on the questions of consistency, quality control, and efficiency. It has also been argued that despite cultural differences product categories have many similar characteristics (especially in B2B markets).

Conclusion

Advertising and direct marketing have the largest impacts on brand value by building relationships with customers. PR (and increasingly MPR—Marketing Public Relations) construct visibility, raise credibility, and ultimately build reputation. Sales promotions can have strategic effects but are largely used for short-term inducements to purchase and, the evidence suggests, with little long-term effect. The process of undertaking a MARCOMS strategy involves conducting an audit, developing the central strategy, and then deciding upon the appropriate creative and media choices. The key issue facing international organizations is the extent to which they can and should standardize or customize their communications.

Summary

MARCOMS primarily consist of four media: advertising, direct marketing, PR, and sales promotions, which can be used in the marketing strategy either singly or holistically with IMC (Integrated Marketing Communications). While MARCOMS can enable organizations to reduce costs in the medium to long term, their main strategic use is in helping to differentiate and position.

KEY TERMS

Advertising A paid-for form of communication using a medium with an identified sponsor. Generally of long-term impact.

Direct marketing An activity involving the recording, tracking, and analysis over time of customers' responses to specific communications. Generally used to build relationships with stakeholders (key ones being customers, suppliers, and staff).

Sales promotions An offer or incentive of extra value for a product or service to staff, distributors, or the buyer. Generally of short-term impact.

Public relations A planned activity to establish and maintain goodwill and mutual understanding between an organization and its immediate and wider stakeholders.

IMC A concept that recognizes the added value of a comprehensive plan that evaluates the strategic roles of a variety of communications disciplines holistically.

Creative brief A summation of the MARCOMS task in order to manage and stimulate the development of creative work to address the task.

Proposition A single-minded and concise statement of what is to be communicated about the product or service in the MARCOMS.

Creative execution Translation of the proposition to a tangible form.

Medium class A type of medium such as TV, newspapers, or direct mail.

Medium vehicle A choice of medium or media within a class such as the *Daily Mail* or the *Daily Telegraph*.

DISCUSSION QUESTIONS

1 What are the pros and cons of approaching the MARCOMS strategy from an IMC perspective?

2 Think of two recent MARCOMS campaigns that featured the organization's values. What sort of insight did the client need to have to use this concept from the Brand Wheel?

3 Identify three brands that you consider to have high awareness but which are performing relatively badly in the marketplace. What would you recommend from a MARCOMS standpoint?

4 Select one of the leading supermarket chains and develop five different potential propositions for the brand based upon: (a) user characteristics, (b) surprising points about the service, (c) price characteristics, (d) disadvantage of non-use, and (e) direct comparison with rivals. Which one would you choose as the basis for developing a campaign and why?

5 You have a local cinema as a client. Examine the case for spending its budget in a concentrated burst in preference to mounting a drip campaign.

ONLINE RESOURCE CENTRE

Visit the Online Resource Centre for this book for lots of interesting additional material at: **www.oxfordtextbooks.co.uk/orc/west/**

REFERENCES AND FURTHER READING

Broadbent, Simon (1999), *When to Advertise* (Henley-on-Thames: NTC).

Erdogan, B. Zater, Michael J. Baker, and Stephen Tagg (2001), 'Selecting Celebrity Endorsers: The Practitioner's Perspective', *Journal of Advertising Research*. 41 (3), pp. 39–49.

Hung, C. L., and Douglas C. West (1991), 'Advertising Budgeting Methods in Canada, the UK and the US', *International Journal of Advertising*, 3 (10), pp. 239–50.

Levitt, Theodore (1983), 'The Globalisation of Markets', *Harvard Business Review*, 61 (3), pp. 92–102.

Ogilvy, David (1980), *Ogilvy on Advertising* (London: Orbis).

Ogilvy, David (1987), *Confessions of An Advertising Man*, 2nd edn (New York: Macmillan).

Piercy, Nigel F. (1986), *Marketing Budgeting* (Dover, NH: Croom Helm).

Piercy, Nigel F. (1987a), 'Advertising Budgeting: Process and Structure as Explanatory Variables', *Journal of Advertising*, 16 (2), pp. 34–44.

Piercy, Nigel F. (1987b), 'The Marketing Budgeting Process: Marketing Management Implications', *Journal of Marketing*, 51 (October), pp. 45–59.

Prescott, Dan (1991), 'Public Relations at General Motors: An Integrated Marketing Communications Approach', MA, University of Colorado School of Journalism and Mass Communication, cited by: Duncan, Thomas R., and Stephen E. Everett (1993), 'Client Perceptions of Integrated Marketing Communications', *Journal of Advertising Research*, 33 (3), pp. 30–40.

Ray, Michael L., and Webb, Peter H. (1986), 'Three Prescriptions for Clutter', *Journal of Advertising Research*, 26 (1), pp. 69–77.

Reeves, Rosser (1961), *Reality in Advertising* (New York: Alfred A. Knopf).

Ries, A., and J. Trout (1981), *Positioning, The Battle for Your Mind* (New York: Warner Books—McGraw-Hill Inc.)

Rossiter, John R., and Larry Percy (1997), *Advertising Communication and Promotion Management* (New York: McGraw-Hill).

Vakratsas, Demetrios, and Tim Ambler (1999), 'How Advertising Works: What Do We Really Know?' *Journal of Marketing*, 63 (1), pp. 26–44.

Ward, Scott, Larry Light, and Jonathan Goldstine (1999), 'What High-Tech Managers Need to Know About Brands', *Harvard Business Review*, 77 (4), pp. 85–96.

West, Douglas C., and C. L. Hung (1993), 'The Organizational Budgeting Processes of Top Advertisers in Canada, the U.K. and the U.S.A', *Journal of Euromarketing*, 2 (3), pp. 7–22.

KEY ARTICLE ABSTRACTS

Percy, Larry (2004), 'Advertising and the Seven Sins of Memory', *International Journal of Advertising*, 23 (4), pp. 413–27.

Effective communication inevitably confronts the problem of memory. This paper examines Schacter's framework and provides a series of suggestions on how to overcome the hurdle. Suggestions include ensuring a consistent look and feel to your advertising over time and using distinctive cues not associated with long-term memory.

Abstract: A positive intention may be formed as a result of exposure to an advertisement, but if a memory malfunction interferes with that intention, the advertising will be ineffective. This paper considers the implications for advertisers of Daniel Schacter's 'seven sins of memory': transience, absent-mindedness, blocking, misattribution, suggestibility, bias, and persistence. Each of the 'sins' is explained in detail and advice provided for advertisers on how to avoid these pitfalls.

Erdogan, B. Zafer, and Michael J. Baker (2000), 'Towards A Practitioner-Based Model of Selecting Celebrity Endorsers', *International Journal of Advertising*, 19 (1), pp. 25–43.

This paper reminds us that the reality of much strategic marketing is cultural and normative in scope and practice. In this case the authors examine the process of selecting celebrity endorsers, which turns out to be a largely unceremonious process.

Abstract: Use of celebrity endorsers has become a widely employed marketing communication strategy. One of the key issues of this strategy is to decide which celebrity to employ. Even though scholars, mostly US-based, have written about the celebrity endorsement strategy and effective endorser characteristics, so far no studies have explored how advertising agencies select celebrity endorsers. To discover the process by which advertising agencies select celebrities and factors considered during this process, semi-structured interviews were carried out. Findings indicate that there is an unwritten and informal process of selecting celebrity endorsers, in which there are a number of factors affecting decisions.

Kitchen, Philip J., and Don E. Schultz (1998), 'IMC—A UK Ad Agency Perspective', *Journal of Marketing Management*, 14 (4/5), pp. 465–86.

This paper explores a number of themes related to Integrated Marketing Communications, in particular the difficulties of measuring its effect, the problems of integrating the PR function, and its value in providing consistency, impact, and continuity.

Abstract: This paper concerns Integrated Marketing Communications (IMC) in terms of its theoretical background, and provides initial findings from an exploratory study of IMC within a judgement sample of UK advertising agencies (total estimated billings—£3.5 billion). The authors consider arguments put forward by academics and practitioners in relation to what IMC is perceived to be, and whether it offers significant value to ad agencies and their clients in the dynamic MARCOMS marketspace leading toward the twenty-first century. Research findings show that IMC is not a short-term managerial fad, nor is it just a re-formulation of existent praxis. Instead, IMC offers a clear response by advertising agencies and their clients driven by a constellation of factors: new forms of information technology (including development and usage of databases), media fragmentation, client desires for interaction/synergy, and global and regional coordination. The paper concludes by stating that IMC is a fundamental, probably irreversible, shift in both the thinking and practice of ad agencies and their clients as reflected by advertising executives. IMC is driven by technological development, customers, consumers, and organizational desire to properly allocate finite resources to the key element of creating exchanges—marketing communications.

END OF CHAPTER 11 CASE STUDY Vauxhall Motors

The task—a summary

You are working in a new business group pitching for the Vauxhall Motors account, a major UK car brand (or 'marque'). You have to prepare a presentation to the main board covering the following topics:

1. A market 'map' showing the marque's position in terms of key image/attribute dimensions of your choosing.
2. Your brief recommendation with reason(s) on whether the marque should be 'rebranded' and use the name 'Opel', a sister brand in Europe.
3. A creative brief describing your advertising strategy for Vauxhall's next campaign.
4. Two or three examples of your initial creative work based on the brief.

UK car market overview

There was a steep decline in new car registrations during the recession in the early 1990s, falling from a peak of 2.3 million registrations in 1989 to 1.59 million in 1991 and 1992. Since then there has been a steady growth reflecting improved economic conditions.

The development of new production facilities by key inward investors, particularly from Japan, has played a major part in boosting production in the UK and reflects the confidence of the industry shown by their substantial investments in the UK. In addition there have been significant changes in the composition of vehicles produced by more established companies.

Toyota announced investment in a second assembly plant, taking its UK total investment to £1.5 billion. Daewoo has invested in a brand-new engineering design facility in the UK. Honda will be making further investment at its UK operation in Swindon and Volkswagen will be investing in the Rolls-Royce Motor Car plant in the UK. Rover has recently ceased trading.

» The UK's largest suppliers, Ford and Vauxhall, have maintained their positions as market leaders. However, long-established players such as Peugeot, Renault, Honda, and Fiat have recorded some of the greatest increases in volumes and have had a major impact on shrinking the leading manufacturers' market shares.

Three key segments continue to dominate the UK car market, the super-mini, lower medium, and upper medium sectors. More recently, there has been a rapid growth in the niche sports car, 4 × 4, and multi-purpose vehicle (MPV) sectors.

Vauxhall

Vauxhall is a long-established UK car marque strongly identified with the town of Luton in Bedfordshire. Now a subsidiary of the American General Motors (GM), it has continued to use its original name. (GM also owns Saab and Opel and has interests in a number of other car companies including Fiat and Daewoo.)

Vauxhall is a 'mass market' brand and produces cars in all the key size sectors: supermini (Corsa), lower-medium (Astra), and upper-medium (Vectra), as well as 'People carriers', four-wheel drives, and sports cars. Its flagship model is the Omega but this does not have the prestige of the equivalent-sized BMW or Mercedes.

Although Vauxhall is still a leading brand, in recent years the company has seen a steady decline in market share (from around 16% in the early 1990s to around 12% in the early 2000s). Further back in time its share was even greater.

This decline is due to a number of factors. There has been a considerable increase in the number of imported cars in the UK (Vauxhall exports are negligible) and in the purchase of 'foreign' brands built in the UK. There has also been a general shift towards premium and lifestyle vehicles, and to brands with more 'sexy' and dynamic images. A strong component of the new car market in the UK has been purchases by corporate 'fleets', with Vauxhall's Vectra frequently seen as the archetypal 'sales rep' special (to the detriment of its overall image). The increase in personal tax on company cars and the move towards 'user chooser' purchasing policies is also threatening to undermine the marque's sales in this area.

It is generally felt that the marque's biggest long-term problem is the lack of a distinctive personality or 'image' in a market where such factors are becoming increasingly important. All cars are now reliable and well built. Consumers now seek out brands that have distinctive product, image, or lifestyle attributes.

Vauxhall is seen as being reliable, trustworthy, but rather dull, an image that some people feel has been exacerbated by a long-running TV campaign featuring the actor and comedian Griff Rhys-Jones as an eccentric professor.

In the words of one expert—'Renault, Citroën and Peugeot are about panache and sex appeal. Volkswagen stands for mainstream dependability, with a Teutonic edge; Fiat has Italian flair. But what is Vauxhall about?'

The task: more detail and guidance

1. A market 'map' showing the marque's position in terms of key image/attribute dimensions of your choosing.

Traditionally such 'maps' are prepared with two 'negative to positive' axes, creating four quadrants. Axes could be combinations of attributes such as performance, prestige, value for money, reliability, quality. You should aim to position Vauxhall in relation to its »

» key competitors. You may wish to produce more than one map or use another method of mapping if this better illustrates your analysis.

2. Your brief recommendation with reason(s) on whether the marque should be 'rebranded' and use the name 'Opel', a sister brand in Europe.

As already mentioned Vauxhall's parent company GM also owns the Opel brand in Europe. There has been some discussion in the media about whether it would be advisable to re-brand Vauxhall as Opel. This would reflect the general move towards global brands and should also provide GM with economies of scale. You should summarize the arguments for and against such a change and make your own recommendation.

About Opel

Opel is a German car marque (named after the founder Adam Opel). Its model range is very similar to that of Vauxhall (the companies share all key components) and Opel's market share in Germany is very similar to if not slightly smaller than Vauxhall's. The brand image is also somewhat similar.

3. A creative brief describing your advertising strategy for Vauxhall's next campaign.

Of most interest will be the general strategic approach you choose to adopt, especially the brand proposition. Please note with regard to media choice that car companies have traditionally been big users of TV and posters.

4. Two or three examples of your initial creative work based on your brief.

Only rough outline ideas are required. Focus on advertising. However, you may briefly explain how your campaign could be translated to other media.

12

E-marketing strategies

LEARNING OBJECTIVES

- Provide an overview of e-marketing strategy
- Examine the impact of e-marketing strategy on industry structure and profitability
- Assess the role of e-marketing on competitive advantage
- Review global issues related to e-marketing

CHAPTER AT A GLANCE

Introduction

In the general excitement over the Internet, many observers have argued that the old rules about marketing strategy have changed. However, the indications are that organizations that treat the Internet as an **evolutionary** force outperform organizations that see it as a **revolutionary** one. A good example would be Avis, Europe's largest car hire company, which has developed newsletter templates used by regional offices across 14 European countries to boost online reservations and reduce costs.

Rosenbloom (2002) has suggested that many of the 'new paradigms' attached to e-marketing have been disproved and Porter (2001) has forcefully argued that the fundamentals of strategy remain unaltered. E-marketing can only be used to create value if companies focus on (1) industry structure, which determines profitability, and (2) sustainable competitive advantage (SCA), which allows a company to outperform the average. Industry structure is determined by the five underlying forces of competition: rivalry, the bargaining power of suppliers and buyers, barriers to entry for new competitors, and the threat of substitutes (see Chapter 2).

When it comes to industry structure and profitability, many of the trends from Internet technology are negative. For example, buyers have more information, there is a reduced need for a salesforce or established channels, barriers to entry are reduced, and there is the potential for greater substitution and intense rivalry with the open system of the Internet. Take the case of the UK. By the end of 2004, 52% of households (12.6 million) could access the Internet from home, compared with just 9% (2.2 million) in 1998 (see Figure 12.1). However, on the positive side, the Internet has dampened the bargaining power of channels as companies go direct to customers, and as overall efficiency has increased many markets

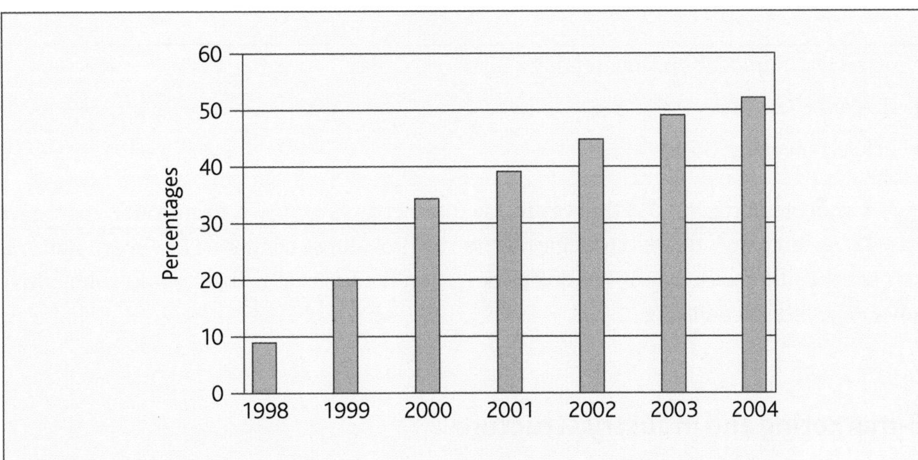

Figure 12.1 Growth in Internet access. *Note*: Proportion of UK households with home access to the Internet. UK Households with home access to the Internet, October to December.

Source: NSO, 2005: **http://www.statistics.gov.uk.**

have expanded. The problem is that while markets have expanded many companies have found Internet technologies have made it more difficult to capture the profits. For example, in the PC market, customers have more information and choice but pure-play online sellers (those with a single business focus) find it extremely difficult to differentiate themselves from competitors as they often lack retail outlets, service departments, or personal selling.

Turning to competitive advantage, the Internet offers considerable scope for operating at a lower cost, commanding a premium price, or doing both. Thus Oxfam has introduced its first online newsletter—*Oxfam Reports Live*—to cut costs on postal services. Meanwhile, the monthly newsletter sent to 250,000 donors is to be personalized to closely match the interests of individual supporters. However, Internet operational advantages are often easily copied and so there has been considerable convergence. Companies do not offer a durable advantage from Internet operational efficiency. Thus, strategic positioning has become increasingly important. If you cannot be operationally more efficient, the only way to generate higher levels of economic value is to gain a cost advantage or price premium by competing in a **distinctive** way. Thus, strategy goes far beyond best practice. The Royal Opera House (ROH) uses SMS and the Internet to boost theatre attendance. As part of the plan, the ROH encourages visitors to **www.royalopera.org** to subscribe to a free e-newsletter and leave their mobile numbers to receive mobile alerts on free open air events, TV broadcasts, special offers, and promotions. Miller Homes' **www.millerhomes.co.uk** uses the e-CRM facility, which automatically notifies customers by e-mail when a new home becomes available that exactly matches their specified criteria. The system is designed to take over the house-hunting process for customers by ensuring that they receive only information which matches their exact needs. It also allows customers to refine their property searches to specific price bands and precise locations, property types, and sizes. In such ways, organizations can use e-marketing tools to deliver a tailored and integrated value chain. The top uses of the Internet as revealed by the National Statistics Office (NSO, 2005: *www.statistics.gov.uk*) are as follows:

- travel, accommodation, and holidays: 55%
- CDs or DVDs: 43%
- tickets for events: 36%

According to Porter (2001) the way to use Internet architecture is to customize packages based on a company's unique strategic position by providing a common IT delivery platform across the value chain. Out-of-the-box packages on the Internet will not work: competitive advantage rests on tailoring.

E-marketing and industry structure

The most successful B2C companies at adapting 'bricks to clicks', such as Tesco, have an ability to integrate marketing, customer service, and use of information and technology in order to deliver a profitable long-term market share or niche strategy (Wilcocks and Plant, 2001). But what are the key characteristics of industry structure in e-marketing?

E- markets

One of the key characteristics of the e-marketing environment is that it is largely 'smart' (Glazer, 1999) as opposed to 'dumb' static markets which are fixed and information poor. Smart markets are dynamic, turbulent, and information rich and are based on new kinds of (1) products, (2) competitors, and (3) customers.

Smart products can adapt or respond to the environment as they interact with customers, such as The Organic Shop, one of the leading organic food and drink e-tailers. It overhauled its site in a rapid response to discovering that people often logged on to make the same order. It decided to incorporate a 'repeat order system' (branded as a 'shopping list'), which enables visitors to have their organic shopping delivered without having to return to the site. A smart competitor is one that is continually changing and in need of constant monitoring, such as with Tesco's entrance into the financial marketplace which caught many established players off guard. Finally, smart customers are also continually changing and require constant information updates. They want convenient one-stop shopping, participation in design, production, and delivery of goods and services and for companies to anticipate their needs. Thus, P&O Cruises encourage interactive activity and one-to-one communications through **www.princess.com**, which includes a 'Plan your Voyage' feature where users choose the cruise most suited to their needs by destination, ship, time of year, or special interest.

The basis of operating in smart markets is to use an individual 'CIF'—a customer information file. A CIF classically covers: customer characteristics; what, when, where, how, and why they buy; what they bought and the cost of goods or services sold; and the potential profit of each customer. Train operator c2c embarked on an online prize promotion to boost its database in a bid to better target its passengers. The website visitors could enter the draw to win a trip to New York including flights and accommodation, after they registered details that would be added to c2c's database of 1.1 million commuters. Data are used for increasingly targeted campaigns.

Many leading bricks to clicks companies see the Internet as central to their strategies as part of a network-centric information-gathering business environment. They are concerned not so much by the technology itself as by what it means for information collection, storage, analysis, and application. Furthermore they realize that their businesses have to operate non-stop all year round and that their websites need constant updating. Learning is quick and they are ready to shift focus. Generally they adopt a top-down route where the top team focuses on the goals and the integration of Web technology, as with Direct Line. Critical business thinking is applied to e-business processes. Companies like Tesco use the Web as part of their multi-channel strategies built upon their established brand and existing business strengths. The Web is seen as part of a larger investment. Thus, Ford and Motorola have made substantial investments in intranet, extranet, and supply chain applications, not just in the front-end. Another B2B case is Friends Provident which has launched an online with-profits bond product for Independent Financial Advisors (IFAs). The new service provided an entirely paperless transaction for IFAs, making it the first fully online with-profits bond. Along with the e-IFA bond product, Friends Provident also launched an online protection product for the IFA market. These online products reduced costs for IFAs by eliminating a great deal of administration and paperwork.

By contrast, laggards tend to put their IT departments in charge of the e-business and their senior business managers generally underfund and undervalue IT and e-business processes. They tend to treat IT and the Web as a cost rather than a profit centre and their Chief Information Officers (CIOs) are often positioned as specialist functional managers.

There are some interesting lessons from B2B exchanges (Day et al., 2003), one of the most hotly contested dotcom areas with nearly 300 formed in 1999 and over 1,500 at the peak in 2000. Most entrants were pure-play sellers such as MetalSite, Chemdex, and Neoforma which offered core services of information exchange, digital catalogues/automated procurement, auctions, logistics, collaborative planning, and value-added services like design and finance. The rush to leave the market began in early 2001 when the cash began to run out. It ran out as many investors realized that few exchanges would achieve the critical mass of buyers and sellers.

Two kinds of B2B exchange market emerged. The **re-formed** market was where the new technology did not change the basic structure, functioning, and purpose of the market, whereas the **breakthrough application** market rewrote the rules by creating new products and services.

The construction industry is a good example. E-marketing has enabled architects, builders, engineers, and general contractors to easily transmit information and drawings amongst multiple firms at different locations. By contrast materials procurement has hardly changed. Most contractors are small businesses with a regional focus and purchasing is typically handled by project managers in the field rather than purchasing departments. Over 20,000 distributors provide materials to customers at a local level the same day or next and generally ordered by mobile. The idea of placing orders by the Internet would have required computers on-site, would not have increased efficiency and would have required significant training amongst the workers. In this case the pay-off was not there and it has not happened.

The reality is that most customers care more about getting the right product at the right time than a good price. E-marketing is more about differentiation than cost advantage. Furthermore, if there is no breakthrough advantage, then incumbent trusted brand-named bricks and mortar companies like John Lewis have the advantage. Most start-ups lack the deep knowledge about their potential customers that the established incumbents have. Another problem was that the range of restraints and protective barriers in many markets was well known to established bricks and mortar players, but hardly understood at first by the dotcoms.

Winners amongst the dotcoms are likely to be companies enhancing rather than replacing traditional industry relationships. Survivors will prosper by purchasing failing dotcoms at bargain prices and leveraging their assets. The also-rans will have either to sell out or to try and find market niches where they can survive the competitive pressures. An example is SciQuest, which has abandoned its goal of connecting 10,000 worldwide life sciences research organizations, preferring to build private exchange networks for the top 20 pharmaceutical companies.

Making a profit?

The ultimate goal of marketing strategy is to aid business viability, of which a major component is making a profit. Despite the potential, the performance so far of most Web-based firms has been dismal (Barsh et al., 2000, and see also: Shama, 2001; Higson and Briginshaw, 2000; Wheale and Heredia, 2003). Businesses have to make money, so how do they generate profits online? The evidence from McKinsey's on e-tailing is that it will be structurally impossible for most purely Web-based retailers ever to make a profit unless they reach the scale of a trader like Amazon.com (which has only just begun to be profitable). Web advantages will go to big and highly skilled traditional retailers that use the Web to extend their existing physical presence. Most pure Web e-tailers might be doomed, but Web-tailing is not.

The simple problem is that most e-tailers lose money. In the USA Amazon, the flagship e-tailer, loses about $7 an order on its non-book sales. Losses can be higher elsewhere, e.g. another US company, Drugstore.com, loses $10 to $15 an order. This is because there are three core weaknesses in Web-tailing operations. (1) Many product categories, such as toys, are difficult to pack, pick, and ship and/or they attract small orders. (2) Simple inexperience in the category and lack of scale inflates fulfilment costs to $12 to $16 an order. (3) Pure Web-tailers are involved in intense price competition and have problems with inventory management and returns that hit gross margins. Add to all this the expense of soaring customer acquisition costs of between $50 and $100 per customer, and low loyalty, and it is no surprise that money is lost. To make comfortable contributions to each transaction, pure e-tailers need efficient order fulfilment, average order sizes of about £50, and gross margins of at least 25%.

The issue is that many so-called 'fixed costs' increase in line with revenues which make large-scale operations hard to create. Furthermore, an 'industrial strength' website and back-end operations can cost millions of pounds per annum and these costs do not decrease over time. Expenses associated with hardware and software (about 30% of total website costs) increase with site traffic, warehousing, and revenue growth.

These issues define e-tailing. Gross margin and fulfilment costs must improve dramatically to make orders profitable. The cost of acquiring customers must drop while their loyalty must rise just to break even. However, the figures for multi-channel players are much better, with break evens typically half those of pure e-tailers. Higher gross margins make the per order economics stronger, lower marketing expenses reduce fixed costs, and many customers use the Web to browse and then purchase with a bricks and mortar company (i.e., e-tailing can add sales to physical channels).

While the overall profitability for pure Web-tailers is poor, there are variations by sector. Books must be sold on a huge scale and can probably only sustain a couple of players with gross margins at just over 20% on orders of around £25. Amazon is the key player and has driven acquisition costs down to about £10 per customer. E-tailers' profits lie with high-end products like cosmetics and hard-to-find items. Somewhat surprisingly, the best product mix for a pure e-tailer would be groceries. With order sizes over £50 and frequent repeat orders, groceries can become viable e-businesses if they reach a sufficient scale. Infrastructure choice is key with models like that of Tesco which involves picking and packing orders in local stores, whereas bespoke warehousing systems are favoured by rivals like Waitrose.

The Tesco model makes sense, but might not be viable were orders to reach a huge scale. Clothing is another surprising sector with promise. Higher per-order economics translate to better gross margins and the potential to lever the brand to reduce acquisition costs. For speciality clothing companies the economics are even better. Yoox.com, an Italian clothing site, has a section called 'The Look' in which outfits are put together for imaginary events, such as 'A date with my literary agent'. On Net-a-Porter, a British high-end clothing site, clothes are grouped according to the latest fashion trends, such as stripes, patterns, or prints, with editors choosing their top ten. These are then linked directly to the page where a purchase can be made. The difficulty is that people need to be measured and like to touch, feel, and try on clothing items so e-tailing of clothing is most likely to develop first with repeat standard items like men's shirts. (See Mini Case Study 12.1.)

Clickstream

Carr (2000) takes a sideways look at profits on the Web and suggests that they will be made incrementally 'a penny at a time' through 'hypermediation'. E-marketing will run on the engine of the 'clickstream'. Carr's premise for hypermediation is based upon the case of an average Internet user who he called 'Bob,' who is interested in a Harry Potter book. Bob might use Netscape to search the phrase 'Harry Potter'. From a list of search services he might chose the GoTo.com site where his search results are posted. From here he picks 'Nancy's Magical Harry Potter Page', a personal and unsophisticated home page with reviews of the books, plot reviews, and discussion boards. There is also a link to a special Harry Potter page at eToys. Bob clicks on this site and decides to buy, using his Visa card, a Harry Potter book at half its list price. Three days later the book is delivered. Who makes money on these transactions?

Obvious suspects are eToys and their book supplier, as well as Visa and the postal service. However, Netscape made a penny from GoTo.com through supplying Bob's click. GoTo.com, in turn, made a penny from Nancy for directing Bob to her home page. However, because GoTo sub-contracts its searches to an outside provider, it had to pay a fraction to them. Nancy, like many individuals, had signed up to be an affiliate of eToys. Every time she supplies a link to eToys that translates into a purchase, she receives a cut of 7.5%. Of course, eToys outsources its affiliate programme to another company, which, in turn, takes a small cut from eToys.

No fewer than nine intermediaries would have had a share of Bob's purchase of the Harry Potter book. At each point that Bob clicked his mouse, value was created and money exchanged. This is hypermediation, the profitability of intermediate transactions rather than the final sale.

Thus, one group that might make profits on the Web is the armies of owners of specialized content sites, as represented by the fictitious Nancy. The second type of intermediary that will make money will be the infrastructure companies that provide the search engines, the advertising networks, the affiliate networks, and the so-called 'backbone' providers. Scale will be important to their profits as every click will only deliver a small amount of revenue. However, these anonymous businesses will quietly collect substantial revenue as the Web develops.

MINI CASE STUDY 12.1

'E-Tailing Comes of Age as Women Spend More than Men'

Women are now spending more money shopping online than men for the first time, with an average annual spend of almost £500.

And spending by women is growing far faster than that of men, according to a new report on e-tailing in Britain from Verdict, the retail consultancy.

The findings are likely to be viewed as a further sign that e-tailing is coming of age, with the figures beginning to reflect the wider spending patterns on the high street. Total retail sales are dominated by women, but until now men have had the lion's share of online shopping because surfing the net was initially very male dominated.

According to Verdict, women shoppers spent an average of £495 online last year, a 71.4 per cent increase on 2002. That growth rate is six times faster than for male online shoppers, who spent £470.

'This is very important for e-tailers,' said Richard Hyman of Verdict. 'Shopping is about women. That is not sexist; it is a matter of fact. In order to build a serious retail business through any channel you have got to understand women.'

He predicts that while male shoppers still outnumber women, accounting for 53.7 per cent of online sales, that balance will soon shift. Women already spend more than men on groceries, furniture and floor coverings, health and beauty, clothing and footwear, homewares and books.

'Women will probably overtake men this year,' said Mr Hyman. 'This is very much a coming of age for the internet.'

The Verdict report found that the total online market in Britain last year rose by 36.1 per cent to £4.9bn. The growth is 10 times faster than that for total retail spending and means that online sales now make up 1.9 per cent of the retail market.

The research also showed a big jump in the use of e-commerce by older shoppers, with spending by those aged over 55 jumping by 129.1 per cent to £747m.

People in this age group now spend more than those in any other, at £527 per head.

'The majority of older customers with internet access are retired ABs,' says the report. 'They have a high disposable income and are able to accept online deliveries during the day. Many more affluent pensioners have adopted the internet as a hobby and enjoy surfing the net for cheap prices and good deals.'

Verdict is predicting that with the changes in the customer base, e-tailers can expect a shake-up of the highly fragmented market. 'There are currently too many retailers and too little to differentiate their offers,' it says. 'Looking ahead, it will be impossible to sustain all of them. Those retailers that establish themselves as mass-market online superstores will be the real winners.'

Source: Susanna Voyle (2004), *Financial Times*, 16 February, p. 5.

Judo

Another distinctive characteristic of e-marketing strategy is the use of 'Judo'. There are similarities between the use of a judo strategy in e-marketing and its use by relatively small companies undertaking product innovation and development (as discussed in Chapter 7). Judo strategy is commonly used as the form of competition amongst e-marketing rivals (Yoffie and Cusumano, 1999). The analogy is made to the art of judo because players attempt to use the strength and weight of their opponents to gain advantage rather than to exchange blows directly. Sumo matches ('wrestling' each other 'face to face' to force the opponent to the ground or 'out of the ring') are what Internet companies try to avoid, as relatively small players tend to lose in sumo.

Judo strategy is where e-marketers set out to turn their rival's size, strength, and resources against themselves using three key principles. First, 'judo players' must be able to move rapidly to uncontested market spaces to avoid direct combat. Next, they must recognize superior force in the market and give way when attacked rather than 'stand and fight'. Finally, and this is the essence of judo strategy, they must use the weight and strength of their opponents against themselves.

Yoffie and Cusumano illustrate the case with Netscape Navigator. It was just about the best browser in the marketplace by 1994, but not by very much. Its spectacular early success was based on the first judo principle—moving the battle to where Netscape had an advantage over its rivals. Netscape's decision was to target early adopters—sophisticated users who already had a high degree of experience of the Internet. By comparison, its rivals offered a complete stack of tools such as dial-up Internet access, a browser, and e-mail. Netscape gave the browser product away by allowing free educational and non-profit use and many people who downloaded it for a trial period of 90 days never paid for it. This facilitated a rapid market penetration. Its final use of judo principle No. 1 was to post a beta version of Netscape on its home page and invite Internet users to try it out and file their comments and complaints. Microsoft was quick to learn judo principle No. 1 and released its own browser, Explorer, as a free product bundled with Windows 95. However, Microsoft raised the ante by making Explorer free to all users, including corporations. Netscape responded by using principle No. 2, being flexible and giving way when attacked directly by a superior force. It decided to target the intranet, and later the extranet markets, and built a deeper e-commerce strategy to shelter from Microsoft's assault. Furthermore, when Microsoft announced it had done a deal with the *Wall Street Journal* to offer special access to Explorer 3.0 users, Netscape rapidly signed up dozens of content providers to deliver interactive Web pages directly to a user's e-mail address. Moreover, when Netscape realized by late 1996 that it could not continue to develop its own platform in competition with Microsoft, it decided to 'embrace and integrate' with all Microsoft's technologies and servers.

Again, Microsoft demonstrated that it too was a master of judo strategy and willingly adopted numerous Internet technologies that Java and Netscape had pioneered, even when they conflicted with Windows. Perhaps the best demonstration of this was Microsoft's decision to bundle AOL online services with Windows 95 in 1996 and undercut the market for its own Microsoft Network (MSN). Later all online services were give open access to Windows 95.

Finally, principle No. 3 represents the essence of judo strategy: use the weight and strength of opponents against themselves. Microsoft's greatest strength was its dominance of the PC operating system market, which enabled it to offer Explorer free on every new PC or network sold in the world. The strategy was to make the operating system, interface, and browser inseparable. One flaw in the strategy was that users with older PCs or networks were unable to use the latest version of Explorer. Thus, Netscape positioned itself as the only browser that supported the entire installed base of Windows—cross-platform support that included Unix users. In another classic judo strategy move, in 1998 Netscape decided to give away the source code to its new browser, Communicator 5.0. This was akin to Coca-Cola giving away its formula! The only proviso was that anyone using the code had to register any changes with Netscape developers. Being unable to match Microsoft's research base, going to the Web potentially provided Netscape with access to thousands of developers, as with Unix. Microsoft was unable to respond in kind because if it opened up its proprietary code it would lose its market hold.

Netscape was finally purchased by AOL in late 1998. One more judo player was counted 'out'. The basic lesson here is that judo strategy can also be played by opponents and that Microsoft is, despite its sumo image, a masterful exponent. As well, judo strategy may be extended beyond the Internet to other markets wherever the potential exists to turn a rival's size and strength against itself.

E-marketing and sustainable competitive advantage

As noted above, some kind of distinctiveness is required to build a SCA in e-marketing. Take the case of Sainsbury's. Dogged by complaints over fulfilment failings and slow delivery times, and overshadowed by the phenomenal e-tailing success of Tesco Online, Sainsbury's has decided to establish 'A Taste for Life', its new website, which differentiates itself online by concentrating on content rather than commerce. Products can still be ordered from the site; however the focus is on dietary information and advice. The site centres on a recipe search engine that helps users find recipes by country, ingredients, and cooking time. When it comes to branding, successful companies use the Internet to reinforce their positions rather than create new sales channels alone.

BMW has aimed to make its site 'drive and feel like a BMW' and uses it to steer potential customers to dealers. Others have used the Web for repositioning, as with Lufthansa, which has repositioned itself as a customer-focused travel agency and information provider, with its InforFlyway service. Brand creation can also be achieved, as with Prudential Assurance and Egg. However, brand creation depends upon consumer motivation and preference.

According to Wolfinbarger and Gilly (2001) consumer motivation on the Web falls into two categories: (1) 'experiential' for fun, or (2) 'goal directed' for efficiency. Experiential behaviour tends to occur when shoppers have a continuing hobby interest. This is as much about the 'thrill of the hunt' as about acquiring items. Goal-oriented shopping is task oriented, efficient, rational, and deliberate. In terms of numbers, a recent Harris survey found that just over 70% of online shoppers said that their most recent purchase had been planned with the remainder saying that they had been browsing and bought on impulse.

Goal-oriented shoppers like convenience and they prefer the anonymity of the Web. Experiential behaviour is quite different from goal oriented. Experiential shoppers are motivated by surprise/excitement/uniqueness, positive sociability, deals, and product involvement. The implications for e-marketing strategy are that shoppers touch and feel items offline and enjoy the experience of being 'out' but they might then buy online. The other key thing to note is that only experiential shoppers are interested in the strategies of content and community (and even so they are the minority). Most shoppers just want the commerce. The goal-focused shopper wants a site that is easy to navigate, is packed with information, has easy transaction processes, and has quick delivery. However, note that Zona Research Inc. suggest that after waiting just eight seconds for a Web page to load 30% of customers will exit and by 12 seconds, 70% have gone.

The one Achilles heel of the Internet is delivering physical products at the right time. When shoppers need products in a hurry, they head for the bricks and mortar outlets rather than their Web counterparts. Moreover, certain experiences cannot be delivered, in particular goods that need touch, such as clothing and furniture, and shoppers that enjoy the social experience of shopping are unlikely to trade this in for the convenience of their computers.

Despite this, many service-focused organizations have successfully harnessed the Web to offer a variety of value-added practices to consumers. They have 'personalized', as with BT Yahoo!, which enables users to tailor their interface and with the use of such things as tiered service levels like Dell's 'platinum' services. They have collected information to provide enhancements, as with FedEx's package tracking, and they 'keep it simple' and respond to what customers 'do not like', as with Direct Line's online car insurance quotes. At the heart of differentiation is **navigation**.

Navigation

Navigation is a term linked to e-marketing: the process of steering between the mass and variety of information in cyberspace. However, navigation also occurs in physical commerce. For example, no one reviews all the possible options in buying a shirt or pair of shoes. Instead consumers rely on suppliers and retailers to help them navigate. However, applied to e-marketing, navigation takes a different form. Over the Internet it is possible to search extensively at negligible cost. Navigation and selection occur independently of physical warehousing and distribution, and bricks and mortar companies no longer have any special advantages. Electronic retailers can focus on navigation and outsourcing and 'pure' navigators like Google, Yahoo!, and Lycos can simply help people make sense of the information without being party to any transactions at all. Navigation is the key to profit potential. Amazon.com is not just an online bookseller, it has broadened its offering to electronics and PCs, gifts, kitchen items, music, movies, software, travel, and toys. The fact that the limits to the domain in which Amazon.com is the preferred navigator are unknown explains why the company is worth more than the entire publishing industry.

Navigation has four dimensions: 'reach', 'affiliation', 'richness' (Evans and Wurster, 1999), and 'range' (Wells and Gobeli, 2003). Reach is about how many customers a business can access and how many products it can offer. Affiliation is about whose interest the business represents. Richness is the depth and detail of information that the business gives the customer and collects about the customer. Range relates to the breadth and depth of the products and services offered. Different combinations offer various advantages.

Reach

'Reach is the degree to which a firm can manage its value chain activities to connect its customers to an accessible product/service offering' (Wells and Gobeli, 2003). In other words, it is not only the ability of customers to reach the firm but also the firm's ability to reach the customer with its products and services. For example, the music industry has traditionally marketed, sold, and distributed its product offering while ignoring the digital transmission element. Napster.com seized the initiative by leveraging the opportunities of reach ignored by the record companies for so long. While Napster was seen as a threat, record companies failed to appreciate that the model of providing digital downloadable music offered a win–win situation for both the industry and consumers given the reduced costs for the companies and the ability for consumers to customize. Where reach is limited through physical incompatibilities, as many supporting processes as possible should be at least digitalized, such as supply-chain management and payment.

Internet reach is phenomenal. The average US physical CD store carries 50,000 titles, whereas companies like EveryCD.com offers prizes to customers who cannot find what they want, the selection is so wide. However, the explosion of reach crosses conventional boundaries with a click of the mouse. E-commerce companies that just mimic conventional physical retailers will find that they lose out to wider navigators. For example, CDNow.com carved out a dominant reach-based position on the Internet only to lose it in a few months to Amazon.com. With hindsight it is clear that consumers do not see CDs as a discrete category and the same may be true for many other categories in the traditional physical marketplace. Electronic retailers will continue to probe the true boundaries of each other's businesses.

For many suppliers, especially the relatively smaller ones, Internet reach is just fine. Small winemakers have increased their business with Virtual Vineyards.com and small publishers have applauded the success of Amazon.com. Most small suppliers do not want to be in the navigation business, so expanded reach is a blessing for them. By contrast, large suppliers have traditionally used navigation tools, like branding and promotion, in the physical marketplace, to good effect. To lose them to Internet retailers is not welcome, but they have to participate in the world of e-commerce. The problem is that whenever the reach extends beyond a supplier's offering, they will always lose. Thus, no book publisher can match Amazon.com. for reach.

One strategy for individual suppliers to achieve critical mass is to form alliances, as when Universal and BMG (two of the world's largest music companies) formed GetMusic.com, a joint venture. They offered their own CDs as well as those of rival companies. Solo efforts would have had no chance of succeeding against the likes of CDNow. Reach has to be pursued in its own right and the lines and identity of the site must make intuitive sense to consumers.

Affiliation

The second issue is affiliation. Affiliation is a product of the Internet culture and the greater transparency of e-commerce. For example, book publishers have long promoted particular books in bookshops and no one has raised a murmur. But when Amazon.com allowed publishers to pay for superior Web page placement, the consumer indignation was so strong that the company was forced to publish the details of these arrangements on its home page (Evans and Wurster, 1999). The issue of affiliation has been compounded by reach. Give a sales agent one sales line and he/she will push it aggressively but as the range increases, the propensity will be to present the range more neutrally. Give the customer the ability to compare sales agents, and the propensity to please the customer more than the supplier will increase, as, for example, in the case of msn.autos which provides buyers with the data and software to compare alternative cars on 80 objective criteria. Microsoft does not need to be paid by the consumer to tilt his/her affiliation in its direction, as the success of the site attracts advertising revenue.

Consequently, pure navigators are best poised to exploit affiliation. Motley Fool is in a better position to navigate mutual funds than Fidelity, because it is not in the business of selling funds. Product suppliers will always lose when it comes to affiliation.

One strategy for product suppliers is to evolve beyond product categories and to use the Internet to offer consumer solutions. Instead the idea would be to provide objective data and decision-support software about content unrelated to your own business. For example, Dell is widening its sales presence with a much broader retailing offering that navigates to peripherals that it does not make and provides objective information about them. Overall, the proposition cements affiliation to Dell while preserving its own product base.

Peripheral manufacturers might form alliances to provide flattering representation of their own products and comprehensive and objective evaluations of computers. Of course, the savvy consumer would use Dell's site for choosing peripherals and the peripheral alliance one to choose computers. To preserve their own businesses, sellers will increasingly commoditize each other.

Richness

The third issue is *richness*. 'Richness is the degree to which a firm can facilitate the exchange of information to deliver products/services that match customers' exact wants and needs' (Wells and Gobeli, 2003). For example, the interaction between a local tailor's shop and its customers is extremely rich as it can easily observe preferences and produce a customized product accordingly. The challenge is to identify the attributes conducive to the digital medium and lever them effectively. Timbuk2 is a good example (see Figure 12.2). Manufacturing custom-made messenger bags leveraging IT, Timbuk2 offers customers control over product design, order entry, and production planning. Only bags designed and purchased are manufactured, and this lowers their overheads while at the same time providing customers with a customized product.

Physical retailers have always had the ability to collect and use information about their customers, but the Internet greatly enhances this aspect. For example 1-800FLOWERS.com maintains a customer-specific file containing anniversary and birthday information and a record of gifts sent. Customers can be alerted about an impending birthday and particular flowers suggested. Furthermore, data-mining techniques can be applied to browsing behaviour as well as purchasing history to build relationships. Purchasing behaviour of similar customers can be compared. Thus, Amazon.com uses 'swarming' technology to compare the titles purchased by two similar buyers and to suggest the different titles purchased by each one to each other. Limitations to richness will evolve, especially with legislation on privacy, and the increasing ability of consumers to manipulate their own information (for example, customizing their own estimation of net worth, and possibly selling it). Furthermore, no

Figure 12.2 Timbuk2

Source: **http://www.timbuk2.com/**. By permission of Timbuk2designs.

single player is likely to have the ideal database, so alliances and markets for swapping information will begin to form. The originators and primary aggregators of such information will extract most of the value.

Richness is one area where producers have an edge in relation to customer information. Retailers, be they physical or electronic, have most information on consumers, but no one knows the goods or services better than suppliers. For example, in the music industry it is the record companies that are best at developing information-rich performer biographies, discographies, recording histories, and chat rooms. Much of this information can be placed on websites, provided to retailers, or placed on enhanced CDs or DVDs. Cross-selling is helped, and the brand image of performers is built. Whether such sites will ever become 'hot' is doubtful as many buyers seem to prefer funky anti-establishment sites. Supplier sites that could become 'hot' are ones involving innovation and rapid product development such as those for mobile phones, hi-fis, and computer technology. But when objectivity and comprehensiveness matter more, they are unlikely to succeed. Furthermore, hot news and excitement about such product categories as groceries are improbable.

Range

The final issue is range. 'Range is the degree to which a firm can offer its customers a value proposition containing a breadth of products/services' (Wells and Gobeli, 2003). It might be category specific (narrow) as with Dell, which can offer high customization. It might be cross-category (broad) like Currys, which offers breadth but minimal specialization or customization. Integrating the digital attributes along the product/service offering is the key to strengthening e-strategy with range. The digital medium allows the seamless integration of complementary products and services that were previously difficult or impossible to manage. Thus, travel portals like Orbitz.com can offer tickets, car hire, and hotel reservations in one cohesive package.

Loyalty

Acquiring customers on the Web is extremely expensive, so unless companies can lock customers in, they will be faced with the prospect of catering solely to price-sensitive buyers. Thus the British Airports Authority has launched two online services designed to produce greater loyalty among its regular customers. One service is a regular newsletter called *Discovery Airside*, whose subscribers receive information on the latest travel news, in-terminal store openings, product introductions, and shopping offers. This is supported by an automated acknowledgement campaign for customers booking travel services online.

If marketed effectively, both B2B and B2C markets can be populated by highly loyal customers. An example of the former has been financial services forum Tank! which launched an e-marketing group called e-tank! that kept participating companies abreast of key e-marketing issues, such as response rates, legislative updates, and case studies through monthly newsletters and an e-tank! microsite.

The Web can be a highly 'sticky' space. New software has enabled the development of virtual advisors (Urban et al., 2000). Virtual advisors are programmed to behave just like an experienced human advisor. They ask questions, record responses, and propose recommendations on the basis of these responses. Clearly not all goods and services need an advisor. Advisors are more likely to be needed when purchases have a high price, are complex (financial planning), have a need for new learning (e.g. digital cameras) and are subject to rapid change (e.g. PCs) or involve risk (e.g. healthcare).

The key element to loyalty on the Web is trust. Thus baby milk substitute manufacturer Wyeth promoted its SMA Nutrition brand through an online campaign featuring a competition and advertorial on Freeserve's parenting portal, **www.Babyworld.co.uk**, which encouraged mothers to register for the SMA careline and apply for a 'New Born Know How' pack. Ocado has rolled out an e-CRM programme, which included special promotions and alerts, to boost loyalty among early adopters of its online home delivery store (see Figure 12.3).

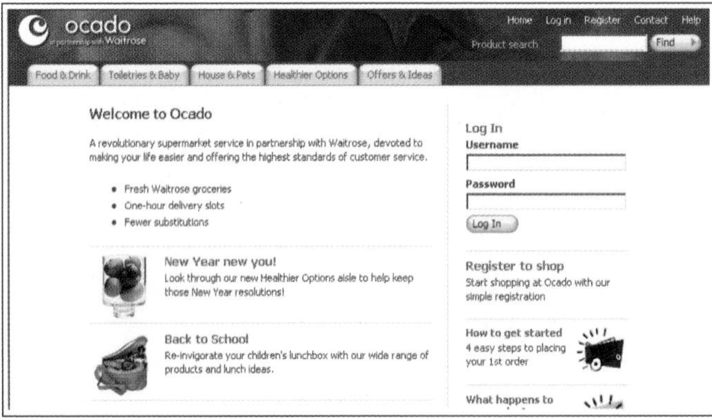

Figure 12.3 Ocado

Source: **http://www.ocado.com**. By permission of Ocado Limited.

The difference online is that customers cannot tangibly evaluate the physical space of the shop or office concerned (Reichheld and Schefter, 2000). Images and promises are all that they have, and if they do not trust the company concerned, they will shop elsewhere. Moreover, when a customer does trust an online company, he/she is more likely to share personal information, and this information can be used by the company to form a more intimate relationship by providing bespoke goods and services. Amazon.com has come to dominate the online book business by creating one of the most reliable and trustworthy of B2C sites. Customers, in their millions, allow Amazon to store their names, addresses, and credit card details so that they can then make repeat purchases with just the click of a mouse. If customers did not trust Amazon to protect their personal details and data, its dominance of the business would be threatened.

Customer relationship marketing (CRM) is a leading example of using information in a smart way. The basis of CRM is to use the information from previous encounters and transactions to influence subsequent encounters and transactions with the same customer. For example, in financial services Fidelity uses CRM strategies to cross-sell a wide range of products to the same customer. 'Event-oriented prospecting' is increasing in importance as an information strategy based on anticipating a customer's life-cycle or other situational needs. Thus, USAA Insurance automatically directs information on driver education (and insurance) to clients with teenagers about to receive their licences.

Related to the issue of trust is the lack of customer focus online. Websites can cost enormous sums to set up, manage, and update, and so to recoup costs too many companies are tempted to appeal to a broad audience. If a company fails to focus, it ends up with an enormously complex website which has to cater to different skills, contents, and service requirements and different levels of price sensitivities. Sites become hard to load and customers rarely return, despite the often widespread early interest.

Focus is the key to loyalty. The Vanguard Group is a good example of a successfully focused site. It was the fastest growing mutual fund company in the USA in the 1990s. It concentrates on a particular kind of person—long-term investors who want low-cost and low-churn index fund investing.

The Web offers companies unprecedented ways of segmenting by observing customer behaviour. For example, people who exit when the price screen appears are probably price sensitive and those who jump from page to page are probably frustrated and unable to find what they want. Basically, the fixation on Web capacity and building visitor counts means that many companies are missing opportunities to sell, cross-sell, and upsell by carefully observing how customers behave.

AOL is a good example of a company that carefully monitors customer behaviour. When it upgraded its software from version 3 to 4 it analysed the key drivers of customer loyalty. Finding that customers were more likely to maintain their accounts when they used AOL as part of their daily routine, they enhanced the software's calendar, scheduling functions, and stock-portfolio tracking capabilities.

One related issue facing bricks and mortar businesses is whether to split off a Web business from the traditional one. In the short run it might be lucrative, but in the longer term it is likely to erode customer loyalty. Customers do not see such differences as tangible, instead they view the holistic company experience. The website must be plugged into the full range of existing corporate capabilities. Take the case of Home Depot, a successful US DIY store. Its website does not cater for everyone. Small contractors form the core of Home Depot's business, and its website focuses on serving their needs better. Contractors can use the website to monitor the progress of their orders. Thus, the website is helping to build loyalty rather than gain new business. The key is to use technology to enhance the customer experience (see Mini Care Study 12.2).

Customization

Customization involves being able, and willing, to change behaviour towards a customer based upon what they tell you, and what you already know about them, and is central to differentiation in e-marketing (Pingjun, 2002 and see also one-to-one marketing: Peppers et al., 1999). E-markets can get smarter with each transaction and increasingly customize their offerings to a customer. Eventually, even if a rival has the same capabilities, a customer is unlikely to defect, as he/she would have to teach a rival everything already learnt by the first seller. National Bicycles provides a good e-marketing example of customization. Customers sit on a smart bike at a dealer's showroom that takes their height, weight, length of leg, etc. This information is relayed to the factory where a customized bike is manufactured in three minutes. For example, Motorola's Pager Division guides telephone customers through a menu of 30 million permutations. There are four key steps to customization: (1) identify your customers; (2) differentiate them; (3) interact with them; and (4) customize your product to fit their needs. The following section will examine each of these in turn.

Identifying customers requires being able to locate and contact a number of customers directly, or at least a large chunk of the most valuable ones, and understand their behaviour. This involves habits and preferences as well as the obvious addresses, phone numbers, and so on, which must be logged at every contact point. This might mean hiring an outside service for scanning or data entry, drip-irrigation dialogue with customers (asking only one or two questions each transaction) and a periodic review of the integrity of the list.

A differentiation strategy via customization requires differentiating customers by recognizing their different levels of value and needs. This is invaluable for deciding on the best e-marketing strategy in any given situation. People will do business with sites that make their lives easier, and are prepared to pay a premium for this. Of course, this does not mean that they do not care about price—simply that they are prepared to trade it off against convenience. Brand choice influences another large group of customers on the Web and, like the convenience seekers, these customers also are looking for longer-term stability in their exchanges on the Web.

E-marketing enables customers to become co-producers (or more correctly co-designers of products and services). In this respect, according to Slywotzky (2000) the future of e-marketing customization belongs to the 'choiceboard'. Choiceboards are online systems that interact with customers so that they can design their own goods and services from a menu of features. Instead of having to haggle over the price of fixed product lines, the Internet changes commerce and enables consumers to describe exactly what they want. Furthermore, suppliers are able to deliver bespoke goods and services without compromise or delay.

MINI CASE STUDY 12.2 'Yahoo Advances into Traditional Territory'

According to Terry Semel, technological change in the media industry used to be smooth, a periodic transition that did not alter the skills needed to succeed in the business: creating great content and assembling a mass audience.

The internet, though, is different. Search, e-mail, blogging and other interactive technologies are changing the relationship between a media company and its audience, and put a premium on command of technology.

'To be a media business, technology is in the core—it's what you must excel at,' the Yahoo chairman and chief executive said earlier this month at the Web 2.0 conference in San Francisco. 'I don't think you can be one without the other: you have to be great at both.'

Under Mr Semel, Yahoo has gone further than any other internet company to define what a new media company should look like. It is, he admits, a work in progress: but with its global audience growing by about 25 per cent a year and revenues increasing by 50 per cent, it is a model that has turned heads. That is particularly the case now that Yahoo has started to produce video and written news and entertainment that in some ways rivals that of the big traditional media groups.

Mr Semel is in no doubt about what it took to bring 379 m unique users to Yahoo's 'network' during the second quarter of this year. 'Everywhere you go in Yahoo, whether it's autos or sport, it's all content,' he said. Delivering more and better content is central to his goal of persuading users to return more often and stay longer. Yahoo generates revenues of only 78 cents per user each month, a figure it hopes to increase by building loyalty.

Yahoo has long used unique content to attract users, even if the internet company produced little of that itself. User-generated material, from personal ads to discussions in chat rooms, has always been core to the 10-year-old portal, along with material aggregated from around the internet. Expanding the reach of its user-generated content, Yahoo recently bought Flickr, a photo-sharing site, and last week acquired Upcoming.org, a social events calendar relying on contributions from users.

The internet company is now producing more of its own content.

In the past month it has launched a series of online columns from financial commentators and begun a one-man news site, called Kevin Sites in the Hot Zone, that combines video news, photos and blogging to report from trouble spots around the world.

In another incursion into old media territory, the portal has tried out distributing shows originally made for television, including taking over a music show, called Pepsi Smash, that was dropped from the air after failing to attract a big enough audience.

Ventures such as these add to a giant experiment in the potential of the interactive medium, according to Mr Semel. 'I don't want to wait 10 years while others experiment with what is the way,' he said.

Source: Richard Waters (2005), *Financial Times*, 18 October, p. 17.

Choiceboard technology is evidenced by Dell's online configuration, Mattell's 'My Design Barbie', and Schwab's mutual fund evaluator. However, the full implications of such technology have yet to be grasped. To lock a customer into a relationship a company must adapt some aspect of its behaviour to meet the customer's needs, such as with mass customizing. A key point is that choiceboards collect precise information about consumer preferences which will enable companies to continually monitor and increase their knowledge and understanding of consumer needs and preferences. Such knowledge can be used to customize the choiceboard interface as well as to potentially point the way for the evolution of entire product lines. Competitors, without matching knowledge, will find it hard to compete with choiceboard players. Furthermore, choiceboards act as magnets for suppliers who appreciate accurate information about demand and preferences.

Three kinds of choiceboard competitor will develop. Companies like Dell and Schwab are the first kind—individual manufacturers. Secondly, consortia of companies will emerge such as MetalSite (a choiceboard launched by a group of leading US metals producers). However, the most threatening kind will be intermediaries. Choiceboards are simply design tools so they need not be controlled by producers. Thus, Point.com uses a choiceboard to help consumers find and buy mobile phones, service plans, and accessories, but does not make anything it offers. Intermediaries are likely to be particularly effective in industries where producers have failed to develop choiceboards.

Communities

A number of consumer goods companies are trying to develop 'community brands' which enable consumers to communicate with each other. Thus Tizer, the soft drink brand, revamped its website **www.tizer.co.uk** to target 13- to 15-year-old boys, aiming to create a 'hangout' zone for teenagers. Visitors to the site can 'stitch up' their friends in Spoof Central, take part in a viral fist fight in Superhero Slam, and place messages on noticeboards. All data from the viral games and prize draws are captured and stored for future marketing initiatives, including e-mail campaigns. The aim is to build differentiation through relationships.

Other leading examples include (McWilliam, 2000), Bosch (**www.boschtools.com**), Pentax (**www.pentax.com**), and Shell (**www.shell.com**) with their forums and discussion groups and Heineken (**www.heineken.com**) with its virtual bars and Nescafé (**http://connect.nescafe.com**) with it virtual café. Will such communities reinforce brands and how willing are consumers to participate?

User groups, of course, have been around for years, especially in B2B markets like banking, insurance, and real estate. Outside of B2B, enthusiasts have formed a variety of clubs, especially around car and motor cycle marques (most notably Harley-Davidson). In Harley's case some of the independent Harley clubs threatened the image of the company and so it formed the official Harley Owners Groups (HOGS). While spontaneous and independently formed user groups pose a risk, they offer a number of attractions. Such groups can be contacted for opinions on things like new designs, product enhancements, and for product tests. As well, they can act as important opinion leaders.

Two leading forms of online communities have emerged (and may coexist): (1) real-time 'chat rooms', and (2) asynchronous discussions that take place over days, weeks, or months. The great thing is that these exchanges provide brands with free content and consumers appreciate the ability to meet like-minded people. The content and exchanges act like magnets and draw people back frequently and regularly. Tools using fuzzy logic, neural networking, and standard statistical analyses (**www.artificial-life.com**) can turn such electronic discussions into useful managerial information.

There are two points of view to successful community sites—the participants and the managers. From the consumer perspective one key aspect is that a site should provide a forum for the exchange of common interests. Women's portal iVillage UK (**www.ivillage.co.uk**) has launched an online campaign in conjunction with Tesco to help parents locate missing children. The online campaign includes live chat sessions with figures closely involved in missing persons campaigns. iVillage UK also added a dedicated missing children discussion board to its site, interviews with the families of missing children and features on topics including child-snatching and support organizations.

Consumers like sites that provide a 'physical sense' of space with set codes of behaviour. It must be a community where people easily grasp what is on offer, what the community norms are, and what is expected of them. Additionally, sites need to promote dialogues and relationships that flow casually and colloquially as in face-to-face contact. Finally it is important to encourage participation by everyone. Too often communities fall into the hands of cliques who dominate the conversation, act as gatekeepers to 'outsiders', and leave most people simply reading the messages rather than participating.

From a managerial perspective, the first requirement is to attract people to the site. Some product groups, like power tools and photography, benefit from their high involvement status and have less trouble attracting people. Other product groups may not be so lucky, so another approach is to focus on associated interests. For example, Disney offers bulletin boards to parents on such issues as health and education and Canada's Molson brewery (**www.molson.com**) attracts ice hockey fans with information and gossip. However, first mover advantage occurs with such sites as there are only so many associated interest sites that are viable. Thus, both Heinz (**www.heinzpet.com**) and Purina (**www.ivillage.com/pets**) have launched pet owner sites and probably either one or the other will dominate.

Another issue for managers is that large communities can lose intimacy, so sub-segments might be encouraged. The problem is that thousands of members simply 'lurk' and do not participate, so a large community may be needed to produce the critical mass of exchange. One thorny issue is whether or not there should be links to other sites. Such links might interest the community, but are they in the brand's interest? Allied to this is the extent to which the brand should control content. The difficulty is that the brand's personality could be adversely affected by 'ugly' comments.

Anonymity is a thorny issue for managers. It is known that some brands use their own moderators to pose as members of the public. Furthermore, members of the public often create false identities for themselves in chat rooms. Rigorous policies need to be set to ensure integrity and quality.

Overall, a new set of skills are needed for managers of online communities. In particular it is necessary to provide leadership and to motivate and reward volunteers in the community and provide them with the right electronic tools. New content needs to be continually developed to keep people's interest. The most difficult task is to link the community strategy to the brand strategy. This is the key challenge.

Global Issues

The World Wide Web has not proved to be as 'global' as was first anticipated (Guillén, 2002). Global standardization on the Web does not deliver the highest profits. For a start, telecommunications and Internet infrastructures differ markedly from country to country. International bandwidths vary considerably between countries, which greatly affects the speed of downloading pages. Websites often need redesigning for particular countries. Limited ownership of PCs and lack of access is another issue. Local costs are also important as many countries do not have flat-fee access rates.

Geographic distance may not be an issue for the Web, but it is for delivering products. It can cost up to £120.00 to deliver a £20.00 CD to certain destinations. Not surprisingly, nearly 50% of foreign orders placed with US websites are never shipped. It is not just distance—processing and restocking returned products can be problematic given the myriad cross-national consumer regulations across the world.

Another factor is that buyers like to purchase products in their own language. Translation objects and browser translation tools provide only partial fixes and do not compare to bespoke local websites. Most search engines and directories are country-specific and operate in one language only. E-business requires staff who are able to handle e-mails, faxes, and phone calls from people in a number of languages.

Buyer behaviour varies in such markets as leisure and entertainment, foodstuffs and clothing, and with such aspects as holidays and festivals. User characteristics vary too: for example, women make up only 10% of users across Latin America but close to 50% in North America or Europe.

E-commerce is largely dependent on the widespread use of credit cards. Even so, it can still prove a challenge in many countries that have a high usage of credit cards as distrust of using them on the Web can run very high, as in Japan. Thus 7-Eleven has established a store-wide system whereby Japanese customers can settle their e-commerce bills in person.

How to quote prices is also a problem. Successful US auction sites have found it hard to compete with local competitors in places like the UK, Germany, France, or Sweden where local currency sites dominate. Currency conversion engines help, but they often frustrate potential buyers. One other consideration is that the time lag between the order and processing often exposes e-businesses to currency risk.

National origin effect is a factor too. It is not very well understood, but it is becoming clear that consumers make judgements about websites partially on the origin of the site. This is particularly so for companies selling financial services or running auctions. However, for many branded goods the origin of the brand is likely to remain more important than the origin of the site.

Conclusion

E-marketing strategy is here to stay and will play an increasing role in both B2B and B2C marketing as it is increasingly doing in C2C as well. The Internet has not changed 'everything' but it has significantly affected industry structure, in particular by intensifying rivalry and empowering buyers. Many B2B markets for such products as forklift trucks have become close to commodity markets as e-marketing has developed. The key to successful e-marketing strategy is to compete effectively on reach, affiliation, richness, and range. Ultimately, the goal is to develop above-average performance through a sustainable competitive advantage. With e-marketing strategy, this is most likely to be achieved through some form of customization and/or development of a community.

Summary

E-marketing strategy is rooted in the classic elements of Porter's five forces and sustainable competitive advantage (SCA). Any e-marketing strategies should be based on businesses run like bricks and mortar companies using classic metrics like gross margin and size of order. However, to achieve e-marketing success it may often be necessary to mentally break down the current business model into its components, understand the new e-business models, and take some risks. Schwab famously reinvented itself when it halved its brokerage fees, committed to navigation as its core business, and started selling its competitors' products. For most companies, such change would be too big a gamble.

KEY TERMS

Internet Global network of computers enabling communication and the sharing of and access to information as well as the ordering and payment for products and the movement of digital products.

E-marketing The use of interactive and digital media to achieve objectives. Objectives may be embedded in strategy (e.g. Direct Line) or tactical (Ford).

Smart market A market based upon customization, the exchange of information, and constant monitoring of change.

Bricks and mortar An organization with a physical presence in the market.

E-tailer A retailer without a physical market presence.

Clickstream A series of mouse click choices between websites, often leading to a purchase and generating income for each mediator.

Hypermediation The series of mediations on a clickstream.

Navigation Steering between the mass and variety of information on the Internet.

Judo strategy Using the Internet strength of a market rival against itself.

Stickiness The degree to which a website holds the attention and clicks of a user.

Co-production The concept of enabling customers to co-design products and services.

Community A group who communicate with each other via a particular website.

DISCUSSION QUESTIONS

1 Evaluate the impact of e-marketing on Porter's traditional five forces analyses.
2 What has been the impact of e-marketing on sustainable competitive (SCA) analyses?
3 What factors might limit the success of an e-marketing judo strategy (i.e. turning a rival's size and strength against itself)?
4 To what extent do you agree with the proposition that e-marketing is more about differentiation than cost advantage?
5 Why is navigation central to developing SCA with e-marketing?
6 Do you agree with Slywotzky that the future of e-marketing customization belongs to the 'choiceboard'?

ONLINE RESOURCE CENTRE

Visit the Online Resource Centre for this book for lots of interesting additional material at: **www.oxfordtextbooks.co.uk/orc/west/**

REFERENCES AND FURTHER READING

Barsh, Joanna, Blair Crawford, and Chris Grosso (2000), 'How E-Tailing Can Rise From the Ashes', *McKinsey Quarterly*, 3, pp. 98–109.

Carr, Nicholas G. (2000), 'Hypermediation: Commerce as Clickstream', *Harvard Business Review*, Jan–Feb, pp. 46–7.

Day, George S., Adam J. Fein, and Gregg Ruppersberger (2003), 'Shakeouts in Digital Markets: Lessons from B2B Exchanges', *California Management Review*, 45 (2), Winter, pp. 131–50.

Evans, Philip and Thomas S. Wurster (1999), 'Getting Real About Virtual Commerce', *Harvard Business Review*, November/December.

Glazer Rashi (1999), 'Winning In Smart Markets', *Sloan Management Review*, Summer, pp. 59–69.

Guillén, Mauro F. (2002), 'What is the Best Global Strategy for the Internet?' *Business Horizons*, May–June, pp. 39–46.

Higson, Chris, and John Briginshaw (2000), 'Valuing Internet Businesses', *Business Strategy Review*, 11 (1), pp. 10–21.

McWilliam, Gil (2000), 'Building Stronger Brands Through Online Communities', *Sloan Management Review*, Spring, pp. 43–54.

Peppers, Don, Martha Rogers, and Bob Dorf (1999), 'Is Your Company Ready For One-To-One Marketing?', *Harvard Business Review*, January–February, pp. 151–60.

Pingjun, Jiang (2002), 'Exploring Consumers' Willingness to Pay For Online Customisation and its Marketing Outcomes', *Journal of Targeting, Measurement & Analysis for Marketing*, 11 (2), pp. 168–84.

Porter, Michael (2001), 'Strategy and the Internet', *Harvard Business Review*, March, pp. 63–78.

Reichheld, Frederick F., and Phil Schefter (2000) 'E-Loyalty: Your Secret Weapon On The Web', *Harvard Business Review*, July –August, pp. 105–113.

Rosenbloom, Bert (2002), 'The Ten Deadly Myths of E-Commerce', *Business Horizons*, 45 (2), pp. 61–6.

Shama, Avraham (2001), 'E-Coms and Their Marketing Strategies', *Business Horizons*, September–October, 44 (5), pp. 14–20.

Slywotzky, Adrian J. (2000), 'The Age of Choiceboard', *Harvard Business Review*, Jan–Feb, pp. 40–1.

Urban, Glen L., Fareena Sultan, and William J. Qualls (2000), 'Placing Trust at the Center of Your Internet Strategy', *Sloan Management Review*, 42 (1), pp. 39–48.

Wells, John D., and David H. Gobeli (2003), 'The 3R Framework: Improving E-Strategy Across Reach, Richness, and Range', *Business Horizons*, 46 (2), March–April, pp. 5–14.

Wheale, Peter R., and Amin L. Heredia (2003), 'Bursting the dot.com 'Bubble': A Case Study in Investor Behaviour', *Technology Analysis & Strategic Management*, 15 (1), pp. 117–37.

Wilcocks, Leslie P., and Robert Plant (2001), 'Pathways to E-Business Leadership: Getting From Bricks to Clicks', *MIT Sloan Management Review*, 42, Spring, pp. 50–9.

Wolfinbarger, Mary, and Mary C. Gilly (2001), 'Shopping Online for Freedom, Control and Fun', *California Management Review*, 43 (2), Winter, pp. 34–55.

Yoffie, David B., and Michael A. Cusumano (1999), 'Judo Strategy: The Competitive Dynamics of Internet Time', *Harvard Business Review*, January–February, pp. 70–81.

KEY ARTICLE ABSTRACTS

Brown, Mark, Nigel Pope, and Kevin Voges (2003), 'Buying or Browsing? An Exploration Of Shopping Orientations and Online Purchase Intention', *European Journal of Marketing*, 37 (11/12), pp. 1666–84. © Emerald Group Publishing Limited. **http://www.emeraldinsight.com**

This paper points out that shopping online is about more than convenience. Therefore, the marketing strategies of e-tailers need to take into account other factors affecting purchase intention such as whether the product or service had been previously purchased.

Abstract: Consumer selection of retail patronage mode has been widely researched by marketing scholars. Several researchers have segmented consumers by shopping orientation. However, few have applied such methods to the Internet shopper. Despite the widespread belief that Internet shoppers are primarily motivated by convenience, the authors show empirically that consumers' fundamental shopping orientations have no significant impact on their proclivity to purchase products online. Factors that are more likely to influence purchase intention include product type, prior purchase, and, to a lesser extent, gender. Findings indicate the existence of similar shopping orientations as in other retail spheres and a possible experience relationship with the intention to purchase. The authors suggest that the Internet is very similar to other forms of non-store retailing. There are challenges to online retailing and profitable Internet retailers are said to be among the minority. Rather than conceptualizing the Internet as a purely convenience-oriented patronage mode, retailers may be better served by taking a more holistic approach with their marketing strategies.

Varadarajan, P. Rajan, and Manjit S. Yadav (2002), 'Marketing Strategy and the Internet: An Organizing Framework', *Journal of the Academy of Marketing Science*, 30 (4), pp. 296–312.

This paper provides an assessment of the role of the Internet within marketing strategy. It examines the key drivers and outputs and points out that building relationships with customers is difficult on the Internet without offline contact.

Abstract: In a growing number of product markets, the competitive landscape has evolved from a predominantly physical marketplace to one encompassing both the physical and the electronic marketplace. This article presents a conceptual framework delineating the drivers and outcomes of marketing strategy in the context of competing in this broader, evolving marketplace. The proposed framework provides insights into changes in the nature and scope of marketing strategy; specific industry, product, buyer, and buying environment characteristics; and the unique skills and resources of the firm that assume added relevance in the context of competing in the evolving marketplace.

Hoffman, Donna L., and Thomas P. Novak (2000), 'How to Acquire Customers on The Web', *Harvard Business Review*, May–June, pp. 179–188.

This paper highlights CDNow's pioneering 'pay-for-performance' marketing strategy which has been emulated by the likes of Amazon.com, REL.com, Dell.com, and Barnesandnoble.com. CDNow offers a revenue-sharing arrangement with affiliated sites: when a customer clicks through from an affiliate's website to the CDNow website and buys a CD, CDNow gives 3% of the revenue from the sale back to the affiliate. In effect, CDNow has turned its affiliates into a virtual commissioned salesforce.

Abstract: Online retail companies, or e-tailers, are finding that it takes enormous marketing expenditures to acquire customers. For most of these companies, the average customer acquisition cost is higher than the average lifetime value of their customers. The authors studied online marketing for seven years, and note the success of music retailer CDNow. CDNow, currently the most powerful online music brand, was one of the first to develop a multifaceted, integrated customer acquisition strategy that reflects a sophisticated understanding of the economics of an online business. The company's BuyWeb programme was the first application of what has come to be known as 'affiliate' or 'associate' marketing programmes. CDNow currently acquires customers using its Cosmic Music Network, which allows unsigned artists to put up a Web page at the CDNow site. In addition, the company also uses radio, television, and print advertising, online advertising, strategic partnerships, word-of-mouth, free links, and public relations. As sophisticated as CDNow's strategy is, the company is finding that, over time, its pure CPM (the number of people who would see an advertisement) buys are disappearing. And this trend is likely to affect other e-tailers. CDNow's experience shows the power of the Internet as it applies to marketing, but it is impossible to say what the best marketing strategy is.

END OF CHAPTER 12 CASE STUDY Persil Gets Playful

Persil is seeking to create a real brand experience online to bond with consumers. Ounal Bailey tells Casper van Vark how detergent can be fun.

Scan the average internet user's favourites list and you'll probably find links to news, entertainment, jobs and travel sites and a currency converter. What you're less likely to find is a washing powder web site.

Although almost every FMCG brand of any kind has an online presence, few go far beyond a shop window, because it's hard to persuade consumers that there's a compelling reason to frequent the sites of products such as toothpaste, margarine or detergent. Although we use them every day, it's hard to get too excited about them.

For this reason, many FMCG brands have opted to 'own' a particular content sector online rather than try to sell a specific product. Pepsi has associated itself with music (**www.pepsi.co.uk**), Kit Kat with 'taking a break' (**www.kitkat.co.uk**) and Huggies with babycare (**www.huggies.com**). Last year, Lever Fabergé joined them with

» the relaunch of its Persil site (**www.persil.com**), changing it from a product-centric to a consumer-focused portal, as part of a £20m integrated TV, press and internet campaign. Persil's long-term digital agency, Modem Media, designed the site.

'We wanted to create a real identity online, making persil.com a hub of information and an online brand experience,' says Ounal Bailey, Persil brand activation manager at Lever Fabergé. The target user is what Persil refers to as 'progressive mums'—busy working mothers with children aged under 10, who have internet access both at home and work. Persil reckons that about half its target market has web access.

Whereas the site used to focus on product information, it now has two main sections: Time In and Time Out. 'We can put our hands up now and admit the old site wasn't a full consumer experience of the brand,' admits Bailey. 'What we had before was just the Time In section—time with the washing machine. The new area is about trying to build a bond with consumers and to show them that we understand what they want.'

Time Out is about lifestyle and the section is divided into time for yourself—relaxation, looking after your skin and diet—and time with the kids. The latter features an activity finder, tips on developing a happy family, and a Get Creative section that encourages artistic pursuits for the kids. 'Get Creative' is an integrated campaign, which aims to promote Persil alongside something important to parents—their children's creativity.

In May last year, the Persil 'Big Mummy' challenge saw 15,000 children's drawings of their parents transformed into one giant mosaic portrait, unveiled at London's Alexandra Palace. In October, an initiative called 'Persil Stars' was launched, continuing the link with kids' creativity, whereby stars could be collected from packs of Persil and exchanged for art materials for use in school. About £7 m worth of art supplies will be given away and teachers can register their schools for the project online.

'We have a core team of about six agencies that work together as a team on Persil,' says Bailey. 'This year we have run a great through-the-line campaign because, for example, Modem Media has worked alongside our offline ad agency, J Walter Thompson. When we have an ad, Modem takes elements from it to use online, so we have that overall consistency.'

However, not all Persil's online activity mirrors its offline work.

One of the features on the site, Messing about, is based on a monthly email newsletter, which goes out to about 75,000 people who have either signed up for it online or responded to earlier promotions. A modern version of the women's weekly staple of things to make and do, it has ideas on occupying kids with cooking, drawing or making silly masks. The email contains text and links, along with a 'make and do' feature at the bottom; for example, a pair of glasses to cut out and colour in.

Content is provided through partners such as IPC's Family Circle magazine, which doesn't have a web site. 'We use partnerships with third parties because we are a washing brand and not in the business of writing recipes,' says Bailey.

According to Modem Media, about 17 per cent of recipients click through to the Persil site, with figures rising as high as 24 per cent for some segments. Users who click through to the site spend 15 to 20 minutes there, although the emails are designed so that customers don't have to visit if they don't want to.

A branded Messing about application sits on partner sites such as Schoolsnet (**www.schoolsnet.com**) and **www.femail.co.uk**. Users can register for the email » and use the activity finder application. There are also 'stain solver' applications, which let users get advice on the removal of a range of stains.

'We've created applications that we've distributed to places where we would expect our consumers to go, so we're not expecting them to just visit our site,' says Bailey. 'We're not kidding ourselves—we are a detergent brand. The aim is for people to have the experience of Persil wherever they are. So there is a variety of places such as Tesco.com, iVillage, Schoolsnet and femail, where Persil now has a presence.'

This level of involvement in customers' lives is hard to imagine without the internet. It seems unlikely, for example, that Persil would have sent out 75,000 Messing about letters in the post every month or that it could have reached its consumers via other brands so readily if it wasn't for their web sites.

However, Camilla Ballesteros, marketing strategy director at Modem Media, says the brand was already forming relationships with its users and that the relaunch of the web site was an opportunity to take this further.

'Persil was becoming more customer-centric anyway, with the launch of "Get Creative" and "Big Mummy". We harnessed that online and added value.'

Persil has a number of sub-brands, such as Persil Capsules and Persil Silk & Wool, all of which are accommodated on the web site. When it launched a new sub-brand last year, Persil Aloe Vera, users were able to ask for samples online, which 46,000 did, making up one-third of all its sample requests.

'Persil Aloe Vera was a big launch last year. People see the ad on TV and wonder what else the product does, and they can't get much information from a 30-second ad. But they can get it online,' explains Bailey. Although the persil.com address was not advertised on the TV ads, visitors to the site still increased when they ran. Overall, traffic to persil.com has increased by 200 per cent since last year, according to Modem Media.

'Traffic went through the roof from the moment the TV ad went out,' says Ballesteros. 'It is because persil.com is an intuitive web address, which is a benefit. They could type in persil.com or co.uk and either way they'd get the Aloe Vera message. From the moment the ad went out, our traffic went up by about 10 times.'

When it comes to interactive TV, Persil was a trailblazer, but iTV is not a cornerstone of its e-marketing strategy. 'With Persil, we were the first to have an interactive quiz on iTV,' says Ballesteros. 'At that time it was incredibly successful, with a high response rate, but no one had ever done it before. What we're saying now is that we'll consider every digital medium, but we're not going to shoehorn a campaign into a medium just because it's digital.'

Bailey insists that the different media have to work together and that's why Persil's agencies co-operate to the extent they do. 'It's really important to have that synergy between different media. We don't look at one medium in isolation; it's the combination and how the consumer responds that's important.'

Another potential area for extending the brand could be a washing and cleaning service, which is an idea that Unilever has experimented with in the past. A separate Unilever scheme that used the Persil brand, called myhome, was initiated in 2000 but is not currently active, though the company is still looking at this area. 'There are some tests going on at the moment for a Persil service,' says Bailey. 'It isn't something that the core brand will go into at the moment, but we're looking at doing something with Sainsbury's.'

» All this added value on the internet makes it easy to forget that people do actually visit persil.com to get information on washing clothes. They can get the phone number of a careline and email their questions as well.

'Washing your clothes sounds really simple, but you'd be surprised what people don't know about getting their clothes clean and how many people use the site for that reason,' says Bailey. 'And the fact that we do what people want us to do means that we have a strong base on which to build. If you don't do the fundamental things right, then you can't go off and do the other things.'

Source: Casper Van Vark (2003), *Revolution*, 1 February.

QUESTIONS

1. To what extent would you agree with the proposition that Unilever treated the Internet as an *evolutionary* rather than *revolutionary* force?
2. Assess the degree to which the relaunched Persil site adhered to Porter's concept of tailoring for strategic advantage?
3. Can the profitability of the Persil site be measured and would it matter if it did or did not make a profit?

Part V Did we get there?

I. Introduction

1. Overview
2. Marketing strategy: analysis and perspectives

II. Where are we now?

3. Environmental and internal analysis: market information and intelligence

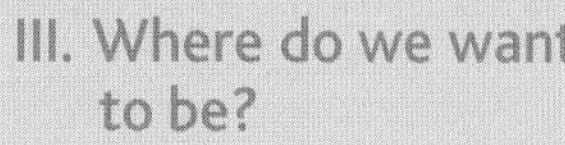

III. Where do we want to be?

4. Strategic marketing decisions and choices
5. Segmentation, targeting, and positioning strategies
6. Relationship strategies

IV. How will we get there?

7. Product innovation and development strategies
8. Branding strategies
9. Service marketing strategies
10. Pricing and distribution strategies
11. Marketing communications strategies
12. E-marketing strategies

V. Did we get there?

13. Strategy implementation and control

VI. Conclusion

14. Social marketing and CSR

13

Strategy implementation and control

LEARNING OBJECTIVES

- Understand the nature of managerial control in a marketing context
- Appreciate the importance of implementation of marketing strategy and why it is frequently the reason for organizational and strategic failure
- Conceptualize competitive advantage as an ongoing process that needs to be measured, managed, and controlled
- Calculate customer lifetime value as an outcome of a competitive advantage process
- Understand the notion of customer equity as a guiding objective for the evaluation of marketing strategy
- Recognize organizational culture as a factor that either helps or hinders the implementation of marketing strategy

CHAPTER AT A GLANCE

Introduction

Marketing management applies the four basic tasks of management, namely, planning, organizing, directing, and controlling to the marketing activities of an organization. Most marketing texts, and indeed marketing practitioners in their work, give considerable attention to the first of these three activities. They spend large amounts of time planning and formulating marketing strategy. They endeavour to direct the actions of marketing personnel, the salesforce, and channel intermediaries, and allocate substantial effort to the organization of marketing activities and human resources. Yet less time is given to the fundamental marketing task of controlling, and its related activity, implementation. As academics, consultants, and marketing practitioners devote more and more time and resources to the formulation of marketing strategy, there is every indication that in future a firm's marketing success will hinge not so much on having a good strategy, but on how well this strategy is implemented and controlled.

The managerial act of control involves three basic steps:

1. Set standards of performance (these are typically in the form of goals or objectives)
2. Evaluate the reality of what occurs against these steps
3. Take corrective or reinforcing action where required

These steps are illustrated in the simple marketing example in Figure 13.1. Let's assume a firm sets a market share objective of 25% (a standard), or step 1 in the control process. In the next step, the manager compares reality against the standard. In the third step, the manager takes either corrective or reinforcing action. If, as in the example, the market share achieved was only 15%, then the manager would need to correct whatever aspects of marketing strategy caused this to happen. On the other hand, if the market share really achieved was 35%, the manager would seek to reinforce whatever actions caused this to happen. As will be seen in the figure, control is a process rather than just a set of steps—the corrective and reinforcing step in turn becomes the source of information for the setting of subsequent standards. Of course, *time* is a critical issue in this regard. In reality outcomes may be either higher or lower than the target figure set, or the objective set established, so most astute managers usually assign a time frame to an objective, e. g., 'Our firm sets a market share objective of 25% to be achieved within a year'. Managers will then either monitor achievement against this standard on a monthly, quarterly, or annual basis (or whatever is deemed appropriate), and it is at this time that the control process and actions will be undertaken.

The act of implementation is the accomplishing of or carrying into effect—in other words, it is the executing of some plan or strategy. If marketing strategy formulation consists of 'thinking' about what will be done, then marketing strategy implementation consists of 'doing' it. When strategic marketing failures occur, it is usually strategy formulation that is blamed—managers say things like, 'Our strategy was wrong'. Too often they overlook the fact that there may have been nothing wrong with their strategy, but that the actual execution of this strategy was flawed. As one executive ruefully put it, 'Our thinking was right. But we did it wrong!' A classic case of this occurred in the United Kingdom in

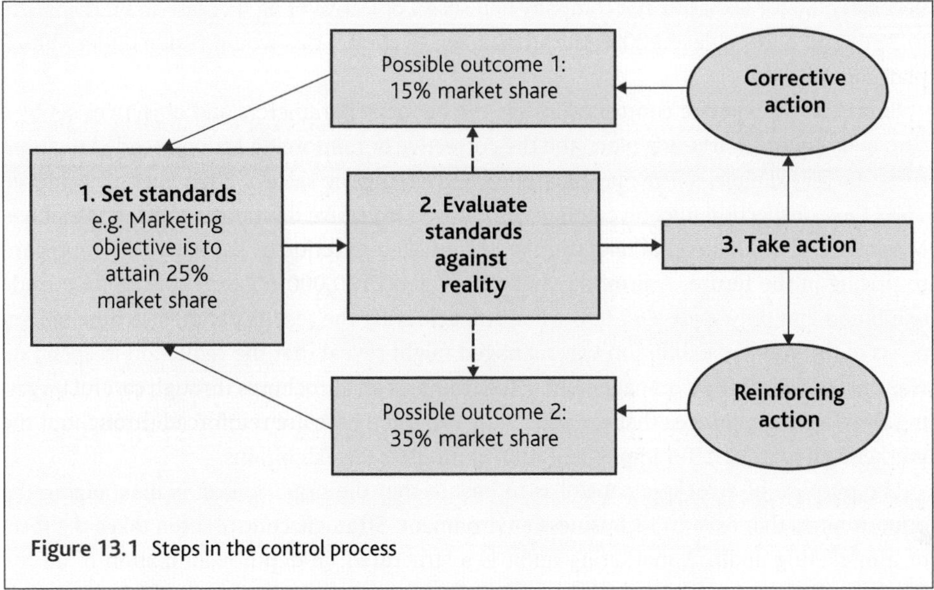

Figure 13.1 Steps in the control process

1995, when Hoover decided to do a sales promotion offering free flights on the purchase of certain products. While the strategy was fine in principle, in implementation it was a disaster that cost the company millions of pounds, as well as a serious loss of reputation. The company 'forgot' to exclude products that cost less than flights from the promotion, and also never made any arrangements to pre-book flights in anticipation of a good response to the promotion!

The following section will consider the task of control in marketing management in more detail. Then it will give greater attention to the implementation of marketing strategy and explore a simple, but powerful tool that permits a diagnosis of the strategy formulation–implementation dilemma. The chapter will also identify reasons why strategic marketing plans are not always implemented successfully in organizations. Next it will synthesize our thinking on the formulation, control, and implementation of marketing strategy by using a well-known framework that considers strategic advantage as a process. An examination of the outcomes of this process will be made as measurable indications of the success or otherwise of marketing strategy formulation and implementation. After giving attention to a particular measure that is regarded by many as the most important outcome of marketing strategy today, namely customer equity, the final part of the chapter will consider the 'people issues'—often referred to as corporate culture—within organizations that can either help or hinder the successful implementation of marketing strategy.

The nature of marketing control

It is useful to distinguish three kinds of control with regard to managing marketing:

Annual plan control looks at the objectives set in the annual marketing plan, evaluates these against the actual results achieved, and takes corrective or reinforcing action when necessary. So for example, if a company had set an objective of an increase in market share to 25%, and only achieved 20%, the steps taken to correct this would reside under annual plan control.

Financial or expense control considers the financial parameters and objectives set by a firm in its annual marketing plan, and the corrective or reinforcing actions needed to attain these. So for example, a firm may have budgeted a return on sales of 20%, but only achieved 15%. Close inspection may reveal that this is due to excessive discounting by the salesforce. Management would need to take steps to ensure less discretion by salespeople with regard to pricing in the future. A firm may have budgeted £100,000 for expenditure on a trade exhibition, but only spent £80,000 while still achieving the results planned. A detailed analysis of the way the exhibition was managed might reveal that the reduction in spending was due to the judicious management of free samples and brochures through careful targeting. Management ensures that the procedures adopted here are reinforced throughout the marketing department for implementation at future trade exhibitions.

The purpose of **strategic** control is to ensure that the organization is maximizing the opportunities that exist in its business environment. Strategic control often takes the form of a marketing audit. A marketing audit is a structured, in-depth examination of all the firm's marketing activities, which identifies those areas of marketing in which the firm is not performing to full potential, as well as those in which the firm is doing well. In order to ensure objectivity, many firms will choose to employ outside consultants to conduct a marketing audit.

Implementation of marketing strategy

It has already been mentioned that many corporate marketing strategies fail not because the formulation of the strategy was faulty, but because the strategy's implementation was less than effective. Most organizations, and most marketing management teams today, spend an inordinate amount of time and effort on the formulation of marketing strategy, which often ensures excellent strategy. Yet the downfall occurs when this strategy is poorly implemented. In simple terms, implementation is the 'doing' of marketing strategy, the putting into action of all that carefully considered and creative marketing thinking.

The problem with poor implementation of strategy is that it is difficult to diagnose. This dilemma was recognized some years ago by Harvard Business School marketing professor Tom Bonoma (Bonoma, 1984). Bonoma suggested that marketers consider two aspects of their strategy when diagnosing (or indeed, controlling for) its success or failure, which are mapped in the grid in Figure 13.2.

On one dimension, the grid in Figure 13.2 considers strategy formulation—which can range from poor to adequate. On the other dimension, the grid considers strategy implementation, which again can range from poor to adequate. Managers should use the grid to think about the formulation of their own marketing strategy, and its implementation. When strategy is well formulated, and well implemented, then it is likely that **success** will follow. Similarly, when strategy is poorly formulated, and also poorly implemented, then, not surprisingly, it generally results in **failure**. It is when one of the other two situations on the

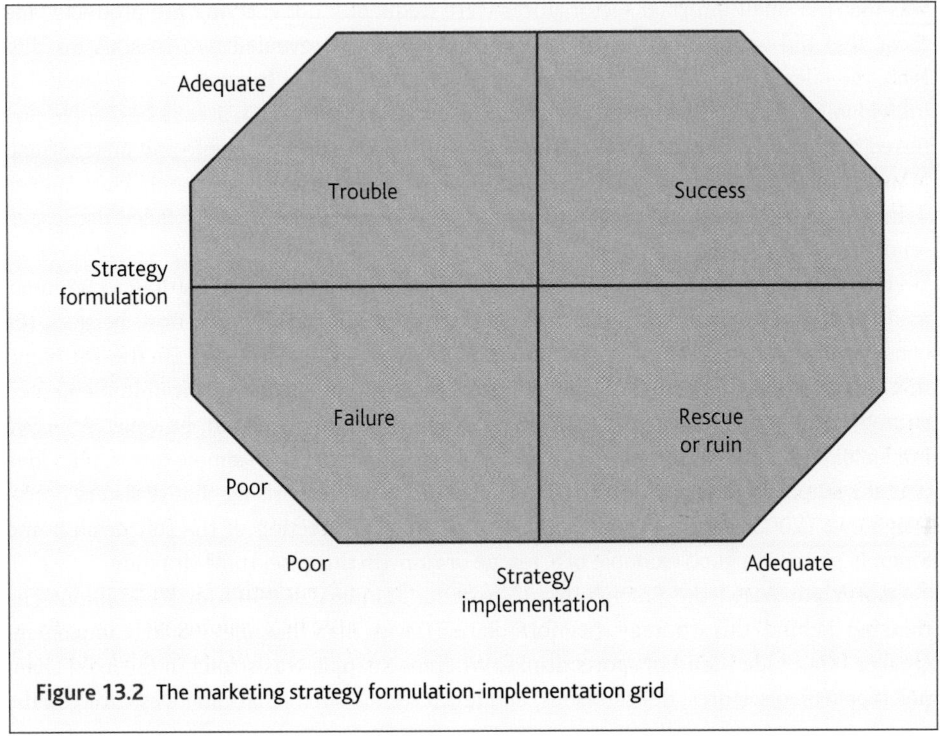

Figure 13.2 The marketing strategy formulation-implementation grid

diagonal in the grid in Figure 13.2 occurs that marketing managers are faced with a real dilemma.

Strategy that is adequately formulated but poorly implemented, according to Bonoma, leads to **trouble**. This is because, very often, poor results will be blamed on the strategy, not on its implementation. 'Our strategy was wrong,' managers will say, 'We shouldn't have done that.' In reality, what they might be saying after a little introspection should be something like, 'We had the right strategy, but we implemented it poorly'. For example, a major consumer goods marketer in Brazil recognized that while they were poor, the consumers in Rio de Janeiro's *favelas* (hillside slums) represented an attractive market segment for inexpensive but high-quality products that the firm was able to supply. The marketing team formulated a strategy that involved designing innovative new products targeted at this market, paying particular attention to issues like packaging (products needed to be portable, durable, and storable). They were also able to price the product range affordably. An innovative approach to promotion involved a tie-up with a popular local soccer team, which produced good results in market research. In order to distribute the products, the firm would rely on the many informal neighbourhood stores (many of which were run from people's homes) that served the slum areas, rather than on large supermarkets that were often far from the consumers.

Six months after the implementation the results in the target market were most disappointing. Rather than simply blame the strategy, the marketing director tasked his team with an in-depth analysis of the entire effort and its implementation. What was discovered was that the small informal sector stores were frequently not carrying the products, and those that did were often out of stock. Further analysis revealed two reasons for this. First, the sales team seldom visited the stores concerned, either because they believed that individually, the small stores didn't matter, or because they were in areas salespeople preferred not to enter. Secondly, deliveries to the stores were unpredictable and intermittent. Many of the *favelas* are situated on steep hillsides, and truck drivers simply chose not to deliver to them because this was difficult. So, a good marketing strategy failed because of implementation issues.

Finally strategy that is poorly formulated but well implemented, according to Bonoma, leads to **rescue or ruin**. This is a particularly complex situation for a firm, because the consequences can frequently be dramatic, and are mostly unpredictable. On the one hand, this situation can rescue a firm's poor marketing strategy, because a well-implemented strategy can overcome weaknesses in formulation. On the other hand, however, effective implementation of a bad strategy can hasten a firm's downfall—in simple terms, if an idea is really stupid, and you do it really well, it shouldn't be surprising that disasters occur! Deighton's (2002) article on the birth, demise, and resurrection of the soft drink brand Snapple provides a good example of a 'rescue or ruin' (in this case, ruin) situation.

Quaker purchased the Snapple brand from its founders in 1994 for $1.7 billion. The thinking behind this strategy (its formulation) was that Snapple would complement Quaker's Gatorade brand of sports drinks. Whereas Snapple was strong in the 'cold channel' (convenience stores, delicatessens, and lunch restaurants), Gatorade was strong in the 'warm channel' (supermarkets).

If Quaker's marketers had formulated their strategy more carefully, they would have realized that Snapple's success was built on certain key issues:

- **The theme of being 'natural':** While not a health drink, Snapple contained few additives, and was seen as an alternative to cola drinks. The 'natural' theme was enhanced through quirky advertising and the use of unconventional spokespersons for the brand, including 'shock jock' radio DJ, Howard Stern.
- **Snapple's range included dozens of different flavours,** some with rather bizarre mixes. While not all of these were successful in terms of sales, product development costs were very low, and the range of flavours made the product 'interesting' in the eyes of the market, and customers always wondered what the next amazing new Snapple flavour would be. The product was also packaged in heavy, chunky, glass bottles, not cans.
- **Snapple was sold at a premium price,** which consumers typically didn't perceive, as the beverage was usually purchased as part of lunch. So, rather than notice that they were paying $2 or $3 for a soft drink, consumers spent $8 on 'lunch', which would typically include a sandwich, and a Snapple.

When it was sold through the 'warm channel', Snapple's new marketing strategy quickly unravelled. In order to cut costs, Quaker ceased the 'natural' and quirky promotional theme, including getting rid of Howard Stern, who had his revenge by calling the product 'Crapple' on his radio show. Supermarkets do not tolerate lots of different product variations, so the Snapple range was ruthlessly pruned, which caused the brand to lose its consumer interest factor. Consumers who considered purchasing Snapple in a supermarket quickly realized that a six-pack of bulky glass bottles was heavy and difficult to carry. Furthermore, when they were buying Snapple in isolation and in comparison to other soft drinks, they also recognized it was expensive—something they had overlooked when they had purchased it as a component of 'lunch'. Gatorade also did not sell well in the cold channel—consumers did not want to drink a sports drink with their tuna mayonnaise on rye sandwich.

Quaker had implemented its Snapple strategy ruthlessly and well. The problem was that the strategy's formulation had been exceptionally poor. So poor in fact that the Snapple brand was sold off to a company called TriArc for $400 million in 1997: a brand equity write-off of $1.3 billion. Not a rescue situation in this case, but very much of a ruin.

In summary, according to Bonoma (1984), marketing managers trying to put marketing strategies into practice often confront structural and personnel problems. Therefore a poor implementation often obscures the effectiveness or ineffectiveness of the marketing strategy itself, so marketing practices should be examined before adjustments are made. The structural problems of marketing involve marketing functions, programmes, systems, and policy directives. Marketing functions often fail because of faulty management assumptions or inattention to marketing basics, while programmes are often contradicted by lack of functional capabilities or insufficient management attention. Systems are limited by errors of ritual and politicization, and marketing policies regularly suffer from lack of a marketing theme and culture. However, good interaction, allocation, monitoring, and organization skills can overcome poor marketing practices.

Why are marketing strategies not implemented well?

The effective implementation of marketing strategy seems an obvious issue: if a firm spends so much time and so many resources on the formulation of good marketing strategy, why wouldn't it implement it well? The clear answer is that it is easier to develop a strategy than to implement one. In too many organizations, marketing strategy is implicit and resides only in the minds of senior marketers. These individuals may have trouble verbalizing their strategy, so most of the other people in the marketing function are therefore forced to guess what the strategy is, and they may guess wrong. Marketing executives who develop their strategy in isolation leave other people without ownership of the strategy and no understanding of the rationale behind it. As many members of the marketing function as possible should be involved in developing a strategy to achieve accurate understanding and proper execution. A good strategic marketing process will help management identify and proactively manage the implications of the strategy for the organization's products, markets, customers, and structure. There are a number of barriers to the implementation of strategy according to Robert (1991) that deserve brief consideration.

The marketing strategy is implicit, not explicit, and people cannot implement what they do not know: when strategy resides in the head of the senior marketing executive, others in the marketing department are forced to guess what it is—and they may guess wrong. This may be referred to as 'strategy by groping' because the strategy only becomes clear over a long period of time, as people test what the strategy might be by trial and error. The lesson from this is, make the marketing strategy explicit!

The marketing strategy is developed in isolation—and people cannot implement what they do not understand: often marketing strategy is developed by a senior marketer or a few senior marketing executives, usually at a retreat at some exclusive resort. Others in the firm, and especially the marketing function, feel divorced from the marketing strategy, and also do not understand it. The lesson here is: involve as many people as possible in the formulation of marketing strategy in order to achieve accurate understanding and proper execution.

Not everyone is a good strategic marketing thinker: many people within the marketing function are involved in day-to-day marketing activities. So they do not spend much time thinking strategically, and have difficulty coping with strategic issues, especially when these are sprung on them. If they are encouraged to understand the differences between strategic processes and everyday operational marketing issues, they will be better able and more willing to implement the formulated marketing strategy. Here the lesson is to encourage the participation of key marketing subordinates in strategy formulation, even if only for its educational value.

The marketing strategy is developed by an external consultant: many firms employ consultants to formulate their marketing strategy for them. While there are roles for consultants in organizations, including conducting marketing audits, conducting research, and other specialist advice, the formulation of marketing strategy is not one of them. The problem caused by having an external consultant(s) formulate marketing strategy is that most members of the marketing function are not committed to this strategy because it is not their strategy! By engaging external consultants to formulate marketing strategy, firms lose out on the commitment that comes from participation. At worst, this will often lead to so-called 'white-anting', where people actively work against and sabotage a strategy that they perceive to be someone else's. The answer is not to use external consultants to formulate marketing strategy—people will not implement a strategy to which they are not committed.

The marketing strategy has unanticipated consequences: when formulating strategy, many marketers do not think it through carefully enough to be able to foresee all the implications the strategy might have. When the strategy is then implemented, many people who initially supported it begin to say things like, 'If we'd known that would happen, we wouldn't have supported it.' A good strategic marketing planning process will anticipate, identify, and proactively manage the implications of a marketing strategy on the organization's products and services, markets, customers, organizational structure, and personnel. Therefore, identify strategic implications beforehand so that people do not give up on a strategy whose repercussions have not been foreseen. (See Mini Case Study 13.1.)

MINI CASE STUDY 13.1 Totally Teen—a new magazine

Avril Hewlett and Delta Hatfield locked the door to Delta's office, took the phone off the hook, and settled down to what both anticipated to be an exhausting afternoon's work that would take them long into the evening. They were in the final stages of completing the marketing strategy for a new magazine, to be called *Totally Teen*, a product of the Argonaut International Publishing Company. As could be expected from the fact that they both played different roles with regard to the new product—Hewlett had been » appointed editor and Hatfield Vice-President, Marketing—their views on how best to target the market for the publication differed considerably.

'I promise to leave content to you!' Hatfield said, 'I think you have great ideas that will make TT a winner. But I have done a lot of research. I think I know the market, and how we can go about making this a success.' Throwing her arms into the air, Hewlett said, 'Shoot! You know what you're doing. We're on the same team. I want to hear what you've got to say, and I want to work with you.'

Totally Teen was to be targeted at teenage girls in the 14–17 age group. Its content would consist of articles and photo-spreads covering issues of interest to teenagers, including music and the movies, fashion, beauty and healthcare, gossip and stories about celebrities, and advice on friendships, relationships, and romance. What made the magazine unique was that it would carry no advertising. As Hewlett said, 'When a girl buys 50 pages of *Totally Teen*, she gets what she's paid for—50 pages of great content. We will carry some paid-for messages, for example, an article on new Nike products that will be exclusive to Nike, and for which they will pay us. But we have the right to refuse copy we don't like; in fact we will do the writing and the editing. And when we do that we will make sure the readers know that it is paid-for editorial—or what is sometimes known as "Advertorial". What they won't find is endless pages of broadcast advertising that simply make the magazine bulkier and more difficult to read.'

Revenue would come from subscriptions and sales, with a minor contribution coming from advertorial. Delta Hatfield summarized her proposed strategy for Hewlett: 'My aim is to tie in a really solid subscription base, rather than to rely on sales from newsagents, book stores, convenience stores, and so forth. Ideally I want to sell two million subscriptions in our first year, even if I have to discount them very heavily. I want to give incentives to girls not only to subscribe, but in subscribing to tell us a lot about themselves. Obviously we will have to get their names and addresses if we are going to mail them the magazine, but I also want to know their ages, their interests and hobbies, their tastes and preferences. That way we can build a better product for them, and help you and your team produce the content they will love to read. As far as I see it, any sales above that—off the shelf from newsagents, convenience stores, and so forth—are just a bonus. But not a very dependable one—someone who buys this month, won't necessarily buy next. I won't even bring these into my calculations. I aim to concentrate on subscription sales exclusively.'

Hewlett nodded, 'I can see why that makes good sense. But how will you get them to subscribe in the first place? I love these kids, but they are fickle. Getting them to subscribe is one thing, getting them to subscribe again is another!'

'That's where Argonaut has really come to the party,' said Hatfield. 'They've agreed to eat distribution costs for five years, so it won't come off our budget or affect our profits. They will print invitations to subscribe and distribute them by mail, through schools where possible, at fashion retail outlets targeted at teens, and at other places where there are large concentrations of teenage girls, such as movie theatres, restaurants, malls, and some clubs. That won't cost us a cent.'

'Terrific! Where's the catch?' asked Hewlett. Hatfield grimaced. 'I thought you'd ask that! I agreed to cut subscription price in the first year by 50% to attract business. My research has shown that after the first year subscribers generally re-subscribe at a high rate, and that they are then far less sensitive to the price of the subscription.'

'Ouch! That means we hardly make money in the first year!' said Hewlett. 'That's true', said Hatfield, 'but the latest corporate thinking in Argonaut is that we shouldn't focus so much on short-term profits, as on customer lifetime value. Greg Moffat, the new finance director, is sold on the fact that investors are increasingly evaluating media and publishing companies by looking at the value of their customer base. So he wants us to manage the marketing of this new product by attempting to maximize the lifetime value of the subscribers.'

Hewlett stuck her fingers in her ears. 'Stop all this business school speak! I don't understand a word! I just write stories that kids want to read. Explain this to me in plain English, please!' she cried.

'OK, its not that difficult to understand. Let me do it using my proposed numbers for TT,' said Hatfield, 'so you can see whether they make sense at the same time. I think we agree we can get two million subscribers in the first year. Our annual subscription for 12 monthly issues will be $96, but we will discount that by 50% in the first year to attract subscriptions. Hopefully, the kids will love what you write, and tell their friends about it, so they'll all subscribe next year and be happy to pay $96. The numbers I've done with Greg suggest that our costs of producing the mag, including editorial, production, and mailing will run to about 40% of real selling price—in other words 40% of $96, or $38.40. Now comes the scary bit. The "life" of one of these kids as a customer is only four years, from 14 to 17—they start to read things like *Cosmo* after that, and grow out of things like TT. Also, the lapse rate is pretty high for publications like this—despite our best efforts, about 35% of our subscribers won't renew at the end of a year.'

'Why so high? We'll produce a really good mag,' said Hewlett. 'I know you will, Av,' said Hatfield. 'But that's the reality of it. First, there are the 17-year-olds who turn 18, and then grow out of it, so we lose about 25% of subscribers, just like that.' Hewlett interrupted: 'Yeah, but we replace them with 13-year-olds who turn 14. And why the other 10%?' Hewlett nodded patiently. 'Yes, you do replace them, but what we are interested in is the lifetime value of one of the original subscribers over a four-year period, so we have to take account of losing the 17-year-olds after only one year. As for the other 10%—as you call it—well that's kids who decide they really don't like the magazine, or they move away, or their parents stop paying for their subscription, or they just forget—or whatever. They just don't resubscribe. Its sad, but it's a fact of life in our business. Actually, I think we are being optimistic if we are only anticipating an additional 10% for that type of failure to resubscribe—in my previous job at Mirror Publishing we used to anticipate at least 20%, and that was for business magazines, which are far less fickle than publications for teenage girls.'

Hewlett fidgeted again, but Hatfield held her hand up in a 'Stop!' motion. 'Hold on. There's one more thing. Greg insists that we discount the net cash flows we get from our subscribers by 20% annually. That is the Internal Rate of Return Argonaut uses to assess new investments, and as we are looking at this investment in the new mag in the same way, we have to apply it.'

'What on earth is that for? Another cheap accounting trick?' exclaimed Hewlett. 'You business types do these things just to confuse us with your gobbledygook.'

'It's to allow for the time value of money,' said Hatfield. 'A dollar's worth of subscription four years from now is not worth a dollar today. So we have to discount future cash flows, and the 20% discount rate allows us to do this.'

'Spare me,' retorted Hewlett. 'I really don't want to know. But what you have said has got me thinking. I know of some ways we can change these numbers! We might be able to put the mag together in a way that will let it appeal to 13-year-olds as well. What if we put in a special effort so that 18-year-olds could be able to subscribe at a discount in their final year, as a "birthday present" for old times' sake? Also, Brenda Massey in our pop music section has been talking to that new label, Valiant Records, and they propose bundling a "Seasonal CD" with the mag four times a year, for only $4 extra, and it will only cost us 50 cents. And we could also. . .'

'Hold on, hold on!, you're going too fast for me! You're much more of a marketer than you said you are,' said Hatfield. 'Those are great ideas, and they will all impact on customer lifetime value. The great thing is Greg has put together a simple little Excel spreadsheet that will allow us to explore them, and see what effect they will have. Why don't we start there? That way we can think of different ways to maximize lifetime value, and see their effects.'

'I hate spreadsheets and I hate the word maximize,' said Hewlett. 'Why don't we have coffee instead?'

'No you don't, and you know this is important,' retorted Hatfield. 'Let's spend an hour or so on this and then it's a Grand Mocha Latte on me.'

Source: This case was prepared by Professor Leyland Pitt, Faculty of Business Administration, Simon Fraser University, as the basis for analysis and class discussion and not to illustrate either effective or ineffective handling of an administrative situation.

Managing competitive advantage as a process: implications for the control and implementation of marketing strategy

In an award-winning article Day and Wensley (1988) alerted us to the management of competitive advantage as a process, rather than as something static, or fixed, and hinting that the aspiration to a competitive advantage that was 'sustainable' was probably a pipe dream for most firms. Their model of the process of competitive advantage is shown in Figure 13.3.

Sources of competitive advantage

According to Day and Wensley (1988), there are only two sources of competitive advantage for a firm—it has either superior skills, or superior resources, and hopefully both. 'Superior skills' is a catch-all phrase for greater resources with regard to human talent, know-how, abilities, or competencies. Superior resources imply greater stocks of financial and other capital, better productive capacity, better location, access to supply and the like.

Positions of competitive advantage

These sources of competitive advantage are used to achieve one of two positions of advantage, or ways of competing. Following Michael Porter (1985), the authors identify two generic competitive strategies, namely the position of low cost, or differentiation. Supposedly the low-cost competitor is able to produce and deliver the product or service at the lowest

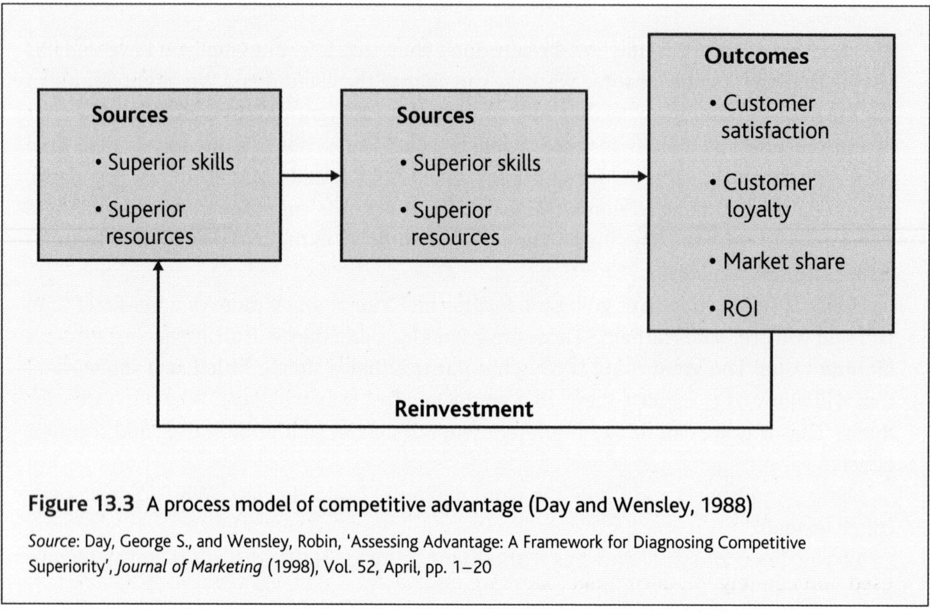

Figure 13.3 A process model of competitive advantage (Day and Wensley, 1988)

Source: Day, George S., and Wensley, Robin, 'Assessing Advantage: A Framework for Diagnosing Competitive Superiority', *Journal of Marketing* (1998), Vol. 52, April, pp. 1–20

cost, with the advantages of margin and pricing flexibility that this confers. For those competitors who are unable to achieve the low cost position, the only other course of action is to differentiate. That is to say, these competitors must make the product or service bigger, smaller, faster, more colourful, of better quality, superior in service, or in a bigger range than other suppliers. In short, they must differentiate their offerings in ways that the customer values and is prepared to pay for in order to compete successfully at best, and survive at least. (See Mini Case Study 13.2.) Porter (1985) implies that the two strategies are mutually exclusive and that to attempt to be a low-cost differentiator is to court the disaster of being stuck in the middle—having increased costs without real differentiation. While that might have been true for the late 1970s and early 1980s, more recently developments such as flexible manufacturing technologies have made these choices less clear-cut. Indeed, recent examples of firms such as Dell and Amazon.com might mean that it may not only be desirable to strive after both positions, but in many situations be the key to survival and success.

MINI CASE STUDY 13.2 **KDC and the Termin8or launch**

Harry Millbury, chief executive of KDC (Pvt) Ltd, thought that 1999 would be the firm's best year ever. As it turned out, for the first time in 12 years, sales had flattened, and profits were down. 'We had been going only one way, and that was up,' Millbury said. 'While the competition was slowly catching up, we were still well ahead. The Termin8or was the most radical product to hit this market in twenty years—it should have revolutionized the business. We had spent countless hours planning our overall strategy, and the marketing strategy for the Termin8or in particular. On paper the plans were perfect. We had left nothing to chance. Now we are looking at dreary sales results, and the Termin8or seems glued to the salesroom floors.'

KDC was a world leader in kiln-descaling equipment and methods. With its head office in Bradford in the United Kingdom, the firm sold and serviced kiln-descaling equipment all over the world, and was a multi-million pound sterling firm with branch offices and operations in Western Europe (Germany); Allentown, Pennsylvania in North America; Newcastle, Australia; Recife, Brazil; and Vereniging, South Africa. The only region of the world where the firm did not have a strong presence was Asia, although its Australian office did serve some customers in that market. However, as Millbury remarked, 'The Termin8or was our first class ticket into the Asian market—there is nothing quite like it, and nothing on the horizon. It is such a superior product that it should run rings around alternatives.'

Kilns, furnaces, and scaling

A kiln is an oven that is used for hardening, burning, or drying anything. Kilns have been used for converting wood into charcoal or to dry green timber so that the timber can be used immediately. Modern timber kilns are also partially depressurized to speed the drying process and reduce fuel usage. Kilns are also used to chemically refine clay objects by heating them until a crystaline matrix of silica and alumina forms, to make them hard and durable. This process is simply referred to as 'firing'. Clays contain aluminium and magnesium silicates which will degrade under high temperatures leaving oxides of aluminium, magnesium, and silica, which can form glass at high temperatures.

A kiln is required to come to a high temperature, and so the design of the ovens normally focuses on insulation, and the ability to add fuel over a course of time. Care must be taken not to heat the kiln too rapidly or to too high a temperature. Products such as cement are produced nowadays in huge rotary kilns that turn out many hundreds of tons a day.

A furnace is a device for heating air or any other fluid. Industrial furnaces are used for many things, such as the extraction of metal from ore (smelting) or in oil refineries and other chemical plants, for example as the heat source for fractional distillation columns. A blast furnace is a type of furnace for smelting whereby the combustion material and ore are supplied with air from the bottom of the chamber such that the chemical reaction does not take place only at the surface. A common example of this is the use of a blast furnace for the production of pig iron from iron ore.

Blast furnaces remains an important part of modern iron production. Modern furnaces include cowper stoves to pre-heat the blast air to high temperatures in order to avoid cooling (and thus having to re-heat) the mix, and use fairly complex systems to extract the heat from the hot carbon dioxide when it escapes from the top of the furnace, further improving efficiency. The largest blast furnaces produce around 60,000 tons of iron per week, enough for about four cars per minute.

Most modern kilns and furnaces are lined with special refractory bricks that can withstand the extreme temperatures required to melt ores and cause the chemical reactions needed to produce various products and raw materials. Over time kilns and furnaces build up scum or scale, which reduces their efficiency, and this scale, or plaque, which is usually very hard, needs to be removed regularly. Because refractory bricks also degrade over time, they also need to be replaced, usually on a maintenance schedule.

Kiln-descaling technologies

Originally, kilns and furnaces were descaled manually, using tools such as pickaxes. This was back-breaking, unpleasant, and perilous work—not only did it involve hard labour under very unpleasant, hot, and dusty conditions, but it was also dangerous as fragments of kiln roof or loose refractory tiles could fall on workers. The advent of pneumatic hammers eliminated much of the really hard manual labour (although it could hardly be called easy), but the unpleasant conditions and danger remained. In the latter years of the twentieth century, further advances were made, and KDC had been at the forefront of these, in the form of mobile descaling machines. The larger models of these were like small construction vehicles, mounted on tracks, and were operated much like a small bulldozer. Pneumatic hammers mounted on the front loosened the scale in a furnace, and automatic shovels could then pick up and clear the debris. This meant that the equipment operator did not have to perform any hard manual labour, but the work in unpleasant and dangerous conditions had not really changed much.

The Termin8or strategy

In 1995, when Harry Millbury took over as CEO of KDC, he embarked on an ambitious growth strategy. 'My vision was that KDC should be the world's leading kiln-descaling technology company,' he said, 'and that we should control at least half of the total world market for kiln-descaling equipment. If we were to achieve this, we could not do it by making minor improvements to products, and being slightly better than our customers. We had to do it by changing the way the market worked, and the way in which customers saw and used our products. In a sense we had to create an entirely new market, and the way to do this would be to create the products that would create the markets. As I saw it, marketing and strategy would be synonymous in KDC. Marketing would be our strategy, and our strategy would be marketing. We built these into a rigorous and regular process of strategic meetings, that focused on new technologies and customer needs. We thought of everything in our strategy—customers, the business environment, and competitors. We gave incredible attention to every detail of our target markets and our marketing activities. That's how the Termin8or was born. It became the focal product in our corporate strategy.'

After weeks of strategic brainstorming and discussion, the KDC senior management team concluded that the reason that descaling technologies had not progressed much over the years was that although hard, manual labour had been eliminated, the most pressing customer problems had remained: the work was still performed in dirty, dusty, hot conditions, and the danger of falling debris was still present. 'We concluded that the only way to make a radical improvement to descaling was to take people out of the process. Somebody asked a flippant question one day, and said, "Why don't we just have a machine that does the job itself, without a human operator?" After some initial scepticism, we invested in a study of robotic systems, and realized that a well-designed machine could go into a furnace or kiln by itself, and do the work. It could be operated remotely, from outside. Humans would no longer have to enter dirty, dusty, dangerous environments.'

After three years of development, the first Termin8or prototypes were successfully tested. 'The name was a bit of a joke,' said Millbury, 'our eighth prototype was the

» most successful. Someone had been to see the Arnold Schwarzenegger movie *Terminator* and said that our product was nearly as clever as the human robots in the film, and that it also "terminated" scale. After that it was a question of formulating a really good marketing strategy. And I think we did that.'

The Termin8or product could enter a kiln or furnace and do an entire descaling job without human presence, apart from a worker stationed outside, who could operate it, and also view what Termin8or was 'seeing' through an onboard camera. Termin8or could also 'climb' walls, and even descale the roof of a kiln or furnace by using a series of telescopic arms and legs to ascend and descend. The firm decided to set a premium price for the new product, and could demonstrate that the premium would be well worth it because of the increases in efficiency and productivity, and of course dramatic improvements in human safety. The product could be distributed and serviced through KDC's existing branch and agency network. 'We also negotiated a great advertising strategy which appeared in all the trade journals and magazines, and on posters at trade shows,' said Millbury, 'It featured Arnold himself, staring stonily at our product. It really got the message across. Cost us an arm and a leg in royalties, but it really made an impression in the target market.'

The technical intricacies of the new product required intensive training of the KDC salesforce. 'We really rely on our sales force,' said Millbury, 'This type of product is quite difficult to sell, and it requires real technical skill as well as great selling techniques. However, because we believed that this new product would be such a winner, we changed the compensation formula for our salesforce. Our policy had been to pay a salary plus 20% commission on sales to a salesperson. We made the decision that because the Termin8or was such a great product, with no competition in the marketplace and none on the horizon, we would pay a 10% commission on its sales.'

Source: This Mini Case Study was prepared by Professor Leyland Pitt, Faculty of Business Administration, Simon Fraser University, as the basis for analysis and class discussion and not to illustrate either effective or ineffective handling of an administrative situation

Outcomes of competitive advantage

When a firm exploits either of the two generic strategies with some success, according to Day and Wensley (1988), the outcomes will be evident in a number of variables, and these variables form the foundations of marketing control, for they are measurable. Obviously the performance of a successful competitor will manifest itself in financial productivity, measured by a return on investment (ROI)—or for that matter ROCE, ROA, RONA, or any of a number of financial acronyms. The successful competitor's performance will also be manifested in the form of increased market share, or at the very least, a maintenance thereof. There are two other outcomes of achieving a position of competitive advantage. One is customer satisfaction: a firm that offers customers the benefits of a differentiated offering, or passes on some of the rents achieved by lower cost, will satisfy customers, all things being equal. The other is customer loyalty: satisfied customers tend to remain loyal to the firm that really fulfils them, and, given the choice, refrain from patronizing competitors.

Most managers give more attention to the outcomes of market share and financial productivity for two obvious reasons: these outcomes tend to be easier to measure, and managers are typically rewarded directly for improvements in these results. Managers are also inclined to agree that customer satisfaction and loyalty are important and that (as loosely implied in the sequence in the diagram in Figure 13.3) they lead to market share and ROI (or other measures). However, they will likewise contend that these concepts are more vague and less easy to measure. To a large extent they are right. While the attempts by consumer psychologists and marketing researchers to improve the measurement of customer satisfaction (cf. Anderson et al., 1994) and service quality (cf. Parasuraman et al. 1985, 1988) have been most laudable, it should not be forgetten that what they are trying to achieve is daunting indeed. They are attempting to 'get inside the heads' of customers and assess complex human cognitive processes such as satisfaction using lamentably inadequate tools like five- and seven-point scales. Customers are required to express enigmatic feelings, impressions, and emotions by circling points on ordinal scales to which marketers attribute interval characteristics.

What makes market share and financial productivity measures appealing as outcomes of a position of competitive advantage is the fact that they are 'hard'—expressed in numbers that can easily be calculated, compared, and tracked. The problem however is that they are historical—a good way of tracking the past, but a rather inadequate indication of the future. Simply, they are not good diagnostics of strategic health. While customers may be capricious at times, all things being equal they are not so fickle as to be satisfied today, and dissatisfied with the same good offering tomorrow, or change the loyalty horse in mid-stream. Indeed, most customers are probably more tolerant of marketers' shortcomings than the latter would give them credit for, and only downgrade ratings or shift allegiances as the result of gross dereliction by supplier firms. Again, the problem with most measures of customer satisfaction and loyalty is that they are soft, and impression based. They are however, about the future.

The logic of the process model presented in Figure 13.3 is that the astute firm will reinvest the financial outcomes of competitive advantage in the sources of competitive advantage itself, namely superior skills and/or superior resources. This activity closes the loop in the model, and suggests that managing for competitive advantage is indeed a process that is continually renewed, revived, and refreshed. Certainly, a marketing strategist's skills may well be distinguished by his/her knowledge of what sources of competitive advantage to invest in, what position(s) to adopt, and the ability to determine the outcome of the process effectively—in simple terms, what was referred to earlier in this chapter as 'control'.

The variables which can be measured and controlled in the outcomes in the model in Figure 13.3 are illustrated in Table 13.1.

But are the outcomes ideal?

It has recently been asked whether the four outcome variables in the process in Figure 13.3 have outlived their usefulness (Pitt et al., Ewing and 2000). In the future, these authors argue, they will be replaced by one overarching outcome variable that will direct all of marketing strategy, and most of corporate strategy. It will undoubtedly be the one variable

TABLE 13.1 The process model of competitive advantage and control variables

Outcome	Operationalization	Typical measure
Customer satisfaction	Customers' overall satisfaction with a firm's products or services.	Customer satisfaction survey, requiring customers to rate satisfaction or various aspects of it on an interval scale.
	Difference between customers' expectations of the quality of a product or service and their perceptions of a particular product or service (also known as 'disconfirmation').	Service quality studies using instruments such as SERVQUAL (Parasuraman et al., 1988).
Customer loyalty	The extent to which customers would be willing to choose an alternative over the firm's offering, given availability.	Surveys of loyalty.
	Customer churn (also known as customer retention rates, or conversely, customer defection rates).	How many customers who are in a firm's customer base at the beginning of a period (usually a year) are still in it at the end of a period? An indication of **retention**. How many customers who are in a firm's customer base at the beginning of a period (usually a year) will not be in it at the end of a period? An indication of **defection**. See Page et al., 1996; Reichheld and Sasser, 1990; Reichheld, 1993.
Market share	The percentage or proportion of the total available market or market segment that is being serviced by a company. Increasing market share is one of the most common objectives used in business. The main advantage of using market share is that it abstracts from industry-wide macro-environmental variables such as the state of the economy, or changes in tax policy.	Can be expressed as: a company's sales revenue (from that market) divided by the total sales revenue available in that market or a company's unit sales volume (in a market) divided by the total volume of units sold in that market.
Measures of financial productivity *All of these measures assess the ability of the firm to make a profit.*	**Sales growth** Analysis: Look for a steady increase in sales.	Percentage increase (or decrease) in sales between two time periods. Formula: Current year's sales – Last year's sales/Last year's sales

(continued overleaf)

TABLE 13.1 *(continued)*

Outcome	Operationalization	Typical measure
	If overall costs and inflation are on the rise, then you should watch for a related increase in your sales. If not, then this is an indicator that your prices are not keeping up with your costs.	
	COGS to Sales Analysis: Look for a stable ratio as an indicator that the company is controlling its gross margins.	Percentage of sales used to pay for expenses that vary directly with sales. Formula: Cost of Goods Sold/Sales
	Gross profit margin Analysis: Compare to other businesses in the same industry to see if your business is operating as profitably as it should be. Look at the trend from month to month. Is it staying the same? Improving? Deteriorating? Is there enough gross profit in the business to cover your operating costs? Is there a positive gross margin on all your products?	Indicator of how much profit is earned on your products without consideration of selling and administration costs. Formula: Gross Profit/Total Sales where Gross Profit = Sales less Cost of Goods Sold
	SG&A to Sales Analysis: Look for a steady or decreasing percentage indicating that the company is controlling its overhead expenses.	Percentage of selling, general and administrative costs to sales. Formula: Selling, General & Administrative Expenses/Sales
	Net profit margin Analysis: Compare to other businesses in the same industry to see if your business is operating as profitably as it should be. Look at the trend from month to month. Is it staying the same? Improving? Deteriorating? Are you generating enough sales to leave an acceptable profit? Trend from month to month can show how well you are managing your operating or overhead costs.	Shows how much profit comes from every dollar of sales. Formula: Net Profit/Total Sales

(continued overleaf)

TABLE 13.1 *(continued)*

Outcome	Operationalization	Typical measure
	Return on Equity (ROE) Analysis: Compare the return on equity to other investment alternatives, such as a savings account, stock, or bond. Compare your ratio to other businesses in the same or a similar industry.	Determines the rate of return on your investment in the business. For an owner or shareholder this is one of the most important ratios as it shows the hard fact about the business—are you making enough of a profit to compensate you for the risk of being in business? Formula: Net Profit/Equity
	Return on assets (ROA) Analysis: ROA shows the amount of income for every dollar tied up in assets. Year to year trends may be an indicator, but watch out for changes in the total asset figure as you depreciate your assets (a decrease or increase in the denominator can affect the ratio and does not necessarily mean the business is improving or declining).	Considered a measure of how effectively assets are used to generate a return. (This ratio is not very useful for most businesses.) Formula: Net Profit/Total Assets

that marketers will want to specify, measure, and take corrective or reinforcing action over. These changes are the result of the most dramatic force impacting on marketing today: information technology.

Customer equity: the single outcome of a process of competitive advantage

While the two sets of outcomes in the Day and Wensley model presented in Figure 13.3 each have their own particular strengths, each set also has its limitations, as pointed out. In summary, the outcomes of ROI and market share are hard but historical, and the outcomes of customer satisfaction and customer loyalty are future oriented but soft. The ideal marketing control variable would be a single outcome that is both hard (a number that can be expressed financially) and future (customer) oriented. Customer Lifetime Value (CLTV), which in turn leads to customer equity, is that single appropriate outcome.

Traditional accounting systems have viewed customers as sources of revenue. Increasingly, firms are beginning to use their accounting systems to view customers as assets, and basing their decisions on customers much as they would base their decisions on investments.

Customer Lifetime Value

Customer Lifetime Value (CLTV) can be calculated using the simple formula below:

$$\mathrm{CLTV} \overset{n}{\underset{i=1}{=}} \Sigma(1+\mathbf{d})^{-i}\pi_i$$

Where:

π_i = sales profit from this customer in period i + any non-sales benefits (e.g. referrals) − cost of maintaining the relationship in period i

d = discount rate

n = final period, estimated to be lifetime horizon for customer

Customer Lifetime Value (CLTV) is the net present value (NPV) of the profit that a firm stands to realize on the average new customer during a given number of years. This is illustrated in the calculations shown in the spreadsheet in Table 13.2.

The spreadsheet in Table 13.2 is a very elementary one indeed: it might be typical of a firm marketing a magazine subscription. If it is assumed that the firm sells 1,000 new subscriptions in Year 1 at $150 each, then the calculation of net revenue and also of net costs at 50% of revenue, are both simple procedures. A further important issue is retention: in simple terms, how many customers at the beginning of a year are still subscribers at the year's end. What has been done in Table 13.2 is to assume a retention rate of 40% at end of

TABLE 13.2 A simple spreadsheet for the calculation of CLTV

Revenue	Year 1	Year 2	Year 3	Year 4	Year 5
Customers	1,000	400	180	90	50
Retention rate	40.00%	45.00%	50.00%	55.00%	60.00%
Ave ann sales	150	150	150	150	150
Total revenue	150,000	60,000	27,000	13,500	7,425
Costs					
Cost %	50.00%	50.00%	50.00%	50.00%	50.00%
Total costs	75,000	30,000	13,500	6,750	3,713
Profits					
Gross profit	75,000	30,000	13,500	6,750	3,713
Discount rate	1.00	1.20	**1.44**	1.73	2.07
NPV profit	75,000.00	25,000.00	9,375.00	3,906.25	1,790.36
Cum NPV profit	75,000	100,000	109,375	113,281	115,072
CLTV	75.00	100.00	109.38	113.28	115.07

Year 1, and then increase this gradually over the five-year period. Thus 400 customers are still subscribers at the beginning of Year 2, 180 at beginning of Year 3, and so forth. Naturally the revenues and the costs for a year are functions of the number of customers at the beginning of that year. Calculation of gross profit is then a simple subtraction procedure, and what follows is perhaps the only, albeit slightly, complex calculation in the entire process. As in all investments, the returns for a customer five years from now are not worth what they are today. Therefore, there is a need to discount gross profits. The discount rate chosen in Table 13.2 is 20%. This figure is discretionary, and its choice will vary from firm to firm: some may choose a premium bank rate, others an internal rate of return, still others some minimum rate of investment acceptability. This is not critical to our discussion, for the principles remain the same. This discount rate is used to calculate the Net Present Value (NPV) of the cumulative gross profit over the years. The final calculation is a simple one: what is the CLTV of a customer who was put on the books in Year 1? The answer is the NPV of the cumulative gross profit for the year divided by the number of customers (in this case 1,000) in Year 1. Thus the CLTV of one of these customers in Year 4 would be $113.28, and in Year 5 $115.07, and so on.

An obvious application of this type of spreadsheet is its use in the calculation of 'What can be done to increase CLTV?' (similar spreadsheets can be downloaded from **www.1to1.com**). The decision-maker can change variables such as price, costs, the discount rate, the number of years an individual will be a customer, and of course the retention rate, to determine the effects these will have on CLTV.

In more general terms however, it is worth considering what can be done from a marketing strategy perspective to:

- **Maximize CLTV:** what marketing strategies need to be formulated?
- **Control:** CLTV is a very powerful control variable that can be used to assess the success or otherwise of a marketing strategy and its implementation. Not only is the overall number a useful metric, but it can be broken down into its components as well, and also be calculated not only by customer group or target market, but right down to the level of the individual customer.

In summary, CLTV can be increased by:

1. Increasing lifetime by either increasing retention rate, or increasing customer life (i.e. the number of years a customer can remain a customer).
2. Increasing sales to, or as a result of, a customer, either by increasing the firm's share of the customer's purchases, or by increasing the customer's referral rate (the number of times that customer refers others to the firm's products and services).
3. Cutting the costs of serving a customer.

Pitt et al. (2000) use a number of cases from well-known firms to illustrate these principles:

- **Increasing retention rates:** Loyalty programmes operate in industries ranging from airlines to restaurants, and supermarkets to hotel chains. Their objective is to raise switching barriers for customers, thereby encouraging their loyalty. Tesco's Club Card in the UK,

FlyBuys in Australia, and the Click's Card in South Africa are some excellent international examples of this strategy.

- **Increasing customer life:** Huggies disposable diapers developed a product extension branded 'Pullups' or 'Trainer Pants' in various international markets. The disposable pants were targeted at infants who were almost 'potty-trained', but whose parents still required the certainty that accidents could be avoided. The product added about six months to the life of a Huggies customer. While this may not seem like much, six months on a life of two years adds 25% to CLTV!
- **Increasing sales of the same product:** Tia Maria is a liqueur usually consumed in small shot glasses after a meal, which limits its sales. The brand has since published recipe booklets encouraging the use of the product in cocktails, as a sauce over ice-cream, and as an ingredient in desserts.
- **Increasing the sales of other products to the same customer:** While Amazon.com began its life in book sales, it quickly moved on to sales of music, VHS tapes, and DVDs as it began to understand its customers' purchasing patterns more effectively.
- **Exploiting customer referral rates:** Palm Corporation's Palm Pilot has been one of the most successful digital products in history. Yet for the first few years of its existence the firm spent very little on advertising. The product was sold almost entirely on 'word-of-mouth' as owners enthusiastically insisted that their friends and colleagues acquire a Palm so that they could beam details to each other.
- **Cutting the costs of serving customers:** The Internet has provided marketers with a wide range of applications to reduce the costs of serving customers without lowering service levels. Customers do their banking online, purchase airline tickets, and check their frequent flyer miles. Most customers welcome the control this gives them over the purchasing situation, yet for the institutions involved, being able to rely on technology and the customer to do the work means very significant cost savings.

From CLTV to customer equity

It has been argued that while the competitive advantage process model of Day and Wensley (1988) offers a powerful and useful tool for the management of organizations, it has become somewhat dated in an important way: the outcomes originally identified are necessary but not sufficient control metrics, and can nowadays be augmented effectively by a single measure. This shift has been driven by information technology to a large extent. CLTV becomes the definitive criterion for controlling the outcome of a process of competitive advantage, and competitive advantage lies at the heart of marketing strategy.

It is important to note that the simple spreadsheet presented in Table 13.2 involves the CLTVs of 'average customers'. However, nothing precludes the firm from recognizing that all customers are individual, and might have their own unique CLTVs. Daily there are the attempts of marketers to capture the data which will enable them to get closer to calculating the CLTV of an individual customer—loyalty cards, warranty registration schemes, customer databases, and the like. If these CLTVs were then summed, the total value of the firm's customer base will be identified—or what Blattberg and Deighton (1996) call **customer equity**. These authors argue that marketing should be managed by the customer equity criterion. If what they say is true (and worldwide interest in the issue suggests it is), then customer equity becomes the ultimate marketing control metric (see also **www.customerequity.com**).

Thus any marketing decision should be evaluated on whether or not it increases customer equity. For example, when thinking about customer acquisition and retention, markets should base their decision on where the next marketing dollar (or pound or yen, or whatever) would be better spent: on getting new customers or keeping the existing ones? The answer is, whichever of the two strategies has the greatest effect on customer equity.

Customer equity and organizational structure

If firms are going to manage for customer equity, there are major implications for how they organize marketing. Whereas in the past many firms have favoured a brand/product management structure, and structured themselves along these lines, nowadays there is a strong argument for the implementation of a customer portfolio management system (Berthon et al., 1997). Rather than structure the firm along product or brand lines where the performance that is evaluated is that of the past (typically market share), the firm's customer base is allocated to portfolios of customers, and each of these is distinctly managed. The performance of a customer portfolio manager is evaluated on the basis of his or her ability to increase the value of the portfolio. This is a future-based measure, for the value of the portfolio is essentially its customer equity, which in turn represents the CLTVs of all the individual customers that make up the portfolio.

There are other issues in the Blattberg and Deighton (1996) article which managers may wish to consider strongly. Rather than merely allocate marketing and advertising budgets according to such variables as media selection and spend, or territories, or even customer markets, in the future managers may wish to consciously split the budget between customer acquisition and customer retention activities. Customer equity becomes the basis upon which this decision can be made. The authors go on to make the somewhat radical suggestion that firms may even wish to consider organizing themselves along the lines of acquisition and retention, and to evaluate the performance of these divisions on their ability to contribute towards customer equity.

Corporate culture, control, and the implementation of marketing strategy

As already noted, writers such as Bonoma (1984) have observed that one of the most important reasons for the failure in implementation of marketing strategy is an inadequate corporate culture. Just as nations, groups, and even local communities have cultures that make them different from others, so do organizations and corporations, and this culture is usually an important determining factor in their success or failure.

When people visit another country for the first time, they are usually struck by the differences (and sometimes, similarities) between the new culture and their own. People may note differences in language, dress, the way food and drink is consumed, attitudes toward time, work and leisure, rituals, music, and religion. The same is true for organizations, which also differ on most of these issues. Culture can be defined as the moral, social, and behavioural norms of an organization based on the beliefs, attitudes, and priorities of its members—in simple terms, corporate culture has often been referred to as 'the way we do things around here'.

Every organization has its own unique culture or value set, whether the organization has consciously tried to create this or not. Usually, the culture of the organization is created unconsciously, based on the values of top management or the organization's founders. Often, members of an organization will be heard to say things like, 'in order to implement that strategy, we would have to change our culture', as if culture can be changed easily and quickly, like bed linen. The reality of corporate culture is that it is usually very deep-seated and embedded. Sometimes it may be easier and better to try to understand the organization's culture, and to work with it, rather than change it, and this has wide and significant implications for the implementation of marketing strategy.

Corporate culture and the marketing function

Marketing academics have long been interested in the effects that an organization's culture will have on its ability to formulate, and more importantly, to implement, marketing strategy. Badovick and Beatty (1987) found that shared organizational values (one aspect of culture) significantly impacted on strategic marketing implementation. Tse et al. (1988) investigated the relationship between national culture and marketing decision-making, finding that an executive's home (national) culture had a significant and predictable effect on decision-making. Qualls and Puto (1989) studied the role that culture's allied concept, climate, has on decision-framing. They found that climate affects choice behaviours through influencing the decision-maker's reference points and decision frames. Webster (1991) investigated cultural consistency within service firms, and found that an employee's position influenced his/her attitudes towards the firm's actual and ideal marketing culture. Slater and Narver (1992) and Narver and Slater (1990) found that market orientation, (a construct comprised of three elements: customer orientation, competitor orientation, and interfunctional coordination) was linked to business performance—and use the concept of organizational culture to explain the relationship.

Meanwhile, Webster (1994) and Deshpandé et al. (1993) found a direct link between organizational culture and business performance, while arguing that market orientation was one sub-component of culture. Specifically, they investigated the relationship between culture and business performance in Japanese companies. They found that companies with cultures that stress competitiveness (Market cultures) and entrepreneurship (Adhocracy cultures) outperform those with cultures that stress internal cohesiveness or rules. More recently, Berthon et al. (2001) looked at the influence of organizational culture and memory development on managers' perceptions of role-related problems. They found that both organizational culture and memory influence managers' perceptions, with externally focused cultures emphasizing strategic problems, and organic process cultures emphasizing unstructured problems.

Conceptualizing corporate culture

A number of authors have attempted to conceptualize corporate culture, and to provide managers with tools to measure it, understand it, and diagnose it.

Goffee and Jones

Goffee and Jones (1996), viewing culture as synonymous with community, argue that business communities are no different from communities outside the commercial arena, such as families, schools, clubs, and villages. Therefore they can (and should) be viewed through the same lens that has illuminated the study of human organizations for nearly 150 years—the lens of sociology. The discipline of sociology divides community along two dimensions: **sociability**, a measure of friendliness among members of a community, and **solidarity**, a measure of a community's ability to pursue shared objectives. Plotting these two dimensions against each other results in four types of business community: networked, mercenary, fragmented, and communal.

To increase **sociability** according to Goffee and Jones (1996), managers can:

- promote the sharing of ideas, interests, and emotions by recruiting compatible people
- increase social interaction among employees by arranging casual gatherings inside and outside the office
- reduce formality between employees
- limit hierarchical differences
- act like a friend, and set the example for geniality and kindness by caring for those in trouble.

To build **solidarity**, managers should:

- develop awareness of competitors
- create a sense of urgency
- stimulate the will to win
- encourage commitment to shared corporate goals.

Charles Handy

Charles Handy (1978) views organizational cultures as having to do with the way in which organizations:

- think and learn
- influence and change
- motivate and reward

With an education in the classics, Handy names his four cultural archetypes after ancient Greek gods, for these cultures do indeed have much in common with the supposed characteristics of the deities.

Zeus—the club culture

Zeus organizations see the 'Big Picture', and typically think intuitively, in wholes. Learning is by trial and error, and members of the organization typically go through an 'apprenticeship' before they fit. A very powerful individual, usually the founder, typically leads Zeus organizations. Control of resources and charisma are what count, and an individual's success usually depends on who they know, not what they know. These types of organizations generally do not respond well to change, and are often vulnerable when the powerful leader (Zeus, the king of the gods) disappears from the scene.

Apollo—the role culture

Left-brain thinkers generally do well in Apollo—or 'role'—cultures, where learning is to do with the acquisition of knowledge and skills. An individual's power stems from his or her role or title, and a role or title generally has rights as well as responsibilities. Apollo cultures are guided by the all-powerful organization chart, which shows the power of an individual relative to others. Most people recognize the Apollo organization as a bureaucracy.

Athena—the task culture

The Athena culture is the culture of the group. It is also known as the Task culture because this type of organization thrives on finding challenging tasks or problems, and completing or solving them. In task cultures, success is desirable if it has been earned, and problems are solved by creativity and logic. Learning is viewed as the ability to solve problems better, and the focus is on resourceful humans rather than human resources. Task cultures love variety and are bored by certainty, which makes them an expensive and luxurious way of running organizations. Typical examples of task cultures are advertising agencies that are working on very exciting and challenging accounts. However, these become very vulnerable (and not very exciting places to work) when the account is lost to a competitor.

Dionysus—the existential culture

The Dionysus culture emphasizes the growth of individualism. In an existential culture, the individual is all that matters, and this individual has nothing much to learn from any other person: learning comes only from immersion. This can be infuriating to others, for it is hard to influence Dionysians—they do not acknowledge the power of the organization! Individuals who like working in existential cultures do so because they value personal freedom most of all. A simple example of a Dionysus culture would be a medical practice: a group of doctors who work together only in order to share resources, and not because they necessarily like each other or want to work together. Anyone who has ever worked at a major research university will also recognize the Dionysus culture: the academics who work in these institutions do so particularly because of the individual freedom they have. Managing this type of organization is extremely difficult, and can usually only be done by consensus or what Handy (1978) refers to as 'Contracted procedures'. As has been said about managing academics: It's like herding cats.

It should not be surprising that Handy (1978) does not acknowledge an ideal culture: each of the above has its advantages, and each its limitations. When managers are asked to describe their organizations in the above terms, most large organizations are described by their members as Apollo, or role cultures, whereas when asked their preferences, most individuals would choose to work in an Athena, or task culture. While this is understandable, as Handy points out, as organizations grow, most tend toward becoming bureaucracies, as the requirements for control and diligence increase.

Deshpandé, Farley, and Webster

Deshpandé et al. (1993) defined corporate culture as the pattern of shared values and beliefs that help individuals understand organizational functioning and thus provide them with the norms for behaviour in the organization. They used two dimensions to identify four culture types. These two dimensions are:

1. organic versus mechanistic processes
2. internal maintenance versus external positioning

The four cultural types they identify are:

- the **Clan** culture, which emphasizes teamwork and cooperation
- the **Adhocracy** culture, which emphasizes entrepreneurship and creativity
- the **Hierarchy** culture, which emphasizes order, regulations, and rules
- the **Market** culture, which emphasizes competitiveness and goal achievement

In a study of customer orientation and innovativeness in Japanese firms, these authors found that market cultures were associated with the best performance, whereas hierarchical cultures were associated with the poorest performance. Deshpandé et al. (1993) adapted their questionnaire to measure and identify corporate culture from the earlier work of Campbell and Freeman (1991) and Quinn (1988).

Conclusion

While most firms spend an inordinate amount of time and effort on the formulation of marketing strategy, it is likely that the reason for many strategic marketing failures and problems lies in implementation, rather than in formulation. The problem with the implementation of marketing strategy is that it can easily mask formulation. When a well-formulated marketing strategy fails, the blame is frequently given to poor formulation, whereas poor implementation was the most likely cause of breakdown. Likewise, when marketing strategy is poorly formulated, good implementation can have two very different possible outcomes. On the one hand, good implementation can disguise a poorly formulated strategy, and make it look good by leading to success. On the other, when a poorly formulated strategy is well implemented, it can simply hasten the downfall.

The managerial task of control lies at the heart of successful strategic implementation. If marketing objectives and goals are carefully and skilfully articulated, and then regularly and systematically compared to actual performance, then corrective action can be taken in time to bring strategy back on track.

The successful implementation of marketing strategy involves many behavioural issues within the organization. It has been demonstrated empirically that the successful implementation of marketing strategy is influenced by the culture of the firm. Managers should therefore strive to understand the cultures of their organizations and the impact this will have on the successful implementation of marketing strategy.

Summary

This chapter defined control as a managerial task that sets standards, evaluates performance against those standards, and then takes corrective or reinforcing action where necessary. Control generally takes one of three forms, namely, annual plan control, profitability control, or strategic control. Implementation is the act of execution of an endeavour, and in the future it is likely that organizations will become as good at strategy implementation as they are at formulation. A number of causes of the inadequate implementation of marketing strategy within organizations were identified.

The implementation of marketing strategy in organizations was viewed through the lens of managing an ongoing process of competitive advantage. This process consists of identifying the sources of advantage, namely, superior skills and superior resources, and turning them into positions of competitive advantage, either a low cost position, or differentiation. If a firm enjoys a position of competitive advantage this will result in measurable, and therefore controllable, outcomes, namely, customer satisfaction, customer loyalty, market share, and measures of financial productivity. The logic of the process of competitive advantage is that the superior returns enjoyed will be reinvested in the sources of competitive advantage.

One of the most significant changes occurring in marketing today is a shift from these four different measures to a single yardstick that overcomes the limitations of the conventional measures and capitalizes on their strengths. Customer Lifetime Value (CLTV) has become a critical metric to use to evaluate and control the successful implementation of a firm's marketing strategy. When all the CLTVs of a firm's customers are summed this is called Customer Equity.

The successful implementation of a firm's marketing strategy is also seen to be a result of a firm's corporate culture, defined simply as 'the way we do things around here'. Three approaches were considered in looking at corporate culture, namely those of Goffee and Jones (1996), Handy (1978) and Deshpandé, Farley, and Webster (1993).

KEY TERMS

Control The managerial task of setting standards, evaluating these standards against reality, and the taking of corrective or reinforcing action where necessary.

Implementation Executing an activity, or putting a plan into action.

Strategy Formulation–Implementation grid A tool for the diagnosis of the successful or otherwise formulation and implementation of marketing strategy.

Process model of competitive advantage An approach to competitive advantage and the implementation of marketing strategy which views competitive advantage not as something static, but as an ongoing process which has to be formulated and controlled.

Customer lifetime value (CLTV) The net present value of all future cash flows from a customer over his/her lifetime.

Customer equity The sum of all of the CLTVs of the customers in a firm's customer base.

Corporate culture The moral, social, and behavioural norms of an organization based on the beliefs, attitudes, and priorities of its members.

DISCUSSION QUESTIONS

1 Briefly outline and describe the steps a marketing manager could take to ensure control of marketing activities at different levels.

2 What are the possible consequences for marketing strategy when a poor strategy is well implemented? Can you think of examples of this occurring other than those mentioned in the text? What are the consequences for marketing strategy when a good strategy is poorly implemented? Can you think of examples of this occurring other than those mentioned in the text?

3 List some of the reasons why marketing strategy is often not implemented successfully, and think of practical examples of this in organizations with which you are familiar.

4 Choose an organization with which you are familiar, and set up a process model of competitive advantage for it. What are the sources of its competitive advantage? How does it compete? What are the outcomes of this process for the organization? What skills or resources will it have to invest in in the future if it is to survive and prosper?

5 Set up a simple spreadsheet and use it to estimate the lifetime values of:

- an infant wearing nappies for two years
- the credit card customer of a bank who takes a card at the age of 20 and is projected to live to the age of 75 (assuming this is a middle income customer)

6 Now use your spreadsheet to predict what might happen if:

- the organizations could extend the lifetimes of their customers by either starting them earlier or ending them later. How might this be achieved?
- the organizations could get customers to use more of the products they already buy
- the organizations could get customers to use their other products or services

7 Using Handy's classification of organizational cultures, identify three organizations under each archetype that are typical of each, and explain why you have placed these organizations under these categories.

ONLINE RESOURCE CENTRE

Visit the Online Resource Centre for this book for lots of interesting additional material at: **www.oxfordtextbooks.co.uk/orc/west/**

REFERENCES AND FURTHER READING

Anderson, Erin, Claes Fornell, and Donald R. Lehmann (1994), 'Customer Satisfaction, Market Share, and Profitability', *Journal of Marketing*, 58 (July), pp. 53–66.

Badovick, G. J., and Sharon E. Beatty (1987), 'Shared Organizational Values: Measurement and Impact Upon Strategic Marketing Implementation', *Journal of the Academy of Marketing Science*, 15 (1), pp. 19–26.

Berthon, Pierre R., James M. Hulbert, and Leyland F. Pitt (1997), 'Brands, Brand Managers, and the Management of Brands: Where to Next?', *Commentary Report No. 97–122*, November (Cambridge, MA: Marketing Science Institute).

Berthon, Pierre R., Leyland F. Pitt, and Michael T. Ewing (2001), 'Corollaries of the Collective: Effects of Corporate Culture and Organizational Memory on Decision-making Context', *Journal of the Academy of Marketing Science* 29 (2), pp. 135–50.

Blattberg, Robert C., and John Deighton (1996), 'Manage marketing by the customer equity test', *Harvard Business Review*, Jul–Aug, 74 (4), pp. 136–45.

Bonoma, Thomas V. (1984), 'Making Your Marketing Strategy Work', *Harvard Business Review*, Mar–Apr, pp. 69–77.

Campbell, J. P., and Sarah J. Freeman (1991), 'Cultural Congruence, Strength, and Type: Relationships to Effectiveness', in R. W. Woodman and W. Pasmore (eds), *Research in Organizational Change and Development*, (Vol. 5) (Greenwich, CT: JAI).

Day, George S., and Robin Wensley (1988), 'Assessing Advantage: A Framework for Diagnosing Competitive Superiority', *Journal of Marketing*, 52, April, pp. 1–20.

Deighton, John (2002), 'How Snapple got its juice back', *Harvard Business Review*, Jan, 80 (1), p. 47.

Deshpandé, Rohit, John U. Farley, and Frederick E. Webster (1993), 'Corporate Culture, Customer Orientation, and Innovativeness in Japanese Firms: A Quadrad Analysis', *Journal of Marketing*, 57, pp. 23–7.

Goffee, Rob, and Gareth Jones (1996), 'What holds the modern company together?" *Harvard Business Review*. Nov–Dec, 74 (6), pp. 133–49.

Handy, Charles (1978), *The Gods of Management* (London: Pan).

Narver, John C., and Stanley F. Slater (1990), 'The Effect of a Market Orientation on Business Profitability', *Journal of Marketing*, 54 (October), pp. 20–35.

Page, Michael J., Leyland F. Pitt, and Pierre R. Berthon (1996), 'Analysing Customer Defections: Predicting the Effects on Corporate Performance', *Long Range Planning*, 29 (6) (December), pp. 821–34.

Parasuraman, A., Valarie A. Zeithaml, and Leonard L. Berry (1985), 'A Conceptual Model of Service Quality and its Implications for Future Research', *Journal of Marketing*, 49 (April), pp. 41–50.

Parasuraman, A., Valarie A. Zeithaml, and Leonard L. Berry (1988), 'SERVQUAL: A Multiple-Item Scale for Measuring Customer Perceptions of Service Quality', *Journal of Retailing*, 64, Spring, pp. 12–40.

Pitt, Leyland F., Michael T. Ewing, and Pierre R. Berthon (2000), 'Turning Competitive Advantage into Customer Equity', *Business Horizons*, September–October, pp. 11–18.

Porter, Michael E. (1985), *Competitive Advantage: Creating and Sustaining Superior Performance* (New York: Free Press).

Qualls, William J., and Christopher P. Puto (1989), 'Organizational Climate and Decision Framing: An Integrated Approach to Analyzing Industrial Buying Decisions', *Journal of Marketing Research*, 26 (May), pp. 179–92.

Quinn, Robert E. (1988), *Beyond Rational Management* (San Francisco: Jossey-Bass).

Reichheld, Frederick F. (1993), 'Loyalty-Based Management', *Harvard Business Review*, March–April, pp. 64–72.

Reichheld, Frederick F., and W. Earl Sasser (1990), 'Zero Defections: Quality Comes to Services', *Harvard Business Review*, Sep.–Oct., pp. 301–7.

Robert, Michel M. (1991), 'Why CEOs Have Difficulty Implementing Their Strategies', *The Journal of Business Strategy*, 12 (2), pp. 58–60.

Slater, Stanley F., and John C. Narver (1992), 'Superior Customer Value and Business Performance: The Strong Evidence for a Market-Driven Culture', *Marketing Science Institute Report No. 92–125* (Cambridge, MA: The Marketing Science Institute).

Tse, David K., K-H. Lee, Ilan Vertinsky, I. Wehrung, and D. A. Wehrung (1988), 'Does Culture Matter? A Cross-Cultural Study of Executives' Choice, Decisiveness, and Risk Adjustment in International Marketing', *Journal of Marketing*, 52 (October), 81–95.

Webster, Cynthia (1991), 'A Note on Cultural Consistency Within the Service Firm: The Effects of Employee Position on Attitudes Towards the Marketing Culture', *Journal of the Academy of Marketing Science*, 19(4), 341–6.

Webster, Frederick E. (1994), *Market Driven Management: Using the New Marketing Concept to Create a Customer-Oriented Company* (New York: John Wiley & Sons).

KEY ARTICLE ABSTRACTS

Noble, Charles H., and Michael P. Mokwa (1999), 'Implementing Marketing Strategies: Developing and Testing a Managerial Theory', *Journal of Marketing*, 63 (4), pp. 57–73.

This paper develops a model that includes important factors which influence the implementation of marketing strategy. The authors have tested their model at the mid-level of marketing management.

Abstract: Implementation pervades strategic performance. It is a critical link between the formulation of marketing strategies and the achievement of superior organizational performance. Research conducted in this area generally has suffered from a lack of conceptual and empirical grounding. Furthermore, implementation research often ignores the mid-level managers, who are intricately involved in most implementation activities. The authors integrate a broad literature review and a grounded theory-building process to develop a model of important factors that influence the implementation of marketing strategies from a managerial perspective. They test this model in a study of mid-level marketing managers in two different organizations. The results provide insights into the nature of implementation in marketing and suggest future research opportunities.

Lane, Nikala (2005), 'Strategy Implementation: The Implications of A Gender Perspective for Change Management', *Journal of Strategic Marketing*, 13 (2), pp. 117–31.

This is a very interesting article, which examines how the managerial style of strategy implementation will vary between male and female sales managers.

Abstract: The implementation of strategic marketing plans remains an elusive goal for many organizations, with many managers knowing what to do but not how to do it. A relevant question relating to the implementation capabilities of managers regards the characteristics of successful implementors. This question highlights several interesting issues, including the impact of manager gender. The current paper reveals the role of female managers in implementing new management techniques in sales organizations, namely, the introduction of behaviour-based management control strategies as an indicator of a possible gender dimension in more general implementation capabilities. The paper summarizes the findings from single company and multi-company studies where the implementation capabilities of male and female field sales managers are examined. The provocative conclusion is that superior implementation capabilities are shown by female sales managers in the implementation of behaviour-based control strategies. The authors suggest this finding may provide insight into implementation capabilities in strategic marketing and more generally.

Raps, Andreas (2004), 'Implementing Strategy', *Strategic Finance*, 85 (12), pp. 48–53.

This paper highlights the low rate of success when it comes to strategy implementation. It encourages business organizations to pay more attention and invest more resources to develop and improve strategy implementation skills as they have done in the past for developing strategic planning skills.

Abstract: The author says that, only a minority of companies have successfully implemented a strategic plan: only 10% to 30% of companies. This low rate is discouraging, especially since a growing number of companies in recent years have invested considerable resources to develop strategic planning skills. Companies obviously need to improve strategy implementation activities, but the pace of these activities and the implementation itself have many problems. Traditional strategy implementation concepts overemphasize structural aspects, reducing the whole effort to an organizational exercise. Ideally, an implementation effort is a 'no boundaries' set of activities that does not concentrate on implications of only one component, such as the organizational structure. The paper says companies should concentrate on four key success factors: (1) culture, (2) organization, (3) people, and (4) control systems and instruments. The author stresses that it is worth the effort. An efficient strategy implementation has an enormous impact on a company's success.

Piest, Bert, and Henk Ritsema (1993), 'Corporate Strategy: Implementation and Control', *European Management Journal*, 11 (1), pp. 122–31.

This is an interesting article, which suggests incorporating the implementation process of corporate strategy with the control system in order for organizations to achieve their strategic objectives more effectively in a dynamic environment.

Abstract: Implementing and controlling corporate strategy is not an easy matter. What is called for is flexible control, combining individual creativity and direction without becoming rigid. In a dynamic environment, change is the only constant factor. Therefore, possibilities for changing the corporate strategy should be incorporated into the control system. This sets specific demands concerning the process of controlling a strategy. Some of the basic issues for implementation and control are discussed. These issues are: (1) using the business mission as a management instrument, (2) developing a control system that is directed toward the future, (3) discovering the limited value of financial figures, (4) finding information that is really meaningful, and (5) making 'what if?' analyses. Regarding the implementation of these management instruments, the control system should be kept simple and the company should be segmented into various entities.

END OF CHAPTER 13 CASE STUDY Corporate culture: from real world firms

Set out below are the espoused corporate cultures of three well-known firms.

Hewlett-Packard

Hewlett-Packard is a company that has, for a long time, been conscious of its culture ('The HP Way') and has worked hard to maintain it over the years. Hewlett-Packard's corporate culture is based on (1) respect for others, (2) a sense of community, and (3) plain hard work (*Fortune* magazine, 15 May 1995). It has been developed and maintained through extensive training of managers and employees. HP's growth and success over the years has been due in large part to its culture.

Google

Google's corporate culture (from **www.google.com/corporate/culture.html**)
Though growing rapidly, Google still maintains a small company feel. At the Googleplex headquarters almost everyone eats in the Google café (known as 'Charlie's Place'), sitting at whatever table has an opening and enjoying conversations with Googlers from all different departments. Topics range from the trivial to the technical, and whether the discussion is about computer games or encryption or ad serving software, it's not surprising to hear someone say, 'That's a product I helped develop before I came to Google.'

Google's emphasis on innovation and commitment to cost containment means each employee is a hands-on contributor. There's little in the way of corporate hierarchy and everyone wears several hats. The international webmaster who creates Google's holiday logos spent a week translating the entire site into Korean. The chief operations engineer is also a licensed neurosurgeon. Because everyone realizes they are an equally important part of Google's success, no one hesitates to skate over a corporate officer during roller hockey.

Google's hiring policy is aggressively non-discriminatory and favors ability over experience. The result is a staff that reflects the global audience the search engine serves. Google has offices around the globe and Google engineering centers are recruiting local talent in locations from Zurich to Bangalore. Dozens of languages are spoken by Google staffers, from Turkish to Telugu. When not at work, Googlers pursue interests from cross-country cycling to wine tasting, from flying to frisbee. As Google expands its development team, it continues to look for those who share an obsessive commitment to creating search perfection and having a great time doing it.

ExxonMobil

Corporate culture (from **www.exxonmobil.com**)
ExxonMobil is a company built from two of the most successful companies in the world. We're a new company with an emerging culture. Since the merger in 1999, we brought together the best of the best ... forming a culture born of excitement, energy and pride. Our culture is one of:

- Coaching, mentoring and continuous learning
- Focusing on doing everything we do better than anyone else
- Developing and applying work processes and new technology to keep us out in front
- Responsible management
- Leadership and success
- High standards of business conduct based on a guiding principle of compliance with all laws and regulations and adherence to the highest ethical standards

Source: This case was prepared by Professor Leyland Pitt, Faculty of Business Administration, Simon Fraser University, as the basis for analysis and class discussion and not to illustrate either effective or ineffective handling of an administrative situation

QUESTIONS

1. How do the corporate cultures of the three firms differ, and in what ways are they similar?
2. What do the descriptions of the corporate cultures tell you about the three firms? If you had a choice, having read the descriptions, which firm would you most like to work for, and which firm would you least like to work for?
3. Then speculate on the implementation of a radical marketing strategy in each firm. In which firm do you think it would be most difficult to implement a radical marketing strategy, and where would it be easiest?
4. ExxonMobil is a firm that resulted from the merger of two companies, Exxon and Mobil. What difficulties would you anticipate from a managerial perspective, with regard to corporate culture when firms merge?

Part VI Conclusion

I. Introduction
1. Overview
2. Marketing strategy: analysis and perspectives

II. Where are we now?
3. Environmental and internal analysis: market information and intelligence

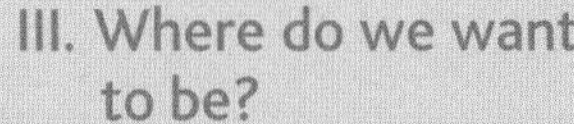

III. Where do we want to be?
4. Strategic marketing decisions and choices
5. Segmentation, targeting, and positioning strategies
6. Relationship strategies

IV. How will we get there?
7. Product innovation and development strategies
8. Branding strategies
9. Service marketing strategies
10. Pricing and distribution strategies
11. Marketing communications strategies
12. E-marketing strategies

V. Did we get there?
13. Strategy implementation and control

VI. Conclusion
14. Social marketing and CSR

Part VI Conclusion

I. Introduction
1. Overview
2. Marketing strategy: analysis and perspectives

II. Where are we now?
3. Environmental and internal analysis: market information and intelligence

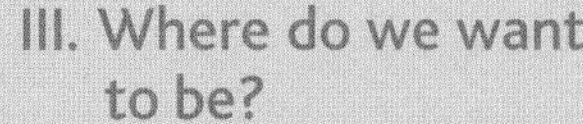

III. Where do we want to be?
4. Strategic marketing decisions and choices
5. Segmentation, targeting, and positioning strategies
6. Relationship strategies

V. Did we get there?
13. Strategy implementation and control

IV. How will we get there?
7. Product innovation and development strategies
8. Branding strategies
9. Service marketing strategies
10. Pricing and distribution strategies
11. Marketing communications strategies
12. E-marketing strategies

VI. Conclusion
14. Social marketing and CSR

14

Social marketing and corporate social responsibility

LEARNING OBJECTIVES

- Examine the various levels of corporate social responsibility (CSR)
- Provide a comparison between the interests of shareholders as opposed to the firm's stakeholders
- Discuss ethics and moral judgement and the firm's actions as a morally responsible organization in society
- Explain philanthropic activities and initiatives and cause-related marketing strategic choices
- Present a discussion of the relevance of environmental responsibility and stewardship and marketing strategic choices
- Illustrate the ways in which a firm can get involved in socially responsible activities to improve its standing as a hands-on and caring community citizen
- Examine the ways in which the CSR strategist can make social responsibility meaningful for the firm by making it a strategic imperative as opposed to an act of compliance
- Discuss ways in which social responsibility can be measured and evaluated

CHAPTER AT A GLANCE

Introduction

In today's world of business, the wants and needs of society are an important contextual consideration. Firms must not only produce excellent goods and services and produce a healthy profit, but also be concerned with their relationship with society at large as well as with the environment. The marketing concept has evolved into market orientation, and firms are more heavily focused on wants and needs of consumers, but this is no longer sufficient. There is a broader context in which the firm operates, and the well-being of society and consumers must be taken into consideration for the firm to be seen as a good community citizen. Not only do consumers expect that corporations will operate legally and fairly, they also want them to act ethically, help charitable causes, clean up the environment, and improve conditions for citizens locally, regionally, nationally, and in some cases internationally. Companies must now be socially responsible. This last chapter serves as a fitting way to conclude this text as everything that was presented in earlier chapters will potentially be enhanced if the company acts as a socially responsible community citizen.

What is corporate social responsibility?

So what exactly is corporate social responsibility? Is it being perceived as a moral and ethical corporation? Is it corporate philanthropy? Is it being 'green'? Is it helping the local community? Is it helping third-world countries? The answer is that all of these are examples of CSR tactics, but each may be insufficient on its own. It is a multifaceted construct that is more complex than once thought. Corporate social responsibility is the actions of the company to act in a socially responsible manner to protect and enhance the various stakeholders that have an interest in the company, the community in which it operates, the environment which surrounds it, and society.

Archie Carroll (1991) presents an excellent graphic to demonstrate the various facets of CSR, which he calls the Pyramid of Corporate Social Responsibility. He envisions the pyramid with the economic aspects of CSR as the foundation since the business's main reason for being is to make money and grow. The second tier then becomes the legal components of CSR that focus on compliance with the rules affecting all business entities. The third tier is the ethical layer, and once the economic and legal facets have been covered, the business must ensure that it acts in a moral and ethically appropriate manner as dictated by human rights requirements and society's expectations. The final level then reflects the highest level, philanthropic activities, which entails those efforts above and beyond the economic, legal, and ethical components. Here the company addresses the needs of the greater community. The idea here is that once lower levels are addressed, the firm can move to the next higher level. The economic and legal aspects of the firm's performance are covered in many ways by other chapters in this book. The ethical and philanthropic levels are covered in this chapter, along with evolutionary additions to the firm's corporate social expectations (beyond philanthropy).

One important caution for global companies at this point is that different cultures may have different perceptions of the use and importance of different levels of the CSR

Pyramid. A recent article by Nabil Ibrahim and Faramarz Parsa (2005) found that there were significantly different CSR responsiveness orientations between American and French managers. The authors found that in general American managers were driven more by legal and ethical considerations in their orientation to CSR while the French were driven more by the economic and philanthropic components. Such cultural differences can have a significant bearing on the success of global CSR initiatives, and understanding the potential for differences in perceptions helps prepare CSR strategists for alliances with foreign firms and organizations. Clearly, this research is in its infancy, and with the growing importance of CSR, more research is needed.

An important starting point for understanding corporate responsibilities is the determination of whom the firm is actually serving with its operations. Is it the shareholder or is it a wider variety of publics? This determination will lead the company to undertake very different strategic initiatives.

Shareholders vs stakeholders

One can see in all of this a potential conundrum in that on the one hand there are those who follow the philosophy that the social responsibility of the firm is to make the most money that it can for its shareholders within legal means. The other side argues that activities undertaken with the aim of being a good citizen, and giving money to needy organizations or undertaking community improvement projects, reduce profits or force firms to increase retail prices to cover the costs incurred. To understand the potential benefits of CSR, one has to be careful to examine all of the relevant constituencies affected by the firm's actions (Snider et al., 2003). The important distinction here really lies in whom the firm sees as its important constituencies. If shareholders are the only public the firm is concerned with, then all actions undertaken must be done in a way that will maximize return for shareholders. This perspective would argue strongly against any expenditure without proven profitability. One could argue that any community investment expenditure or donation to a charitable organization would be seen as a potential drain on company financial performance. If, on the other hand, the firm considers that there are a variety of publics that must be considered, then it might strategically make a very different set of choices.

Stakeholders are all those groups or publics that interact with and are affected by the operations of the firm. These publics include employees, partners, suppliers, customers, community members, governmental agencies, and social activist groups (see Figure 14.1). If the firm takes the view that all of these groups have a stake in the operations of the firm, then their concerns must also be considered in corporate strategies and CSR initiatives. It may be that value perceived by some of these stakeholder groups may precede and in some cases drive improvements in shareholder wealth (Snider et al., 2003). As a result, stakeholder theory serves as a better framework for examining CSR.

Understanding the various stakeholder groups and their concerns, the firm is in a stronger position to examine an array of CSR components to see which ones are most appropriate. While the CSR Pyramid placed philanthropic activities at the top level, philanthropy as a tactic is only one of a number of different possibilities for CSR initiatives. The following sections will present discussions of corporate ethicality, philanthropy, environmental or green marketing, and social activism (see Figure 14.2).

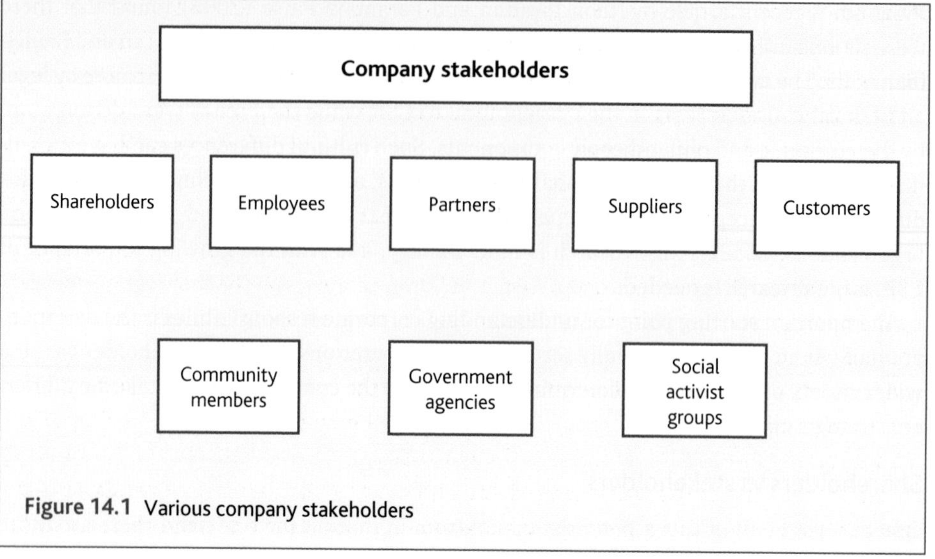

Figure 14.1 Various company stakeholders

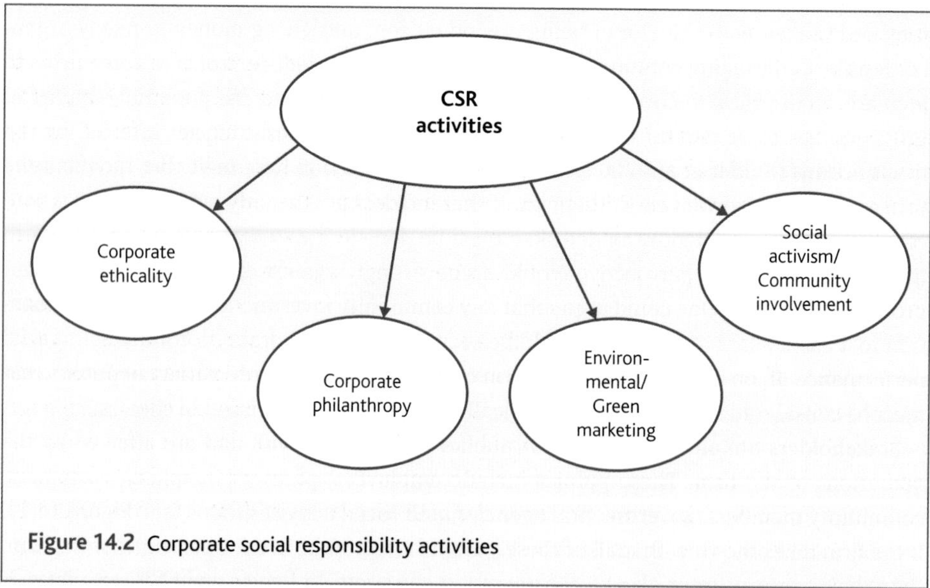

Figure 14.2 Corporate social responsibility activities

Corporate ethicality

What is clear is that CSR is more complex than originally thought. At one time being a good corporation meant operating in a reasonable manner, adhering to laws and regulations, but as corporations like Enron, MCI, Parmalat, and Credit Lyonnais have been seen to violate public trust, the issue of ethicality has been added to the set of firm requirements. Charles Handy in a 2002 article in *Harvard Business Review* discussed how serious this loss of trust had become in the USA and the UK. He reported that a 2002 Gallup poll found that 90%

of the Americans surveyed felt that those running corporations could not be trusted to look after the best interests of their employees. In this same study it was also reported that only 18% of those surveyed believed that companies spent a significant amount of effort looking after their shareholders, and 43% perceived that senior executives were only concerned with their own well being. Seeing the enormous amount of money being paid as salaries to senior executives when their companies were seriously underperforming presents supporting evidence of this problem. In fact Handy reports that a British survey found that 95% of those British respondents surveyed believed that senior executives were looking out for their own self-interests. This is representative of a serious problem, and the first step in eliminating the problem involves companies taking a harder stand on acting in an ethically responsible manner.

What is ethics? It is the set of moral principles or values that shape the actions of either an individual or a group of individuals. Ethical principles therefore set a standard for behaviour in a society. Legality sets the foundation for what behaviours are seen as lawful or unlawful, but ethics focuses more on moral judgement, and in particular on whether an action is the right thing to do from a moral standpoint as opposed to whether it is lawful or not. The difficulty is that certain activities that are seen as lawful may not actually be seen as ethical or as morally appropriate, and certain activities that are seen as unlawful may not be morally inappropriate.

Why do we need ethics? Because there are a number of examples of businesses that have acted in ways that have damaged public trust. Scandals throughout the global business community have served to weaken consumer trust and belief in big business. Ethicality and the adoption of codes of ethical conduct serve to signal to the public that the companies that adopt them will not abide by unethical behaviour. With ethics the question is not whether an action is legal or not, but whether the action is morally right or wrong. Morals are basically sets of rules derived from cultural norms. Moral judgement is the framework of beliefs upon which the individual makes judgements on whether an action is morally appropriate or not. Different cultures have achieved different levels of moral judgement, which affects their views on whether certain actions are ethical or unethical. Cultural differences in ethical predisposition can be seen clearly when collectivist cultures are compared to individualistic cultures (Ford et al., 1997). Japanese managers having a collectivist orientation must undertake actions that benefit the group as a whole before they can even think about their own personal aggrandizement. Individualistic American managers look towards benefiting themselves first and secondarily looking to benefit the group. These differences in perspective and expectation can create difficulties when addressing the issue of the ethicality of certain actions. As an example, a Japanese firm may use individuals to do intelligence-gathering about competitors' actions using any means necessary to find information that will help their company, but if the organization is put in a better position as a result of the information-gathering, even if the actions were not morally defensible, the group benefits, and the individual benefits because the group benefits. The danger would be that, if the Japanese employees were actually caught in the act of using inappropriate means to get the information, they would actually bring shame upon the company and be fired. This shows the potential complexity in the determination of right or wrong when judging the ethicality of certain actions or practices. Does the end justify the means, or do the means justify the ends? These are fundamental philosophical arguments, and different cultures may approach ethical responsibility from different perspectives. In some cultures if the group benefits as a result of the action, that is the only thing that matters. In other cultures, doing things the right way will ensure that the outcome is also morally defensible. What is ethical is a complex subject.

So how does a company approach ethical actions and ensure that it acts in an appropriate manner? It sets up a set of ethical guidelines for behaviour. All employees of the organization are asked to adhere to these guidelines in their actions. These guidelines often become formalized into a code of ethical conduct. It is expected that all individuals who are employed by the company will follow the code. Lamb et al. (2005) suggest that developing ethical guidelines or codes of conduct provides companies with the following advantages:

1. Employees learn to identify what the company recognizes as acceptable business practices.
2. The guidelines can serve as an effective internal behavioural control mechanism.
3. A written code eliminates any confusion as to whether a practice is ethical or not for decision-making purposes.
4. The formulation of the code of ethical conduct allows for discussion among the firm's employees of what is appropriate or not and produces better decision-making.

But is being ethical sufficient? If we look back to the Pyramid of CSR, we see it is a step in the right direction, but it does not go far enough. The fourth level involves corporate philanthropic activities.

Corporate philanthropy

Corporate philanthropy is primarily focused on corporate giving to charitable organizations. Michael Porter and Mark Kramer (2002) suggest that while most companies feel that they should give to charities, most do not know how to do it well. They argue that what is considered to be strategic philanthropy by many corporations is often far more opportunistic than strategic, or worse, done for the sake of doing it rather than trying to give anything meaningful. They suggest that philanthropy is actually more like public relations or advertising that works to enhance a company's image by attaching the name to cause-related marketing or charitable sponsorships. Porter and Kramer ask whether corporations should even consider giving philanthropically. If by philanthropy one is referring to a variety of small cash payments to local charities or universities, this may not be appropriate, especially if the giving is more a function of the interests of certain executives in the organization. What is needed is the connection of these payments to a series of sound social or business objectives. What Porter and Kramer (2002) suggest is that charitable giving can be used to improve an organization's 'competitive context', which entails the actual quality of the business environment in the locations where the company does business. They suggest that philanthropy be used to merge social goals and economic goals, thus allowing the company both to give money but also leverage relationships and capabilities in the active support of charities. To accomplish this, changes would have to be made in the way that the business approaches charitable giving. The business needs to refocus on where it should spend its money, as

well as how. The first requirement is to choose the most suitable recipients for charitable donations. Who will benefit most from the company's donations? Who fits with the company's mission and capabilities? These are important questions to be answered first before anything else is attempted. The second step entails alerting other funders to the choice of recipient for donations. By attracting the interest of other donors, the organization ensures that overall philanthropic spending is increased and spread more effectively across a number of givers. Step three involves the improvement of recipient performance, which will not only benefit society but also increase the impact of the monies given. This will then lead to the fourth step, the advancing of knowledge and practice, setting up what Porter and Kramer identify as a 'virtuous cycle'.

Another variant of charitable giving is what has become known as cause-related marketing or CRM (not to be confused with customer relationship management). Cause-related marketing involves a linking up between the corporation and a particular charitable cause. There are two ways that this can happen: the company can make unconditional donations on a regular basis to a particular charitable cause, or it can link its donations to customer purchase behaviour. The company that makes a donation to charity once a consumer has made a particular purchase allows the company to receive its benefit before the charitable organization receives its donation. Intuitively, one would expect that this could leave the consumer feeling that the activity is not as altruistically motivated as unconditional donations would be; however, a study done in 2003 (Dean, 2003/2004) found that when consumer perceptions of conditional and unconditional donations to charitable causes were compared, there was little negative effect found for the use of conditional donations. This study also examined whether long-term relationships with charitable causes and corporate donations were more important than single donations to charities, and the findings indicated that:

- firms with excellent reputations for social responsibility gain little from single-instance charitable donations
- firms with poor reputations for social responsibility may significantly improve consumer perceptions from single-instance charitable giving
- firms with average reputations may or may not see improvements in consumer perceptions with single-instance giving
- firms that are perceived to be irresponsible socially will not be thought of as excellent community citizens with a single charitable donation. This will take time and effort to significantly change

Ultimately, if the firm is interested in charitable giving, it must note that there are concerns associated with donations (Endacott, 2004). One is that causes like products or services may be subject to changing consumer preferences. What is the 'hot' cause or charity today may lose resonance with a company's consumers tomorrow, so the donor company must be careful to track the perceptions of its consumers periodically to see if their views of a particular charity or cause have changed. Significant events like hurricanes, terrorist attacks, tsunamis, and other disasters can divert consumer interests and force the company to shift its focus to a different charitable organization. The selection of a cause must be done carefully since the cause or causes must resonate with the company's consumers and have a logical association with the company brand. Finally, for multinational companies, there are very few global charities but there are many global causes, so the multinational must be careful to choose wisely and realize that consumers in different countries may have significantly different perceptions of the same charitable organization or cause.

Merely giving to or affiliating with a charitable organization may not be sufficient. Another possibility involves focusing on improving the environment. This may have social consequences certainly, but the concern is for the improvement of the environment. Strategically this may be a better choice for companies that have been criticized for polluting the environment or cutting down forests. It may be a necessary step to improving a damaged image.

Environmental/green marketing

Environmental concern is another important aspect of CSR. Environmental/green marketing involves the actions undertaken by the firm or donations that are aimed at improving or preserving the environment surrounding the firm. Green marketing focuses on the idea of keeping the environment clean and green. This often entails reducing or eliminating corporate pollution. There is certainly support for the statement that 'it pays to be green'. One can see many examples where the concerns of the environment are being strategically built into corporate plans. Take the visible example of McDonald's. McDonald's was criticized for using styrafoam packaging for its hamburgers that was not biodegradable. Strategically turning to improving its image, McDonald's began to replace the plastic packaging with paper packaging so that they were seen as more environmentally friendly. The New Zealand government decided that since it was already known for its clean and green environment, anything made or connected with New Zealand would benefit from that association, so fruit, vegetables, lamb, agricultural equipment, and other products were automatically tagged with the 'Made in New Zealand' label, which signalled environmental responsibility. There was great synergy strategically in undertaking this since New Zealand found that its competitive advantage lay in its excellent agricultural industry.

Recently, Kia attempted the green strategy in the UK by offering a free bicycle with the purchase of a Sedona Car ('Brands that Play the Green Card', 2005). Since most car trips in the UK were found to be less than one mile in distance, Kia's concern was to give a free bicycle so that any short trips could be done on the bicycle, while longer trips could be handled using the Sedona. Kia also utilized a 'walking bus' campaign to promote the escorting of children to school. However, while the company was able to take 1% of the competitive car market, its cars were not seen by the public to be environmentally responsible, so the company was forced to use an aggressive pricing advertising strategy. The mistake here was that its product did not live up to its green strategic orientation and thereby raised concerns among consumers that the image was inconsistent with the company's actions.

A more successful example may be seen in the environmentally responsible campaign undertaken by ABB Corporation. ABB invented a variable-speed drive unit that could allow a factory to operate in much the same way as a hybrid automobile, by slowing the emissions output and saving energy when the plant was not needed at full capacity production.

In 2002 ABB ran a global campaign that claimed that it could stop 50 million tons of carbon dioxide from being produced. The campaign was quite successful, allowing the company to repeat the campaign in 2005 but now suggesting that it can stop 68 million tons ('Brands that Play the Green Card', 2005).

Corporate social responsibility strategists have taken particular notice of the Toyota Corporation's support for the UN World Food Program. Toyota has put its brand soundly behind the United Nation's World Food Program by supplying fleets of trucks to help with food deliveries. They have simply done this and not promoted their actions to the maximum. This is just one more piece of evidence of Toyota's environmental concern, and it has long supported this UN initiative. A clear CSR partnership was formed which works to the benefit of both parties. The UN is aided by the use of the trucks, and Toyota gains increasing credibility for its environmental stewardship. This is an example of a win–win proposition. But what makes this so successful is that this activity is perfectly consistent with Toyota's mission, image, capabilities, and strategic context ('Brands that Play the Green Card', 2005).

Forest Reinhardt, in a 1998 *California Management Review* article, outlined key strategic considerations when attempting to use environmental product differentiation. Reinhardt presented the following requirements for both industrial and consumer marketers (Reinhardt, 1998):

1. Will the customer pay a premium for this environmental product differentiation?
2. Do the customers have credible information about the claims that you are making for these environmentally responsible products?
3. Are there sufficient barriers to imitation to keep competitors from eroding the perceived advantage or your environmentally responsible products?

But environmental causes and actions may not by themselves be sufficient or fit with corporate strategy, and it may make more sense to get involved in social issues and become an activist to improve social conditions. A more hands-on presence may be required in this case.

Social activism and community involvement

One important type of CSR activity involves the firm in an activist role in attempting to improve the community in which it operates. Social activism includes the actions undertaken by a firm, individuals, or a group that are aimed at making the quality of life in society better for all the inhabitants (see Figure 14.3). From a firm strategy perspective, this often involves some kind of proactive role in improving the community in which the firm operates. An important approach to this can be seen in what is known as corporate social initiatives or CSI. Many companies in the UK as well as in the USA are now focused on building corporate images as good community citizens. Major financial resources are being invested in community involvement projects. These projects range from locally focused education and training for youth and adults to improve their employment potential, to global projects involving aid for developing countries.

An example of this social involvement can be seen in the USA in the efforts of the home improvements chain of stores, Home Depot, to bring company employees into community service. In 2004 50,000 of Home Depot's 325,000 employees donated two million hours to

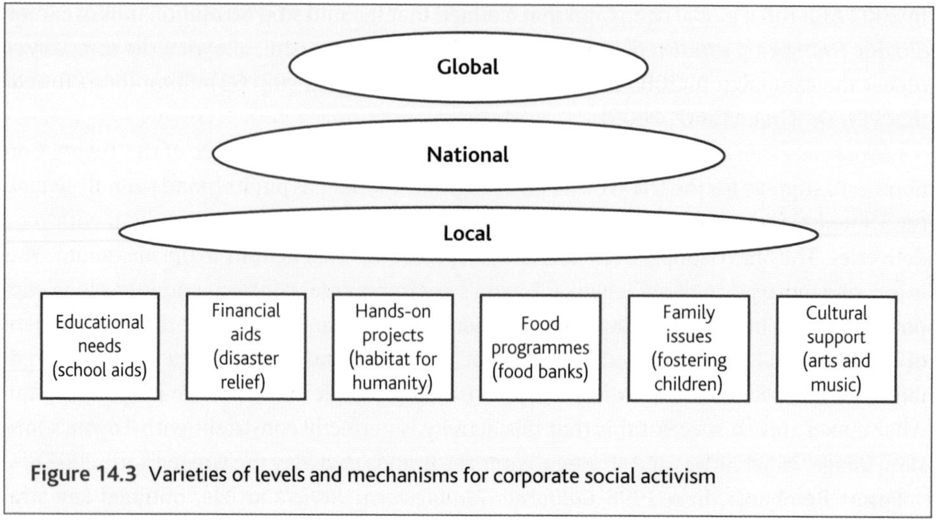

Figure 14.3 Varieties of levels and mechanisms for corporate social activism

community service (Grow et al., 2005). Home Depot's CEO, Robert L. Nardelli, is trying to encourage other companies to follow Home Depot's lead. In May 2005, he invited executives from 24 different companies and foundations to come to Home Depot's headquarters in Atlanta, Georgia to discuss community service initiatives. In September 2005 these executives initiated a 'Month of Service', a plan developed with a community group known as the Hands-On Network, which entails 2,000 different community projects across the United States using corporate volunteers. This is certainly a reflection of the importance of changing the focus from shareholders to stakeholders, as Nardelli argues that the firm must be accountable to its suppliers, customers, employees, community members, and social activists.

The use of the Hands-On Network reflects the fact that partnering possibilities with NGOs (non-governmental organizations) are increasingly important. NGOs are organized around shared values, principles, or beliefs (Spar and LaMure, 2003). They are activist organizations that work for particular causes of interest. Examples include Greenpeace, Earthwatch, PETA (people for the ethical treatment of animals), and the Free Burma Coalition. These organizations can bring strong pressure to bear upon target organizations. When faced with NGO pressure, companies have three strategic options: (1) pre-emption, (2) capitulation, and (3) resistance (Spar and LaMure, 2003). Some firms become proactive and develop a dialogue with NGOs which can lead to a partnership, while others give in to pressure, or fight. The costs of resistance can be high, both from the standpoint of financial costs and from potential damage to images. A good example of partnering with NGOs can be seen in the recent partnership announced between Cadbury Schweppes and two NGOs to work together on a project to improve biodiversity levels of cocoa farms in Ghana and help the country establish its first cocoa farm eco-tourism initiative ('Communication Key to Cadbury-NGO Partnership', 2005). The key to success for this kind of proactive partnering is to understand what each party wants to get from the partnership and see how this can be accomplished. Cadbury paired up with Earthwatch and the Ghana Nature Conservation

Research Centre (NCRC), and the three worked together to find common ground. The partnership helped ensure benefits for each of the three partners. It helped develop strong relationships for Cadbury with cocoa farmers in Ghana, improved the conditions for the farmers, fostered agricultural improvements that aided the environment, and created new natural habitats for wildlife. All round, it was seen as a beneficial relationship. It seems clear that social activism, social projects, and community involvement are important mechanisms for CSR. Mini Case Study 14.1 provides further discussion of this issue.

Hess et al., Rogovsky and Dunfee (2002) argue that these new social projects are a significant departure from previous community relations projects, which were often opportunistically undertaken. The authors suggest that these new Corporate Social Initiatives, as they call them, or CSI are actually closely tied to core competencies and long-term corporate strategies. They cite such companies as United Parcel Service (UPS), which has collected packaged food products from Europe and the United States, stored these donated products in distribution centres, and then delivered those goods to aid refugees and natural disaster victims in impoverished countries. This type of corporate aid represents a major shift from the isolated philanthropic gestures of the 1980s when firms made donations without truly building on their core values, competencies, and long-term strategies. What effective companies now realize is that corporate investments in community development build strong community trust, goodwill, and partnerships, which in turn lead to stronger local economies as well as corporate profitability.

MINI CASE STUDY 14.1 'Big Business Pitches Itself on Fair Trade Territory'

Nestlé's decision to enter the fair trade market by launching its Nescafé Partners' Blend coffee earlier this month has been hailed as a powerful endorsement of moves to give producers in the developing world a better deal. However, it also poses a significant marketing challenge for the smaller, independent groups that have pioneered the fair trade business model.

'While we have always argued that to really impact on world poverty we need the involvement of big commercial companies, the flipside is that we are now conjuring up significant new competitors,' says Paul Chandler, chief executive of Traidcraft, which sells a portfolio of fair trade products through the internet, catalogues and community groups. It also supplies mainstream supermarkets.

Over the past 18 months a number of large retailers, including supermarkets Sainsbury, Tesco and Wal-Mart-owned Asda, have introduced own-label fair trade products—a development that has put pressure on existing fair trade brands. 'We must all work harder now to differentiate ourselves,' says Mr Chandler.

Nestlé is launching its Nescafé Partners' Blend brand in the UK against 107 other coffee brands carrying the Fairtrade mark, spanning 364 different Fairtrade coffee products.

But according to the Fairtrade Foundation, the UK's certification body, there is plenty of room for all because the market, although growing fast, remains far from saturated.

'One of our priorities is ensuring new players grow rather than cannibalise existing sales, so when we are working with a company seeking Fairtrade certification we look » for clear evidence of careful targeting and distinctive market positioning,' says Ian Bretman, deputy director of the Fairtrade Foundation.

'Supermarket own-label Fairtrade products are a discrete brand proposition with their own defined customer base: own-label customers,' he adds. 'Nescafé Partners' Blend, meanwhile, is a mass market proposition that we firmly believe will complement and grow the sector by bringing new consumers in.'

Pearse McCabe, planning director of global brand design consultancy Fitch, adds that Nescafé's appeal may not stretch to some fair trade customers because of the high profile criticisms Nestlé has faced from pressure groups that claim it has aggressively marketed baby milk in Africa.

'In the short term, smaller, independent fair trade products are likely to benefit from the cynicism some consumers may have about Nestlé's move into fair trade, given recent criticism it has attracted for some of its other activities,' says Mr McCabe.

The company has argued that it firmly believes breastfeeding is the best way to feed a baby and that when it does market its infant formula to mothers in the developing world who cannot or choose not to breastfeed, it does so in accordance with World Health Organisation guidelines.

The big commercial brands may also face consumer cynicism because they are moving into the expanding fair trade coffee market at a time when international sales of conventional coffees are in decline. A cynical consumer could therefore view the strategy as defensive as well as socially responsible.

'Consumers are cynical and understand that an organisation like Tesco is driven by delivering shareholder value, so they will closely inspect any established player moving in that direction,' says Jonathan Hall, client managing director of global marketing consultancy Added Value. 'If there is a logical fit and demonstrable proof of their commitment then it will be accepted; without that it will not.'

According to new research conducted by Fitch, today's consumer expects unprecedented levels of integrity from the companies behind the brands they buy. The consultancy found that 83 per cent of British consumers it surveyed believe brands should be more open in their actions; and 41 per cent believe transparency is the best way for a company to demonstrate its honesty.

Fitch's Mr McCabe warns that if consumers can be persuaded of Nestlé's commitment to fair trade, existing fair trade brands will face tough competition backed by a significantly higher brand presence and marketing spend. 'In the longer term, Nestlé could pose a real and substantial threat if consumers believe buying a Nestlé fair trade product has the same positive social impact as buying any other fair trade brand,' he says.

Mr Hall at Added Value notes that as consumers get more choice they tend to grow lazier. 'The last thing any brand wants is for a consumer to have to think too hard about whether to buy, which is why a strong brand relies on a package of different offers,' he says. 'Green & Black's chocolate launched with a clear organic market positioning but care was taken to interweave other attributes into the brand—associations with quality and self-indulgence—which ensured a solid platform for growth.'

In this respect, established fair trade brands are well positioned to defend their territory because marketing fair trade products has always required a delicate balancing act. Penny Newman, chief executive of Cafédirect, the UK's first Fairtrade brand and after 14 years the country's sixth largest coffee brand, explains that marketing fair trade brands

» depends on juggling a number of key messages: 'You can't just rely on the fair trade message. In the early days of fair trade the quality of the first coffees was interesting as the focus was on producer needs rather than customers. But the danger with that was that a consumer wouldn't come back for more if the coffee wasn't up to scratch.'

Mr Bretman of the Fairtrade Foundation adds that today's fair trade brands must communicate not only what they do, but also how they can have a social impact, in addition to the message that what's inside is a great product. 'It's not as easy as it is with other [non-fair trade] products to use the brand as a shorthand,' he claims.

While a better articulation of their ethical credentials is certainly one route for established fair traders to head off the challenge posed by big commercial groups, some suggest a more combative approach is needed. In this respect, companies could try to communicate the distinction between fair trade products and fair trade business.

'Big players coming into fair trade are not necessarily behaving ethically across 100 per cent of their supply chain,' explains Traidcraft's Mr Chandler. 'So it is important for consumers to understand that a company that has a fair trade product is not the same as a company that is a fully fair trade business.'

Ms Newman agrees. 'Consumers look for demonstrations of integrity,' she says. 'Cafédirect has always gone beyond the minimum requirements the Fairtrade mark demonstrates, so it is essential we articulate this along with our commitment to balancing consumers' and producers' needs, product quality, innovation and integrity throughout everything we say and do.'

Kate Nicholas, organizer of last week's International Communications Consultancy Organisation summit on the globalization of public relations and associate publisher of *PR Week*, says: 'Given that many consumers still have only a vague notion of what fair trade is, clear differentiation could be gained by established fair trade brand owners highlighting the activities of their larger, commercial rivals. They might highlight how the major supermarket chains who have recently moved into fair trade treat their suppliers closer to home—in the UK, for example. There's much ammunition there if these longer-standing fair trade businesses chose to take so bold a stand.'

Source: Meg Carter (2005), *Financial Times*, 25 October.

Hess et al. (2002) examined a number of recent successful corporate social initiatives (CSI) and found that they had three things in common:

1. they were all connected to core values of the firms involved
2. they were all built upon the core competencies of the firm
3. the CSI programmes undertaken were systematically reviewed and evaluated and were reported regularly to all relevant firm stakeholders

This represents a shift from seeing only company shareholders as important to viewing all relevant stakeholders (e.g., communities, employees, and governments) as important. The authors argue that the change has been driven by three factors: competitive advantage (community involvement and the resulting positive image create a new source of less-tangible and hard to imitate corporate competitive advantage), the new moral marketplace (companies must adhere to the moral expectations and standards of their stakeholders), and the comparative advantage of private firms (intense competition has enabled private firms to be better positioned to assist in solving social problems than either governments or non-profit organizations).

The authors caution that firms designing corporate social initiatives should be aware of possible criticisms that they may face. Shareholders (rather than stakeholders) may raise concerns about the costs inherent in CSIs that might reduce potential dividend payouts. Even some of the firm's stakeholders may be concerned with the particular causes that are chosen. Finally they caution that CSIs may involve difficult judgements involving such things as the reaction of consumers to the initiatives as well as the nature of the expected market impact. Will the consumers buy into the cause? Will they buy more of the company's products and services as a result?

Hess et al. (2002) present four critical suggestions for companies when approaching the development of Corporate Social Initiatives:

1. The firm must connect the CSIs to its mission statement and core values, with top management integrally involved in the CSI programme development, implementation, and evaluation.
2. The firm's management must be attuned to marketplace expectations of social responsibility so that alienation and reputation loss do not occur.
3. CSIs must be tied directly to the core competencies and primary resources of the company.
4. The company must set clear objectives for CSI programmes and have specific mechanisms for measuring the success of these programmes.

So how do companies measure and communicate their successes in terms of their CSR initiatives? They must be careful to do thorough social audits. There is a growing concern in Europe as well as the United States over the need for social auditing, accounting, and reporting (SAAR). This is a necessary evolutionary development, as a firm's success in terms of social performance must be measured so that this performance can be effectively reported to stakeholders. Social reporting improvements have recently been seen in the creation of the Global Reporting Initiative (GRI) and AccountAbility, the Institute of Social and Ethical Accountability (ISEA). These types of initiatives will help companies better communicate their successes with important stakeholders.

If CSR is so important and widespread, why is there still so much confusion? Because too many firms are doing it just to say that they do it, and they do not have any true commitment to it. CSR must be made an integral part of the strategic planning process.

Moving CSR from compliance to strategic imperative

If the company is to move beyond the use of CSR to pretend it is a community citizen, it becomes imperative to find ways in which the firm can truly live out what it is preaching. This, like strategic planning itself, can be done so that the organization can say that it has completed the process to mark one more box off on the list of things to do. As has been discussed previously in this chapter, CSR is not just giving money to charitable organizations. It incorporates such important issues as human rights, environmental stewardship, family-friendly work conditions, and community development and nurturing. It is a multifaceted construct, which should be thought of as an integral part of business strategy. What firms are now finding is that corporate citizenship leads to competitive advantage. Marc Epstein and Bill Birchard present a convincing argument for this in their groundbreaking 1999 book, *Counting What Counts: Turning Corporate Accountability to Competitive Advantage*. The authors suggest that intense competition in a variety of industries presents companies with the possibility that all of them will be seen as comparable, potentially undermining perceived competitive advantages. A reputation for good corporate citizenship serves as an effective point for differentiation. One can certainly argue that firms like Ben & Jerry's and The Body Shop have made names for themselves with their corporate citizenry. As the authors argue, good reputations attract investors, customers, better job candidates, and nurturing environments help keep employees from leaving. There are also tax benefits that can accrue to those good corporate community members, and, above all else, a strong reputation is not easily undermined by competitors. Well, how do we know that corporate citizenship really pays? Epstein and Birchard (1999) tried to find some evidence to support these claims. They discuss the results of two surveys that were done in 1998 to demonstrate the relevance of CSR. The first was done in the UK by MORI, and the main finding was that one-third of the analysts and institutional investors surveyed believed that community citizenship does positively affect financial performance. The other survey was done by the Conference Board in New York City which involved interviews with 25,000 consumers across 23 countries and found that two-thirds of the consumer respondents felt that businesses should address social issues. Even more enlightening was the fact that 23% of the respondents actually took personal actions to punish those companies that they believed were not being socially responsible.

The problem is that even though this argument has been made, many managers still seem to remain somewhat sceptical about the importance of CSR. The Conference Board went further in its assessment, and found that in the period from 1995 to 1997 those asset management firms that were socially conscious and invested accordingly grew 227% as opposed to growth of only 84% for assets managed across all funds (Epstein and Birchard, 1999). There is at least evidence that being a responsible corporate citizen can be a profitable strategy. What is helping at present is that increasing numbers of firms are actually touting their financial successes from pursuing social responsibility initiatives. In a recent *Marketing Week* article ('Corporate Social Responsibility', 2005), Sainsbury's CEO, Justin King, was reported as telling the company's investors that the company's support of Comic Relief's Red Nose Day generated an extra 0.3% sales in the first quarter of 2005. People were visiting Sainsbury's specifically to buy a red nose (he reported that almost four million were sold) and remaining in the stores to buy other items. As a result, Sainsbury's, which had been struggling financially, was able to increase store sales while also raising £6.5 million for Comic Relief's charities. It seems as though CSR is resonating much more visibly with consumers as well.

If community citizenry is to help the firm gain a competitive advantage, CSR must be integrated into everything that the company does. Epstein and Birchard (1999) examined a number of companies, and they found that the following steps were important in ensuring that this integration actually takes place within the firm:

1. Engage the stakeholders through dialogue ('What would they like us to do?').
2. Define and codify values, codes, and policies ('What does citizenship entail?').
3. Assign executive responsibility ('Who will champion the process?').
4. Integrate social issues into strategic planning ('Is it really important to the company?').
5. Communicate and train ('Are our people on board and committed?').
6. Measure what really counts ('What are meaningful measures for social performance?').
7. Report and verify ('Have we effectively told our story to our stakeholders?').

Companies are increasingly reporting that the pursuit of CSR initiatives is paying back in significant ways. An analysis was carried out by the Work Foundation and The Virtuous Circle in the UK in 2003 to assess whether CSR activities generated higher performance, and the report of this study, published on 25 March 2004, 'Achieving High Performance: CSR at the Heart of Business', indicated that high-performing businesses did show a strong correlation between CSR activities and stronger performance in terms of productivity as well as profitability when compared with other firms ('CSR Activities Generate Higher Performance—Official', 2004). The key as has already been demonstrated is to make CSR a part of corporate planning so that it is pursued meaningfully, carefully, and synergistically. See Mini Case Study 14.2.

MINI CASE STUDY 14.2 'Nike Shows the Way to Return from the Wilderness'

In the 1990s Nike became the clear global market leader in sportswear with high global brand awareness. Phil Knight, the innovative founder and chief executive officer, had built an incredible global empire with a highly-focused brand architecture making lucrative use of the recognizable company 'swoosh' logo and a series of tie-ins with recognizable sports figures like Michael Jordan and Tiger Woods. In order to compete in the highly competitive clothing industry, Nike had been moving its production facilities from developed to developing countries for decades. While the strategic choices that Phil Knight had made had created a global brand giant and made him the sixth richest man in the United States, these great strengths eventually became the company's biggest problems.

In 1992, *Harpers* magazine ran a story which contrasted the global sports figure, Michael Jordan, with a poor young factory worker in Indonesia by the name of Sadisah. The article reported that Sadisah worked six days a week, 10 hours a day, earning 14 cents per hour making Nike running shoes. It would take Sadisah 30 days to be able to afford a single Nike shoe at the US retail selling price. The article then went on to claim that it would take Sadisah more than 44,000 years to earn as much money as Michael Jordan had received from Nike for signing his endorsement deal.

This article started a strong public backlash, and intense criticism was directed at Nike. Publications such as *The Economist* began to take aim at Nike, and even »

» charitable organizations such as Oxfam and Christian Aid began to join the ranks of the outraged. In a number of countries when Nike retail stores were opened during this time period, protesters would clash with police and often these protests would become violent. On American university campuses students protested against Nike's slave-labour practices and argued for their university sports programs to sever all connections to the Nike brand. The criticism became so widespread that a number of anti-Nike websites began to appear using such clever vehicles as the 'swooshtika', an altered variation of the swoosh, and such slogans as 'Nike: Just Don't' as opposed to the company's recognizable 'Just Do It'. By 1998 Nike became synonymous with slave labour and worker abuse.

The way in which Nike handled the problem was a perfect example of what should not be done in handling corporate social responsibility (CSR). The company did not respond effectively to the criticisms, and went on its way carrying out business as usual. It became particularly noticeable that the company had no concern over its tarnished community citizen image when Phil Knight was interviewed about the use of underage workers in sweat shops in a documentary film, entitled *The Big One*, made by the social activist Michael Moore and responded that Moore should 'Tell it to the United Nations'.

The backlash was so problematic that Phil Knight finally responded in 1998 with a Corporate Social Responsibility program that included a six-point plan, establishing a new independent monitoring system to oversee operations, the raising of minimum worker age requirements in all company plants, and setting formal targets for improving overseas worker conditions. A large CSR department was also established which reported directly to Phil Knight, and Nike went on the offensive to actively seek out and work with its biggest critics to build a better company image. In April of 2005 Nike published its second formal Corporate Responsibility Report. This document is remarkable in that it is the first document of its kind to reveal all of its factory locations, the labour policies for each of these locations, and the manner in which it intends to systematically improve the employment practices of its suppliers. This document is being hailed as a model for UK firms that are mandated by law to produce an Operating and Financial Review that is to include CSR information, practices and policies. Nike provides an excellent example of how a company can improve its brand image by acting in a socially responsible manner and making its operations transparent to a global public.

Source: Mark Ritson (2005), *Marketing*, 20 April, p. 21.

Lessons learnt by key CSR practitioners

An insightful article was recently published in *Corporate Responsibility Management* that provided important strategic lessons learnt by five, experienced CSR practitioners (Longshaw, Roper, May, Hastings, and Patterson, 2005). Paul Longshaw is a CSR consultant who has worked with a number of major corporations including British Petroleum, Cancer Research UK, Orange, Oxfam, and Vodafone. One particularly relevant lesson related to his experiences with BP, which tasked him and three others with the responsibility of implementing a global volunteering initiative for 100,000 employees. He found out that it is not possible to do this virtually through the intranet. He found that this kind of communication really had to be done face to face. He had to be able to convince them, but this could not be done from a distance. He also recommends that global programmes of this kind have to allow for cultural adaptations since different cultures have different ways of dealing with community involvement. His last recommendation was that if a company attempts to implement this kind of global initiative, it should ensure that it is seen to be strongly backed by senior management. Their names and endorsement should be readily visible.

Another practitioner interviewed in the article is Anita Roper who was hired as the director of sustainability at Alcoa. Her recommendation is to take the time to talk to the relevant stakeholders. Nothing is better than outright personal consultation, but the process takes time and should be planned for. All relevant stakeholders should be included and given sufficient time to understand the issue and give their informed opinion.

Brendan May, head of CSR at Weber Shandwick, a UK public relations company, also participated. May suggests that the greatest lesson he learnt was to actively engage NGOs. The people who work for NGOs work for low salaries because they are so strongly committed to the cause that they are focused on. They tend to be well trusted by the public, and entering into dialogue and eventual partnerships is the best approach to take.

Further suggestions were made by Michael Hastings, head of corporate social responsibility for the BBC, who provides three main lessons: (1) it is essential to get ownership of the CSR agenda you are interested in undertaking from the CEO, (2) CSR is most importantly about ingraining processes into an organization rather than a PR proposition, and (3) if the process is to be incorporated into the fabric of the organization, you have to show people how it will improve performance.

Moreover Lynn Patterson, senior manager in charge of CSR at RBC Financial group cautioned CSR practitioners that they should take care to slow things down a bit since things are changing quite quickly in CSR. She suggests that rushing in may be a mistake because fads appear and go, and implementing an initiative without knowing who all the key players are and without a network of trusted sources may be disastrous.

The latest thinking: the Virtue Matrix

Roger L. Martin (2002), in *Harvard Business Review*, provided an excellent tool for corporate strategists to allow them to calculate the potential profitability of acting socially responsibly. He called this tool the Virtue Matrix. Martin argues that corporate management must deal with a series of obstacles when attempting to position their companies as better community citizens. If companies commit to community projects that are not undertaken by competitors, they risk losing their competitive position. If they welcome the involvement of the government in overseeing the projects, they face the possibility of new regulations being passed, forcing the company to spend a considerable amount of money in compliance with limited social benefits being realized. Finally, if companies adopt wage scales and working conditions that match those in developed nations, they may force jobs to be outsourced to countries with less restrictive standards. Martin presents CSR as a product or service that is subject to market forces, and his Virtue Matrix allows the user to understand the forces that affect supply and demand.

Martin (2002) divides CSR into two components: instrumental and intrinsic. Instrumental CSR involves such activities as the support of charities and arts/cultural organizations, either by choice or by regulation, that serve both the interests of shareholders as well as the interests of society and the community. Intrinsic CSR includes those actions and initiatives that are altruistic by nature but which may or may not resonate with shareholders. These are actions which are undertaken because management believes that they are the right thing to do but they may not sufficiently serve shareholder interests. By incorporating both of these aspects into the matrix, Martin provides a better framework for managers to evaluate CSR opportunities.

The matrix is divided into four quadrants. The two lower quadrants of the matrix comprise the **civil foundation**, which incorporates laws, regulations, customs, and norms. The left lower quadrant includes conduct that is undertaken **by choice** to adhere to norms or customs, while the right lower quadrant includes those actions that are mandated by regulations or laws. These actions are therefore labelled actions of **compliance**. Martin suggests that many CSR actions begin by entering in the bottom left quadrant, but as they become more the norm rather than the exception, they eventually become the basis for laws or regulations and move to the lower right quadrant. Martin suggests that the key aspect to the civil foundation is that the upper limit is not fixed. It will move over time. In developed economies it may be expected that new social initiatives will often become norms and are later codified. The point is that the upper limit will move. In developed economies it may be expected to move upwards while it might actually move downwards in less healthy economies.

The upper quadrants involve those activities that are intrinsic by nature, which may or may not be seen as beneficial by shareholders over time. These actions are undertaken because management feels they are the correct actions to take. Certainly it would be expected that if these are seen as valuable to shareholders, other companies would imitate those behaviours, and as a result upper quadrant initiatives may move downwards into the civil foundation over time. The upper left quadrant is the **strategic frontier**, which includes activities that may actually add to shareholder value if supported by customers, employees, and governmental agencies. The upper right quadrant is the **structural frontier**, which includes those actions that are intrinsic and clearly not in the interests of shareholders. Here the idea is to bring benefits to society rather than immediately to the company. The line separating these two upper quadrants is shown as a wavy line because some CSR initiatives fall in the middle between actions that would be seen as beneficial and those that would be seen as inappropriate. It becomes clear when examining the matrix that potentially innovative and beneficial initiatives might be stifled because management would not want to take the risk of attempting something which competitors would not emulate and which shareholders would not value.

Martin (2002) argues that the biggest barrier to corporate virtue is the lack of vision inherent in company management. This stems from a lack of vision, but this can be corrected by providing support for businesses and leaders who undertake innovative and risky actions. Martin suggests that **consumer agitation** can help in this regard. Consumer pressure can support corporate actions. Martin also suggests that **peer encouragement** can help as businesses that achieve success can communicate that success and encourage other companies to follow suit. Martin also argues that the lack of any economic incentives is problematic in relation to corporate initiatives that fall within the structural frontier because here the rewards are not necessarily visible to consumers, so consumer agitation will not help and peer encouragement will not be found since the risks may appear to be too high. As a result, it may need government agencies to step in and validate the actions undertaken, in order to help initiatives shift from the upper quadrants to the lower quadrants.

The Virtue Matrix is one of the most interesting and innovative approaches that have been developed to help corporate managers understand the forces inherent in positioning their companies as good community citizens. Companies and their innovative managers can indeed find ways in which to better both society and their own shareholders as well as to create for themselves a competitive advantage and greater profitability if they understand the forces involved and the potential barriers that have to be overcome. The Virtue Matrix provides an excellent tool for strategic decision-making.

Conclusion

Corporate Social Responsibility is a key to corporate success. Firms can no longer think of themselves in isolation from the forces and publics around them. Gone are the days of simply satisfying shareholders. The company of today must pay attention to a number of relevant publics including employees, suppliers, partners, community groups, and social activists. CSR managers must weave initiatives into the basic fabric of the organization, and CSR must be a process that is endorsed by top management. When done the right way, it will improve not only the image of the firm, but also productivity and profitability. Good corporate citizenship is well worth the effort, but it must be tied to the skills, abilities, competencies, and values of the firm.

Summary

Corporate social responsibility is comprised of a number of important components. The firm has an economic responsibility in that it must maximize shareholder value. The firm also has a legal responsibility to operate according to society's rules and regulations. Beyond law and economics, social responsibility also encompasses ethics. The firm must act in a fair, just, and moral way in its operations. Finally corporate social responsibility entails a discretionary/philanthropic level that entails such diverse social responsibilities as donating money and hands-on help to charities, the community, the environment, and in some cases developing nations. Being a good community citizen carries great responsibilities with it. It signifies being a good steward of the investments made by the shareholders; it means operating within the legal system of not only the location of the headquarters but also wherever else the firm has operations; it entails ensuring that the firm, its employees, and its management always do what is fair and morally defensible; and it demands that the firm act in a responsible way to help the local community, make the environment cleaner and safer, and protect community citizens. But being a good citizen is not just doing things that appear to be altruistic for the sake of being able to say that you are a good community citizen. The things that are done, the aid given, the corporate presence in different activities and initiatives must be tied to the mission, values, and essence of the organization and its leadership. Corporate social responsibility must be treated as an integral part of strategic market planning. Only when the company sees itself as a vital member of its various communities will it act in the most appropriate ways and ensure its viability. Hopefully with the strategic knowledge that this text provides the reader will be better prepared to make the most informed decisions as the firm operates in its various markets.

KEY TERMS

Corporate social responsibility The actions of the company to act in a socially responsible manner to protect and enhance the various stakeholders that have an interest in the company, the community in which it operates, the environment which surrounds it, and society.

Shareholders Those individuals who have purchased stock in the company. They have a vested interest in the operation of the firm. They expect the company to be a good steward of their investments.

Stakeholders All the groups or publics that interact with and are affected by the operations of the firm. These publics include employees, partners, suppliers, customers, community members, governmental agencies, and social activist groups.

Ethics The set of moral principles or values that shape the actions of either an individual or a group of individuals. Ethical principles therefore set a standard for behaviour in a society. Legality sets the foundation for what behaviours are seen as lawful or unlawful, but ethics focuses more on moral judgement, and the focus becomes the right thing to do from a moral standpoint as opposed to whether it is lawful or not.

Moral judgement The framework of beliefs upon which the individual makes judgements on whether an action is morally appropriate or not.

Corporate philanthropy The act of giving to charitable organizations. This might include donations of monies, physical labour, or marketing expertise.

Cause-related marketing (CRM) The commitment of a corporation to a particular charitable cause. There are two ways that this can happen: the company can make unconditional donations on a regular basis to a particular charitable cause, or it can link its donations to customer purchase behaviour. The company that makes a donation to charity once a consumer has made a particular purchase allows the company to receive its benefit before the charitable organization receives its donation.

Environmental/green marketing The actions undertaken by the firm or donations that are aimed at improving or preserving the environment surrounding the firm. Green marketing focuses on the idea of keeping the environment clean and green. This often entails reducing or eliminating corporate pollution.

Social activism The actions undertaken by a firm, individuals, or a group aimed at making the quality of life in society better for all the inhabitants. From a firm strategy perspective, this would often involve some kind of proactive role in improving the community in which the firm operates.

Non-governmental organizations (NGOs) Organizations organized around shared values, principles, or beliefs. They are activist organizations that work for particular causes of interest. Examples include Greenpeace, Earthwatch, PETA (people for the ethical treatment of animals), and the Free Burma Coalition. These organizations can bring strong pressure to bear upon target organizations.

Instrumental CSR The types of activities undertaken by the company in support of charities and arts/cultural organizations, either by choice or by regulation, that serve both the interests of shareholders as well as the interests of society and the community.

Intrinsic CSR Actions and initiatives that are altruistic by nature but which may or may not resonate with shareholders. These are actions which are undertaken because management believes that they are the right thing to do but they may not sufficiently serve shareholder interests.

DISCUSSION QUESTIONS

1 What is the difference between company shareholders and stakeholders, and why would this matter when determining appropriate CSR strategy?

2 What is moral judgement, and how does it affect ethical decision-making?

3 How do French and American managers differ in their views of corporate social responsibility, and why would this be important for a CSR strategist?

4 What is cause-related marketing, and what are the two variations of cause-related giving that were discussed in the chapter?

5 What are the three primary requirements for using environmental product differentiation as suggested by Forest Reinhardt, and why is this important for the CSR strategist?

6 What are corporate social initiatives, and what are important considerations when they are being developed?

7 Does corporate social responsibility create firm profits? How do we know?

8 What is the Virtue Matrix, explain how it works, and why is it important for the CSR strategist?

ONLINE RESOURCE CENTRE

Visit the Online Resource Centre for this book for lots of interesting additional material at: **www.oxfordtextbooks.co.uk/orc/west/**

REFERENCES AND FURTHER READING

Carroll, Archie (1991), 'The Pyramid of Corporate Social Responsibility: Toward the Moral Management of Organizational Stakeholders', *Business Horizons*, (July–August), pp. 39–48.

'Brands that Play the Green Card' (2005), *Campaign* (15 July), pp. 26–7.

'Communication Key to Cadbury-NGO Partnership' (2005), *Corporate Responsibility Management*, Vol. 1, No. 4, pp. 8–9.

'Corporate Social Responsibility: Show Them You Care' (2005), *Marketing Week* (5 May), p. 41.

'CSR Activities Generate Higher performance—Official' (2004), *Women in Management Review*, Vol. 19, No. 5/6, p. 280.

Dean, Dwayne Hal (2003/2004), 'Consumer Perception of Corporate Donations: Effects of Company Reputation for Social Responsibility and Type of Donation', *Journal of Advertising*, Vol. 32, No. 4 (Winter), pp. 91–103.

Endacott, Roy William John (2004), 'Consumer and CRM: A National and Global Perspective', *Journal of Consumer Marketing*, Vol. 21, No. 3, pp. 183–9.

Epstein, Marc J., and Bill Birchard (1999), *Counting What Counts: Turning Corporate Accountability to Competitive Advantage* (New York: Perseus Books).

Ford, John B., Michael S. LaTour, Scott J. Vitell, and Warren A. French (1997), 'Moral Judgment and Market Negotiations: A Comparison of Chinese and American Managers', *Journal of International Marketing*, Vol. 5, No., 2, pp. 57–76.

Grow, Brian, Steve Hamm, and Louise Lee (2005), 'The Debate Over Doing Good', *Business Week*, Issue No. 3947 (15 August), p. 76.

Hess, David, Nikolai Rogovsky, and Thomas W. Dunfee (2002), 'The Next Wave of Corporate Community Involvement: Corporate Social Initiatives', *California Management Review*, Vol. 44, No. 2 (Winter), pp. 110–25.

Joachimsthaler, Erich, and David A. Aaker (1997), 'Building Brands Without Mass Media', *Harvard Business Review*, (January–February), pp. 39–50.

Lamb, Charles W., Jr., Joseph F. Hair, Jr., and Carl McDaniel (2005), *Essentials of Marketing*, 4th edn (Mason, Ohio: South-western Publishing).

Longshaw, Paul, Anita Roper, Brendan May, Michael Hastings, and Lynn Patterson (2005), 'What I've Learned as a CSR Practitioner', *Corporate Responsibility Management*, Vol. 1, No. 5, pp. 34–7.

Martin, Roger L. (2002), 'The Virtue Matrix: Calculating the Return on Corporate Responsibility', *Harvard Business Review*, Vol. 80 (March), pp. 68–75.

Porter, Michael E., and Mark R. Kramer (2002), 'The Competitive Advantage of Corporate Philanthropy', *Harvard Business Review*, Vol. 80 (December), pp. 56–67.

Reinhardt, Forest L. (1998), 'Environmental Product Differentiation: Implications for Corporate Strategy', *California Management Review*, Vol. 40, No. 4 (Summer), pp. 43–73.

'Ripping Holes in Big Brands' (2005), *Marketing Week* (28 April), p. 26.

Ritson, Mark (2005), 'Nike Shows the Way to Return from the Wilderness', *Marketing* (20 April), p. 21.

Snider, Jamie, Ronald Paul Hill, and Diane Martin (2003), 'Corporate Social Responsibility in the 21st Century: A View from the World's Most Successful Firms', *Journal of Business Ethics*, 48 (2), pp. 175–84.

Spar, Debora L., and Lane T. LaMure (2003), 'The Power of Activism: Assessing the Impact of NGOs on Global Business', *California Management Review*, Vol. 45, No. 3 (Spring), pp. 78–102.

KEY ARTICLE ABSTRACTS

Hess, David, Nicolai Rogovsky, and Thomas W. Dunfee (2002), 'The Next Wave of Corporate Community Involvement: Corporate Social Initiatives', *California Management Review*, 44 (2), pp. 110–25.

Many organizations are finding that corporate community involvement is a key to success. This helpful article discusses the concept of CSI or corporate social initiatives for guiding community involvement. Critical factors for success are presented to help companies achieve the most effective community image.

Abstract: The practice of corporate philanthropy has evolved significantly over the past few decades and has now become an integral part of corporate strategy. This article identifies an emerging form of corporate community involvement called corporate social initiatives (CSI). CSI programmes differ from their predecessors in that they are connected to the firm's core values, and have clear objectives and means of measurement. This article explicates the drivers behind the increased interest in CSI, relates CSI to changes in the environment of social expectations for business, reviews potential challenges to CSI programmes, and suggests critical factors in the design of successful CSI programmes.

Reinhardt, Forest L. (1998), 'Environmental Product Differentiation: Implications for Corporate Strategy', *California Management Review*, 40 (4), pp. 43–73.

This paper focuses on the strategic use of product differentiation to create a sound corporate reputation for being environmentally concerned. A series of requirements for success in both industrial and consumer goods segments are presented and discussed.

Abstract: Political demands for environmental improvement create obligations for managers that can conflict with shareholder value creation. While differentiating products along environmental lines is a conceptually straightforward way of reconciling these apparently conflicting demands, not all attempts to do so have succeeded. This paper describes three requirements for successful environmental product differentiation: (1) firms must discover or create a willingness in consumers to pay for public goods. (2) Firms must overcome barriers to the dissemination of credible information about the environmental attributes of their products. (3) Firms must defend themselves against imitation. More broadly, environmental strategy must be integrated with the overall strategy of the business. The appropriate environmental strategy depends, like the overall strategy of the business, on the fundamental economics of the industry and the internal capabilities of the business—basic constraints that have often been obscured in the academic debate about business and the environment.

Martin, Roger L. (2002), 'The Virtue Matrix: Calculating the Return on Corporate Responsibility', *Harvard Business Review*, 80 (March), pp. 68–75.

This insightful article provides marketing strategists with a tool for assessing the possible returns from being socially responsible. The Virtue Matrix is presented as an effective mechanism for balancing the costs of social responsibility with the opportunities.

Abstract: Many consumers and investors, as well as a growing number of business leaders, have added their voices to those urging corporations to remember their obligations to their employees, their communities, and the environment, even if they pursue profits for shareholders. But executives who wish to make their organizations better corporate citizens face significant obstacles. If they undertake costly initiatives that their rivals do not embrace, they risk eroding their competitive position. These dilemmas, which have long bedevilled business thinkers, were the focus of discussion among a group of executives, academics, and public-sector policy-makers, Martin included, who gathered at the Aspen Institute in Colorado under the auspices of its Initiative for Social Innovation Through Business. It would be going too far to say the group arrived at any solutions to these urgent problems. But prodded by the discussion, an analytical tool that helps executives think about the pressing issue of corporate responsibility is presented.

END OF CHAPTER 14 CASE STUDY 'How Wal-Mart is swapping tired for tidy'

Supercenter number 1,794 is everything that Wal-Mart wants it to be. The retailer's better-quality George brand women's clothing is showcased at the front of the store, with ample space to browse between the racks. The aisles are neat, the shelves well-stocked. A Wal-Mart employee offers friendly assistance to customers at the automated self-check out. The store, opened last year outside the college town of Bloomsburg, Pennsylvania, has modern-looking sinks and automatic taps in its tidy bathrooms

About 100 miles to the west, Wal-Mart Supercenter 2,129 tells a different story. It sits outside the small town of Clearfield in the wooded mountains of a depressed former coal-producing region. The vast store is open 24 hours a day but it too gives the impression of faded glory. On a recent night-time visit, it had tired-looking fruit and vegetables in its grocery section, jumbled and crowded clothing racks, shelves in need of stacking, messy toilets and a sticky spillage near the milk coolers.

The two stores reflect something of the challenge facing the world's largest retailer in its biggest market. This year, Wal-Mart is expected to record sales of more than $310bn, 80 per cent of which will come from its US operations, with after-tax earnings of more than $10bn [See Figures C14.1 and C14.2]. But, after years of dramatic sales growth and expansion—it has more than 3,000 Supercenters and discount stores spread across the US—Wal-Mart seems to some in Wall Street to have lost its edge. Sales at established stores are sluggish, return on invested capital has diminished and its shares are down 10 per cent so far this year, having touched levels not seen since 1999.

Internationally, too, there have been problems. Asda, which accounts for about half of its international sales, has been losing ground in the UK grocery market to Tesco. Wal-Mart Germany continues to lose money, as do Japan's Seiyu department stores, in which the group has a stake.

At the same time, the retailer is embroiled in a bitter battle over its labour practices that has brought together union-led critics and local activists in the biggest and most expensive campaign facing a single corporation in America (see below). Its headquarters in Bentonville, Arkansas, have also been rocked by a scandal involving Tom Coughlin, its former vice-chairman, who has been accused by the company of embezzling over $400,000 in false expense claims and is under investigation by a federal grand jury.

Last month, after a detailed review of its operations, the retailer laid out its response to the range of challenges it faces. A series of radical changes to the way it does business in America include abandoning its centralised management structure and a

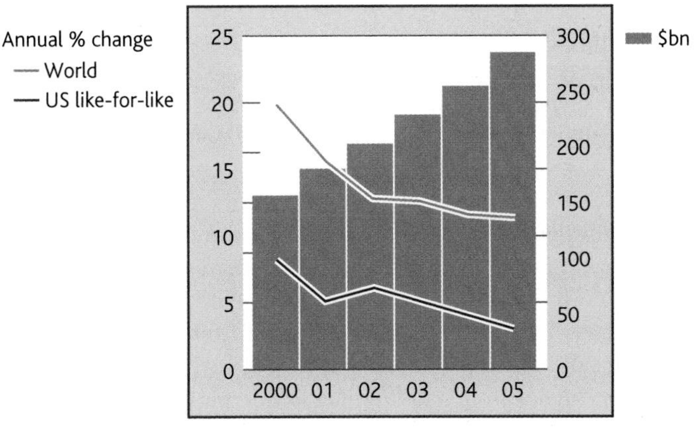

Figure C14.1 Net sales

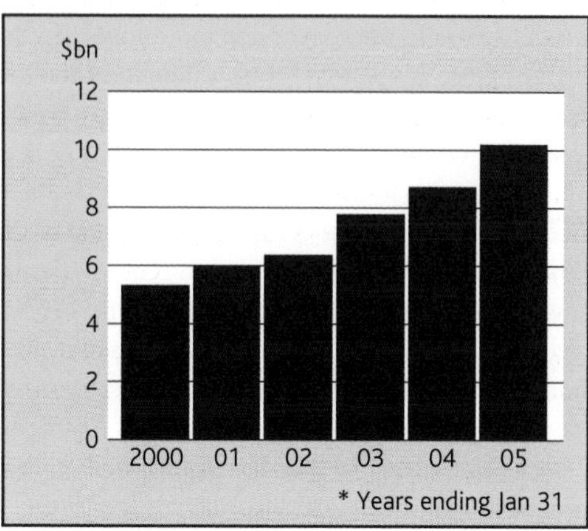

Figure C14.2 Income from continuing operations

marketing strategy aimed at extending its appeal beyond its traditional low-income core customers.

At the same time, Lee Scott, chief executive, has announced changes to Wal-Mart's positioning on environmental and social issues that could eventually reshape its public image, including a commitment to invest $500 m a year in developing environmentally-friendly stores and moves to improve and monitor its global supply chain.

'We are at an inflection point,' says John Menzer, who was last month appointed vice-chairman responsible for Wal-Mart's US operations after six years heading its international division. He compares the changes under way to important moments in the retailer's past such as the opening of the first Supercenter selling both food and merchandise in 1988, its move into Mexico in 1991 and the acquisition of Asda in 1999. He dismisses the idea that Wal-Mart's glory days are gone.

'Ten years ago we were growing at 40 per cent a year, and just the law of numbers means you're not going to keep growing at 40 per cent a year,' says Mr Menzer. 'But growing in strong, low double-digit numbers is still do-able for this company.'

Expansion of the store network remains central to Wal-Mart's growth strategy. The retailer has announced plans to add about another 60 m square feet of retail space worldwide in the year to January 2007—roughly equivalent to Tesco's total and in line with its target of 8 per cent growth in square footage. International store growth will accelerate, while in the US it is planning to add 270–280 Supercenters selling both general merchandise and groceries, of which 160 will be converted from existing stores.

Wal-Mart executives say the retailer still has plenty of room for growth in the US—which delivers higher profit margins than its international operations—and that its property department has identified and approved sites for 900 to 1,000 Supercenters. They also say the political campaign against the retailer has shown no sign of slowing expansion or affecting sales. In the current year, Wal-Mart expects to open 266 Supercenters—more than the 240–250 initially projected.

'The fact of the matter is that customers actually get it, and the best performing openings have been in precisely those "difficult markets" where people thought we wouldn't succeed,' says Eduardo Castro-Wright, head of Wal-Mart's US stores.

Store expansion alone has not been enough to convince the stock market, with analysts focusing on profits that, as a result of increased operating costs, have not been keeping track with sales—one of the company's objectives. Wal-Mart's profits in the three months ending on July 31 grew by 6 per cent, while sales increased 10.2 per cent.

'Our largest operation, Wal-Mart US, has not been growing its earnings at the same rate of sales . . . That is the difficult news,' Tom Schoewe, chief financial officer, told analysts in Arkansas last month, noting that, as a result, Wal-Mart's return on investment had deteriorated this year. But he argued that the trend would flatten out and within 12 to 18 months would reverse.

For Wal-Mart, the principal challenge is to increase sales and profit margins at its US stores to offset cost pressures such as rising wages and healthcare expenses. This year, comparable store sales growth is running at about 3.3 per cent. Wayne Hood, an analyst at Prudential Equity, argues that Wal-Mart needs sales to grow by at least 4 per cent annually to fully offset costs.

Embarrassingly for Wal-Mart's management, the retailer's sales growth has also trailed that of its main rival, Target, whose more prosperous customer base has recently been less affected by higher fuel prices. Target's comparable store sales have risen more than 6.3 per cent this year.

Wal-Mart's management believes that the solution is relatively simple: persuading some of the millions of Americans who shop at its stores for food also to buy products such as clothes and electronics, which bring in higher profits. The retailer estimates that 84 per cent of the US population shops at its stores. But of those who shop there frequently, nearly a third focus only on foods and consumables, which have lower profit margins. [See Figure C14.3.]

'The growth will come from selling more to our core customers,' says Mr Castro-Wright. 'Selling more based on the fact that we know that a lot of the customers already in our stores are shopping for basics but not moving to the other side of the box to shop for general merchandise, apparel and electronics.'

This strategy provides the key to most of the changes. To begin with, Wal-Mart carried out its first wide-ranging customer research last year. While the retailer has collected terabytes of data on what its customers buy, it had traditionally left market research to its suppliers.

'We are a lot more customer-centric than we have ever been,' says Mr Castro-Wright. 'We have a much better understanding of what drives our customer behaviour in our stores and in our competitors' stores. And we're applying that to everything we do.'

The research, involving 13,000 customers, led to the launch in October of a more up-market fashion brand, Metro 7, aimed at the group Wal-Mart dubs 'selective shoppers'—essentially those who might go to Wal-Mart for groceries or household goods but who would not previously have thought of buying clothing.

The strategy has been backed up by a shift in Wal-Mart's advertising style. Traditionally, it has used newspaper inserts to highlight its low prices. Its national television advertising was shot inside its stores and either focused on prices or featured employees extolling the benefits of working for the retailer.

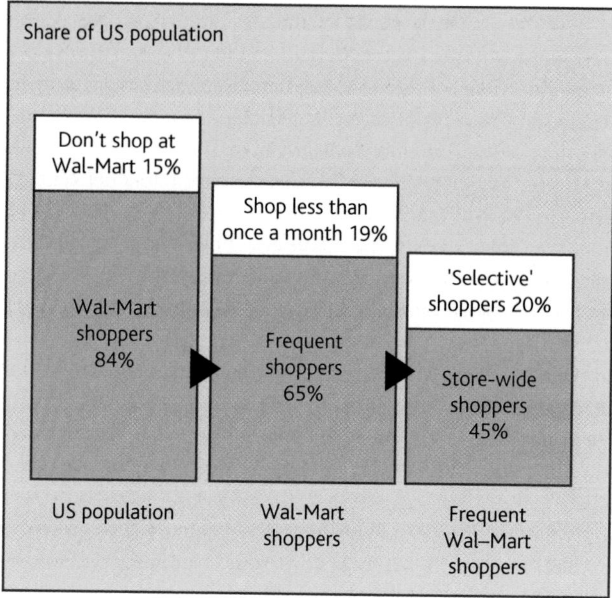

Figure C14.3 US market penetration

Since John Fleming, a former Target executive, took over this year as head of marketing, Wal-Mart's campaigns—including fashion advertising in *Vogue*—have switched their focus to lifestyle rather than pricing. The current Christmas advertising campaign uses celebrities on a scale unprecedented for the retailer. Those appearing include Garth Brooks and Martina McBride, the country and western singers, Destiny's Child, the R&B group, and Queen Latifah, the rapper and actress.

The marketing strategy is linked to a drive to deliver consistency across Wal-Mart's store network. Mr Castro-Wright, the former head of Wal-Mart de Mexico, says the annual sales growth of the 800 best-performing Wal-Mart stores is on average 10 times better than that of its worst performing stores, with clear correlations between staff morale and customer satisfaction. So he is changing the way that district store managers operate, concluding after studying stores' performance over three years that weak management is the principal factor behind underperformance.

'By and large, underperforming stores happen in clusters, and the commonality there is the district manager,' he says. Wal-Mart is appointing fashion and food merchandizers to assist each of its district managers—now called 'market managers'—who will advise on the look and feel of stores.

The changes at that tier of operational management are only part of a larger restructuring. Since it expanded nationally in the 1970s and 1980s, Wal-Mart has been known as a heavily centralised organisation. Every Monday, the heads of its five divisions and 30 regions would take off from Bentonville in the company's private fleet of aircraft

» to visit stores across the US, flying back in time for the weekly Friday meeting at company headquarters. Now the five divisional heads will instead be based around the country and join the meeting by video-conference. Wal-Mart has announced that it will open a Midwest office in Chicago. Mr Menzer says the divisional heads will have the kind of autonomy enjoyed by the heads of Asda or Wal-Mart de Mexico.

'We're emulating the international model,' says Mr Menzer. 'Those five divisional heads will almost be country presidents within Wal-Mart. We'll empower them . . . make them accountable, and we think that will help run the store size that we have today. It's been very successful internationally and we're basically importing it to the US.'

Wal-Mart is also moving nine of its 30 regional managers 'to the field', initially focusing on strategic markets including New York and California, where it is facing some of its strongest political opposition. Mr Castro-Wright says the regional managers are being prepared for their changed responsibilities with business training at Duke University. They will come to Bentonville only every month.

Wal-Mart executives identify other ways they can increase returns, including further expanding the volume of imports handled by its global procurement office. Analysts estimate this accounts for only about 10 per cent of the imported goods Wal-Mart sells, the remainder being acquired through middlemen or suppliers. Mr Menzer also says that further acquisitions remain on the agenda, with Wal-Mart planning to expand international business to about 30 per cent of total sales.

According to Mr Castro-Wright, 'there are no sacred cows' as the retailer seeks to squeeze value from everything from its logistics programmes to staff scheduling. At the same time, the retailer is trying to attract promising outside talent from companies such as PepsiCo's FritoLay and McDonald's.

'We are reviewing everything where we can make an improvement. We're not set in the way that we operate . . . that's not the mindset of the organisation today,' he says.

'Change is something that this company always did very well,' Mr Castro-Wright adds. 'We are changing the way that we are organised and the way that we go to market to become much more relevant to a broader customer.

'That's the direction we're taking. Does that mean we're decentralising? Oh yes, we are, absolutely so.'

Activists join the battle of 'prebuttal' and initiate the 'site fight'

The battle lines were drawn at the JW Marriott Hotel in Washington DC. At 9.30am last Friday, Wal-Mart was due to open a meeting there of academics and media to discuss the retailer's economic impact. So at 8.45am, the Wake Up Wal-Mart campaign launched a pre-emptive strike. At a news conference called in the same hotel, it announced it was setting up a 'Wal-Mart Workers of America Association' to fight for improved conditions for employees.

The tactic worked. Newspapers across the US included a paragraph or two on Wake Up Wal-Mart in their reports of the corporate event. It was the latest skirmish in the most bitter and high-profile battle currently being fought against a single US company, pitting the country's largest private employer against a coalition of activist critics. Their campaign is funded to a large extent by the UFCW, the grocery workers' union that Wal-Mart refuses to recognize. »

» Both sides have adopted the tactics of an American political campaign—hiring professionals adept in the art of the 'prebuttal' and spin. Paul Blank, Wake Up Wal-Mart's director, and Chris Kofinis, its head of communications, worked respectively on Howard Dean's and Wesley Clark's unsuccessful bids for the Democrats' 2004 presidential nomination. Wake Up Wal-Mart has embraced strategies of the Dean campaign, using the internet to build an activist network.

Wal-Mart has countered by hiring Edelman, the public relations group, which runs a 'war room' at the retailer's headquarters to direct media strategy. Advisers include Michael Deaver and Leslie Dach, past media consultants respectively to Ronald Reagan and Michael Dukakis. The sharpened response was demonstrated a few days before the Washington conference. Facing the release of a film called Wal-Mart: the High Cost of Low Price, it detailed what it said were factual errors in the polemic and pointed to scathing reviews of earlier work by Robert Greenwald, the filmmaker.

'This company has spent a long time being quiet, hoping that things would go away, and it hasn't really worked for us . . . If there was going to be a story written, we wanted our point of view in that story as well,' says Bob McAdam, the co-ordinator of Wal-Mart's fight-back campaign.

Behind the media war lies a struggle focused on two areas. Having abandoned its effort to unionise Wal-Mart workers, the UFCW has sought allies to bring pressure on the retailer by slowing its expansion, challenging applications to open stores through dozens of 'site fights' in local communities. At the same time—with support from some of Wal-Mart's unionised competitors—the campaign is targeting the retailer's healthcare record, accusing it of using Medicaid, the state and federal government supported health insurance safety net, to subsidize its reliance on low-wage labour.

Wal-Mart has responded on both fronts. Lee Scott, chief executive, last month surprised its environmental critics with a commitment to invest $500 m a year in reducing greenhouse gas emissions. He also outlined objectives including independent monitoring of its supply chain and setting environmental standards for its suppliers—issues it used to dismiss. Wal-Mart's public image had already been boosted in September by its response to Hurricane Katrina, heading corporate donations and dispatching its trucks to get initial assistance to the victims.

But Wal-Mart knows it remains vulnerable to criticism on healthcare—which a recently leaked report to its board by Susan Chambers, head of benefits administration, described as 'one of the most pressing reputation issues' facing the retailer. Conceding that Wal-Mart's critics were 'correct in some of their observations', she added: 'Specifically, our coverage is expensive for low-income families, and Wal-Mart has a significant percentage of associates and their children on public assistance.'

This year, the state legislature in Maryland, dominated by Democrats, approved a bill that would require private-sector employers with more than 10,000 staff in the state to spend at least 8 per cent of their local revenue on healthcare—Wal-Mart spends only 0.5 per cent nationwide. The state's Republican governor vetoed the bill but a push to overturn the veto may follow. Similar bills are being discussed in other states. 'Proposals such as these, if successful, will bring added costs to Wal-Mart,' Ms Chambers' memo noted, while the legislative battles were 'contributing to the decline of Wal-Mart's overall reputation'. »

» The retailer has since approved a plan to offer healthcare for a lower monthly payment by its workers—although the $1,000 deductible on claims led Wake Up Wal-Mart to dismiss it as 'a sham'. Wal-Mart executives argue, however, that the problems lie beyond the company. 'We cannot solve the healthcare crisis in the US by ourselves', says Mr McAdam.

Source: Jonathan Birchall (2005), *Financial Times*, 8 November.

QUESTIONS

1. What are the specific problems that Wal-Mart is facing here?
2. How does Corporate Social Responsibility fit into Wal-Mart's image improvement strategies?
3. Is this important for Wal-Mart? Why?
4. What other CSR activities would you recommend for Wal-Mart in its image enhancement strategies?

End of book Case I

Tesco: the customer relationship management champion

Our mission is to earn and grow the lifetime loyalty of our customers.

Sir Terry Leahy, Chief Executive Officer (Tesco), quoted in Tesco's 1998 Annual Report.

They (Tesco) know more than any firm I have ever dealt with how their customers actually think, what will impress and upset them, and how they feel about grocery shopping.[1]

Jim Barnes, Executive Vice President of Bristol Group, a Canada-based Marketing Communications and Information firm, and a CRM expert.

The whole philosophy is in balancing the business in favor of the customer. That comes down to a mixture of company culture and customer insight.[2]

Crawford Davidson, Director (Clubcard Loyalty Program), Tesco.

A Master at CRM

Every three months, millions of people in the United Kingdom (UK) receive a magazine from the country's number one retailing company, Tesco. Nothing exceptional about the concept—almost all leading retailing companies across the world send out mailers/magazines to their customers. These initiatives promote the store's products, introduce promotional schemes and contain discount coupons. However, what set Tesco apart from such run-of-the-mill initiatives was the fact that it mass-customized these magazines.

Every magazine had a unique combination of articles, advertisements related to Tesco's offerings, and third-party advertisements. Tesco ensured that all its customers received magazines that contained material suited to their lifestyles. The company had worked out a mechanism for determining the advertisements and promotional coupons that would go in each of the over 150,000 variants of the magazine. This had been made possible by its world-renowned customer relationship management (CRM) strategy framework (see Exhibit I for a brief note on CRM).

The loyalty card[3] scheme (launched in 1995) laid the foundations of a CRM framework that made Tesco post growth figures in an industry that had been stagnating for a long time. The data

1. 'How a Supermarket can be a Corner Shop,' **www.crmguru.com**, January 23, 2003.
2. 'How a Supermarket can be a Corner Shop,' **www.crmguru.com**, January 23, 2003.
3. Loyalty cards are a part of 'loyalty programs,' which fall under the domain of customer retention strategies. These cards reward customers when they make purchases from the company in the form of points that accumulate over time. These points can later on be redeemed for cash/gifts/discounts. Thus, they provide incentives to customers for remaining a particular company's customers.

EXHIBIT I A brief note on CRM

Customer Relationship Management (CRM) deals with learning about the needs and behaviour of customers in order to develop stronger relationships with them. It involves the use of technology to enable organizations to continue attracting new and profitable customers while forming ever tighter bonds with existing ones—and optimizing on these relationships over time. With CRM, it becomes possible to launch mass-marketing activities on a one-to-one basis and treat each customer as an individual.

CRM involves the use of various tools, technologies and business procedures to attract and retain customers, prospects and business partners. These include Contact Management, Sales Force Automation (SFA), Opportunity Management, Relationship Management, Marketing Automation, Company Websites, Telesales and Telemarketing Systems. Technologies such as eCRM, iCRM, and Enterprise Relationship Management (ERM) are also tools of CRM. Essentially, any and all technologies, processes and procedures that facilitate or support the sales and marketing functions can be regarded as CRM tools.

CRM software is designed to help companies keep track of their customers and boost revenues (by increasing customer loyalty). Applications range from sales and field-service automation to call center and customer-database management. More than its technological components, CRM is a process that helps bring together various pieces of information about customers, sales, marketing effectiveness and market trends. It helps companies provide better customer service, make call centers more efficient, cross sell products more effectively, close deals faster, simplify marketing and sales processes, find new customers and increase customer revenues. Typically, CRM software collects the following information:

- Responses to campaigns
- Sales and purchase data
- Web registration data
- Demographic data
- Shipping and fulfillment dates
- Account information
- Service and support records
- Web sales data

CRM not only helps reduce overall business costs, it helps companies provide better customer service and earn long-term customer loyalty. It allows companies to

- Gain a better understanding of customer needs and build individual customer solutions.
- Establish a dialog with customers (using the Internet).
- Improve marketing efforts by using readily accessible customer information.
- Link departments, giving them access to the same information (updated in real time).

Source: ICMR.

collected through these cards formed the basis for formulating strategies that offered customers personalized services in a cost-effective manner. Each and every one of the over 8 million transactions made every week at the company's stores was individually linked to customer-profile information. And each of these transactions had the potential to be used for modifying the company's strategies.

According to Tesco sources, the company's CRM initiative was not limited to the loyalty card scheme; it was more of a company wide philosophy. Industry observers felt that Tesco's CRM initiatives enabled it to develop highly focused marketing strategies. Thanks to its CRM initiatives, the company became UK's number one retailer in 1995, after having struggled at number two behind arch rival Sainsbury's for decades (see Exhibit II for a brief note on the UK's retailing industry). In 2003, the company's market share was 26.7%, while Sainsbury's market share was just 16.8%.

Background note

The Tesco story dates back to 1919 when Jack Cohen (Cohen), an ex-army man, set up a grocery business in London's East End. In 1924, Cohen purchased a shipment of tea from a company named T. E. Stockwell. He used the first three letters of this company's name, added the 'Co' from his name and branded the tea 'Tesco.' Reportedly, he was so enamored of the name that he named his entire business Tesco. The first store under the Tesco name was opened in 1929 in Burnt Oak, Edgware. The company grew rapidly in the years that followed, and evolved into a general food retailing outfit. By 1930, around 100 stores were operating under the Tesco label.

Realizing that the self-service mode of running supermarkets prevalent in the US worked out much cheaper than the traditional mode and enabled companies to offer their merchandise at low prices, Cohen decided to adopt the same for Tesco stores. In 1948, the first self-service Tesco store was opened in St Albans. Over the next few years, Tesco grew to over 400 stores—many of which were purchased by Cohen from other smaller shopping store chains in the country.

In the early 1960s, the company began selling clothing, household goods and fresh food in addition to groceries. Tesco pioneered the large format stores concept in the UK with the launch of a 16,500 sq. ft. store in Leicester in 1961. By now, Tesco had become a household name in the UK and was renowned for its competitive prices. However, due to the Retail Price Maintenance (RPM) system prevalent in the country during that time (which prohibited larger retailers from pricing goods below a price agreed upon with the suppliers), companies such as Tesco were not able to compete on price with small retailing outfits.

To overcome this problem, Tesco came up with the idea of 'trading stamps.' These stamps were given to customers in return for making purchases at its stores. After the customers collected a specified number of stamps, they could exchange them in return for cash or gifts. This scheme became very popular and Tesco's popularity and sales soared substantially. While other players in the industry were busy copying this scheme, Cohen worked towards getting the RPM abolished. The RPM was abolished in 1964, following which Tesco was able to offer competitively priced merchandise to its customers. Meanwhile, it decided to continue the trading stamps scheme.

Throughout the 1960s, Tesco continued to grow through the acquisitions route. It acquired a network of 212 stores in the north of England, and during 1964–65, acquired 144 more stores. Another chain, Victor Value, came under the company's fold in 1968. In the same year, Tesco became the first retailer to formally introduce superstores to the British retailing industry with the launch of its Crawley, West Sussex store.

Though Tesco owed its success till now to its cheap prices model (referred to as the 'pile it high and sell it cheap' model by Cohen as well as industry observers), it had to rethink its pricing strategy in the 1970s. This was primarily due to the fact that customers across the UK were becoming more affluent and were no longer looking only for bargains. There was a growing need for costly, luxury merchandise.

EXHIBIT II A brief note on the UK's retailing industry

The retailing industry is one of the UK's primary service sector industries. In 2002, its sales amounted to £234 billion. That year, there were over 322,000 retail outlets in the country (December 2002 figure) employing around 2.9 million people (11% of the country's total workforce). Despite the sluggish growth since the 1990s, the industry remains one of the biggest job creators in the UK. The industry has gone through major structural changes since the mid-1980s. These include the growing importance of technology in the business, an increasing influx of foreign players, overseas expansion by UK firms, and a focus on price cutting by leading chains due to intensifying competitive pressures. The top 10 players ranked according to their 2001–02 turnovers (in descending order) are listed in the following table:

Rank	Company	Rank	Company
1.	Tesco	6.	Dixons Gp.
2.	Sainsbury's	7.	Somerfield
3.	Asda	8.	John Lewis Partnership
4.	Safeway	9.	Boots
5.	Marks & Spencer	10.	Wm Morrison Spmkt

For the 12 weeks ending May 25th 2003, Tesco was the market leader with a 26.7% market share. During that period, the market share of Sainsbury's had fallen from 17.5% to 16.8%. Asda (which is owned by the world's largest retailer, the US-based Wal-Mart) was at number three with a market share of 16.3%. Sainsbury's used to be the market leader till 1995, but by 1995, Tesco outstripped it and continued to grow at a scorching pace (Refer to the following table for market share information).

UK retailing industry—market shares

	1997	1998	1999	2000
Tesco	22.0	22.9	23.4	24.2
Sainsbury's	19.7	19.8	19.1	18.6
Asda	13.3	14.1	14.8	16.3
Safeway	10.3	10.2	10.0	10.1
Morrisons	3.9	3.9	4.5	5.1

Safeway, a leading player once, was struggling to stay afloat in 2003. The competition in the industry was on these fronts: price cuts, store modernization, product-mix expansion and premium image creation. All the stores were working towards creating an image in the minds of customers. While Tesco and Asda focused on price cuts, players such as Waitrose focused on building a high quality image for themselves. As far as price cutting was concerned, Asda was the champion (its prices were 3% less than Tesco's), followed by Tesco and then Sainsbury's.

Source: Compiled from information available on **www.brc.org.uk** and other sources.

To factor in these changes sweeping the industry, Tesco's management carried out a strategic overhaul of the company's operations. The company closed down many of its stores to concentrate on superstores. The stores that were not closed down were refurbished through better layouts (such as wider aisles) and improved atmospherics (including better lighting). The product mix was also changed and Tesco now began offering a much wider range of goods. In addition, the company renewed its focus on customer service and quality. In line with the product diversification drive, Tesco began operating petrol pumps in 1974. Since trading stamps did not fit in with its efforts to go up-market, Tesco discontinued them in 1977.

Even though Tesco went up-market, it tried to retain its image as a company offering competitive prices. In 1977, the company successfully launched a price cutting campaign named '*Checkout at Tesco.*' By the end of the 1970s, the company had emerged as one of the leading companies in the UK. In 1979, its annual turnover crossed £1 billion. In 1985, Tesco launched the '*Healthy Eating*' initiative, a path breaking move that aimed at conveying the nutritional value of the company's merchandise to the customers. By now, Tesco had also emerged as the largest independent retailer of petrol in the UK.

The 1990s were a period of many large-scale changes at the company. For the first time in many years, Tesco began experimenting with newer store formats. Three new formats, Tesco Metro, Tesco Express and Tesco Extra Store, were launched during the 1990s. While Tesco Metro was a city center store that served the local community of a particular region, Tesco Express was a combination of a petrol pump and a convenience store. Tesco Extra Store was a hypermarket that focused equally on food and non-food merchandise.

This decade also saw the company entering global markets. It entered France in 1994 and Hungary and Poland in 1995. In 1995, Tesco launched the Clubcard loyalty scheme. In the same year, it diversified into a new business through a joint venture (for the first time in its history) with the Royal Bank of Scotland to launch the Tesco Personal Finance (TPF) venture. TPF offered customers a wide array of personal finance services, including the Tesco Visa card, cheque on current account deposits, car loans, life/auto/pet/home/travel insurance, loans, bonds, mortgages and pension savings programs. Tesco classified TPF under the 'Retailing Services' division.

In 1996, the company entered the Czech Republic, and in 1998, it entered Northern Ireland and Thailand. Even in international markets, Tesco adopted the policy of offering its services to customers in innovative ways. For instance, in Thailand, its customers could buy 'tescooters' (scooters) and have them delivered to their homes.

In 1998, after the utilities business was deregulated in the UK, Tesco began offering electricity and telecommunications products and services. In 2000, Tesco established Tesco.com as a wholly-owned subsidiary functioning under the retailing services division. Besides covering all the e-commerce activities for Tesco's customers in general, Tesco.com gave special emphasis to the sale of groceries over the Internet. This service was later extended to customers in Ireland and South Korea.

In 2000, Tesco began operations in Taiwan. The following year, the company tied up with a leading supermarket chain from the US, Safeway Inc., to launch an online grocery shopping service for US customers. In the same year, Tesco entered into an agreement with a leading US automobile company, General Motors (GM). Under this agreement, customers could buy GM cars through Tesco.

In an innovative move, the company began offering a large number of organic food products in 2001. In addition, a host of new ranges of food products (such as 'The Food Doctor,' 'Finest

Dips,' 'Grab and Go,' 'Unwind Range,' and 'Finest') were launched in the early 21st century. During this period, the company also gave a lot of importance to its non-food businesses. It carried a wide range of merchandise like toys, sports equipment, lighting, furnishing, electrical items and clothing. Many new brands in the non-food segment were successfully launched (such as Cherokee and Florence & Fred).

Continuing its thrust into global expansion, Tesco launched its first store in Malaysia in May 2002. In July 2002, it expanded its presence in Poland by acquiring a chain of hypermarkets named 'HIT.' Tesco's store network in the UK grew further in January 2003 when it acquired 870 convenience stores operating under the T&S label (the company planned to convert 450 of these stores into Tesco Express stores by 2006–07). For the accounting period ending April 2003, TPF had over 3.4 million customer accounts and earned profits of £96 million. Also, tesco.com had proven to be one of the rare, profitable dotcom ventures. In 2003, it earned a profit of £12 million.

By mid-2003, the company was operating 2,291 stores in the UK, Hungary, Poland, the Czech Republic, the Slovak Republic, Thailand, South Korea, Taiwan, Malaysia and the Republic of Ireland. Employing around 296,000 people across these countries, Tesco was earning profits in at least eight of the ten countries. The group's strong financial performance was reflected in the healthy growth in revenues and net profits over the years. While revenues and net profit stood at £18.46 billion and £842 million in 1999, they were £28.61 billion and £1.36 billion in 2003 (see Exhibit III for Tesco's key financial statistics).

CRM—the Tesco way

Tesco's efforts towards offering better services to its customers and meeting their needs can be traced back to the days when it positioned itself as a company that offered good quality products at extremely competitive prices. Even its decision to offer premium end merchandise and services in the 1970s was prompted by growing customer demand for the same (See Table I

TABLE I Tesco—core purpose & values

Core purpose

Creating value for customers, to earn their lifetime loyalty.

Values

1. No one tries harder for customers:
Understand customers better than anyone
Be energetic, be innovative and be first for customers
Use our strengths to deliver unbeatable value to our customers
Look after our people so they can look after our customers

2. Treat people how we like to be treated:
All retailers, there's one team—The Tesco Team
Trust and respect each other
Strive to do our very best
Give support to each other and praise more than criticize
Ask more than tell and share knowledge so that it can be used
Enjoy work, celebrate success and learn from experience

Source: **www.tesco.com.**

EXHIBIT III Tesco—key statistics

(in £ million)

Year ended February	**1999**	**2000**	**2001**	**2002**	**2003**
Group sales	**18,456**	**20,358**	**22,773**	**25,654**	**28,613**
Turnover					
UK	15,835	16,958	18,372	20,052	21,615
Rest of Europe	1,167	1,374	1,756	2,203	2,689
Asia	156	464	860	1,398	2033
Total turnover	**17,518**	**18,796**	**20,988**	**23,653**	**26,337**
Underlying operating profit (1)					
UK	919	993	1,100	1,213	1,297
Rest of Europe	48	51	70	90	141
Asia	(2)	(1)	4	29	71
Total profit	**965**	**1,043**	**1,174**	**1,332**	**1,509**
Underlying pre-tax profit*	881	955	1070	1221	1401
Profit before tax	**842**	**933**	**1,054**	**1,201**	**1,361**
Retail statistics					
UK					
Number of stores	639	659	692	729	1,982
Total sales area (000 sq.ft.)	15,975	16,895	17,965	18,822	21,829
Turnover per full time employee (£)**	151,138	156,427	161,161	165,348	162,457
Weekly sales per sq.ft. (£)***	21.05	21.43	22.01	22.33	22.16
International					
Number of stores	182	186	245	250	309
Number of hypermarkets	22	38	68	102	152
Total sales area (000 sq.ft.)	5,378	7,144	10,397	13,669	18,115

*Excluding net loss on disposal of fixed assets, integration costs and goodwill amortization.
**2003, 2002 and 2001 statistics have been calculated based on the adoption of FRS 19, 'Deferred Tax.'
***2003 ratios have been impacted by the acquisition of T&S Stores Plc.
Source: **www.tesco.com.**

for the company's 'core purpose' and 'values' that highlight the importance given to customer service).

Various initiatives were undertaken by the company over the years to improve customer service. For instance, in 1993–94, Tesco launched the *'First Class Service'* initiative. Under this initiative, the company gave customer service training to over 90,000 store staff. The program was an innovative one in that it involved store managers in behavioural service training for the very first time. Instead of being passive participants of a training program, employees were asked to work out the right approach for their training needs. Based on the above approach, Tesco made work teams to carry out regular training programs focusing on customer service improvement.

In 1994, the company launched the '*One in Front*' scheme to reduce the time customers had to spend waiting at check-out counters. Under this scheme, Tesco store personnel ensured that if there was more than one person at any counter, another counter would be opened for the person second in line. This way, no customer would have to wait at the check-out counters. Of course, it was not possible for Tesco to adhere to this policy during peak traffic hours. Nevertheless, this effort to improve customer service was appreciated by customers.

The biggest customer service initiative (and the first focused CRM drive) came in the form of the loyalty card scheme that was launched in 1995. This initiative was partly inspired by the growing popularity of such schemes in other parts of the world and partly by Tesco's belief that it would be able to serve its customers in a much better (and profitable) manner by using such a scheme. Tesco knew that at any of its outlets, the top 100 customers were worth as much as the bottom 4,000 (in terms of sales). While the top 5% customers accounted for 20% of sales, the bottom 25% accounted for only 2%. The company realized that by giving extra attention to the top customers (measured by the frequency of purchases and the amount spent), it stood to gain a lot.

Work in this direction began in 1994, when Tesco tied up with Dunnhumby,[4] a marketing services outfit, to develop its loyalty program. In May 1994, Tesco began testing of the Clubcard loyalty scheme at two of its stores for a period of six months. The scheme started off like any other loyalty card scheme. Customers became members by paying a joining fee and providing personal details such as name, address, date of birth, e-mail, family composition, dietary requirements and product preferences.

To ensure the program's success, it was essential that all Tesco employees understood the rationale for it as well as its importance. So, the company distributed over 140,000 educational videos about the program to its staff at various stores. These videos explained why the initiative was being undertaken, what the company expected to gain out of it, and why it was important for employees to participate whole-heartedly in the program.

Impressed with the program's results over six months, the company introduced the scheme in all its stores by February 1995. The stores captured every one of the over 8 million transactions made per week at Tesco stores in a database. All the transactions were linked to individual customer profiles and generated over 50 gigabytes[5] of data every week. Dunnhumby used state-of-the-art data mining[6] techniques to manage and analyze the database. Initially, it took a few weeks to analyze the vast amount of data generated. To overcome this problem, Dunnhumby put in place new software that reduced this time to just a few days. As a result, it became possible to come up with useful and timely insights on customer behaviour in a much faster way.

The analysis of the data collected enabled Tesco to accurately pinpoint the time when purchases were made, the amount the customer spent, and the kinds of products purchased. Based

---

4. Dunnhumby, established in 1989 by Edwina Dunn and Clive Humby, offered marketing and employee related services to corporate clients. The company offered its services through its divisions: Dunnhumby Cinnamon (direct marketing division) and Dunnhumby Crucible (data division). Dunnhumby operated in the UK and the US, and had clients such as Virgin Mobile, Wella, Unilever, Lever Fabergé and Gillette.

5. A byte is a unit that is capable of storing a single character of data in a computer system. It is an abbreviation for 'binary term' and is equal to 8 bits. Large amounts of data are classified as kilobytes (1,024 bytes), megabytes (1,048,576 bytes), and gigabytes (1,073,741,824 bytes).

6. Data mining refers to the process of using database applications to look for hidden patterns in a group of data and using it to predict future behaviour. This is done through specialized software that not only presents the existing data in new ways, but discovers hitherto unknown relationships among the data.

TABLE II Tesco—classifying customers (A)

<table>
<tr><td></td><td></td><th colspan="6">SHOPPING FREQUENCY</th></tr>
<tr><td></td><td></td><th>Daily</th><th>Twice weekly</th><th>Weekly</th><th>Stop start</th><th>Now & then</th><th>Hardly ever</th></tr>
<tr><th rowspan="3">EXPENDITURE</th><th>High spend</th><td colspan="2">PREMIUM</td><td colspan="2">STANDARD</td><td colspan="2">POTENTIAL</td></tr>
<tr><th>Medium spend</th><td colspan="2">STANDARD</td><td colspan="2">POTENTIAL</td><td colspan="2">UNCOMMITTED</td></tr>
<tr><th>Low spend</th><td colspan="2">POTENTIAL</td><td colspan="4">UNCOMMITTED</td></tr>
<tr><td></td><td></td><td colspan="2">FREQUENT</td><td colspan="2">INFREQUENT</td><td colspan="2">RARE</td></tr>
</table>

Source: **www.ecrnet.org**.

on the amount spent and the frequency of shopping, customers were classified into four broad categories: Premium, Standard, Potential and Uncommitted (Table II). Further, profiles were created for all the customers on the basis of the types of products they purchased. Customers were categorized along dimensions such as, Value, Convenience, Frozen, Healthy Eating, Fresh and Kids.

Tesco also identified over 5,000 need segments based on the purchasing habits and behaviour patterns of its customers. Each of these segments could be targeted specifically with tailor-made campaigns and advertisements. The company also identified eight 'primary life stage' need segments based on the profiles of its customers. These segments included 'single adults,' 'pensioners' and 'urban professionals' among others. Another classification of customers developed from the insights generated through data mining is given in Table III.

Using the information regarding customer classification, Tesco's marketing department devised customized strategies for each category. Pricing, promotion and product related decisions were taken after considering the preferences of customers. Also, customers received communications that were tailored to their buying patterns. The data collected through the Clubcard scheme allowed Tesco to modify its strategies on various fronts such as pricing,

TABLE III Tesco—classifying customers (B)

Category	Classification	Characteristics
Up-market	Finer Foods	Foodies who are time poor, money rich and choose everyday luxury items.
Mid-market Cost conscious	Healthy	Organics shoppers, fruits and vegetables, weight watchers, etc.
	Convenience	People on the go who have not got the time or inclination for scratch cooking.
	Traditional	Traditional housecraft with time to buy and prepare ingredients.
	Mainstream Price sensitive	Family type meals, Popular brands, Kids' products. Cost conscious customers who tend to buy cheapest on display.

Source: **www.ecrnet.org**.

TABLE IV How Tesco used the information generated by the Clubcards

Pricing	Discounts were offered on goods that were bought by highly price-conscious customers. While the company kept prices low on often-bought goods/staples, for less familiar lines, it adopted a premium pricing policy.
Merchandising	The product portfolio was devised based on customer profiles and purchasing behaviour records. Depending on the loyalty shown by customers towards a particular product, the substitutes available for the same, and the seasonality, the product ranges were modified.
Promotion	Promotions were aimed at giving special (and more) rewards to loyal customers. Few promotions were targeted at the other customers.
Customer service	Extra attention was given to stocking those products that were bought by loyal customers.
Media effectiveness	The effectiveness of media campaigns could be evaluated easily by noticing changes in the buying patterns of those customers whom the said campaign was targeted at.
Customer acquisition	The launch of new ventures (such as TPF and Tesco.com) went off smoothly since Tesco targeted the 'right' kinds of customers.
Market research	While conducting marketing research, Tesco was able to tap those customers that fit in accurately into the overall research plan.
Customer communication	It was possible to mass-customize communication campaigns based on individual customer preferences and characteristics. Tesco began holding 'Customer Evenings' for interacting with customers, gathering more information, and gaining new customers through referrals.

Adapted from an article on **www.clarityblue.com**.

inventory management, shopping analysis, customer acquisition, new product launches, store management, online customer behaviour and media effectiveness (Table IV).

Tesco began giving many special privileges, such as valet parking and personal attention from the store manager, to its high-value customers. Special cards were created for students and mothers, discounts were offered on select merchandise, and the financial services venture was included in the card scheme. The data generated was used innovatively, e.g. special attention given to expectant mothers in the form of personal shopping assistants, priority parking and various other facilities. The company also tied up with airline companies and began offering Frequent Flyer Miles[7] to customers in return for the points on their Clubcards.

Reaping the benefits

Commenting on the way the data generated was used, sources at Dunnhumby said that the data allowed Tesco to target individual customers (the rifle shot approach), instead of targeting them as a group (the carpet bombing approach). Since the customers received coupons that matched

7. Frequent Flyer Miles are customer retention programs originally adopted by airline companies. Under this program, customers are awarded points for each mile they flew with a particular airline. After accumulating a certain number of points, customers can 'cash' them for air tickets, discounts and cash rewards. The concept was adopted by many industries later on as a tool for customer retention.

Figure I Tesco—increasing number of loyal customers

Source: www.clarityblue.com.

their buying patterns, over 20% of Tesco's coupons were redeemed—as against the industry average of 0.5%. The number of loyal customers increased manifold since the loyalty card scheme was launched (Figure I).

The quarterly magazine Tesco sent to its customers was customized based on the segments identified. Customers falling in different categories received magazines that were compiled specifically for them—the articles covered issues that interested them and the advertisements and discount coupons were about those products/services that they were most likely to purchase. This customization attracted third-party advertisers, since it assured them that their products/services would be noticed by those very customers they planned to target. Naturally, Tesco recovered a large part of its investment in this exercise through revenues generated by outside advertisements.

The data collected through the cards helped the company enter the financial services business as well. The company carried out targeted research on the demographic data and zeroed in on those customers who were the most likely to opt for financial services. Due to the captive customer base and the cross-selling opportunity, the cost of acquiring customers for its financial services was 50% less than what it cost a bank or financial services company.

Reportedly, the data generated by the Clubcard initiative played a major role in the way the online grocery retailing business was run. The data helped the company identify the areas in which customers were positively inclined towards online shopping. Accordingly, the areas in which online shopping was to be introduced were decided upon. Since the prospective customers were already favorably disposed, Tesco.com took off to a good start and soon emerged as one of the few profitable dotcom ventures worldwide. By 2003, the website was accessible to 95% of UK's population and generated business of £15 million per week.

By sharing the data generated with manufacturers, Tesco was able to offer better services to its customers. It gave purchasing pattern information to manufacturers, but withheld the personal information provided by customers (such as names and addresses). The manufacturers used this information to modify their own product mixes and promotional strategies. In return for this information, they gave Tesco customers subsidies and incentives in the form of discount coupons.

The Clubcards also helped Tesco compete with other retailers. For instance, if players such as Asda or Sainsbury's reduced prices on certain low-margin products to pull customers into the store so that they may be motivated to purchase high-margin products later on, Tesco was quick to reduce its own prices on such products. This way, the company ensured that the footfalls in its stores did not decline on account of competitive pressures.

When Tesco found out that around 25% of its customers, who belonged to the high income bracket were defecting to rival Marks & Spencer, it developed a totally new product range, 'Tesco Finest,' to lure back these customers. This range was then promoted to affluent customers through personalized promotions. As planned, the defection of customers from this segment slowed down considerably.

Analysis of the data revealed that Tesco customers were not happy with in-store stands that displayed candy. These stands attracted children, who forced their parents to buy the candy. Similarly, many customers did not like off-shelf displays that were aimed at fuelling impulse purchases. Going against traditional retailing wisdom, Tesco decided to reduce the number of such displays, while doing away completely with the candy shelves. The company hoped that what it stood to lose in unit sales would be offset by increased customer loyalty (and thereby increased overall sales). Proving its decision right, the holiday season sales for 2002 were the best ever for Tesco, despite the removal of these impulse purchase drivers.

As a result of the above strategies, Tesco was able to increase returns even as it reduced promotions. Dunnhumby prepared a profit and loss statement for the activities of the marketing department to help assess the performance of the Clubcard initiative. Dunnhumby claimed that Tesco saved around £300 million every year through reduction in expenditure on promotions. The money saved thus was ploughed back into the business to offer more discounts to customers.

By the end of the 1990s, over 10 million households in the UK owned around 14 million Tesco Clubcards. This explained why as high as 80% of the company's in-store transactions and 85% of its revenues were accounted for by the cards. Thanks largely to this initiative, Tesco's turnover went up by 52% between 1995 and 2000, while floor space during the same period increased by only 15%.

Not only was Tesco's program the biggest CRM program in the UK, it was one of the most sophisticated and extensive CRM programs in the whole world. Commenting on the reasons for Tesco's success, Clive Humby said, 'I think one is that they make sure that consumers get things that really matter to them. So the relevancy of the communication. And two, it was the first one to really use data powerfully. And, as a result, they have got a march on their competitors.'[8]

From customer service to customer delight

To sustain the growth achieved through the launch of Clubcards, Tesco decided to adopt a four pronged approach: launch better, bigger stores on a frequent basis; offer competitive prices (e.g. offering everyday low prices in the staples business); increase the number of products offered in the Value range; and focus on remote shopping services (this included the online shopping venture). To make sure that its prices were the lowest among all retailers, Tesco employed a dedicated team of employees, called 'price checkers.' This team checked and compared Tesco's prices with those of other companies on a weekly basis. The company even helped its customers compare prices by providing the information on tesco.com.

---

8. 'Tesco Tests Loyalty Programs,' **www.abc.net.au**, June 19, 2003.

By late 1998, even though Tesco's CRM efforts had resulted in superior financial performance and market share, the company was still not satisfied with its customer service standards. Commenting on the need to improve on this front, Chris Reid, Customer Initiatives Manager, said, 'We have spent so much time improving the way our stores look, the range of products we sell and our service processes that we may have temporarily overlooked the impact that our people can make on customers through their behaviour. We need to redress that.'[9]

The above realization culminated in the launch of the '*Every Customer Offered Help*' (ECOH) initiative. As part of ECOH, all employees were given clear instructions about the way in which they were expected to deal with customers. Employees posted at the check-out counters, for instance, were asked to be very particular about greeting the customers, offering them help and finally, wishing them a good day. Store managers, who were responsible for making the ECOH initiative successful, participated whole-heartedly in the scheme.

In mid-2001, Tesco acquired a 53% stake in Dunnhumby. Analysts said that this was a clear indication of Tesco's realization that its growth during the 1990s had occurred largely because of Dunnhumby's expertise. According to a **www.1to1.com** article, 'Tesco knows the customer data managed by Dunnhumby is its most valuable asset.'[10] In the same year, Dunnhumby created a separate retailing division to provide market research services to Tesco, as well as its suppliers.

Tesco knew that the loyalty card initiative was just one part of the overall thrust on CRM and that customer service enhancement was needed to survive and excel in the intensely competitive British retailing market. The company therefore took a host of other initiatives to sustain its leadership position. In 2001–02, Tesco introduced Customer Champions in its stores to further the thrust given to customer service.[11] The company also successfully implemented a new scheduling scheme for store employees to increase customer satisfaction levels.

Tesco required all employees (including top level executives) to spend some time every year in the stores to help them get acquainted with the nuances of customer service. This program not only helped ingrain customer service as a company philosophy in all employees, it also resulted in the development of many innovative ideas. Unlike Asda's customer service program, Tesco's program did not require employees to get 'too personal' with customers (reportedly, Asda posted employees at the doors just to greet customers).

To ensure that its CRM efforts were backed by a strong operational framework, the company paid special attention to controlling costs and streamlining its supply chain. In association with its suppliers, Tesco strove to eliminate all non-value adding costs. It also collaborated with suppliers to develop a 'Lean Thinking' approach, which focused on smart and efficient working. The company also followed a continuous stock replenishment policy to ensure at least 99% stock availability. As a result, not only were store shelves stocked adequately at all times, the chances of merchandise getting spoilt in the store backrooms was also reduced.

Commenting on Tesco's approach towards business, an April 2001 issue of *The Economist* stated, 'Irritating though it is to its detractors, Tesco's success comes from consistently good management and close attention to what customers want.'

---

9. 'Once You Get to the Top, How do You Stay There?' **www.axia.com**.

10. The customer champions aimed at providing the customers with an overall better shopping experience. This move was similar to the concept of 'customer assistants' introduced by Tesco in 1996. These specially trained employees assisted customers in a friendly manner while they shopped at the company's stores.

11. The customer champions aimed at providing the customers with an overall better shopping experience. This move was similar to the concept of 'customer assistants' introduced by Tesco in 1996. These specially trained employees assisted customers in a friendly manner while they shopped at the company's stores.

Tesco identified long-term growth as the broad strategic goal to be achieved in the future. To do so, it focused on four aspects of its business: 'Core UK Business,' 'Non-Food Business,' 'Retailing Services,' and 'International Business'. The 'Core UK Business' addressed the company's commitment to continue serving its UK customers in an increasingly better manner, while the 'Non-Food Business' business aimed at increasing the company's focus in new areas. In 2003, the non-food business in the UK was estimated to be worth £75 billion, of which Tesco had a 5% share. Tesco believed that the market held a lot of growth potential and hence planned to focus strongly on this segment.

The success of TPF and tesco.com prompted the company to seek other avenues for further leveraging of the retailing services business. Accordingly, the company decided to launch a fixed line telephone service in the UK in September 2003, followed soon after by a mobile phone service. As far as the focus on international business was concerned, by 2003, Tesco was already earning 45% of its revenues from non-UK operations. The company planned to explore the possibilities of entering new, profitable markets and expanding its global network further.

In February 2003, Tesco launched a new initiative targeted at its women customers. Named '*Me Time*,' the new loyalty scheme offered ladies free sessions at leading health spas, luxury gyms and beauty saloons and discounts on designer clothes, perfumes and cosmetics. This scheme was rather innovative since it allowed Tesco customers to redeem the points accumulated through their Clubcards at a large number of third party outlets. Company official Crawford Davidson remarked, 'Up until now, our customers have used Tesco Clubcard vouchers primarily to buy more shopping for the home. However, from now on, "Me Time" will give customers the option of spending the rewards on themselves.'

In April 2003, Tesco cut a total of £60 million off a vast range of products to continue offering competitive prices to UK customers. This was the latest addition to the price cuts that it had been carrying out since 1998. Commenting on the price cuts, Tim Mason, Tesco's Marketing Director, said, 'Many families will find some of their costs have increased recently, including their National Insurance contributions. By lowering prices we are doing our bit to help.'[12]

Not surprisingly, Tesco was the only retailing outfit that managed to get a place in the 'Top 10' of the prestigious 'The Euro BW 50' list in July 2003. The company was at number 10 in the list of the 50 top businesses in Europe compiled by *BusinessWeek*.

An invincible company? Not exactly . . .

Tesco's customer base and the frequency with which each customer visited its stores had increased significantly over the years. However, according to reports, the average purchase per visit had not gone up as much as management would have liked to see. Analysts said that this was not a very positive sign. They also said that while it was true that Tesco was the market leader by a wide margin, it was also true that Asda and Morrison were growing rapidly (Exhibit II).

Given the fact that the company was moving away from its core business within the UK (thrust on non-food, utility services, online travel services) and was globalizing rapidly (reportedly, it was exploring the possibilities of entering China and Japan), industry observers were rather skeptical of its ability to maintain the growth it had been posting since the late-1900s. *The Economist* stated that the UK retailing industry seemed to have become saturated and that Tesco's growth could be sustained only if it ventured overseas. However, it also cautioned that UK retailers had usually not fared well abroad and mentioned that Tesco needed to act carefully.

---

12. **www.tesco.com.**

Tesco's growth was based largely on its loyalty card scheme. But in recent years, the very concept of loyalty cards was being criticized on various grounds. Some analysts claimed that the popularity of loyalty cards would decline in the future as all retailing companies would begin offering more or less similar schemes. Critics also commented that the name loyalty card was a misnomer since customers were primarily interested in getting the best price for the goods and services they wanted to buy.

Research conducted by Black Sun, a company specializing in loyalty solutions, revealed that though over 50% of the UK's adult population used loyalty cards, over 80% of them said that they were bothered only about making cheaper purchases. Given the fact that many companies in the UK, such as HSBC, Egg and Barclaycard, had withdrawn their loyalty cards, industry observers were skeptical of Tesco's ability to continue reaping the benefits of the Clubcard scheme. Black Sun's Director (Business Development), David Christopherson, said, 'Most loyalty companies have a direct marketing background, which is result-driven, and focuses on the short-term. This has led to a "point for prizes" loyalty model, which does not necessarily build the long-term foundations for a beneficial relationship with customers.'[13]

However, Tesco and Dunnhumby refused to accept the above arguments. Dunnhumby sources said that provided loyalty cards were made a part of an overall CRM strategy framework (like Tesco had done), the chances of failure would be minimal.

Commenting on the philosophy behind Tesco's CRM efforts, Edwina Dunn (Edwina) said, 'Companies should be loyal to their customers—not the other way round.'[14] Taking into consideration the company's strong performance since these efforts were undertaken, there would perhaps not be many who would disagree with Edwina.

QUESTIONS TO BE ANSWERED

Where Tesco is now

1. Perform a SWOT analysis and discuss Tesco's current situation. What does the SWOT indicate?
2. Examine the customer service efforts undertaken by Tesco prior to the loyalty card scheme's launch. Why do you think the company felt the need to launch Clubcards?

Where Tesco is going

3. Analyse Tesco's Clubcard scheme in depth and comment on the various customer segmentation models the company developed after studying the data gathered.
4. How did Tesco use the information collected to modify its marketing strategies? What sort of benefits was the company able to derive as a result of such modifications?
5. What are Tesco's objectives as indicated in the text? Are these appropriate? Why or why not?

How Tesco will get there

6. What measures did Tesco adopt to support the CRM initiatives on the operational and strategic front? Is it enough for a company to implement loyalty card schemes (and CRM tools in general) in isolations? Why?
7. With Tesco moving away from its core business of grocery retailing towards non-grocery and globalization, what do you think the future has in store for the company?
8. What do you think Tesco should do to retain its growth pace and leadership status?

---

13. 'Loyalty Cards vs. Price Cuts: Which is More Persuasive?' **www.blacksun.co.uk**, February 15, 2002.
14. 'Loyalty Cards vs. Price Cuts: Which is More Persuasive?' **www.blacksun.co.uk**, February 15, 2002.

REFERENCES AND FURTHER READING

1. 'Tesco: Piling Up the Profits', *The Economist*, 12 April 2001.
2. Breese, Allan, 'Tesco', **www.kamcity.com**, 9 June 2000.
3. Rogers, Martha, 'High for Tesco and Dunnhumby', **www.1to1.com**, 6 August 2001.
4. Retail Brand Value, 'The Case of Tesco', **www.crm-forum.com**, 27 September 2001.
5. Millar, Bill, 'Is Customer Loyalty in the Cards?', **www.1to1.com**, 1 October 2001.
6. 'Marketer Masterclass', *Pharmatimes*, December 2001.
7. 'Loyalty Cards vs. Price Cuts: Which is More Impressive?', **www.blacksun.co.uk**, 15 February 2002.
8. Rowe, Deborah, 'Customers That Count', **www.cimcroydon.co.uk**, 21 March 2002.
9. Cannon, Jeff, 'How a Supermarket Can be a Corner Shop', **www.crmguru.com**, 24 March 2003.
10. Tso, Karen, 'Tesco Tests Loyalty Programs', **www.abc.net.au**, 19 June 2003.
11. 'The Mediocre Middle', *The Economist*, 28 June 2003.
12. Lowenstein, Michael, 'Tesco: A Retail Customer Divisibility Champion', **www.customerloyalty.org**.
13. 'Tesco—The Brand Experience is Everything', **www.brandingasia.com**.
14. 'Tesco Clubcard and Dunnhumby', **www.clarityblue.com**.
15. 'Once You Get to the Top, How do You Stay, There?', **www.axia.com**.
16. **www.ecrnet.org**.
17. **www.brc.org.uk**.
18. **www.datamonitor.com**.
19. **www.dunnhumby.com**.
20. **www.tesco.com**.

End of book Case II

Nike: evolution of marketing strategy

Introduction

For the year ended 31st May 2004, Nike, a leader in the global sports shoe industry announced a vastly improved performance, earning almost $1 billion on sales of $12.3 billion. Earnings had increased by 27% while orders worldwide went up by 10.7%. Nike's return on invested capital was 22%, up from 14% four years ago. Having completed a $1 billion share repurchase, Nike had plans to buy back shares worth $1.5 billion over the next four years.

Nike had faced a crisis in the late 1990s. Many analysts felt this was because its creativity had not been backed by operational discipline. Nike had operated on instinct, often guessing how many pairs of shoes to produce and hoping it could offload them in the market. In the past few years, Nike had tried to balance creativity with a strong business focus. Nike had overhauled its information systems to get the right number of shoes to the market more quickly. The company had also streamlined logistics and strengthened its management team. It focused on more efficient management of its portfolio of brands—Cole Haan dress shoes, Converse retro-style sneakers, Hurley International skateboard gear, and Bauer in-line and hockey skates. As 2004 drew to a close, Nike realized that it could not underestimate powerful competitors such as adidas. When founder Phil Knight resigned on 18th November 2004, it marked the beginning of a new era at Nike under the leadership of William D. Perez. Perez had earlier been president and chief executive of S. C. Johnson & Son.

Nike's business

Nike was involved in the design, development and worldwide marketing of high quality footwear, apparel, equipment, and accessory products. The largest seller of athletic footwear and athletic apparel in the world, Nike offered its products through approximately 18,000 retailers in the US and various independent distributors, licensees and subsidiaries in nearly 200 countries around the world. Independent contractors manufactured most of Nike's products. Footwear products were mostly produced outside the US, while apparel and equipment were made both in the US and abroad.

Nike's athletic footwear products were worn for both casual and leisure purposes. Running, basketball, children's, cross-training and women's shoes were Nike's top-selling product categories. Nike also offered shoes designed for outdoor activities like tennis, golf, soccer, baseball, football, bicycling, volleyball, wrestling, aquatic activities, hiking, and other athletic and recreational uses.

Nike sold sports apparel, athletically inspired lifestyle apparel, as well as athletic bags and accessory items. Nike often marketed footwear, apparel and accessories in 'collections' of similar design or for specific purposes. Nike also marketed apparel with licensed college and professional team and league logos.

Nike sold sports balls, timepieces, eyewear, skates, bats, gloves, and other equipment designed for sports activities, swimwear, cycling apparel, maternity exercise wear, children's clothing, school supplies, timepieces, and electronic media devices. Nike also sold various plastic products to other manufacturers through its wholly owned subsidiary, NIKE IHM, Inc. and plastic injected and metal products to other manufacturers through its wholly-owned subsidiary, BAUER Italia SpA.

Nike sold a line of dress and casual footwear, apparel and accessories for men and women under the brand names Cole Haan®, CH, Gseries by Cole Haan, and Bragano through its wholly-owned subsidiary, Cole Haan Holdings. Nike's wholly-owned subsidiary, Bauer NIKE Hockey Inc., offered ice skates, skate blades, in-line roller skates, protective gear, hockey sticks, and hockey jerseys, licensed apparel and accessories under the Bauer® and NIKE® brand names. Bauer also offered various products for street and roller hockey. Another wholly-owned subsidiary Hurley International offered a line of action sports apparel (for surfing, skateboarding, and snowboarding) and youth lifestyle apparel and footwear under the Hurley brand name.

Background note

Early history

In 1958, Phil Knight, a keen athlete and an undergraduate at the University of Oregon, and his track coach Bill Bowerman realized the need for a good running shoe. The leading track shoes of the time were being produced by European companies, adidas and Puma. These shoes were made of leather, had little cushioning, and used steel spikes for traction. Knight and Bowerman started designing shoes that were lighter, better padded, and featured waffle like patterns in their rubber soles. However, these models did not become commercially successful.

While studying in the business school at Stanford University, Knight figured out that with cheap Japanese labor, an American distributor could sell track shoes that offered the same quality as adidas but at significantly lower prices. Knight was confident that he could sell more than 20,000 pairs of shoes (mainly to high school and college track team members) within three years of operation.

In 1964, Knight and Bowerman formed the Blue Ribbon Sports (BRS) Company. Bowerman's job was to test the shoes, offer design ideas, and endorse the shoes with coaches he knew. The two men signed a contract with a Japanese shoe manufacturer, Onitsuka Tiger, to make 1,000 pairs of a high quality, low-cost shoe called Tiger. This model was called Tiger Limber-Ups and resembled the then popular adidas Italia model. Their initial investment of $500 each and 'track-to-track' sales techniques paid off. These shoes were initially stored in the basement of Knight's home and sold out of the trunk of his Plymouth Valiant during the local track meets. By the end of 1965, the company had sold Tiger shoes worth $20,000 and made a profit of $3,240.

In 1966, Bowerman designed a lightweight shoe made of nylon-and-suede leather with a cushioning sole and good foot support. It resembled one of adidas' models. BRS named it Aztec (in anticipation of the 1968 Olympics in Mexico City). adidas, which traditionally launched a major new model at each Olympics had already developed a model called the Azteca Gold and threatened to take legal action against BRS. To get around the problem, BRS chose the name

'Cortez', which went on to become one of the company's best-selling brands. In 1967, the company introduced the Tiger Marathon, which marked the beginning of the use of nylon in athletic shoes.

In the early days, the BRS staff worked enthusiastically without following any rules and procedures. Inventory figures did not add up. Shipments were not matched with orders. Company expenses were met using personal credit cards—Knight's or Jeff Johnson's (BRS's first actual employee). Nike often ran into delivery problems because Onitsuka's shipments would get delayed, or would be incomplete, and filled with shoes that BRS had not ordered.

To meet their overdues to Onitsuka, Knight decided to offer 30% of the company's equity holding to the public on May 18, 1970 at $2 a share. The public offering was aborted owing to tight credit, recession and a slowing market in the US. Consequently, Knight privately placed debentures worth $200,000.

The 1970s

In 1971, Knight and Bowerman decided to develop a distinctive trademark and a new brand name 'Nike', inspired by the Greek winged Goddess of Victory. A local Portland student, Carolyn Davidson, who was paid $35 for the design, created the Nike symbol or 'Swoosh.' The new shoes were launched at the 1972 Olympics Trials held in Eugene, Oregon. Knight and Bowerman quickly cashed in on the publicity by advertising that Nike was worn by 'four of the top seven finishers.' During the same year, the company also severed its already shaky ties with Tiger after a dispute over distribution rights. Nike began to involve itself with a Japanese trading company called Nissho Iwai.

During the early 1970s, Nike's sales grew from $10 million to $270 million. The growth was driven by a patented waffle sole and the cushioning system, known as Nike Air. In 1975, Bowerman stumbled accidentally upon an idea for a new sole, which he tested by stuffing a piece of rubber into a waffle iron. The result was the waffle shoe, which Nike added to its running shoes. When running became popular during this time, Nike quickly improved its line of running shoes to appeal to this new market. These innovations rapidly helped Nike to become a leading player in the athletic shoe industry, so much so that over half of the running shoes sold in the US were Nikes.

In the late 1970s, almost every athletic shoe manufacturer followed the trend which Nike had created. Soon there were hundreds of models of lightweight, technically innovative running shoes on the market. When physical fitness began to grow in popularity, the market for athletic shoes expanded dramatically from a small number of serious athletes to hundreds of thousands of joggers.

The 1980s

In the early 1980s, Nike replaced adidas as the leading athletic shoe company in the American market. When Nike went public, Knight became one of the richest men in the world. But in the mid-1980s, after five years of rapid growth at an annual rate of 44%, Nike failed to anticipate the emerging market for aerobic shoes, having concentrated its efforts on casual shoes. Reebok began selling large numbers of its fashion-oriented aerobic shoes to women.

During the 1980s, Knight focused his attention on international operations and left daily decision making to other managers. With top managers moving from job to job, there was poor coordination among the design, marketing, and production efforts. In 1985, an excess inventory of 22 million pairs of shoes forced Nike to cut prices and also release some of its manufacturing capacity in the Far East. Reebok picked up much of this capacity.

Knight took several steps to try to re-establish Nike's dominance in the industry. He created small management teams to focus on niche markets. New advertising campaigns were developed that highlighted the technology of the shoes. Focus groups were used to determine the athletic shoe needs of customers. The company also began to make its products more fashionable by adding colour to many of its new products. All these changes helped Nike improve its position marginally in the industry in 1988.

In the late 1980s, Nike launched several new brands. Air Jordan (named after basketball superstar Michael Jordan of Chicago Bulls) in 1985, the Cross-Trainer in 1987, Air Pressure (Basketball shoes with inflatable soles) in 1989, and Aqua Sock (water shoes) in 1990. Nike paid $64 million[1] to acquire New Hampshire based Cole-Haan, which owned several popular brands including Country, Sporting, Classic, Bragano, and Cole-Haan. In 1990, Nike introduced a new footwear category, Tensile Air, a dress shoe with the Nike air-cushioning system. Led by Cole-Haan, the business grew by 16% the following year. In 1990, Nike also acquired the Cole-Haan Accessories Company, a distributor of premium quality belts, braces, and small leather goods.

Recent history

In the 1990s, Nike made more acquisitions including Tetra Plastic Inc., (1991) and Sports Specialties Inc (1993). Tetra manufactured plastic film used in the manufacture of Nike's Air-sole cushioning components. Sports Specialties distributed licensed headwear. Both companies operated as subsidiaries of Nike. In 1991, Nike became the world's first sporting goods company to surpass sales of $3 billion. A year later, Nike opened its first Nike Concept Shop at Macy's supermarket in San Francisco. The company also launched NikeTown, a concept retail store that combined innovative products with endorsements and image selling by top athletes.

In 1994, Nike launched PLAY (Participate in the Lives of American Youth), a multimillion-dollar initiative aimed at addressing the need for recreation for kids. PLAY included Reuse-A-Shoe, a program that diverted more than one million used shoes. In 1995, the company also received a license to place its logo on the National Football League (NFL) uniforms.

In the mid-90s, Nike moved ahead of its competitors such as Reebok and adidas. Its sales grew from $3.8 billion in 1994 to $9.2 billion in 1997. Investors benefited from a 320% increase in the stock price from 1st January 1995, to a high of $75 in early 1997.

But in the late 1990s, the teenage market suddenly switched from Nike Air Jordans to hiking boots and casual leather shoes. In 1994, athletic shoes accounted for 38% of all shoes sold in the US. Four years later[2], this figure dropped to 31%. Nike's own sales slide was accelerated by its lingering association with arrogant millionaire athletes and overseas sweatshops. As the company underestimated the anti-Nike sentiment about its overseas workers, the damage to the brand was significant.

Nike also misread the importance of the shift from a white-shoe, athletic look to a more urban, brown-shoe trend—largely because of its long-held insistence on performance at the expense of fashion. That blunder gave space to competitors such as New Balance Athletic Shoe Inc, Reebok and upstarts like And1 and Skechers which offered flashy, well-priced shoes that trend-setting urban teenagers desired. Nike also neglected the crucial 'kill zone,' the $60-to-$90-a-pair sneaker segment that accounted for most domestic sales[3].

---

1. In 1988.
2. According to industry researcher Footwear Market Insights.
3. Robson, Douglas, 'Just Do . . . Something,' *BusinessWeek*, 2 July 2001, pp. 70–71.

The crisis and restructuring

Knight, who had detached himself from Nike in order to travel and pursue other interests, joined the company back in 1999 after Bowerman's death, at a time when Nike was struggling. While addressing employees at a meeting, Knight admitted that there had been a management failure. Knight put together a new executive team that was comprised of a few Nike veterans who carried the heritage and culture of Nike's early years, along with several outsiders.

The new executive team sent out signals that the time had come to solve all the problems. Traditionally, the Nike culture had encouraged local managers to spend heavily and increase market share aggressively without worrying about profitability. Years of breakneck growth had encouraged unchecked spending. Managers had plenty of big-picture goals but no hard budget numbers to control them. Under the new scheme of things, managers had to hold expense increases to about 3% below revenue increases. Nike also began to streamline manufacturing and logistics.

Because Nike pumped out 120,000 products every year in four different launch cycles, many things could go wrong. Nike put in place a matrix structure that broke down managerial responsibility both by region and product. Under the matrix, Nike headquarters established which products to push and how to do it. However, regional managers were allowed some leeway to modify those rules.

Nike overhauled its supply-chain. In the past, retailers either desperately awaited delivery of fast moving shoes or struggled to get rid of non-moving stocks. The company used 27 different computer systems worldwide, most of which could not connect with the others. Nike spent $500 million to build a new system to facilitate faster design and shorter manufacturing times. The percentage of shoes it made without a firm order from a retailer fell from 30% to 3%. The lead-time for getting new sneaker styles to market was cut to six months from nine.

An automatic replenishment system was introduced to ship out basic, high-volume merchandise without waiting for retailers to place orders. In the past, retailers often ran out of simple apparel items. That also hurt sales of higher-priced items like halter tops, since consumers frequently purchased basic and fashion items together. Nike began selling merchandise worth $100 million a year through auto-replenishment. These improvements smoothed out many of the supply problems that had dogged Nike in the late 1990s.

Nike also realized the need to manage its acquisitions more effectively. After buying Cole Haan almost 15 years ago, Nike had struggled to add any real value to the dress-shoe outfit. Nike's managers realized that by giving their acquired brands some independence, rather than tightly integrating them and imposing Nike's corporate culture, they could achieve better results.

Nike announced it would acquire complementary brands as they became available. In mid-August, it paid $43 million for Official Starter Properties, licensors of sneakers and athletic apparel whose brands included the budget-level Shaq label.

In 2003, for the first time, sales overseas exceeded that in the US. Nike was also seriously looking at sports fashion as a core business, a clear departure from the past. Nike's worldwide apparel sales reached $3.5 billion in fiscal 2004. In June 2003, Nike announced that it would acquire Converse[4] in a $305 million deal.

---

4. In 2003, Nike completed the acquisition of Converse, the globally recognized footwear brand with nearly a century of sports heritage, and home of the perennially popular Chuck Taylor All-Star and Jack Purcell footwear.

Product development

Nike had attempted to keep itself on the cutting edge of technology. The company's broad game plan was to launch new technically advanced shoe models from time to time. In 1964, it launched the lightweight shoe with reduced weight but better performance. Nike developed the waffle shoe in 1975. High traction and lightweight were characteristics of this model. Nike's Air sole model, which appeared in the market in 1979, incorporated an air-cushioning system that lessened the impact of heels on pavements and minimized the possibility of injury. In 1980, the company formed the Nike Sports Research Laboratory (NSRL), which used video cameras and traction testing devices to research several types of concerns including children's foot morphology. In addition, NSRL evaluated ideas from Nike's product development group. The group developed various products keeping a five-year time horizon in mind—cross-training shoes, the Nike Footbridge stability device, inflatable fit systems, and the Nike 180 air-cushioning system. Researchers made shoe molds in the model shop and evaluated shoe characteristics such as tension and adhesion in the testing lab.

During the late 1980s, Nike continued with its technological improvements. In 1987, Nike launched the Visible Airline model with a gas-cushioning system. The Air pressure model introduced in 1989 incorporated a separate device to pump up the shoe. In 1990, Nike introduced the Air 180 model that provided air cushioning in the heel and front of the shoe. Nike also launched the built in pump shoe that provided better fit. A year later, Nike developed a shoe that combined neoprene and lycra spandex materials and provided runners with a form fitting, supportive and lightweight shoe. Nike pioneered the Air Max technology in 1993 that provided 30% more cushioning.

In 1999, Knight split off a part of the business which made products for non traditional sports into an autonomous unit called ACG (all-conditions gear). ACG had its own staff, budget, and marketing plan. The decision to form a separate unit was prompted by Nike's failure to build credibility among fans of nontraditional sports, a small but important demographic segment that tended to originate fashion trends among teens. Knight put the business under the charge of Gordon O. McFadden, a 17-year veteran of Norwegian outdoor-apparel maker Helly Hansen. Four of the five top ACG executives were outsiders.

A keen sportsman himself, McFadden began developing new products, such as a $175 snowboarding jacket with a dozen pockets designed to hold gloves, goggles, and headphones. He began putting 15 or 20 designers in a studio close to the action in Southern California, the center of the skateboarding and surfing worlds. ACG began to develop a clog-like shoe, the Rufus, that it hoped would slow the onslaught of 'brown shoes,' the hiking boots and other casual footwear that many young customers preferred to athletic shoes.

ACG quickly realized the need to create a new image. It introduced new print ads and in-store promotions and decided to open dozens of stores at ski lodges and outdoor resorts. The new stores and products would bear ACG's logo: an inverted triangle with the letters ACG underscored by a swoosh. ACG expected sales of action-sports products to grow by about 20% annually, compared with an 8% rate before the unit was given its independence.

Nike's worldwide apparel sales had shrunk from $2.9 billion in fiscal 1998 to $2.7 billion in 2000 as customers discarded its athletic styles in favor of more fashionable, street-worthy gear. Nike treated the business as an accessory, even though it accounted for some 30% of total revenues. But gross margins for Nike's apparel were among the highest for the company. They rose from around 38% to nearly 43% in the 12 months ended February 2002. So Nike began to lay greater emphasis on fashion apparel.

In October 2000, Knight recruited Mindy Grossman from Polo Jeans. Grossman radically changed Nike's approach to designing, manufacturing, and merchandising. She slashed apparel lead times from 18 months to about 11 while launching a three-tiered labeling system for Nike's clothes: black for hard-core athletic gear, silver for sports-inspired active wear, and white for fashion apparel.

When Nike acquired skateboard equipment marketer Hurley International for $95 million in 2002, it was another inroad to the desired youth market. Nike had initially failed to make an impact on 9-to-21-year-old skateboarders for its skateboard shoes. Nike went back and redesigned the shoe, adding thicker tongues and a different insole from famed sneaker designer Marcus Tayui. It also recruited an insider to bring it all together and provide insight on trends: Kevin Imamura, editor of TransWorld Stance, a skateboarding pop culture magazine published by Time Inc.'s TransWorld Media. Serving as the communications manager, Imamura helped the shoe and apparel giant connect with competitive skateboarders through the development of two new performance shoes.

In 2004, adidas unveiled the adidas 1, a $250 shoe slated for December that had a computer chip that automatically adjusted the fit as the wearer ran. Nike responded with Nike Free, that made runners feel as if they were barefoot. The idea was drawn from the barefoot runners of Kenya, who had proved that shoeless training built strength and improved performance. Meanwhile, the company continued to refine its Shox technology—a special cushioning system first developed for runners, and a top seller in categories from running to basketball to cross-training. The shoes, which sold for up to $135 a pair, helped put to rest the idea that high-priced sneakers no longer sold well in the US.

Just before the 2004 European soccer championships, Nike launched its Total 90 III, a sleek shoe that drew inspiration from cars used in the Le Mans 24-hour road race. Nike realized that millions of kids around the globe played casual pickup soccer games in the street and developed the shoe especially for them.

In November 2004, Sony PlayStation and Nike were developing a video game designed to encourage the 'PlayStation generation' to do more physical exercise. EyeToy Kinetic, which was being created through a partnership between Sony Computer Entertainment Europe and Nike's training experts, Motionworks, was intended to provide a personal fitness training schedule. The interactive game, which was due to be released early in 2005, would feature a variety of fitness activities to be carried out via the EyeToy, which projected the exerciser's image onto the television screen.

Nike believed video games 'might provide another long-term access point' for the brand to encourage young people to be more active.

Advertising & promotion

Nike positioned its products as high performance shoes designed with high technology features. Nike athletic shoes were targeted at men and women aged between 18 and 34 years.

Until 1976, except for the routine purchase of space in running publications, Nike's advertising was largely in the form of cooperative arrangements with retailers who inserted ads in local newspapers. These ads, while spreading the Nike name, did little to enhance Nike's image as a quality shoe manufacturer among general consumers. Retailers most often put Nike shoes on sale, giving the company the image of a cheap, all-purpose product.

In 1976, Nike did not have an advertising agency. Knight hired a Portland based advertising agency, which came up with the tagline: 'Keeping your feet in touch with what's new.' These ads, which predominantly occupied the back covers of sports magazines, were considered by the company 'to be flat and uninspired.' The company decided to communicate more effectively to emphasize quality and innovation in design.

Later, Nike's advertising agency, Weiden & Kennedy, developed advertisements that tended to focus on the technical advantages of the products. Nike positioned itself as the brand for serious athletes. Recreational runners, sportsmen and women bought Nike's products because they were comfortable and it suggested they were knowledgeable about the particular sport.

In the 1980s, Nike attempted to broaden its appeal and become a part of the youth culture surfacing in the US. Achieving the balance in communications between fashionability and sports performance required Nike to rethink the way in which its advertising worked. In 1986, when it launched Nike Air, the company came up with the idea of a series of black and white clips of everyday Americans interspersed with athletes wearing Nike products to the tune of the Beatles' 'Revolution.' The advertisement captured the mood of the times and the fast spreading fitness revolution. It also suggested technical excellence.

Nike spent $20 million on a huge campaign before the Los Angeles Olympics in 1984. That year, Nike's US sales decreased by 12% and profits dropped by 30%. Between 1985 and 1987, Nike's problems worsened. Its share in the US market dropped from 27.2 to 16%—mostly because of Reebok, whose share grew from nothing to more than 32% of the market. Nike was undeterred, however, and aggressively increased its annual advertising spending to $45 million by 1989 and $150 million by 1992.

In a breakout campaign in the mid-1980s, Nike quickly created a dominant media presence in several trend-setting US cities. TV ads linking Nike to a city were used, but the real drivers were huge, oversized billboards and murals on buildings that blanketed cities with messages featuring key Nike-sponsored athletes (not products). Carl Lewis's legs extended past the natural frame of billboards, to draw the attention of people. This visual presence was supported by an in-store effort to translate the advertising into sales.

The centerpiece of the program was Los Angeles during the 1984 Olympic games. The effort included an 'I love LA' commercial with clips of key sponsored athletes in action—Carl Lewis leaping through the sky and landing in the sands of Venice Beach and John McEnroe arguing with a traffic cop. These scenes were also captured on billboards and murals. The resulting visibility and presence for Nike spilled over into the Olympic media coverage. Nike's perceived association with the Olympic games turned out to be several times that of Converse, the official sponsor. Though Converse spent a lot of money on sponsorship, it was Nike which captured the attention of the consumers.

Nike's celebrity spokespersons included Michael Jordan, Bo Jackson, Pete Sampras, Andre Agassi, Jim Courier and John McEnroe. Michael Jordan's contract to market the Air Jordan basketball shoe was the most lucrative endorsement contract in sports at that time. Jackson was featured in Nike's cross-training advertisements. Agassi was offered a lucrative contract to endorse Nike athletic shoes and apparel, including the Challenge Court tennis shoe.

Nike's ads were meant to be viewed as a stylish piece of communication rather than a sales pitch. Nike's positioning was also based on real sporting credentials aimed at 'in the know' consumers. Nike did not believe in projecting an athlete as more interesting or benign than he actually was. Nike believed knowledgable consumers would easily spot this. For example, Bo Jackson was signed up to promote Nike and appeared in a series of humorous ads with the theme 'Bo Knows.' However, when he suffered a hip injury, which prevented him from playing, Nike decided to continue using him and began to use ads which talked about his hip replacement. Similarly the basketball star, Charles Barkley, had the reputation of a bruiser on court. Rather than play this down, Nike created a TV ad featuring Barkley in an aggressive animation style knocking down competitors and pulling down the basket.

Often Nike depended more on intuitive understanding of customers than detailed market research. While Nike did use marketing research from time to time, it sometimes ignored the results of the research. One research study indicated that Nike was well advised to go back to its roots as a serious sports brand. Nike went against the advice and prepared a film which showed striking sports images revolving around the famous Beatles singer John Lennon's composition, 'Instant Karma.'

When it came to women's products, Nike used a different style. Historically, Nike had lagged behind Reebok in this market. When the aerobics revolution started, Nike decided it would be a fad. Nike was also worried that advertising which appealed to women might undermine the product's appeal to men. Having given Reebok a headstart, Nike later put together a strong women's range. Nike realized that if it communicated with women in a personalized way, there would be no impact on its core men's market. The campaign developed by Weiden & Kennedy took an introspective look at women's lives. Using double-page, black and white spreads, the ads empathized with women and simply said: 'We understand the way you feel.' The success of these ads was reflected in the increasing sales. Nike's sales to women began to grow faster than those to men bringing the shoemaker on par with Reebok in the women's market. The campaign won widespread acclaim in the ad industry, winning the Magazine Publishers of America Kelly Award for 1991.

Nike inserted TV ads during professional and college sports events, prime time programs, and late night programs. Prime time ads were intended to reach a broad range of adults and late-night advertising was geared towards younger adults. Print media such as *Sports Illustrated*, *People*, *Runner's World*, *Glamour*, *Self*, *Tennis*, *Money*, *Bicycling* and *Weight Watchers* were also very important advertising vehicles.

Over the years, Nike had come up with campaigns that attempted to capture the attention of customers with media weight and quality of execution. For example, an early Michael Jordan commercial showed him soaring through the air on the way to dunking the ball, with the tagline, 'Who says man was not meant to fly?' This image became the symbol of Michael Jordan and was one of the most popular posters ever developed. The personal side of Jordan was exposed in a series of humorous ads developed by Spike Lee, at that time a relatively unknown avant-garde director.

Nike's 'Just do it' campaign launched in 1988 was named the fourth best advertising campaign in the century by *Advertising Age.* The first 'Just do it' ad showed wheelchair racer Craig Blanchette and the slogan in white letters on a black background. The tagline was never spoken. However, it resonated with an entire generation.

As Nike's advertising director, Scott Bedbury, noted[5]:

> We can't put it on pencils and key chains; this thing has become much more than an ad slogan. It's an idea. It's like a frame of mind.

It connected with overweight men putting off an exercise program, busy executives becoming diverted from fitness, and people of all types with a dream on hold. It associated Nike with making fitness actually happen, setting the right priorities, and living (as opposed to thinking) the dream.

5. Aaker, David A., and Joachimsthaler, Erich, *Brand leadership*, The Free Press, 2000, p. 179.

The 'Just do it' slogan had a long run. It was supplemented for a short time in 1997 by the 'I Can' slogan, which challenged athletes to set their own limits and suggested that achievement was up to the individual. The new slogan attempted to influence consumer perceptions and to align Nike with the major trends of caring and sharing of the 1990s. But this campaign failed to make a big impact.

Nike had been successful in its attempts to build loyalty by licensing Nike gear to college sports teams. Some of the institutions that signed agreements to wear Nike gear during 1993 and 1994 included the University of Miami, Pennsylvania State University, University of Michigan, and University of Nevada-Las Vegas.

In 1996, Nike focused on the soccer market with a series of expensive advertisements. The firm vied with adidas and Reebok for customer attention at the 1996 Summer Olympics in Atlanta.

For the 1998 World Cup Football tournament in France, Nike signed contracts with six leading teams, including the 1994 champions, Brazil, to whom it agreed to pay $400 million over the next ten years. This money went towards funding the Brazilian Football Federation (CBF), buying training equipment and building a new soccer center. Apart from this, the company also entered into individual contracts with 14 of the 22 players of the Brazilian National team. The other five contracted teams included the Netherlands, South Korea, Nigeria, Italy and the United States.

In mid-2003, Jordan, a division of Nike, unveiled its most ambitious national marketing campaign since the launch of the brand in 1997. Centered on the theme of 'Love,' the major initiative was a multi-faceted extension of the brand's Fall/Holiday 2002 print advertisements. The 'Love' program was launched in Atlanta in February 2003. It continued throughout the year, reaching many major markets in the US.

On February 25, 2004, Nike launched its 'What If?' Spring advertising campaign, featuring Andre Agassi, Lance Armstrong, Randy Johnson, Marion Jones, Brian Urlacher, Michael Vick and Serena Williams. These seven world-class athletes stepped outside their own sport to display their tremendous talents in sports such as boxing, baseball, hockey, volleyball, gymnastics and bowling.

The six-week campaign provided consumers with images of athletes including Andre Agassi as a member of the Boston Red Sox fielding a ground ball and throwing out a speedy runner at first base, Lance Armstrong battling toe-to-toe with Fitz Vanderpool in the ring and Marion Jones speeding toward the vault and executing a perfect flip.

A senior Nike executive remarked,[6]

> Nike athletes such as Michael Vick and Brian Urlacher prove each time they hit the field how powerful talent, speed and desire can be. The 'What If' campaign asks the question, 'What if Lance Armstrong was given a pair of boxing gloves instead of a bike as a child?' Our belief is that a passionate athlete's drive to win would translate into success in any sport.

While developing the vignettes, elite coaches and trainers worked with the Nike athletes to ensure authenticity to the last detail. In addition, Nike secured participation from athletes from each of the respective sports to appear with the seven stars. Serena Williams was partnered with AVP Tour Professional Nancy Mason as she hit a powerful crosscourt spike playing against Jenn Meredith and Carrie Busch; and Randy Johnson bowled against the legendary and recent US Open winner, Pete Weber.

---

6. Aaker, David A., and Joachimsthaler Erich, *Brand leadership*, The Free Press, 2000, p. 179.

In September 2004, Nike extended its ties with grass-roots sport with the launch of a DVD documenting the UK's one-on-one street football scene. The film, produced by Nike's ad agency, Wieden & Kennedy, showed the company's search for the UK's first Panna KO champion. 'Panna' was the Dutch word for 'nutmeg'—the term that described the move of knocking the ball between an opponent's legs. Three hundred thousand copies of the DVD were distributed in football and music magazines in October 2004. It was the second piece of branded content W&K had created for Nike in 2004. In May 2004, Nike had created a magazine titled, *Goodbye Hoof, Hello Nutmeg*, to tie in with Euro 2004.

After acquiring companies Nike typically gave them a makeover. Nike had 'swoosh-ified' the hockey-equipment maker Bauer, for example, and highlighted Nike Air technology in its Cole Haan shoe subsidiary. Many feared the same would happen when Nike bought Converse. Nike made pricey, high-tech sneakers like the $165 Air Jordans. Converse was known for cheap, low-tech sneakers. The *Wall Street Journal* sounded an ominous note when the deal broke in July 2003: 'The Swoosh is swallowing Chuck Taylor.' With Converse, Nike departed from tradition. Nike executives mentioned they had always intended to leave Converse alone.

In October 2004, Nike hired advertising agency executive Ben Moore as its head of brand communications for the UK and Ireland. He took on the role vacated by Jack Gold, who moved to director of communications for the Americas region, based at Nike's global headquarters in Portland, Oregon. Gold's move was part of a restructuring of Nike's global marketing operation, which also saw European advertising director Stefan Olander relocating to the US.

The road ahead

By September 2004, Nike's Soccer sales were nearly $1 billion, or 25% of the global market. For the first time, Nike's share of the soccer shoe market in Europe (35%), exceeded that of adidas (31%). Nike had achieved rapid growth in part by using the aggressive marketing tactics that made it big in the US. Nike paid the prestigious Manchester United club an unprecedented $450 million over 14 years to run its merchandising and uniform operations.

Nike faced many challenges in the fall of 2004. After several years of fast growth, European sales of higher-priced shoes had started to slide. In the US, retro-sneaker makers like K-Swiss, Diesel, and Puma were doing well. adidas had redoubled efforts to penetrate the North American basketball market, where Nike had a 60% share. Taking a leaf from Nike's book, adidas had just signed three NBA all-stars: Tracy McGrady, Tim Duncan, and Kevin Garnett to endorse its products. Nike executives wondered what they needed to do to strengthen the company's competitive position.

QUESTIONS TO BE ANSWERED

Where Nike is now

1. Using the Porter Framework (cost–differentiation–focus), describe Nike's current strategic orientation. Would you say that this has been successful? Why or why not?
2. Has Nike done a good job in environmental scanning? Why or why not?
3. Do a SWOT analysis and discuss Nike's current situation. What does the SWOT indicate?
4. How would you characterize the role that marketing has played in Nike's development to date in this case?

Where Nike is going

5. How would you describe the current positioning of Nike?

6. Where does Nike appear to be heading strategically? Does this direction make sense given their present positioning?
7. Using the Ansoff matrix, how would you characterize Nike's recent actions and decisions?
8. Has Nike done an effective job of segmenting its markets? Why or why not?

How Nike will get there

9. What specific strategic suggestions would you make to Nike management regarding the various components of the marketing mix to help it improve its performance?
10. How can Nike compete effectively against such competitors as adidas, K-Swiss, Diesel, and Puma?
11. What do you think that the Nike brand actually stands for in the minds of its various target segments? Is this viable? Why or why not?
12. Is Nike running 'out of gas' in the marketplace? Can it return to its former glory? Why or why not?

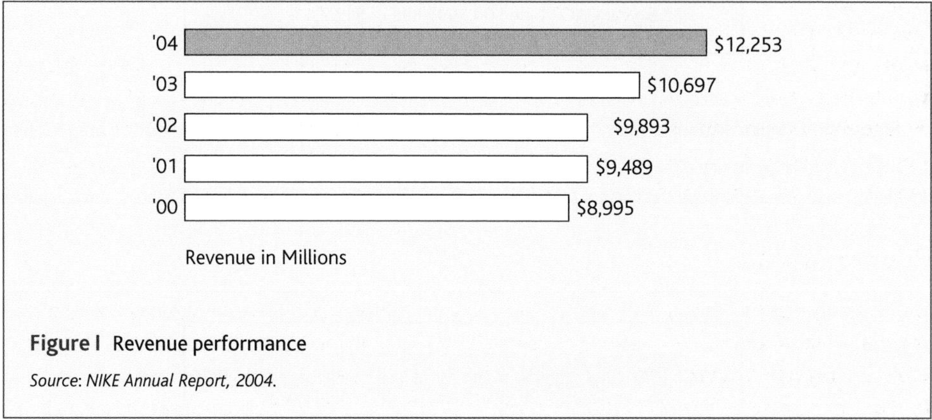

Figure I Revenue performance

Source: NIKE Annual Report, 2004.

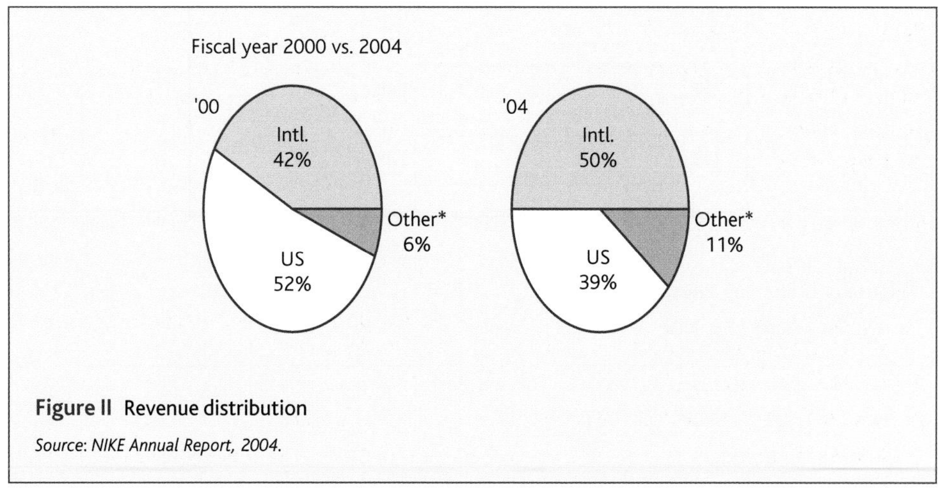

Figure II Revenue distribution

Source: NIKE Annual Report, 2004.

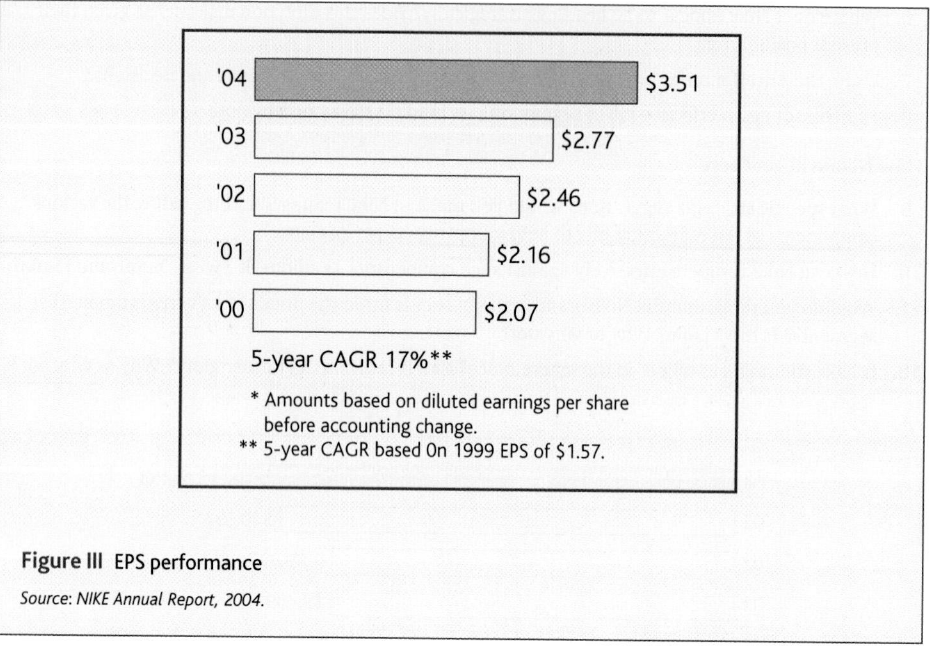

Figure III EPS performance

Source: NIKE Annual Report, 2004.

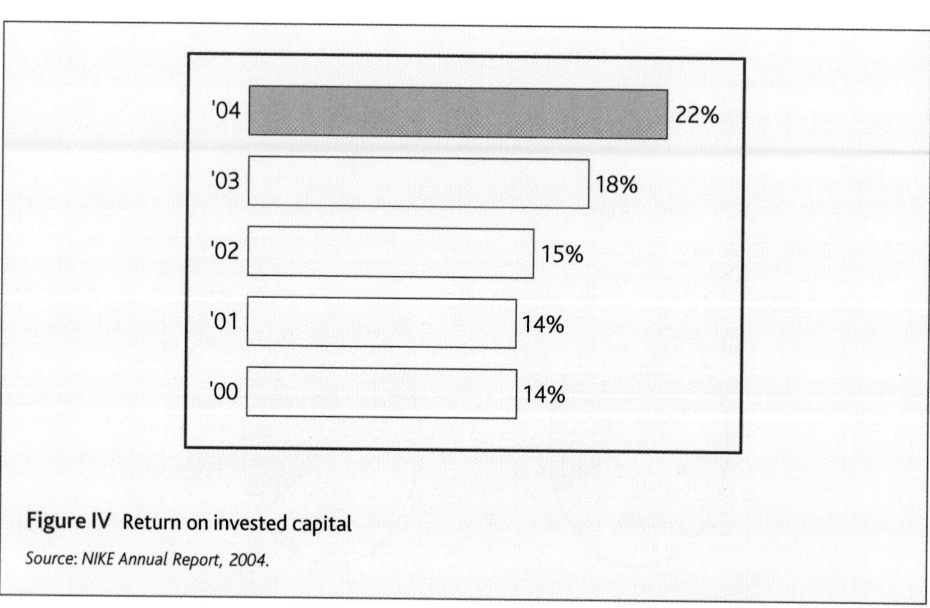

Figure IV Return on invested capital

Source: NIKE Annual Report, 2004.

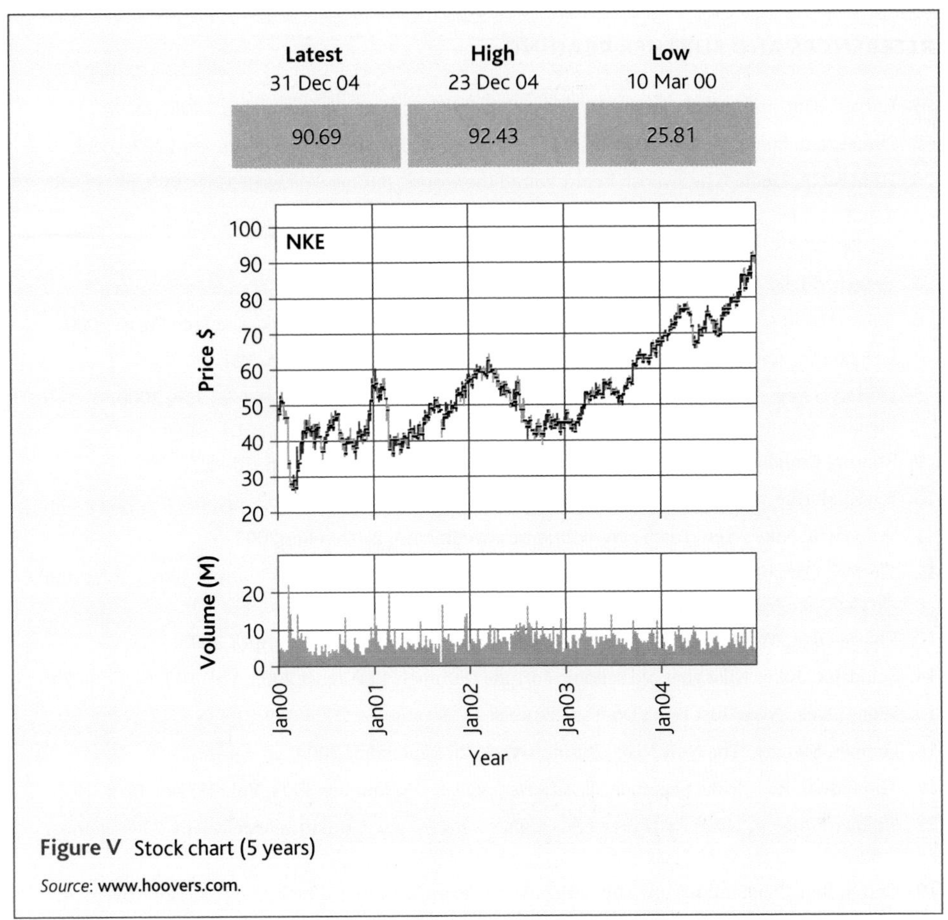

Figure V Stock chart (5 years)

Source: www.hoovers.com.

	May 04	May 03	May 02
Revenue ($ mil.)	12,253.1	10,697.0	9,893.0
Net income ($ mil.)	945.6	1,006.2	663.3
Net profit margin	7.7%	9.4%	6.7%
Employees	24,667	23,300	22,700

Figure VI Income statement

Source: www.hoovers.com.

REFERENCES AND FURTHER READING

1. Carvell, Tim, and Labich, Kenneth, 'Nike vs. Reebok', *Fortune*, 18 September 1995, pp. 90–8.
2. Himelstein, Linda, 'The game's the thing at Nike now', *BusinessWeek*, 27 January 1997, p. 88.
3. Himelstein, Linda, 'The swoosh heard 'round the world', *BusinessWeek*, 12 May 1997, pp. 76–8.
4. Schiff, Lenore, and Sellers, Patricia, 'Four reasons Nike's not cool', *Fortune*, 30 March 1998, pp. 26–27.
5. Branch, Shelly, 'The Brand Builders', *Fortune*, 10 May 1999, pp. 132–4.
6. Aaker, David A., and Joachimsthaler, Erich, *Brand leadership*, New York: The Free Press, 2000.
7. Lee, Louise, 'Can Nike Still Do It?', *BusinessWeek*, 21 February 2000, pp. 121–6.
8. Lindsay, Greg, 'I want a Unique Logo—Just Like Theirs', *Fortune (Europe)*, 24 July 2000, pp. 204–5.
9. Robson, Douglas, 'Just Do. . .Something', *BusinessWeek*, 2 July 2001, pp. 70–1.
10. Boyle, Matthew, 'How Nike Got Its Swoosh Back', *Fortune*, 24 June 2002, pp. 16–17.
11. 'A Jog with Nike's New Team', **www.businessweek.com**, 28 October 2002.
12. Tierney, Christine, and Holmes, Stanley, 'How NIKE Got Its Game Back', *BusinessWeek*, 4 November 2002, pp. 129–31.
13. Kharif, Olga, 'When to Run with Nike?', **www.businessweek.com**, 18 April 2003.
14. Schlosser, Julie, 'Nike goes old school', *Fortune (Europe)*, 11 August 2003, Vol. 148, No. 3, p. 74.
15. Wong, Alex, 'Nike: Just Don't Do It', *Newsweek*, 20 September 2004, Vol. 144, No. 12, p. 39.
16. Holmes, Stanley, 'The New Nike', *BusinessWeek*, 20 September 2004, pp. 59–66.
17. Thomaselli, Rich, 'Nike Skateboard', *Advertising Age*, 1 November 2004, Vol. 75, No. 44, p. 19.
18. Holmes, Stanley, 'Nike: Can Perez Fill Knight's Shoes?', **www.businessweek.com**, 22 November 2004.
19. Carter, Ben, 'PlayStations links up with Nike for 'exercise' game', *Marketing (UK)*, 24 November 2004, p. 1.
20. Holmes, Stanley, and Sager, Ira, 'Phil Knight kicks off his CEO shoes', *BusinessWeek*, 20 December 2004, p. 13.
21. *NIKE Annual Report, 2004.*
22. **www.nike.com**.
23. **www.hoovers.com**.

End of book Case III

Samsung: the making of a global brand

Now they're in consumers' consideration set. After Sony, they have the potential to be the No. 2 brand globally.

Jan Lindermann, Global Director for Brand valuation, Interbrand in 2001.

Emerging giant?

In 1998, South Korea's leading consumer electronics major, Samsung Electronics Corporation (Samsung), entered into an agreement with the International Olympic Association to sponsor the 1998 Seoul Olympics. According to company sources, Samsung wanted to sponsor the Olympics to establish itself as a global brand. Analysts felt that by associating itself with the Olympics, Samsung would increase its brand visibility and brand recall among its consumers worldwide. They also pointed out that to become the next Sony (Exhibit I) of the consumer electronics market, Samsung would have to invest heavily in marketing.

EXHIBIT I Sony Corporation

The history of Sony dates back to 1946 when Masaru Ibuka, Tamon Maeda and Akio Morita formed a company called Tokyo Tsushin Kogyo (Tokyo Telecommunications Engg. Co) with an initial capital of 19,000 yen in the city of Nagoya with just 20 employees to undertake research and manufacture of telecommunications and measuring equipment. The company's main objectives were as follows: to establish an ideal factory, free, dynamic and pleasant where technical personnel of sincere motivation can exercise their technological skills to the highest level.

The first product of the company was an electric rice cooker, which failed to generate sales for the company. Since its first product was a failure, the company entered into the replacement parts business for electric phonographs. In 1950, the company produced Japan's first tape recorder. The machine was bulky and heavy; however, it performed excellently. But, tape recorders could not find sufficient markets, as it was a totally new concept in Japan and people were not ready to pay a high price for it even if they liked its performance. Soon Morita realized that unique technology and unique products were not enough to keep a business going.

In 1955, the company produced its first transistorized radio and in 1957 it produced a pocket radio. These two products were a huge hit in the market and the company expanded to US markets. In 1958, Tokyo Tsushin Kogyo was renamed Sony, and in 1960 it established its first overseas sales subsidiary, the Sony Corporation of America, with a capital of $500,000. In the following year it expanded its operations to Switzerland through Sony Overseas SA.

In 1972, Sony became the first Japanese company to set up manufacturing facilities in the US, and in 1973, Sony received an Emmy award for its Trinitron technology. In 1976, Morita took over as CEO from Ibuka, and in 1979, Sony produced an innovative product—the Walkman—which achieved a cult following and high sales, boosting the company's profits during the 1980s. In 1981, Sony came up with the 3.5-inch floppy disk.

In 1989, Norio Ohga took over as CEO and Chairman of Sony from Morita. During Ohga's regime, Sony emphasized process innovations to improve efficiency and control production costs. During Morita's period, the emphasis was on product development.... In the same year [that Ohga tookover], Sony acquired Trans Corn Systems Division and Columbia pictures. In 1994, Sony was restructured to improve the speed and quality of its corporate decisions. It formed eight new internal companies and focused on specific markets. In the same year, Sony established SW Networks (SWN), a full service radio network with more than 600 affiliate stations catering to both domestic and international markets.

In 1995, due to the lack of new products and an unfavorable exchange rate between the dollar and the yen, Sony ran into problems. In the same year, Noboyudki Idei took over as president from Ohga. Under Idei, Sony strengthened its market position. In the late 1990s, it developed an innovative product—the PlayStation (computer game machines). More than six million PlayStations were sold within 3 years of its introduction. In 1998, Sony restructured its consumer electronics business to make operations more efficient and better adaptable to networks, which were becoming increasingly important.

In 1999, Sony signed a joint venture with Royal Philips Electronics and Sun Microsystems to develop networked entertainment products. In early 1999, Sony again announced that it would restructure its businesses into four autonomous units. In the same year it introduced the world's most sophisticated robot called AIBO (the Japanese word for companion and the English abbreviation for Artificial Intelligence Robot). For 2001, Sony reported net income of $134 million. By this time it had a presence in more than 61 countries and offered products and services in the categories of consumer electronics, games, pictures and music.

Source: **www.sony.net.**

In the late 1990s, Samsung entered into various marketing alliances with companies worldwide and sponsored events to enhance its brand awareness. Due to its marketing efforts, its brand value appreciated by 200% from $3.1 billion in 1999 to $8.3 billion in 2002. Consequently, in 2002, Samsung emerged as the only non-Japanese brand from Asia to be listed in the global top 100 brands valued by Interbrand Inc[1] (Table I). The company was ranked 34th in Interbrand's list of the world's top 100 brands.

1. Interbrand is a leading brand consultant established in 1974. Interbrand lists the top 100 brands of the world in association with *BusinessWeek* magazine.

TABLE I Brand value of Samsung

(in $ billions)

Year	Rank	Brand Value
1999	—	3.1
2000	43	5.2
2001	42	6.4
2002	34	8.3

Source: **www.samsung.com**.

In spite of the worldwide downturn in 2002, Samsung posted a net profit of 1.7 trillion won[2] for the third quarter of 2002–03, which was much higher than its net profit of 425 million won in 2001 for the same period. In 2002–03, Samsung emerged as the number three player in the global cell phone market after Motorola and Nokia. It also emerged as the world leader in the $24.9 billion memory chip market.

According to industry sources, Samsung's innovative advertising strategies, improvements in product design and focus on global markets helped it achieve an increase in earnings over the years.

Background note

Samsung was established in 1969 as the flagship company of Samsung Corporation (Exhibit II). It was the third largest player in the Korean electronics market after Lucky Goldstar (LG) and Daewoo.[3] Samsung achieved fast growth through exports, which constituted around 70% of its total production. Most of the exports were to the USA on an Original Equipment Manufacturer (OEM) basis. It supplied components for high tech industries in the USA. In the early 1970s, Samsung decided to venture into the television market, and in 1972 it started production of black and white television sets for the local market. After its success in the television market, Samsung set up its home appliances plant in 1973. By 1974 it started manufacturing refrigerators and washing machines.

EXHIBIT II About Samsung Corporation

The history of Samsung's parent company—Samsung Corporation—dates back to 1938. Initially, the group exported dried fish, vegetables and fruit to China. By 1948 it owned flour mills and confectionery machines. Subsequently, it expanded its businesses and diversified into various fields. In 1951, Samsung Moolsan (Samsung Corporation) was formed, and by 1953, the company ventured into the manufacture of sugar through the

2. As on March 3, 2003, US$ 1 = 1, 188.60 won (KRW).
3. LG and Daewoo are the largest Korean conglomerates. General Motors bought a stake in Daewoo, when it was liquidated in 2002 due to financial problems.

Cheil Sugar Manufacturing Co, which was the only sugar manufacturing company in South Korea at that time.

In the early 1960s, the company diversified into the textile, banking and insurance sectors. In 1965, it entered the print media by acquiring Saechan Paper Manufacturing. And in 1969, it established the group's flagship company Samsung Electronics. The 1970s saw the group diversifying into the heavy engineering, chemicals and petrochemical industries. Later in the 1980s, the company diversified into the high technology area and the aerospace industry. In 1983, Samsung developed its first chip, the 64K Dynamic Random Access Memory (DRAM) chip, through its subsidiary Samsung Semiconductor & Telecommunications, and emerged as an Original Equipment Manufacturer (OEM) for companies such as Intel.

In 1985, it set up Samsung Data Systems (renamed Samsung SDS), which was involved in consulting, business integration and data center services. In 1987, on the death of Lee Byung Chull, Lee Kun Hee (Hee), his son, was appointed chairman of the group. In 1994, the group diversified into the automobile industry. This move has been regarded as one of the biggest mistakes committed by the group. In the same year, due to economic reasons, the 'New Management' philosophy was introduced. This philosophy laid emphasis on qualitative rather than quantitative growth. In 1995, the Samsung Corporation diversified into the financial services business through Samsung Finance, which was renamed Samsung Capital. In 1996, Samsung Electronics developed the world's first giga-bit DRAM, and in the same year, Samsung established its commercial vehicles plant.

In 1997, the company faced a severe cash crunch due to the South Asian crisis. This crisis resulted in a high exchange rate for the South Korean currency (won). In order to generate cash for its investments and decrease debts, Samsung restructured the organization. It initiated cost cutting measures on a large scale; it also hived off non-core businesses such as the Samsung Construction Equipment Business to generate cash. It also hived of its forklift business and sold off real estate and other assets (amounting to $300 million) and decreased its global investments by 30%. It sold 10 of its business units to overseas companies for around $1.5 billion dollars. It also laid off around 50,000 people. In February 1998, Samsung Corp produced its first passenger car. By 1999, Samsung Corp had lowered its high debt–equity ratio from 365% in 1997 to 148%. In 1999, Samsung Corp closed down its passenger and commercial vehicle business and its chairman, Kun Hee Lee, covered the group's debt through personal stock worth 2.8 trillion won.

In 2000, Samsung Corp announced a new management program to stay ahead of the competition in the digital age. According to the new management program, the company aimed at devoting 'human resources and technology to create superior products and services, thereby contributing to a better global society.' By 2000, it employed around 174,000 employees all over the world. Its net income in 2000 was $ 7.3 billion on net sales of $119.5 billion.

In 2001, Samsung announced its vision—'continuously striving to conquer new era in digital technology and products.' By 2002, Samsung Corp was involved in heavy engineering, consumer electronics, financial services and chemicals. It had a presence in more than 60 countries.

Source: ICFAI Center for Management Research.

By the mid-1970s, Samsung started production of color TVs (CTVs) and energy efficient high cold refrigerators. By the late 1970s, the company's exports to the US markets exceeded US$100 million. During the same period, it established a marketing subsidiary in the USA. In the 1980s, it started manufacturing microwave ovens and air conditioners. In 1980, it acquired Korea Telecommunications Corp, which was renamed Samsung Semiconductor & Telecommunications Co in 1982. In the same year, Samsung established a sales subsidiary in Germany and its first overseas plant in Portugal to cater to European markets. In 1986, research labs were established in Santa Clara (California) and Tokyo to improve the product line. In 1988, the Samsung Semiconductor business was merged with Samsung. By the end of 1989, Samsung was ranked 13th in semiconductor sales worldwide.

Though Samsung was able to establish its brand image in the Korean market, it was regarded as an OEM in global markets. Since Samsung had a poor brand image in global markets and its products had a high defect rate, many consumers associated Samsung's products with poor quality.

To change this perception of its products, Samsung Corporation initiated a restructuring process across the group in 1994. Samsung Electronics, the flagship company of the group (contributing around 90% of the group's profits), was the main focus of this restructuring.

In 1994, a business restructuring process—'New Management'—was initiated to transform Samsung into a global brand. This process identified three major focus areas: quality, globalization and multifaceted integration. The company shifted its focus from quantity to quality, and set up manufacturing units across the world to bring down costs, tap global markets efficiently and employ the best talent. The group also implemented various quality initiatives such as Six Sigma and manufacturing initiatives such as assembly manufacturing to enhance output through the optimum utilization of resources.

This change in focus enabled Samsung to become one of the top global brands and also the world leader in around 17 product categories (Exhibit III). Due to the emphasis on continuous innovation, it launched technologically superior products, and by 2001 it posted a net income

EXHIBIT III Market position of Samsung in various product categories worldwide*

(Figures for 2001)

Product	Product Category	Market Share	Market Position
Monitor	Digital Media Network	21%	First
VCR	Digital Media Network	20%	First
DVDP	Digital Media Network	17%	Third
ODD	Digital Media Network	13%	First
D-RAM	Digital Solution Network	29%	First
S-RAM	Digital Solution Network	26%	First
TFT-LCD	Digital Solution Network	20%	First
Microwave Oven	Digital Appliance Network	25%	First
CDMA Mobile Phone**	Telecommunications	27.3%	First
GSM Mobile Phone**	Telecommunications	9.1%	First

*Figures are for 2002.
**This list is not exhaustive.
Source: **www.samsungelectronics.com.**

EXHIBIT IV Income statements of Samsung Electronics from 1997 to 2001

(in thousands US$)

	2001	2000	1999	1998	1997–
Sales: Domestic	7,926,014	8,222,763	7,029,885	5,380,693	5,663,406
Export	16,493,575	17,632,254	13,714,980	11,259,056	7,386,318
Total sales	24,419,589	25,855,017	20,744,865	16,639,749	13,049,724
Cost of sales	18,487,732	16,586,258	14,027,936	11,578,914	8,976,018
Gross profit	5,931,857	9,268,759	6,716,929	5,060,835	4,073,706
Selling expenses	4,200,836	3,661,553	3,157,358	2,492,518	2,055,176
Operating profit	1,731,021	5,607,206	3,559,571	2,568,371	2,018,530
Non-operating income					
Interest & dividend	95,365	117,969	180,890	279,383	120,977
Gain on foreign currency transactions	180,429	225,543	212,448	863,231	1,321,352
Gain on foreign currency translation	35,736	25,733	207,638	—	—
Gain on valuation of investments (equity method)	591,848	657,109	236,888	—	—
Other	469,551	489,779	470,591	371,563	290,965
	1,372,929	1,516,133	1,308,455	1,514,177	1,733,294
Non-operating expenses					
Interest expense	154,709	258,949	572,835	924,894	536,428
Amortization of deferred charges	—	—	—	1,559,267	1,117,517
Loss on foreign currency transactions	183,196	210,444	222,768	857,732	1,478,708
Loss on foreign currency translation	68,999	179,365	84,666	—	—
Loss on valuation of inventories	40,821	—	—	—	—
Other	331,484	481,508	576,914	375,354	508,878
	779,209	1,130,266	1,457,183	3,717,247	3,641,531
Ordinary profit	2,324,741	5,993,073	3,410,823	365,247	110,293
Extraordinary income	—	115,863	—	235,068	46
Extraordinary loss	—	—	211,484	259,920	1,773
Net income before taxes	2,324,741	6,108,936	3,199,339	340,395	108,556
Income tax expense	102,316	1,573,091	681,148	80,895	21,283
Net income	2,222,425	4,535,845	2,518,191	259,500	87,283

Source: **www.samsungelectronics.com.**

of $2.2 billion (Exhibit IV). By 2002, Samsung's product range included digital media networks, device solution networks, digital appliance networks and telecommunications (see Table II for Samsung's product profile). It had manufacturing bases worldwide, a presence in around 47 countries, and approximately 64,000 employees. Samsung also had around 24 production subsidiaries, 35 sales subsidiaries and 20 branch offices worldwide (Table III).

TABLE II Product profile of Samsung Electronics

Product category	Products
Digital Media Network	TVs, Monitors, Laptops, Mobile Hand PC, DVD Player, Digital Camcorder, Laser Printer, ODD: 32X DVD/CDRW Combo Drive, HDD.
Digital Solution Network	512 Mb DDR, 32 Mb UtRAM, 1 Gb Nand Flash, Smart Card IC, Compact LCD Driver IC, Embedded ARM, 40" TFT-LCD, 1.8" TFT-LCD.
Digital Appliance Network	Refrigerators, Air Conditioners, Washing Machines, Microwave Ovens, Vacuum Cleaners.
Telecommunication	Mobile Phones: TFT Color LCD, X-4200, PDA: I-300, CDMA 2000 1x EV-DO, AceMAP Solution Softswitch.

Source: **www.samsungelectronics.com**.

TABLE III Global network of Samsung*

	Continent	Country
Production subsidiaries	North America	Mexico, Brazil, USA
	Europe	England, Spain, Hungary
	Asia	China, India, Malaysia, Philippines, Thailand, Vietnam, Indonesia, South Korea
Sales subsidiaries	North America	USA, Canada, Mexico
	South America	Colombia, Argentina, Republic of Panama
	Europe	England, Germany, France, Italy, Sweden, Portugal, Poland, The Netherlands, Russia
	Asia	Ukraine, Japan, China, Singapore, Philippines, UAE, South Korea
	Australia	Australia
	Africa	South Africa
Branch Offices	South America	Brazil, Colombia, Peru
	Africa	Egypt, Morocco, Ivory Coast, Tunisia
	Asia	Iran, Saudi Arabia, Jordan, Turkey, China, Malaysia, South Korea, Kazakhstan
	Europe	Austria, Russia, Latvia

*This list is not exhaustive.
Source: **www.samsungelectronics.com**.

The making of a global brand

In 1993, as a first step in its globalization drive, Samsung acquired a new corporate identity. It changed its logo and that of the group. In the new logo, the words Samsung Electronics were written in white color on a blue color background to represent stability, reliability and warmth. The words Samsung Electronics were written in English so that they would be easy to read and remember worldwide. The logo was elliptical in shape, representing a moving world—symbolizing advancement and change. The first and last letters 'S' and 'G' broke out of oval shape partially, in order to connect the interior with the exterior. According to company sources, this design represented the company's wish to connect itself with the world and serve society as a whole.

Product initiatives

Samsung realized that to become a global brand, it had to change the perceptions of consumers who felt that it was an OEM player and associated its products with low technology. Generally, consumers in developed markets (such as the US) opted for Samsung when they could not afford brands such as Sony and Panasonic. To change consumer perceptions, Samsung decided to focus on product design and launch innovative products.

Samsung decided to revamp its image by:

- Moving away from cheap imitated products.
- Offering innovative and technologically advanced products.
- Initiating marketing activities worldwide to increase the visibility of the Samsung brand.

In 1994, Samsung restructured its design department. It integrated all its design activities under four design groups. These groups formed the 'Samsung Electronics Design Institute.' (Earlier, the design department was called the 'Industrial Design Center'.) Samsung established design institutes in Seoul (South Korea), Palo Alto (California, US) and Middlesex (England). The Samsung Electronics Design Institute set about designing new products that would appeal to consumers worldwide.

In 1996, Yun Jong Yong (Yun) was appointed as the CEO of Samsung. He brought about major changes across the organization. After holding a brainstorming session with senior executives, he decided to base Samsung's design philosophy on the principle of 'Balance of Reason and Feeling.' In other words, Samsung's designs should balance technological excellence with human adaptability. Yun also declared the year 1996 as the 'Year of Design Revolution' and initiated a program for building a complete global design with a budget of $126 million.

Samsung product designs won Industrial Design Excellence Awards (IDEA)[4] in 1996. The products that won the awards were the NETboard computer (which targeted US students between 16 and 25 years); the 'Weeble' phone that shook from right to left when the phone rang, to get the attention of the consumer, and 'Junior TV,' which had a wearable remote.

In the late 1990s, Samsung realized the importance of customization over mass production. It therefore developed innovative products (considered fun and high end products) for the mobile phone sector in accordance with customer preferences in local markets.

Samsung used 'Lifestyle segmenting' instead of 'technological segmentation' to market its products since consumers generally bought electronic products which reflected their lifestyle instead of those that had specific technological features. Using lifestyle segmentation, the company divided the market and positioned its products. Samsung invested around $3 million in market research to identify the lifestyle and purchasing patterns of Generation Y (13–25 years old) and Generation N (Internet-friendly) consumers. The lifestyle-based product designing strategy was successful at Samsung due to the effective coordination of the activities of

4. IDEA Awards are sponsored by *BusinessWeek* magazine and awarded by the Industrial Designer Society of America for excellence in product design.

the company's geographically disposed design teams. Its team of designers in North American, European and Korean markets undertook surveys to understand the lifestyles of consumers. Then workshops were conducted so that all teams could share ideas for product design.

Samsung established a Lifestyle Research Group for studying consumer behavior and a Materials and Finishes Group for deciding on the materials, colors and product finishing for all product lines. In addition to the above two groups, it also established an Advanced Design Group, enabling exploration of new product concepts by interdisciplinary teams. And in order to encourage innovation, it announced an annual design competition for its designers.

In 1999, Samsung announced its plan to become one of the top three digital product suppliers in four markets: personal multimedia, mobile multimedia, home multimedia and component business. It set a sales target of $58 billion by 2005 for those markets. Samsung also announced the launch of various digital products in different categories. To achieve its targets, the company announced R&D investment of around $1.4 billion spread over the next 10 years.

In 1999, Samsung launched products such as the SCH-3500, the world's first CDMA PCS portable telephone combining voice activated dialing and Internet access, and a portable digital audio player with MP3 audio compression format (with a removable SmartMedia card). According to Yun, 'our new product portfolio reflects a basic shift in strategy, demonstrating our deep conviction that digital connectivity is the future of our industry, especially in terms of personal and mobile multimedia products.'

By the early 21st century, Samsung emerged as one of the biggest brands in the mobile phones segment. In the cell phone market, it changed its focus from low-end mass markets to high-end markets. The selling price of Samsung's mobile phones was higher than that of Nokia's products because of the high technology and additional features that Samsung offered to customers. A typical Samsung mobile phone allowed consumers to dispatch e-mail, access dictionaries, the Bible, and Buddhist songbooks, and play electronic games. Samsung also launched a 50-gram phone, which was said to be world's lightest phone. It could be worn as a wristwatch and it had the facility for giving voice commands. Analysts felt that though this kind of product did not generate volumes, it helped Samsung project itself as a high-technology company.

Consolidating its presence in different markets

To change its brand image, Samsung decided to associate itself with global sport events. In 1998, when Seoul hosted the Olympics, Samsung became the official sponsor of the wireless technology to the games. This move helped it boost its image worldwide.

In 1999, Erick Kim (Kim), a Korean American working with IBM, took over as the marketing head of Samsung. He focused on capturing the US retail market for consumer electronic goods, such as TVs, washing machines and microwave ovens, through partnerships with US retailing giants.

Samsung entered into a partnership with Best Buy, one of the top US retailers. Best Buy executives conducted customer research to analyze consumer buying behavior. This information was passed on to Samsung's engineers, who tried to create gadgets that would meet customer expectations. This relationship resulted in the creation of two best selling products—a DVD/VCR player and a cell phone, which could function as a Personal Digital Assistant. In 2001, sales of Samsung products through Best Buy were reported to be around $500 million. For 2002, the company expected sales of $1 billion through Best Buy. Samsung also entered into alliances with US retailers such as CompUSA and Sears, Roebuck & Co to increase its market presence in the USA.

In countries like Nigeria, Samsung focused on providing value for money and high-technology products. It tried to build its image by providing information about the company through TV and radio commercials and media events. It also invited Nigerian journalists to Korea to provide them with a detailed picture of the company. Samsung also improved its communication with distributors, as they could provide the company with customer feedback. It also planned to build close relationships with dealers and distributors to push its products in Nigerian markets (as dealers and distributors play a major role in initial product sales).

Due to its brand building activities across the world, Samsung reported a net profit of 2.95 trillion won in 2001 on total revenues of 32.4 trillion won. In July 2001, Samsung entered into a marketing alliance with AOL Time Warner to work together on an AOLTV set-top box[5] with the TiVo recording service.[6] In return, Samsung products would be promoted in AOL Time Warner's marketing initiatives. Due to this alliance, Samsung products were promoted in AOL Time Warner's magazines *People, Entertainment Weekly* and *Sports Illustrated*.

In early 2003, Samsung announced that it would concentrate on the US and European markets, where its brand was considered weak in product categories other than mobile phone handsets. Kim said, 'Our brand is weaker in Europe and the US, but in cell phones we're pretty strong. In those regions we'll be even more focused. Wireless and digital TV are the two areas we'll focus on in Europe and the US.'

Samsung emphasized brand building when entering new markets. When entering India, one of the world's largest markets, Samsung realized that its products were unknown [there]. In India, as elsewhere in the world, Japanese goods were considered to be of better quality than Korean goods. To project itself as a high-technology company, Samsung undertook a two-month corporate campaign, which highlighted the company's strengths in semiconductors, color picture tubes, color televisions and mobile phone handsets.

In addition to strengthening the Samsung brand in specific markets, the company also launched global advertisement campaigns to enhance its brand image worldwide.

Advertising and promotional strategies

In 1997, Samsung launched its first corporate advertising campaign—the Nobel Prize Series. This ad was aired in nine languages across Europe, the Middle East, South America and the CIS countries. The advertisement showed a man (representing a Nobel Prize Laureate) passing from one scene to another. As the man passes through different scenes, Samsung products are transformed into more advanced models. According to company sources, the idea was to convey the message that Samsung uses Nobel Prize Laureates' ideas for making its products. Samsung also signed an agreement with the Nobel Prize foundation to sponsor the Nobel Prize Series program, worldwide. The program was developed by the Nobel Foundation, Sweden to spread [knowledge of the] achievements of the Nobel Prize Laureates.

Initially, Samsung's advertising activities were decentralized. The company employed various ad agencies to design campaigns for its products. However, in 1999, Kim forfeited Samsung's agreements with around 55 advertising firms and signed a $400 million contract with a US

---

5. A set-top box is a device that enables a television set to become a user interface to the Internet and also enables a television set to receive and decode digital television (DTV) broadcasts.

6. TiVo is an American company offering a branded subscription-based interactive television service that lets viewers program and control which television shows they watch, and when.

based ad agency, Foote, Cone & Belding (FCB).[7] FCB created global campaigns for the company (featuring models carrying the company's gadgets), which highlighted the superior technology of Samsung products.

In 1999, Samsung unveiled a new campaign in the US with a new slogan—'Samsung DIGITall: Everyone's invited'—on the eve of its 30th anniversary. Samsung redesigned its logo to convey its objective: making life filled with convenience, abundance and enjoyment through innovative digital products. The new slogan, Samsung DigitAll, expressed the company's aim of providing digital products 'For all generations, For all customers and For all products.'

In April 2001, Samsung launched its new brand campaign, which was created by True North Communications' FCB Worldwide. This campaign was aired in around 30 countries with a budget of $400 million. As part of the brand campaign, the company advertised 30-second TV spots on various channels such as CNN, VH1, ESPN, TNT and NBC during NBA games. The first advertisement in the series—'Anthem'—was set in UK. The advertisement showed different Samsung products—a flat screen TV monitor, MP3 Player, watch phone—being used by people from different ethnic backgrounds. The voice over was:

> There is a world where you see, hear and feel things like never before, where design awakens all your senses. This is the world of Samsung and everyone's invited.

At the end of the commercial the company's tagline 'DigitAll, Everyone's invited' appeared.

The 'DigitAll' campaign was launched across all countries where the company had a presence and across all product lines. The campaign involved the sponsorship of events at global and regional levels. Reportedly around 30 people from Samsung's Seoul and North America offices worked with FCB on the campaign.

In 2001, Samsung added the word 'WOW' to its marketing campaigns to show the admiration of consumers for its innovative but affordable products. It was reported that Samsung's 2001 global brand campaign increased consumer awareness about Samsung from 83.7% in 2000 to 91.2% in 2001, and in the US, brand awareness and preference for Samsung increased from 56.4% to 74.1% in the same period.

In April 2002, Samsung adopted Internet marketing to reach high-profile consumers. It concentrated on increasing brand awareness, web traffic, and gave product information with every advertisement. It bought ad space on more than 50 websites such as Fortune.com, Forbes.com and BusinessWeek.com. At same time, Samsung continued to advertise in the print and television. Said Peter Weedfald, vice president, marketing communications and new media, 'We are integrating all forms of media; it allows us to articulate the demand for our products and manage promotions in real time.' As part of its outdoor advertising initiative, Samsung bought a 65-foot-tall electronic billboard in New York's Times Square.

In May 2002, Samsung announced its plans to extend its 'DigitAll' campaign, by launching new global campaigns with different taglines—'DigitAll Passion,' 'DigitAll Escape,' and 'DigitAll Wow.' The new ads promoted existing products, like mobile phones, color LCD mobile phones, entertainment products, and future products like the Internet refrigerator. These advertisements highlighted the flexibility and user-friendly nature of Samsung products. The campaign, for which the company had budgeted around $200 million, was aired on TV spots across US, Europe, CIS, Southeast Asia, South America, Africa, the Middle East and China. According to Kim, 'Many consumers think of digital technology as an elite experience that's inaccessible

---

7. Founded in 1873, US based FCB is one of the world's top ten ad agencies. It has a presence in around 28 countries. The agency offers integrated services to its clients, with interactive CRM solutions across both online and offline channels.

to them. Samsung prides itself on developing revolutionary technology that meets everyone's needs—business or personal.'

Beating Sony?

In 2001, Samsung declared that it would beat Sony in the consumer electronics market by 2005. Kim said, 'We want to beat Sony. Sony has the strongest brand awareness; we want to be stronger than Sony by 2005.' However, analysts felt that it would be difficult for Samsung to beat Sony so soon as Samsung was regarded as an OEM player till the mid-1990s.

In 2002, while Samsung was ranked 34th with a brand value of $8.1 billion, Sony was ranked 21st with an estimated brand value of $13.90 billion. However, while Samsung's rank had moved up from 42 in 2001, Sony's had slipped down from 20th in 2001. In the third quarter of 2002, Samsung emerged as the world's number three player in the mobile market, beating Siemens and Ericsson, with a market share of 36.4%. In CDMA technology, it was the world's number one player (Table IV).

However, analysts felt that though Samsung's brand building initiatives had improved its brand value and image in the global market, it was not yet in a position to overtake Sony. According to analysts, the company needed to concentrate on manufacturing high technology products. Though Samsung offered televisions, digital cameras, MP3 players and DVD/VCRs, its product range did not include stereos and personal computers, which enjoyed high demand in the US, the world's largest market for consumer electronics. Moreover, Sony's Walkman and DVD player were still considered benchmarks of quality in consumer electronics market.

Though initially Sony downplayed the rivalry, in 2001, it accepted it. Sony Chairman, Nobuyuki Idei, said, 'The product design and the product planning—they're learning from us. So Sony is a very good target for them.' Since Sony was Samsung's largest customer for chips, analysts felt that Samsung could not risk direct combat with Sony in international markets. Analysts also pointed out that both Samsung and Sony needed each other for their survival.

Since digital technology was replacing analog technology, Samsung felt it was in a position to produce high technology products. With the digitalization of consumer electronics, Samsung's expertise in chip making would enable it to offer technologically advanced products to its consumers.

However, analysts were skeptical about the company's performance due to the falling prices of PCs, cell phones and PDAs. They also expressed doubts about the company's ability to pump

TABLE IV Mobile phone vendor market share for 3Q 2002 (in %)

	GSM Handset	CDMA Handset
Nokia	44.4	9.4
Motorola	14.1	18.7
Siemens*	11.9	0
Samsung Electronics	9.1	27.3
Sony Ericsson	6.5	2.1
LG Electronics	1.2	19.2

*Siemens does not make CDMA mobile phones.
Source: **www.nordicwirelesswatch.com**

more money into R&D. Since chips generated most of the company's profits, falling chip prices would affect its R&D investment.

QUESTIONS TO BE ANSWERED

Where Samsung is now

1. Using the Porter Framework (cost–differentiation–focus), describe Samsung's current strategic orientation. Would you say that this has been successful? Why or why not?
2. Do a SWOT analysis and discuss Samsung's current situation. What does the SWOT indicate?
3. By 2002, Samsung was rated as one of the top 3 players in the global mobile handset market. Analysts attributed Samsung's success to its marketing initiatives. Discuss the role of marketing in Samsung's success.
4. Compared to established rivals like Sony, Matsushita and Nokia, Samsung was a late entrant in the global consumer electronics market. Comment on Samsung's brand building initiatives in the global consumer electronics market.

Where Samsung is going

5. How would you describe the current positioning of Samsung?
6. What are Samsung's objectives at this point? Do they make sense given Samsung's current position?
7. Using the Ansoff matrix, which strategic direction does Samsung appear to be heading at this point?
8. Who are the important market segments for Samsung as it heads into the future?

How Samsung will get there

9. What specific strategic suggestions would you make to Samsung management regarding the various components of the marketing mix to help it reach its objectives?
10. Analysts felt that it would not be easy for Samsung to beat Sony, which was known for technologically superior products like the Trinitron television, PlayStation and Walkman. Do you think Samsung can beat Sony only through aggressive marketing, without bringing out any technologically advanced products?
11. What important branding lessons come out of this case analysis?
12. Can Samsung achieve its objectives? Explain why or why not.

REFERENCES AND FURTHER READING

1. Nussbaum, Bruce, 'Korea's Samsung: The Hungriest Tiger', *BusinessWeek*, 2 June 1997.
2. 'Samsung Celebrates 30 Years and New Products', **www.twice.com**, 11 September 1999.
3. Brown, Heidi, 'Look Out, Sony', *Forbes*, 16 April 2001.
4. 'Samsung: No Longer Unsung', *BusinessWeek*, 6 August 2001.
5. Holstein, J. William, 'Samsung's Golden Touch', *Fortune*, 17 March 2002.
6. Elkin, Toby, 'Samsung Massively Boosts Online Advertising', **www.adage.com**, 29 April 2002.
7. Orr, Deborah, 'The Rise of Samsung', *Forbes Global*, 11 November 2002.
8. Van, Marc, 'Samsung to Sell 43 Mln Handsets in 2002', **www.nordiacwirelesswatch.com**, 21 November 2002.

9. **www.idsa.org.**
10. **www.samsung.com.**
11. **www.samsungelectronics.com.**
12. **www.adage.com.**
13. **www.internetnews.com.**

Index

Pages that include tables and figures are highlighted in **bold**.

I

J

K

L

M

N

O

P